HISTORIC U.S. COURT CASES
AN ENCYCLOPEDIA

SECOND EDITION

HISTORIC U.S. COURT CASES
AN ENCYCLOPEDIA

SECOND EDITION

John W. Johnson
Editor

Volume I

Routledge
Taylor & Francis Group

NEW YORK AND LONDON

Published in 2001 by
Routledge
Taylor & Francis Group
270 Madison Avenue
New York, NY 10016

Published in Great Britain by
Routledge
Taylor & Francis Group
2 Park Square
Milton Park, Abingdon
Oxon OX14 4RN

Printed in the United States of America on acid-free paper
10 9 8 7 6 5 4 3 2

International Standard Book Number 0-415-93019-7 (Set)
International Standard Book Number 0-415-93755-8 (Vol.1)
International Standard Book Number 0-415-93756-6 (Vol. 2)
Library of Congress Card Number 2001031651

Library of Congress Cataloging-in-Publication Data

Historic U.S. court cases : an encyclopedia / John W. Johnson, editor.—2nd ed.
    p. cm.
    Rev. ed. of: Historic U.S. court cases, 1690–1990. 1992.
    Includes bibliographical references and index.
    ISBN 0-415-93019-7 (set : alk. paper— ISBN 0-415-93755-8 (v. 1 : alk. paper—
ISBN 0-415-93756-6 (v. 2 : alk. paper)
    1. Law—United States—History. 2. Law—United States—Cases. I. Title: Historic U.S.
court cases. II. Johnson, John W., 1946- III. Historic U.S. court cases, 1690-1990.
KF385.A4 J64   2001
349.73'0264—dc21   2001031651

Taylor & Francis Group is the Academic Division of T&F Informa plc.

**Visit the Taylor & Francis Web site at
http://www.taylorandfrancis.com

and the Routledge Web site at
http://www.routledge-ny.com**

To the memory of
Paul L. Murphy, C. Herman Pritchett, and Mary K. Bonsteel Tachau:
esteemed teachers, scholars, and mentors

Preface to Second Edition

———◄○►———

The content and spirit of *Historic U.S. Court Cases: An Encyclopedia*, second edition, reflect the blend of popular interest and specialized attention recently paid to American law. The volume is designed to serve both the student and layperson interested in learning about important American court cases as well as the legal specialist looking for a convenient repository of case information, analyses, or references.

The original edition of *Historic U.S Court Cases*, published in 1992, was compiled between 1987 and 1991, a period bounded by the bicentennial celebrations of the U.S. Constitution and the Bill of Rights. During these years a media spotlight was focused on America's founding legal document and the first ten amendments. This provided a welcome civics lesson to the nation and offered encouragement and visibility to those of us who teach and write about American law. The revised edition of this volume was assembled in the late 1990s, at a time when much of the nation's attention was fixated on less lofty legal events than in the 1987–91 years. The scandals of the Clinton administration and the ensuing impeachment crisis, depressing as they were, also focused attention on the rule of law.

This volume, like the 1992 edition, is not an "encyclopedia" in the most common sense of the word. Generally, when we think of an encyclopedia, we think of a comprehensive, exhaustive, or complete compendium of information on a subject. No single volume, no matter how large, could present a comprehensive, exhaustive, or complete treatment of the thousands of U.S. court cases that experts might call "historic." However, there is another level for understanding the term "encyclopedia." Dictionaries and thesauruses note that an encyclopedia may also be a volume that offers an extensive, thorough, or sweeping treatment of a subject. Readers familiar with the old *International En-*

cyclopedia of the Social Sciences (IESS), published in 1968, and the even older *Encyclopedia of the Social Sciences (ESS)*, published in 1930, will understand this meaning of "encyclopedia." The essay/entries in the *IESS* and the *ESS* offer extensive treatments of important social scientific concepts, written by experts. Obviously not all social science concepts could be defined even in a multivolume set, so the editors of the two projects selected some of the most important concepts in the social sciences and commissioned the entries. The results are two sets of volumes that, although now dated, are remarkably readable and provocative. They remain classic reference tools in academic and public libraries.

It would be arrogant (and erroneous) to compare *Historic U.S. Court Cases* to the *IESS* or the *ESS*. My volume is far less ambitious. But it is fair to say, I believe, that this legal encyclopedia bears some resemblances to the two well-known reference sets. Like the *IESS* and the *ESS*, it is selective and not comprehensive. The essays are meant to highlight major legal issues and concerns by concentrating attention on selected court cases, rather than occupying the entire field of American law.

I have employed no single criterion for selecting a case for an essay/entry in this volume. Some cases are obvious choices by virtue of their great impact as precedents in American law. Likewise, some cases are featured because of their fame as important historical events in and of themselves. In addition, some cases have been selected because they are representative of a large body of important litigation. A few cases have been selected for treatment because they are decidedly *not* typical; these cases reveal interesting eccentricities in the American legal past. Other cases have been selected because they raised or continue to raise significant historical or legal issues. Finally, a few essays examine cases that showcase the role of a particularly famous jurist, lawyer, or litigant.

A large number of the essays in this volume concern U.S. Supreme Court decisions. The importance of the U.S. Supreme Court as the final arbitrator for legal disputes in this country is obvious. However, some of the most influential cases in American history were decided in the lower federal courts, the state courts, and (in the pre-Constitutional era) in the colonial courts. Accordingly, some of these non–U.S. Supreme Court decisions are the subjects of essays in the volume.

As was the case with the two aforementioned social science encyclopedias, the essays in this volume were composed by individual contributors who were not hamstrung by lock-step formulas or formats. The contributors were allowed, within the bounds of stylistic consistency and the number of words prescribed, to sound their own voices and stake out their own conclusions. There is no party line or standard of orthodoxy. If there is a thematic thread to the volume, it is as a result of my charge that essayists focus on the narrative, dramatic dimension of legal disputes within their larger social and historical contexts. Hence, the contributors were encouraged to stress the factual bases of disputes and to emphasize provocative issues raised by litigation. They were also asked to place their case (or cases) within the broader social milieu. How they chose to respond to these general suggestions was left largely to their own devices. I provided model essays to the contributors and, when asked, ventured suggestions or offered feedback. Then I edited the contributions. For the most part, the only substantive changes I made in the submissions were to correct factual errors. It is important to note that all of the essays that appear in the *Encyclopedia* are original compositions; none were published elsewhere prior to their appearance in this volume or the 1992 edition.

Based upon the advice of an advisory board, the suggestions of senior American legal experts, and the serendipity of professional and personal contacts, I selected about eighty scholars to prepare essays for the original volume. For the new essays in the revised volume I contacted many of the same individuals plus a handful of new authors. In total, eighty-five different authors are represented in the revised edition. As was the case in the assignments for the *IESS* and the *ESS*, efforts were made to cast the net widely. Because some of the best writing about the law continues to be accomplished by nonlegal experts, I did not want lawyers or legal historians preparing all the entries. Thus, I designed the *Encyclopedia* to reflect thoughtful contributions to an understanding of the law from a variety of scholars and writers.

The authors of essays in the first edition of the *Encyclopedia* were given the occasion to revise and update their contributions. Most took advantage of this opportunity. In addition, I reviewed and re-edited all the essays from the first edition that appear again here in this revised format. A few essays from the first edition have been deleted in this volume, and a number of essays appear in different sections of the volume.

Of the 201 total essays, forty-three are new to this revised edition. Of the new essays, about half treat cases of the 1990s and the other half pick up legal cases from earlier periods. I have made special efforts to include essays in this edition on very recent cases of major importance—for example, the federal district court decision in the Microsoft antitrust case (May 2000), the U.S. Supreme Court holding on the Nebraska "partial-birth" abortion statute (June 2000), the U.S. Supreme Court's rulings in the high-profile Florida election cases (December 2000), and the PGA–Casey Martin case ruling of May 2001. Given the pressure of deadlines, there inevitably were some recent cases of historic interest that could not be treated in this volume.

A bit of prosopography on the eighty-five contributors to *Historic U.S. Court Cases,* second edition, may be of interest to users of the volume. Slightly more than half (54 percent) qualify as legal experts. These include historians with constitutional or legal specialties (30 percent), political scientists who specialize in public law (13 percent), and law professors or practicing attorneys (11 percent). The other essayists (46 percent) fall into the following categories: historians with other than legal specialties (24 percent); other social scientists or humanities professors (11 percent); unaffiliated scholars (9 percent); and academics in government service (2 percent). Of the individuals who eventually committed to the project, 41 percent, reside in the South; 29 percent live in the Midwest; 18 percent make their homes in the West; and 12 percent hail from the East. Those conversant with American legal scholarship will recognize the names of many distinguished senior legal scholars in the roster of contributors. But there were also quite a few essays prepared by scholars new to the profession who already have developed an interest or expertise on a particular case or area of the law. Of the many people I solicited for contributions to the *Encyclopedia*, most kindly accepted the commission(s). Those who did not usually recommended others to serve in their stead.

The revised edition of the *Encyclopedia* consists of essays of varying lengths. Cases deemed to be of monumental importance were afforded about 5,000 words. Cases of what I term medium-level significance tend to be about 2,000—the modal length of selections in the volume. And a sample of lesser cases are treated in essays of about 1,000 words. The original volume consisted of six parts. Tighter organization in the revised edition has led to the elimination of what was formerly Part VI. Most of the essays that originally appeared in the now defunct Part VI have been allocated to appropriate places in Parts I through V. Part I offers a selection of twenty-eight essays on crime and criminal law. Part II presents thirty selections on governmental organization, power and procedure. Part III offers fifty-three contributions on economics and economic regulation. Part IV tenders forty-three essays dealing with the important issues of race, gender, sexual orientation, and disability. And Part V, on civil liberties, includes forty-seven essays keyed to some of the most important individual freedoms in the national Bill of Rights. All the parts are slightly expanded from their original status in the 1992 edition of the *Encyclopedia*. In particular, Part IV contains new subsections on gay/lesbian issues and the law affecting Americans with disabilities.

Each of the five parts begins with a brief introduction. Within each introduction is a short

rationale for the subsumed topics and a very brief synopsis of the cases covered. The introductions do not explain the holdings of the cases or engage in much rhetoric about how the cases fit into their historical context. These tasks the contributors accomplish themselves in their own essays. Given the storylike composition of most of the essays, extensive editorial commentary on my part would be superfluous.

Within each part of the volume, the essays are arranged in thematic sections according to the chronology of the cases covered. Under the title of each essay is the name and affiliation of the contributor. This is followed by the title of the case(s) discussed in the essay. For those interested in consulting the cases directly, the official legal citations are included (except for cases that were not published in court reports). The name of the court that decided the case(s) is noted. In the left-hand column on the first page of each essay is a short box entitled "The Case in Brief," which outlines the date, location, court, principal participants, and significance of the case that follows. This brief overview serves as a convenient preview as well as a tool to refresh the reader's memory after the essay has been read. Each essay is followed by a brief "selected bibliography." Each bibliography notes the sources that the contributor felt to be most useful in constructing his or her selection and in offering relevant information and analyses on the case(s) treated. Many of the authorities cited are books or journal articles that can be found in good academic or public libraries. For legal specialists and others with access to law libraries or on-line legal services, there are also many references to law review articles.

Who might use this volume and how might it be used? General readers with legal questions should probably begin by consulting the name and subject index. If a case name is known, the *Encyclopedia*'s case index should be the starting point. For someone with an interest in a broad legal topic, the table of contents or the introductions to the five parts would be places to begin. Then the focus could be narrowed by reading selected essays or by consulting the indexes. Legal specialists might want to enter the volume through any or all of these portals, checking what they already know against the accounts of the cases offered in the essays. For all users, however, the selected bibliographies should be particularly suggestive for additional reading.

Another approach to the use of the *Encyclopedia*—one that might appeal to the informational browsers among us—would be to start paging through the volume, searching for essays on cases that appear interesting. Given the quality of the writing and the inherent drama of historic judicial decisions, I suspect that it will not take the curious intellectual shopper long to find several essays to peruse with care.

John W. Johnson

Acknowledgments

———◀◦▶———

Almost ten years ago, I took the opportunity to thank the many scholars, colleagues, and friends who provided assistance and encouragement in producing the original edition of *Historic U.S. Court Cases: An Encyclopedia*. If anything, I received more help the second time around.

First and foremost, I want to thank the more than eighty contributors. Despite busy schedules, these teachers, scholars, attorneys, and public citizens produced well-written and authoritative essays in a timely fashion. In most instances their work required little substantive editing. I hope that when they see the final product of their labors they will feel that the time they lavished on their essays was well spent. I am privileged to be personally acquainted with about four-fifths of the contributors to this volume—a slightly higher percentage than was the case with the contributors to the 1992 edition of the *Encyclopedia*. With the remaining one-fifth, I have communicated by phone, letter, and e-mail. It is, of course, gratifying to be able to count on one's friends and to be able to thank them directly for their contributions. But the professionalism demonstrated by scholars whom I have not yet met is especially welcome; I hope someday to make the acquaintance of these remaining authors and express my appreciation, in person, for the privilege of including their work in this volume. Of all the contributors, I want to single out for special mention the following individuals who accepted particularly difficult commissions under the pressure of tight deadlines: Bill Lasser, Steve Lowe, Christine Nemacheck, David Walker and, especially, Tinsley Yarbrough. I profoundly regret that a few prominent contributors passed away since producing essays for the original edition of the *Encyclopedia*. I have dedicated this volume to the memory of three such contributors—distinguished teachers/scholars whom I was fortunate to have as mentors early in my career.

My home institution, the University of Northern Iowa (UNI), has been supportive of my work on this and other scholarly writing projects for over a decade. At UNI, I want to thank two of my bosses, Dean Julia Wallace and Provost Aaron Podolefsky. I also want to express appreciation to my history department colleagues for their interest in my work, especially Dick Broadie, Bob Martin, Chuck Quirk, Roy Sandstrom, Don Shepardson, David Walker, and Carol Weisenberger. Once again, the history department's senior secretary, Judith Dohlman, provided wide-ranging clerical assistance on a project of mine; without her formatting of essays, typing of contracts, and general record keeping, this project would have been immensely more difficult to complete.

Members of the staff at Routledge are old hands at producing reference volumes. A number of Routledge editors devoted time and energy to this second edition. I want to thank especially Richard Steins, Mark O'Malley, and Daniel Yacavone. Two reviewers retained by Routledge provided useful advice on reorganizing the revised volume, and a team of copy editors saved me from an embarrassing number of errors and awkward sentences. Other individuals at Routledge rendered the professional formatting, printing, and marketing necessary to turn a long manuscript into a handsome and, I hope, once again useful reference work. Finally, I thank my good friend and distinguished legal historian, Kermit L. Hall, for suggesting back in 1986 that I might possess the skills and stamina to produce a book of this type.

None of the generous and hard-working individuals named above should be held to account for any errors or shortcomings of the

Encyclopedia. As the person whose name appears on the title page, I bear that responsibility.

While not working on this project or engaging in other academic tasks, I occasionally sought diversion and stress relief with a diverse group of fellow golf fanatics: Kitty and Murray Austin, Jim Bodensteiner, Dick Broadie, Dick Followill, Laura Hoistad, Steve Gaies, Lee Luther, Kirk Manfredi, Dennis Nebbe, Steve Olerud, Roger Sell, Bob Sherwood, Tim Von Tersch, Russ Wiley, and Jack Wilkinson. I wish fairways and greens to all of them.

Once again I thank my children—Matt, Noah, Barb, Steve and Chris—for their understanding and support. They may not always have known what I was up to when I was occupied on this project, but they respected the fact that I was doing something I considered important. Finally, I can acknowledge but in no way repay the considerable obligations I owe to my wife, Charlotte Mull-Johnson. She patiently listened to me talk about court cases, she adapted to my sometimes strange work schedule, and she tolerated stoically most of my moods. No author could ask for more.

Contents

——◁○▷——

HISTORIC U.S. COURT CASES
An Encyclopedia

SECOND EDITION

PART I

CRIME AND CRIMINAL LAW

- Pre–1900
- 1900–1959
- 1960–2000

It is only appropriate to begin a volume on law with a section on crime. The great jurist and legal philosopher Oliver Wendell Holmes Jr., in his famous 1897 address titled "The Path of the Law," counseled his listeners that "[i]f you want to know the law and nothing else, you must look at it as a bad man, who cares only for the material consequences which such knowledge enables him to predict." Of course, Holmes went on to emphasize that the bad man's perspective is not enough by itself for one to understand and appreciate the place of law in a society. But it is a good starting place. The twenty-eight selections in Part I offer a sample of cases throughout American history that stem from criminal acts but also illuminate some of the larger historical issues or problems of their eras. As is true for many selections in this volume, some of the cases are well known and are important historical events. Others cases, however, are not important *per se*; rather, they offer representative or curious examples of legal issues presented outside the glare of contemporary publicity.

Pre–1900

For the colonial era, the first selection, "Witchcraft and the Law," deals with the most notorious example of the prosecution of the crime of witchcraft in American history. It is followed by two other selections on colonial crimes—"Pirates Walk the Plank in Charleston" and "New York on Fire"—that touch upon historical conflicts, one involving piracy and the other a racial riot.

The next two selections provide an examination of cases that figured prominently in the American Revolution. The first, "The Writs of Assistance Cases," deals with a set of disputes in the 1760s concerning practices of colonial customs officials operating under the authority of the English Crown. The second, "The Boston Massacre Trials," examines the legal proceedings for the British soldiers charged with the killings of a group of Massachusetts protesters in 1770 that had inflamed the American colonies.

For the early national era, two essays of historical note are presented. "Treason and the Whiskey 'Insurrection'" presents the first case prosecuted under the definition of *treason* in the U.S. Constitution. "Defective Indictment" discusses the importance of a small technical issue in a state court to the prosecution of a violent crime.

For the mid-nineteenth century, four essays involving crime are offered: "A Double Standard of Justice" discusses a bizarre case from Louisiana dealing with violence, sex and honor; "Death for Grand Larceny" examines an early California death penalty case; "The Constitution: A Law for Rulers in War and Peace?" considers the fate of two notorious critics of the federal conduct of the Civil War; and "Public Opinion, Expert Testimony, and 'The Insanity Dodge'" probes the criminal trial of Charles Guiteau, the assassin of President James Garfield.

1900–1959

For the first half of the twentieth century, four essays dealing with criminal matters that raised important historical or constitutional issues are included. "The Fruits of the Poisonous Tree" examines the birth in the federal courts of the "exclusionary rule," which holds that illegally seized evidence cannot be used against a defendant. "Two Nations: The Case of Sacco and Vanzetti" discusses the murder and bank robbery prosecution of two Italian immigrants in the 1920s that became an American cause célèbre. "Are Bootleggers Entitled to Privacy?" analyzes a prosecution for the violation of Prohibition that turned upon the government's use of wiretap evidence. And "Showdown Over Gun Control" examines a 1939 U.S. Supreme Court decision on gun control legislation that set a precedent that is still viable over sixty years later.

The final selections in this section consider two of the most noteworthy trials of the Cold War. "Icons of the Cold War: The Hiss-Chambers Case" probes the perjury trial of a former state department official, Alger Hiss, accused of lying about passing top secret government documents to communist couriers. "A Crime Worse than Murder" examines the trial and appeal of Julius and Ethel Rosenberg, the so-called "atom spies."

1960–2000

For the late twentieth century, several selections on cases from the 1960s discuss Supreme Court decisions involving the constitutional rights of those accused of crimes. "The Exclusionary Rule Binds the States" reviews the landmark decision that "federalized" the exclusionary rule. By contrast, "'Good Faith' and the Exclusionary Rule" presents an example of a partial retreat from the exclusionary rule by the 1980s Supreme Court under Chief Justice Warren Burger. Three other essays in this subsection— "'Incorporation' and the Right to Counsel," "Lawyer? You Want a Lawyer?," and "You Have the Right to Remain Silent"—deal with the right of a defendant to an attorney under the Fifth Amendment to the Constitution.

"The Death and Resurrection of Capital Punishment" discusses the two leading Supreme Court cases on the constitutionality of capital punishment, and "Plea Bargaining and the 'Vindictive' Exercise of Prosecutorial Discretion" offers an example of a state case involving the common practice of plea bargaining in the courts.

The remaining four essays in this section treat a potpourri of headline cases in the last quarter century. "Will the Real Patty Hearst Please Stand Up?" considers the role of excessive publicity in the criminal trial of a famous heiress. "For Pure Cold Cash: The Walker and Ames Espionage Cases" reviews one of the most infamous espionage cases of the late Cold War. "Surrogate Motherhood: Womb for Rent" discusses the recent and continuing legal controversy surrounding surrogate parentage. And "Narratives in Black and White: The O. J. Simpson Trials as Social Drama" offers an examination of the criminal and civil trials of athlete and celebrity O.J. Simpson, judicial proceedings that had little legal importance but bulked large on the cultural landscape of the United States in the 1990s.

Pre–1900

Witchcraft and the Law

—◄◦►—

David Thomas Konig

Department of History
Washington University in St. Louis

The Salem Witchcraft Trials (1692) [Massachusetts colonial court]

◄◦► THE CASE IN BRIEF ◄◦►

Date
June–November 1692

Location
Boston, Massachusetts Bay Colony

Court
Massachusetts colonial court

Principal Participants
Governor William Phips
Lieutenant Governor William Stoughton
141 accused, 26 convicted,
   19 sentenced defendants
Reverend Cotton Mather
Reverend Increase Mather

Significance of the Case
The law of precedence (English or colonial) was debated as accusations from Puritans resulted in a trial that culminated in the hanging of 19 for practicing witchcraft.

From the perspective of three hundred years, it is hard to comprehend how an entire society—that of Massachusetts Bay in 1692—could plunge into a frenzied fear of the devil. Unable fully to recapture the thinking of the people involved, we tend to see the episode known as the Salem witchcraft trials of 1692 as a thinly veiled, cynical mass assault on nonconformists, dissidents, or other powerless groups.

The people of New England were no different from good Christians anywhere in the late seventeenth century: they had no doubt of Satan's existence, and they implicitly believed in his relentless assault on the kingdom of God. According to their beliefs, Satan, the former archangel Lucifer, had attempted to usurp God's rule and, for such rebellion, had been flung from heaven. Not content to accept such banishment, Satan had begun a remorseless campaign to destroy the kingdom of God denied to him and, as prince of darkness, to establish his own rule. Not even New England—and Puritan New England at that, where the saints preserved the holy errand of the Reformation—was immune to the threat. Indeed, the Puritan colony was all the more likely a target. As explained by Reverend Deodat Lawson of Boston (formerly of Salem), God allowed Satan to practice his evil "to serve [God's] own most Holy Ends." The devil's temptations were a test for the believer and a warning to the backslider. "Their Graces are hereby tried," Reverend Cotton Mather said of the New England saints in 1689, and "their Uprightness is made known."

In 1689, God seemed to have good reason to test the faithful. In the minds of many, New England had departed from its original godly purpose. Boston, the holy "Citty upon a Hill" of John Winthrop in 1630, was now a thriving commercial center, with ships traveling all over the Atlantic community. Approximately one in six men took part in the colony's overseas trade; church membership had never approached that figure in the seventeenth century. A once pious, holy experiment now seemed given over to Mammon; the Christian communalism now seemed supplanted by a more secular character and an incipient individualism. Worse, many approved of the changes and pushed them forward. Young people, it appeared, had no interest in reformation and only used the new openness of society to go their own way. Parents, complained one minister, were letting their children "have their swinge, to go and come where and when they please, and especially in the night."

How had these changes come about? Many agreed with Cotton Mather in 1689 when he warned, "Go tell Mankind, that there are Devils and Witches; and that tho those night-birds least appear where the day-light of the Gospel comes, yet New-England has had examples of their Existence and Operation."

The message reached a jittery and insecure people all over New England, but it had special meaning for those of Salem, just north of Boston. This small seaport had experienced all of the pervasive social and economic changes affecting the region as a whole. Older even than Boston, Salem was one of the Puritans' first New World settlements and had long held the reputation of being a very devout community. But Salem had grown rapidly in the past generation and had become a thriving—and worldly—commercial center with ties to London and other European cities. The old unity of its founders had faded, and merchants had replaced ministers as the town's leaders.

There were, in fact, two Salems: next to the bustling port of Salem Town was a traditionalist, and much poorer, outlying parish known as Salem Farms, or Salem village. The village encompassed a scattering of homesteads, most of them residences of families who did not share in the wealth or participate in the new ways of life in Salem Town. Humble families barely getting by on their own farm production, they adhered to older notions of communal behavior and religious conservatism.

They also clung to older notions of folk practice, including the use of magic to improve or ameliorate their hard and uncertain lives. For the young, the future held as much fear as promise, and they not infrequently resorted to folk magic to foretell the future and give them some assurances. Young women, in particular, looked anxiously to the future, in which the wealth or trade of their husbands would determine their own standing in the community. Largely powerless to control their own lot in life, many young women turned to magic as a source of information or as a way to guide their lives. For a small group of adolescent girls in the Salem Village household of Reverend Samuel Parris, the future might be revealed in the white of an egg—much like the image in a crystal ball. But when a murky image resembling a coffin appeared at one of their sessions, it so terrified them that they reacted physically, with violent and uncontrollable contortions. With their hopes turned to horror, they shrank back in fear that they had "tampered with the devil's tools so far that hereby one door was opened [to the devil] to play those pranks."

The anxieties of change in seventeenth-century Salem turned the petty fortune-telling of the girls into a major crisis for the entire colony. Like nearly everyone else at that time, the people of both Salems believed in the reality of Satan and in his never-ending efforts to induce Christians to betray God. The two Salems were as distrustful of one another as any feuding villages ever were, but their resentments were made worse by the wide gap between their two ways of life. After Reverend Parris told others about the "afflictions" of the girls, these tensions erupted into a firestorm of witchcraft accusation when the girls, including Parris's nine-year-old daughter Elizabeth, began to attribute their convulsive torments to the satanic acts of three local women. The effects spread into neighboring towns in Essex County suffering from the same kind of divisions. Traditionalists in the village believed that the people of the town had sold their souls to the devil in return for their wealth. On the other side, residents of the town feared that their poorer neighbors were enlisting Satan and his tools in revenge and resentment against their prosperous way of life.

Horror followed shock when it became apparent that some people *were* using magic and witchcraft. Pins and dolls were found in the home of one woman suspected of being a witch. Parris's efforts to overcome Satan's wiles with prayer failed dismally, and—more disturbing still—others were turning to magic as a cure for the bewitchments. Parris was aghast to learn that a village woman had persuaded Parris's West Indian servant Tituba and her husband John Indian to attempt an old English folk remedy by baking a "witch cake." This concoction of ordinary meal and the urine of a victim was fed to a dog (presumably, a "familiar" of the witch), which would then injure the witch and reveal his (or, more likely, her) identity. Parris roundly rebuked this attempt as "going to the Devil for help against the Devil."

But where else could they go for "help against the Devil"? When the first accusations were made in February 1692, the people of Salem found themselves in an odd position because they had no legitimate government from which to seek aid. In 1684, the Crown had revoked the colonial charter of 1629 in its consolidation of all the New England colonies (with New York) into one huge Dominion of New England. For five years, New England functioned without its customary legal institutions until, emulating England's Glorious Revolution against James II, its residents rose in rebellion in 1689 and ousted James's royal officials. Hastily reconstituting their former charter institutions, they attempted to operate government as they had known it until a new charter could bring them the properly constituted legal institutions needed to establish law and order.

The governor, Sir William Phips, arrived with that charter on May 14, 1692. However, until then, a legal vacuum existed and accelerated the sense of panic. Moreover, war had broken out when Catholic France declared its enmity for the Protestants William and Mary, who now ruled England and its colonies. Salem—exposed on the northern frontier against French Canada—was gripped with fear. Villagers in Marblehead, a few miles away, rioted when colony officials tried to remove that town's cannon for the defense of Boston, and rumors swirled of a combined French and Indian invasion, to be abetted by an uprising of local black slaves.

Helpless against these external threats, the people of Salem begged their acting magistrates to take quick action against the internal threats they perceived. They were not alone in panicking amid the insecurity and fear. The provisional court of assistants at Boston, sensitive to any imputations against its legitimacy or its capacity to meet violations of the law, had condemned thirteen pirates to death in 1689—an unprecedented crackdown that far exceeded the customarily more lenient treatment of felons. Although the reconstituted court pardoned eleven of these men, the sternness of the government had sent an implicit but reassuring message to a frightened people. For those who needed a more explicit message, complained an indignant observer, the assistants ordered the execution of another man "to frighten the people into submission."

The two resident magistrates at Salem, John Hathorne and Jonathan Corwin, found a village rife with accusations on February 29, 1692, when they traveled to its meetinghouse to examine the first three persons accused of witchcraft. Despite having little authority, upon which they remanded the three—Sarah Good, Sarah Osborne, and Tituba—to Boston jail. They also had little notion of how to proceed, for such examinations had been a rarity in the colony before 1692. Until that year, only seventy indictments had been handed up in all of New England, but most had been dismissed, and only eleven accused witches (five in Massachusetts Bay, the remainder in Connecticut) had been executed. Even so, Hathorne and Corwin continued to examine and imprison suspects for what they anticipated would be a trial as soon as the new government was established. Martha Corey, Dorcas Good (Sarah's four-year-old daughter), and Rebecca Nurse followed the others to Boston jail. So widespread were the accusations that the two magistrates had to continue their examinations in Salem Town, with the aid of Deputy Governor Thomas Danforth and four other magistrates (James Russell, Isaac Addington, Samuel Appleton, and Samuel Sewell). From their seats in the town meetinghouse, they continued to commit suspects to jails in Boston, Salem, and Ipswich, now overflowing with inmates. By the time Governor Phips sailed into Boston harbor on May 14, probably more than a hundred people languished under indictment.

Phips confronted a puzzling judicial situation for, unless he was to release them all, trials had to be scheduled. According to the new charter, the legislature (but *only* the legislature) of Massachusetts Bay had the authority to create courts. Before any courts could be established, therefore, elections had to be held, and Phips had expected that no court could thus be set up until January 1693. Such a delay was unthinkable; already, one prisoner (Sarah Osborne) had died from the conditions in Boston jail, and others were sure to follow during the course of the winter.

Acting in haste, Phips, therefore, constituted a special court of a type that, in England, was commissioned to deal with criminal activity, a court of "oyer and terminer"—literally, to hear and determine. There were two problems with his decision. First, it created a court without proper statutory authority; in that sense, it rendered all prosecutions legally improper. The second problem was more tangled, for Phips worded his commission in a way that created ambiguity about the court's jurisdiction. Courts of oyer and terminer might be special (that is, they might deal with a particular class of crimes in a particular area) or general (in which they might determine all crimes in the area). Phips issued his commission to a "Special Court of Oyer and Terminer," but in the body

of the commission he authorized it "to inquire of, hear and determine for this time, according to the law and custom of England and of this their Majesties' Province, all manner of crimes and offenses had, made, done or perpetrated within the counties of Suffolk, Essex, Middlesex, and each of them." Did this mean that a *special* court had *general* jurisdiction? Phips evaded the question by busying himself in preparations to lead New England troops into battle against the French and Indians. He left the answer to the court, led by Chief Justice William Stoughton (the new lieutenant governor), who was assisted by John Richards, Nathaniel Saltonstall, Wait Winthrop, Bartholomew Gedney, Samuel Sewall, Peter Sergeant, and the two former examining magistrates, Hathorne and Corwin. Perhaps the answer, when it came, was the product of clerk Stephen Sewall (the judge's brother) or King's Attorney Thomas Newton: either might have prepared the indictments, which were drawn up in advance and specified witchcraft, leaving only the names of the victim and the accused to be added. If any crime at all were to be prosecuted before January 1693—that is, if the province were to have any weapon against any form of social disorder—the act would have to involve satanic collusion, and the person named would thus become a witchcraft defendant.

Moreover, the commission had specified trial "according to the law and custom of England and of this their Majesties' Province." Two models—English and local—thus competed for application. The difference was great. If the court followed Massachusetts Bay practice, the Bible would greatly influence the trials. As to substance, the Massachusetts Bay *Laws and Liberties* of 1648 followed the biblical definition of witchcraft as merely consulting with spirits; it did not require actual harm (*maleficium*) to a victim. In this regard, colonial law matched that of England, which Sir Edward Coke defined as consulting spirits "for any purpose . . . without any other act or thing."

Despite this agreement in substance, a major procedural difference separated the law of Massachusetts from that of England. New England criminal procedure required two witnesses to any capital crime. A legacy of ecclesiastical law but not a common-law rule, this requirement had been enacted in 1641 and enjoyed a powerful standing in the colony's trial practice. According to the Book of Numbers, "[O]ne witness shall not testify against any person to cause him to die," a point emphasized many years earlier by Reverend Charles Chauncey in answer to Plymouth governor William Bradford, that "God would not put our lives into the power of any one tongue." By contrast, the common-law rule permitted conviction on the testimony of a single witness. (The English requirement of two witnesses was a statutory rule applying only to treason.)

English and local law also differed on the matter of forfeiture of a felon's estate. The common-law rule that a felon's property be confiscated by the state upon conviction was not followed in Massachusetts.

A precise reconstruction of the Salem witchcraft trials is impossible: no actual trial records survive, and historians must rely on the pretrial examinations of suspects, the accounts of observers (usually complaints by those opposing the prosecutions), and the petitions of the suspects themselves. Nevertheless, it is possible to reconstruct the trials with some measure of certainty. In the first place, it is clear that the court decided to adhere scrupulously to English practice. In part, this decision revealed the overweening ambition of Chief Justice Stoughton, whose political aspirations inclined him to seize every opportunity to impress royal officials with his trustworthiness as lieutenant governor. As it became ever more clear after 1684, those officials who would occupy the highest judicial offices in the colony would be those men who conformed to the systems of royal justice and the needs of imperial administration. Stoughton, however, did not have to impose this decision on an unwilling local leadership. No one had forgotten that Massachusetts Bay had lost its charter in 1684 largely because of the colony's many departures from English law. Of course, its rejection of toleration for the Church of England stood as the most serious example of repudiating English law, but other areas, too, figured in the decision by the Court of King's Bench to vacate the charter. The colony's leaders had protested the in-

nocuous nature of their departures from a complicated system "which wee pretend not to a thorow acquaintance with," but their disingenuous claim to unsophisticated provincialism neither convinced the Crown nor gave them confidence for its usage in a later conflict. Moreover, Stoughton and Bartholomew Gedney had served on the superior court established under the Dominion of New England—a court that adhered strictly to common-law principle and practice—and they would follow that path in 1692.

The oyer and terminer court that convened on June 2, 1692, for the first trial therefore had a strong, internally imposed mandate to honor English law. That some measure of uncertainty still remained, however, became clear immediately after the trial. As the first defendant to stand trial, Bridget Bishop was probably the easiest case. Her own husband had accused her of witchcraft, the girls of the Parris household had accused her of urging them to sign a covenant with the devil, two women had testified to seeing her with the devil, and workmen renovating a wall in a house she once occupied discovered "several puppets made up of rags and hogs' bristles with headless pins in them." The jury returned a guilty verdict, and she was hanged on June 10. The court's uncertainty was apparent, however, in its prompt adjournment and consultation with the area's ministers on a vital point of law before conducting any more trials.

Their question concerned "spectral evidence," the acceptance of testimony that described actions by a specter, or devil, in the image of the accused witch. Already, Cotton Mather had urged Judge John Richards not to allow such evidence. Mather's reasoning was hardly modern or secular in the sense of rejecting specters as unnatural and thus impossible. Instead, Mather was acting on a theological imperative; namely, that the devil's powers were so awful that he might, in his horrid dissembling, use the specter of an innocent person to confound God's children and harm someone. Deodat Lawson agreed, although perhaps because his own deceased wife was being accused by such "proof." Warning of immense trouble for innocent persons, Mather argued that if spectral evidence were admitted as conclusive proof, "The Door is opened!"

A wary Phips asked for advice from the local ministry. He did so despite the admissibility of spectral evidence at common law; used in English trials since 1593, it was justified in the widely used handbook for justices of the peace, Michael Dalton's *Countrey Justice*. So convinced of its admissibility was Chief Justice Sir John Holt of King's Bench that he accepted it in English trials *after* those in Salem, admitting such evidence in trials in 1695 and 1696. But would the people of Massachusetts Bay accept trials that used it?

The clergy of the colony answered promptly. Three days later, Phips received the *Return of the Several Ministers* with their advice to exercise "exquisite caution, lest by too much credulity for things received only upon the Devil's authority there be a door opened for a long train of miserable consequences." Squarely confronting the issue, they reported that capital convictions for witchcraft "ought certainly to be more considerable than barely the accused person being represented by a specter unto the afflicted, inasmuch as 'tis an undoubted and a notorious thing that a Demon may, by God's permission, appear even to ill purposes in the shape of an innocent, yea, a virtuous man." It is ironic that this episode, the last ever in which a governor of Massachusetts consulted the clergy for legal advice, saw the ministers taking what would be (for different reasons, of course) the modern position against a secular institution that chose the opposite. Only three ministers (including Samuel Parris) disagreed, but Chief Justice Stoughton pressed onward against their advice and ordered that spectral evidence be admitted. In protest, a "very much dissatisfied" Judge Nathaniel Saltonstall resigned from the bench.

The acceptance of spectral evidence opened the door for the "long train of miserable abuses" about which the ministers had warned. When the court resumed on June 30, it condemned five more women (Sarah Good, Rebecca Nurse, Susannah Martin, Elizabeth Howe, and Sarah Wildes), all of whom were hanged on July 19. Most shocking—and most puzzling to historians—was the case of Re-

"Witch Hill" or "The Salem Martyr," a nineteenth-century painting by Thomas Satterwhite Noble depicting a woman who was found guilty of witchcraft en route to the gallows. *AP/Wide World Photos.*

becca Nurse. A respected member of the community, she was not at all like the mostly poor or obscure defendants that had been sent to Gallows Hill. Judge Hathorne's sister and brother-in-law had testified for her as character witnesses, and thirty-nine of her neighbors had petitioned the court on her innocence. In fact, the jury acquitted her at trial. But no one had yet been acquitted and dismissed; Stoughton, ruling the courtroom with an iron hand, ordered Nurse interrogated about an ambiguous remark she had made in court. Exhausted by her ordeal and hard of hearing, she failed to respond. The jury, sent back to deliberate further, returned with a guilty verdict.

Nurse's acquittal and then conviction turned, perhaps, on a peculiar evidentiary test employed at the trials. According to the practice of witch-hunting, a witch might be identified by physical signs of suckling a demon, or "familiar." As Dalton described what to look for, the court should be watchful for "some big or little

Teat upon their body, and in some secret place, where he (the Devil) sucketh them. And besides their sucking, the Devil leaveth other marks upon their body, sometimes like a blew spot or red spot, like a flea-biting; sometimes the flesh sunk in and hollow." At Salem in 1692, it appears that a jury of women, including midwives, examined suspects for such marks. Given the primitive state of gynecological examination in the seventeenth century (physicians almost never examined genital areas), it is not surprising that any mark or growth might appear to be the "preternatural excrescence" they were seeking. Under such circumstances, who could definitively say whether a growth was natural?

Rebecca Nurse made precisely that point at her trial, arguing that what the jury found when examining her was nothing unnatural; in fact, as she pleaded to the court, one of "the Moaste Antiente skilfull, prudent" women of the examining jury dissented from the others "and Did then declare that she saw nothing in or about yoer Honor's poare pettissioner But what Might arise from a Naturall cause." Nurse's petition apparently convinced the jury, for they returned a not-guilty verdict. At that point, however, Stoughton reopened the interrogation and sent the trial back for more deliberation, whereupon they changed their verdict. Not only Nurse but also five other women discovered with such marks were executed.

As the trials reached their peak in the summer of 1692, Nurse's treatment was not unusual, but it, too, bespeaks the lingering uncertainty attaching to trial procedure. The court preferred confessions above all else, for such an admission of guilt would, in its view, corroborate other flimsier evidence (such as the questionable spectral proof). Moreover, a confession might be used as an indication that the accused had repented of his or her crime and was acknowledging both Christ and the court. Every person who confessed, in fact, was spared upon conviction. Only one confessing suspect, Samuel Wardwell, went to the gallows, but he renounced his confession. For these reasons, the court did everything it could to extract a confession. After all, James VI of Scotland (later James I of England) had "warmly" recom-

mended its employment, even if his purpose was to gain proof for execution.

Torture need not be so brutal, and the court also used a less overtly atrocious method in seeking confessions. "There are numerous instances," reported one opponent of the trials, ". . . of the tedious Examinations before private persons, many hours together; they all that time urging them to Confess (and taking turns to perswade them) till the accused were wearied out by being forced to stand so long, or for want of Sleep, etc. and so brought to give an Assent to what they said; they then asking them, Were you at such a Witch-meeting, or have you signed the Devil's Book, etc. upon their replying, yes, the whole was drawn into form as their confession." Some of these episodes lasted eighteen hours and included the "most violent, distracting, and draggooning methods."

An adjournment of more than a month, from June 30 to August 5, did not abate the fury of the prosecutions. While the court was in recess, court officials forced the confessions of two men, Richard and Andrew Carrier, tying them "neck and heels" until "the blood was ready to come out of their noses." A third victim of this torture, William Proctor, refused to admit his guilt even though he was tied "neck and heels till the blood gushed out at his nose." Tying a person "neck and heels" was of dubious legality, though used in both England and New England (and Virginia, where it was legal).

At its August session, the court tried six more defendants and condemned them all, including Reverend George Burroughs, once minister at Salem Village and now serving a parish in Maine. Five of the condemned were hanged on August 19, and only Elizabeth Proctor escaped the gallows. Pregnant, she was able to gain a temporary reprieve until she would deliver her child, on the grounds that her execution would also take the life of an innocent person. (By the time she gave birth, the witch-hunt had ended, and all had been reprieved or released.)

Despite (or perhaps because of) the continued popular frenzy, signs of opposition to the trials and sympathy for the accused began to appear among the general population. When

Burroughs stood before the gallows, his appeal for mercy was so eloquent, and his recital of the Lord's Prayer so dramatic, that the crowd stirred and seemed ready to demand his release. Escapes became more frequent, and letters of support for the defendants arrived steadily. From Salisbury on August 9, magistrate Robert Pike wrote to Jonathan Corwin, his Essex County court colleague now serving on the oyer-and-terminer court, that accepting spectral evidence was succumbing to Satan's trickery. Such a practice, he reported, "do disquiet the country." Later in August, a member of the governor's council in Boston complained to Cotton Mather that spectral evidence was so unreliable that anyone accused on that basis ought to have the right of bail, and anyone convicted by it should be banished rather than executed.

This trend appears only to have emboldened those pushing the prosecutions forward. At the court's sessions on August 9 and 17, fifteen persons were condemned; eight were hanged on August 22. When the court adjourned, it gave no sign of slackening its determination. While in recess, in fact, the court continued to pressure suspects for evidence and confessions. In doing so, it perpetrated what remains the most extraordinary episode of the trials, an event that remains ultimately impossible of definitive explanation. This was the treatment accorded Giles Corey in what is commonly (though incorrectly) described as an execution. Corey, whose wife Martha had been condemned on September 9 and would be executed thirteen days later, was brought before the magistrates and asked to plead guilty or not guilty. He pleaded not guilty, but when asked the routine question of how he wished to be tried (the proper answer being, "By God and this court"), Corey balked.

Why did Corey refuse? It is possible that he wished to preserve his estate from forfeiture: if he was not tried, his estate would descend to his heirs. The estates of others already had been confiscated under the common-law rule, but at least one defendant had made a will, in the hope that New England practice would prevail. Yet another reason may have operated: Corey was quite possibly entering his own

form of protest against the court and its practices. It is unlikely he was protesting his wife's conviction, since he had offered incriminating testimony against her. Whatever his reason, the court followed the normal—though rarely invoked—procedure in such cases, the application of *peine forte et dure,* or strong and hard punishment. On September 18, Corey was placed on the ground, and heavy stones were placed on his chest, literally to press from him the required plea to be tried by the court. Corey never yielded, and survived ever more weight for another day until he died. Reputedly, his last words were "More weight."

The accusations of the Salem Village girls only grew wilder as time went on. Opponents of the trials, such as Nathaniel Saltonstall, found themselves accused. So, too, did prominent individuals on the governor's council. No one was safe from being identified as an instrument of the devil. The girls were being summoned to other villages to identify witches, where, it seemed, any illness might be attributable to witchcraft. When the father of a sick child brought it to Salem for the girls to locate the offending witch, a disgusted Reverend Increase Mather chastised the man and asked "whether there was not a God in Boston, that he should go to the Devil in Salem for advice."

By autumn, popular revulsion against the accusations and the manner of conducting trials finally led opponents to take more assertive action. On October 3, Increase Mather took a more emphatic and insistent public stand against spectral evidence, reading to his ministerial colleagues his statement of "Cases of Conscience Concerning Evil Spirits Personating Men." Although admitting the reality of witchcraft, Mather lashed out at the reliance on spectral evidence, which the devil himself probably was using to send innocent people to the gallows. "It were better that ten suspected witches shall escape," Mather urged, "than that one innocent person should be condemned."

Governor Phips, beset by doubts from the first, acted soon, too, ordering the court adjourned until further advice might be obtained from England. Before an answer could be received, the legislature in late October called for a day of fasting and counsel from the clergy "so that [we] may be led in the right way as to the witchcrafts." Their purpose, only thinly disguised by this request, was, according to Judge Sewall, "that the Court of Oyer and Terminer count themselves thereby dismissed." By then, 141 persons had been arrested and twenty-six convicted; nineteen had died by the gallows, one by pressing, and two of natural causes while in jail.

In January 1693, the properly constituted Superior Court of Judicature replaced the oyer and terminer court and began its own trials—but without spectral evidence. Stoughton continued to preside, although the lack of spectral evidence made convictions difficult. No one, in fact, was convicted upon trial by that court: except for three who confessed, all were acquitted. Phips reprieved the three confessors, as well as five persons convicted by the old court. His clemency outraged Stoughton, whose "passionate anger" revealed his frustrated ambition. Soon, all remaining in jail were freed.

The divided opinion that had existed during the trials continued, although clearly the public had had enough of the trials and wished them over. On the one hand, the judges who served on the oyer and terminer court did not suffer politically: all were elected to the governor's council later in 1693. On the other hand, a wave of remorse ultimately washed over Salem. Judge Sewall publicly repented at church in 1697, and that same year the jurors admitted to having been "under the power of a strong and general delusion." Asking forgiveness, they repented of "bring[ing] upon ourselves and this People of the Lord the guilt of innocent blood." Anne Putnam, major accuser among the girls, recanted the accusations she had made "ignorantly, being deluded by Satan."

Other steps followed. The Salem Town church revoked its excommunication of several of the convicted, and in 1703 the legislature reversed many of the attainders created by the felony convictions (although only for those requesting it). Confusion continued to the end: the legislature voted to reverse the remaining attainders in 1711, but its list was not complete, and several remain technically in effect to this day.

Selected Bibliography

Boyer, Paul, and Stephen Nissenbaum. *Salem Possessed: The Social Origins of Witchcraft*. Cambridge, MA: Harvard University Press, 1974.

Breslaw, E. *Tituba, Reluctant Witch of Salem: Devilish Indians and Puritan Fantasies*. New York: New York University Press, 1996.

Demos, John P. *Entertaining Satan: Witchcraft and the Culture of Early New England*. New York: Oxford University Press, 1982.

Godbeer, R. *The Devil's Dominion: Magic and Religion in Early New England*. Cambridge, Eng.: Cambridge University Press, 1992.

Hoffer, Peter C. *The Salem Witchcraft Trials: A Legal History*. Lawrence, KS: University Press of Kansas, 1997.

Karlsen, Carol F. *The Devil in the Shape of a Woman: Witchcraft in Colonial New England*. New York: Norton, 1987.

Konig, David T. *Law and Society in Puritan Massachusetts: Essex County, 1629–1692*. Chapel Hill, NC: University of North Carolina Press, 1979.

Rosenthal, B. *Salem Story: Reading the Witch Trials of 1692*. Cambridge, Eng.: Cambridge University Press, 1993.

Weisman, Richard. *Witchcraft, Magic, and Religion in Seventeenth-Century Massachusetts*. Amherst, MA: University of Massachusetts Press, 1984.

Pirates Walk the Plank
in Charleston

——◄◦►——

Bonnie S. Ledbetter
Clemson, South Carolina

The King v. Stede Bonnet (1718) [South Carolina colonial court]

◄◦► THE CASE IN BRIEF ◄◦►

Date
October and November 1718

Location
Charleston, South Carolina

Court
Vice-Admiralty (South Carolina colonial)
Court

Principal Participants
Major Stede Bonnet
Judge Nicholas Trott

Significance of the Case
An educated colonial man of wealth
turned pirate, was caught, tried for his
crimes and hanged, marking the beginning
of the end of piracy in America.

In the early years of the eighteenth century, the waters of the Atlantic swarmed with pirates. An estimated 1,700 roved the coast of North America. One of the most unusual pirates was Stede Bonnet, who had abandoned a respectable life in middle age to take up an outlaw career on the high seas. A man of education and wealth who had retired as a major, in the army, he knew nothing of the sea and was a bumbling pirate. Nevertheless, in 1717, in his ship *Revenge*, he plundered ships from New England to South Carolina. In 1718, he formed an alliance with the notorious buccaneer, Edward Thatch, otherwise known as "Blackbeard."

Together, Blackbeard and Bonnet terrorized Charleston, taking hostages from ships and threatening to send their heads to South Carolina governor Robert Johnson if the pirates were not sent supplies. They got their supplies and sailed away after setting the hostages ashore nearly naked.

When word reached Charleston in August that an unidentified pirate was lurking in the Cape Fear region, South Carolina sent two sloops to raid the pirate den. After a nip-and-tuck battle, the victorious South Carolinians were surprised to learn that they had captured the despicable Stede Bonnet. They brought him and his crew back to Charleston for trial before the noted jurist, Nicholas Trott. Judge Trott wrote an account, *The Tryals of Major Stede Bonnet and Other Pirates* (1719), which is the major record of the trials.

Judge Trott immigrated to South Carolina in 1699 and held numerous government posts, some of them simultaneously, which aggravated some prominent South Carolinians. Trott was a versatile man, the first lawyer in South Carolina, a biblical scholar, the codifier of South Carolina laws, and chief justice at the time of the Bonnet trial. In the political struggles between the supporters of the proprietors and those who wanted South Carolina to become a royal colony, Trott, a strong advocate of proprietary interests, came down on the losing side of the debate and after 1719, his influence declined dramatically.

Although Stede Bonnet had escaped by bribing his guards, the trial of his crew began before the vice-admiralty court as scheduled on October 28. Judge Trott delivered the charge to the jury, a learned historical exposition on the laws against piracy. The attorney general conducted the prosecution. The accused had no lawyers, since the South Carolina bar considered it "a base and vile thing to plead for money or reward." In their defense, the prisoners claimed they had been forced into piracy, but Judge Trott cut them off and denounced them from the bench. On November 8, twenty-nine men were hung and then buried in a marsh below the low-water mark.

Bonnet was recaptured on November 6 and stood trial before the vice-admiralty court. Once again, Judge Trott showed no patience with the defendant. He not only condemned Bonnet in this life, but also consigned him "to the lake that burneth with fire and brimstone" in the next.

Bonnet maintained his dignity and composure until Trott sentenced him to hang. Then Bonnet collapsed into a quivering coward who pleaded most pitifully with the governor for mercy. Governor Johnson rejected his pleas and set the date for his execution on November 10. Bonnet was hung and then buried with his men below the waterline.

Shortly before the hangings of Bonnet and his men, the South Carolinians rounded up another group of pirates. In the bloody battle, twenty-four were captured, most of whom were severely wounded. They were hurriedly tried, so they could be executed before they died of their wounds.

The trials of Stede Bonnet and his fellow pirates marked the beginning of the end of piracy in colonial America.

Selected Bibliography

Hughson, Shirley Carter. *The Carolina Pirates and Colonial Commerce, 1670–1740*. New York: Johnson Reprint Corporation, 1973.

Johnson, Herbert A. *South Carolina Legal History*. Spartanburg, SC: Reprint Company, Publishers, 1980.

Rankin, Hugh F. *The Golden Age of Piracy*. New York: Holt, Rinehart and Winston, 1969.

New York on Fire

—◄◦►—

Bonnie S. Ledbetter
Clemson, South Carolina

The King v. John Hughson and Over 150 Residents of New York City (1741)
[New York colonial court]

—◦► THE CASE IN BRIEF ◄◦—

Date
May–August 1741

Location
New York City

Court
New York (colonial) Supreme Court

Principal Participants
John Hughson
Mary Burton
John Ury
Chief Justice James DeLancey
Othello (a slave)

Significance of the Case
Judges also served as examiners of slaves
and others in a racially charged trial
about a conspiracy to burn New York City.

In the spring of 1741, New York City was in turmoil. A series of fires and a string of thefts appeared too numerous to be coincidental. While authorities were investigating the thefts, ten fires broke out over a period of three weeks. The first fire began on March 18 at the governor's house in the fort. The house, chapel, secretary's office, and several other buildings burned to the ground, but the efforts of the citizens passing buckets of water, plus a timely shower, prevented the fire from spreading beyond the fort to the city. A week later, the roof of Captain Warren's house caught fire. The next week, Mr. Van Zandt's warehouse was destroyed. Three days after that, a fire was discovered in Quick's stable. As the people trudged home from that fire, another alarm sounded for a fire at Ben Thomas's house. The next day, a haystack blazed near Joseph Murray's stables, and the following day Sergeant Burns's house burned, Mrs. Hilton's roof caught fire, and Colonel Philipse's storehouse ignited. When the storehouse fire was nearly out, another alarm sounded, and most of the firefighters left to attend to the new fire.

However, one man who remained behind on the roof of Philipse's storehouse saw a black man jump out a window of one of the storehouses and go leaping across several garden fences, evidently in a great hurry to leave the scene. The firefighter cried out, "A negro, a negro!" and quickly a crowd was on the heels of the fleeing man. They chased him to his master's, dragged him out, and carried him off to the jail. His name was Cuffee, and he belonged to Mr. Philipse, whose storehouse burned.

Inspection of the sites revealed evidence that looked suspiciously like arson. By the time a grand jury assembled at the city hall on April 21, many citizens were convinced there was a conspiracy, including the judge who charged the jury to uncover the plot. The grand jury summoned a sixteen-year-old servant girl, Mary Burton, who had hinted to neighbors that she knew of criminal activities at her master's tavern. She appeared extremely frightened and refused to be sworn or give evidence. Neither threats of punishment nor promises of rewards moved her to reveal anything, but being led to jail caused her to change her mind quickly. Now she told the grand jury she would talk about the stolen goods, but would not answer questions about the fires. Nothing could have intrigued the grand jury more, and they began to pressure her to tell everything or risk having to answer on the day of judgment for "a most damnable sin." Reluctantly, she agreed.

Mary Burton claimed that her master, John Hughson, illegally entertained slaves at his tavern near the New York waterfront, and that he received stolen goods. In fact, two slaves, Prince and Caesar, had recently brought him items related to the investigation. Moreover, Mary said Hughson presided over meetings of slaves at his tavern, where he encouraged the slaves to set their masters' houses on fire and to kill the white people while they extinguished the fires. After killing the masters, she claimed, the slaves planned to take the white women for themselves, while Hughson would become king. Mary also implicated Cuffee, along with Caesar and Prince, as ringleaders of this plot. She accused Hughson's wife, Sarah, and an

Irish prostitute, Peggy Kerry, who lived at Hughson's, of being in on the conspiracy. The grand jury was "astonished" and "amazed" at the revelation that white people would stoop to such villainous activities, but two days later their surprise diminished, because they maintained that blacks were not capable of such a design on their own. Peggy Kerry and the Hughsons were arrested and jailed.

The grand jury met on April 23 with two of the three judges of the New York Supreme Court who would hear the cases, Judges Frederick Philipse and Daniel Horsmanden. Chief Justice James DeLancey was occupied with other business, but joined the deliberations in July. Leading lawyers were invited to advise the judges and grand jury. There was general agreement that they should move swiftly and secretly.

An interesting aspect of the legal procedures in these cases was that the judges were the chief examiners of the accused and the witnesses, and the chief recorders of their depositions. Philipse and Horsmanden began their investigation by going to the jail to question Peggy Kerry. Despite hints of a pardon, or at least mercy, Peggy denied any knowledge of the fires.

On April 24, Caesar and Prince, and Mr. and Mrs. Hughson and Peggy were indicted and arraigned. They all pleaded not guilty. On May 1, Prince and Caesar were tried on two counts of theft. The prisoners had no legal counsel, and their defense consisted of protests of innocence. Prince and Caesar were found guilty, and a week later were sentenced to hang. "They died very stubbornly" on May 11, denying their guilt to the end. Caesar's body was left hanging in chains in a prominent location.

While Peggy Kerry and the Hughsons, now joined in jail by their daughter Sarah, waited for their trial, an opportunistic prisoner, Arthur Price, charged with stealing from his master, told one of the jailers that Peggy Kerry and young Sarah Hughson had confided their guilt to him in jail. Price was brought before a judge, who took his testimony. Price was so skillful in pumping information out of the inmates that the judges ordered him put in the same cell as Cuffee, the slave who had fled from the fire at the Philipse storehouse, and allotted "a tankard of punch now and then, in order to cheer up their spirits, and make them more sociable."

Price said Cuffee told him that Quack, a slave of John Roosevelt, had set the fire at the governor's house. Quack was arrested and tried with Cuffee. At the trial, witnesses said that Quack's wife was a cook at the governor's house, but that the governor had forbidden Quack ever to come into the fort. Thus, on one occasion when a sentry refused to let him enter, Quack attempted to push past the sentry. However, he was clubbed with a gun and thrown out of the fort. Two other slaves testified that Quack set the fire and that Cuffee had vowed to burn his master's storehouse. The owners of both Quack and Cuffee spoke in defense of their slaves, saying they were not out of their sight at the times the fires were supposedly set, but their words carried little weight with the jurors. Quack and Cuffee were found guilty and ordered burned at the stake the next day, May 30.

The terrified convicts were led to the stakes where the authorities attempted one last time to extract confessions from them. With hints of reprieve, the interrogators told Cuffee that Quack had confessed and vice versa, which prompted them both to confess. The officials considered postponing the executions until the governor could be consulted, but the sheriff declared he could not move the prisoners through the crowd, which was in a dangerously ugly mood, so the executions proceeded.

In their confessions, Quack and Cuffee confirmed the guilt of several other accused slaves and named seven more. All were arrested before the day was over. The judges tried to examine each of the accused, but each one implicated more supposed conspirators until there were so many that the two judges could not keep up, but required assistance from several of the king's counselors to write down the testimony. Ultimately, more than 150 people were arrested. Not even Chief Justice DeLancey's Othello was exempt from accusation. Othello, who was well known in New York, was considered to have "more sense than the common rank of negroes." His master "took a great deal of pains with him, endeavoring to persuade him to confess," but Othello stubbornly in-

sisted he knew nothing of any plot. Nevertheless, he was jailed "some time before any evidence came to light," apparently because he was a leader among blacks.

On June 10, the governor issued a proclamation offering a pardon to anyone, white or black, who would confess by July 1. There was a wholesale rush to confess. This saved some from execution, but not Othello. The recorder noted that Othello's confession was "neither voluntary nor free," but that he had behaved "with a great deal of composure and decency, with an air of sincerity which very much affected the recorder." Othello confessed to almost nothing, and when the judges decided that there should be no special consideration for him just because he belonged to the chief justice, he was sentenced to hang. With nothing to lose, he retracted the little he had admitted.

After the central characters—John Hughson; his wife, Sarah; and Peggy Kerry—were hung on June 12, attention began to focus on a different factor. England was at war with Spain. Most of the action took place at sea, and the previous year a captured Spanish vessel was brought to New York as a prize. On board were a number of blacks who claimed they were free men, but nevertheless they were sold to citizens of New York. About half a dozen of these Spanish Negroes were among those accused of being accomplices in the plot to burn New York. Depositions began to mention that the conspirators were waiting for the Spanish and the French to attack the city, at which time the blacks were to put the plot into action.

In this web of fear and suspicion, a schoolmaster named John Ury, or Jury, had the misfortune to become entangled. A newcomer to New York, he knew Latin and liked to take part in discussions about religion, which promoted the idea that he was a Roman Catholic priest in disguise. He was arrested, and Mary Burton immediately recognized him as one of the leaders who attempted to influence the blacks to kill their masters. Numerous blacks also testified that he led them in mysterious ceremonies.

Ury's defense was significantly undermined by the arrival of a letter from General James Ogelthorpe of Georgia alerting authorities to watch out for Spanish agents operating under the cover of physicians, dancing masters, and the like. Ury defended himself very feebly, and subsequently he was sentenced to hang. In his final words at the gallows, he maintained his innocence, forgave his accusers, and exhorted them to confess their "horrid wickedness."

Ury was the last victim to die in the frenzy surrounding the conspiracy to burn New York City. Between May 11 and August 29, 1741, thirteen blacks were burned at the stake and sixteen blacks and four whites were hung, while over seventy blacks and seven whites were transported to foreign countries. Mary Burton collected a reward and disappeared from history.

There were people at the time who questioned the validity of the charges. Judge Daniel Horsmanden, a participant in the interrogations and trials, found it incredible that anyone could doubt the existence of a conspiracy. To demonstrate what he considered the overwhelming evidence, he collected the records of the trials and compiled the eyewitness accounts in a book. Ironically, generations that followed have used Horsmanden's work to condemn his conclusions.

From today's perspective, it is difficult to judge the extent of a conspiracy, if there was one. It is not difficult to believe that slaves might want to burn their masters' property and might talk about a combined effort to burn the city. If there was such talk, the record indicates the plot was not well planned. There was no definite timetable. There were no specific tasks assigned, other than that each slave was to set fire to his own master's house. The fires that broke out were scattered on various days, which was not an effective method for burning the whole city. There was no real plan for what to do if the plot was successful.

On the other hand, the record does show that at least some innocent people suffered horrible deaths as sacrifices to the fears of the white citizens. Even Judge Horsmanden was "moved to compassion" by the pleas of Othello and others, but their sincerity worked against them. The judges thought it illustrated how crafty slaves could be.

The black conspiracy to burn New York does demonstrate that a judicial process can go awry under pressures of fear and prejudice. Judging by their standards, not twentieth-century standards, there were flaws in the procedure. The preponderance of the testimony came from a single witness, Mary Burton, whom even the judges described as having "a warm hasty spirit" and "a remarkable glibness of tongue." To give so much weight to the words of such a young and dubious witness raised questions then—and raises them now.

A second white witness, Arthur Price, was a felon and a planted informer. The testimony of slaves was not accepted under colonial law, but, in this case, the confessions of slaves were used against all of the accused. Suspects were jailed on suspicion without evidence. Liquor was used to loosen tongues. The accused were "prompted" to help them "remember" their part in the plot. Promises of mercy were given to encourage confessions, and after the confessions were made, the promises were discarded. As this case makes obvious, grave injustices can occur in the name of justice.

Selected Bibliography

Headley, Joel Tyler. *The Great Riots of New York: 1712–1873*. New York: Bobbs-Merrill, 1970.

Hoey, Edwin. "Terror in New York—1741." *American Heritage* 25 (June 1974): 72–77.

Horsmanden, Daniel. *The New York Conspiracy*. Boston: Beacon, 1971.

The Writs of Assistance Cases

———◀◉▶———

David Thomas Konig

Department of History
Washington University, St. Louis

Petition of Lechmere (1761) [Massachusetts colonial court]

◀◉▶ THE CASE IN BRIEF ◀◉▶

Date
1761

Location
Boston, Massachusetts Bay Colony

Court
Massachusetts (colonial) Superior Court

Principal Participants
Chief Justice Thomas Hutchinson
James Otis Jr.
Okenbridge Tacher

Significance of the Case
Customs officials' power to seize evidence at will were challenged in an effort to restrain Parliament's authority over colonial law: a struggle noted as one of the earliest expressions of American constitutional thought.

On September 10, 1760, Chief Justice Stephen Sewall of the Massachusetts Superior Court of Judicature died in Boston. A little more than a month later, King George II died in London. Individually, each death left a gap—Sewall's as chief magistrate, George's as monarch of the world's greatest empire. Together, however, they produced a crisis in Massachusetts politics and provided the setting for a legal struggle that yielded one of the earliest expressions of an American formulation of constitutional thought. John Adams was doubtless exaggerating when, in 1817, he looked back on the episode and said, "Then and there the child Independence was born"; but he did not err in identifying it as a landmark on the route toward Revolution.

Sewall's death produced a dilemma for Governor Francis Bernard. In office for only five weeks since his arrival in the province, Bernard learned that his predecessor, William Shirley, had promised to appoint Col. James Otis Sr. to the next opening on the province's highest court. An ambitious politician from the small Cape Cod town of Barnstable, Otis had been

22

spurned in his attempt to gain election to the Governor's Council in 1757 and only reluctantly had returned to the colonial legislature. Now that a Superior Court vacancy appeared—and the chief justiceship, at that—Otis looked to achieve the capstone of his political career.

Governor Bernard had misgivings about honoring Shirley's pledge, however. As governor, his salary depended in part on moneys collected in the process of justice. By statute, he received a third of all moneys collected from forfeitures of smuggled goods. Moreover, Otis's son James Jr.—no less ambitious a politician—was serving as advocate-general of the Vice-Admiralty Court, where forfeitures were supposed to be handled. Eager to cultivate the support of Boston's mercantile community, young Otis was notoriously diffident in prosecuting forfeiture cases, and Bernard was justifiably suspicious of the problems Otis might create for his personal finances and political success.

The new governor, therefore, made what he believed to be the safest choice possible when he overlooked the elder Otis and turned instead to Thomas Hutchinson. Scion of one of the province's oldest families, Hutchinson was as different from his ancestor Anne—of Antinomian fame—as anyone in Massachusetts. A man who once described himself as "a quietist, being convinced that what is, is best," Hutchinson was viewed by Bernard as "much prudenter man than I ever pretended to be." Reliably pro-British in mercantile matters and a stalwart upholder of the status quo, he had risen to the provincial lieutenant-governorship and was considered a leader in the Governor's Council, the upper house of the legislature. The loyal Hutchinson thus stood as a sturdy political foundation upon which Bernard might build a prosperous and successful governorship.

Instead, the Hutchinson appointment was the rock upon which his administration foundered. Holding multiple posts was legal, but Hutchinson's occupying such powerful and lucrative posts as these—executive, legislative, and now judicial—was certain to arouse resentment in patronage-conscious Boston, where he already had the reputation of belonging to a clique that included a brother-in-law as province secretary. Such accumulation of offices spurred the antigovernment faction to protest. Young Otis resigned from his Vice-Admiralty position even before Hutchinson took office as chief justice on December 30, 1760.

Only three days earlier, news of George II's death had reached Boston. Amid the mourning for a king who had ruled for more than three decades and the celebration for the succession of a young and vigorous King George III, a normally routine matter was ignored. Writs—the formal, written warrants that ran in the name of the monarch—had validity only during the life of the monarch whose name had legitimized them, and for six months thereafter. All writs in George's name, therefore, would shortly have to be reissued.

Ironically, the writ that would set James Otis Jr. against Thomas Hutchinson was not a very common writ. In fact, the Superior Court had issued them to only eight men in Massachusetts between 1755 and 1760. This was the customs writ of assistance, a warrant that authorized a customs official to command a local constable or justice of the peace, during daytime, to assist him in entering "any house, shop, cellar, warehouse or room or other place, and in case of resistance to break open doors, chests, trunks and other packages, there to seize, and from thence to bring, any kind of goods or merchandize whatsoever, prohibited and uncustomed." For this reason, the writ was also known as a "writ of assistants."

This authority was vital to customs enforcement in a seaport where the illegal importation of goods was a mainstay of mercantile success. By the Staple Act of 1663, nearly anything shipped to the colonies from the European continent, India, or the East had to pass through Great Britain, there to pay a tax and be retransported to North America. Boston traders detested this law as an infringement on their rights and a drain on their profits, and they evaded it through every species of subterfuge imaginable.

They also fought the Staple Act legally. One stratagem was to remove forfeiture cases from the Vice-Admiralty Court, which used no jury and relied on civil law principles, to the Superior Court, where common law procedural guarantees obtained and where sympathetic local jurors would acquit them. This required a writ of prohibition from Superior Court judges, taking the case to their jurisdiction. By the 1750s judges on the Superior Court were less willing to grant writs of prohibition, and other techniques were needed.

Would-be evaders of the Staple Act might also hide their goods once on shore and move them as soon as a customs officer applied for a search warrant. Aware of this ploy, customs officers retaliated with a writ that enabled them to search likely hiding places—a writ of assistance. This writ, as authorized by the Act of Frauds of 1662 and extended to the colonies by another Act of Frauds in 1696, had the potent advantage of being a *general* writ: as issued in Massachusetts by the governor, it did not have to specify place or the precise nature of the goods. Always ready, it enabled swift application and bolstered customs enforcement greatly.

But the writ, when issued by the governor, violated the law: by statute, it was to be issued by the Court of Exchequer, not ex officio by the governor. Ironically, it was Thomas Hutchinson who pointed this out to his friend Governor Shirley in 1755; unknowingly, he had taken upon himself a thorny problem. In Massachusetts there was no exchequer court, and the Superior Court was the only forum comparably close to serve in that capacity for this purpose. Some question existed as to whether it was close enough in jurisdiction to serve the exchequer purpose of issuing a writ of assistance, and in the 1754 case of *McNeal v. Brideoak* the Superior Court had refused to exercise exchequer jurisdiction. But in that case, it was the *chancery* side of exchequer that was declined, not the common law side pertaining to writs of assistance. The issue of the Superior Court's authority to issue a writ of assistance, therefore, was still not settled when, in 1761, Boston port officials applied to the Superior Court for a new writ of assistance under the name of King George III. The chief justice to whom they addressed their request was, of course, Thomas Hutchinson.

The need for new writs quickly attracted the attention and talents of partisans on both sides.

On the Crown's side, no less a personage than the surveyor-general of His Majesty's customs for the Northern District of America, Thomas Lechmere, took over for the port officers in petitioning for the writs; opposing him, a group of merchants led by Thomas Greene challenged the request. Arguing for the former was Jeremiah Gridley, perhaps Boston's most eminent attorney and a teacher of many leaders of the Boston bar; opposing him were his former student James Otis Jr., and Oxenbridge Thacher (possibly he, too, had been a Gridley student).

Gridley and Thacher drew the issue neatly on the question of the Superior Court's exchequer jurisdiction. To the former, such authority rested securely on statute: Parliament had conferred such power on the Exchequer, and by a province statute of 1699 the Superior Court had been given exchequer jurisdiction. Thacher denied any exchequer jurisdiction in Massachusetts by referring to the 1754 *Brideoak* case and pointing out other differences between the provincial court and Exchequer. No court in Massachusetts, he argued, possessed the authority to issue writs of assistance.

Their arguments, though properly to the point, are now forgotten, buried by the fallout from Otis's pyrotechnics. As described by John Adams in 1817, "Otis was a flame of fire! With the promptitude of Clasical [sic] Allusions, a depth of Research, a rapid Summary of Historical Events and dates, a profusion of legal Authorities, a prophetic glare of his eyes into futurity, and a rapid Torrent of impetuous Eloquence, he hurried away all before him; American Independence was then and there born. . . . Then and there was the first scene of the first Act of Opposition to the arbitrary Claims of Great Britain. Then and there the child Independence was born." There is, of course, some reason to question this distant recollection: Adams was writing to William Tudor, then at work on a biography of Otis, and he was trying to supply Tudor with information that would elevate a Massachusetts patriot over those of the Virginian Patrick Henry, whose biography was also then in progress.

That motivation aside, Adams was correct in singling out Otis for having set forth a vital Revolutionary principle. Rather than addressing the statutes or the common law for that matter, Otis had chosen to rest his case on a "higher law" argument. General writs were unconstitutional simply because they violated "the fundamental Principles of Law." Special writs, issued on probable cause for a specific location on sworn application, were legal as a matter of state necessity, but the general writs could not be so justified. "A Man, who is quiet, is as secure in his House, as a Prince in his Castle," said Otis, who maintained that general writs were an arbitrary exercise of state power that permitted wanton abuses by unrestrained officers who did not even have to account for their actions by returning the writ to the issuing court for examination and trial. Statutory empowerment did not matter. In the most controversial statement of the case, Otis attacked the writs and the authority of the legislature that had created them: "An Act against the Constitution is void: and if an Act of Parliament should be made, in the very Words of this Petition, it would be void. The executive Courts must pass such Acts into disuse."

Otis's argument was as confused as it was radical, for it was not at all clear what he meant by the requirement to "pass such Acts into disuse." He probably meant no more than that principles of statutory interpretation be applied to interpret the law in such a way as to make it consistent with common law procedures. For this he was drawing on the English Lord Coke's decision in the 1610 *Bonham's Case*, in which Coke had written, "When an Act of Parliament is against Common Right and Reason, or repugnant, or impossible to be performed, the Common Law will control it, and adjudge such Act to be Void." Otis, therefore, was attempting to impose a rule of interpretation to limit the power of Parliament by restricting the writ to that of a special, not general, warrant. Although he went further in his 1764 pamphlet, "The Rights of the British Colonies Asserted and Proved," Otis in 1761 was nonetheless making a radical point by invoking a power to restrain Parliament within prescribed constitutional bounds. Unfortunately, by 1761 Coke's view of judicial control of the legislature had been eclipsed by Sir William Blackstone's elevation of Parliamentary omnipotence, which would overwhelm any argument for limitation.

So, too, would English practice. Convinced that the Superior Court did have exchequer jurisdiction, Chief Justice Hutchinson needed to know only if general writs were issued in England. He therefore asked the province agent, William Bollan, for information on English practice and continued the case until an answer arrived. When the Superior Court resumed in November, Bollan's answer settled the question: general writs were, in fact, issued in England. Unanimously, the Superior Court agreed that Lechmere's petition be approved, and that general warrants be issued when requested. When such were requested in 1762, Otis's argument had some effect, however: they were made out to named officers rather than to anyone bearing them.

Otis attempted to keep his constitutional argument—and his political career—alive through pamphlets, but a head injury suffered in a barroom fight with an English officer aggravated a mental instability already beginning to appear, and he steadily withdrew from politics. Hutchinson, later governor of the province, also withdrew from politics prematurely. He came to be seen as a hated symbol of British rule amid the collapse of royal government brought on, or at least hastened, by the ferment that had impelled Otis to oppose general writs of assistance.

Selected Bibliography

Dickinson, Oliver M. "Writs of Assistance as a Cause of the American Revolution." In *The Era of the American Revolution*, ed. Richard B. Morris. New York: Harper & Row, 1965.

Frese, Joseph. "James Otis and Writs of Assistance." *New England Quarterly* 30 (1957): 496–508.

Konig, David Thomas. "The Theory and Practice of Constitutionalism in Pre-Revolutionary Massachusetts: James Otis on the Writs of Assistance," in *Law in a Colonial Society*, ed. John A. Yogis. Toronto, Canada: Carswell, 1984.

Smith, Maurice Henry. *The Writs of Assistance Case.* Berkeley: University of California Press, 1978.

Ubbelohde, Carl. *Vice-Admiralty Courts and the American Revolution.* Chapel Hill: University of North Carolina Press, 1960.

Waters, John J. *The Otis Family in Provincial and Revolutionary Massachusetts*. Chapel Hill: University of North Carolina Press, 1968.

Wroth, L. Kinvin, and Hiller B. Zobel, eds. *The Legal Papers of John Adams*. 3 vols. Cambridge, MA: Harvard University Press, 1965.

The Boston Massacre Trials

—◄◦►—

Harold B. Wohl
Emeritus Professor of History
University of Northern Iowa

Rex v. Preston, Rex v. Weems et al., and *Rex v. Manwaring et al.* (1770)
[Massachusetts colonial court]

◄◦► THE CASE IN BRIEF ◄◦►

Date
October–December, 1770

Location
Boston, Massachusetts Bay Colony

Court
Massachusetts (colonial) Superior Court

Principle Participants
John Adams
Samuel Quincy
Captain Thomas Preston
Samuel Adams and the Sons of Liberty

Significance of the Case
A British officer and five soldiers were tried for shooting a colonist who taunted them, and a subsequent brawl ensued resulting in five resident's deaths, and in the fueling of a local and national independence movement.

While no single riot by itself can make a revolution, people taking to the streets in the years after 1763 played an important part in the coming of the American Revolution. In almost every instance, the anger of the crowd was directed against British policy and the people who served it. One incident in particular sent shock waves through the colonies, fanning the flames of anti-British sentiment. It was the climax of a season of violence.

In early 1770 British troops had been quartered in Boston for more than a year. Traditionally Boston had no British garrison, and many townspeople resented their presence and demanded their removal. On Monday evening, March 5, in the square before the Custom House, a mob of toughs armed with clubs began taunting Private Hugh White, who was on duty in the sentry box, and began hurling icicles and chunks of ice at him. Pushed to the breaking point by this goading, the soldier struck one of his tormentors with his musket. Soon a crowd of fifty or sixty gathered around the frightened soldier, prompting him to call for help. The officer of the day, Capt. Thomas

Preston, and seven British soldiers hurried to the Custom House to protect the sentry.

Upon arriving at the Custom House, Captain Preston must have sensed the precariousness of his position. The crowd had swelled to several hundred, some anxious for a fight, others simply curiosity seekers. Still others had been called from their homes by the town's church bells, a traditional signal that a fire had broken out. Efforts by Preston and others to calm the crowd proved useless. And because the crowd had enveloped Preston and his men as it had the lone sentry, escape was nearly impossible. The riotous crowd began striking at the troops with sticks and stones and finally knocked Private Hugh Montgomery down. He rose to his feet and fired into the crowd. Others fired too, and when the smoke had cleared, five people lay dead or dying and eight more were wounded. Preston and his men quickly returned to their barracks, where they were placed under house arrest. They were later taken to jail and charged with murder. The cause of resistance now had its first martyrs.

Provocative encounters between British soldiers and civilians were a common source of irritation and the cause of an increasing number of incidents around town. This was the first time, however, that soldiers had killed civilians. Those killed were Crispus Attucks (an Indian or mulatto seaman in his forties, who also went by the name of Michael Johnson), James Caldwell (a sailor), Patrick Carr (an immigrant from Ireland who worked as a leather breeches maker), Samuel Gray (a rope maker), and Samuel Maverick (a seventeen-year-old apprentice). Anti-British "Patriots" in Boston promptly referred to the killings as "the Boston Massacre." Col. William Dalrymple, the English commander, preferred to call it a "scuffle."

The morning after the fatal shooting on King Street, John Adams was retained to defend Captain Preston. Adams did not know that it was the acting governor, Thomas Hutchinson, who had recommended him to Preston, along with another young patriot lawyer, Josiah Quincy. Although Hutchinson was a leading Tory figure, he apparently believed Adams was the best lawyer for so important a case. Adams detested both the Boston mob and the sight of

British troops on Boston Common. But he firmly believed in the right of an accused person with his life at stake to have the counsel of his choice. It was Adams's and Quincy's devotion to the law that led them to put the cause of justice above their politics and join the defense team, which also included the Tory attorney, Richard Auchmuty.

Apparently Samuel Adams and the leading Sons of Liberty also influenced the selection of the defense team. They signaled their approval of their young friends' acceptance of the assignment. Despite the political benefits the patriots derived from the massacre, they had, in the past, supported orderly demonstrations and expressed distaste for uncontrolled mobs, of which the Boston Massacre was a prime example. Confident that local jurors would return a verdict of guilty, they were willing to let the military have the best available lawyers. That way no one could later claim the proceedings were unfair or make martyrs of the soldiers. The patriots failed to consider the possibility of an acquittal.

Samuel Quincy, Josiah's elder brother and a Tory, was appointed one of the Crown's prosecutors. However, fearing that the Tory leanings of the prosecutor might soften the prosecution, the selectmen of Boston engaged Robert Treat Paine, John Adams's longtime rival at the bar, as a kind of special prosecutor to represent the families of the murdered and to assist the king's attorney.

Meanwhile, as John Adams and the Quincy brothers were preparing their respective cases, publicity about the deaths of March 5 soon enshrined the "massacre" in Whig legend. The patriot leaders of Boston used the episode as proof to other colonists that their earlier reports of oppression by the troops were not exaggerated. The *Boston Gazette*'s account of the "massacre," complete with black border and featuring four coffins, circulated through the colonies and was widely copied. Within weeks all the colonies knew that "the streets of Boston have already been bathed with the BLOOD of innocent Americans! Shed by the execrable Hands of the diabolical Tools of Tyrants!" Pamphleteers whipped up the townspeople by writing incendiary newspaper articles as well as letters

A painting by Paul Revere (1735–1818) showing the Boston Massacre. Five people were killed after British troops opened fire into a crowd. *Hulton Getty Collection/Archive Photos.*

and pamphlets portraying the victims as martyrs and memorializing them in extravagant terms. In one eulogy, Joseph Warren of the Sons of Liberty addressed the dead men's widows and children, dramatically re-creating the gruesome scene in King Street. "Behold thy murdered husband, gasping on the ground . . . take heed, ye orphan babes, lest whilst your streaming eyes are fixed upon the ghastly corpse, your feet slide on the stones bespattered with your father's brains." To propagandists like Warren it mattered little that the five civilians had been bachelors!

For the great majority of colonists the description of the massacre in the Boston newspapers was reinforced by Paul Revere's famous engraving of the scene. Inaccurate in many details but dramatic in its overall effect, the engraving was a masterful piece of propaganda. Appropriately splattered with blood, it became an instant best-seller. In Revere's representation, Preston, with his sword drawn, seems to be ordering the soldiers to fire on peaceful, unarmed, well-dressed men and women. The Custom House has been labeled Butcher's Hall, and smoke drifts up from a gun barrel sticking out of a second-floor window. In subsequent editions, the blood spurting from the dying Americans became more conspicuous. To the propagandists, what actually happened mattered little. Their job was to inflame emotions; they performed their work well.

The grand jury indicted Preston and his men in five separate indictments of murder and, for good measure, had indicted four Customs employees, accused of firing out of a window of the Custom House. Samuel Adams and the Sons of Liberty preferred that the trial begin promptly, while memories were fresh and emotion ran high. But the trials of Captain Preston and the soldiers were postponed until the fall session of the Superior Court to allow time for the preparation of the defense and to permit the town's passions to cool. It was not until September, six months after the shooting, before Preston and his men were arraigned. Each pleaded not guilty. The court then adjourned, and on October 24, 1770, John Adams rose to defend Captain Preston.

Legally, the Massacre was interesting because of British legal constraints on the military. Everyone knew that the soldiers could not use lethal force against unarmed civilians unless ordered to do so by some civil, not military, authority. Everyone, including the Sons of Liberty, Hutchinson, and General Thomas Gage, commander in chief of all the British troops in North America, agreed that Captain Preston had no orders to fire from a civil magistrate. Yet a soldier, like anyone else, also retained the right of self-defense. Therefore, were the soldiers' lives actually in danger? Did they fire only as a last resort to save their own lives?

As the time for the trial approached, the defense realized it had a possible conflict of interest on its hands. Were Preston to be tried in the same proceeding as the men, mutual finger-pointing might well convince the jury to find all the defendants guilty. If the defense failed to show that the killings were justifiable, then Preston would have to argue that the men fired without his orders. The men, on the other hand, would likely argue that they had only obeyed their officer's command to fire. To avoid this difficulty, the defense moved for separate trials. First they would prove that Preston gave no order to fire. Then they would consider the defense of his troops.

The case of *Rex v. Preston* began at 8:00 A.M. on Wednesday, October 24, 1770. The first item was impaneling the jury. A murder case could not be heard by a judge alone. The Tories feared that the jury would be packed with Sons of Liberty. After nineteen challenges, Preston's lawyers seated a jury of twelve, only two from Boston, and five of Tory persuasion.

Samuel Quincy opened for the Crown and handled the evidence, while John Adams did the same for Preston. Auchmuty and Paine closed for the defense and prosecution, respectively. It was usual practice for the junior counsel to open the case and examine the witnesses with the senior man closing the argument. Josiah Quincy, although active in the pretrial preparations, did not participate in the trial itself.

By the standard of the day the trial was a long one. With a break for the Sabbath, the court was done in six days. The trial of Captain Preston thus became the first criminal trial in Massachusetts history to run more than one day.

Opening the argument against Preston, Quincy set out to establish that even if Preston had not given the order to fire the first shot, he had sufficient time to call "Recover" before the volley began. One witness swore to that. But the testimony soon became as chaotic as the night itself. Adams set out to prove that Preston gave no order to fire. Since the law forbade the accused to take the stand, Preston did not speak in his own defense. His best witness was Richard Palmes, the merchant and Son of Liberty, who said that Preston had been facing him and that he had had his hand on Preston's shoulder when someone shouted "Fire!": it had not come from Preston. Three black witnesses also bolstered Preston's defense. Two slaves, one belonging to a Son of Liberty, and a freeman from the West Indies testified to the provocation of Crispus Attucks and the crowd, who were swinging their sticks at the soldiers. The case went to the jury at 5:00 P.M. on Monday, October 29. The jury took only three hours to reach its verdict: not guilty. The vast weight of the evidence exonerated the captain; the Crown had failed to prove that he ordered his men to shoot. The British officer was quickly packed off to England, where he received a pension of £200 per year from George III "to compensate him for his suffering."

With Preston freed, attention now turned to the trial of the soldiers, which began three weeks later on November 27. Preston's acquittal actually made the soldiers' defense more difficult. Even if Preston had not given the order to fire the first shot, there was no question that shots had been fired and that the soldiers had fired them. That being the case, the soldiers must have fired without orders. If they fired without orders, so the thought ran, they must be murderers and "blood required blood."

Robert Treat Paine and Samuel Quincy again conducted the prosecution; John Adams, Josiah Quincy, and Sampson Salter Blowers were the attorneys for the defense. For some unknown reason, Auchmuty was not retained to defend the soldiers. Adams now stepped into the senior counsel's role, while Josiah Quincy assumed the task of cross-examining the Crown's witnesses and presenting the defense's case. With a touch of irony, Samuel Quincy, a staunch Tory, shaped the argument to help hang the soldiers, whereas his younger brother Josiah, a fiery Whig, attempted to save their lives.

The first move of the defense attorneys was to exercise their peremptory challenges in the selection of the jury. Every man on the jury panel from Boston or its immediate vicinity was struck. The jury that was finally seated consisted of country men who would presumably be less apt to sympathize with the Boston mob or feel pressures to return a guilty verdict.

The prosecution's trial strategy was simple: it need only prove that the defendants had fired their weapons. The burden was on the defense to prove that the provocation the soldiers faced justified the killings. The prosecution paraded a string of witnesses who testified that the crowd was "standing orderly and making no outcry" when the soldiers fired upon them in cold blood. In its turn, the defense produced witnesses who gave a rather different version of the night's events, testifying to the violence of the mob's attack, first against the sentry and then against the file of soldiers. The soldiers' best defense came from beyond the grave. Dr. John Jeffries, who treated Patrick Carr for his wounds until the Irish boy died four days after the shooting, testified that Carr repeatedly told him that the soldiers would have been injured

if they had not fired. Asked by Jeffries if he believed the soldiers had fired in self-defense or purposely to kill civilians, Carr replied: "in self-defense."

It was all hearsay evidence, but when Josiah Quincy put the next question, "Was he apprehensive of his danger?," it became admissible. Massachusetts law permitted unsworn testimony from someone who knew he was dying; presumably no man facing the ultimate judgment would use his last breath to lie. Samuel Adams was heard to remark that since Carr, an Irishman, had probably died a Roman Catholic, Protestant Boston could discount the worth of his last words.

In his summation John Adams blamed the riot on "outside agitators" who invited their own deaths: "a motley rabble of saucy boys, Negroes and mulattoes, Irish teagues and outlandish jack tars. And why should we scruple to call such a set of people a mob . . . unless the name is too respectable for them. The sun is not about to stand still or go out, nor the rivers dry up, because there was a mob in Boston on the fifth of March that attacked a party of soldiers."

Rex v. Weems was an even longer trial than Preston's, lasting from November 27 to December 5: five days were devoted to impaneling and taking testimony, and two and a half days were expended for argument and charges. But the jurors were out for only two and a half hours. Cpl. William Weems and Privates James Hartigan, William McCauley, Hugh White, William Warren, and John Carroll were found not guilty. However, the jury also decided that the soldiers had fired before it was absolutely necessary to their defense. Since Matthew Kilroy and Hugh Montgomery were the two soldiers whom witnesses had actually seen firing, the verdict for them was "not guilty of murder, but guilty of manslaughter." Those two men were held for sentencing and the others were released.

One last trial remained. Edward Manwaring, a Customs officer, and three of his friends were charged with firing from the windows of the Custom House. *Rex v. Manwaring* began on December 12. The case against the four civilians was so thin and so riddled by the testimony of witnesses for the defense that by noon the jurors "acquitted all the Prisoners, without going from their Seats." In fact, the prosecution's principal witness, Manwaring's fourteen-year-old French servant boy, was himself indicted for perjury, convicted, and sentenced to an hour in the pillory and twenty-five lashes at the whipping post.

On December 14, nine days after the *Weems* trial ended, John Adams was back in court to hear Kilroy and Montgomery sentenced. They were asked whether there was a reason they should be spared the death penalty, manslaughter being a capital offense. Each man pleaded "benefit of clergy," a remnant of medieval law that removed those in holy orders from civil jurisdiction. Defendants who could prove they were clergymen might insist on being tried by an ecclesiastical tribunal as the church's punishments were far less severe than those of a secular court. Since the law dated from the time when the clergy were the only literate class, a man could establish his status merely by reading Psalm 51:1. It came to be called "the neck verse." By claiming the benefit the two soldiers would escape the death penalty. They would be branded "by fire on the thumb," the necessary judicial price for ensuring that the life-saving plea could not be claimed a second time. Kilroy and Montgomery held out their hands and Sheriff Greenleaf seared their thumbs. The two prisoners were then released from custody and so nine months after the shooting the Boston Massacre, legally speaking, passed into history.

Those acquainted with the modern courtroom would find the proceedings of these trials quite unusual. Witnesses were not sequestered but remained in open court during the taking of other testimony! Witnesses were also called out of order: for example, Crown witnesses were called in the middle of the defense's case; rebuttal witnesses were called immediately to refute specific segments of testimony. And when addressing the jury, counsel not only argued law but read directly from law books. Today a lawyer's closing speech concentrates exclusively on the facts, leaving the law to be summed up in the judge's charge. Throughout the *Weems* trial there is not even the sign of an

objection to a question, or a motion to strike an answer. Many witnesses apparently took the stand, were asked what they knew of the events on the night in question, then stepped down without being cross-examined.

Popular feeling did not rejoice in the triumph of justice over prejudice. Samuel Adams was so pained by the outcome of the trials that he demagogically retried the case in a series of heated newspaper articles, continuing to call the shootings a massacre and claiming that justice had not been done. But John Adams considered his participation in the defense "one of the most gallant, generous, manly and disinterested Actions of my whole life, and one of the best Pieces of Service I ever rendered my Country." The death sentence, he wrote in 1773, "would have been as foul a Stain upon this Country as the Executions of the Quakers or Witches, anciently. As the evidence was, the Verdict of the Jury was exactly right."

Of all the incidents leading to the American Revolution, many stand out as significant. The Boston Massacre is one such event. But its singular importance must not be overblown. After all, the redcoats were exonerated. The verdict was, in John Adams's words, "exactly right." And the colonists and the mother country did not finally resort to arms until five years after this dramatic event. By that time, only an inflated and inflamed rhetoric kept the incident from being forgotten.

Yet the Massacre, taken together with other events, did help to shape the popular attitude that the British were heartless tyrants who terrorized a peaceful citizenry. As a symbol of British oppression, it bolstered what their political theory told them—that a standing army was the greatest danger a people's liberty could face. For the next thirteen years Bostonians would gather each March 5 to commemorate the event. Only when the Peace of Paris in 1783 brought the final guarantee of American independence would they begin celebrating July 4 instead.

The site of the Boston Massacre is now on a traffic island in the midst of the city's financial district. Every day thousands of Bostonians and tourists stand on this historic spot waiting for the traffic to abate.

Selected Bibliography

Bailyn, Bernard. *The Ordeal of Thomas Hutchinson.* Cambridge, MA: Harvard University Press, 1974.

Butterfield, Lyman H., ed. *Diary and Autobiography of John Adams.* 4 vols. Cambridge, MA: Harvard University Press, 1961.

Countryman, Edward. *The American Revolution.* New York: Hill and Wang, 1985.

Maier, Pauline. *From Resistance to Revolution.* New York: Knopf, 1972.

Middlekauff, Robert. *The Glorious Cause.* New York: Oxford University Press, 1982.

Smith, Page. *John Adams.* 2 vols. Garden City, NY: Doubleday, 1962.

Wroth, L. Kinvin, and Hiller B. Zobel, eds. *Legal Papers of John Adams.* 3 vols. Cambridge, MA: Harvard University Press, 1965.

Zobel, Hiller B. *The Boston Massacre.* New York: Norton, 1970.

Treason and the Whiskey "Insurrection"

——◄◦►——

Mary K. Bonsteel Tachau

Deceased Professor of History
University of Louisville

United States v. Mitchell, 2 Dallas 348 (1795) and *United States v. Vigol*, 2 Dallas 346 (1795)
[U.S. Circuit Court of Appeals]

◄◦► THE CASE IN BRIEF ◄◦►

Date
May 1795

Location
Philadelphia, Pennsylvania

Court
U.S. Circuit Court of Appeals

Principal Participants
George Washington
Alexander Hamilton
Philip Vogol
John Mitchell
Associate Justice William Patterson

Significance of the Case
Farmers opposed to the whiskey tax resorted to violence and were convicted of treason; the first case prosecuted under a constitutional definition of treason that has never been overruled.

Philip Vigol and John Mitchell were the first to be tried and convicted of treason after the Constitution, with its new and narrow definition of that crime, had been adopted. Their trials set a precedent that led soon after to the convictions of John Fries. Yet it is clear that none of these men had been engaged in "levying War against them [the United States] or in adhering to their Enemies, giving them Aid and Comfort," as those words are commonly understood.

Vigol and Mitchell were among the thousands of trans-Appalachian farmer-distillers who strongly opposed the whiskey tax of 1791 because they considered it oppressive and, as it was not uniformly applicable throughout the nation, unconstitutional. Secretary of the Treasury Alexander Hamilton, who had devised the excise, adamantly refused to make substantive changes in the law or to advocate its repeal. When three years of largely peaceful protests punctuated by occasional intimidation of excise officers proved unsuccessful, western Pennsylvanians turned to violence in July 1794. They harassed the United States marshal, robbed the mail, and burned the estate of the revenue inspector, a wealthy Federalist slave owner who had been a general during the Revolutionary War. Until the moderates took control about two weeks later, bands of angry farmers roamed the countryside, frightening those they suspected might cooperate in carrying out the law.

Alarmed, the administration of President George Washington decided to use force to end the violence and gain compliance. U.S. Supreme Court Associate Justice James Wilson provided a statement that the laws were opposed and their execution obstructed "by Combinations too powerful to be suppressed by the ordinary Course of judicial Proceedings, or by the powers vested in the Marshal." Judicial proceedings had not been tried, nor the powers of the marshal tested, but the declaration gave the president authority to call out the militia under the Militia Act of 1792. The administration delayed until receiving the report of three appointed commissioners, who were surprisingly successful in obtaining 12,950 troops from four states.

Henry Lee was the nominal commander of the militia army, but Washington and Hamilton rode at its head as it proceeded westward in late September. The officers were generously wined, dined, and housed along the way, and farmers waved at the troops. No resistance was encountered; the only indications that the procession was not welcome were a dozen liberty poles and a few taunts in taverns. The president left the army at Bedford to return to Philadelphia for the opening of Congress, where he reported that an insurrection had been suppressed.

A month later, Hamilton reported the arrest of 150 men who were charged with treason—although in No. 84 of *The Federalist*, he himself had defended the Constitution against critics who wanted a bill of rights by emphasizing the protections already contained in the document. Among those provisions, he specifically named its narrow definition of treason. As he knew, the Framers had intentionally adopted a stringent version of the fourteenth-century English Statute of Treasons, keenly aware of the abuses that had resulted in England from "constructive treason" (broadly construing what constituted treasonous acts).

The prisoners were marched three hundred miles to Philadelphia in bitter winter weather and jailed pending trial. However, in April 1795, grand jurors returned only forty-eight indictments: one for assault and battery, two for unspecified felonies, fourteen for misdemeanors, and thirty-one for treason. Vigol and Mitchell were in the last group and were given court-appointed attorneys.

Before the cases were tried the following month, William Lewis argued for the insurgents that selection of the jury panel had been illegal under both Pennsylvania and federal law. He claimed that the large number summoned from the eastern counties made it highly unlikely that any of the defendants would have a majority of jurors from his own district on his trial jury. Lewis was overruled by Associate Justice William Paterson and District Judge Richard Peters, who comprised the federal circuit court bench.

Philip Vigol was charged with high treason for levying war against the United States by trying to prevent the execution of the excise law by force. As "one of the most active insurgents," he had joined in attacking two revenue collectors in their homes and requiring them to relinquish their offices. He had also been at Couche's Fort, from which the mob had gone to burn the inspector's estate, and had been among those who harassed the marshal.

Attorneys William Lewis and Moses Levy did not question the law but agreed with the prosecution that the case rested on proof of the overt acts by two witnesses. Justice Paterson ruled that the law arose from evidence and intention. Regarding the former, he said that "the current runs one way"; regarding the latter, that there was not "the slightest possibility of doubt." Lewis and Levy then argued that Vigol had acted under duress and that the indictment was in error regarding the dates of the offenses and the number of participants. Their contention was overruled by Justice Paterson, who instructed the jury that "the crime is proved." Nevertheless, the jury deliberated five hours before reaching its verdict that Vigol was guilty. The court sentenced him to be hanged.

John Mitchell was also charged with high treason for having levied war against the United States. He, too, had been at Couche's Fort and, according to one witness, at the attack on the inspector's estate. Moreover, Mitchell had participated in an inflammatory assembly that was said to have threatened Pittsburgh and he had refused—admittedly, while intoxicated—to sign an oath of submission to the laws.

U.S. Attorney General William Bradford and U.S. District Attorney William Rawle asserted that raising a body of men to obtain the repeal of a law by intimidation or violence, or opposing and preventing by force and terror the execution of a law, constituted an act of levying of war. Theirs was a doctrine of "constructive levying of war"; it loosely interpreted the narrow meaning of the words that the framers had so consciously adopted only eight years earlier.

Defense counsel Edward Tilghman and Joseph Thomas protested that interpretation of the constitutional language. They contended that while using violence or intimidation to compel Congress to repeal a law might be treasonous, the crimes with which Mitchell was charged were of far less magnitude—at most, arson or misdemeanor. Finally, they asserted that Mitchell's notorious drunkenness might mark him as a "bad man," but was not sufficient to maintain a charge of high treason.

Bradford and Rawle countered that if the defense attorneys' arguments prevailed, Vigol should have been acquitted and all the prisoners in jail released. Further, they said, if the insurgents' illegal conduct was *intended* to force Congress to repeal the whiskey tax, the excise *would* be suppressed throughout the Union, thus accomplishing the purpose of levying war against the United States.

However strained the prosecution's arguments seem today, they carried weight at the time. Justice Paterson instructed the jury that

Mitchell "must be pronounced guilty," and the jury complied. Mitchell, too, was sentenced to be hanged.

After all the arrests, indictments, and a dozen trials, only Mitchell and Vigol were convicted of high treason. Nothing in the records explains why they were singled out from the thousands who had opposed the whiskey tax. Neither owned a still, and both were described as "simple." Soon after their convictions, President Washington received petitions and memorials pleading for mercy. Washington pardoned them in June, and a month later, he pardoned all of the other "insurgents" as well.

Mitchell's and Vigol's trials are nonetheless significant in American constitutional and legal history because of the prosecution's success in establishing the doctrine of constructive levying of war. That precedent was followed in the treason trials of John Fries and Aaron Burr. Only Chief Justice John Marshall's insistence upon a strict interpretation of the standard of proof required by the Constitution has obscured the fact that the doctrine has never been overruled. The existence of a "whiskey insurrection" has become an accepted fact, although there never was an organized resistance that made war or threatened the government—and even sending an army to western Pennsylvania did not achieve compliance with the law.

Selected Bibliography

Boyd, Steven R., ed. *The Whiskey Rebellion: Past and Present Perspectives*. Westport, CT: Greenwood, 1985.

Slaughter, Thomas P. *The Whiskey Rebellion: Frontier Epilogue to the American Revolution*. New York: Oxford University Press, 1986.

Tachau, Mary K. Bonsteel. "George Washington and the Reputation of Edmund Randolph." *Journal of American History* 73 (June 1986): 15–34.

Defective Indictment

—◄◦►—

Yasuhide Kawashima

Department of History
University of Texas at El Paso

The State v. John Owen, 5 N.C. 452 (1810) [North Carolina Supreme Court]

◄◦► THE CASE IN BRIEF ◄◦►

Date
1810

Location
North Carolina

Court
North Carolina Supreme Court

Principal Participants
Attorney General Oliver Fitts
Five court justices
John Owen

Significance of the Case
The case established a precedent establishing individuals' rights to be fully informed of charges against them and shows the importance of a legal technicality in a state case prosecuting a violent crime.

On the night of April 21, 1809, in the city of Raleigh, North Carolina, John Owen, a cabinetmaker of the county of Wake, struck one Patrick Conway with a pine stick, causing several wounds, from which Conway died instantly. The superior court of law for the county of Wake tried the case, and the jury found the defendant guilty of murder as charged in the bill of indictment prepared by Oliver Fitts, North Carolina attorney general.

The defendant appealed to the North Carolina Supreme Court for a ruling on whether sentence of death could be pronounced against him on the bill of indictment. Seawall, the defendant's counsel, challenged the validity of the indictment, arguing that (1) the stroke that caused the mortal wounds was only laid by implication and (2) the indictment did not mention the length and depth of the mortal wounds.

The attorney for the state rejected the notion of implication. He argued that the words *then and there* indicated the time and place of the assault, and the same words following the word *giving* indicated that the mortal wounds occurred at the time and place of the assault and striking. He interpreted, therefore, that the first allegation of assaulting and striking was carried on throughout the sentence.

The state also maintained that the only reason given for describing the dimensions of the wound was so the court might understand that the wound was mortal. Where it was impossible to describe the wound, the description was dispensed with. There were exceptions, but bruises were not mentioned as one of them. Yet, it was held to be unnecessary to describe such wounds. The state insisted that wounds inflicted with sticks were very different from those caused by axes and swords but were very similar to bruises, and therefore, the description of these wounds might not be necessary.

The state supreme court that heard the appeal in 1810 consisted of five judges. The judges were unanimous in their opinion that the first exception taken to the indictment could not be supported. Judge Taylor, who delivered the opinion of the court, explained that the indictment contained a direct allegation of a stroke. Also, all the sentences were connected together by the words *and then and there*, so that, in all these respects, it carried the criminal charge forward from one sentence to another. Further repetition might have obscured but could not have illustrated the charge, the judge stated, nor could it have brought the indictment nearer to the most approved precedents.

In regard to the second exception, the judges were divided. Three judges (Henderson, Lowrie, and Hall) maintained that the exception was fatal to the indictment and that sentence of death could not be pronounced against the prisoner. Judge Henderson had some doubt about the propriety of requiring the dimensions of a wound charged to be mortal in an indictment, but he could find no authority for a death charged in an indictment to be produced by a wound, the dimensions of which were omitted. It was not for the court to determine why this description was required, he reasoned, but it was enough to know that the law required it.

Judge Lowrie added that it was probable that Conway had died due to the strokes stated to have been given, but the dimensions of the wounds, being required, could not be dispensed with. All the exceptions to this rule, he pointed out, were cases where the wound could not be described, such as where a limb is cut off or the body run through. Judge Hall examined the position of English common law on this issue at the time it was adopted by the United States. He found that whenever death was said to be produced by a wound, the dimensions of the wound had to be given. Thus, it could not now be dispensed with.

The two dissenting judges (Taylor and Locke), on the other hand, concluded that wherever death was caused by a cut with a sword, dagger, or other edged instrument, it was necessary to state the dimensions of the wound. However, when death was due to a wound with a club, cudgel, or stick, it was sufficient to state the wound without the dimensions. They therefore asserted that the exception to the indictment could not be sustained.

By a narrow majority of the court (3 to 2), the indictment was judged to be insufficient, and the prisoner was remanded to jail to answer the same charge once a new bill of indictment was prepared. *The State v. John Owen* clearly set forth the rule that when death is caused by a wound, an indictment for murder should contain a clear description of the wound's length, breadth, and depth. The omission of such description is fatal to the indictment.

This case established an important precedent in guaranteeing the right of individuals to be fully informed of the charges against them. The court concluded that the "want of the requisite precession and certainty" in the indictment, which might at one time "postpone or ward off the punishment of guilt," might at another time "present itself as the last hope and only asylum of persecuted innocence."

Selected Bibliography

"Ninth Annual Survey of North Carolina Case Law." *North Carolina Law Review* 40 (1961–1962): 482–602.
"Thompson v. Loyal Protective Ass'n." *Northwestern Reporter* 132 (August 4–November 24, 1911): 554–558.

A Double Standard of Justice: Is Adultery by a Wife Worse Than Murder by Her Husband?

———◁◦▷———

Marie E. Windell

Special Collections
University of New Orleans

John François Cortes v. Maria Emilie de Russy (1843) [Louisiana state court]

◁◦▷ THE CASE IN BRIEF ◁◦▷

Date
October 1843

Location
Alexandria, Louisiana

Court
Louisiana Supreme Court

Principal Participants
Judge Henry Adams Bullard
John François Cortes
Marie Emily de Russy

Significance of the Case
A divorce case with accusations of an illegitimate birth, challenges to duels, wife abuse, attempted abortion, suicide, and premeditated murder; the judge's rulings on limitation of divorce actions, reconciliation, and payment of costs were cited in later Louisiana cases.

Between 1843 and 1934 this suit for divorce was hidden behind the cryptic initials, "J.F.C. v. M.E." in the *Louisiana Reports*, because the antebellum court reporter considered it too scandalous for normal reporting. The case file contains incriminating letters in a drama filled with accusations of an illegitimate birth, challenges to duels, wife abuse, attempted abortion, suicide, and premeditated murder.

This was the only case cited in its category (and still by initials) in the centennial edition of the *American Digest*. In 1934 two Louisiana attorneys, without benefit of the original documents, identified the litigants but contradicted the record. An accurate and complete history can now be determined from the early manuscript appeals of the Louisiana Supreme Court.

This marital tragedy arose in northwestern Louisiana, at Natchitoches, an eighteenth-century frontier outpost that in the 1840s was an important shipping point on the route to Texas and Mexico. The testimony not only illuminates the position of women on the frontier and the social problems of violence and divorce, but also gives insight into the workings of the antebellum Louisiana Supreme Court.

A double standard of justice for husbands and wives had usually been defined for adultery alone: wives received harsh treatment, and husbands, forgiveness, for essentially the same offense. According to the Louisiana law (1827) permitting divorce, a single act of adultery by a wife was sufficient grounds for the husband to sue for divorce, but the wife could stake her claim on the same grounds only if her husband kept a mistress in their home, or openly and publicly elsewhere. By the law of 1832, flight from an infamous offense was added as grounds, but in this case Cortes's attorneys argued that his wife's adultery barred her plea on the grounds of murder committed by her husband. Which of the two spouses had the morally superior position, and thus the stronger claim for divorce?

The suit was brought in March 1842, in the Natchitoches District Court for the husband, J.F.C., after he had murdered his wife's alleged lover and had fled the state to join the army of Mexico, which was then at war with the Republic of Texas. In 1843 the Louisiana Supreme Court granted a divorce and custody of their small child to the husband, on the grounds of his wife's adultery.

In 1934 two Louisiana attorneys published the diary of a Natchitoches lawyer, William Long Tuomey, who referred to the 1842 murder of the alleged lover, James M. Giles. In an explanatory note, the editors correctly identified the couple, but denied any adultery on the mistaken assumption that Judge Henry Adams Bullard, writing for the Supreme Court, had cleared the wife and had given her the divorce.

Out of the original manuscript file of the case, heard in the Supreme Court session in Alexandria in 1843, arise several figures preoccupied with honor, control, or endurance, surrounded by a crowd of witnesses. It is remarkable that these manuscript pages survived the Civil War, for the legal archives of the Western District were moved about during the war, in part by federal troops, and were even shipped to Washington, D.C., before their return to the Court a generation later.

Nachitoches was composed of French-speaking Catholics and an increasing number of English-speaking Protestants when John François Cortes and Marie Emilie de Russy were married in 1834. Cortes, then in his early twenties, was the eldest son of a well-to-do merchant and former mayor, who had died while the son was a minor. His father's partner had warned about their armed customers: on the frontier, he wrote, "Might makes right."

Emilie de Russy was the daughter of Major Louis G. de Russy, of the U.S. Army, who was a Whig candidate in 1838 for the Louisiana State Senate. He later served in the Mexican War and was a noted colonel of engineers in the Confederate forces. Fort de Russy on the Red River was named for him.

Cortes, a steamboat agent, land speculator, and later director of a local steamboat company, had mutual interests with his father-in-law in Fort Jesup, twenty-five miles to the west. In 1839 Cortes had accompanied Major de Russy, a second in the most famous duel in the Western District. Eleven men were killed before the chain of honor ran its course in the affair between Gen. Pierre E. Bossier and François Gaiennie. Cortes himself boasted in 1841 that he had received and accepted challenges to three duels in a single day.

Throughout the seven years of marriage, Cortes drank heavily, abused his wife, and was consumed by bouts of jealousy, followed by moments of remorse, a typical pattern in twentieth-century research on violent husbands trying to maintain supremacy in a marriage. At times he was affectionate; at others, so abusive, even in her father's presence, that her uncle once ordered Cortes out of the house.

One of the strongest antebellum controls over married women was the social stigma of divorce. Mrs. Cortes had "long meditated a separation from the plaintiff because of his outrageous conduct," but she hesitated to take "so harsh a step." Had she been able to steel herself to petition for a separation or divorce, she had sufficient grounds based on cruel treatment. For example, in 1837 Cortes threatened his wife with a pistol "if she did not immediately go to bed," and on another occasion she was rescued from being strangled by him while in bed.

Also, when they were boarding in a New Orleans hotel, according to a witness in the next room, he dragged her around on the bedroom floor. About two years after the marriage, he pretended to take poison to create the false impression among their friends that she had driven him to this step. In 1838, in New Orleans, he threw her out of their hotel room into the public hallway after midnight, like a prostitute. A witness, James Waddell, heard her pleas but was restrained by his own wife's caution. Members of Cortes's circle, even his father-in-law, rarely opposed him.

Cortes justified his abuse and violence by allegations of his wife's adultery. Around 1840 he accused an acquaintance of improper intercourse with her, but afterward admitted his error and apologized. In 1840 or 1841 his jealousy centered on a young bachelor attorney and neighbor of Mrs. Cortes's aunt, James M. Giles, who lent books to her and her friends in an informal reading circle. Always suspicious, Cortes arranged another scheme to "injure his wife in the good opinion of the public." He invited Giles to accompany his wife to the theater, pretending that his own business interfered. However, after all were seated, Cortes arrived and by "scowling looks" indicated that he was displeased with Giles's attention to his wife.

Cortes, whose emotional problems were compounded by financial embarrassments, was frequently a defendant in lawsuits over debt. His wife often mediated for him with her friends to extricate him from difficulties. Such frustrating episodes must have threatened him with a further loss of control, despite her patience, mildness, and ladylike qualities that his own witnesses praised.

Her one defiant act described in the testimony took place in 1838, while she was caring for a dying child. When her husband demanded that she leave the child's bedside and come to bed with him (cursing the child—"I wish it was in Hell"), Mrs. Cortes refused.

Following the deaths of her mother and the child, Mrs. Cortes chose passive resistance by a visit to relatives in Texas in 1838, the year of her father's political campaign. Although Major de Russy had never seen his daughter "guilty of light conduct," he gave way to Cortes's insistence that he write a letter urging her to return and adapt more closely to the "Disposition" of her husband.

The direct cause of their separation in March 1841 was a ridiculous scene: Mrs. Cortes refused to permit her husband, who was drunk, to carry her across a muddy street to a ball. After she escaped for protection to her father's house, Cortes vowed to "crush her and her whole family." Was he jealous of the attorneys and judges who regularly visited the major at Grande Ecore on the bluff? Cortes refused to acknowledge in writing, as his father-in-law recommended, that his accusations had been groundless. He tore away their young son, Edward, and confronted the major in a liquor store, pushing and threatening him.

Suddenly Cortes changed his conduct, remained sober, expressed the deepest penitence, and promised to reform. Acceding to pleas by his friends, his wife returned to town in September, to live with her aunt, the wife of the deputy clerk of the court, Thomas P. Jones. Against her better judgment, she rejoined her husband in October, with the understanding that she would leave permanently if mistreated.

Almost immediately Cortes abandoned his changed conduct, became abusive, and whispered suspicions to his friends that she was unfaithful. In December he deliberately provoked a quarrel with Giles, but was caught in the toils of his own plot. Giles threatened to publish their correspondence, and was able to extract an abject apology from him. Cortes, humiliated and knowing that his wife, then pregnant, was planning a permanent separation, vowed their utter ruin.

On the night of February 10, 1842, the Cortes family and two slaves, Emma and Emmeline, were at home. A twenty-foot passage lay between their house and that of their neighbors, the Fearings, who also let a room to one John D. Martin. The Fearing household usually retired around 10 P.M.; the Cortes, not until midnight.

That evening Giles and Benjamin Valcour Cortes, a brother of John Cortes and also the sheriff, sat drinking in the coffeehouse-tavern of Patrick Shelly. Giles, the last customer, drank alone and left between midnight and 1 A.M., apparently intoxicated.

A little past midnight, Fearing and Martin were awakened by loud talking next door. Shortly after, John Cortes walked down the alley and forced open the shutter of his dining room window, which was opposite Martin's bedroom window. Swearing and hitting the sash to open it, he broke the glass, went back inside, and loud talking resumed in the Cortes house. The slave Emmeline knocked on Fearing's window and said her master had sent her for a candle. For about an hour the Fearing and Martin men watched Cortes walking back and forth in the front room.

Around 1 A.M. a knocking at the front door of the Cortes house was followed by Cortes's voice "in a passion" in French, which the two neighbors did not understand. Apparently the racket was the noisy arrival of Giles, although the two witnesses heard only Cortes, who continued to talk loudly until nearly daybreak, keeping them awake the balance of the night. According to Mrs. Cortes, Giles had come at the invitation of her husband to end the quarrel, but had arrived intoxicated. Cortes shouted for arms and various people, and declared that he had caught his wife and Giles in bed together, which both denied. Giles left, forgetting his hat, cane, and cloak.

Cortes twice sent Emmeline for his brother, but the sheriff refused both requests because he thought it was one of the "Plaintiff's foolish quarrels with his wife," one of his "foolish frolics." In the meantime, according to Mrs. Cortes, her husband, while awaiting his brother, placed a cloak and pillow wrapped in a lady's shawl on the dining room floor—in order, she said, to give color to the accusations he had been making against her. A candle, candlestick, and cane lay nearby. A man's hat sat on the pillow. A piece of cloth hung from a nail at the broken window.

Around 4 A.M. Emmeline awakened the jailer, Edward Brenan, and brought him to the house. Cortes showed him the stage set in the dining room and asked him to put the slave Emma in jail and to bring his brother.

The sheriff found his pregnant sister-in-law, wan and passive, in a black dress, in mourning for her mother-in-law. Cortes walked up and down, charging that a lady (her aunt?) had been the cause of her "ruin in this Town." Like many abused and helpless wives, she claimed that "no one was to blame but herself." This attempt to maintain self-respect was interpreted by the sheriff, and later by the Supreme Court, as an admission of guilt.

When she had somewhat recovered, Mrs. Cortes insisted to her brother-in-law that (though appearances were against her), she was not guilty. In cross examination on this conversation, he admitted that his brother was a jealous man and that Mrs. Cortes's conduct ever since her marriage until this occurrence had always been proper and unexceptionable.

Shortly after, Cortes wrote letter no. 3 to his wife: "I must see you, alone . . . it is to *save you* if I *can*, *Compatibly with my honour* . . . no one shall ever Know it." What violence was he contemplating? Was he implying an abortion to save his "honour"? His wife declined this interview also.

Major de Russy proposed that the two brothers and their friends agree to a future separation for the couple. For this, Mrs. Cortes would return to her husband until the scandal died down; she would give up her son to Cortes's sister, and write a letter of apology to her husband.

Four years earlier Major de Russy had written a letter to appeal to his son-in-law. He now composed her apology, which she copied and signed as her own. Although it was letter no. 4, it was labeled "A" as if in anticipation of Hawthorne's *Scarlet Letter*: "I find the evidences [circumstantial evidence] against me such as must crush me, my child, my friends." Cortes's avowed goal against his wife had been achieved, and at great cost to her future suit.

Although his efforts had not crushed Giles or his friends, Cortes's erratic behavior frightened them, and the attorney left town. In his absence, Cortes alternated between threats against Giles and denials of an attack upon him, ending with a "sacred promise" in early March to his brother and their friends. Giles, reassured, returned to Natchitoches but never appeared in public again.

A few days later, on the afternoon of Sunday, March 13, around 4 P.M., Cortes entered the rooms of Giles and his partner, John E. Rothrock, where they were at dinner, and shot and killed Giles in cold blood. Afterward he calmly walked down the street; "no one pursued of course."

Convinced that his wife would never return, Cortes brought suit for divorce in the Natchitoches District Court, but was persuaded by his friends to flee to Mexico; and his attorneys filed for him. He was defended by seven attorneys from leading local firms. Mrs. Cortes, who had only ten days to file an answer, apparently was unprepared for the suit. After two weeks Judge James G. Campbell, a friend of her father, issued a judgment by default. When it was set aside, her ten days had stretched into five weeks.

Her answer summarized the cruel treatment she had received, but the reconciliation had invalidated all her prior evidence on those grounds. She claimed an immediate divorce according to the law of 1832, without the usual delay of two years. Mrs. Cortes also asked for custody of Edward during this suit; a court order for her clothes, "which are withheld from her"; and an allowance for support, because she had "no income whatever." Judge Campbell continued the case until the November term of 1842, at Natchitoches, to permit her to collect testimony in and outside the state.

In the meantime, Mrs. Cortes and Mrs. Samuel Kathrens left by steamboat to visit relatives in Kentucky. En route, on June 1, Mrs. Cortes fell from the hurricane deck; a healthy male child was born that evening. Apparently it was stillborn, for no witness saw it longer than five minutes. Jumping overboard from steamboats was a common method of suicide at the time, but her leap seems rather to have been an attempt to bring about a premature birth. Or was Mrs. Cortes trying to make the birth seem premature when it actually was close to term (i.e., conceived in September, when she was living with her aunt in Natchitoches)? According to Louisiana law, without proof to the contrary, the husband was the father of a child born in a marriage.

During the November term, the plaintiff, the defendant, and her witnesses all were out of the state. Major de Russy, representing his daughter, had located Cortes in Mexico City only two weeks earlier. He hoped to have the suit dismissed because the plaintiff was now a resident of a foreign country, and to receive a continuance to collect testimony that was vital to her case.

The District Judge for this term was not the major's friend, James G. Campbell, but George R. King, a former district attorney who was soon to join the Court of Errors and Appeals in Criminal Matters. He would not grant a continuance, and reproached the absent defendant for not having used "even ordinary diligence" to procure witnesses or their testimony by commissions. Without the deposition by Cortes, his wife was left without corroboration of her version of the events, and her defense suffered a fatal weakness during the appeal.

The major question before the District Court was the alleged adultery on February 10–11 and, as a corollary, the legitimacy of the stillborn infant. Cortes's attorneys interpreted her passivity that night as evidence of her guilt, not the exhaustion of a pregnant woman after an all-night vigil. Her statement on blame and the copy of her father's letter, "A," written to secure Cortes's agreement to a separation, were interpreted by them as her admission of adultery. In order to prove infidelity, they also dated the reconciliation two weeks later than did her counsel.

Her attorney's defense rested on the arguments that Martin's and Fearing's testimony proved that no adultery had taken place on the night of February 10–11, and that the birth was premature. The evidence of four physicians supported her claim: none of them believed that Mrs. Kathrens could determine the age of the newborn "in the dark, wrapped up in a blanket, and for only five minutes."

Judge King instructed the jury to find for a separation from bed and board if not for divorce. An immediate divorce could be granted only on the grounds of flight from justice or proven adultery. The jury, following King's charge, found in favor of a separation and custody for Mrs. Cortes. Having lost the suit, her husband was ordered to pay the costs.

At the same term Cortes was also a defendant in a case over the bankruptcy of his steamboat company. Unless he won the divorce suit on appeal, his seven attorneys might not be paid. In fact, when he died in Mexico in 1846, his debts in Louisiana exceeded his estate.

During the trial one juror, Elijah Clark, out of court and against explicit judicial instructions, told witnesses there was insufficient evidence for adultery. Unfortunately for Mrs. Cortes, the comments of the loquacious juror provided her husband's attorneys with a ground for appeal. The appeal was heard in the Louisiana Supreme Court during the October term of 1843, in Alexandria. Cortes's lawyers had to counter his crime and overturn the verdict for Mrs. Cortes. Felix Sherburne, a native of France, argued that adultery was a criminal offense under French law, a primary source for Louisiana civil law. He thereby neatly juxtaposed the husband's crime of murder and the wife's alleged adultery, although the latter was not a criminal offense in the state.

Her attorneys, now four, marshaled a convincing argument, supporting her good conduct by witnesses, among them her brother-in-law and the doctors, all sustaining her point of view. Giles, a longtime friend of the deputy clerk, had lived with his partner Rothrock, opposite the Jones household. Rothrock had once seen Giles and Mrs. Cortes in the Jones's sitting room at twilight without a candle, but never in "Circumstances to excite the suspicion of anything wrong." One attorney suggested that Giles had come to visit the slave Emma, who had been (inexplicably) jailed the next morning by Cortes, a jealous man. Judge King's ruling had prevented Mrs. Cortes from acquiring a deposition from her husband, and the two slaves present that night were not eligible witnesses. But as a final authority, her attorneys quoted the *Digest* of Bullard and Curry on infamous crime as grounds for divorce.

Judge Henry Adams Bullard—the Bullard who coedited the *Digest*—was a handsome man, noted for his melodious speaking voice and his gift for languages. He had attracted the attention of the learned Reverend Timothy Flint in his travels, and he would become the first professor of civil law in the United States. As a young attorney from Massachusetts, he had participated in 1813 in a disastrous border

raid from Natchitoches for Texas independence, and was one of a few officers to escape the Mexican army ambush of his men. Bullard's pride was easily injured even before the Texas fiasco, and after he retired from the Louisiana Supreme Court in 1846 and went into politics, his temper and self-esteem were the butt of newspaper ridicule.

Since 1839 Judge Bullard had been involved in a long and acrimonious divorce trial. His wife accused the judge of adultery with a young neighbor who shared his taste for German Romantic poetry. He won a separation on the grounds of public defamation, and his wife's appeal was then before the Court in 1843. Was Bullard more willing to believe in adultery by Mrs. Cortes and Giles in their reading circle because of his own experience? Furthermore, his brother Charles had been a fellow defendant with Cortes in a lawsuit.

Contrary to his usual practice, Bullard annotated the Cortes case file with phrases that show he was convinced of her adultery. He misread the testimony on their life after the reconciliation: "there is no evidence that the parties lived unhappily, or that the husband was guilty of any cruelty or outrage." It was not the duty of the Court, he said, "to give any analysis of the evidence," and then discarded the jury's verdict. Bullard refused to believe that Cortes, whose letters were filled with references to his honor, could stoop to dishonorable stratagems. All the circumstances, remarked Bullard, "repel such a charge," despite the pattern of Cortes's schemes to humiliate his wife. The judge's preoccupation with honor surfaces in his description of the murder as "unmanly."

Bullard was also offended by the use of his *Digest* on behalf of a woman who, he was convinced, had been surprised by her husband "in his own house, in flagranti delicto" with her paramour. Speaking for the Court, he granted a divorce and child custody to Cortes, then a captain in the Mexican army, and ordered his wife to pay the costs in both courts.

The judge had not only ignored Louisiana jurisprudence that required adultery to be proved and that a spouse's admission was not sufficient proof, but also had denied the evidence of cruelty against Mrs. Cortes after the reconciliation. His rulings on limitation of divorce actions, reconciliation, and the payment of costs were cited in later Louisiana cases, and they carried this suit into the federal *American Digest* as the classic case of denial of divorce to a wife whose husband had murdered her paramour.

Selected Bibliography

Bonquois, Dora J. "The Career of Henry Adams Bullard, Louisiana Jurist, Legislator, and Educator." *Louisiana Historical Quarterly* 23 (October 1940): 999–1106.

Cortes, John François, v. Marie Emilie de Russy, Alexandria, 1843. ["*J.F.C. v. M.E.*" Original case file in Supreme Court of Louisiana Collection of Legal Archives. Archives & Manuscripts/Special Collections, University of New Orleans.]

Tuomey, William Long. "A Young Lawyer of Natchitoches of 1836; the Diary of William S. Toumey [sic]." *Louisiana Historical Quarterly* 17 (January, 1934): 64–79; (April 1934): 315–326.

Death for Grand Larceny

———◄◦►———

Gordon Morris Bakken

Department of History
California State University, Fullerton

People of the State of California v. George Tanner, 2 Cal. 257 (1852)
[California Supreme Court]

◄◦► THE CASE IN BRIEF ◄◦►

Date
 April–July 1852

Location
 California

Court
 California Supreme Court

Principal Participants
 George Tanner, defendant
 California Chief Justice Hugh C. Murray

Significance of the Case
 The rough-and-tumble environment of the California gold rush set the stage for capital punishment for grand larceny and for the court-upheld exclusion of a juror opposing the death penalty from serving on a capital case.

The gold rush in California, by creating instant wealth and instant cities, provided lawmakers with the challenge of crime in the streets and vigilance committees operating in place of legitimate authority. As part of the legislative effort to stem popular justice and bring statutory law in accord with the culturally accepted penalties for certain crimes, the California legislature provided in 1851 for the death penalty for grand larceny. George Tanner became the first to appeal his death sentence under this statute.

The 1851 statute amended the 1850 penal code by giving the jury discretion in robbery cases of either setting prison sentences from one to ten years or sentencing the robber to death. Grand larceny received the same treatment. Petit larceny—stealing property worth less than fifty dollars—had the penalty of "imprisonment in the County jail not more than six months, or . . . fine not exceeding five hundred dollars, or . . . any number of lashes not exceeding fifty upon the bare back, or . . . such fine or imprisonment and lashes in the discretion of the jury." The legislature put into formal law what the people had been putting into action in the rough-and-tumble environment of the gold fields.

The narrow legal issue in the *Tanner* case involved a juror's declaration against the death penalty. The California Supreme Court decided that a juror's declaration of conscientious scruples against the death penalty was sufficient under the current statute to exclude the person from a jury in a grand-larceny case. The accused, George Turner, had stolen fifteen hundred pounds of flour, six sacks of potatoes, five kegs of syrup, two and one-half barrels of meal, one keg of powder, and one-half barrel of mackerel, thus running afoul of the amended 1850 California penal code. The court of sessions jury brought in a verdict of "guilty of grand larceny, punishable with Death." Tenth District Judge Gordon N. Mott upheld the verdict with the death penalty, and Tanner appealed to the California Supreme Court.

Chief Justice Hugh C. Murray delivered the opinion for a unanimous court. The statutory challenge of the judge's order excluding the juror was rejected on statutory interpretation grounds. Legislators had provided that in cases where "the offence charged by [is] punishable with death," a juror would "neither be permitted nor compelled to serve as a juror." Given that the penal statute provided for the death-penalty option, the challenge to the juror and the judge's order excluding the juror from service were sustained.

Beyond the narrow ruling on this important issue of criminal justice administration, the court commented upon the penal statute and public policy. First, Murray wrote that "it was not" the court's "purpose to discuss the policy of the law." Then he went on to do so, criticizing the legislature's actions "in the face of the wisdom and experience of the present day," and to characterize the death penalty for crimes less than murder as "alike disgusting and abhorrent to the common sense of every enlightened people."

Regardless of their personal distaste for such a penalty, the judges recognized that their role was limited. First, the court was to support legislatively defined public policy. This was needed "to correct the administration of the law." Correct administration would, in turn, "secure a due enforcement of the penalties ordained for its violation." Finally, the court was to implement the public-policy declarations of the people through their duly elected representatives. "The law has ordained," Murray wrote, "that this offence shall be punished with death, and to allow jurors to sit upon a trial for larceny who declared that they would not impose this penalty, would defeat the intention of its framers, and practically work a repeal of its provisions." Such a result would be "a mockery to justice." It was the court's duty to prevent "the administration of justice from becoming a mockery." The judicial function was to be supportive of the statements of public policy in law, regardless of personal philosophy.

The *Tanner* case contained several elements common in western criminal cases of the frontier period. The death penalty for property crimes, commonly associated with horse stealing, was broad and part of jury discretion. Justice was often swift. Tanner committed the crime on April 3, 1852, was brought to trial on April 14, lost his appeal in the district court on April 24, won a petition for rehearing before the supreme court on May 24, lost on the hearing on the petition on July 16, and was executed on July 23, 1852. Finally, western appellate opinions often were communicated to the bar and the populace by the media. On May 16, 1852, the *Alta California*, San Francisco's daily newspaper, published the entire text of the supreme court opinion. In the days before advance sheets, and with bound volumes frequently following opinion by many months, western newspapers often informed the people of the developing state of the law.

SELECTED BIBLIOGRAPHY

Bakken, Gordon Morris. "The Influence of the West on the Development of Law." *Journal of the West* 44 (1985): 66–72.

McKanna, Clare V., Jr. *Homicide, Race, and Justice in the American West, 1880–1920.* Tucson, AZ: University of Arizona Press, 1997.

Senkewicz, Robert M. *Vigilantes in Gold Rush San Francisco.* Stanford, CA: Stanford University Press, 1985.

The Constitution: A Law for Rulers
in War and Peace?

—◄○►—

Thomas D. Morris
Emeritus Professor of History
Portland State University

Ex parte Vallandigham, 1 Wallace 243 (1864) and
Ex parte Milligan, 4 Wallace 2 (1866) U.S. Supreme Court

◄○► THE CASE IN BRIEF ◄○►

Dates
1864 and 1866

Location
Washington, D.C.

Court
U.S. Supreme Court

Principal Participants
Lambdin P. Milligan
Justice David Davis
U.S. Representative Clement L.
  Vallandigham
Judge Advocate General Joseph Holt

Significance of the Case
Two cases examining federal conduct of
the Civil War, especially the powers of
the president and military during war,
producing opposite rulings on civil
liberties.

Early in 1866 some suggested that the case involving Lambdin P. Milligan was closed. U.S. Supreme Court Justice David Davis observed that "the presumption is that Milligan was hanged." Davis, however, countered that the Supreme Court would presume him alive because his counsel would not otherwise bother the Court to hear his case. Davis knew full well that Milligan, a strong antiwar Democrat from Indiana, was alive even though he had been condemned to death after a trial by a military commission in Indianapolis in 1864. Indeed, Milligan, who did not die until December of 1899, was a respected lawyer in Huntington, Indiana. The story of another antiwar Democrat, the Negrophobic U.S. congressman from Ohio, Clement L. Vallandigham, who also was tried by a military commission in the North, ended differently. Vallandigham had been ordered confined for the duration of the war, but President Lincoln changed the sentence to banishment into the Confederacy. After the war he tried to revive his influence in the national Democratic Party, but the effort faltered. He then turned to a full-time law practice. He died in June 1871.

The constitutional results of the trials of these two antiwar Democrats ended as differently as did their lives. After his banishment, Vallandigham escaped through the Union blockade. He first went to Canada, and eventually he found his way back to Ohio. He then appealed to the U.S. Supreme Court for a writ of certiorari directed to the judge advocate general, Joseph Holt, to void the proceedings of the military commission and set aside its sentence on the ground that he had committed no crime and that he could not be tried by a military commission. Holt responded that the Court could not exercise jurisdiction to revise the proceedings of a military commission because such a commission did not exercise any judicial power under Article III of the Constitution. It exercised a military power in time of war, and this belonged to the military commander "to the exclusion of the civil authority." This was necessary for the common defense and the safety of the public. Vallandigham's offense, for which he was arrested and tried in the spring of 1863, was an expression of sympathy for the Confederacy and, specifically, for having delivered a speech in which he expressed "disloyal sentiments and opinions" with the intention of "weakening the power of the government in its efforts for the suppression of an unlawful rebellion." As required by the Habeas Corpus Act of 1863, the military informed the federal district court judge that it had arrested Vallandigham and was proceeding with a trial by a military commission. The judge refused to grant a release. His ground was that the military commander alone was competent to determine what was required for security. What followed in the U.S. Supreme Court was anticlimactic, and, given the decision in the *Prize Cases*, likely predictable. The Court was not about to restrict the powers to wage war against the Confederacy during the rebellion itself. Justice James M. Wayne, for the Court, held that a military trial was not a trial under the judicial power of the United States, and the Supreme Court possessed no certiorari or habeas power to review, reverse, or revise the proceedings. Even Chief Justice Roger B. Taney acquiesced, in despair. One view of the case is that Lincoln and others agreed with the notion

of "adequacy" constitutionalism, that is that not all legitimate authority came from the precise words of the Constitution or statutes. Especially during a time of war was this so?

The next time around, in *Ex parte Milligan*, the Court produced one of the "bulwarks of American liberty," a "landmark of constitutional liberty." Among the allegations against Lambdin P. Milligan, and others, was the charge that they were involved in a secret military organization that had as its purpose the overthrow of the government. While the Court overturned Milligan's conviction, Justice David Davis could not forbear comment on Milligan's alleged activities. "Open resistance to the measures deemed necessary to subdue a great rebellion . . . is wicked." Worse, such "resistance becomes an enormous crime when it assumes the form of a secret political organization, armed to oppose the laws, and seeks by stealthy means to introduce the enemies of the country into peaceful communities, there to light the torch of civil war, and thus overthrow the power of the United States." Whether Davis really understood the so-called secret lantern societies with which Milligan was allegedly associated is of little moment. The fact is they were more a fiction born of a "war psychosis" than anything else. They were never large, effective, or even particularly dangerous. For the most part they did nothing whatever.

Authorities, whether out of conviction or political opportunism, moved vigorously against the likes of Milligan. His case was argued by counsel before the Supreme Court in March 1866. The decision was announced on April 3, 1866, but the opinions were not delivered until December 17 of that year. The arguments of counsel helped frame the responses of the justices, and in some respects the arguments echoed those presented in the *Prize Cases*. One of the critical lines of analysis concerned the powers and duties of the president and the military during a time of war.

James Speed, the attorney general, Henry Stanbery, and Benjamin F. Butler appeared for the government. Among the points they made were that a military commission "derives its powers and authority wholly from martial law," and martial law "is the will of the commanding officer . . . expressed in time of war within the limits of his military jurisdiction, as necessity demands and prudence dictates, restrained or enlarged by the orders of his military chief or supreme executive ruler." Moreover, the president had ordered the suspension of the writ of habeas corpus, and this had been ratified in the act of Congress of 1863. But the most expansive points made by counsel for the government were that the powers of the president during the war "must be without limit," and that the Fourth, Fifth, and Sixth Amendments to the Constitution were "peace provisions" that were silenced during war, when "*salus populi suprema est lex!*"

David Dudley Field, counsel for Milligan and brother of Supreme Court justice Stephen Field, hit hard at both of these claims. The critical question, he contended, was whether the president "by his own mere will and judgment of the exigency" could bring any person in the land before military officers for a trial. There was no such power granted in the Constitution, Field argued. There was no "authority beyond or above the law," and the president possessed no "prerogative as representative of the people or as interpreter of the popular will." These, of course, were the same claims made earlier in the *Prize Cases*. The president had no power "without limit." He was charged with enforcing the law of the land, and under no circumstances could he create military commissions for the trial of civilians absent an act of Congress. Moreover, the bill of rights was not silent during the war: the amendments were "passed for a state of war as well as a state of peace."

Justice David Davis wrote for five members of the Court, and Chief Justice Salmon P. Chase wrote a concurrence for the others. The question framed by Davis was whether or not the military commission had the "*jurisdiction, legally to try and sentence*" Milligan. One possible ground would be that jurisdiction derived from martial law, but that claim did not avail in the case before the Court. "Martial law cannot arise from a threatened invasion," in Davis's view. Rather the "necessity must be actual and present; the invasion real, such as effectually closes the courts and deposes the civil administration." Martial law, he concluded, "can never

HON. CLEMENT L. VALLANDIGHAM.

Page 818

Clement L. Vallandigham (1820–1871). *Archive Photos.*

exist where the courts are open, and in the proper and unobstructed exercise of their jurisdiction." Davis's opinion is filled with ringing affirmations of the protections afforded citizens by the Constitution, even in time of war. To the sweeping claim of government counsel that martial law was necessary for the safety of the country, for instance, he responded that if it were the case, "it could be well said that a country, preserved at the sacrifice of all the cardinal principles of liberty, is not worth the cost of preservation." But his most often quoted maxim was that "the Constitution of the United States is a law for rulers and people, equally in war and in peace, and covers with the shield of its protection all classes of men, at all times, and under all circumstances." He then rejected the doctrine, whose results would be "pernicious," that any provisions of the Constitution were suspended during "any of the great exigencies of government." To accept such a doctrine would lead to either anarchy or despotism. Despite these profound affirmations of civil liberties, however, there was something slightly disingenuous about Davis's opinion. He opened it with an admission that during the "wicked Rebellion," the temper of the country precluded a calmness vital to a judicial resolution. Once the war ended and the public safety was secured, he maintained, the issues could be discussed and resolved. This was nearly an admission that during the war itself, "adequacy" constitutionalism necessarily prevailed. But if that were so, all his assertions in favor of violated rights (such as the right to a jury trial) and against martial law have a hollow ring. Nonetheless, the holding was that Lambdin P. Milligan should be discharged on the habeas petition. The military commission in Indiana had had no jurisdiction to try and sentence him.

Chief Justice Chase agreed with the latter two points, but his analysis differed. He focused upon the congressional law on habeas corpus of 1863 and concluded that Milligan's case came within its terms. The Habeas Corpus Act allowed the president to suspend the writ, required lists of prisoners to be sent to the judges, and if a grand jury adjourned without finding an indictment, a prisoner was entitled to be discharged, and, finally, if no list had been supplied, a prisoner would likewise be entitled to a discharge. There had been no list of prisoners supplied, and there had been no grand jury indictment against Milligan. According to Chase, the critical point was that the Habeas Corpus Act was drafted to "secure the trial of all offenses of citizens by civil tribunals" in those states where civil courts were open. For Chief Justice Chase and Justices James M. Wayne, Noah H. Swayne, and Samuel F. Miller that was enough. The real point of disagreement with the majority, however, turned on the power of Congress to authorize trials of civilians by military commissions, even in states like Indiana. Davis's view was that it lacked such power, while Chase held that it possessed it. It was a judgment to be made by Congress whether there was an "imminent public danger" that warranted the use of military trials of civilians.

For security against the abuse of this power, Chase reasoned, one should depend upon the virtue of the people, "on their zeal for public and private liberty, upon official responsibility secured by law," and upon elections. This was an argument that would reappear in the opinion of Justice Robert Jackson during World War II in the *Japanese Internment Cases* and in Justice Felix Frankfurter's concurrence in *United States v. Dennis*, the case affirming the convictions of the top leaders of the Communist Party under the Smith Act. Even though there is a point to the argument, it has proven to be a thin foundation for the protection of civil liberty in the face of the fears and passions of war, hot or cold.

But there was still more at stake in *Milligan* than a libertarian protection of dissent during war. The case must be seen within the context of Reconstruction as much as that of Civil War. Throughout the South during 1865 and 1866 federal authorities used the military to prevent a resurgence of power by conservative Southern whites and to protect blacks and their allies from violence and oppression. Throughout the South, trials were held by military commissions, or in military provost courts, or in the courts of the Freedmen's Bureau, an agency largely run by military personnel. What was the relationship between the *Milligan* opinion and the use of military trials in controlling the South? President Andrew Johnson argued that the opinion prohibited the use of military courts. Justice Davis, in an extensive letter, tried to explain his view of the relationship. There was none, he wrote. There was "not a word said in the opinion about reconstruction & the power is conceded in insurrectionary States." He was particularly stung by charges in Republican newspapers that *Milligan* was a second *Dred Scott* opinion in that it stripped the federal government of the power to protect blacks and carry out an effective reconstruction policy. *Dred Scott*, Davis retorted, "was in the interest of Slavery, & the Milligan opinion in the interest of liberty." But he immediately gave away the game when he added the next sentence: "I did not suppose the Republican party would endorse such trials after the war is over. Yet they do it." Davis was determined to assure the protection of civil liberties (in theory at least) in war, peace, *and* reconstruction. But, as is often the case, there was a price: "Civil liberties" for most Southern whites during the early years of Reconstruction could also mean oppression of blacks.

Selected Bibliography

Fairman, Charles. *History of the Supreme Court of the United States: Reconstruction and Reunion 1864–88 Part One.* [Volume 6 in the Holmes Devise History of the Supreme Court.] New York: Macmillan 1971.

Hyman, Harold M., and William M. Wiecek. *Equal Justice Under Law: Constitutional Development, 1835–1875.* New York: Harper & Row, 1982.

Klement, Frank L. *Dark Lanterns: Secret Political Societies, Conspiracies, and Treason Trials in the Civil War.* Baton Rouge: Louisiana State University Press, 1984.

Swisher, Carl B. *History of the Supreme Court of the United States: The Taney Period, 1836–64.* [Volume 5 in the Holmes Devise History of the Supreme Court.] New York: Macmillan, 1974.

Public Opinion, Expert Testimony, and "The Insanity Dodge"

——◁◦▷——

Elisabeth A. Cawthon
Department of History
University of Texas at Arlington

The United States v. Charles J. Guiteau, 1 Mackey 498 (1882)
[District of Columbia court]

◁◦▷ THE CASE IN BRIEF ◁◦▷

Date
October 1881–January 1882

Location
Washington, D.C.

Court
District of Columbia court

Principal Participants
Charles J. Guiteau, defendant
Judge Walter Cox

Significance of the Case
Controversies remain in cases where responsibility for criminal acts are at stake, specifically, the plea of not guilty by reason of insanity, a case stemming from the trial of Charles J. Guiteau, who assassinated President James A. Garfield in 1881.

In the early 1880s, Charles Julius Guiteau was one of the most widely discussed individuals in the United States and perhaps the world. After shooting President James Garfield, Guiteau became a public figure, much to his delight. As the central character in the resulting murder trial, Guiteau took on even greater significance. Yet even attentive scholars of late-nineteenth-century American politics often fail to appreciate the furor that surrounded Guiteau's trial. Guiteau is remembered best as a disappointed office-seeker, whose killing of the president led to calls for civil-service reform. That historical understanding of Guiteau's modest political impact, however, does not capture his importance in either a contemporary or a long-term sense. Around Guiteau's rather pathetic persona raged several fundamental legal, medical, and ethical controversies—controversies that, over a century later, still pervade trials at which questions of individual responsibility for criminal acts are decided.

The facts surrounding Guiteau's criminal actions were not much in dispute during his trial for the murder of President Garfield. On Saturday, July 2, 1881, in front of several witnesses in a Washington, D.C., railway station, the unexceptional-looking Guiteau had calmly fired two shots at the president, gravely injuring him. When Guiteau tried to leave the station, a district policeman detained him; Guiteau's only comments were that he had shot Garfield and he expected to go to jail as a result. The president lingered for several months before dying, and Guiteau was held in custody during that time. Public interest in Garfield's fate was intense, as was fascination with his background and motivation.

Expressions of some sympathy for Guiteau during the late summer and early fall of 1881 were related to the widespread hope that the president might recover. If Garfield could regain his health, then most commentators thought Guiteau would simply be sent to an insane asylum. That is, many observers postulated that Guiteau must have been insane to have committed such an irrational crime in an unremorseful manner, and he ought to be institutionalized. (This was not the rosiest fate that could befall a defendant in the nineteenth century.) But the climate of opinion altered with Garfield's death. In an effort to make sense of the loss of the president, both Garfield's political allies and moralists with other axes to grind tried to draw lessons from Garfield's death and Guiteau's life. In the wake of Garfield's funeral, Guiteau was cast less as an object of pity than as a villain. Increasingly, Guiteau came off in descriptions in print, in song, and from the pulpit, as a calculating attention-seeker, a legal huckster, a man who had not summoned sufficient moral fiber to rise above an unpromising family history. A brief association by Guiteau's father with the Utopian Oneida Community was widely discussed, for example, as an indication of a hereditary tendency toward depravity.

Guiteau was formally arraigned on October 14, 1881. His trial stretched over two and one-half months in the late fall of 1881, and a guilty verdict was returned after just over an hour's deliberation by the jury on January 5, 1882. The major issue of the trial, in the minds of the American public, was Guiteau's character.

The conduct of the trial, of course, revolved around a more traditional legal question—that of the defendant's state of mind at the time of the assassination. Since it was apparent that Guiteau had pulled the trigger—indeed, he had admitted often and openly that he had meant to kill Garfield—the only substantive question before the jury was whether to accept the argument by Guiteau's counsel that Guiteau had been acting while "legally insane." Guiteau made his lawyers' position rather tricky. He maintained, throughout the trial, that he was technically, or legally insane, because he had acted according to God's will in shooting the president. Yet Guiteau's brother-in-law, whose testimony on the Guiteau family history played a key role in the defense, insisted that the family's reputation should not be unduly sullied through the presenting of evidence that suggested the family's unstable emotional legacy. When Guiteau's lawyers argued that he should be judged not guilty by reason of insanity, they sought, with their case, to make an important clarification in the Anglo-American law on criminal responsibility. Guiteau's trial ultimately became the leading example in the United States in the nineteenth century of the "defense of insanity"—or, as it was popularly known, "the insanity dodge."

The branch of law dealing with the plea of "not guilty by reason of insanity" had been murky, at best, in the United States, ever since a set of standards for insanity, the M'Naghten Rules, had been formulated by a panel of English judges in 1843. After a series of acquittals of defendants in England in the early 1800s, and the resulting furor over courts allowing juries to be "lenient" toward criminals, the M'Naghten Rules created a relatively simple set of standards that judges could state to trial juries to help them assess the state of mind of an accused person. The gist of the M'Naghten "test" for insanity was whether, at the time of the commission of the crime, the accused person knew that what he or she was doing was a crime, and was aware of the practical and legal consequences of his or her actions.

Among legal authorities in England and the United States (where the M'Naghten Rules were widely admired, although not uniformly or universally adopted from state to state), the M'Naghten standard for insanity was regarded as a kind of compromise between two earlier "tests" of criminal responsibility. The M'Naghten test included a requirement that the defendant either had to be acting without reason (as if he or she were a wild beast, incapable of reason), or must have been unaware that what he or she was doing was wrong. Furthermore, when a defendant according to the M'Naghten Rules wished to argue that at the time of the crime he or she did not know right from wrong, he or she also was required to show that the incapacity to distinguish right from wrong resulted from a disease of the mind, rather than from ignorance or mere crankiness. Thus, the M'Naghten Rules almost necessitated the use of medical testimony to illustrate the extent to which defendants were diseased rather than simply misguided shen they committed the acts for which they were on trial. Although the guilty verdict reached in Guiteau's trial settled his case and seemed to indicate some preference in judicial and legal circles for a rather strict (that is, narrow) legal interpretation of insanity, the insanity defense remained quite controversial in the wake of Guiteau's conviction.

The trial of Guiteau served not only as a legal watershed in the adaptation of the M'Naghten Rule to the United States, but also as a forum for the airing of a bitter dispute among several groups of professionals interested in the question of insanity and criminal responsibility. Neurologists, psychiatrists and psychologists, criminologists, and state bureaucrats, all of whom served as "expert witnesses" in the Guiteau case, expressed vital disagreements about the causes of crime, the hereditary bases of insanity, the effectiveness of cures for mental disease, and other issues about which they had been battling within their professional journals for years. Among the most vocal expert witnesses in the Guiteau case were John P. Gray, superintendent of New York State's Utica Asylum and editor of the *American Journal of Insanity*, and Edward Spitzka of the New York Neurological Society. Gray and Spitzka were professional antagonists long before the Gui-

teau case pitted them against one another. In the Guiteau trial, Gray's testimony was vital to the prosecution, and Spitzka lent valuable assistance to the defense.

Gray held to a narrow definition of *insanity*, which was compatible with a strict application of the M'Naghten Rules. He was unwilling to accept the idea of "moral insanity," which was gaining currency among some medical professionals, as a way of understanding social nonconformity that had led to criminal actions. To Gray and a number of his colleagues concerned with the supervision of asylums, true insanity was a recognizable but comparatively rare phenomenon; most individuals who fell outside a "wild beast" test were depraved, sinful, willful, or even momentarily deluded. Some accused persons who claimed to be insane, Gray would have admitted, had come from unfortunate environments, which made it more difficult for them to resist temptation; but he still argued against their being classified for legal purposes as "insane." Gray's examinations of Guiteau were of great weight during the Guiteau trial; the trial itself was an excellent opportunity for Gray to state his views to a wide audience.

On the other side of the debates about the causes of insanity and its prevalence as a disease, were neurologists such as Edward Spitzka. Spitzka, with his grounding in European psychological theory and his respect for the possibilities of anatomical causation, argued during the Guiteau trial for a broader definition of *insanity*, albeit based on his understanding of insanity as primarily hereditary and organic in origin. Thus, the Guiteau trial brought to public attention disagreements—which professionals had been airing among themselves, and which continue to rage—around the roles individual choice, environmental influence, and genetics play in criminal behavior. The debate between neurologists such as Spitzka and asylum superintendents such as Gray, however, was not a simple disagreement over nature versus nurture or environment versus heredity. In a larger sense, conflicts among the experts at Guiteau's trial raised in a public forum the issue of how expert testimony should be integrated into a criminal trial, a subject that had not come fully under legal discussion in the United States until the Guiteau case.

Guiteau's conviction and execution (which was carried out on June 30, 1882) also brought into the realm of legal and public discussion quandaries concerning the impact of public opinion on the conduct of trials. During the trial itself, very few organs of public opinion (from newspapers to popular songs) expressed much sympathy for Guiteau. In fact, public opinion was distinctly hostile, not only to Guiteau, but also to anyone who was perceived as too lenient toward him. Judge Walter Cox, who presided at the trial, had decided that Guiteau's jury ought to be given every opportunity to see the defendant's mental state, so he allowed Guiteau to participate actively in his own defense. That comparative permissiveness caused Cox no end of threatening letters and professional criticism. And when one of Guiteau's regular prison guards, Sergeant William Mason, took a shot at Guiteau, the less respectable Washington newspapers started a subscription for the expenses of Mason's defense. Several editorial commentators took the opportunity to suggest that lynching Guiteau would be in order, noting that Mason had been merely public-spirited.

In the midst of the heated atmosphere surrounding Guiteau's trial, most newspaper columnists, ministers, and even writers for legal and medical journals argued that because the judicial process was being used in a reasonably orderly fashion, American society was committed to the rule of law. In the months and years after Guiteau's death, however, few writers disagreed that public opinion had played a part in Guiteau's conviction and execution. Had Guiteau killed a less important figure, the argument ran, the insanity defense probably would have been accepted. Guiteau's singing of a strange, childlike song in his last moments, more than any of his odd actions, convinced several sober professionals that he should have been declared legally insane at his trial. And some anatomists made much of autopsy findings indicating that Guiteau may have had syphilis—a disease that, in addition to its terrible moral connotations, was known to cause insanity in a recognized physiological sense.

Despite the softening of at least professional opinion on Guiteau's physical condition, however, the view of the insanity defense as a "dodge" for crafty defendants and their cunning lawyers persisted as a cherished belief among Americans. For example, in the 1981 trial of John Hinckley Jr. for the attempted assassination of President Ronald Reagan, a number of parallels to the Guiteau trial could be observed: significant portions of the M'Naghten Rules were still being invoked as appropriate standards for determining the defendant's state of mind; public opinion polls indicated that Hinckley's plea of not guilty by reason of insanity was perceived to be calculating and manipulative of the legal process; indeed, some members of Congress argued for the elimination of the insanity defense in almost all instances; an array of expert witnesses testified for each side in the case, often contradicting one another and leaving the jurors confused. The Hinckley case, although its outcome (incarceration in a mental hospital) was more favorable to the defendant, showed the extent to which the difficult issues raised in the trail of Charles Guiteau have yet to be resolved by the American judicial system.

Selected Bibliography

Caplan, Lincoln. *The Insanity Defense and the Trial of John W. Hinckley, Jr.* Boston: D. R. Godine, 1984.

Clyne, Peter. *Guilty but Insane: Anglo-American Attitudes to Insanity and Criminal Guilt.* London: Nelson, 1973.

Finkel, Norman J. *Insanity on Trial.* New York: Plenum, 1988.

Maeder, Thomas. *Crime and Madness: The Origins and Evolution of the Insanity Defense.* New York: Harper and Row, 1983.

Rosenberg, Charles E. *The Trial of the Assassin Guiteau.* Chicago: University of Chicago Press, 1968.

Simon, Rita James, and David E. Aaronson. *The Insanity Defense: A Critical Assessment of Law and Policy in the Post-Hinckley Era.* New York: Praeger, 1988.

Walker, Nigel. *Crime and Insanity in England.* Edinburgh: Edinburgh University Press, 1968.

1900–1959

The Fruits of the Poisonous Tree

—◄○►—

William Lasser

Department of Political Science
Clemson University

Weeks v. United States, 232 U.S. 383 (1914) [U.S. Supreme Court]

◄○► THE CASE IN BRIEF ◄○►

Date
1914

Location
Washington, D.C.

Court
U.S. Supreme Court

Principal Participants
Justice William R. Day
Fremont Weeks

Significance of the Case
The case established the federal exclusionary rule under the Fourth and Fifth Amendments of the Constitution and banned the use in a criminal trial of illegally seized evidence.

One of the most controversial rules ever laid down by the U.S. Supreme Court is the so-called exclusionary rule, which bans the use in a criminal trial of illegally seized evidence. Although most of the controversy surrounding the rule has been generated in the past forty years, the rule itself dates back to the 1914 case of *Weeks v. United States.*

Weeks was arrested by a U.S. marshal and charged with the transportation of lottery tickets through the U.S. mails. His arrest was based on two searches of his house, the first by local police officials and the second by the federal marshal himself; neither search was authorized by a search warrant. The searches yielded a variety of incriminating papers and articles, including lottery tickets and documents resulting to the lottery. They were seized by the marshal and held for use in Weeks's upcoming criminal trial in the U.S. district court.

At this point, the case took an interesting procedural twist. Before the trial, Weeks brought an action in federal court demanding that his property be returned to him, on the grounds that it had been obtained in violation of the Fourth and Fifth Amendments to the Constitution. If the incriminating material was returned to Weeks, of course, it would effectively eliminate the government's case against him. Weeks's demand for a return of his property eventually reached the U.S. Supreme Court.

Justice William R. Day wrote the opinion of the Court. The meaning of the Fourth Amendment, he began, was made clear by the Court in the 1886 case of *Boyd v. United States*, which involved a suit by the government to take possession of thirty-five cases of plate glass allegedly imported into the United States fraudulently, in violation of federal customs revenue acts. As part of this action, the government requested that E. A. Boyd & Sons be ordered to produce certain papers tending to implicate them in this alleged fraud. Under the federal statute, the Boyd's failure to produce such papers was to be taken by the court as "confessed, unless his failure or refusal to produce" the documents "shall be explained away to the satisfaction of the Court." The Court held that such a rule constituted an illegal search and seizure under the Fourth Amendment and violated the self-incrimination guarantees of the Fifth Amendment. In doing so, the Court held that "constitutional provisions for the security of person and property should be liberally construed. A close and literal construction deprives them of half their efficacy, and leads to gradual depreciation of the right as if it consisted more in sound than in substance. It is the duty of courts to be watchful for the constitutional rights of the citizen, and against any stealthy encroachments thereto."

The specific right guaranteed by the Fourth and Fifth Amendments—which, the *Boyd* court said, "throw great light upon each other"—was the right of the citizen in a free society to be free from "the invasion of his indefeasible right of personal security, personal liberty, and private property, where that right has never been forfeited by his conviction of some public offense." Therefore, the Court said in *Boyd* that the only searches permissible under the Constitution were those "founded on affidavits, and made under warrants which described the thing to be searched for, and the person and

place to be seized." The federal statute authorizing the production of evidence "by a mere service of notice upon the party," the Court concluded, failed to meet that test, and the court below was not permitted to draw incriminating conclusions from Boyd's refusal to produce the material in question.

Under the standards of the Fourth Amendment, as interpreted in *Boyd*, it seemed clear that the seizure of evidence in *Weeks* was unconstitutional. The Supreme Court focused its attention on the second search of Weeks's home—the one by the U.S. marshal. The first search, because it was performed by nonfederal officers, was beyond the reach of the Fourth Amendment, the Court said, because that amendment reaches only "the Federal Government and its agencies." (The Fourth Amendment was not extended to the states until *Mapp v. Ohio* in 1961.) The second search, however, was performed by a federal agent and was clearly unconstitutional. The marshal, the Court concluded, had acted "without authority of process," nor was it clear whether "such could have been legally issued."

The Court's determination that the search of Weeks's house and the seizure of his property were illegal did not resolve the case, however. The Court still needed to act on Weeks's motion that the evidence in question be returned to him. And here the problem facing the Court was trickier, since the Fourth Amendment provides no specific remedy to enforce its guarantees.

Nevertheless, the Court proceeded to decide the case. The Fourth Amendment, wrote Justice Day, "puts the courts of the United States and federal officials, in the exercise of their power and authority, under limitations and restraints as to the exercise of such power and authority, and to forever secure the people, their persons, houses, papers and effects against all unreasonable searches and seizures under the guise of law." The "tendency of those who execute the criminal laws of the country to obtain convictions by means of unlawful seizures and enforced confessions," Day concluded, "should find no sanction in the judgments of the courts which are charged at all times with the support of the Constitution and to which people of all conditions have a right to an appeal for the maintenance of such fundamental rights."

Weeks, therefore, turned on a very specific issue, "the right of the court in a criminal prosecution to retain for the purposes of evidence" the letters and papers illegally taken from Weeks's house. Could the Court, as an agency of the federal government, keep such documents in its possession? "If letters and private documents can thus be seized and held and used in evidence against a citizen accused of an offense," Day answered, "the protection of the Fourth Amendment declaring his right to be secure against such searches and seizures is of no value, and, so far as those thus placed are concerned, might as well be stricken from the Constitution." The evidence in question had to be turned back to the defendant, and therefore could not be used at trial.

In later years, as the exclusionary rule was expanded and modified and as the controversy surrounding it grew, a great deal of attention would be paid to the theoretical justification for this extraordinary remedy. Some justices on the modern Supreme Court believe that the exclusionary rule is simply a means to the end of enforcing the Fourth Amendment through the deterrence of police misconduct. For them, it is derived from, but not a part of, the Fourth Amendment, and it can be discarded in circumstances where it is counterproductive or where other ways of enforcing the amendment exist. Others argue that the exclusionary rule is a part of, and required by, the Fourth Amendment. The remaining justices fall somewhere between these poles.

Scholars have attempted to find support for both positions in the *Weeks* decision. And, in fact, there is language to support both positions in Justice Day's argument. On the one hand, Day declared that the district court's order denying Weeks's application for the return of his possessions was itself "a denial of the constitutional rights of the accused." At other times, however, Day seemed to treat the exclusionary sanction as a means to an end—in other words, as a remedy. "If letters and private documents can thus be seized and held and used in evidence," he wrote, "the protection of the Fourth Amendment . . . is of no value."

It seems clear, however, that Day's opinion leaned toward the view that the Fourth Amendment directly required the suppression of the evidence in the *Weeks* case, at least given the particular circumstances involved. Early on in the opinion, he tipped his hand: "The case in the aspect in which we are dealing with it involves *the right of the court* to retain the letters and correspondence of the accused, seized in his house in his absence and without his authority" [emphasis added]. For a court to "sanction such proceedings," Day concluded, "would be to affirm by judicial decision a manifest neglect if not an open defiance of the prohibitions of the Constitution." The Fourth Amendment, in other words, was directed toward the federal courts as well as to federal law-enforcement officials.

Day's conclusion in *Weeks* was influenced by a number of factors not usually present in modern exclusionary-rule cases. In the first place, he was asked to decide directly on a motion to the federal court to return the papers in question. Thus, the Court was not being asked to impose a rule on law-enforcement officials, but on the judiciary itself. This conclusion was reinforced by the decision in *Boyd*, in which the Supreme Court specifically stated that a court's use of private books and papers produced by compulsion is "the equivalent of a search and seizure" under the Fourth Amendment. "Though the proceeding in question is divested of many of the aggravating incidents of actual search and seizure, yet . . . it contains their substance and essence, and effects their substantial purpose."

Whatever Day's motivation, *Weeks v. United States* remains a landmark among the Supreme Court's decisions explicating and enforcing the Fourth and Fifth Amendments. Its legacy, both in protecting constitutional rights and in generating controversy for the Supreme Court, is considerable.

Selected Bibliography

Kamisar, Yale. "Does (Did) (Should) the Exclusionary Rule Rest on a 'Principled Basis' Rather Than an 'Empirical Proposition'?" *Creighton Law Review* 16 (1982–1983): 565–667.

Schlesinger, Stephen R. *Exclusionary Injustice: The Problem of Illegally Seized Evidence*. New York: Marcel Dekker, 1975.

Two Nations:
The Case of Sacco and Vanzetti

——◄◉►——

Wayne K. Hobson

American Studies Department
California State University, Fullerton

Commonwealth v. Sacco and Vanzetti, 255 Mass. 369 (1926)
[Supreme Judicial Court of Massachusetts]

◄◉► THE CASE IN BRIEF ◄◉►

Date
May 12, 1926

Location
Boston, Massachusetts

Court
Supreme Judicial Court of Massachusetts

Principal Participants
Nicola Sacco
Bartolomeo Vanzetti
Judge Webster Thayer

Significance of the Case
The conduct of the trial judge and ensuing appeals of the guilty-of-murder verdict divided public opinion—and spurred massive street protests—on the fate of two anarchists in postwar Massachusetts; for many, the trial revealed a dark side of intolerance toward "foreigners" in the United States.

In *The Big Money*, published nearly a decade after the August 1927 execution of Nicola Sacco and Bartolomeo Vanzetti, John Dos Passos angrily defined the meaning of the case in terms of the division within the United States that it laid bare: "America our nation has been beaten by strangers who have turned our language inside out and who have taken the clean words our fathers spoke and made them slimy and foul their hired men sit on the judge's bench they sit back with their feet on the tables under the dome of the State House they are ignorant of our beliefs they have the dollars the guns the armed forces the power-plants they have built the electric chair and hired the executioner to throw the switch all right we are two nations."

In more measured terms, literary critic Edmund Wilson made a similar point in 1928, declaring that the case "revealed the whole anatomy of American life, with all its classes, professions, and points of view . . . it raised almost every fundamental question of our political and social system." The most memorable epitaph was provided by Vanzetti himself, who, in his ungrammatical but eloquent English, anticipated correctly that his execution would make him a martyr for justice: "If it had not been for these thing, I might have live out my life talking at street corners to scorning men. I might have die, unmarked, unknown, a failure. Now we are not a failure. This is our career and our triumph. Never in our full life could we hope to do such work for tolerance, for joostice, for man's understanding of man as now we do by accident."

The two men had been arrested in Massachusetts on May 5, 1920, on suspicion of two payroll robberies—a failed attempt in Bridgewater on December 24, 1919, and a successful one in South Braintree on April 15, 1920, during which the paymaster, Frederick Parmenter, and a guard, Alessandro Berardelli, were killed. Vanzetti was convicted of both crimes. Sacco, who had an alibi for the Bridgewater crime, was convicted only of the South Braintree murder.

Today, few believe Vanzetti was guilty of either crime. His July 1, 1920, conviction for the Bridgewater crime was based on highly questionable eyewitness testimony that his inept lawyer did not challenge. The evidence against him for the South Braintree crime was equally tenuous, and it is apparent that, had he not entered that trial, which lasted from May 31 to July 14, 1921, as a convicted felon and as a close friend of Sacco, there would have been virtually nothing to tie him to it. Several questionable eyewitnesses placed him at or near the robbery scene, but none who witnessed the murders identified him. The prosecution also argued that the gun he was carrying when he was arrested had been taken from the dead payroll guard, Berardelli. However, documents released by state police in 1977—fifty years after the executions—show that the prosecution knew that the serial numbers on Berardelli's gun did not match those on Vanzetti's. As in several other instances during the trial, the prosecutors, who were not required to share their evidence with the defense, willfully introduced evidence they knew was incorrect or misleading.

The other key element in the prosecution's case against Vanzetti, as well as against Sacco, was that the two men were heavily armed

when arrested and that they gave false and evasive answers when questioned about their movements, associates, and beliefs. To the police and prosecution, this behavior indicated guilty knowledge. The defense, on the other hand, explained their behavior in a way that most later students have accepted. The two men, who were not informed that they were suspects in a murder case, were trying to protect anarchist friends and associates from antiradical prosecution and trying to protect themselves from deportation as anarchists. The federal government, aided by state and local officials, had spent the previous two years investigating, arresting, and attempting to deport leftist aliens. Many of Sacco and Vanzetti's closest associates in the anarchist movement had already been deported. Furthermore, Vanzetti learned on the day before he was arrested that a colleague, Andrea Salsedo, had died under suspicious circumstances in federal custody in New York. It is also possible that Sacco and Vanzetti were making arrangements to hide stockpiled dynamite when they were arrested. They later claimed, however, that they were trying to get rid of incriminating radical literature (it was a deportable crime for an alien anarchist to possess such literature).

The case against Sacco for the South Braintree crime has always seemed stronger than the case against Vanzetti. More eyewitnesses reported seeing Sacco at the crime scene, including several who said he was the triggerman. Definitive ballistics retests in 1982 linked the gun he was carrying when arrested to a bullet and a shell introduced into evidence at the trial. According to these tests, the four shells found at the crime scene and the six bullets taken from Parmenter's and Berardelli's bodies came from two separate weapons, a Colt .32 and a Harrington and Richardson .38 revolver. Sacco's gun, the Colt, was responsible for one bullet and one shell. The Harrington and Richardson produced the others. For some students of the case, this evidence proves Sacco's guilt and confirms rumors that have surfaced from time to time that people close to the defense knew all along that he was guilty. To other scholars, including the authors of the most recent authoritative reexamination of the case, it is far more likely that Sacco was framed, that some-one substituted the incriminating bullet and shell. Comparing autopsy reports on bullet tra-jectories with the most trustworthy eyewitness testimony convinced these scholars that a sin-gle gunman shot both Berardelli and Par-menter, using the same gun for both murders.

Beyond these matters of eyewitness testi-mony and physical evidence, many people in the 1920s based their assessment of the two men's guilt or innocence on judgments about their backgrounds and character. Sacco and Vanzetti were demonized during their trial as men with no sense of social responsibility or re-spect for authority, as slackers during wartime, and as dangerous foreign anarchists during the postwar years. As such, they were seen as men who would not feel any compunction about committing armed robbery and murder. Al-though both men had emigrated from Italy in 1908, they had not yet become American citi-zens, had not bothered to learn English beyond a rudimentary level, had left the country dur-ing World War I, probably to escape the draft, and as anarchists, they were openly contemp-tuous of capitalism and the American govern-ment. We can see why Sacco and Vanzetti were vilified if we place these facts in the context of emotions and fears generated by large-scale immigration from southern and eastern Europe during the previous two decades; by American involvement in World War I; by the postwar se-ries of labor strikes, bombings, and attempted bombings presumably carried out by leftist radicals; and by the widely reported crime wave of the 1920s, with Italian names fre-quently linked to organized criminal activity. Sacco and Vanzetti symbolized dangerous new trends that needed to be unequivocally branded as illegitimate and treated with all the harsh-ness that the law allowed. In short, prosecuting and executing Sacco and Vanzetti was equated with restoring respect for authority and Ameri-can institutions. In the absence of public opin-ion polls, it is difficult to know precisely how many Americans saw Sacco and Vanzetti in these terms, but it seems likely that a majority did. Certainly this was so in Massachusetts.

On the other side, Sacco and Vanzetti's sup-porters saw their prosecution as symbolic of wartime and postwar intolerance and repres-sion. Their arrest came on the heels of the in-famous "Palmer Raids," in which federal officers, led by Attorney General A. Mitchell Palmer, arrested more than three thousand alien radicals whom they had marked for de-portation, detaining them under brutal condi-tions and affording them only the most mini-mal due process. For many American liberals and radicals, these arrests, detentions, and de-portations signified that they were living through a period when the repressive appara-tus of the state was being dispatched against the least powerful. The attitude that had de-manded 100 percent Americanism during wartime was being carried forward into peace-time.

Fortunately for their supporters, Sacco and Vanzetti were appealing human beings whose qualities and character seemed to refute the ab-stract and demonized image advanced by their persecutors. Sacco emerged, based on stories of his life and the many letters he wrote from prison, as a devoted husband and father, a hardworking and skilled shoe-factory opera-tive, and a man who regularly used the im-agery of flowers to express his emotions. In particular, Sacco's farewell letters to his two children have a dignity and tenderness that conveyed his essential character to those who believed him innocent. Vanzetti also possessed a sociable and affectionate temperament. But in other ways he differed markedly from Sacco. He was unmarried, had no known romantic attachments, had never developed a skilled trade, and lived the itinerant and uncertain life of an unskilled laborer. When arrested, at age thirty-one, he was making his living as a fish peddler. But Vanzetti had an intellectual cast of mind and early in life had developed an in-satiable appetite for knowledge. His wide-ranging reading led him by 1912 to embrace anarchism.

Although their supporters downplayed their ideological beliefs, preferring to convey the image of Sacco as a simple man devoted to his family and of Vanzetti as a philosophical ideal-ist, both men emphasized that their commit-ment to anarchism explained not only why they had been unjustly convicted, but explained who they were. Recent research on the connections between the two men and the Italian American anarchist movement underscores this point. They were followers of Luigi Galleani, the leading Italian anarchist in the United States during the first two decades of the century. Galleani preached and practiced an uncompromising and militant, even violent, anarcho-communism. Galleanists believed that the modern capitalist state was inherently tyrannical and oppressive, that it could not be reformed, and must be replaced. And they were willing to use dynamite to defend their cause.

After many prominent socialists, labor activists, and anarchist leaders had been arrested and jailed and their publications suppressed during World War I, Galleani called for a direct action response. Arming themselves and working in small, close-knit groups that acted on their own, his followers planned and carried out retaliatory bombings. We do not know what role Sacco and Vanzetti played. The terrorist activities of several of their closest associates have been documented, and it is reasonable to assume that they were involved, at least in a backup or logistical role, although there is no direct evidence linking them to any specific bombing. Furthermore, there is absolutely no evidence linking Galleanist violence to armed robbery.

Recognizing the inherent implausibility of the robbery and murder charges against Sacco and Vanzetti, and determined to resist this latest chapter in the ongoing government campaign against radicalism, the remaining Galleanists quickly organized a defense committee in 1920 and reached out to others for money and assistance. Fred Moore, who had a national reputation as a defender of labor and radical activists, led the defense team for the 1921 trial. His participation greatly increased the public visibility of the case, convincing labor and left liberal journalists and activists that a major test of the American judicial process lay ahead.

In retrospect, we can see that the Sacco-Vanzetti case marked the culmination of fifty years of political trials involving labor and radical activists, beginning with the executions of twenty alleged Molly Maguires in the late 1870s. Other cases in this series include the trial of eight anarchists for the 1886 Haymarket bomb blast in Chicago; the federal prosecution of Eugene Debs for defying a court injunction during the 1894 Pullman strike; the 1906–1907 prosecution of Big Bill Haywood for the murder of former Idaho governor Frank Steunenberg; the 1911 trial of the McNamara brothers for bombing the *Los Angeles Times* building; the trial of Arturo Giovannitti and Joseph Ettor for a murder during the 1913 Lawrence textile strike; Joe Hill's 1915 conviction and execution for murder, and his consequent martyrdom as the troubadour of the Industrial Workers of the World; the conviction and likely frame-up of Tom Mooney and Warren Billings for the 1916 Preparedness Day bombing in San Francisco; the 1918 trial and imprisonment of Debs for violating the wartime Sedition Act; and the trial in 1920 of Communist Benjamin Gitlow for criminal anarchy.

Taken together, this is a remarkable series of symbolic trials with a common subtext, raising questions of power and limits: How far beyond the bounds of fairness and justice was the state willing to go to destroy labor and radical movements? How extensive and irresponsible was the labor or radical movement's willingness to use dynamite and other forms of coercion and violence to achieve its aims? Was the case at hand a frame-up, as labor and radical leaders invariably claimed, often with great justification? Or was the case an exposé of yet another labor radical who believed the end justified any means, as the prosecution and the opponents of labor regularly claimed?

In an impressive mobilization of its forces, the Sacco-Vanzetti Defense Committee raised eight hundred thousand dollars to support the defendants' appeals. Liberal journals, such as the *New Republic*, publicized the case for years, emphasizing the prejudices of the authorities and providing a positive reading on the character of the two defendants. But Massachusetts authorities were unmoved, and very likely they were strengthened in their convictions by this show of strength from the left, as the story of the unsuccessful appeals undertaken by defense lawyers between 1921 and 1927 suggests.

According to the procedure in Massachusetts, all appeals were to be heard by the judge who had tried the case, although his rulings on matters of law, but not on matters of fact, were subject to review by the supreme judicial court of the commonwealth. Therefore, Judge Webster Thayer, who had presided at both trials, was the final authority on all matters of fact. The defendants' supporters found this rigid and unrealistic form of judicial review maddening, particularly since it was so obvious to them that Judge Thayer was implacably prejudiced against the defendants. In 1939, the Massachusetts legislature finally expanded the supreme judicial court's powers to include review of all facts in capital cases.

Defense lawyers for Sacco and Vanzetti filed eight appeals for another trial on the facts, relying primarily on new evidence that substantiated their claims of prosecutorial and jury misconduct and that pointed to the strong probability of the defendants' innocence. In fact, the defense made a much stronger case for their clients during the appeals process than they had during the murder trial itself. For example, a major exculpatory witness—a man who had received a shot through his overcoat at South Braintree and who had looked the killer directly in the face—was found. He was absolutely certain that Sacco was not the shooter. The prosecution, led by District Attorney Frederick G. Katzmann, had known about the witness, but kept him from the defense. In addition, it was disclosed that the jury foreman had declared before the trial began, in response to a friend who expressed doubt about the two men's guilt, "Damn them, they ought to hang them anyway." Finally, the Commonwealth's leading ballistics expert, police captain William Proctor, swore an affidavit stating that he had repeatedly told Katzmann that he would have to answer in the negative if he were asked whether he had found positive evidence that Sacco's pistol had fired any of the recovered bullets. Therefore, Katzmann had framed his question in court so that Proctor could say the bullet was "consistent with being fired by [Sacco's] pistol" while failing to clarify that all he really knew was that any Colt .32 could have fired the bullet. In October 1924, Thayer denied this and all other appeals, arguing that the jury had known perfectly well what Proctor had

Sacco and Vanzetti at the time of their trial. *Hulton Getty Collection/Archive Photos.*

meant, even though in his own charge to the jury he had stated that Proctor had identified Sacco's gun as one of the murder weapons.

Rebuffed by Thayer, the defense team, now led by eminent Boston defense attorney William G. Thompson, made two appeals to the supreme judicial court. In the first appeal, they argued that, throughout the murder trial, Judge Thayer had abused his discretionary power with incorrect or prejudicial rulings and statements. Their underlying argument was that Thayer's violent personal hostility to the defendants had poisoned the atmosphere in the courtroom and had led him to deny the posttrial motions for a new trial. In May 1926, in a unanimous ruling, the supreme judicial court denied the appeal, holding that Thayer had acted properly and within his discretionary power as a trial judge.

Thompson then filed a second appeal with the high court, based on evidence that had come to light just as the first appeal was being finalized. On November 18, 1925, Sacco's fellow inmate, Celestino Madeiros, sent him a note confessing his own participation in the South Braintree robbery and declaring that Sacco and Vanzetti had no involvement in the crime. Madeiros belonged to the Morelli gang from Providence, Rhode Island, which had committed a number of armed robberies. Realizing the inherent unreliability of such a confession, the defense undertook a thorough investigation of Madeiros and the Morelli gang. They learned that Joe Morelli bore a striking resemblance to Sacco. He, in fact, had been identified as the shooter by several South Braintree eyewitnesses who were shown his photograph. The defense, however, was not able to secure any other confessions or physical proof linking the Morelli gang to the South Braintree crime. Madeiros's story was correct on many details that he could not possibly have known about except through his own involvement, although it was weakened because he failed to remember any landmarks around the crime site. Because this new evidence involved questions of fact, it was appealed to Thayer, who ruled against the defense, declaring that he did not believe Madeiros. Appealing this ruling to the supreme judicial court, Thompson attacked Thayer's competence and bias, pointing out that a jury, not a judge, should determine the truth or falsity of Madeiros's confession. He urged the justices to overturn the convictions on the grounds that Thayer should have used—that is, that the confession was new evidence that would unmistakably be a real factor in a jury's decision-making process were it to be presented at trial.

Recognizing that time was running out and in a conscious effort to broaden the base of the defense's public support, Harvard Law School professor Felix Frankfurter wrote a scathing attack, published in the March 1927 issue of the *Atlantic Monthly*, one month before the supreme judicial court's decision on the Madeiros confession was handed down. Frankfurter skillfully detailed weaknesses in the case against the two men, the evidence of prosecutorial misconduct, and judicial prejudice. His aim was to appeal to middle-class professionals and other leaders of public opinion who had remained aloof from the controversy. Although he enjoyed a measure of success, as evidenced by the growing list of newspapers calling for a new trial, his intervention was very late in the game. This became evident one month later when the supreme judicial court denied the defendants' final appeal, arguing that Thayer was the proper judge of the relevance of any new facts. Defense lawyers then sought to move the case into federal court. But they were thwarted by the long-standing deference of the federal judiciary to state courts in criminal justice matters.

After these failures, the only remaining recourse was to appeal to Governor Alvan T. Fuller to commute the death sentences. Frankfurter's intervention and intense lobbying had generated sufficient pressure so that Fuller had to at least make a show of seriously considering this step. He appointed a three-member special advisory commission, headed by A. Lawrence Lowell, the conservative president of Harvard University, to investigate and report to him. The committee took testimony and issued a report upholding Thayer's conduct of the murder trial as "scrupulously fair," no matter what opinions the judge had indiscreetly voiced in conversation with outsiders. The committee dismissed the defense's new evidence as unconvincing and as unlikely to produce a different result. In retrospect, it seems clear that Lowell's mind was made up from the beginning. The report eased Fuller's task, and he quickly rejected the clemency request. On August 23, 1927, shortly after midnight, Nicola Sacco and Bartolomeo Vanzetti were taken to the electric chair in Charlestown prison and executed. Thousands of people in Boston, around the United States, and in cities around the world held vigil and protested, often angrily, on that final night when the two nations later memorialized by Dos Passos were dramatically on display.

Selected Bibliography

Avrich, P. *Sacco and Vanzetti: The Anarchist Background.* Princeton, NJ: Princeton University Press, 1991.

Joughin, L. G., and E. M. Morgan. *The Legacy of Sacco and Vanzetti*. Princeton, NJ: Princeton University Press, 1948.

Parrish, M. E. "The Two Italians." In *Felix Frankfurter and His Times: The Reform Years,* 176–196. New York: Free Press, 1982.

Russell, F. *Sacco & Vanzetti: The Case Resolved*. New York: Harper & Row, 1986.

Young, W., and D. E. Kaiser. *Postmortem: New Evidence in the Case of Sacco and Vanzetti*. Amherst, MA: University of Massachusetts Press, 1985.

Are Bootleggers Entitled to Privacy?

Department of Political Science
Brooklyn College–City University of New York

Olmstead v. United States, 277 U.S. 438 (1928) [U.S. Supreme Court]

◄o► THE CASE IN BRIEF ◄o►

Date
1928

Location
Washington, D.C.

Court
U.S. Supreme Court

Principal Participants
Roy Olmstead
Chief Justice William Howard Taft
Justice Louis D. Brandeis
Justice Oliver Wendell Holmes Jr.

Significance of the Case
The U.S. Supreme Court affirmed the legality of wiretaps installed without warrants and used to convict a bootlegger; until the 1960s this decision limited individual rights to those specifically mentioned in the Constitution.

In 1919, the states ratified the Eighteenth Amendment, prohibiting the manufacture, sale, transportation, and importation of intoxicating liquors. Acting under its mandate, Congress passed the National Prohibition Act, which set out criminal sanctions for trafficking in liquor. "Bootlegging," or importing and selling liquor illegally, quickly became a major industry in the United States, as the American people decided they wanted alcoholic beverages to be readily available (a preference that resulted in the repeal of this amendment by the Twenty-First Amendment in 1933).

Roy Olmstead put together a bootlegging business that, according to the Supreme Court, had three offices in Seattle, employed at least fifty people, and used two seagoing ships and a number of smaller boats to transport liquor to British Columbia and throughout the state of Washington. This illegal business exceeded two million dollars in sales a year.

The federal government discovered what the High Court called this "conspiracy of amazing magnitude" by wiretapping the telephone line in one of the company's offices as well as the telephone lines leading into the homes of four of its employees. The taps continued for many months, during which stenographers took notes of the conversations they overheard. Eventually, seventy-five people were indicted. Olmstead and two others, who were among those convicted of conspiracy to violate the National Prohibition Act, appealed to the Supreme Court on the grounds that (1) the wiretaps violated the Fourth Amendment ("The right of the people to be secure in their persons, houses, papers, and effects, against unreasonable searches and seizures, shall not be violated") and (2) such searches and seizures are unreasonable unless the law-enforcement officials undertaking them have been granted warrants for "probable cause." He also relied on the Fifth Amendment's guarantee that "No person . . . shall be compelled in any criminal case to be a witness against himself."

The case raised two major issues. One was the extent to which the Court would interpret the Fourth Amendment's search-and-seizure clause in light of technological developments. That is, would the amendment be held to prohibit government wiretapping, which obviously could not have been foreseen at the time the amendment was written? The second was whether the Court would follow in this case the doctrine it established in *Weeks v. United States* (1914), in which it held that illegally obtained evidence could not be used in federal courtrooms. The *Weeks* decision was based on the Court's belief that the most effective way to prevent the government from obtaining evidence illegally in violation of the people's rights was to render the evidence useless by preventing it from being introduced in court. One of the dissenting justices also raised the issue of privacy.

Chief Justice William Howard Taft, writing for himself and four other justices, upheld the convictions. He expressed agreement with the *Weeks* doctrine, but he did not believe that the evidence gathered had been obtained illegally. Distinguishing the case from others in which homes and offices had been entered and searched by law-enforcement officers who had no warrant, Taft noted that in those cases there

was "actual entrance" into private premises "and the taking away of something tangible." But in the *Olmstead* case, Taft said, "we have testimony only of voluntary conversations secretly overheard. . . . There was no searching. There was no seizure. . . . There was no entry of the houses or offices of the defendants." It was "reasonable" to assume, said Taft, that "one who installs in his house a telephone instrument with connecting wires intends to project his voice to those quite outside, and that the wires beyond his house, and messages while passing over them," are not protected by the Fourth Amendment. Congress could, if it chose, pass a statute making evidence derived from wiretaps inadmissible in the courtroom, but the courts had no right to add such "an enlarged and unusual meaning to the Fourth Amendment," which had not been violated here. The chief justice also maintained that the Fifth Amendment's privilege against self-incrimination had not been breached. No one had made the defendants talk on the telephone, so they had not been forced to incriminate themselves. Responding to the argument that a Washington State law made it a crime to intercept telephone messages, Taft noted that the statute did not make the evidence obtained from such interceptions inadmissible in court, and so there was no reason to overturn the convictions.

Justice Louis D. Brandeis dissented. Reiterating the extent of the wiretaps, which involved eight telephones, at least seven government agents, and 775 typewritten pages of conversations overheard, he challenged the government's contention that this was not an unreasonable search and seizure. Brandeis reminded the Court that its own decisions had permitted constitutional phrases regarding government powers to be "updated" to meet "modern conditions," and he argued that no less could be done for "clauses guaranteeing to the individual protection against specific abuses of power." When the Fourth Amendment was written, the search-and-seizure clause could be violated only by the physical intrusion of government agents into a home. But the privacy that the clause was designed to protect could now be invaded by "subtler and more far-reaching means." They were subtler because no physical intrusion was necessary for wiretapping; and they were more far-reaching because wiretapping invaded the privacy of people at both ends of every telephone call made or received by the person being tapped, no matter what the subject of the conversation. This, Brandeis believed, violated the intention of the Constitution's framers, who "sought to protect Americans in their beliefs, their thoughts, their emotions, and their sensations. They conferred, as against the government, the right to be let alone—the most comprehensive of rights and the right most valued by civilized men." Brandeis added that, in order to protect the right of privacy, every "unjustifiable intrusion by the government . . . whatever the means employed" had to be seen as a violation of the Fourth Amendment, and the use of evidence gathered during it as a violation of the Fifth.

Brandeis's impassioned defense of privacy was not surprising. In 1890, Brandeis and his law partner Samuel Warren had written an article entitled "The Right to Privacy," published in the *Harvard Law Review*, that has been credited with alerting the legal profession to the importance of the right to privacy and its necessity in a democratic society. It was in that article that Brandeis and Warren had first called privacy "the right to be let alone," and had written that public scrutiny of private lives was a deprivation of the dignity to which human beings are entitled. They warned against the dangers of technology, including "instantaneous photographs" and "numerous mechanical devices" that could be used to invade privacy. In *Olmstead*, Brandeis added that "Discovery and invention have made it possible for the Government . . . to obtain disclosure in court of what is whispered in the closet. . . . The progress of science in furnishing the Government with means of espionage is not likely to stop with wire tapping." And he foresaw accurately that "Ways may some day be developed by which the Government, without removing papers from secret drawers, can reproduce them in court, and by which it will be enabled to expose to a jury the most intimate occurrences of the home." This

was of major concern to Brandeis, who believed that democracy was impossible unless each member of the electorate was free to try out various ideas in order to decide what he or she believed would be the best possible governmental system and policies. "Freedom to think as you will and to speak as you think are means indispensable to the discovery and spread of political truth," Brandeis would write in the 1927 case of *Whitney v. California*. Thus, privacy and democracy were inextricably linked. And so he viewed wiretaps, used to supply evidence in *Olmstead*, as a threat not only to the defendants but to the entire democratic process.

Brandeis saw Fifth Amendment difficulties as well because he believed that wiretaps violated the right against self-incrimination, initially meant to negate the use of torture, but the spirit of which had consistently been construed by the Court to be "as broad as the mischief against which it seeks to guard." The government's admirable purpose, which was to enforce the law, was no excuse for its violating the Constitution: "Experience should teach us to be most on our guard to protect liberty when the government's purposes are beneficent. . . . The greatest dangers to liberty lurk in insidious encroachment by men of zeal, well-meaning but without understanding."

Aside from the constitutional issue, the government had gathered the evidence in clear violation of the Washington law against wiretapping. The government itself had "[laid] bare the crimes committed by its officers on its behalf." By introducing the tainted evidence in court, the Justice Department had sanctioned the illegal behavior of the police officers, and the Court was now giving further sanction to government criminality. "A federal court should not permit such a prosecution to continue," Brandeis protested. Nothing in the Eighteenth Amendment was designed to give government officials the power to break the law. It was an established rule of law that courts would not hear plaintiffs who came with "unclean hands." The need for the Court to follow that rule was particularly important here, since the party that had appeared with "unclean hands" was the government. This was a threat because of the educational role played by the government. "Our government is the potent, the omnipresent teacher. For good or for ill, it teaches the whole people by its example. . . . If the government becomes a law-breaker, it breeds contempt for law; it invites every man to become a law unto himself; it invites anarchy." Accepting tainted evidence was tantamount to a declaration by the Court that "the end justified the means." "Against that pernicious doctrine," said Brandeis, "this court should resolutely set its face."

Justices Oliver Wendell Holmes Jr. and Harlan F. Stone agreed, with Holmes adding that it is "a less evil that some criminals should escape than that the government should play an ignoble part" in capturing them. Holmes shared Brandeis's distaste for the lesson being taught by the Court's acceptance of government criminality. While it was undoubtedly desirable for criminals to be detected, it was equally desirable for the government to use only methods that did not require the government itself to "foster and pay for other crimes, when they are the means by which the evidence is to be obtained."

Justice Butler dissented separately, stating that the case should be retried with the understanding that wiretapping violated the Fourth and Fifth Amendments. He, too, disagreed with the Court's statement that telephone calls were not to be treated as private, saying not only that people contracting for telephone service assume they will have "the private use of the facilities employed in the service," but also that "the communications belong to the parties between whom they pass." Butler noted that many telephone conversations "includ[e] communications that are private and privileged—those between physician and patient, lawyer and client, parent and child, husband and wife." The invasion of privacy was sufficiently distressing for Butler, who was known for his insistence on construing the words of the Constitution literally when the government threatened to regulate business, to add in *Olmstead* that "The direct operation or literal meaning of the [constitutional] words do not measure the purpose or scope of its provisions" and that the Fourth Amendment was clearly designed to safeguard the people "against all evils that are like and equivalent to those embraced within the ordinary meaning of its words."

Thus, in addition to the question of how the Court would construe the Fourth and Fifth Amendments in criminal cases, *Olmstead* involved the concept of privacy. The word *privacy* itself is not to be found in the Constitution, but defenders of a constitutional right to privacy have found it implied not only in the sections of the Fourth and Fifth Amendments discussed above but in the First Amendment's guarantee of free speech and association, the Third Amendment's provision that soldiers shall not be quartered in homes without the permission of the owners, the Fifth and Fourteenth Amendments' prohibition of the government's taking of a person's liberty without due process of law, and the Ninth Amendment, which says that "The enumeration in the Constitution, of certain rights shall not be construed to deny or disparage others retained by the people." The form and degree of privacy protected by the Constitution has remained a major issue in constitutional law, affecting such disparate areas as the right to reproductive freedom and the right to die.

The *Olmstead* case also involved two competing approaches to constitutional interpretation: that which tended to limit individuals' rights to those specifically mentioned by the framers, and the competing approach that emphasized enforcing the spirit of the framers' intentions. *Olmstead* was eventually overruled by the Supreme Court's 8–1 decision in the 1967 case of *Katz v. United States*, which adopted the second form of jurisprudence in holding that "unreasonable searches and seizures" had to be defined in light of the government's ability to use methods for searching that could not have been foreseen at the time of the writing of the Constitution.

Selected Bibliography

Brandeis, Louis D., and Samuel D. Warren. "The Right to Privacy." *Harvard Law Review* 4 (1890): 193–220.

Glancy, D. J. "The Invention of the Right to Privacy." *Arizona Law Review* 21 (1979): 1.

Hixson, R. F. *Privacy in a Public Society: Human Rights in Conflict.* New York: Oxford University Press, 1987.

Landynski, Jacob W. *Search and Seizure and the Supreme Court.* Baltimore: Johns Hopkins Press, 1966.

Murphy, Walter F. *Wiretapping on Trial: A Case Study in the Judicial Process.* New York: Random House, 1965.

Seipp, D. J. *The Right to Privacy in American History.* Cambridge, MA: Harvard University Press, 1978.

Strum, Philippa. *Privacy: The Debate in the United States Since 1945.* Fort Worth, TX: Harcourt Brace & Company, 1998.

Showdown Over Gun Control

Department of History
Northwestern Oklahoma State University

United States v. Miller, 307 U.S. 174 (1939) [U.S. Supreme Court]

◄◦► THE CASE IN BRIEF ◄◦►

Date
January–May 1939

Location
Washington, D.C.

Court
U.S. Supreme Court

Principal Participants
Jack Miller and Frank Layton
Associate Justice James C. McReynolds

Significance of the Case
The right to bear arms and the National Firearms Act were challenged setting a 60-year precedent that still holds in the courts. The decision supported power of Congress to regulate weapons and underscored that the "right of the people to keep and bear Arms" is not absolute.

Few issues in recent decades have been the subject of as much volatile debate in the United States as has that of gun control. Those who want American citizens to have the unlimited (or almost unlimited) ability to own guns and other weapons have become highly organized. Led by the National Rifle Association (NRA), pro-gun advocates have spent millions of dollars fighting any effort by the national and local governments to restrict access of ordinary people to weapons. They have become one of the most vocal and powerful lobbying groups in the country. They contribute money to so-called pro-gun candidates for office, and they try to defeat those who do not support their proposals. Proponents of governmental gun control have accused the NRA not only of using scare tactics to foster its agenda, but also of distorting the law while stirring up a large segment of the population to fear and even hate the government.

The crux of the dispute lies in the Second Amendment to the U.S. Constitution. That oft-quoted provision states that "A well regulated Militia, being necessary to the security of a free

State, the right of the people to keep and bear Arms shall not be infringed." Whole forests have been felled to make the paper used by those on the opposing sides of the gun-control issue to disseminate their interpretations of the twenty-seven words in the Second Amendment. The U.S. Supreme Court's most important construction of the Second Amendment was in *United States v. Miller,* a decision that the Court has shown no inclination to reverse in the more than sixty years since that 1939 holding.

In 1934, Congress passed a law commonly known as the National Firearms Act. Among its provisions was language making it illegal to carry certain weapons across state boundaries. Authorities in Arkansas arrested Jack Miller and Frank Layton for transporting an unregistered, double-barreled, 12-gauge sawed-off shotgun from Claremore, Oklahoma, to Siloam Springs, Arkansas, in violation of the law. The two men moved to dismiss the indictments against them, alleging that the National Firearms Act was unconstitutional because it denied them their Second Amendment rights. U.S. Federal District Judge Heartsill Ragon of the Western District of Arkansas agreed with the defendants and dismissed the indictments. The United States appealed the decision to the nation's highest court.

The U.S. Supreme Court, in an 8–0 opinion, reversed the district court, upheld the validity of the National Firearms Act, and reinstated the indictments. In writing for the unanimous panel, Associate Justice James C. McReynolds left no doubt as to the Court's interpretation of the Second Amendment. Quoting the statutory definition of a sawed-off shotgun, McReynolds wrote: "In the absence of any evidence tending to show that possession or use of a 'shotgun having a barrel of less than eighteen inches in length' at this time has some reasonable relationship to the preservation or efficiency of a well regulated militia, we cannot say that the Second Amendment guarantees the right to keep and bear such an instrument."

During the years since the Supreme Court's ruling in *Miller,* opponents of gun-control legislation have attacked it in several ways. One of the more sophisticated challenges to *Miller* is that the first thirteen words of the Second

Amendment ("A well regulated Militia, being necessary to the security of a free State") merely explain the right that follows them. This argument holds that "the right of the people to keep and bear Arms" is not related in any way to the government's maintenance of a militia (which has, since the Second Amendment was drafted, been supplanted by the National Guard). Those who cling to this line of reasoning, however, either ignore *Miller* or refuse to accept its legitimacy as a definitive precedent.

Some anti–gun control spokespersons have argued that *Miller* actually supports rather than refutes their pro-gun position. They have seized upon a statement Justice McReynolds wrote in explaining why Congress could ban Miller's shotgun. McReynolds noted that the weapon was not "part of the ordinary military equipment" nor "that its use could contribute to the common defense." Therefore, some gun advocates contend, the *Miller* decision supports a person's "right" to bear any military weapon he or she chooses; all that is required to pass the *"Miller* test" is to prove that a weapon being possessed is "ordinary military equipment" that "could contribute to the common defense." While some may hope that this is what *Miller* means, most constitutional scholars—even pro-gun ones—disagree. Pro-gun commentators usually concede that the Second Amendment (together with the power granted to Congress in the body of the Constitution to organize and arm the militia) allows the U.S. government to restrict access to military weapons. Nevertheless, they usually argue that ordinary citizens have the right to possess as many nonmilitary weapons as they desire.

These conflicting theories clashed in 1982 in the case of *Quilici v. Village of Morton Grove,* a case decided by the Seventh Circuit of the U.S. Court of Appeals. The citizens of Morton Grove, Illinois, passed an ordinance banning handguns within their village limits. Victor D. Quilici and other pro-gun advocates challenged the provision on several grounds, including that it violated the Second Amendment. The appeals court disagreed. Referring to the Second Amendment, Judge William J. Bauer, writing for the unanimous three-judge panel, stated: "Construing this language according to its plain meaning, it seems clear that the right to bear arms is inextricably connected to the preservation of a militia." This is precisely the interpretation that the Supreme Court gave to the Second Amendment in *United States v. Miller*. The Court refused to hear the case, in effect approving the circuit court's decision and reaffirming the *Miller* interpretation of the Second Amendment.

Despite more than sixty years of judicial deference to the *Miller* decision, the debate over gun control remains intense. The views of some commentators notwithstanding, *United States v. Miller* clearly supports the power of Congress to regulate weapons. Unless the Supreme Court should reverse that decision, the "right of the people to keep and bear Arms" is not absolute. Consequently, the showdown over gun control—regardless of what the pro-gun lobby says—is really about whether new limitations on gun ownership should be enacted, not about whether such restrictions are constitutional.

Selected Bibliography

Barnett, R. E., and D. B. Kates. "Under Fire: The New Consensus on the Second Amendment." *Emory Law Journal* 45 (1996): 1139–1259.

Denning, B. P. "Can the Simple Cite Be Trusted?: Lower Court Interpretations of *United States v. Miller* and the Second Amendment." *Cumberland Law Review* 26 (1996): 961–1004.

Levinson, Sanford. "The Embarrassing Second Amendment." *Yale Law Journal* 99 (1989): 637–659.

Volokh, E. "The Commonplace Second Amendment." *New York University Law Review* 73 (1998): 793–821.

Icons of the Cold War:
The Hiss-Chambers Case

—◄○►—

John W. Johnson
Department of History
University of Northern Iowa

United States v. Alger Hiss, (1950) [U.S. Federal District Court]

◄○► THE CASE IN BRIEF ◄○►

Date
January 1950

Location
New York City

Court
U.S. Federal District Court

Principal Participants
Alger Hiss
Whittaker Chambers

Significance of the Case
Post–World War II fears of Communism
and of Soviet espionage formed the
background of this case, in which a high-
ranking official of the State Department
was convicted of having perjured himself
about his role in passing top-secret
government documents to the Russians.

On a humid Washington day in August 1948, a short, heavyset man named Whittaker Chambers testified before the House Committee on Un-American Activities about his radical activities and associations in the 1930s. Seldom has an explosive case involving crime, politics, espionage, and famous people had such an unimpressive beginning. Chambers wore a rumpled suit and spoke in a quiet, phlegmatic fashion. He stated that he was a former member of the underground wing of the American Communist Party. On first appearance, Chambers was a decidedly uninspiring witness (it would later be revealed that he had a history of mental instability). The accusations of Whittaker Chambers, however, spawned a singular legal, political, and ideological mystery that still baffles American historians.

Few members of HUAC (as the committee was generally termed) attended the August 1948 hearing at which Chambers testified. The claims that the committee had been making since the end of World War II about Communists in America were beginning to sound stale and empty. President Truman, a Democrat, had

77

recently blasted HUAC for its transparent attempts to besmirch the legacy of the New Deal by branding liberal Democrats as Communist-inspired. Near the end of the summer of 1948, most Americans were beginning to agree with the president that HUAC's accusations were just "red herrings."

If HUAC was going to be able to convince the country that Communists posed a significant danger, it was going to have to come up with a credible witness and at least one sensational villain. Chambers, despite his appearance and background, would ultimately prove to be that witness. Personal appearance notwithstanding, he was an accomplished writer, translator, and editor who was acquainted with many major figures in American arts and letters from the twenties through the forties. At the time of his HUAC testimony he was a senior editor for *Time* magazine. He also had an excellent memory for details. The villain that Chambers identified as a possible candidate for the anticommunist opprobrium of HUAC was named Alger Hiss.

A man of impeccable intellectual and political credentials, Alger Hiss graduated with honors from Harvard Law School, was selected as a legal assistant for the great Supreme Court justice Oliver Wendell Holmes, served as a staff member for an important congressional committee, performed with distinction for a decade in the Department of State, and was currently president of the Carnegie Endowment for International Peace. Notably, while in the State Department Hiss attended the Yalta Conference with President Franklin Roosevelt and had directed the arrangements for the foundation of the United Nations. It would have been difficult for an American of forty-four years of age to have constructed a better résumé of public service than the one that Alger Hiss had assembled by 1948. Moreover, Hiss looked the part of a respected statesman: he was tall and handsome, wore tailored suits, was a polished public speaker, and was married to an attractive woman. He also had a roster of distinguished friends in the federal government. There were some in the forties who said that Alger Hiss, that young rising star of foreign policy, would one day become secretary of state. If Hiss was a Communist, there was something decidedly wrong in the country. If a person as accomplished and poised for greatness as Alger Hiss was not a loyal American, who could be trusted?

Chambers's fingering of Alger Hiss not only provided HUAC with weeks of spectacular headlines, but it also helped establish the climate of fear that would lend credence to the charges of political conservatives in the late forties and early fifties that the country was being undermined by Communists and their unwitting sycophants. The Chambers testimony, in short, helped advance the Cold War.

Hiss promptly rebutted the charges of Chambers. He appeared before HUAC a few days after Chambers's initial broadsides and vehemently denied being a Communist. He also denied knowing someone named Whittaker Chambers. Most of the reporters covering the hearing tended to believe Hiss and branded Chambers as a liar. Even some of the members of HUAC itself began to doubt whether they had been wise to allow Chambers to testify publicly before investigating fully his accusations. One of the members of HUAC who expressed such second thoughts was a young congressman from California, Richard M. Nixon. But Nixon and the Republican leadership of the committee decided to press forward and arranged a confrontation before HUAC of Hiss and Chambers.

At this public encounter, Hiss again denied knowing a man named Whittaker Chambers. But he acknowledged that the man calling himself Chambers looked like someone he had known in the mid-thirties named "George Crosley." Hiss then made a bizarre request: he asked the committee's permission to examine closely "Crosely's" teeth because he said that the man he had known by that name had bad teeth. Apparently satisfied that the man before him was that dentally defective person, Hiss acknowledged that he and his wife had known Crosley in the thirties but that neither he nor Priscilla had ever passed any confidential State Department papers or documents to Crosley. Hiss also testified that he had broken off his acquaintanceship with "Crosley" in early 1937. There the matter might have died. If it had just

Alger Hiss denies that he was a Communist as he testifies before the House Un-American Activities Committee in Washington, D.C. *Hulton Getty Collection/Archive Photos.*

been Chambers's words versus Hiss's—the words of a disturbed, self-described former Communist opposed to that of the country's rising star in foreign policy—there would have been little question who should have been believed. When Chambers repeated his charges on the radio show *Meet the Press,* Hiss brought suit against Chambers for slander.

Claiming that being slapped with a libel suit prompted his memory, in November Chambers produced a set of confidential State Department documents from the thirties that he had kept hidden away for over a decade. They could only have come from someone who had had official access to them, someone like Alger Hiss. Most were typewritten: Chambers claimed that they were typed on a Woodstock-brand typewriter that belonged to the Hiss family. Among these documents were also four confidential memoranda in Hiss's own handwriting. Chambers alleged that these materials had been passed to him by Alger Hiss in 1937 and

1938 and that copies had been sent on their way to the Soviet Union by a communist courier. These materials were turned over to the U.S. Department of Justice's Criminal Division since they appeared to incriminate Hiss in an elaborate espionage scheme.

In early December Chambers gave to HUAC several roles of microfilm that he had hidden in a hollowed-out pumpkin in a field on his Maryland farm. The "pumpkin papers"—more copies of confidential State Department documents from the thirties bearing Hiss's name or allegedly typed on the Hiss Woodstock—further inflamed the passions of the defenders of Hiss and Chambers. Finally, the Department of Justice subpoenaed Hiss and Chambers to testify before a federal grand jury. Essentially, Hiss and Chambers repeated the same stories before the grand jury that they told before HUAC. The grand jury accepted the face validity of Chambers's testimony, found that there was probable cause that Hiss had lied when he had denied passing state secrets to Chambers, and, on December 15, 1948, indicted Alger Hiss on two counts of perjury.

The first count claimed that Hiss had lied when he testified under oath that he had not stolen State Department documents and passed them to Chambers. The second count claimed that Hiss had testified falsely when he swore that he had not seen Chambers since the end of 1936. Were it not for the fact that the statute of limitation had expired and that several witnesses who might have corroborated Chambers's allegations were not available to testify, Hiss would have been charged with espionage for the illegal release of State Department documents in the thirties.

The trial took place in the Foley Square Courthouse in New York City in the summer of 1949. While the Hiss trial was proceeding in the same building, eleven members of the "open" portion of the American Communist Party were being tried for allegedly violating the Smith Act, a federal law that made it a crime to belong to an organization that advocated the violent overthrow of the U.S. government. The trial of the Smith Act defendants was a stormy affair, complete with scores of angry harangues by lawyers and defendants and the issuing of numerous contempt citations by Judge Harold Medina. It would eventually become one of the longest trials in American history and, on appeal, result in the important Supreme Court decision of *Dennis v. U.S.* (1951), which upheld both the constitutionality of the Smith Act and the conviction of the defendants. The Hiss trial was not, on the surface, as turbulent as the Dennis trial. Nor would the Hiss trial raise constitutional issues as important as those presented in the *Dennis* case. But the place of the Hiss trial in American history would prove to be at least as large as that of Eugene Dennis and his codefendants.

To many politically informed liberals in 1949, Hiss appeared to have been a victim of the scare tactics of the right wing of the Republican Party. In addition, many Democrats felt that the hostility that Hiss faced resulted from the fact that Hiss was seen, by conservative Republicans, as a symbol of what was wrong with the Democratic reform of the thirties. By attacking Hiss, Republicans were thought to be getting in their licks at Franklin Roosevelt's New Deal.

Hiss was represented at the federal court trial by a legal team led by Lloyd Paul Stryker, a flamboyant attorney. Hiss, an attorney himself, had many friends and associates with legal expertise who rendered advice and provided volunteer research assistance. At the trial, the Hiss defense team pursued four main lines of argument. First, they presented witnesses to suggest that Chambers was mentally unstable. To advance this line of inquiry, the Hiss attorneys emphasized Chambers's admitted homosexuality, thus playing upon the homophobic prejudices of the time. Second, Hiss's attorneys stressed that Hiss and Chambers barely knew each other and seldom met. Third, they maintained that Hiss's Woodstock typewriter had been given away long before Priscilla Hiss could have retyped the State Department documents. In fact, the defense attorneys even suggested the possibility that the FBI or other unknown parties could have typed the documents to frame the Hisses. Finally, the defense attorneys presented many distinguished friends of Alger Hiss who testified that the defendant was a man of complete integrity and would not have associated himself with Communists. Among the character witnesses were Supreme Court Justices Felix Frankfurter and Stanley Reed.

The prosecution's strategy was essentially to allow the testimony of Chambers and the allegedly stolen documents to speak for themselves. The prosecution, with forensic evidence, attempted to show that Priscilla Hiss retyped the purloined State Department papers on the Hiss Woodstock. Throughout the trial, the prosecution objected to what it perceived as favoritism toward Hiss and the defense's case. For example, the prosecution was incensed that the trial judge, Stanley H. Kaufman, came down from the bench to shake hands with the two Supreme Court justices who testified on Hiss's behalf.

Finally, after six weeks, the case went to the jury. After more than two days of deliberations, the jury reported that it was hopelessly deadlocked and could not reach a verdict. The judge reluctantly dismissed them. When reporters queried the jurors, they found that the panel favored conviction by a vote of 8-4. The four favoring acquittal were not convinced that Mrs. Hiss typed the stolen documents on the Woodstock.

Prosecutor Thomas Murphy and his superiors in the Justice Department elected to retry the case. With Murphy again leading the prosecution, a second trial took place in November. In the four-month interval between the two trials the world had changed: the Soviet Union had exploded an atomic bomb, the Communist Chinese had succeeded in taking over all of mainland China, HUAC had begun investigating alleged Soviet espionage in the wartime Manhattan Project, and U.S. public opinion polls showed an increasing concern over the threat of domestic communism. In short, the Cold War was heating up.

For the second trial, Hiss retained a new attorney, Claude B. Cross. In contrast to Lloyd Stryker, the Hiss attorney in the first case, Cross was much less flamboyant. The judge this time around was the circuit's second-most senior jurist, Henry W. Goddard, a tough, no nonsense judge. The conduct of the second trial was more professional than the first. Unlike Stryker, Cross did not attempt to goad the prosecution or play upon the emotions of the jurors.

In fact, attorneys for both sides were consistently polite. The case went to the jury on the afternoon of January 20, 1950. The jury deliberated all night and returned the next afternoon with a verdict of guilty on both perjury counts. Hiss was then sentenced to five years in federal prison.

On appeal his sentence was upheld by the Circuit Court. In 1951 the U.S. Supreme Court voted 4-2 not to hear the case. Three Supreme Court justices—Frankfurter and Reed and Thomas Clark—did not participate in the decision declining to review the Hiss verdict. Frankfurter and Reed disqualified themselves because they had testified on Alger Hiss's behalf at the first trial, and Clark disqualified himself because he had been U.S. attorney general at the time of the bringing of the indictment against Hiss. Hiss surrendered to the U.S. marshall on March 21, 1951, and began serving his sentence in a federal penitentiary. Subsequent appeals for review of his conviction were turned down.

Less than three weeks after Hiss's January 1950 conviction, Senator Joseph McCarthy delivered his Wheeling, West Virginia, speech alleging personal knowledge of Communists in sensitive government positions. McCarthy stated in part: "The reason why we find ourselves in a position of impotency is . . . because of the traitorous actions of those who have been treated so well by this Nation . . . those who have had all the benefits that the wealthiest nation on earth has had to offer—the finest homes, the finest college education, and the finest jobs in Government we can give. This is glaringly true in the State Department. There the bright young men who are born with silver spoons in their mouths are the ones who have been the worst." Clearly, McCarthy had in mind Alger Hiss. Comments such as these served as the springboard to launch the Wisconsin senator's four-year campaign of allegations and undocumented attacks that constituted what has been termed "McCarthyism." In fact, in one speech during the 1952 presidential campaign, McCarthy cleverly appeared to stumble and confuse Hiss with the Democratic candidate for the presidency, Adlai Stevenson: "Strangely Alger—I mean Adlai . . ." The point

was not lost on his sympathetic listeners: McCarthy believed that Adlai Stevenson, a liberal Democrat, was much like the convicted perjurer Alger Hiss.

After serving three years and eight months of his five-year sentence, Hiss was released from prison in November 1954. Throughout his incarceration and during the remainder of his long life, Hiss has professed his innocence. In 1957 he published *In the Court of Public Opinion*. Rather than an autobiography, this book is a lawyerly defense of his innocence, alleging fraud and forgery on the part of the federal prosecutors and the FBI. After his release from prison, Hiss attempted without success to work in a small business. He also spoke occasionally on the Cold War to academic audiences. For liberals, Hiss came to be seen as one of the principal casualties of the Cold War—a bright, accomplished, and ambitious man cut down in his prime by demagogues of the political right.

For conservatives, Hiss was the embodiment of what was wrong with America and was, thus, vilified for decades. Richard Nixon, for example, in his *Six Crises* and in other accounts of his life, cited his success in "getting Hiss" as one of his greatest political accomplishments. By contrast, for Nixon and other conservatives, Alger Hiss's accuser, Whittaker Chambers, became a virtual hero. His Communist past notwithstanding, Chambers became a favorite of conservatives after he testified against Hiss. Chambers told his fascinating life story in a popular book, simply titled *Witness*, published in 1952. Named a Book of the Month Club selection, his eight hundred-page memoirs was more personal and revealing than Hiss's *In the Court of Public Opinion*.

In the years since the 1948 HUAC hearings, there have been scores of books and articles on the Hiss-Chambers case. Ironically, just as the case began to fade from memory it was resuscitated in the early seventies by the Watergate scandal. Richard Nixon, who began his national political career attacking Hiss, now was the object of a sensational investigation of his own alleged wrongdoings. In fact Hiss himself wrote an article for the *New York Times* in 1973, titled "My Six Parallels." The title of Hiss's piece was, of course, an allusion to *Six Crises*, the title of Nixon's book, which included a chapter on the Hiss case. The article drew comparisons between his case and the break-ins of the Nixon years, suggesting that the Watergate fiasco and similar "dirty tricks" had been foreshadowed by government tampering with evidence in his own case. Thus, as Nixon's stock when down, Hiss's seemed to rise.

Then the worm turned again. In 1975, as a result of a lawsuit under the Freedom of Information Act, a liberal historian named Allen Weinstein was successful in forcing the FBI to release its voluminous files on the Hiss-Chambers case. Drawing on the FBI's materials, hundreds of interviews, and the files of Hiss's own attorneys, Weinstein in 1978 published a book titled *Perjury*, which came to the conclusion that Hiss was guilty of lying under oath and, by implication, had committed several counts of espionage.

The ending of the Cold War in the early 1990s led to the opening of Russian and East European archives to American scholars and to interviews with former Soviet-bloc officials. The consensus that emerged from the documents in the archives and the testimony of aging spies and bureaucrats was that Hiss was almost certainly the perjurer and Communist agent that Whittaker Chambers had alleged him to be.

Alger Hiss died in 1996 at the age of 92. With virtually his last breath, Hiss persisted in denying his guilt in the matter that has been termed by his dwindling roster of advocates as the "American Dreyfus affair."

Selected Bibliography

Caute, David. *The Great Fear: The Anti-Communist Purge Under Truman and Eisenhower*. New York: Simon and Schuster, 1978.

Chambers, Whittaker. *Witness*. New York: Random House, 1952.

Cooke, Alistair. *A Generation on Trial: U.S.A. v. Alger Hiss*. New York: Knopf, 1950.

Haynes, John Earl, and Harvey Klehr, *Venona: Decoding Soviet Espionage in America*. New Haven, CT: Yale University Press, 1999.

Hiss, Alger. *In the Court of Public Opinion*. New York: Knopf, 1957.

Hiss, Tony. *A View from Alger's Window: A Son's Memoir*. New York: Knopf, 1999.

Latham, Earl. *The Communist Controversy in Washington: From the New Deal to McCarthy*. New York: Atheneum, 1969.

Nixon, Richard. *Six Crises*. New York: Warner Books, 1962.

Tannenhaus, Sam. *Whittaker Chambers: A Biography*. New York: Random House, 1997.

Weinstein, Allen. *Perjury: The Hiss-Chambers Case*. New York: Knopf, 1978.

A Crime Worse Than Murder

——◄◦►——

Joseph Glidewell

Social Sciences Department
Truett-McConnell College

United States of America v. Julius and Ethel Rosenberg (1951)
[U.S. Federal District Court]

◄◦► THE CASE IN BRIEF ◄◦►

Date
March–April 1951

Location
New York City

Court
U.S. Federal District Court

Principal Participants
Julius and Ethel Rosenberg
Morton Sobell
Klaus Fuchs
Judge Irving Kaufman

Significance of the Case
Espionage charges during the
"Second Red Scare" culminated in
the controversial executions of two
Americans for selling U.S. secrets of the
atom bomb.

At 12:00 noon on April 6, 1951, Federal Judge Irving Kaufman faced Julius and Ethel Rosenberg in the largest federal courtroom in the Southern District of New York. His purpose was to impose sentence. For the past month the Rosenbergs, along with Morton Sobell, Anatolia Yakovlev, and David Greenglass, had been on trial, charged with conspiracy to commit espionage in wartime. However, Yakovlev, who had left the country years before, and Greenglass, who had pleaded guilty, were granted severances for purposes of the trial. Therefore, the main defendants were the Rosenbergs and Sobell.

What had transpired from March 6 through April 6, 1951, was the nation's first trial for the theft of the atomic bomb secrets. Found guilty of the charge on March 29, the defendants waited to hear their fate. As they stood facing Judge Kaufman, little could they know that their trial would spark worldwide demonstrations, protests, and a controversy that still rages fifty years later.

The Rosenberg trial occurred during what has been called the "Second Red Scare" in

83

American history. The period has been characterized as a time of anticommunist furor that developed into a "Communist witch hunt." Numerous organizations as well as individuals were publicly accused of being Communist sympathizers simply because of their associations with left-wing political beliefs. This hysteria occurred because of the ideological conflict that had arisen at the end of World War II between the Soviet Union and the United States. Labeled the "Cold War," this ideological confrontation had America in its grip and it permeated all areas of American life.

Following World War II, Americans had witnessed Communist military advances and success in Eastern Europe and in other areas of the world. These and the revelations of espionage within the U.S. government that surfaced during the Alger Hiss trial threw the United States into a mood of fearful anticipation of what would occur next. The years 1949–1950 saw the fall of China to the Communist forces of Mao-Tse-tung and the explosion of an atomic device by the Soviet Union years ahead of the timetable that had been predicted by Western scientists. Then, in June 1950, the Korean War erupted and the initial success of the North Koreans' invasion of the South set the stage for a major "Red Scare." It was amid this atmosphere that the Rosenberg trial took place.

The arrests of the Rosenbergs and the other defendants were the result of an intensive investigation that had lasted over four years. The investigation began in 1945 when a Soviet consul named Govzenko, in Ottawa, Canada, defected to the West. His tales of espionage took the combined efforts of the Canadian Mounties, Scotland Yard, and the FBI four years to unravel. The key break occurred in early 1950, when British scientist Klaus Fuchs confessed his espionage activities to a Scotland Yard agent. Fuchs's confession led the authorities to Harry Gold, a chemist from Philadelphia, who in turn confessed to the FBI. It was Gold's confession that led to David Greenglass, Ethel Rosenberg's brother.

The government's case rested on the alleged scenario that, during the 1930s, the Rosenbergs became members of the Communist Party in New York City and were active party members until the time of their arrest. During the summer of 1944, Ethel's brother David Greenglass, while in the U.S. army, began work as a machinist at the atomic weapons center in Los Alamos, New Mexico. In January 1945, Greenglass, after being recruited by Julius to help the Soviet Union, gave the Rosenbergs sketches of the high-explosive lenses that were used to detonate an atomic bomb. Later, Harry Gold was sent to Los Alamos to obtain more information from Greenglass. Through this meeting and others more sketches were passed on, even one of the atomic bomb itself.

When World War II ended in August 1945, the espionage activities of Greenglass also ended. He was released from the army and returned to New York City, where he and Julius Rosenberg, along with Bernard Greenglass, opened a machine business. The next several years passed quietly for both the Greenglasses and the Rosenbergs. But unknown to them, the Soviet spy ring to which they had belonged had been unraveled by the combined efforts of British and American intelligence.

According to the government, when Julius Rosenberg read of Harry Gold's arrest he immediately began to make plans for the Greenglasses to leave the country. However, Ruth Greenglass, David's wife, refused to leave, and eleven days after Gold's arrest, on May 23, the FBI arrested David Greenglass. Several days later, on July 17, Julius Rosenberg was arrested, and one month later, on August 11, Ethel was taken into custody.

The U.S. attorney given the task of prosecuting the "Atom Spies" was Irving Saypol. Known as the nation's number one legal hunter of Communists, Saypol was assisted by Myles Lane, Roy Cohn, James Kilsheimer, and James Branigan Jr.

The trial was to be presided over by Judge Irving Kaufman, who at forty years of age was the youngest judge on the federal bench. Kaufman had a distinguished record as he had served as special assistant to the U.S. Attorney for the Southern District of New York and later advanced to assistant U.S. attorney. After several years of private practice, he became special assistant to the attorney general of the United

States. Following this position he accepted an appointment as a federal judge.

For the defense, the Rosenbergs were represented by Alexander Bloch and his son Emmanuel, better known as Manny. Manny Bloch, though he liked to be portrayed as just "people's lawyer," was an accomplished attorney who had handled several national cases involving Communist Party leaders and had a reputation as a crusader for left-wing causes. Ethel's attorney, Alexander Bloch, had legal experience in dealing with unions but was on unfamiliar ground with the type of case he was being asked to handle. However, he remained as Ethel's attorney until the end, and she never questioned this arrangement.

The first day and a half of the trial was spent selecting a jury. Over three hundred prospective jurors were called as the importance of the case made jury selection a "tedious business." Judge Kaufman led the questioning, and within a surprisingly short time a jury of eleven men and one woman was chosen. With this and other formalities out of the way, late in the second day of the trial, the U.S. attorney gave his opening statement.

Prosecuting Attorney Saypol immediately set the tone of the trial as he endeavored to tie Julius and Ethel Rosenberg to communism. Immediately, Defense Attorney Manny Bloch objected, arguing that communism was not on trial, but Judge Kaufman allowed the remarks to stand. Saypol then proceeded to equate conspiracy with treason by promising to show "evidence of the treasonable acts of these three defendants" and that "they have committed the most serious crime which can be committed against the people of this country." This point was important in the government's case as it wanted a charge of treason against the defendants so that stiff penalties could be obtained, possibly the death penalty for Julius Rosenberg. However, treason would be almost impossible to prove. Conspiracy, though, would be very easy to prove. But it did not carry as stiff a penalty as treason. Therefore, Saypol linked the two together in hopes of getting both a conviction and severe punishment.

From the beginning, the trial took on the aura of a historic event. The prosecution had hinted that possibly 123 witnesses would be called, including such notables as atomic scientist Robert J. Oppenheimer and General Leslie Groves, head of the atomic research at Los Alamos. Yet only a handful of witnesses were called; none of whom were household names.

The government's first witness was Max Elitcher, a close friend of defendant Morton Sobell. Elitcher's testimony linked himself, Sobell, and Julius Rosenberg together as he testified to numerous attempts by Rosenberg to get information about military equipment and of Rosenberg's constant desire for him to recruit engineering students who might be able to obtain military information. Elitcher further testified about a trip he made to Morton Sobell's home in which Sobell told him about information in his home that was "too valuable to be destroyed and yet too dangerous to keep around." He then told how he and Sobell drove to meet Rosenberg and give him what he identified as a thirty-five-millimeter film can.

The prosecution's second witness was David Greenglass, Ethel's brother and the main witness for the government. Greenglass told of how Julius and Ethel during the 1930s had told him how they preferred Russian socialism to capitalism, how Julius convinced David's wife, Ruth, to ask him to get information that would be of value to the Soviet Union, of the sketches he made for Julius, of his meeting with Harry Gold, and how Ethel typed up the information he had given to the Rosenbergs.

Greenglass testified that the jurors were given an insight into the allegedly simply ingenuity of the agents involved in espionage when he described the method used by Ruth to meet her contact. According to Greenglass, after an evening meal with the Rosenbergs, it was decided that Ruth would go to live in Albuquerque and be used to pass information to a Soviet operative. For identification, Julius went into the kitchen along with Ethel and Ruth and cut a box of gelatin into two irregular sections. Julius kept one piece and gave Ruth the other to use to identify her contact. With this testimony David Greenglass forever linked Julius and Ethel Rosenberg to a piece of physical evidence that, unlike implosion theories, high-explosives lenses, and isotopes, the jury and public could understand. Greenglass went on to testify regarding a meeting in Albuquerque with Harry Gold and plans made by Julius for his family to leave the country.

The government's next witness was David Greenglass's wife, Ruth. Most of her testimony corroborated the essentials of her husband's story. However, she did add two crucial pieces of the puzzle that her husband had failed to mention. The testimony that further threw suspicion on the Rosenbergs was Ruth's statements about various sums of money paid to David by Julius and about the existence of a mahogany console table. Ethel said this table was a gift from Julius that was hollow underneath for photographic purposes; he said it was to be used to take pictures on microfilm of the typewritten notes. On cross-examination Ruth repeated her story nearly word for word.

The Greenglasses were the government's main witnesses, and no doubt it was their testimony that led to the conviction of the Rosenbergs. However, five minor witnesses were called to corroborate the Greenglass testimony. Dorothy Printz Abel, Ruth's sister, corroborated the story of the Rosenbergs meeting with the Greenglasses at the Rosenbergs' home; Lorin Abel, Ruth's brother-in-law, testified that he held the money Julius gave to David Greenglass; a doctor, confirmed that Julius called him about inoculations needed for a trip outside the country; an army intelligence officer, confirmed that David Greenglass was accurate in his description of the security measures at Los Alamos; and Harry Gold corroborated the trip to Albuquerque and his meeting with David Greenglass with the famous remark "Julius sent me."

After Gold's testimony the prosecution called eight minor witnesses to prove that Morton Sobell had taken "flight" to Mexico to avoid capture by the authorities. The final witness was Elizabeth Bentley, the famous "Red Spy Queen." Bentley more than likely was called for effect rather than for the testimony she could deliver. However, she did relate her past history as a Soviet courier and gave suspicious testimony when she testified to telephone calls she received "in the small wee hours" and how the conversation always started with the

saying, "This is Julius." Shortly after her testimony the prosecution rested.

The defense called as its first witness Julius Rosenberg. He was questioned about his youth, his political beliefs, his family relationships, dealings with the family business, and the charges made by his brother-in-law and sister-in-law. He denied that he had anything to do with espionage. Throughout his questioning and cross-examination Julius remained calm and cool.

After several minor witnesses were called, the final defense witness was Ethel Rosenberg. She also denied all allegations regarding espionage. After Ethel denied the securing of passport pictures, the defense rested its case. Morton Sobell elected not to take the stand.

The prosecution then recalled several rebuttal witnesses. Evelyn Cox, a household domes-

Ethel Rosenberg and her husband, Julius Rosenberg (fourth from left), in custody during their trial for espionage. They were convicted as atomic spies and executed in the electric chair in 1953. *Corbis.*

tic, testified regarding the console table and its removal from its usual place in the Rosenberg home. Then Ben Schneider, the owner of a small photo shop, testified it was the Rosenbergs who came into his photo shop sometime in May or June and ordered three dozen passport-size pictures. Following Schneider's testimony, the lawyers made their final arguments, the judge delivered his charge, and the case went to the jury. The jury retired on Wednesday, March 28, at 4:30 P.M. and one day later they reached verdicts of guilty against all three defendants. One week later the three convicted defendants faced Judge Kaufman to hear their fate.

The law under which the three had been found guilty, the Espionage Act of 1917, carried a maximum of twenty years' imprisonment with the exception of violation during wartime, where the punishment was death or imprisonment for not more than thirty years. With these guidelines in mind, Kaufman proceeded. He began by explaining the reason for the sentence he was about to impose and his opening remarks left no doubt of his decision. "I consider your crime worse than murder." Kaufman then explained that he had no doubt of the couple's guilt, that their actions had directly led to the Korean War, and that their deed changed the history of the United States for the worse.

After explaining that Julius was the "prime motivator" in the crime, and Ethel was "a full-fledged partner," he told the Rosenbergs: "It is not in my power to forgive you. Only the Lord can find mercy for what you have done." He then imposed sentence. "The sentence of this court is . . . the punishment of death." Later Morton Sobell received the thirty-year maximum penalty with the judge's recommendation for no parole.

What followed for the next three years was one unsuccessful appeal after another. Following a final refusal by the U.S. Supreme Court to hear the case, the only avenue left for the defendants to pursue was a presidential pardon. But this was also denied amid worldwide protests to spare their lives. On June 18, 1953, almost three years after their arrest, the Rosenbergs went to the electric chair at New York's Sing Sing Prison.

Controversy persists about the Rosenberg case. While most scholars have supported the official verdict of the case, numerous questions have been raised as to whether the penalty was just or the depth of involvement of the Rosenbergs in Soviet espionage. A number of Americans have even maintained that the Rosenbergs were completely innocent, the victims of an elaborate government frame-up.

The reasons for the skepticism are many. This was a case that had no disinterested eyewitnesses, and the prosecution offered no clear evidence, such as a "smoking gun," that could tie the defendants together. The sketches, the box of gelatin, and hotel receipts of supposed espionage travels did not link the Rosenbergs to Greenglass or any other espionage agent. Much of the physical evidence, such as the console table, the sales ticket for its purchase, or the negatives of the purported passport photos were never located. From these points, many believe that the Rosenbergs were found guilty only because of the hysteria of the times.

Arguments that support the verdict have emphasized that the defense offered no major witnesses other than the defendants. Furthermore, none of the defendants offered a foolproof alibi to refute any of the charges, and no physical evidence or witness testimony was given on their behalf. Following the sentencing, 112 judges heard the appeals of the case over a three-year period. While 16 disagreed as to whether a stay of execution should be granted or further review allowed, none concluded that the Rosenbergs were denied due process or that they were innocent. Recently, the National Security Agency (NSA) released forty-nine partially decoded Rosenberg-era cables. These reveal that Julius Rosenberg did actively spy for the Soviet Union, though he gave the Soviets very little hard information. According to one source, "Julius Rosenberg had more in common with Inspector Clouseau than with James Bond." In 1996, former Soviet spy Alexander Feklisov stated that Julius Rosenberg did indeed spy for the Soviet Union but that the assertion that "the Rosenbergs delivered atomic secrets to the Soviets is absurd." Feklisov insisted that "Ethel Rosenberg never had direct contact with Soviet intelligence, but she was probably aware of her husband's activities."

Despite the recently released cables and interviews, some Americans see Julius and Ethel Rosenberg as representing an era of Red Scare hysteria in which the rights of many were violated. In their struggle to assert their rights as U.S. citizens, they became Cold War casualties. To others, the Rosenberg trial remains a symbol of justice done to those who committed "a crime worse than murder."

Selected Bibliography

Latham, Earl. *The Communist Controversy in Washington*. New York: Atheneum, 1969.

Nizer, Louis. *The Implosion Conspiracy*. New York: Doubleday, 1973.

Pilat, Oliver. *The Atom Spies*. New York: G.P. Putnam Sons, 1952.

Radosh, Ronald, and Joyce Milton. *The Rosenberg File: A Search for the Truth*. New York: Holt, Rinehart and Winston, 1983.

Root, Jonathan. *The Betrayers: The Rosenberg Case—A Reappraisal of an American Crisis*. New York: Coward-McMann, 1963.

Schneir, Miriam, and Walter Schneir. *Invitation to an Inquest: Reopening the Rosenberg "Atom Spy" Case*. Baltimore: Penguin, 1973.

1960–2000

———◦———

The Exclusionary Rule Binds the States

————◄०►————

Stephen Lowe
Greenville, South Carolina

Mapp v. Ohio, 367 U.S. 643 (1961) [U.S. Supreme Court]

◄०► THE CASE IN BRIEF ◄०►

Date
1961

Locations
Ohio, Washington, D.C.

Court
U.S. Supreme Court

Principal Participants
Justice Thomas Clark
Dollree Mapp

Significance of the Case
A then-controversial Supreme Court decision bound state and local authorities to adopt the federal law prohibiting unreasonable search and seizure; landmark decision thus "federalized" the exclusionary rule.

When the Supreme Court decided *Mapp v. Ohio* in 1961, it reversed *Wolf v. Colorado*, a decision tendered only twelve years earlier. In *Wolf*, the Court had determined that the Fourth Amendment's prohibition against "unreasonable searches and seizures" only applied to the federal government, not to the states. To a bare 5–4 majority of the Warren court of 1961, however, it was determined that the "exclusionary rule" should apply to the states as well as to the federal government if the principle were to have an element of common sense. Not only is logic an important element in the law, said Justice Thomas Clark, but common sense as well.

Dollree (Dolly) Mapp had been convicted following a 1957 arrest under an Ohio law that forbade the possession of lewd and lascivious material. The facts of her arrest are a perfect example of the extent to which state and local police forces could technically go prior to the 1960s, although many states adhered to the exclusionary rule of their own volition. On the afternoon of May 23, 1957, several Cleveland police officers, acting on a tip, demanded entrance to Mrs. Mapp's home, where they hoped to find a suspect in a local bombing. After contacting her lawyer, Dolly Mapp denied admission to the police unless they could produce a search warrant. Since they did not have a warrant, the officers left and began to watch the house. About three hours later, the policemen, reinforced by a lieutenant carrying what he claimed was a valid warrant, again demanded entrance to the house. When Mrs. Mapp again refused, the officers forced open a side door and entered. Once inside, they produced a warrant, which Mapp grabbed and "placed . . . in her bosom." A struggle followed, during which the police handcuffed Mapp for her belligerence. They then began to search the house. During the search, the materials that were later used to convict her were discovered. At the trial, the prosecution failed to produce the warrant, and according to the Supreme Court decision, "the failure to produce one [was not] explained or accounted for."

The Ohio Supreme Court admitted that the argument could very well be made that the evidence was unlawfully seized, but it still upheld Mrs. Mapp's conviction on two grounds. First, the fact that the evidence was not seized violently was considered important, because the U.S. Supreme Court held in *Rochin v. California* (1952) that only evidence seized in a "shocking" manner fell under the exclusionary rule. Second, the Court pointed to *Wolf v. Colorado*, saying that even if the search was unreasonable, states are not prevented from using evidence gained in such a manner in court.

Mapp's attorneys did not address the issue of illegal search and seizure before the Supreme Court; instead, they sought to have the Ohio law forbidding possession of lewd material declared unconstitutional. The Ohio Supreme Court ruled by a vote of 4–3 that the statute was ill-advised, but Ohio's constitution required at least a 6–1 ruling to strike down a state law. Also, Mapp's attorneys sought to invoke *Rochin v. California* by arguing that the search of Mrs. Mapp's home was a "shocking" display of disregard for her rights.

The American Civil Liberties Union filed an amicus curiae brief in the *Mapp* case at the U.S. Supreme Court level. The ACLU, however, did not address search and seizure until the final paragraph of its brief. Instead, the ACLU argued that the Ohio law was illogical and unreasonable, because it served no rational purpose. Also, the ACLU argued for an interpretation of the Fourth and Fourteenth Amendments to guarantee a right of privacy, and argued that certain aspects of the Ohio law violated the equal protection clause of the Fourteenth Amendment.

Finally, in the last paragraph of the ACLU brief, the Court was asked to "re-examine this issue and conclude that the ordered liberty concept guaranteed to persons by the Due Process Clause of the Fourteenth Amendment necessarily requires that evidence illegally in violation thereof, not be admissible in state criminal proceedings."

In its decision, the U.S. Supreme Court stuck to the search-and-seizure issue and ignored the privacy matter. Justice Thomas Clark, writing for himself and four other justices, pointed out that many states already adhered to the exclusionary rule and did not allow illegally seized evidence to be admitted in their courts. "Moreover," said Clark, "our holding that the exclusionary rule is an essential part of both the Fourth and Fourteenth Amendments is not only the logical dictate . . . , but it also makes very good sense. There is no war between the Constitution and common sense."

The Court's decision in *Mapp v. Ohio* received a great deal of criticism. It was immediately assailed because of the Court's reliance upon the search-and-seizure ground when that issue had hardly been raised in the lower court or discussed in oral arguments. The decision was seen as devastating to the police and an unreasonable restriction of state power. Many questions were left unanswered until subsequent cases clarified and restricted the decision.

The decision in *Mapp v. Ohio* had the far-reaching effect of binding all states henceforth by the exclusionary rule. As Justice John Marshall Harlan said in a 1969 concurring opinion in *Chimel v. California*, "every change in Fourth Amendment law must now be obeyed by state officials facing widely different problems of local law enforcement."

Selected Bibliography

Graham, Fred. *The Due Process Revolution: The Warren Court's Impact on Criminal Law*. New York: Hayden, 1970.

Howard, A. E. Dick, Jr., ed. *Criminal Justice in Our Time*. Charlottesville: University of Virginia Press, 1965.

Sowle, Claude R., ed. *Police Power and Individual Freedom: The Quest for Balance*. Chicago: Aldine, 1962.

"Good Faith" and
the Exclusionary Rule

———◄○►———

Tinsley E. Yarbrough

Department of Political Science
East Carolina University

United States v. Leon, 468 U.S. 897 (1984) [U.S. Supreme Court]

◄○► THE CASE IN BRIEF ◄○►

Date
   1984

Locations
   Burbank, California; Boston,
   Washington, D.C.

Courts
   U.S. Ninth Circuit Court of Appeals
   Massachusetts Supreme Court
   U.S. Supreme Court

Principal Participants
   Albert Leon
   Justice Byron R. White

Significance of the Case
   The Constitution's guarantee against
   unreasonable search and seizure was
   again subjected to the Court's scrutiny
   as the admission of evidence on good-
   faith grounds was questioned.

The language of the Fourth Amendment to the U.S. Constitution does not specifically provide that unconstitutionally seized evidence must be excluded from trials. But the U.S. Supreme Court's decisions in *Weeks v. United States* (1914), applying the exclusionary rule in federal cases, and *Mapp v. Ohio* (1961), extending it to state trials, clearly rested on the proposition that the exclusionary rule was an essential ingredient of the constitutional guarantee against "unreasonable searches and seizures" and necessary to assure that courts would not become parties, in effect, to police misconduct. The *Mapp* court, speaking through Justice Tom C. Clark, expressly held, for example, that "all evidence obtained by searches and seizures in violation of the Constitution is, *by that same authority*, inadmissible in a state court" [emphasis added]. Nearly fifty years earlier, moreover, Justice William Rufus Day had reasoned in *Weeks* that the admission of illegally seized evidence in court would mean that the Fourth Amendment was "of no value, and . . . might as well be stricken from the Constitution. The efforts of the courts and . . . officials to bring the

94

guilty to punishment, praiseworthy as they are, are not to be aided by the sacrifice of those great principles established by years of endeavor and suffering which have resulted in their embodiment in the fundamental law of the land."

However firmly grounded in the Constitution and the imperative of judicial integrity the exclusionary rule might have been in the eyes of its defenders, *Mapp* became a major target for outspoken critics of the Warren court's civil liberties rulings, including President Richard M. Nixon and the conservative federal appeals court judge, Warren E. Burger, who Nixon selected to replace retiring Chief Justice Earl Warren in 1969. In *Bivens v. Six Unknown Named Agents* (1971) and other cases, the new chief justice vehemently attacked the exclusionary rule, charging that it had no basis in the Constitution's language; did little to deter misconduct by police (who were rarely sanctioned as a result of their Fourth Amendment violations); constituted a sort of "universal capital punishment" in which the sanction (exclusion of evidence from trial) was the same whether police misconduct was minor or extreme; and worst of all, in Burger's eyes, exacted a terrible social cost in returning felons to the streets. Recommending that the exclusionary rule be retained for only the most egregious Fourth Amendment violations, Burger was optimistic that abandonment of the rule would encourage government to focus on other ways (such as civil suits against offending officers and stricter police disciplinary policies) to protect against official lawlessness.

A majority refused to join Chief Justice Burger, Associate Justice William H. Rehnquist, and others in scrapping the exclusionary rule. They did agree, however, to substantially curtail its use. Rejecting the argument that the rule was required by the Constitution, the Court recast it as simply a judicially created device intended to deter police from violating the Fourth Amendment. Its future application in specific settings was, thus, to depend on a judicial balancing of the deterrent interests the rule was said to further against the social costs it exacted in the freeing of guilty defendants. Following this balancing approach, the Court held

that illegally seized evidence could be used in grand jury proceedings (*United States v. Calandra*, 1974), and civil cases (*United States v. Janis*, 1976). In *Stone v. Powell* (1976), a majority further concluded that the rule's deterrent effect would not be substantially enhanced by permitting a state defendant to raise suppression claims in a federal-court habeas corpus proceeding after being given a "full and fair" opportunity to raise such claims in the state courts. And in 1984, the Court recognized an "inevitable discovery" exception to the rule, holding in *Nix v. Williams* that illegally seized evidence (such as the body of a murder victim) was admissible if it would have been discovered anyway through lawful means during the police investigation of the crime.

That same year, the Court embraced yet another, and potentially far-reaching, modification of the exclusionary rule—the "good faith" exception to its application. Based upon a tip from an anonymous informant of unproven reliability, the police in Burbank, California, conducted surveillance of Alberto Leon and others suspected of extensive drug trafficking. The police later secured a warrant to search their residences and automobiles. When the ensuing searches produced large quantities of cocaine and other evidence, Leon and his confederates were indicted on federal drug charges. On the defendants' motion, however, a U.S. district judge suppressed some of the evidence seized, on the ground that the information provided by an informant of unproven reliability had not established probable cause for issuance of the warrant on which the searches had been based. While agreeing that the police had acted on a reasonable belief that the warrant was valid, the judge also refused to recognize a good-faith exception to the exclusionary rule. When the U.S. Court of Appeals for the Ninth Circuit affirmed the district court, the Supreme Court granted the government's petition for a writ of certiorari to review the good-faith issue.

On the same day the Court heard oral arguments in the *Leon* case, the justices also heard *Massachusetts v. Sheppard*, which raised the same issue. In *Sheppard*, Boston police investigating a homicide applied to a judge for an arrest warrant, as well as a warrant authorizing a search of a suspect's residence. Attached to the warrant application was a supporting affidavit listing items for which the police wished to search, including the victim's clothing and the murder weapon. Because the local court was closed, police had difficulty finding an appropriate warrant application form and finally altered one used in another district for drug searches. When a detective located a judge at his residence, he informed him that the warrant form might need further modification. The judge agreed that the supporting affidavit established probable cause and indicated that he would make the necessary changes in the application form. Although he did make a number of changes, the judge neglected to modify the form to authorize a drug search before signing the warrant and informing police it was sufficient to authorize their search. At a pretrial hearing to suppress evidence seized in the search, the trial judge acknowledged that the warrant failed to conform to the Fourth Amendment's requirement that warrants "particularly" describe "the things to be seized." Even so, he upheld the admission of the evidence on good-faith grounds. Following Sheppard's conviction, however, Massachusetts' highest court reversed, holding that the evidence should have been suppressed and rejected the good-faith claim.

In *Illinois v. Gates* (1983), decided the previous term, the Supreme Court had asked the parties to address the good-faith issue. But the Court ultimately declined, holding instead that no unconstitutional seizure had occurred in *Gates*. The *Gates* court had also relaxed considerably the standards for judging the validity of searches based on tips furnished by anonymous informers, holding that the reasonableness of such searches should depend merely on a judicial assessment of the "totality of the circumstances," rather than on the stricter requirements imposed in two earlier cases.

During oral arguments in *Leon* and *Sheppard*, the questions of several justices indicated that the Court might also decide those cases without resolving the good-faith claim. At one point during argument in *Leon*, for example, Justice Byron R. White suggested that the Court perhaps should follow *Gates*, reversing the lower

court on the ground that no illegal search had occurred in *Leon*. But Solicitor General Rex E. Lee—who was eventually to resign from the Reagan administration in the wake of complaints he was not pursuing the administration's conservative civil-liberties agenda with sufficient zeal—urged the justices to adopt the good-faith exception to the exclusionary rule. An attorney for Leon, on the other hand, condemned the good-faith standard as "unconstitutional, unmanageable, illogical." He argued that it was bound to encourage "magistrate shopping" by police who had insufficient evidence to justify issuance of a valid warrant, but who were hopeful that the fruits of a search conducted with a bad warrant would fall within the good-faith exception. Leon's counsel also contended that probable cause was lacking in the case, to which Justice Rehnquist retorted, "There's nothing magic about [probable cause]. Surely some association with a drug dealer is an indication that you have some proclivities that way yourself."

When the Court issued its decisions in *Leon* and *Sheppard* on July 17, 1984, Solicitor General Lee and counsel for Massachusetts got the broad ruling they had sought. Speaking for the majority, Justice White concluded that the exclusionary rule did not bar the prosecution's use at trial of evidence seized by police in an objectively reasonable reliance on a search warrant ultimately found to be invalid. White agreed that judges must not be mere rubber stamps for police and that evidence should continue to be suppressed (1) if police officers knowingly or recklessly mislead a magistrate, (2) if they rely on a warrant based on information grossly inadequate to establish probable cause to justify its issuance, or (3) if a warrant is so deficient on its face (i.e., fails to conform to the Fourth Amendment's requirement of particularity) that police could not reasonably presume its validity. White maintained, however, that the exclusionary rule was designed to deter police misconduct rather than penalize the errors of judges. Excluding from trial evidence seized by police in a good-faith belief that their conduct was lawful would hardly serve that deterrent function. Instead, "[i]ndiscriminate application of the exclusionary rule," declared White, "may well 'generat[e] disrespect for the law and administration of justice.'"

In a brief concurring opinion, Justice Harry A. Blackmun emphasized the decision's "unavoidably provisional nature." This latest exception to the exclusionary rule was based on the Court's "empirical judgment" that application of the rule in good-faith situations would have little appreciable deterrent impact on the police. But such assumptions, added Blackmun, should not be "cast in stone." Should the good-faith exception result "in a material change in [the extent of] police compliance with the Fourth Amendment," the justice warned, "we shall have to reconsider what we have undertaken here."

Chiding the majority in a separate opinion (in part concurring and in part dissenting) for its recognition of the good-faith exception to the exclusionary rule, Justice John Paul Stevens contended that a search and seizure could not be "both 'unreasonable' and 'reasonable' at the same time." In his judgment, the Court could not "intelligibly assume . . . that a search was constitutionally unreasonable but that the seized evidence is admissible because the same search [since conducted in 'good faith'] was reasonable." Yet, that was precisely what the Court was holding in *Sheppard* and *Leon*. Because he found the search at issue in *Sheppard* clearly reasonable and the warrant on which it was based at worst a merely technical violation of the Fourth Amendment's particularity requirement, Stevens concurred with the Court's judgment, though not its good-faith rationale, in *Sheppard*. He favored remand of *Leon* to the court of appeals, however, for reconsideration in light of the *Gates* decision.

As the Court's staunchest supporters of the exclusionary rule, Justices William J. Brennan and Thurgood Marshall vigorously dissented. In an opinion joined by Marshall, Justice Brennan drew on the Court's opinions in *Weeks* and *Mapp* in contending that the exclusionary rule was a constitutional requirement binding on courts as well as police, not a mere judicially created tool to be applied or withheld at the discretion of judges. Cases establishing the rule as an implicit command of the Fourth Amendment had emphasized its role in assuring that courts would not permit the introduction of illegally seized evidence and thereby become parties to official lawlessness. "[T]he question whether the exclusion of evidence would deter future police misconduct," declared Brennan, "was never considered a relevant concern." Given the judicial integrity rationale that originally underlay the rule's adoption, Brennan found it alarming that the Court could condone a search based on a warrant that a judge had illegally issued. Nor would he accept the majority's assumption that application of the rule in good-faith contexts would have no appreciable deterrent effect on police. "[T]he deterrence rationale for the rule," the justice observed, "is not designed to be . . . a form of 'punishment' of individual police officers for their failures to obey the restraints imposed by the Fourth Amendment. . . . Instead, the chief deterrent function of the rule is its tendency to promote institutional compliance with Fourth Amendment requirements on the part of law enforcement agencies generally." The majority's concern that application of the rule in good-faith situations would be "unfair" to police, contended Brennan, was thus based on a fundamental misunderstanding of the rule's deterrence function. Finally, the justice drew on statistics in charging that the majority had grossly exaggerated the social costs the rule had exacted. He cited, for example, a 1979 study by the General Accounting Office that reported that only 0.2 percent of all federal felony arrests were declined for prosecution because of potential exclusionary-rule problems. According to a four-year study of the rule's impact in California, moreover, only 0.8 percent of all arrests there were rejected for prosecution because of illegal-search concerns. Indeed, added Brennan, in the *Leon* case itself, the defendants had lacked standing to challenge the bulk of the drug evidence to be used in their prosecution; application of the rule in that case was thus hardly likely to prevent their convictions.

Brennan's arguments, like those on which *Weeks* and *Mapp* were based, have largely fallen on deaf ears in the Burger and Rehnquist courts. While not formally rejecting the exclusionary rule, a post-*Leon* majority has continued to embrace good-faith and related exceptions to its application. *Illinois v. Krull* (1987), for example, upheld evidence seized in good-faith reliance on a statute that unconstitutionally authorized warrantless administrative searches. That same year, in *Maryland v. Garrison*, the justices condoned use of heroin evidence seized by police who, armed with a warrant to search one third-floor apartment, mistakenly searched an adjoining apartment instead. And in *Arizona v. Evans* (1995), a computer error indicating an outstanding misdemeanor warrant led to a good-faith seizure of

evidence from a defendant's vehicle. Only Justices Stevens and Ruth Bader Ginsburg dissented from the Court's decision upholding use of that evidence. "Good-faith" violations of the Fourth Amendment thus appear very secure on the current Supreme Court.

Selected Bibliography

Bloom, R. M. "United States v. Leon and Its Ramifications." *University of Colorado Law Review* 56 (1985): 247–263.

"Incorporation" and the Right to Counsel

—◁◦▷—

Tinsley E. Yarbrough
Department of Political Science
East Carolina University

Gideon v. Wainwright, Corrections Director, 372 U.S. 335 (1963) [U.S. Supreme Court]

◁◦▷ THE CASE IN BRIEF ◁◦▷

Date
1963

Location
Florida, Washington, D.C.

Courts
Florida Circuit Court of Appeals
U.S. Supreme Court

Principal Participants
Clarence Earl Gideon
Justice Hugo L. Black

Significance of the Case
In a rare decision reversal, the Court upheld an indigent's petition seeking court-appointed counsel; landmark case decided that states are required to appoint counsel to defendants who cannot afford it in non-capital as well as capital cases.

Clarence Earl Gideon was not one of God's nobler creatures. In 1961, when he was hauled into a Florida circuit court to be tried for breaking into Panama City's Bay Harbor Poolroom, his "rap sheet" already included three burglary convictions, one for possession of government property, and a twenty-day jail term for public drunkenness. He was fifty, but looked at least ten years older. His voice and hands trembled; his face was wrinkled. "Anyone meeting him for the first time," journalist Anthony Lewis later wrote, "would be likely to regard him as the most wretched of men."

But Clarence Gideon was not yet drained of spirit. Because he had no funds for a lawyer, he asked Judge Robert L. McCrary Jr. to appoint counsel for his defense. Although obviously sympathetic to Gideon's plight, Judge McCrary denied the request: "Mr. Gideon, I am sorry, but I cannot appoint Counsel to represent you in this case. Under the laws of the State of Florida, the only time the Court can appoint Counsel to represent a Defendant is when that person is charged with a capital offense. I am sorry, but I will have to deny your request to appoint Counsel to defend you in this case."

Gideon was hardly persuaded. "The United States Supreme Court," he replied defiantly, if inaccurately, "says I am entitled to be represented by Counsel." But the judge had made his ruling, and Gideon was obliged to defend himself before a six-man jury. He "conducted his defense," Justice Hugo L. Black would conclude, "about as well as could be expected from a layman," making opening and closing statements, cross-examining prosecution witnesses, presenting witnesses in his own behalf, and declining to testify himself.

Gideon was a layperson, however, not a lawyer, and he made mistakes no reasonably competent attorney would have made. The principal witness for the prosecution testified, for example, that he had seen Gideon in the poolroom and then saw him leave at five-thirty on the morning the break-in was discovered. On cross-examination, Gideon asked the witness what he had been doing outside the poolroom at that hour, but the defendant did not pursue that potentially fruitful line of questioning. Nor did he probe the witness's reputation, relationship with the defendant, or related areas a lawyer surely would have explored. Apparently, because the prosecution's chief witness had also testified that Gideon was carrying a pint of wine when he left the poolroom, the defendant did question witnesses closely in an effort to establish that he had been intoxicated on the fateful morning. Yet under Florida law—law with which any attorney would have been familiar—evidence of intoxication could have served as a defense for the crime with which Gideon was charged. Finally, Gideon did not ask the judge to define the elements of the crime for the jury and did not challenge numerous errors Judge McCrary arguably committed over the course of the trial.

Following Gideon's conviction, Judge McCrary sentenced him to five years in prison, the maximum sentence allowable under state law for the felony of breaking and entering with intent to commit a misdemeanor. From his cell in the Florida State Prison at Raiford, Gideon then filed a petition for a writ of habeas corpus with the state supreme court, contending that the

trial judge's failure to appoint him defense counsel violated rights "guaranteed by the Constitution and the Bill of Rights by the United States Government." When the Florida high court denied his petition without opinion, he turned to the U.S. Supreme Court, seeking review via an in forma pauperis petition, a procedure allowing indigents to petition a federal court for relief without complying with the rules or meeting the expenses ordinarily connected with the filing of a case.

The law clerk who initially screened Gideon's petition for Chief Justice Earl Warren decided that it at least merited some response from the state. He had the Court's clerk request a reply to the petition from Florida authorities. Citing the Supreme Court's 1942 decision in *Betts v. Brady*, Florida's attorney general urged the Court to deny Gideon a hearing. Under *Betts*, he argued, the Sixth Amendment guaranteed the right to counsel only in federal cases, and it was not per se binding on the states through the due process clause of the Fourteenth Amendment. Instead, indigent state defendants were entitled to appointed counsel only when "special circumstances" in a case, such as the gravity of the offense or the accused's limited mental capacity, required appointment of a lawyer to assure the defendant a "fair trial." Gideon, who apparently was unaware of *Betts*, had claimed no "special circumstances" and thus had no right to appointed counsel.

In his response to the state's reply, as in his original petition, Gideon continued to maintain that "a citizen . . . cannot get a just and fair trial without the aid of counsel," whatever the circumstances. "It makes no difference," he added in a slap at the *Betts* rationale, "how old I am or what color I am or what church I belong too [sic] if any." Ultimately, the Supreme Court determined that *Betts* should indeed be given further scrutiny. On June 4, 1962, the Court granted Gideon's motion to proceed in forma pauperis and petition for a writ of certiorari. In addition to other issues raised by the case, the Court's order stipulated that the parties were to discuss the following question in their briefs and oral argument: "Should this Court's holding in *Betts v. Brady* . . . be reconsidered?"

Since Gideon was a pauper, the Supreme Court also granted the petitioner what the state of Florida had denied him, a Court-appointed attorney—and very distinguished counsel at that. No doubt in recognition of the tremendous significance of the *Betts* reconsideration and possible reversal, the Court appointed prominent Washington attorney Abe Fortas, a close friend of several justices, confidant of presidents, and himself a future member of the Court, to represent the petitioner. Since his principal responsibility was to represent Gideon, not do battle with Supreme Court precedent, Fortas and his staff first reviewed the record of Gideon's case to determine whether he might be entitled to counsel under the *Betts* "special circumstances" doctrine. They quickly determined that no such claim could be made; instead, Gideon's case was an ideal one in which to challenge what they considered the *Betts* myth—the assumption that *any* layperson can receive a fair trial when obliged to act as his own counsel, whatever his background or the circumstances of his case. In briefs and oral argument, Fortas pressed that position before the Court. The ACLU and the attorneys general of twenty-two states supported Fortas's stance in amicus curiae briefs, while officials of only two states, Alabama and North Carolina, supported Florida's contentions.

Now the matter was in the Court's hands. The Supreme Court rarely overturns its own decisions. But *Betts* had always rested on a fragile foundation, and the Court's post-*Betts* counsel rulings had steadily weakened the precedent's underpinnings. Ten years before *Betts* was decided, in *Powell v. Alabama* (1932), the first of the infamous "Scottsboro cases" to reach the high tribunal, the Court had stopped short of automatically requiring appointed counsel for indigent state defendants. Instead, it had held merely that appointed counsel was necessary to assure the Scottsboro defendants a fair trial, given the gravity of their offense, the possible imposition of the death sentence, their youth and limited education, their isolation from friends and family, and the moblike atmosphere in which they were tried. Justice George Sutherland's opinion for the *Powell* court did

include the dictum, however, that the provision of counsel was a "fundamental" right of the sort earlier cases had found implicit in the Fourteenth Amendment's due process clause. A dictum in Justice Benjamin N. Cardozo's opinion for the Court in *Palko v. Connecticut* (1937) assumed the same position, as did dicta in several other cases decided between *Powell* and *Betts*. Thus, when the *Betts* court limited *Powell* strictly to its facts and rejected any per se right of appointed counsel for state defendants, it ignored a significant body of developing dicta.

In the years after *Betts,* the difficulty of applying its "special circumstances" formula in individual cases had also become increasingly apparent. In two 1948 cases in which the absence of counsel had allowed significant errors of the trial judge to go unchallenged, for example, the Supreme Court reversed one defendant's conviction, yet affirmed the other's, for reasons difficult if not impossible to fathom. No doubt partly because of such difficulties, the Court by 1945 had begun distinguishing noncapital and capital cases, invariably requiring counsel in the latter. More significantly, after 1950, the Court had invariably found "special circumstances" requiring the appointment of a lawyer in all state criminal cases, capital or noncapital. All that appeared to remain, it seemed, was *Betts*'s formal reversal.

On March 18, 1963, the Supreme Court, speaking through Justice Hugo Black, took that final step. Black, who had registered a dissent in *Betts* and had long urged application of the Sixth Amendment right of counsel in all state cases, was a fitting choice to write the Court's opinion. As the Court's spokesman, however, he was unable to reiterate his long-stated view that the framers of the Fourteenth Amendment had intended its first section to embody all the guarantees of the Bill of Rights, including the right to counsel, a position that had never acquired majority support on the Court. Instead, he drew on *Palko v. Connecticut* and other earlier opinions to conclude that the Fourteenth Amendment embodied "fundamental" guarantees of the Bill of Rights and that the *Betts* majority had erred in refusing to include the right to counsel among safeguards of that character. Citing *Powell* and other pre-*Betts* cases that characterized the right to counsel as a fundamental guarantee, he concluded that "the Court in *Betts v. Brady* made an abrupt break with its own well-considered precedents." He added, "In returning to these old precedents, sounder we believe than the new, we but restore constitutional principles established to achieve a fair system of justice." Rejection of *Betts*, Black asserted, was also compelled by "reason and reflection." He continued:

> [I]n our adversary system of criminal justice, any person haled into court, who is too poor to hire a lawyer, cannot be assured a fair trial unless counsel is provided for him. This seems to us to be an obvious truth. Governments, both state and federal, quite properly spend vast sums of money to establish machinery to try defendants accused of crime. Lawyers to prosecute are everywhere deemed essential to protect the public's interest in an orderly society. Similarly there are few defendants charged with crime, few indeed, who fail to hire the best lawyers they can get to prepare and present their defenses. That government hires lawyers to prosecute and defendants who have the money hire lawyers to defend are the strongest indications of the widespread belief that lawyers in criminal courts are necessities, not luxuries. The right of one charged with crime to counsel may not be deemed fundamental and essential to fair trials in some countries, but it is in ours. . . . Twenty-two States, as friends of the Court, argue that *Betts* was "an anachronism when handed down" and that it should now be overruled. We agree.

Although Justice Black was unable to advance his "total incorporation" thesis regarding the relationship of the Bill of Rights to the Fourteenth Amendment, Justice William O. Douglas, who had also dissented in *Betts*, was not subject to such strictures. Douglas drafted a brief separate opinion in which he noted that ten justices over the years had expressed support for total incorporation; then he added: "Unfortunately [that view] has never commanded a Court. Yet, happily, all constitutional questions are always open. . . . And what we do today does not foreclose the matter." After circulating his draft to Justice Black for his colleague's approval, Douglas filed the concurrence.

Two other justices also registered concurrences in the case. Justice Tom C. Clark, who typically favored a more flexible approach to the Fourteenth Amendment's meaning than certain of his brethren, declined to join Justice Black's opinion because it suggested that incorporated rights were to have equal application in federal and state cases. In his brief *Gideon* concurrence, however, Clark observed that the Fourteenth Amendment's due process clause applied to the deprivation of "liberty" as well as "life." He then asserted that he could "find no acceptable rationalization" for the Court's continuing to require counsel in all state capital cases, as it had been for many years despite *Betts*, yet refuse to apply such a per se rule in noncapital state cases. To eliminate this incongruity, Clark joined the Court's decision.

While agreeing that *Betts* should be overruled, Justice John Marshall Harlan considered the precedent "entitled to a more respectful burial than has been accorded," adding, with a nod to Black and Douglas, "at least on the part of those of us who were not on the Court when the case was decided." *Betts*, Harlan contended, was not, as Black had argued, "an abrupt break" with the Court's precedents. In *Powell*, the Court had ordered counsel for the Scottsboro defendants because of "the particular facts there presented," not as a requirement for all state cases, or even all state capital cases. The *Betts* "special circumstances" rule was thus consistent, Harlan contended, with *Powell*; indeed, it was modeled after the Court's approach in the earlier case. Over the years, however, *Betts* had been gradually undermined, first in capital cases and then in all state prosecutions involving serious offenses. "The Court has come to recognize that the mere existence of a serious criminal charge constituted itself special circumstances requiring the services of counsel at trial." Overruling *Betts*, therefore, would do "no more than to make explicit something that has long been foreshadowed in our decisions." Failure to do so, on the other hand, would "in the long run . . . do disservice to the federal system," especially since many state courts had not yet fully grasped the reality of *Betts*'s erosion.

In his *Gideon* concurrence, Justice Harlan also rejected the notion that Bill of Rights safeguards found to be "implicit in the concept of ordered liberty," and thus binding on the states through the Fourteenth Amendment due process guarantee, should be given the same force in federal and state cases. In his view, the Fourteenth Amendment did not "incorporate" the terms of the Sixth Amendment or other Bill of Rights safeguards "as such," only guarantees approximating Bill of Rights provisions. Considerations of federalism demanded greater judicial deference, moreover, to the states than to the federal government.

However, as additional Bill of Rights safeguards were applied to the states via the Fourteenth Amendment after *Gideon*, the Court rejected Harlan's position, embracing instead the view, as put by Justice Douglas in his *Gideon* concurrence, that "rights protected against state invasion by the Due Process Clause of the Fourteenth Amendment are not watered-down versions of what the Bill of Rights guarantees." With the exception of its decision in *Apodoca v. Oregon* (1972), permitting nonunanimous state jury verdicts while forbidding them in federal cases, the Court remained largely faithful to that approach to the incorporation question. In such cases as *Argersinger v. Hamlin* (1972), the Court also carried *Gideon* beyond felonies to all cases in which any prison or jail sentence is im-

posed. Employing a variety of constitutional rationales in cases decided before and after *Gideon*, moreover, the justices extended the right of indigent defendants to counsel to all "critical stages" of a criminal case, including custodial police interrogation, postindictment lineups, preliminary hearings, arraignments, and obligatory appeals.

The constitutional ruling that Clarence Earl Gideon's minor run-in with the law had spawned, however, was to remain the Court's most significant decision regarding the scope of the right to counsel. Certainly for Gideon it was. On August 5, 1963, he was retried, represented on this occasion by counsel. After a little more than an hour's deliberation, the jury returned an acquittal verdict. That evening, Gideon paid a last visit to the Bay Harbor Poolroom.

Selected Bibliography

Beaney, William M. *The Right to Counsel in American Courts*. Ann Arbor, MI: University of Michigan Press, 1955.

Carter, Dan T. *Scottsboro: A Tragedy of the American South*. Baton Rouge, LA: Louisiana State University Press, 1969.

Lewis, Anthony. *Gideon's Trumpet*. New York: Random House, 1964.

Lawyer?
You Want a Lawyer?

—◁◦▷—

Delane Ramsey

Taylors, South Carolina

Escobedo v. Illinois, 378 U.S. 478 (1964) [U.S. Supreme Court]

◄◦► THE CASE IN BRIEF ◄◦►

Date
1964

Locations
Chicago, Washington, D.C.

Courts
Illinois Supreme Court
U.S. Supreme Court

Principal Participants
Danny Escobedo
Warren Wolfson
Justice Arthur Goldberg

Significance of the Case
A defendant's right to counsel from his
first encounter with the law bound the
Fourth and Fifth Amendment's guarantees
and set a ground-breaking precedent for
citizens' rights under the law.

"You're under arrest."
"I want my lawyer."

These phrases have a staccato rhythm and familiarity that popular entertainment has burned into the collective American conscious. However, the right to counsel has not always been an American tradition.

The right to counsel has evolved slowly within American jurisprudence. Many state constitutions did not even mention counsel. The Sixth Amendment to the U.S. Constitution states, in part, "In all criminal prosecutions, the accused shall . . . have the assistance of counsel for his defense." Until fifty years ago, this was interpreted as *allowing* defendants to provide their own counsel, not *compelling* provision of counsel by an outside agency. The Supreme Court found, in 1938, that the Sixth Amendment required all defendants in federal criminal cases to have an attorney (at the defendants' expense) or to intelligently waive that right. In 1963, federal legislation provided counsel for indigent defendants in federal cases.

The Constitution originally protected civil rights only from federal intrusion, not from state interference. Because federal constitutional protections had not yet been applied to the state courts, the suspect's rights in state criminal cases were comparatively unprotected. Although the Scottsboro case in 1932 drew attention to state courts' denial of counsel, not until 1961 did the Supreme Court rule that states must allow or provide counsel to defendants in state capital cases. In the 1963 decision, *Gideon v. Wainwright*, the High Court went one step further and required the states to allow or provide counsel if necessary in any state criminal case that could result in imprisonment or loss of freedom. Since life and liberty are fundamental human rights, counsel necessary to protect a defendant's life, in one criminal case, is equally necessary to protect a defendant's liberty in another. *Gideon* answered the question of *why* counsel should be provided in state criminal cases. The remaining issue was *when*: at what point before the trial does counsel become necessary for the protection of a defendant's rights?

On January 20, 1960, Danny Escobedo, twenty-two and of Mexican background, was arrested in Chicago for the murder of his brother-in-law. Escobedo was interrogated, said nothing, and was released later that day on a writ of habeas corpus. Ten days later, Escobedo was again arrested and taken to police headquarters. He was told that someone had identified him as the murderer. Escobedo was then taken to interrogation. He asked for his lawyer, Warren Wolfson, repeatedly during the interrogation, but he was told that his lawyer did not want to see him. Wolfson arrived at the station house shortly after the police brought in Escobedo. He asked to see Escobedo, but was told that the interrogation was under way. When told that he would have to wait until it was completed, Wolfson complained to the chief on duty, but was still not allowed to talk to Escobedo. Wolfson then "had a conversation with every police officer that I could find," trying to get to his client. Wolfson only saw Escobedo briefly through an open door, but the police prevented any communication.

Escobedo was interrogated in Spanish by an officer who knew his family. Escobedo denied any criminal knowledge. He was then confronted with his accuser. Escobedo told his accuser, "You're lying. I didn't shoot Manuel; you did it." This remark showed complicity in the murder, which under Illinois state law was as serious as the violent act itself. Escobedo then made other statements that further incriminated himself. A state's attorney was called in to take Escobedo's statement. The state's attorney did not tell Escobedo of his right to remain silent or that his statement would be used against him at the trial.

At his trial, Escobedo's statement was admitted into evidence over the objections of his counsel. Escobedo was convicted. He appealed to the Illinois Supreme Court to have his statement suppressed. The state supreme court ultimately reaffirmed his conviction. Escobedo then petitioned the U.S. Supreme Court to hear his case on the grounds that his Sixth Amendment right to counsel had been violated. The appeal was argued before the Court on April 29, 1964.

On June 22, by a 5-4 majority, the Court reversed Danny Escobedo's conviction. The Court found two legal principles prevailing or controlling. The suspect under interrogation had been denied his request to see counsel. And the police had not warned Escobedo of his constitutional protection to remain silent during the interrogation. Under Illinois state law, admission of "mere" complicity in a murder was as damaging as active participation in the violent act. "The guiding hand of counsel was essential" in protecting the defendant's rights, particularly in this specific case. Deprived of this guiding hand, the defendant had effectively been denied his Sixth Amendment protection of access to counsel and his Fourteenth Amendment right of due process.

The Court held that a suspect must have the protective assistance of counsel whenever that suspect becomes the specific focus of an investigation; in practical terms, at the time of arrest. "Where a police investigation is no longer a general inquiry into an unsolved crime but has begun to focus on a particular suspect," the right to counsel must be allowed or provided. Any lack of such counsel, the Court concluded, would result in the exclusion of evidence obtained from the unprotected interrogation.

The *Escobedo* decision was announced in June 1964. This was in the midst of a hot, tension-filled summer in the country's largest cities. The civil rights movement was provoking extremists to violence. Serious racial riots erupted in several northern cities, while antiblack violence rose in the South. The first opposition to the Vietnam War appeared. The Supreme Court added to the heat with several emotional decisions. Reaction was shrill from groups offended by decisions on apportionment, obscenity, and racial desegregation. However, there was little general reaction to *Escobedo*, as it was almost lost among these more controversial rulings. Still, a group of California women circulated petitions to overturn *Escobedo*. Legislation restricting the Court's jurisdiction was introduced in Congress, although it later died of neglect. The general public seemed more concerned with bigger issues in 1964.

Escobedo left at least one major legal question unanswered. Implicit within *Escobedo* is a Fifth Amendment value involving protection from self-incrimination. For this Fifth Amendment protection to be operative, the Sixth Amendment right to counsel must be available. Defendants deprived of counsel would incriminate themselves. Defendants had an additional right, the right to remain silent during interrogation in order to avoid self-incrimination. But, in order to exercise this right of silence, defendants must be aware of it, and if not already aware of that right, must be told about it. The question remained: who would tell them? The police had denied Escobedo this information. Who would advise future suspects? The Court did not specifically address this Fifth Amendment matter in the *Escobedo* ruling.

The Supreme Court's ruling in *Miranda v. Arizona* in 1966 answered this question. Suspects in custody or under arrest must be told that they have the right to remain silent and that anything they say can be used against them during a trial. In addition, they have the right to an attorney before questioning, and an appointed attorney will be provided if they cannot afford their own. Suspects can stop an interrogation at any time. It was now the responsibility of the police to advise suspects of

their rights. The prosecution must demonstrate in court that the suspect was advised of these rights, including any informed waivers of these rights to which the suspect agreed.

Miranda finally changed the relationship between citizen and state, between suspect and police. Citizens/suspects now had the right to be told, in a way that they understood, that their rights and person were protected from the abuse of institutional power. Citizens/suspects standing alone could now tell the assembled police power of county, city, state, or nation that they had nothing to say—and make it stick.

The general public is more familiar with *Miranda* than it is with *Escobedo*. But many experts in the legal fraternity consider *Escobedo* to be the more significant decision. *Escobedo* extends the range of constitutional protection farther. *Miranda* was the ultimate extension of a citizen/suspect's rights. *Escobedo* was the penultimate step, the stepping-stone to *Miranda*. *Miranda* merely stated *who* advised suspects of their rights. *Escobedo* had already stated that these rights must be protected. *Miranda* can be considered the icing on *Escobedo*'s cake. *Escobedo* did the work, *Miranda* got the credit.

Escobedo and *Miranda* were criticized as "coddling criminals," as unnecessarily restricting the police in their effort to control a rising crime rate. The passage of twenty-five years has changed that earlier response. Recently, the chief of police in a major southern city remarked that these decisions have actually strengthened the police. Unable to rely on unprotected confessions, the police have become more professional in the thoroughness and scope of their investigations. The police themselves seem pleased that convictions are now based on hard evidence, not questionable confessions.

Escobedo and *Miranda* produced paradoxical results. Suspects are better advised of their rights and consequently speak less freely than they did before 1966. Police professionalism has made impressive advances since then. The public is better served by a more professional police and by the knowledge that the citizen/suspect has an "even break" in court. The final winner, then, is the citizen. Citizens know that whenever they need them, their Fifth and Sixth Amendment rights of silence and counsel are protected and available.

After his release in 1964, Danny Escobedo had several scrapes with the Chicago police. By 1968, he was serving concurrent twenty- and twenty-two-year sentences at the Leavenworth Federal Penitentiary for multiple federal drug violations. Twenty years later, Escobedo was again incarcerated, this time for child molestation.

Selected Bibliography

Enken, Arnold N., and Sheldon H. Elsen. "Counsel for the Suspect: *Massiah v. U.S.* and *Escobedo v. Illinois.*" *Minnesota Law Review* 49 (1964): 47–91.

Michaux, Roy H., Jr. "Right to Retained Counsel at Time of Arrest." *North Carolina Law Review* 43 (1964): 187–199.

"You Have the Right to Remain Silent"

—◄◦►—

B. Keith Crew

Department of Sociology, Anthropology, and Criminology
University of Northern Iowa

Miranda v. Arizona, Vigner v. New York, Westover v. United States, and
California v. Stewart, 384 U.S. 436 (1966) [U.S. Supreme Court]

◄◦► THE CASE IN BRIEF ◄◦►

Date
1966

Locations
Arizona, California, New York,
Washington, D.C.

Courts
Supreme Courts for Arizona, New York,
California
U.S. Supreme Court

Principal Participants
Miranda, Vigner, Westover, Stewart
Chief Justice Earl Warren
President Richard M. Nixon

Significance of the Case
The Supreme Court wrestled with a
defendant's right to remain silent while
law enforcement officials raged in controversy over the Court's cumulative-case
decisions in its "due process revolution."

"You have the right to remain silent."

"If you give up the right to remain silent,
anything you say can and will be used against
you in a court of law."

"You have the right to an attorney, and to
have the attorney present during questioning."

"If you cannot afford an attorney, one will be
appointed for you."

By now most Americans are familiar with
these "*Miranda* warnings" from police
shows on television if not from civics classes or
practical experience. After a generation of routine use, they are an accepted ritual of police
work, as much a part of a typical arrest as the
placing of handcuffs on the suspect.

The *Miranda* rules can still stir up controversy in those rare cases where an officer's failure to read a suspect his or her rights allows an
apparently guilty person to go free; however, it
is difficult now to appreciate the consternation
on the part of the public and law-enforcement
officers that this decision originally sparked.
There are few today who seriously argue that
requiring the police to "read them their rights"

results in thousands of guilty criminals being released. Nevertheless, *Miranda* still symbolizes to many "law and order" politicians and commentators an allegedly misguided concern with the rights of criminals.

Perhaps no decision has come to symbolize an entire era in Supreme Court decisions to the extent that this case symbolizes the Warren court's approach to criminal justice. Although it is far from being the most important or far-reaching decision of that court, *Miranda* is in many ways the classic Warren court decision. Warren himself authored the lengthy opinion of the Court, and it contains examples of all the major elements of his jurisprudence. Warren seldom followed a narrow or literal reading of the Constitution. Rather, he believed that the Constitution contained imperative ethical principles, which were progressively realized as society's "standards of decency" evolved. Armed with this evolutionary theory of democratic values, Warren was not bashful about breaking with precedent or imposing new rules on the other branches of government. Warren's opinion in *Miranda* has been criticized precisely because it emphasized substantive issues of fairness and justice over legal reasoning and precedent.

Miranda was the culmination of a series of decisions by the Warren court, collectively referred to as the "due process revolution." Basically, each of these cases depended on the logic that the Fourteenth Amendment placed the same restrictions on the states' use of criminal law that the Bill of Rights, especially the Fifth and Sixth Amendments, placed on the federal government. Furthermore, the Court repeatedly imposed new rules not specifically mentioned in the Constitution, on the argument that they were essential to realize the ethical imperatives of the Constitution. For example, in *Mapp v. Ohio* (1961), the Court applied this logic when it extended the exclusionary rule, preventing the use of illegally obtained evidence in court, to the states.

Several of these key due process cases, including *Miranda*, involved extending and defining the right to counsel. In *Gideon v. Wainwright* (1963), the Court extended the right to counsel to noncapital felonies in state courts. In

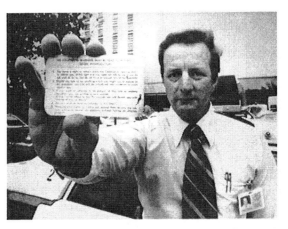

A police officer in Miami, Florida, shows his "Miranda card," which contains the warnings that must be read to a subject before he or she is questioned by the police. *AP/Wide World Photos.*

doing so, the Court had articulated the position that, in our complex criminal justice system, access to legal counsel was essential to assure due process. *Gideon*, however, addressed only the right to be represented at trial. Then, in *Escobedo v. Illinois* (1964), the Court extended the right to counsel to the investigative phase of criminal justice.

Escobedo set the stage for *Miranda*. The *Escobedo* case provided further illustration of the linkage between the Sixth Amendment right to counsel and the Fifth Amendment protection against self-incrimination. Escobedo had not confessed outright; he had unwittingly incriminated himself in a manner that would have been unlikely had his lawyer been present to advise him. Escobedo had been denied contact with his lawyer while in custody and under interrogation. He had specifically requested that he be allowed to see his attorney; furthermore, his attorney was at the police station and repeatedly asked to be allowed to see his client. By limiting its decision to these narrowly defined circumstances, the Court had left open the question of precisely at what point in the investigative process an individual's right to be represented by legal counsel begins.

The *Escobedo* decision created a furor among the nation's prosecutors and police, who complained loudly that the Court was "coddling criminals." Law-enforcement officials were concerned that the Court was moving toward effectively banning the use of confessions altogether. Justice Arthur Goldberg, author of the Court's opinion, had argued that a "law enforcement system that depends on the confession" was inherently "less reliable and more subject to abuses than a system which depends on extrinsic evidence independently secured through skillful investigation."

In a 1965 article in the *New York Times Magazine,* former federal prosecutor Sidney Zion summed up the concerns of law-enforcement officials as follows: "Does this mean that in the future the Court may rule that all suspects have a right to see a lawyer before the police can talk to them, whether they request counsel or not, and whether they can afford one or not? No one can be sure, but the question itself is enough to turn district attorneys gray. If that should ever happen, most lawyers agree, confessions would disappear, because any lawyer worth his salt would advise his client to remain silent."

In the *Miranda* decision, the Court did precisely what prosecutors feared: it ruled that the right to counsel began with police interrogation. Furthermore, it did away with the existing "voluntariness" standard, under which confessions were usually admissible in court as long as there was no evidence of coercion. Law-enforcement officials now had a positive duty to inform suspects of their rights; any incriminating statements made under interrogation without such warnings would henceforth be presumed to be involuntary, and therefore inadmissible as evidence. The Court did limit the new rules to interrogation initiated by investigators; it explicitly excluded the situation where a person "enters a police station and states that he wishes to confess to a crime."

The facts of *Miranda* and its three companion cases are relatively simple. On March 13, 1963, Ernesto Miranda was arrested and taken into custody at the Phoenix police station, where he was identified by the complaining witness. He was then questioned for two hours by police detectives. Miranda had signed a written confession, at the top of which was a typed paragraph stating that the confession was made voluntarily, "with full knowledge of my legal rights, understanding any statement I make

may be used against me." One of the interrogating officers testified that he had read this paragraph to Miranda, but apparently only after Miranda had already confessed orally. In a jury trial, Miranda was convicted of rape and kidnapping, and sentenced to twenty to thirty years in prison. In the trial, the written confession and the officers' testimony regarding the oral confession were admitted as evidence over the objections of the defense attorney. On appeal, the Arizona Supreme Court upheld the conviction, emphasizing the voluntariness of the confession and the fact that Miranda did not explicitly request an attorney.

The U.S. Supreme Court reversed the decision of the Arizona Supreme Court. According to the Court's interpretation of the record, Miranda had not been "apprised of his right to consult with an attorney and to have one present during the interrogation." That Miranda had not himself initiated a request for an attorney (as had Escobedo) was deemed irrelevant. Further, his right "not to be compelled to incriminate himself" was not protected in any other manner. The Court did not accept the signed typed statement that the defendant had "full knowledge" of his legal rights as sufficient; the forfeit of a defendant's constitutional rights required proof of a "knowing and intelligent waiver."

This reasoning was applied to similar circumstances in each of *Miranda*'s companion cases. In each one, the Court noted that there was no evidence in the record that the defendant had been apprised of his rights to counsel and against self-incrimination before or during interrogation; hence, the defendant's self-incriminating statements should not have been allowed at trial. Thus, the Court went well beyond its previous ruling in *Escobedo*. The burden was no longer on the suspect to assert his or her right to see counsel or remain silent; now it was the state's duty to establish that a suspect had been fully informed of his or her rights and the consequences of waiving them. What most galled law-enforcement officials was that in none of these cases were the police accused of violating existing rules of conduct.

Critics of the legal reasoning Warren used in the *Miranda* decision have focused on two issues in the wording of the Constitution. The first relates to the Sixth Amendment right to legal counsel. Strictly read, the amendment seems to establish only a right to have the "assistance of counsel" in trials. Obviously, *Escobedo* and *Miranda* extended that right to pretrial phases of criminal prosecution.

Considerably more controversial was the Court's interpretation of the Fifth Amendment clause regarding self-incrimination. The Fifth Amendment states that no person "shall be compelled in any criminal case to be a witness against himself." Much of the ensuing debate revolved around the meaning of *compelled*. Traditionally, it was taken to refer only to the use, or threatened use, of physical force. Warren's opinion in *Miranda* stressed the psychological intimidation of being held in custody by the police, particularly if the arrestee is "incommunicado," as were each of the defendants in the instant cases.

To understand why the Court ruled the way it did in *Miranda*, as well as the controversy that the decision engendered, it is necessary to understand the history of the police in the twentieth-century United States. The role and image of the police changed drastically between 1920 and 1965. Warren saw his opinion in *Miranda* as contributing to that evolutionary process.

The police have not always enjoyed the legitimacy and respect from the public that they generally have today. Well into the twentieth century, the police were more commonly (and accurately) characterized as at best inefficient and poorly trained, and at worst brutal and corrupt. In 1931, President Herbert Hoover's National Commission on Law Observance and Enforcement (more commonly referred to as the Wickersham Commission after its chair, George Wickersham) investigated the state of law-enforcement in the nation. Various "Wickersham reports" documented the extensive police corruption, brutality, and the use of the "third degree" to extract confessions. Warren cited the Wickersham reports extensively in his opinion in *Miranda*, particularly their comments that reliance on extracting confessions "makes police and prosecutors less zealous in the search for objective evidence" and "brutal-

izes the police." Worst of all, such conduct by the police was said to reduce public respect for law and order, thus actually leading to more crime.

The Wickersham reports set the agenda for police reform, stressing expert leadership, centralized command, political neutrality, and higher personnel standards. One of its primary authors was August Vollmer, the pioneering chief of police of Berkeley, California, from 1905 to 1932. It is interesting to note that Earl Warren was the district attorney of Alameda County, which includes Berkeley, from 1920 to 1938. Although it is not clear how much, if any, Vollmer may have directly influenced Warren, it is obvious that Warren had firsthand knowledge of the dangers of unchecked police power, as well as an optimistic view of the ability of a professionalized police force to operate within constitutional limits of fair play. As a prosecutor, Warren made his own contribution to the growing reform movement in law enforcement. He expanded and professionalized the district attorney's investigative and legal staff, and he improved cooperation among the various local law-enforcement agencies. He also established his reputation early by successfully prosecuting several corrupt local police officials.

Nationally, the reforms begun by Vollmer and publicized by the Wickersham commission began to improve the image and reality of police work. Change was slow, however; older police could not simply be replaced overnight by highly trained, professionally oriented officers. Most big-city police departments were still controlled by local political machines as late as the 1950s, when the next major phase of police reform occurred. In the 1950s, several of the largest police departments were racked by scandals of police brutality and corruption. The typical response to these scandals was to hire a new, reform-oriented chief of police to "clean house." Some of these reformers, such as O. W. Wilson, who became Chicago's chief of police in 1960, were protégés of Vollmer. Ironically, these reformers were among the loudest critics of the Warren Court's due process agenda. The very success of their reforms depended on their demonstrated ability to reform from within.

They believed they had shown that the police could police themselves.

Furthermore, the reformers' model of professionalization stressed the law-enforcement role of the police. They redefined the main purpose of the police as "fighting crime." Historically, neither the police nor the public had defined the primary function of the police this way. It was not until after World War II and the introduction of patrol cars, better telephone service, two-way radios, and the use of forensic science to solve cases that the image of police as crime fighters began to take hold.

Just as police departments across the country were successfully portraying their main duty as controlling crime, the United States began to experience an unprecedented increase in crime. Although the increases, which began in the early 1960s, had more to do with demographic changes than lack of effective police work, the police had raised public expectations about their ability to control crime. The due process decisions of the Warren court provided a convenient scapegoat.

As far as many prosecutors and police were concerned, as long as they were not beating confessions out of people or threatening to do so, statements by defendants like Miranda were voluntary and should be admissible. They operated on the assumption that no innocent person would confess; if suspects incriminated themselves because of ignorance or fear, well, that was their tough luck and a victory for public safety. To place further restrictions on police interrogation would reduce the number of confessions, thus depriving the police of an important weapon in the fight against crime.

The Court, however, remained skeptical of the utility of confessions. It also saw custodial interrogation as the ultimate test of the rights of individuals against the power of the state. Although the types of abuses documented in the Wickersham reports, such as dangling a suspect by his heels from a fifth-story window, were acknowledged to be the exception rather than the rule, the rough treatment of detainees was still common enough that Warren could cite several cases on which he himself had ruled.

Even without brutality, the Court argued, custodial interrogation was designed to intimi-date suspects into incriminating themselves. Chief Justice Warren quoted extensively from police manuals to illustrate the point. He noted that the goal of the instructions given police in these manuals was, quite frankly, to get the subject to relinquish the right to remain silent or seek legal counsel. Suggested tactics for accomplishing this included isolating the subject, tiring him or her by questioning nonstop for hours, and even deceit (such as giving the suspect false legal advice).

The assumption that only the guilty would confess was called into question in a dramatic way by the case of George Whitmore. Whitmore was a young black man who confessed while in custody to a rape and two murders in New York City in 1964 (shortly after the *Escobedo* decision). Prosecutors pointed to the case as an example of a serious crime that could not have been solved without the confession. Instead, the case turned out to illustrate just the opposite: the unreliability of custodial confessions. Another man was later charged and convicted of the murders; Whitmore's confession was shown to be phony. There was some evidence that the police had beaten Whitmore, but no follow-up investigation was conducted.

The Court also had another model to contrast to the claims of local police and prosecutors that confessions were an essential tool of law enforcement. For years, the FBI had downplayed the use of confessions in its investigations, relying on new forensic techniques to solve cases with objective evidence. In fact, the FBI had for years been giving detained suspects warnings very similar to those outlined in the *Miranda* decision.

The Court was also aware of changes in the nature of crime in recent years. Crime was seen to be connected to social conditions such as urban poverty and racism. Typical defendants who confessed while in custody and without the aid of an attorney were, like Whitmore and Miranda, likely to be undereducated, poor, and members of a minority group. In other words, they were members of social groups that had been discriminated against by other social groups and who had the fewest resources to defend themselves.

A number of studies have been conducted to assess the impact of *Miranda* on law enforcement. Almost uniformly, they show that the impact of this decision, in terms of unsolved cases, or lost convictions, has been minimal. The fact that most cases are solved by confessions does not mean that they can only be solved by them. As an example, Ernesto Miranda himself was convicted on other evidence upon retrial, as were each of the defendants in the companion cases. Nevertheless, the symbolic power of the case outweighed by far its actual impact. Richard Nixon made the "liberal" Supreme Court decisions an issue in his 1968 presidential campaign, which featured a heavy appeal to "law and order." He promised to appoint Supreme Court justices who would overturn *Miranda* and other rulings that favored the rights of "criminals" over the police. The Supreme Court under Warren's successors, Warren Burger and William Rehnquist, did chip away at *Miranda* in some decisions, but for the most part the police have learned to live with the duty of reading suspects their rights. As recently as June 2000, in *Dickerson v. United States*, the Rehnquist court by a vote of 7-2 reaffirmed the constitutionality of the *Miranda* warning.

Earl Warren, of course, did not view his decision as antipolice. It infuriated him that Nixon portrayed it that way. He was not trying to hamper police work, but to "ennoble" it. Whether his Court's due process revolution contributed to better law enforcement is still a matter of debate. Predictions that suspects would not confess after being informed of their rights have not been borne out, however. Today, the overwhelming majority of felony cases are decided by guilty pleas, which require a confession as a matter of course.

There is an ironic postscript to the case. Miranda was paroled in 1972. In 1976, he was murdered in a fight over a card game. When the police arrested his killer, they dutifully read him his rights, as required by *Miranda v. Arizona*.

Selected Bibliography

Ayres, Richard. "Confessions and the Court," in *The Ambivalent Force: Perspectives on the Police*, Arthur Niederhoffer and Abraham S. Blumberg, eds. Hinsdale, IL: Dryden, 1976.

Grahm, Fred P. *The Due Process Revolution: The Warren Court's Impact on Criminal Law*. New York: Hayden, 1970.

Inciardi, James A. *Criminal Justice*. 6th ed. San Diego: Harcourt Brace Jovanovich, 1999.

Manning, Peter K. *Police Work*. Cambridge, MA: MIT Press, 1977.

Walker, Samuel. *The Police in America*. New York: McGraw-Hill, 1983.

Wasby, Steven L. *The Impact of the United States Supreme Court: Some Perspectives*. Homewood, IL: Dorsey, 1970.

Weaver, John D. *Warren: The Man, The Court, The Era*. Boston: Little, Brown, 1967.

White, G. Edward. *Earl Warren: A Public Life*. New York: Oxford University Press, 1982.

The Death and Resurrection of Capital Punishment

———◁◦▷———

B. Keith Crew

Department of Sociology, Anthropology, and Criminology
University of Northern Iowa

Furman v. Georgia, 408 U.S. 232 (1972) and *Gregg v. Georgia*, 428 U.S. 153 (1976)
[U.S. Supreme Court]

◁◦▷ THE CASE IN BRIEF ◁◦▷

Date
1972, 1976

Locations
Georgia, Washington, D.C.

Courts
Georgia Supreme Court
U.S. Supreme Court

Principal Participants
William Furman
Troy Leon Gregg
Justices Thurgood Marshall and John
Paul Stevens

Significance of the Case
The Supreme Court's rulings on two
Georgia cases scrutinized the
constitutionality of the death penalty;
after a temporary suspension, the death
penalty was ruled constitutional in 1976.

The use of capital punishment in the United States peaked during the 1930s. Although most states still had "death rows" in the 1960s, actual executions had declined. Society appeared to be moving away from capital punishment. The American Civil Liberties Union (ACLU) and the National Association for the Advancement of Colored People (NAACP), convinced that the death penalty was reserved for poor and black offenders, began providing legal assistance to virtually every death-row inmate, hoping that an appeal would eventually result in the abolition of capital punishment. Actual executions ceased in 1967, as states anticipated just such a move by the Supreme Court.

In 1972, the Court agreed to decide whether capital punishment, as imposed in the cases of three petitioners, constituted "cruel and unusual punishment in violation of the Eighth and Fourteenth Amendments." The 5-4 decision of the Court in *Furman v. Georgia* effectively abolished capital punishment in the United States, by declaring unconstitutional most existing state laws authorizing the death penalty. It was not, however, the Court's final word on the death penalty: four years later, in *Gregg v. Georgia*, the Court upheld new state capital-punishment statutes, in effect reviving the death penalty. Actual infliction of capital punishment resumed shortly afterward, with the execution of Gary Gilmore in Utah in 1977. What accounts for the Court's apparent about-face on this most controversial of legal issues? An examination of the opinions of these two cases sheds some interesting light on the Supreme Court's task of interpreting the Constitution.

It might at first be tempting to attribute the Court's turnaround on the issue of capital punishment to a simple change in personnel, because the votes in *Furman* had fallen neatly along ideological lines. The five justices who voted to invalidate existing capital-punishment statutes in *Furman* were all holdovers from the liberal Warren Court (William O. Douglas, Potter Stewart, Byron White, William Brennan, and Thurgood Marshall); the dissenting votes were cast by the four conservative justices appointed by Richard Nixon: Chief Justice Warren Burger, and Justices Harry Blackmun, Lewis Powell, and William Rehnquist. Each of these men had been nominated to the Court for, among other qualities, their "hard-line" positions on crime. Four years later, the liberal Douglas had been replaced by another conservative, John Paul Stevens, who added his vote to the pro–capital punishment side.

Although the shift toward a more conservative Court was certainly real and important, it does not by itself explain the reinstatement of capital punishment. There is more to the story than the pro– or anti–capital punishment sentiments of the judges. Indeed, two of the dissenters expressed a personal distaste for capital punishment. Chief Justice Burger and Justice Blackmun each asserted that if they "were possessed of legislative power," they would vote to abolish, or at least severely restrict, the use of capital punishment. Although the unofficial moratorium on executions from 1967 to 1972 indicates that the country was looking to the Court for moral leadership on the question of the death penalty, *Furman* was decided on

grounds other than the morality of capital punishment per se. The arguments made in *Furman* set the stage for *Gregg*. Given those arguments, trends in both public opinion and professional debate about crime and punishment in the 1970s made the decision in *Gregg* inevitable, even if the composition of the Court had remained liberal. In *Furman*, the Court declined to address the constitutionality of the death penalty itself (except for two opinions) and instead focused its attention on the procedures used to impose the death penalty.

In the fall of 1971, the Court agreed to review three death-penalty cases to address the issue of whether capital punishment constituted cruel and unusual punishment. The leading case was *Furman v. Georgia*. William Furman, a 26-year-old black man, killed the owner of a home he was burglarizing in the middle of the night. The victim awoke and startled Furman as he was making his escape; Furman tripped, and his gun fired accidentally. The bullet passed through a closed door, striking and killing the victim who was standing on the other side. Here is Furman's version of the murder: "They got me charged with murder and I admit, I admit going to these folks' home and they did caught me in there and I was coming back out, backing up and there was a wire down there on the floor. I was coming out backwards and fell back and I didn't know nothing about no murder until they arrested me, and when the gun went off I was down on the floor and I got up and ran. That's all to it."

The prosecution basically accepted Furman's account of the accidental nature of the shooting. But because it occurred during the commission of a felony, it met the statutory definition of "premeditated murder," thus making Furman eligible for the electric chair.

In the two other cases, *Jackson v. Georgia* and *Branch v. Texas*, the defendants were convicted of raping, not killing, their victims. Jackson, a 21-year-old black man, was convicted of raping a white woman. He threatened her with a pair of scissors; she was bruised and abrased, but did not require hospitalization. Branch, a mildly retarded young black man, raped a 65-year-old white widow, holding his arm against her throat. Other than the trauma of the rape itself (which should not be minimized), the victim suffered no injury requiring medical attention.

These three cases contained elements that typified the argument that the death penalty was used as an instrument of racial discrimination. All three defendants were black, and in each case the victim was white. The race of the offenders and their victims was important, because the discriminatory application of the death penalty became the central issue of the Court's decision. From 1930 through 1967, more than half of the 3,859 people executed in the United States were black.

Discrimination was especially apparent in the imposition of capital punishment for rape. For example, criminologist Marvin Wolfgang and law professor Anthony Amsterdam (who helped argue *Furman* before the Supreme Court) found that of defendants convicted of rape in eleven Southern states, 13 percent of blacks were sentenced to death, but only 2 percent of whites. Overall, in the United States, 90 percent of the 455 men executed for rape from 1930 through 1967 were members of nonwhite racial minorities.

Furman's case, which did involve a murder, also typified an important issue. A popular assumption about capital punishment is that it is, or should be, reserved for the most extreme crimes. Although any murder is tragic, Furman's crime was no more heinous, outrageous, or vicious than were hundreds of murders that resulted in less severe punishments; however, the defendant was black, the victim was white, and the crime occurred in the South.

The Court's decision in *Furman* was unusual in that it was published per curiam (unsigned). The majority could not agree on a single argument to support its decision; therefore, each justice published a separate concurring opinion. Only Brennan and Marshall were willing to argue that the death penalty was essentially "cruel and unusual." Douglas, Stewart, and White focused on the narrower issue of the wording of the state laws in question and on the effects of those laws on the administration of the death penalty.

In arguing that the death penalty was "cruel and unusual punishment," Brennan and Marshall had to overcome several logical pitfalls.

The first is that the Constitution implies that capital punishment is permissible: the due process clause of the Fifth Amendment reads that no person shall "be deprived of life, liberty or property, without due process of law," a statement that implies that a person can be "deprived of life" with due process. Previous Supreme Court rulings had only restricted the type of crimes to which capital punishment could be applied and prohibited specifically gruesome or shocking methods of execution.

Nevertheless, Brennan and Marshall felt there were compelling reasons to define capital punishment as cruel and unusual. In the case of *Trop v. Dulles*, former chief justice Earl Warren had developed and applied the principle that the constitutional prohibition against cruel and unusual punishments must be interpreted in light of the "evolving standards of decency" of society. Marshall and Brennan believed that the death penalty failed the test of "evolving standards." Brennan specified four principles for defining a punishment as cruel and unusual under the "evolving standards" doctrine: (1) if a punishment is "unusually severe" (by which he meant disproportionate to the crime committed); (2) if there is a likelihood that it is inflicted arbitrarily; if it is inconsistent with social standards of human dignity; and (3) if it serves no penal purpose more effectively than would less severe punishments. Each of Brennan's four principles, implicitly accepted by Marshall, refers to the social effects of the law as it is actually applied, rather than to the logic of the written law.

This line of reasoning reflected a type of "sociological jurisprudence," a judicial philosophy characterized by three elements: (1) a distinction between "law in the books" and "law in action"—in other words, a focus on the practical application of law rather than an abstract definitions; (2) a willingness to bring social-science data to bear on legal questions; and (3) the assumption of the "living law,"—in other words, the idea that the law must be interpreted according to the contemporary norms and values of society. Each of the justices who voted against capital punishment in *Furman* cited sociological data showing that capital punishment was apparently inflicted in an arbitrary manner, that it provided no better deterrent than did life imprisonment, and that social support for the death penalty had declined in recent decades.

This last idea does not mean that the Court should base its decisions on public opinion polls. As Justice Marshall pointed out in his opinion, the public may be misinformed or even misled about the realities of capital punishment. Marshall's use of the idea of contemporary standards is thus based on what a "reasonable" person must conclude from applying contemporary standards to complete information in a logical manner; this is the job of the judiciary, not pollsters.

Justices Douglas, Stewart, and White also applied the "evolving standards of decency" approach, but limited their opinions in *Furman* to the arbitrary and thus discriminatory application of the death penalty rather than to the idea of capital punishment. Looking at the evidence provided by criminologists Marvin Wolfgang and Marc Reidel and others, the justices concluded that black and poor offenders were disproportionately selected for capital punishment. For these justices, what made the death penalty "cruel and unusual" was the lack of rational criteria for deciding who was to be executed and who was not. The lack of standards or guidelines allowed juries and judges to exercise their prejudices against certain classes of people. Thus, the constitutionality of the death-penalty statutes was decided on the basis of their effects (disparities in punishment meted out) rather than on the formal, logical relationship of capital punishment to received constitutional law.

The four dissenting judges rejected the sociological jurisprudence of the majority in favor of a more formalistic or positivist approach. Finding nothing in the wording of the Constitution to imply that capital punishment is cruel and unusual, these justices then turned to previous Supreme Court decisions and other comments on the legal prohibition against cruel and unusual punishments. There were precedents for restricting the use of capital punishment to the most serious crimes; likewise, there were prohibitions against particular methods of execution. However, the Court had repeatedly up-

held the use of capital punishment. Furthermore, in a case decided just one year before *Furman*, the Court had upheld the unlimited discretion of juries that the majority now cited as the main reason for abolishing the existing death-penalty laws.

Its conclusion that the lack of guidelines rendered the death penalty unconstitutional was a new direction for the Court. Barely a year earlier, the Court had held in *McGautha v. California* that "committing to the untrammeled discretion of the jury the power to pronounce life or death in capital cases" was well within the bounds of constitutionality. *Furman* made that very "untrammeled discretion" the grounds for abolishing capital punishment. Yet, that logic left the door open for the reinstatement of capital punishment.

Several states immediately began rewriting their death-penalty statutes in an attempt to meet the standards laid down in *Furman*. Two strategies were possible. One was to make the death penalty mandatory for certain types of crimes. For example, Rhode Island had a law mandating capital punishment for murder committed by a prisoner serving a life sentence. The second strategy was to provide juries with guidelines to determine when a person should receive a death sentence.

The approach taken by Georgia and other states was to institute two-stage trials in capital cases. In the first stage, the jury determined the guilt or innocence of the defendant. Upon conviction, the jury would then decide on the sentence to be given. At the sentencing stage, the judge is required to instruct the jury about the legal guidelines for inflicting capital punishment: the case must include at least one of a list of "aggravating" circumstances before capital punishment can be recommended. Further, these must be weighed against a list of potentially "mitigating" circumstances. Finally, all cases that result in a sentence of death are automatically appealed to the state supreme court, which must compare each case to other capital cases to ensure that the death penalty is not being inflicted in an arbitrary or discriminatory manner.

The Georgia statute was challenged in the case of Troy Leon Gregg. Gregg had been convicted of robbing two men and shooting them to death. At the sentencing stage of the "bifurcated trial," the jury considered three aggravating circumstances: (1) whether the murder was committed while the offender was committing another felony; (2) whether the murder was committed for the purpose of receiving money or property; and (3) whether the murder was "outrageously and wantonly vile." The jury agreed that the first and second circumstances were present, and returned four death sentences, two for the murders and two for the robberies.

It is interesting to compare Gregg's conviction with Furman's. Whereas Furman committed murder mainly because of his own incompetence as a burglar, Gregg deliberately and cold-bloodedly shot two men in order to take their property. Although one should be careful about drawing conclusions on the basis of only two cases, this comparison illustrates one intent of the new guidelines: to reserve capital punishment for the most heinous murderers.

On review, the Georgia Supreme Court overturned the two death penalties for robbery. The Georgia Supreme Court noted that capital punishment was rarely inflicted for that crime in Georgia and that the jury could not properly consider the murders as aggravating circumstances for the robberies, after first defining the robberies as aggravating circumstances for the murders. The end result for Gregg, of course, was the same whether he received one death penalty or several.

The U.S. Supreme Court agreed to review once again whether capital punishment was cruel and unusual and thus in violation of the Eighth and Fourteenth Amendments. Although, as in the *Furman* case, the Court was unable to agree on a single opinion, by a 7-2 vote it upheld Georgia's capital-punishment statute. On the theory that legislatures represent the "will of the people," Justices Stewart, Powell, and Stevens overcame the "evolving standards of decency" criterion, by noting that Congress and thirty-five states had enacted new death-penalty laws since *Furman*. They also suggested that capital punishment is not necessarily "disproportionate" to the crime of murder. Furthermore, they stated that retribu-

tion (vengeance) was a valid purpose of criminal law; thus, there was no need to weigh the deterrent effect of capital punishment against lesser punishments.

Of the *Furman* standards, then, the only remaining question was whether the penalty was inflicted in an arbitrary manner. Given the specific guidelines and automatic review imposed by the new Georgia law, it is difficult to imagine how the "arbitrary" argument could have been made. If the liberals—Douglas, Stewart, and White—had truly been opposed to capital punishment, they had painted themselves into an ideological corner in *Furman* from which they could not escape. Douglas was no longer on the Court when *Gregg* was decided; Stewart and White joined with the new majority in upholding the death penalty. The four conservatives, joined by Justice Stevens, applied the same formalistic approach as before. Only now, with *Furman* as precedent, the ironic result of that approach was that they voted for the death penalty by invoking arguments that they had rejected as invalid in the previous case.

In effect, the *Furman* decision made the *Gregg* decision inevitable, by shifting the debate over the death penalty from substantive to procedural issues. The extent of the dominance of procedural over substantive concerns is further evidenced in *Woodson v. North Carolina* (1976), decided the same day as *Gregg v. Georgia*. In *Woodson*, the Court struck down state laws that had taken the alternative strategy of making capital punishment mandatory for certain types of offenses. The Court ruled in that case that mandatory death sentences merely "papered over" the problem of jury discretion, shifting it to the prosecutor. The result of *Gregg v. Georgia*, then, is that the death penalty is constitutional if it is imposed in a two-stage procedure accompanied by specific guidelines that take into account differences in individual defendants and their crimes.

The terms under which the *Gregg* decision reintroduced capital punishment are consistent with a general trend of reform that dominated criminal justice policy in the 1970s. Disillusioned by the failure of prisons to either rehabilitate or deter criminals, liberals and conservatives joined forces in calling for a return to fixed or "determinate" sentences. Sentences were to be determined primarily by the nature of the crime, not the offender. This return to a policy of making the punishment fit the crime was supported by the reintroduction of retribution as a legitimate—indeed, the main—rationale for punishment. Various states began making retribution official policy by adopting either fixed-sentencing schemes or sentencing guidelines.

Central to both of these approaches is the weighing of punishments for a crime to fit the degree of seriousness of the offense, resulting in a reduction in the discretionary power of judges and juries. Supreme Court rulings on the death penalty since *Gregg* have primarily consisted of a fine tuning of such guidelines. For example, in *Coker v. Georgia* (1977), the Court ruled that the death penalty is excessive for the crime of rape. Following this standard of proportionality, most state laws now permit the death penalty only for crimes that involve the death of a victim. In yet another case from Georgia, *Godfrey v. Georgia* (1980), the Court ruled that the aggravating circumstances contained in death-penalty laws must be given fairly specific interpretations.

Opponents of the death penalty may look back on *Furman* as an opportunity lost. Had the other liberals on the Court joined ranks with Brennan and Marshall in declaring the death penalty per se to be cruel and unusual under the "evolving standards" doctrine, it is possible that the challenge of *Gregg* would never have taken place. At the least, the reinstatement of the death penalty would have had to overcome a strong precedent. Instead, the moral and political debate over the death penalty was reframed as an issue of legal formalism. In other words, capital punishment will, for some time, be considered legitimate as long as clearly stated rules for its imposition are followed; the question of its moral correctness or practical effectiveness as a deterrent has been rendered moot.

Shortly after the *Gregg* decision, executions resumed when Gary Gilmore was killed by firing squad in Utah in January 1977. By 2000, the number of inmates on death row exceeded three thousand; there have been 635 executions since 1977. As of 2000, thirty-eight states have capital-punishment statutes on the books.

Recent Supreme Court rulings on death-penalty cases have revolved around procedural questions, rather than reviving the philosophical debate over cruel and unusual punishment. For example, the form of execution was recently challenged in an appeal from the state of Florida. The petitioner in *Bryan v. Moore* (2000) argued that Florida's use of the electric chair constituted cruel and unusual punishment. Ultimately, the Court dismissed the appeal when Florida stipulated that it would carry out execution by lethal injection unless the death-row inmate himself elected death by electrocution.

In another development, researchers Radelet, Bedau, and Putnam published a study in 1992 in which they claimed that at least twenty-three innocent people have been executed. More recently, the Death Penalty Information Center documented eighty-three cases, since 1973, of death-row inmates who were found innocent when granted new trials. New evidence in the form of DNA analysis has played a key role in many of these reversals. The average time between the original conviction and clearance is just over six years. This is somewhat disturbing to those opposed to the use of the death penalty, because recent Supreme Court rulings have tended to shorten the time between conviction and execution.

The Court is unlikely to reverse *Gregg*, however, as long as it practices a formalistic jurisprudence. Abolitionists will have to marshal public opinion and legislation if they are to succeed in doing away with capital punishment.

Selected Bibliography

American Friends Service Committee. *Struggle for Justice*. New York: Hill and Wang, 1971.

Bowers, William J. *Executions in America*. Lexington, MA: D. C. Heath, 1974.

Bowers, William J., and Glenn L. Pierce. "Arbitrariness and Discrimination under post-Furman Capital Statutes." *Crime and Delinquency* 26 (1980): 563–635.

Hawkins, Richard, and Geoffrey P. Alpert. *American Prison Systems: Punishment and Justice.* Englewood Cliffs, NJ: Prentice Hall, 1989.

Inciardi, James A. *Criminal Justice.* 6th ed. New York: Harcourt Brace Jovanovich, 1999.

Radelet, M. L., H. A. Bedau, and C. E. Putnam. *In Spite of Innocence.* Boston: Northeastern University Press, 1992.

Wolfgang, Marvin E., and Marc Riedel. "Race, Judicial Discretion and the Death Penalty." *Annals of the American Academy of Political and Social Science* 407 (1973): 129–148.

Plea Bargaining and the "Vindictive" Exercise of Prosecutorial Discretion

—◄◦►—

B. Keith Crew

Department of Sociology, Anthropology, and Criminology
University of Northern Iowa

Bordenkircher v. Hayes, 434 U.S. 357 (1978) [U.S. Supreme Court]

◄◦► THE CASE IN BRIEF ◄◦►

Date
   1978

Locations
   Kentucky, Washington, D.C.

Courts
   U.S. District Court of Eastern Kentucky
   U.S. Supreme Court

Principal Participants
   Paul Lewis Hayes
   Justice Potter Stewart

Significance of the Case
   The case was part of the process by which the acceptable parameters of plea bargains were defined; it gave increased legitimacy to the power of a prosecutor to use his or her authority to bring charges to encourage defendants to plead guilty.

The vast majority of criminal convictions are the result of guilty pleas; estimates vary from 80 to 95 percent, depending on the jurisdiction. Many of these guilty pleas in turn are the result of plea bargains, where a defendant pleads guilty in the expectation of some leniency in sentencing. The central figure in all this plea bargaining is the prosecuting attorney, sometimes referred to as the district attorney or state's attorney. The prosecutor has virtually unchecked discretion in deciding what charges to bring against a suspect. In 1977, the U.S. Supreme Court had the opportunity to consider one aspect of this discretionary power: the extent to which the state may go to induce a defendant to waive his or her constitutional right to a jury trial.

So-called plea bargains usually take the form of "charge bargains." A suspect who has been charged with one or more crimes is offered the chance to plead guilty to fewer charges, or to less serious charges. For example, a charge of first-degree robbery might be reduced to one of second-degree robbery. In exchange for the reduced charges, the prosecution is assured of a conviction, and the state is spared the trouble and expense of a trial. Can the converse occur? In other words, can the prosecutor threaten to increase the charges if the suspect refuses to plead guilty? That was the question facing the Court in *Bordenkircher v. Hayes*.

In 1973, Paul Lewis Hayes was arrested in Fayette County (Lexington), Kentucky, and charged with a forgery in the amount of $88.30. If convicted, he faced a possible sentence of two to ten years in prison. Under Kentucky law at the time, a person with two prior felony convictions could also face the additional charge of being a habitual offender. Upon conviction as a habitual offender, the original sentence could be enhanced to as much as life in prison (with possibility of parole).

Hayes and his attorney attended a pretrial conference with the assistant prosecutor who was handling the case. The prosecutor offered to recommend a sentence of five years in exchange for a guilty plea. With a five-year sentence, Hayes would have been eligible for parole in two years. Instead, Hayes elected to take his chances with a jury trial.

The prosecutor's office then prepared a new indictment, charging Hayes with the original forgery charge and with being a "persistent felony offender." The jury convicted Hayes on the forgery charge and, in a separate hearing, subsequently added a conviction as a habitual offender. Upon determining that Hayes had been convicted of two prior felonies, the jury sentenced him to life in prison (with possibility of parole).

Hayes filed a petition in federal court for a writ of habeas corpus, on the grounds that the second indictment was an act of prosecutorial vindictiveness, undertaken solely to punish him for exercising his right to trial. The U.S. District Court for Eastern Kentucky upheld the conviction, but it was overturned by the Court of Appeals for the Sixth Circuit. The circuit court ruled that Hayes had to serve only the sentence for the original forgery conviction.

In its ruling, the court of appeals drew a distinction between "concessions relating to prosecution under an existing indictment," and threats to bring more severe charges not contained in the original indictment. Although the distinction between promises to decrease charges and threats to increase charges by prosecutors may not seem important, it points up two issues that are raised by the practice of plea bargaining. The first is the issue of voluntariness. A plea of guilty involves the waiver of constitutional rights: the right to a trial by jury, and the right not to be compelled to incriminate oneself. A long series of previous decisions by the Court, highlighted by *Miranda v. Arizona* (1966), had emphasized that any waiver of constitutional rights places a burden on the state to show that the defendant's decision was voluntary and made with full knowledge of the consequences.

The second issue is whether it is fair to punish an individual for exercising a constitutional right. The Court previously ruled that prosecutors could not punish an appellant for successfully attacking an original conviction by either seeking more severe sentences or filing more serious charges in a new trial. Such actions were defined as impermissible "vindictiveness" on the part of the prosecutor.

The U.S. Supreme Court reversed the court of appeals and upheld Hayes's conviction as a habitual offender. In an opinion written by Justice Potter Stewart, the Court ruled that the prosecutor's threats and actions against Hayes did not violate his rights to due process under the Fourteenth Amendment. As long as the prosecutor had probable cause to file the additional charges, his or her discretion in the selection of charges was not open to challenge.

In overturning Hayes's habitual-felon conviction, the court of appeals had argued that the prosecutor's actions violated principles that protected "defendants from the vindictive exercise of prosecutorial discretion." Neither of the cases enunciating these principles, however, arose from the context of plea negotiations.

The Supreme Court asserted that plea bargains were different. Although plea bargains have been a common feature of criminal justice since the nineteenth century, the practice has been openly acknowledged only recently. "Copping a plea" has an unsavory quality to the public, because it implies that a guilty criminal is getting away with less punishment than he or she deserves. Legal principles traditionally required that confessions be "free and voluntary"—that is, not the result of any threats or promises. As the practice of plea bargaining became more widely accepted, it resulted in courtroom charades that were often humorous. In many states, the judge was required to ask defendants, for the record, if they had been offered any benefits in exchange for pleading guilty. The defendants were supposed to answer no, but often they would blurt out something like, "Yeah, they told me I'd only get two years if I copped a plea."

The Court had, as recently as 1970 in *Brady v. United States*, secured the legitimacy of plea bargains. That case did involve direct plea negotiations, however. Brady had changed his plea to guilty after his codefendant pled guilty and was available to testify against him. His lawyer advised him that a jury trial might result in the imposition of the death penalty. The Court merely ruled that the possibility of a jury trial resulting in a more severe sentence, or any other opportunity or offer of leniency, did not render a guilty plea involuntary. In so ruling, however, the Court did acknowledge and accept the existence of plea bargains, stating that they were justified by the "mutuality of advantage" between the defendant and the state. As long as the plea negotiations were conducted without coercion, and the defendant's plea was made with full knowledge of the possible consequences of going to trial, the defendant's Fifth and Sixth Amendment rights were not violated.

The *Brady* decision left open the question of what rules prosecutors had to follow in plea negotiations. These were developed in subsequent cases. In *Santobello v. New York* (1971), the Court held that prosecutors must keep promises they make during plea negotiations. In *Henderson v. Morgan* (1976), the Court reinforced the idea that to be valid, a guilty plea must be made with the defendant having "full knowledge of its consequences." *Bordenkircher v. Hayes* can be interpreted as part of this process of defining the acceptable parameters of plea bargains. As such, it put an apparently permanent stamp of legitimacy on the power of prosecutors to use their authority to bring charges to encourage guilty pleas.

In a dissenting opinion in this case, Justice Harry Blackmun argued that the prosecutor's only motive for seeking a conviction on additional charges was to "discourage the defendant from exercising his right to trial." The majority opinion held that, in the context of plea negotiations, this was a perfectly legitimate motive. The very concept of plea bargains depended on the "mutuality of advantage" cited in *Brady*. The state's advantage was in avoiding the inconvenience of a trial.

Selected Bibliography

Heumann, Milton. *Plea Bargaining*. Chicago: University of Chicago Press, 1978.

Inciardi, James A. *Criminal Justice*. 6th ed. San Diego: Harcourt Brace Jovanovich, 1999.

Utz, Pamel J. *Settling the Facts*. Lexington, MA: Lexington, 1978.

Will the Real Patty Hearst Please Stand Up?

——◄○►——

Nancy Isenberg

Department of History
University of Tulsa

United States v. Patricia Hearst, 466 F. Supp. 1068 (1978) [U.S. District Court]

◄○► THE CASE IN BRIEF ◄○►

Dates
September 24, 1976
November 7, 1978
February 1, 1979

Location
San Francisco

Court
U.S. District Court

Principal Participants
Patricia Hearst
Chief U.S. Attorney James R. Browning
Judge Oliver Carter

Significance of the Case
The case revolved around the way the media shaped a defendant's identity and exploited the defendant Patty Hearst's contrasting images in and out of the courtroom.

The criminal trial of Patricia "Patty" Hearst is significant because it demonstrates the distorting role that the mass media frequently have in shaping a defendant's identity. The case is also compelling because it reveals how gender expectations can influence a jury. Unlike most criminal defendants, Patty Hearst became a media celebrity long before her trial. Her kidnapping by the Symbionese Liberation Army (SLA) in 1974 sparked a cottage industry in books, news coverage, and films. Hearst herself contributed *Every Secret Thing* in 1982. By then, her ex-fiancé, Steven Weed, had published his 1976 tell-all narrative, *My Search for Patty Hearst*. And F. Lee Bailey, her self-promoting lawyer, had demanded exclusive rights to publish his version of the Hearst case as part of his fee. The Hearst case contained all the elements of a feature-length film; indeed, it became one in 1988 with the release of *Patty Hearst*.

Kidnapped from her Berkeley, California, apartment on February 4, 1974, the "beautiful heiress"—granddaughter of newspaper magnate William Randolph Hearst—became worldwide news when she was taken by the SLA as a "prisoner of war." From the beginning, this crime did not fit the pattern of a typical kidnapping. In exchange for Hearst's parents setting up a food-distribution program for the poor, the SLA promised her release. The SLA was essentially using Hearst as a weapon to advance its version of class war. The kidnapping took another strange twist on April 3 when the SLA released a communiqué detailing Hearst's conversion to the revolutionary identity of "Tania." Next, the SLA robbed the Hibernia Bank in San Francisco, where "Tania" identified herself on the surveillance camera, dramatically demonstrating that she had joined the revolutionary struggle.

Two days later, the SLA provided another taped communiqué in which "Tania" claimed she willingly participated in the robbery. She protested that any talk of her being brainwashed was "ridiculous." She dismissed ex-fiancé Weed as a "clown" and a "sexist, agist pig," asserting that she was a revolutionary feminist. One month after this stunning message, police stormed the Los Angeles hideout of the SLA and, in a televised shootout, killed all of the group's members except Patty Hearst and Emily and John Harris. After the shootout, Hearst and the Harrises went into hiding. In a June 7 communiqué, "Tania" eulogized her dead comrades, declaring her feelings for slain SLA member William Wolfe, known as "Cujo," whom she described as "the gentlest, most beautiful man I've ever known."

Hearst and the Harrises were not arrested until September 17, 1975. The long-sought Hearst then underwent weeks of psychological testing to determine her mental competence. Finally, on February 4, 1976, Patty Hearst's trial for bank robbery and use of a firearm in the commission of a felony began. The San Francisco trial quickly became a national media event. From February to March 1976, the press corps filled the courtroom. Judge Oliver Carter, sixty-five, presided over the trial despite failing health. James R. Browning Jr., chief U.S. attorney for the Northern District of California, led the prosecution team. The lead counsel for the defense was F. Lee Bailey, who had a national reputation for taking high-profile cases.

Legal scholars have generally failed to appreciate the role of embedded media biases in criminal proceedings. According to Jean Baudrillard, the media often mutate reality into simulated images, effectively creating a "hyperreality." The simulated personalities of Hearst played a major role in the trial and contributed the narrative guidelines and visual images used by the jury to evaluate her gestures, appearance, and testimony. At the time, Harvard law professor Alan Dershowitz, drawing a distinction between rules of law and the theatricality of criminal proceedings, described the Hearst trial as a "major dramatic-political-theatrical event," but not a "major legal event." However, such a distinction does not necessarily exist in the courtroom. All trials, and the reception of evidence, testimony, or legal argumentation, rest on staged performances. Whoever has the best script and most effectively captures the "culturally mediated" imagination of the jury will have the best chance for a favorable verdict. That, along with the visual performance of the accused, comprise the narrative cues used by the jury to decide a defendant's guilt or innocence.

The Hearst case underscores why narrative scripts and theatrical performances have legal implications. The prosecution's use of the bank surveillance film, taped messages, and the "Tania Interview" (a manuscript drafted by the Harrises and Hearst during their year in hiding) introduced important evidentiary questions. How, for example, does the court decide what written, oral, or visual documents prove volition? Rejecting defense objections, Judge Carter ruled that "statements made by the defendant after the happening of the bank robbery, whether by tape recording, or oral communication, or in writing, were made voluntarily." While the prosecution aimed to convict Hearst based on words that were not completely her own and on filmed footage of the robbery, the defense introduced expert testimony on "stylistics," suggesting that Hearst's authorship of the "Tania Interview," or her taped messages, were not her own invention. Carter ruled against the introduction of this testimony, dismissing the value of literary analysis, even though volition was a contested issue.

Patty Hearst's "mediated personality" was on trial, and the members of the jury, perhaps,

A bank surveillance camera captures a picture of heiress Patty Hearst as she participated in a robbery in San Francisco. She was kidnapped by the Symbionese Liberation Army in 1974 but later joined her kidnappers in a bank raid. *Hulton Getty Collection/ Archive Photos.*

found themselves drawn to interpret Hearst's culpability through her sexual behavior. The seven women and five men focused on the story of her "romance" with the SLA's William Wolfe. Although Hearst denied that the relationship was consensual, testifying to rape, the jury believed she was "lying through and through," convinced by a "love trinket" of Wolfe's that she carried in her purse. Hearst's mediated words also undercut her claim of rape: she had, after all, called Wolfe "the gentlest, most beautiful man I've ever known." The news media spun this into a full-blown love story. Yet this tale of true love, like the carefully crafted performance on the surveillance film, and Patty's portrayal in the "Tania Interview," were all produced by the SLA.

The SLA's conscious manipulation of Hearst's identity, in particular the manufacturing of "Tania," were presented in the mass media and adopted during the trial by the prosecution.

The leaders of the SLA were the real literary stars of the case. They generated the performance, artifice, and scripted narratives of Hearst's identity as a form of guerrilla theater, cleverly anticipating the response of the mass media and inevitably contributing to the legal narratives that in the end persuaded the jury.

The prosecution's main goal was to prove that Hearst was a willing member of the SLA. Browning and his team did everything possible to paint the defendant as a "rebel in search of a cause." They exploited her image as a criminal celebrity, beginning their case by screening the surveillance film, cropping frames to offer close-ups that "convey personality." The prosecution also used photographs of Hearst that highlighted a "criminal personality," such as making the black-power fist on her arrest. The "Trish Tobin tape," a recorded conversation between Hearst and a friend while incarcerated, showed Patty voicing radical statements interspersed with expletives. She *appeared* guilty: visual performances on film, testimony by the bank guard—who claimed that she looked, spoke, and acted like a criminal—and her jailhouse patter on tape suggested a criminal personality.

In response, Bailey attacked Hearst's visual performance as staged, providing three psychiatric experts to testify that Hearst was a victim of brainwashing, or "coercive persuasion." By the time Hearst appeared for trial, her external image had been radically altered: looking pale and drained of emotion, she wore baggy clothes and pink fingernail polish. She even went by a different name, "Pat," shedding her former identity as the antisocial and hostile "Tania." "Pat" was now a shy, docile, tearful young woman on trial.

The prosecution challenged the brainwashing story in two ways. First, Browning and his team introduced experts who portrayed Hearst as a sexual deviant, highlighting her relationship with Steven Weed, her former high school teacher, rendering Hearst as "Lolita" before she became "Tania." Next, Browning dismissed the defense's "coercive persuasion" strategy by contrasting Hearst's situation to that of young male soldiers imprisoned by the Chinese Communists during the Korean War. Not only was she comfortably situated in her own country, but the SLA was not a real guerrilla force; indeed, it was "overwhelmingly female." Near the end of the trial, Browning introduced the love trinket, providing further evidence that Hearst had a reason—romance—to remain with the SLA.

Expert psychological testimony failed to persuade the jurors. It fell short of capturing their imaginations. Most jurors found Hearst's court performance unconvincing, comparing her to a robot. They believed that she had failed to tell them what they wanted to hear. While one juror expected the trial to possess the excitement of television, most looked for Hearst to comply with their media-informed understanding of female behavior. Hearst's decision to exercise her Fifth Amendment privilege (against providing testimony that might incriminate her)—which she did forty-two times—only made her more distant, increasing jurors' distrust and leading some to conclude that she was lying. The jurors had hoped to find the real Patty Hearst, an authentic and whole personality whose actions made sense; they never had the chance. They found her guilty because she did not give a natural performance; she did not provide the emotionally intense bond, the intimate confessions, that they expected. Hearst was the "girl in the box," and the jurors wanted her to offer a conventional love story. They wanted her personality to be "universally legible" in a way that followed what they knew best: the formula of news melodrama or television soap opera.

As a writer for the *Nation* concluded, "The question of who she was seemed to matter more than what she was," regardless of her guilt or innocence. Jurors' attempts to find an authentic Hearst led them to rely on narratives spun from evidence that hinted at a hidden romance or a story of criminal rebellion drawn from visual images. Browning's decision to use the love trinket came from Emily Harris, who gave an interview while in prison, and virtually directed him to this piece of evidence, suggesting how it should be interpreted. Thus, even from prison, the SLA dictated how Hearst's identity should be explained.

On September 24, 1976, Patty Hearst was sentenced to seven years' imprisonment. Re-

leased on $1.5 million bail pending the appeal of her robbery conviction, she returned to jail a year later when the U.S. Supreme Court refused to hear her appeal. She then fired Bailey and hired George C. Martinez, who filed motions in federal court, requesting that her sentence be reduced and her conviction overturned. Martinez argued that Bailey's interests in writing a book on the case, together with his constant attempts to keep himself and the trial in the news, conflicted with his duty to give Hearst the best defense possible. He also argued that the pretrial and ongoing publicity made it impossible for her to find an impartial jury, particularly in the media-saturated environment of San Francisco. Finally, Martinez contended that Hearst's right of due process had been violated through the acquisition of the Trish Tobin tape.

All of these concerns focused on Hearst's celebrity status. The district court acknowledged the unusual degree of national publicity surrounding her trial, but it still ruled that her jurors were not "unfairly prejudiced." Hearst's notoriety also contributed to the dispute over the Trish Tobin tape. At stake was whether her jailers were justified in secretly taping her conversations. The court followed the precedent that prisoners can be monitored as a security precaution. Yet, while Hearst was held in San Mateo County Jail, she was not placed in a maximum-security area, nor were all her conversations recorded. As the sheriff admitted, highly detailed records were kept of Hearst during her incarceration. Rather than a security threat, Hearst was the subject of exceptional scrutiny because she was a criminal celebrity in custody.

On November 7, 1978, the court denied all the motions Martinez raised. Fittingly, a "Committee for the Release of Patricia Hearst" worked to refashion her image one more time, organizing a popular letter campaign to persuade President Jimmy Carter to commute her sentence. This strategy worked, and Carter commuted her sentence on February 1, 1979. Over two decades later, in January 2001—in literally the final hour of his second term—President Bill Clinton granted Hearst (now Patty Hearst Shaw) executive clemency for her robbery conviction in the 1970s.

The principal legacy of this trial is the success that a radical group had in exacting a form of media terrorism. It generated the narratives, images, and confessional disclosures that served to convict the defendant. The prosecution succeeded, in part, because of Judge Carter's rulings on the evidence. But, perhaps more importantly, government had an unlikely partner—the Symbionese Liberation Army—helping to prepare its case against Patricia Hearst from beginning to end.

Selected Bibliography

Alexander, Shana. *Anyone's Daughter: The Times and Trial of Patty Hearst*. New York: Viking, 1979.

Castiglia, Christopher. *Bound and Captured: Captivity, Culture-Crossing, and White Womanhood from Mary Rowlandson to Patty Hearst*. Chicago: University of Chicago Press, 1996.

Isenberg, Nancy. "Not 'Anyone's Daughter': Patty Hearst and the Postmodern Legal Subject." *American Quarterly* 52 (December 2000):639–681.

Menicucci, Jeffrey D. "Stylistic Evidence in the Trial of Patty Hearst." *Arizona State Law Journal* 2 (1977): 387–410.

Schuetz, Janice. *The Logic of Women on Trial: Case Studies of Popular American Trials*. Carbondale: Southern Illinois University Press, 1994.

For Pure Cold Cash:
The Walker and Ames Espionage Cases

———◄○►———

Joseph Glidewell
Social Sciences Department
Truett-McConnell College

United States v. John A. Walker, Jr., 624 F. Supp. 99 (1985)
[U.S. Federal District Court]

◄○► THE CASE IN BRIEF ◄○►

Dates
1985, 1994

Locations
Baltimore, Washington, D.C.

Court
U.S. Federal District Courts

Principal Participants
John Anthony Walker Jr.
Judge Alexander Harvey
Aldrich Ames

Significance of the Case
In the closing years of the Cold War, two spies—who betrayed their country for greed—were tried in cases that have led to stricter national security efforts to combat espionage.

It began with a phone call in November 1984 to the FBI Office in Boston. Barbara Walker, ex-wife of John Anthony Walker, told the FBI agent on the phone that she believed her former husband had been selling secrets to the Soviet Union. She was particularly concerned that he had attempted to gain their children's assistance in his traitorous activities. The Walker family espionage ring, which included John Walker, his son Michael, a brother Arthur Walker, and a close friend named Jerry Whitworth was one of the most notorious of several episodes of espionage uncovered late in the Cold War. The Walker ring was ultimately found to have supplied the Soviets with highly classified communications and encryption material, plus the names of U.S. agents and Soviet double agents. As a result of information supplied to them by the Walker ring, the Soviets were able to decode some of the most sensitive communications transmitted by U.S. military forces, as well as deprive the United States of vital information for many years. As the case unfolded in public view, it brought back memories of the days of the early Cold War and the

"Red Scare" rhetoric. Though national security was at stake, this case also illustrated how rights of the accused were threatened as the public clamored for the strictest of punishments.

In 1967, John Walker, command watch officer on the staff of Commander, Submarine Forces Atlantic at the Norfolk, Virginia, Naval Station, "volunteered" his services to the Soviets. At the time he sold his first classified information Walker needed money to dig himself out of a large financial hole. For the next ten years, Walker's contact with the Soviets consisted mainly of a series of exchanges or "dead drops." In total, Walker conducted about thirty drops and had thirteen face-to-face meetings with his KGB (Soviet secret police) handlers. For his efforts Walker was paid between $1 million and $1.5 million. After several years of solitary espionage activity, John Walker recruited his son Michael, his brother Arthur (a retired navy lieutenant commander working for a military contractor), and Jerry Whitworth (a senior chief radioman in the navy). Together these individuals provided Walker with classified material to sell to the Soviets.

Following Barbara Walker's 1984 phone call, the FBI began to investigate. After several interviews with his ex-wife, a wiretap was installed on Walker's phones. Within a month, the FBI overheard several conversations that led them to believe that a meeting with a Soviet handler was about to take place. Walker was then placed under constant surveillance. Finally, on the evening of May 19, 1985, the FBI followed Walker to a drop site. Walker left a package for his Soviet counterpart to retrieve. As Walker prepared to leave the area, the FBI moved in. The package was picked up by the agents and taken to their field office and examined. Inside it were classified documents from the USS *Nimitz*. Walker, who was still under surveillance, was arrested later that night.

After Walker was arrested he was taken to the Baltimore FBI office. There he was photographed, fingerprinted, and taken to a conference room where he was questioned. The next day Walker was taken to a hearing where the magistrate found that probable cause had been shown by the government and remanded Walker to a U.S. marshall without bond. At the hearing, Walker told the magistrate that he was indigent and wanted a court-appointed attorney. Thomas B. Mason and later Fred Warren Bennett, both federal public defenders, were appointed.

Once information in the Walker case became public, newspapers, television, and radio representatives crowded every court proceeding. The publicity became so intense that Walker's attorneys filed a motion in the Baltimore United States District Court asking to hold the assistant director of the FBI in contempt of court because of the many statements that he had made to the media about the case.

The FBI had in its possession the contents of the package that Walker had dropped on the evening of May 19. The contents included, besides some garbage, a U.S. navy study of the problems with the Tomahawk Cruise Missile, schematics of missile defense systems of the USS *Nimitz*, and a study of how U.S. satellites could be sabotaged. The FBI lab found eighty-three of John Walker's fingerprints and sixty-three of his son, Michael's, on the contents of the package. The FBI also conducted a search of Walker's home. This led to the discovery of three-by-five cards bearing the first name of each member of the espionage ring. Also obtained from this search were sophisticated espionage paraphernalia, calendars of every act of espionage Walker had committed, an expensive camera used to photograph naval documents, and pictures of the drop sites. Other items were found that implicated Jerry Whitworth. The FBI also obtained a sheet of paper that showed how much Walker had paid Whitworth for his part in the espionage activities ($332,000 over a ten-year period). Later the FBI conducted other searches that turned up additional evidence. At the same time that the FBI investigation was taking place, the Internal Revenue Service became involved because Walker had not paid any taxes on the money he had earned from his espionage business.

Five days after John Walker was arrested, his son Michael, who served as a yeoman on the USS *Nimitz*, was apprehended. Michael immediately confessed to his part in his father's espionage business. After continually failing polygraph tests, Arthur Walker confessed his role in the espionage ring to a federal grand jury in Baltimore on May 28, 1985. John Walker's friend, Jerry Whitworth, turned himself in on June 3, 1985.

The U.S. government elected to try Arthur Walker first. The trial was held in the eastern district of Virginia; it was presided over by Judge Calvitt Clarke Jr. Judge Clarke had been a federal judge for over eleven years and had a reputation as a no-nonsense jurist. The federal government chose Tom Miller and Robert Seidel Jr. from the U.S. attorney's office to prosecute the case. Since Arthur Walker claimed he could not afford to hire an attorney, Judge Clarke appointed two attorneys for him, Samuel Meekins and J. Brian Donnelly. For Arthur Walker to avoid conviction his attorneys had only two options: either they had to succeed in getting his confession thrown out or they had to convince Judge Clarke that no testimony regarding John Walker's espionage activities should be allowed into the record. In the pretrial hearings Walker's attorneys failed on both issues. The trial was set for August 5. Several days before the trial was to begin, the government made an offer to Arthur Walker to plead nolo contendere to the espionage charge, which carried a life sentence. In return Walker would agree to cooperate fully with the federal government in its investigation and prosecution of the other members of the Walker espionage ring. However, bureaucratic problems ensued and the offer for the plea was withdrawn. Walker then waived his right to a trial by jury and agreed to be tried by Judge Clarke.

The Arthur Walker trial lasted four days. The prosecution presented all the evidence that it had acquired, and the defense team attempted to attack the credibility of the written reports that the FBI had taken in its investigation. No witnesses were presented for Walker's defense. On August 9 Judge Clarke made his decision. He found Arthur Walker guilty on seven counts of espionage. On November 12, Judge Clarke sentenced Arthur Walker to three life terms plus four ten-year terms and a fine of $200,000. Walker's attorneys appealed the verdict to the United States Court of Appeals for

the Fourth Circuit. On July 7, 1986, Arthur Walker's appeal was denied.

The trial of John Walker and his son followed next. John Walker and his attorneys had watched Arthur Walker's trial very closely. The decision was made by John Walker's attorneys to attempt to raise various motions challenging the government's case. The defense's first challenge involved asking the court to suppress certain statements made by John Walker during a conversation with an FBI agent immediately after he was arrested. Walker's attorneys argued that the statements in question were obtained in violation of rights secured to him by the Fifth Amendment to the Constitution of the United States. Walker's attorneys claimed that, although the statements were voluntarily made, the law enforcement officers did not issue the proper "Miranda warning." According to the defense, when Walker was taken into custody, an FBI agent informed Walker of his Miranda rights. Walker stated that he understood his rights and would sign the portion of the form that would show he had been informed of his rights. However, he also stated he did not wish to waive his rights. In fact, during the day in question, Walker invoked his Miranda rights a second time. Later when approached by an FBI agent, Walker himself initiated a conversation with the agent. Walker's attorneys asked the court to suppress the entire set of conversations that he had with the FBI.

Judge Alexander Harvey, a former assistant attorney general for the state of Maryland and a U.S. district judge since 1966, heard the motions. According to Judge Harvey, once a suspect has been "Mirandized" and expresses his desire to consult with an attorney, the subject "can not be subjected to further interrogation until counsel has been made available to him." Judge Harvey went on to state that the U.S. Supreme Court has repeatedly reaffirmed this restraint on police interrogation. In addition, Judge Harvey noted that "interrogation under Miranda refers not only to express questioning but also to any words or actions on the part of the police . . . that the police should know are reasonably likely to elicit an incriminating response . . . from the suspect." Judge Harvey thus ruled that the statements in question could not be used by the government as a part of its case.

With this victory in hand, the defense attempted to suppress evidence seized at the drop site as a violation of the Fourth Amendment. The government opposed this motion on two grounds. First, the prosecutors insisted that a search of the bag could be justified on the basis of probable cause coupled with "exigent circumstances." Judge Harvey agreed. Then the prosecutors argued that the defendant had abandoned the bag and all its contents when law enforcement authorities came upon it. The judge agreed that "the location of the bag, discovered on a roadside in a sparsely populated rural setting, clearly supports a finding of abandonment." Judge Harvey ruled that "a person who would leave at such a location what had all the appearance of a bag of trash could hardly have retained a reasonable expectation of privacy with regard to the contents of the bag."

Having lost their pleas for suppression of evidence, John Walker's attorneys offered the U.S. attorneys a plea bargain. They said that Walker would volunteer to plead guilty and offer information in return for leniency in his son Michael's sentencing. The government accepted this offer. Walker pleaded guilty to attempting to deliver national defense information to a foreign government and unlawful receipt of national defense information in violation of U.S. laws. In addition Walker pleaded guilty to conspiring to deliver national defense information to a foreign government from 1968 to 1985. Furthermore, he agreed to cooperate fully with the government on questions about his knowledge of espionage and espionage-related activities. In return for full cooperation in this agreement, Walker was promised that all other counts of the indictments against him would be dismissed, that the maximum sentences that he would receive would run concurrently, and that no other charges of other violations of federal criminal law for his involvement in espionage or espionage-related activities would be brought at a later date. Michael Walker pleaded guilty to five espionage charges. Though the maximum penalty

was life imprisonment, the government agreed to a deal that essentially gave Michael Walker a sentence of twenty-five years in prison.

On March 24, 1986, the final member of the Walker espionage ring, Jerry Whitworth, went to trial. The "show-stopper" of that trial was the ten-day testimony given by John Walker, in which he described in full detail both his own espionage career as well as Whitworth's. On July 11 a jury returned a guilty verdict on all seven counts of espionage and on five counts of income tax evasion. On August 28 Whitworth was sentenced to a total of 365 years in prison and a fine of $410,000 dollars.

At 9:30 A.M. on November 6, 1986, John Walker appeared before Judge Harvey to be sentenced. After stating to Walker that his espionage activities had caused tremendous harm to the national security of the United States, the Judge intoned: "Your motive was pure greed." He went on to say that "throughout history spies have been moved to betray their country for ideological reasons, you and the others . . . were traitors for pure cold cash." Throughout the trial, John Walker's facial expression had seldom changed. However, what Judge Harvey said next clearly upset Walker's stoic demeanor. Mentioning that there had been suggestions of parole, the judge stated: "it is difficult for me to believe that any parole commissioner could ever agree to an early release for you, and I shall do everything in my power to see that this does not occur." Walker was then given his sentence: life imprisonment.

The end of the Cold War in the early 1990s did not mean the end of espionage or espionage prosecutions. The Aldrich Ames case, although it never reached trial because the defendants pleaded guilty and accepted a plea bargain, illustrated once again the danger to American national interests of clandestine spying in exchange for money. Taking place in the mid-1990s, the Ames case was arguably even more serious than the Walker case.

In February 1994 the FBI arrested Aldrich Ames, a counterintelligence officer of the Central Intelligent Agency, and his wife, Rosario Ames. Aldrich Ames, who had worked for the CIA for more than thirty years, admitted to revealing to the Soviet Union (and later Russia)

Former CIA agent Alton Ames leaves federal court in Alexandria, Virginia, on April 28, 1994. *Associated Press AP.*

the names of virtually every Western agent, including U.S. agents and Soviet double agents, who had worked against the Soviet Union during the height of the Cold War. By Ames's own account, at least twelve double agents had been executed by the Soviets as a result of his betrayals. In return for his services, Ames was paid more than $2 million by the Soviet and Russian governments between 1985 and 1994.

The U.S. government built its case by using video surveillance of Ames and his wife as they crossed the Potomac to a residential neighborhood in northeast Washington in an attempt to verify that materials left at a drop site had been successfully retrieved. Also, the FBI obtained evidence against Ames and his wife by taps on their telephones and computers, by rummaging through their garbage, and by electronically monitoring their bank accounts. On an annual government salary of about $70,000,

Ames and his wife were somehow able to live in an expensive home, invest heavily in stock and securities, and buy two condominiums and a farm in his wife's native country of Columbia.

Although Ames and his wife were not arrested until February 22, 1994, the FBI had been suspicious of their activities as far back as the mid 1980s, when Ames's occasional meetings with Soviet agents attracted government attention. After the arrest, with the freezing of their assets, Aldrich and Rosario Ames had to rely on court-appointed attorneys. Former U.S. Attorney William Cummings was appointed to represent Rosario Ames, and Plato Cachesis was appointed to represent Aldrich Ames.

In April 1994, Cachesis informed the government that he was prepared to raise numerous evidentiary challenges to the government's case against Ames. Besides arguing that the searches of the Ames home, car, office, and computer were illegal, Cachesis pointed out to the government prosecutors that it had yet to be established that Ames had passed even one secret document to a Russian agent. However, rather than take the risk of fighting the charges against him on technical grounds, Cachesis announced that Ames would plead guilty to several charges. In exchange for the promise that the prosecutors would seek a lenient sentence against his wife, Ames admitted to committing espionage and tax evasion and received a life sentence in prison. Rosario, whose espionage activities were considerably less destructive than her husband's, was sentenced to five years in prison. Both defendants forfeited their remaining assets. Following the sentencing, U.S. Attorney Helen Fahey stated that the Ames espionage case was "the most damaging spy case in the history of the country." Prosecutors believed that, because Ames compromised American penetrations of the Soviet military and intelligence services, the United States "was deprived of extremely valuable intelligence for years to come."

As a result of the Walker and Ames spy cases, stricter security measures were instituted to protect against similar acts of espionage. However, as long as military and diplomatic secrets are kept by the United States, and as long as rival governments are willing to pay for those secrets, there remains the possibility that there will be individuals like John Walker and Aldrich Ames willing to accept cold cash for giving up those secrets.

Selected Bibliography

Barron, John. *Breaking the Ring*. Boston: Houghton Mifflin, 1987.

Hunter, Robert. *Spy Hunter: Inside the FBI Investigation of the Walker Espionage Case*. Annapolis, MD: Naval Institute Press, 1999.

Kneece, Jack. *Family Treason*. New York: Stein and Day, 1986.

Maas, Peter. *Killer Spy*. New York: Warner Books, 1995.

Surrogate Motherhood:
Womb for Rent

—◄◦►—

Elizabeth E. Traxler

Department of Social Sciences
Greenville Technical College

In re Baby M, 109 N.J. 396 (1988) [New Jersey Supreme Court]

◄◦► THE CASE IN BRIEF ◄◦►

Date
1988

Location
New Jersey

Court
New Jersey Supreme Court

Principal Participants
William Stern
Mary Beth Whitehead

Significance of the Case
New Jersey's highest court declared surrogacy illegal after a much-publicized trial that involved contracts, parenting, and the issue of custodial rights; despite this case, no national standard has emerged concerning the legality and details of surrogacy motherhood.

The case of *Baby M* garnered nationwide attention when its facts were made public in 1986. Included in the story were elements of a drama guaranteed to rival the hottest soap opera: a baby passed through a window to escape "the law," charges of alcoholism and sexual abuse, flights to other states, a nomadic existence in motels, and a six-week trial involving the testimony of thirty-eight witnesses and generating a half million dollars in legal fees.

The *Baby M* case was by no means the first use of surrogate motherhood contracts, or even the first legal challenge to such agreements. The history of surrogacy can be traced at least as far back as the story told in the Bible of Sarah urging Abraham to enlist her maid Hagar as a surrogate mother. No doubt through the years there were cases of friends and relatives who provided this service for couples unable to bear children. The use of legal surrogacy contracts emerged in the mid-1970s, and several hundred children had been born as a result before the *Baby M* case arose. Yet, none of the previous contracts or challenges in court attained the notoriety of this particular one. The publicity accorded this case and trial guaranteed extensive consideration of the unresolved issues raised by this method of procreation. The court's decision and resulting commentary generated legislation to address the issue, and also provided a precedent for cases subject to future litigation. Initially, however, there appeared to be nothing particularly unusual with this contract or the circumstances surrounding its creation.

The agreement entered into by William Stern and Mary Beth Whitehead was a fairly typical surrogacy contract. Whitehead agreed to be artificially inseminated with Stern's sperm and to surrender the baby and all parental rights to Stern at birth so that his wife could then adopt the child. Contact with Whitehead after that point was to be limited to an annual picture and progress report. In return, Stern agreed to pay all expenses of insemination, pregnancy, and childbirth, as well as a fee of $10,000 at the time of termination of parental rights by Whitehead. Should the baby be born with abnormalities, Stern agreed to accept legal responsibility for it after birth. The contract also included stipulations that Whitehead would undergo amniocentesis and leave to Stern any decision regarding abortion.

Nor were the circumstances surrounding the agreement out of the ordinary. The Sterns, he a biochemist and she a pediatrician, decided on surrogate childbirth after they learned that Mrs. Stern had a mild case of multiple sclerosis. Fearful that pregnancy would exacerbate her condition, they decided that surrogacy was their best route to parenthood. Their ages and differing religions, as well as Stern's desire to carry on his family bloodline after the death of his last living relative, led them to rule out adoption as an alternative. They turned to the Infertility Center of New York in search of a surrogate. There they came into contact with Mary Beth Whitehead, who sought to provide such services. Whitehead maintained that she turned to surrogacy as a way to provide money for her two children's future education and out of a desire to provide happiness for a childless couple. She and her husband considered their family complete, and he, in fact, had had a vasectomy nine years earlier. Yet what began over a celebratory dinner at the time of conception

had soured even before Whitehead gave birth to a baby girl on March 27, 1986.

Indications of second thoughts surfaced during the pregnancy as Whitehead resisted Stern's medical advice and insistence on amniocentesis. Whitehead signed the papers acknowledging Stern's paternity after much hesitation. The issue came to a head at "Baby M's" birth when Whitehead began to voice her uncertainty over giving up the baby. Contrary to provisions of the contract, she both named the baby and identified her husband as the father on the birth certificate. Though she did relinquish the baby to the Sterns on the day of her release from the hospital, she successfully convinced them the following day to allow her to take the baby for a week's visit. Fearful for Whitehead's emotional state should they refuse her request, the Sterns grudgingly consented. Unknown to the Sterns, Whitehead took the baby out of state during that time to visit her parents in Florida. After much ambivalence, Whitehead finally told the Sterns that she would not give up the child and would not terminate her parental rights by honoring the contract. The Sterns obtained a court order granting them temporary custody of the baby when it appeared that the Whiteheads were planning a move to Florida before the issue could be litigated. They arrived at the Whitehead home accompanied by the police to enforce the decree, but were stymied in their efforts when the Whiteheads spirited the baby away from the residence via a window. Thus began a lengthy period during which the Whiteheads, complete with baby, were on the move constantly to evade the authorities' efforts to enforce the court order. Finally, after eighty-seven days, the Florida police were able to take custody of the baby and returned her to the Sterns in New Jersey. The legal battle culminated in a nonjury trial before Judge Harvey R. Sorkow in the Superior Court of New Jersey.

The trial resulted in a lengthy decision which touched on most of the major unresolved issues surrounding surrogate motherhood contracts. Essentially, the case turned on whether the contract was a valid one, enforceable by the state; and, if it was, what remedies were available, given Mary Beth Whitehead's breach. At the time, there existed no state or federal law regarding such arrangements. It was left, therefore, to the court to determine the legality of the contract. Though New Jersey statutory law was silent on surrogacy, other statutes, especially those concerning adoption, child custody, and termination of parental rights, could have been construed to govern the matter. That, in fact, is what had occurred in a 1981 Michigan case when that state's adoption laws were used to declare the fee payment aspect of surrogacy contracts illegal. Five years later, in a Kentucky case, that state's supreme court accepted a fee as payment for services, thus avoiding the anti-baby selling elements of their laws. However, Kentucky applied its adoption statutes to allow the surrogate mother a five-day grace period after the baby's birth in which to change her mind concerning surrender of the baby and parental rights.

The New Jersey court argued that surrogacy had not been medically perfected at the time of these statutes' passage and rejected them as irrelevant to these proceedings. Judge Sorkow applied only principles of common and constitutional law in his assessment of the contract's legality. He argued that contracts are protected under common law unless they are against public policy. After brief consideration of the major critiques of surrogacy, he held that such contracts were not void from a public policy standpoint. In so doing, he rejected the following objections to surrogacy on public policy grounds: (1) that it degraded women by treating them only as reproductive machines; (2) that it could lead to exploitation of women of lower socioeconomic status by women in a financial position to rent another's womb; and (3) that the fee payment provisions amounted to buying and selling a child, an act illegal in all fifty states.

Judge Sorkow also found support for surrogacy contracts in principles of constitutional law, most notably in the right to privacy grounded in the Fourteenth Amendment's Due Process Clause and in the same amendment's Equal Protection Clause. Tracing the case history affirming the existence of a right to privacy, the judge asserted that such a right included within it a right to procreate. If that were the case, he maintained, the chosen means

of procreation must also be protected. From this, he argued that the state could not deny men and women the right to enter into surrogacy contracts for the purpose of procreation unless a compelling reason for restriction could be shown. He found none of the reasons advanced by others (essentially the same ones used to argue that these contracts were harmful to public policy) sufficiently compelling to justify state restrictions.

Judge Sorkow further argued that the constitutionality of the surrogacy contract was grounded in the Fourteenth Amendment's Equal Protection Clause. He maintained that a woman offering her services for pay as a surrogate was substantially the same as a man being paid as a sperm donor. The 1976 U.S. Supreme Court case of *Reed v. Reed*, a gender discrimination case, was cited to support the proposition that the Equal Protection Clause forbade differential treatment of the sexes unless a compelling reason could be offered. In the absence of such a reason, he insisted that women must be accorded the same rights as men. Since the various public policy arguments were not found convincing enough to void the contract on common-law principles, they were also not held to be sufficient justifications for state restriction of constitutional rights lodged in both clauses of the Fourteenth Amendment.

Because Judge Sorkow found the contract valid and Whitehead to have breached it, a determination of the remedies available to Stern was next made. Generally, contract law allows for two remedies: payment of monetary damages to the aggrieved party or an order for specific performance of the terms of the contract—the latter to be used when money cannot adequately compensate. Judge Sorkow maintained that although contract law principles would seem to mandate specific performance, this could not be ordered unless it was also in the best interest of the child. At this point, he asserted the common law principle of *parens patriae*, whereby the state acts as a guardian to protect the interests of those with legal disabilities—in this case Baby M. After a review of the testimony from experts on the meaning of "best interests," as well as their evaluations of the relative abilities of each couple to fulfill those interests, Judge Sorkow ordered that the terms of the contract be specifically performed, thereby terminating Mary Beth Whitehead's parental rights and lodging all such rights with the father, William Stern. He then proceeded to an immediate hearing in which Elizabeth Stern became the baby's adopted mother.

Given the emotions of the parties to this case, it is not surprising that it did not end at that point. Ten days later, the New Jersey Supreme Court, pending outcome of the appeal, ordered visitation privileges for Mary Beth Whitehead. On February 3, 1988, the state's highest court handed down its opinion, in which much of the lower court's decision was reversed. Surrogacy contracts were found to be contrary to existing New Jersey statutes forbidding payment for babies and regulating termination of parental rights. They were also held to be against the public policy of protecting the best interests of the child, which included being raised by both of her natural parents. Although the court acknowledged a constitutional right to procreate, it held that this pertained only to the right to conceive a child, not to the right to contract away parental custody and rights. On these bases, surrogacy contracts were declared illegal and unenforceable in New Jersey.

The court then proceeded to a determination of custody of Baby M, using only the principle of best interests of that child. Drawing on the expert testimony at the trial and on an assessment of the child's previous year and a half with the Sterns, the court awarded custody to Mr. and Mrs. Stern. The issue of visitation was remanded to the trial court with the admonition that some form of visitation be allowed Whitehead.

In the years since the *Baby M* case, the issue of surrogacy motherhood has become more, rather than less, tangled. No federal legislation or federal court decision governs disposition of the issue. Instead, each state, either through state court decisions or state legislation, has dealt with the issue. A few states recognize surrogate motherhood contracts, others have laws making them unenforceable, and still others provide for civil or criminal penalties for those who enter into such contracts. In fact, in the majority of states, no law, either judicial or statu-

tory, has emerged on surrogate motherhood. Efforts to convince states to adopt a uniform act on surrogate similar to those dealing with other issues of family law have been unsuccessful.

The issue is further complicated by the advances in reproductive medicine since 1988. The traditional surrogacy of the *Baby M* case has been joined by gestational surrogacy, where the woman carrying the baby to gestation has no genetic link to the child. As can be imagined, this opens the door to differing legal attitudes toward surrogacy contracts. In fact, a 1998 Massachusetts Supreme Court case suggested that gestational surrogacy might be acceptable where traditional surrogacy contracts were unenforceable.

The New Jersey Supreme Court assertion at the close of its decision in the *Baby M* case remains relevant today: "The problem is how to enjoy the benefits of the technology—especially for infertile couples—while minimizing the rise of abuse. The problem can be addressed only when society decides what its values and objectives are in this troubling, yet promising area."

Selected Bibliography

Bacin, James F. "A Matter for Solomon: Rights and Obligations of Surrogate Mothers after *Baby M.*" *Western State University Law Review* 15 (Fall 1987): 297–317.

Coleman, Malina. "Gestation, Intent, and the Seed: Defining Motherhood in the Era of Assisted Human Reproduction." *Cardozo Law Review* 17 (January 1996): 497–530.

Field, Martha A. *Surrogate Motherhood.* Cambridge, MA: Harvard University Press, 1988.

Kerian, Christine L. "Surrogacy: A Last Resort Alternative for Infertile Women or a Commodification of Women's Bodies and Children?" *Wisconsin Women's Law Journal* 12 (Spring 1997): 113–166.

Klinke, Katy Ruth. "The *Baby M* Controversy: A Class Distinction." *Oklahoma City University Law Review* 18 (Spring 1993): 113–151.

Recht, Steven M. "'M' Is for Money: Baby M and the Surrogate Motherhood Controversy." *American University Law Review* 37 (Spring 1988): 1013–1050.

Stark, Barbara. "Constitutional Analysis of the *Baby M* Decision." *Harvard Women's Law Journal* 11 (Spring 1988): 19–52.

Narratives in Black and White:
The O. J. Simpson Trials as Social Drama

——◦——

Wayne K. Hobson

American Studies Department
California State University, Fullerton

California v. Simpson, No. BA097211 (1995) and *Rufo, et al. v. Simpson*, No. SC031947 (1997)
[California Superior Court]

◦ THE CASE IN BRIEF ◦

Date
October 3, 1995; February 12, 1997

Locations
Los Angeles, Santa Monica

Court
Los Angeles County Superior Court

Principal Participants
Orenthal James (O.J.) Simpson
Johnnie L. Cochran; F. Lee Bailey
Marcia Clark; Christopher Darden

Significance of the Case
The jury acquitted O.J. Simpson of homicide in a criminal trial, but he was ordered to pay $33.5 million in damages in a civil trial that found him responsible for murder. The case polarized the nation along racial lines.

Two juries, two verdicts. On October 3, 1995, a Los Angeles County Superior Court criminal trial jury found Orenthal James (O.J.) Simpson not guilty of the June 12, 1994, homicide of his former wife, Nicole Brown Simpson, and her friend Ronald Goldman. On February 12, 1997, a Los Angeles County Superior Court civil trial jury held O.J. Simpson responsible for those same murders and assessed him $33.5 million in compensatory and punitive damages. Explaining the conflicting verdicts is only the first step in making sense of the Simpson case. Behind the courtroom dramas is a much larger social drama, as the competing legal teams, the media, interest groups, and the general public struggled for control of the narrative that would define the larger cultural meaning of the case. In the end, as is so often true in celebrated criminal cases, underlying social and cultural conflicts were more evident than consensus or resolution.

How can we explain the intense public interest in the case? O.J. Simpson was a celebrity, a football star who had parlayed his fame into lucrative endorsements and then into a broadcasting and acting career. In 1994, at age forty-seven, he was earning about $1 million a year, primarily from endorsements, autographs, and celebrity engagements. But, as O.J. Simpson's legal problems unfolded, race became more important than celebrity in shaping the meaning of the social drama. It mattered that the two victims were white. It mattered even more that O.J. Simpson was African American.

At the criminal trial, prosecutors tried to present a race-neutral narrative. With a wealth of physical evidence tying the defendant to the murders, the prosecution told a story of domestic violence, stalking, intimidation, and public humiliation escalating to murder. The couple—Nicole Brown and O.J. Simpson—met in 1977 when she was eighteen and he thirty; they married in 1985 and had two children, then they divorced in 1992. Nicole called police to their residence eight times before Simpson was finally prosecuted, in 1989, for wife battering. In 1993, she made a dramatic 911 call for help. However, her call to a women's shelter five days before the murder to report that Simpson was stalking her was declared inadmissible as hearsay. When Nicole's safety deposit box revealed photographs of her battered face, the prosecution claimed that she was testifying from the grave. As Prosecutor Christopher Darden explained to the jury, "She left him. She was no longer in his control. He could not stand to lose her, and so he murdered her."

To substantiate this narrative, the prosecution, led by Deputy District Attorney Marcia Clark, introduced evidence that Simpson had opportunity to commit the crimes, which occurred between 10:15 and 10:45 P.M. on the night in question. He was alone after 9:40 and not seen again until approximately 10:55, at his home a ten-minute drive from Nicole's condominium. Physical evidence at the crime scene at Simpson's home and in his car tied him directly to the crime. A trail of blood on the left side of the path, on the gate, and on the driveway at the murder scene led to Simpson. DNA testing, which yields results in terms of statistical probabilities, showed that the odds were very small that anyone other than Simpson had left that blood: 1 in 170 million for the blood on the pathway, 1 in 57 billion for the blood on the

gate. A knit cap and an expensive glove from the crime scene were tied to him. The knit cap contained African American hairs and carpet fibers from the model of sport utility vehicle that Simpson drove. The glove was Simpson's size, and there was evidence that Nicole had purchased one of only 200 pairs ever sold. Photographs showed Simpson wearing such gloves at public events in earlier years. Goldman's shirt bore traces of African American male hair as well as cotton fibers similar in color to a jumpsuit Simpson wore earlier that evening. A bloody footprint at the scene came from an expensive Bruno Magli shoe, in size twelve, Simpson's size. Simpson's vehicle, a white Ford Bronco, contained bloodstains consistent with Simpson and the two victims. A bloody glove found at Simpson's home matched the crime scene glove. It contained the same Bronco carpet fibers and the cotton fibers found on Goldman's shirt. It also had hair fibers and blood consistent with the defendant and the two victims. Finally, socks found in Simpson's bedroom contained fibers and blood consistent with that of Simpson and his ex-wife.

In response, O.J. Simpson's lawyers constructed a counternarrative designed to make the apparently overwhelming physical evidence irrelevant. Simpson's wealth enabled him to retain a multiracial "dream team" of highly skilled defense lawyers and forensics experts. Dominant among the defense counsel was veteran Los Angeles attorney Johnnie L. Cochran, who had long battled racism in law enforcement. The defense narrative portrayed a racially biased Los Angeles Police Department (LAPD) planting and contaminating physical evidence such that none of it could be taken at face value. The police criminalist admitted that one of the most apparently conclusive blood samples, from the rear gate at the crime scene, had been collected three weeks after the killings and that he could not account for 1.5 mm of the blood sample taken from Simpson. Taken together, these two facts, along with the fact that forensic photographs could be interpreted to show no blood on the gate immediately after the murders, suggested that the highly positive DNA match for that blood sample resulted from police fabrication of evi-

In a dramatic moment—and one that devastated the prosecution—American football hero and murder defendant O.J. Simpson tries on one of the gloves that prosecutors said he wore the night of the murders of his ex-wife Nicole Brown Simpson and her friend Ron Goldman. *Reuters/Sam Mircovich/Archive Photos.*

dence. Detective Mark Fuhrman was accused of planting evidence: the bloody glove he "found" behind the guest house at Simpson's home, the bloody sock found in Simpson's bedroom, and the blood evidence found in Simpson's Bronco. These accusations gained credence when the defense turned up a witness who had tape-recorded twelve hours of Fuhrman expressing his hatred of African Americans and bragging about planting evidence and committing other racially motivated injustices under the cover of police authority.

To buttress their narrative, defense lawyers presented expert forensic testimony implying that someone had tampered with the blood samples. They also presented witnesses to challenge the prosecution's time line, shortening the time between the murders and when Simpson was next seen. Finally, they suggested that

Nicole's death was incident to a drug deal gone wrong. Defense lawyers worked hard to portray her as living a dissolute lifestyle, one that could lead to violent death.

Celebrated criminal trials are often likened to dramas. More to the point, two different dramas typically compete for the jury's attention, a crime drama and a courtroom drama. The crime drama, which the prosecution usually emphasizes, asks the jury to imaginatively reconstruct the crime, placing the defendant at the center of action. The courtroom drama, which the defense usually emphasizes, asks the jury to focus on the conflict emerging before their eyes in the courtroom, to see the defendant as he appears to them rather than as he might appear in their imaginations under murderous circumstances. Frequently, the courtroom drama seeks to unmask the face of authority, revealing official misconduct and questionable but all-too-human motives. Often, the defense will try to stage dramatic courtroom moments. In the Simpson criminal trial, the courtroom drama frequently overrode the crime drama; most memorably, Cochran goaded Darden into "testing" the bloody glove Fuhrman had "found" by trying it on the defendant's hand. Simpson, not surprisingly, found the glove "too tight" and visibly struggled to force it on his hand. Cochran would return to this moment in his summation, telling the jury, "if the glove doesn't fit, you must acquit."

Shifting the focus from the crime drama to the courtroom drama, Simpson's lawyers were fortunate that trial judge Lance Ito believed in airing all issues fully. Ito's unwillingness to assert control allowed the defense to disrupt the prosecution's presentation of the crime drama, which contributed to the excruciatingly slow pace of the trial. The judge unintentionally helped the defense shift the focus to the courtroom drama and their narrative.

Nevertheless, when the jury quickly announced its verdict at the end of the more than eight-month trial, a majority of the media and public responded with incredulity. How could the jury acquit a man most Americans believed guilty? The trial's every moment had been televised, with that coverage regularly supplemented by reactions from pundits. It had been

"O.J. every day, all day." And most media coverage strongly implied that Simpson was almost certainly guilty, his history of domestic violence transforming him from a nice guy celebrity into an abusive husband, with the physical evidence clinching the case. Significantly, while the victims' families appeared often in media coverage, the defendant's family seemed absent even though his two sisters were in constant attendance at the trial.

Critical observers quickly concluded that the jury had been influenced by racial considerations more than by evidence presented in court. The final jury (during the course of the trial ten original jurors were replaced by alternates) consisted of eight African American women, one African American male, one Hispanic male, and two Caucasian women. This racial composition reflected where the trial was held—downtown Los Angeles, rather than Santa Monica, whose courthouse was closer to the murder scene. Whereas African Americans constitute eleven percent of Los Angeles County's population, they make up thirty-one percent of the jury pool for the downtown courts and a mere 7 percent of the Santa Monica jury pool. Twenty-eight percent of the nine hundred jurors summoned at the beginning of the Simpson criminal trial were African American. That percentage increased to approximately fifty percent after the judge dismissed 304 jurors for hardship reasons. A second reason for the racial composition of the final jury was that the defense, far more than the prosecution, relied on consultants to guide the questions it asked and the decisions it made during voir dire (preliminary period of questioning to qualify jurors). By and large, the defense got the jury it wanted. In contrast, the final jury in the civil trial, held in Santa Monica, had no African Americans. But what does it mean to say that race influences a jury's verdict? The jurors themselves denied that race explained their decision. In books and interviews, they emphasized the LAPD's sloppy handling of physical evidence, the glove that didn't fit, and the unreliability of the prosecution's key time line eyewitness. Critics of the Simpson jury, on the other hand, point to the extremely limited and perfunctory review the jury gave to the evidence, discussing it for fewer than four hours after receiving the case.

More important than the controversy over the jury's verdict is the racial divide among the public that the Simpson trial revealed. When the verdict was announced, television showed African Americans around the country cheering the verdict and whites expressing shock and dismay. Missing from these news reports was the crucial information that some whites agreed with the jury while some blacks did not. Nevertheless, poll data had consistently shown wide splits between blacks and whites on Simpson's likely guilt. In early July 1994, before DNA evidence was available, the Gallup poll found that sixty-eight percent of whites believed Simpson was guilty while sixty percent of blacks believed him innocent. After the verdict, seventy-four percent of whites told *Newsweek* that Simpson committed the murders, whereas sixty-six percent of blacks said that they agreed with the jury.

The poll results reflect two contrasting narratives circulating in the public, a white narrative and a black narrative. These contrasting storylines define the social drama of the Simpson case. The white narrative presumed that when the ex-wife of a physically abusive husband has her throat slashed, the ex-husband is the likely suspect. Whites found it easier than African Americans to surrender the presumption of innocence, especially when physical evidence tending to confirm the presumption of guilt began to find its way into the media. In addition, victims' rights advocates and domestic violence activists used the Simpson case to publicize their causes, adding two crucial emotional components—women's anger and men's guilt—to the narrative supporting a presumption of guilt.

For many whites, the essential drama now became overtly racial: Would African Americans put aside race thinking and approach the Simpson case rationally, as many whites believed they had done in a recent case involving the LAPD beating of an African American man, Rodney King? In March 1991, white police officers were videotaped viciously beating King, whom they had stopped after a high-speed car chase. When an all-white jury in a white suburb of Los Angeles found the officers not guilty of criminal assault, the overwhelmingly black and Hispanic population of south central Los Angeles answered with a complex and sustained urban riot. Many whites found the riot understandable, although quite frightening. Having realized that people of color had long been victimized by law enforcement, they shared the rioters' anger at the Simi Valley verdict, which seemed to ignore the physical evidence of the videotaped beating. When a civil court jury in 1994 found that the beating violated King's civil rights and ordered the city of Los Angeles to pay him $3.8 million in compensatory damages, it seemed to many whites that the legal system had shown its capacity for justice.

White thinking about the Simpson and King cases was based on an optimistic, if selective, reading of recent history that stressed declining white racial prejudice and impressive social and economic gains for blacks who were moving into the middle class. Of course, some "rogue" whites remained, but they were a despised minority, not a serious threat to racial progress. Believing the race problem now largely "solved," whites who once supported affirmative action programs withdrew that support, taking comfort that in California a conservative African American, Ward Connerly, was leading the antiaffirmative action movement. In this atmosphere, the Simpson case became a test of black willingness to live up to their side of an emerging implicit racial bargain. Whites seemed to say, "we won't be racists any longer, but you will have to act like you believe us and stop thinking and acting in racially conscious ways." After all, hadn't Rodney King himself responded to the riots that erupted in his name by pleading, "Can't we all get along?"

Many, perhaps most, African Americans saw the white view sketched above as arrogant or irrelevant. Black response to the case revealed two interrelated concerns: (1) that the presumption of innocence must be maintained, and (2) that, as Representative Eleanor Holmes Norton stated, "for many black Americans, every black man is on trial." These perspectives reflected that African Americans understood

the Simpson case in a very different historical perspective than did white Americans. Black Americans noticed racial progress in some areas, little if any progress in other areas. The criminal justice system was one such area where blacks felt as vulnerable as ever to racism.

African American distrust of the criminal justice system in general and the police in particular is rooted in a long history of differential treatment. Black males routinely swap stories about being stopped by police for "Driving While Black." The long American history of lynchings, of differential racial patterns in capital punishment, of white juries freeing obviously guilty whites accused of racial crimes, and of black exclusion from or token representation on police forces and juries is well known. Most major urban race riots in the 1960s, including the Watts riot of 1965, were set off by law enforcement mistreatment of black citizens. The LAPD had a reputation in minority communities for responding too quickly with violence. That racial thinking inspired police violence seemed confirmed in 1982 when Police Chief Daryl Gates blamed black physiology rather than police misconduct for a recent spate of choke-hold deaths among African Americans in police custody: "[their] veins or arteries do not open up as fast as they do on normal people." Gates's standard of "normality" was clear.

In the late 1980s and throughout the 1990s, police in Los Angeles and other urban areas often resorted to massive paramilitary tactics in organized assaults on youth gangs. These assaults found support outside minority communities from a public in a "law and order" mood. Rates of African American incarceration shot up so that in 1994 almost seven percent of adult black males were in prison, as compared with one percent of adult white males. Studies of sentencing patterns revealed that when age, type of crime, and prison record were controlled, blacks and other racial minorities received considerably longer prison sentences than did whites. One-half the prisoners in American prisons were African American, while blacks were only twelve percent of the national population. More than one-third of

African Americans in their twenties were under some kind of court supervision (prison, parole, or probation), a significantly greater percentage than were enrolled in college. In sum, when African Americans looked at the criminal justice system in the 1990s, they saw not progress but a continuation of differential treatment. Black citizens and black defendants did not receive the same presumption of innocence as did white citizens and defendants.

But O.J. Simpson was not a typical black defendant, as everyone knew. He could afford to hire high-priced lawyers. He had worked at crafting an image of himself as "not black, just O.J." He had distanced himself from the black community. Nevertheless, he was a symbol of black achievement. If he could be presumed guilty and treated like any other black defendant—not only in the courtroom, but also in assumptions that the police, the media, and the general public brought to the case—then, many blacks feared, historical patterns of racial discrimination and hatred would be reinforced.

And it seemed that the presumption of innocence was being taken away from Simpson. Within a week of the murders, *Time* ran a cover picture of Simpson, with his skin darkened. On June 13, four days before the famous Bronco "chase" and his arrest, Simpson was handcuffed at his home by officers who were taking him downtown for questioning. Blacks read volumes into the handcuffing, as coverage in the black press shows. According to many blacks, the police and the national media were relying on racist assumptions to portray Simpson. He was assumed to be a man who could not control his violent impulses. This image of the black male had been at the root of historic injustices such as lynching, and continued to influence unequal treatment in the criminal justice system. It seemed that if Simpson were to be convicted under these circumstances, the negative and violent image of black males would be reinforced in the white psyche. In this context, it was easy for the insistence that Simpson be accorded the *presumption* of innocence to become the desire that Simpson be *found* innocent.

When defense lawyers attacked the prosecution's physical evidence by developing a counternarrative predicated on a police conspiracy, many African Americans were ready to accept that the defense story was as plausible as the prosecution's story; that is, they had grounds for reasonable doubt about the prosecution's story. Critics argued that, to discount the overwhelming physical evidence pointing to Simpson, one had to believe in a massive conspiracy involving many police officers. Such a conspiracy seemed inconceivable to most whites, even those appalled by Fuhrman's racism and aware of the so-called code of silence within the LAPD. By contrast, many blacks found such a conspiracy plausible, and they pointed out that the reasonable doubt standard did not require the defense to conclusively prove all details of the conspiracy.

Hence, African Americans cheered the verdict because they read it as a victory for the presumption of innocence. Stunned by the racial divide the verdict revealed, many whites devised their own conspiracy theory, imagining a black plot to free Simpson and score a victory over whites. The widespread reference to Cochran "playing the race card" invoked a game metaphor that structured the way the public and the media discussed the trial. African Americans, for their part, were outraged at this "race card" discussion, viewing it as tantamount to saying that Fuhrman's own unabashed racism was irrelevant. Talk about the race card was also seen as denigrating Cochran's intellectual abilities. Cochran, whom many whites saw as a cynical race-mongering criminal lawyer, was a source of pride in black communities. His long career in the Los Angeles courts prosecuting rogue white cops and defending black victims of police misconduct established him as someone with the courage and skills to tell truth to power and to achieve results.

The civil trial was something of an anticlimax. A wrongful death suit rarely follows acquittal in a criminal trial, but in this case public outrage over the criminal verdict helped insure that a civil trial would occur. A combination of circumstances made a judgment against Simpson much more likely in the civil case. Whereas the criminal jury had to find the defendant guilty beyond a reasonable doubt, the civil jury had only to find that the preponderance of evidence pointed to the defendant's "liability" for the deaths of the plaintiffs. Also, the venue was changed, from downtown Los Angeles to Santa Monica. The criminal trial had not been held in Santa Monica because the courthouse there was undergoing repairs and lacked the elaborate security and press facilities available downtown. In addition, after the Rodney King case, the district attorney's office considered holding the trial anywhere but downtown as politically unviable. These factors did not apply to the civil trial.

Another difference between the two trials was that O.J. Simpson—with his acquittal at the criminal trial removing his Fifth Amendment privilege against self-incrimination—could be compelled to testify in a civil trial. The plaintiffs' lawyer, Daniel Petrocelli, was thus able to get into the record Simpson's personal version of his relationship with Nicole and then attack it with evidence from phone records, witness recollections, and Simpson's own prior statements. Petrocelli's theory of the case was very similar to that advanced by the prosecution in the criminal trial; that is, he portrayed Simpson as narcissistic, as so obsessed with getting his own way that he was driven to kill what he could not have. With the advantage of hindsight, Petrocelli avoided mistakes that the criminal prosecutors had made in presenting the physical evidence. In addition to the predominantly white jury and Simpson's testimony, Petrocelli benefited from a new piece of evidence: photographs in which Simpson wore the rare Bruno Magli shoes that he had denied owning. Finally, Petrocelli had the advantage of a different judge, Hiroshi Fujisaki, who ruled that Fuhrman's racism was irrelevant to the civil case unless Simpson's lawyers could show that the detective's racial views had a discernible impact on the investigation. Simpson's new legal team, headed by Robert Baker, could not show this, so it had to devise a new narrative to explain Simpson's innocence. Without Fuhrman's evidence to support the supposition of a police conspiracy and without a jury sympathetic to that view, Baker raised only a perfunctory defense against the DNA and other physical evidence. Instead, he attacked the plaintiff's theory of Simpson's motivation, arguing that he was too grand a celebrity and too irresistible to women to have suffered over Nicole's departure. Indeed, she, not he, had been the pursuer throughout their marriage and separations. Her reports of domestic violence reflected her state of mind and her provocation, not the other way around. Baker, like the criminal trial defense team, implied that the real killer came out of the victim's allegedly sordid world of drugs and sex. But the jury was not convinced. It took a week to deliberate, which some trial observers took to be a commentary on the rush to judgment of the Simpson criminal trial jury. For some, the civil verdict "evened the score." For others, the racial divide was dramatized once again.

Selected Bibliography

Abramson, J., ed. *Postmortem: The O.J. Simpson Case.* New York: Basic Books, 1996.

Gibbs, J.T. *Race and Justice: Rodney King and O.J. Simpson in a House Divided.* San Francisco: Jossey-Bass, 1996.

Hunt, D.M. *O.J. Simpson Facts & Fictions: News Rituals in the Construction of Reality.* New York: Cambridge University Press, 1999.

Toobin, J. *The Run of His Life: The People v. O.J. Simpson.* New York: Simon and Schuster, 1997.

PART II

GOVERNMENTAL ORGANIZATION, POWER, AND PROCEDURE

- Separation of Powers
- Federalism
- Judicial Procedure
- Political Questions
- Governmental Scandals

The selections in Part II examine thirty cases that concern the powers of government, most often those of the federal government, during the more than two hundred years of the United States' existence. The U.S. Constitution of 1787 provided a grand outline for the new American government, but it would be necessary for the courts, usually the U.S. Supreme Court, to act to add flesh to the constitutional skeleton. Since the Constitution is a living document, its meaning has been evolving since the 1780s. Many of the cases discussed in Part II were decided during the great era of constitutional definition under the chief justiceship of John Marshall (1801–1835). But some selections treat cases decided as recently as the late 1990s, thus illustrating the point that the Constitution is still capable of being stretched and tightened by the judiciary.

Separation of Powers

This section presents selections on the separation of powers among the three branches of the federal government. Even before the Constitutional Convention, there was "A Hint of Judicial Review" in a 1784 decision of the New York Mayor's Court. The major case, however, establishing the judicial right to pass on the constitutionality of the acts of Congress, was *Marbury v. Madison*; it is discussed in "The Supreme Court Declares Its Independence: Judicial Review of Federal Statutes." The next selection examines a twentieth century case, "The High-Water Mark of Presidential Power," in which the Supreme Court purported to extend a virtually unlimited grant of power to the president in the sphere of foreign affairs. The following selection, "How One Immigrant Shook the U.S. Government to Its Very Core," illustrates how long-standing understandings of the separation of federal power—in this case the "legislative veto"—can be upset and redrawn by modern judicial construction. The final selection, "Contemporary Lessons in the Separation of Powers: Congressional Standing and the Line-Item Veto," examines two recent cases in which the U.S. Supreme Court considered whether Congress could extend a power to the president not specified by the framers of the Constitution.

Federalism

The U.S. Constitution, pursuant to the principle of federalism, permits a sharing of power between the states and the national government. If state and federal laws conflict, however, how should the conflict be resolved? Article VI of the U.S. Constitution—the supremacy clause—stipulates that, when federal law and state law come into conflict, federal law is supreme. Two selections, "Judicial Review of State Court Decisions" and "Judicial Review of State Court Decisions: Yet Another Round," illustrate how the Supreme Court of John Marshall first interpreted the supremacy clause. Another selection, "Implied Federal Powers: Pandora's Box?" examines the landmark case of *McCulloch v. Maryland* (1819) in which the Marshall court interpreted the supremacy clause and the necessary and proper clause of Article I. The fourth selection, "Federalism Writ Large: The Eleventh Amendment and State Sovereign Immunity," discusses how a Supreme

Court decision handled a sticky issue of federalism involving a two-hundred-year-old amendment to the U.S. Constitution.

Judicial Procedure

Over the years, various state and federal court decisions have dealt with technical matters of legal procedure that ultimately had great consequences. Several of the more interesting of these cases are addressed in this section. "A Rebuke to the Court" concerns an early Supreme Court case that was so unpopular that it sparked a constitutional amendment. The second selection, "California Rejects the Mandatory Conciliation Formerly Required under Mexican Law," provides an example of what can happen in an American state court when the laws of another country conflicts with the laws of the United States. The next three selections—"Congress Should First Define the Offenses and Apportion the Punishment: Federal Common-Law Crimes," "Federal Common Law of Crimes," and "Federal Common Law?"—deal with the arcane but historically important issue of whether there is a general common law applicable to the federal courts that parallels or complements the common law of the states. "A Leg to Stand On: Taxpayer Lawsuits Against the U.S. Government" presents a modern case that determined when an individual has "standing to sue" in a federal court.

The final two selections—"A Nicaraguan Feast: Having the Jurisdictional Cake and Eating It Too" and "From Court Side to Courtroom"—do not deal with the powers of any units of U.S. government. Instead, they concern procedures of nongovernmental bodies that affect or may potentially affect Americans. The former selection examines a decision of the World Court of Justice of the United Nations involving American interests, and the later concerns the legality of rules of procedure adopted by a private sports organization.

Political Questions

Traditionally, U.S. courts have gone to great lengths to avoid deciding cases involving disputes over the legitimacy of elected government officials. In explaining their reasoning, judges and justices traditionally maintained that they did not want to enter the "political thicket." "The *Right* of Revolution v. the Right of *Revolution*" reveals how the mid-nineteenth-century U.S. Supreme Court refused to determine which elected government of the state of Rhode Island did in fact have power. The following three selections—"When Was a War a War, and What If It Was?," "More than a Trojan Horse: The Test Oath Cases," and "Indestructible Union, Indestructible States"—review notable U.S. Supreme Court decisions growing out of the American Civil War. As each selection demonstrates to one degree or another, the justices of the High Court were loathe to admit that the rule of law had broken down in the 1860s. As a result, all of these decisions reviewed suffer from extremely tortured judicial reasoning.

Political questions continued to vex the courts in the twentieth century. "The White Primary" and "From the 'Political Thicket' to 'One Man, One Vote'" discuss in detail how the U.S. Supreme Court moved, albeit glacially, to assert its power over state legislatures for the purpose of promoting equal treatment of the races in state elections. Finally, the controversial judicial resolution of the many political questions in the presidential election of 2000 are examined in "The 2000 Florida Election Cases: Politics over Principles."

Governmental Scandals

One way to determine the legitimacy of a government is to see how effectively it deals with alleged corruption or notorious scandals. U.S. constitutional government, judged by this standard, has been remarkably resilient. One of the first great impeachment trials that occurred under the U.S. Constitution involved the controversial and haughty Justice Samuel Chase, discussed in "Can Intemperate Behavior Be a 'High Crime or Misdemeanor'?" The impeachment trial of President Andrew Johnson is examined in "The Right To Remove a President from Office Is Tested." The famous Watergate tapes case of the early 1970s, treated in "The Court Topples a Presidency," provides an illustration of how well the American system endured and dealt with a dishonesty that reached to the very pinnacle of government. By contrast, "Credibility and Crisis in California's High Court" offers a state analogue to the Watergate crisis in which the taint of scandal could not be eradicated by the actions of the judiciary. Finally, the profoundly embarrassing sexual and ethical lapses that led to the impeachment (but not conviction) of President Bill Clinton are analyzed in "Justice Delayed Is Justice Denied" and "The Travails of William Jefferson Clinton."

Separation of Powers

A Hint of Judicial Review

---◄○►---

Robert S. Lambert

Emeritus Professor of History
Clemson University

Rutgers v. Waddington, (1784) [New York state court]

◄○► THE CASE IN BRIEF ◄○►

Date
 1784

Location
 New York

Court
 New York state court

Principal Participants
 Elizabeth Rutgers
 John Lawrence
 Joshua Waddington
 Alexander Hamilton

Significance of the Case
 A case concerning property seized during
 the Revolutionary War allowed for a
 judicial interpretation of legislative intent
 of statute provisions.

As a British colony, New York had functioned under the restraints of its charter and the principles of the English common law as interpreted by British authorities in the colony and in England. After independence was declared, the New York Constitution of 1777 stated that colonial acts or British statutes and common-law principles contrary to it were of no force. For practical purposes, this gave state courts jurisdiction over constitutional questions. The Council of Revision, a panel composed of the governor, the state chancellor, and judges of the supreme court, was given a qualified veto over legislative enactments that did not conform to the "letter and spirit" of the constitution.

One authority has called *Rutgers v. Waddington* "a marker on the long road that led to the ultimate formulation of judicial review." The case had its origins in the disputes over property rights that arose because New York City was occupied by the British army during most of the American Revolution. As the British occupation drew to a close, the state legislature enacted a series of laws designed to punish those who had supported the British and to give citizens of the state recourse against persons who had injured them or their property. The Rutgers case was brought under the Trespass Act of March 1783, allowing persons forced from their property as a result of the occupation to bring suit against those who had occupied, received, or purchased that property during the war. Defendants might not plead "any military order or command whatever of the Enemy," as justification for using the property; and such suits, once brought in any inferior court of the state, might not be moved to another court. The act was passed just as the preliminary articles of the peace treaty between Great Britain and the United States arrived from Paris.

Elizabeth Rutgers would seem to be an ideal person to seek redress under the Trespass Act. When the British captured New York in 1776, she abandoned her property on Maiden Lane, in which she held a life estate, and fled the city. In 1778, under permission granted by the commissary general of the British army, two British merchants residing in the city occupied the Rutgers property and put in working order a malthouse and brewhouse for the use of the army. The authorization to use the Rutgers property commenced in 1780 and was continued by the British commander in chief until peace was declared in 1783. During the latter period, the merchants paid an annual rent of £150 that went to a relief fund for the city's poor.

When it was known that the British army would evacuate the city, the merchants offered to return the property with improvements to the Rutgers family, but negotiations were broken off when the family demanded the improvements plus £1,200 in back rent. After fire destroyed the brewery and the British army left the city, the merchants turned over the keys to the property and once again offered to settle; they were answered in February 1784 by a suit under the Trespass Act brought against Joshua Waddington, their agent, for £8,000 in back rent.

Rutgers v. Waddington drew much public notice because it was tried at a time of intense anti-British feeling in New York, a result of the long occupation of the city and the refusal of the British, in defiance of the treaty of peace, to withdraw from military installations in upstate New York. Its importance is further revealed by the fact that it attracted such established members of the New York bar as Attorney General Egbert Benson for the plaintiff, and Morgan Lewis and Brockholst Livingston for the defense. But two relatively new men, Alexander Hamilton for Waddington, and John Lawrence for Rutgers, undertook most of the burden of preparing and arguing the case.

Lawrence's strategy for the plaintiff was clear: the Trespass Act permitted anyone who had abandoned property, because of the enemy invasion, to "bring an action of Trespass against any Person" who had "occupied" it. But because Lawrence failed to include in his argument the act's clause that forbade the occupier from pleading, "in Justification, any military order . . . , of the Enemy," Hamilton was able to shift the grounds of the argument from those of a simple trespass to the constitutionality of the statute itself.

Hamilton's argument admitted the occupation of Rutgers's property, but on two grounds pleaded justification. First, the state constitution made the common law of England, including the law of nations and thus the laws of war, the law of New York. Therefore, Waddington's occupation of Rutgers's property was lawful between 1778 and 1780 under a license from the commissary general of the British army ("as by the laws usages and Customs of nations in time of War he might lawfully do"); between 1780 and 1783, the occupation was lawful due to the authority of the commander in chief, for the same reason. Second, under the definitive treaty of peace between Britain and the United States, the nations agreed that claims by their citizens for "compensation, recompence, retribution or indemnity," as a result of the war were "mutually and reciprocally . . . renounced and released to each other." Lawrence then demurred, citing the Trespass Act's prohibition of of "military orders" as a justification.

The trial was held June 29, 1784, before Mayor James Duane, the recorder, and the five aldermen who composed the Mayor's Court of the City of New York, a part of the judicial system carried over from colonial times. Counsel for the plaintiff opened by arguing that the court had no power to interpret anything beyond state law. The law of nations, he maintained, did not apply because the use of land for private purposes, even when authorized by the enemy, did not relate to the war, and the law of nations was not part of the common law but only civil law that could not bind a sovereign state. As to the treaty, property rights were an internal matter not covered by the treaty power under the Articles of Confederation, and New York's ratification of the articles, a simple legislative act, could be rescinded.

Hamilton answered that the Trespass Act violated the law of nations and of the state, a power that could reside only in Congress. As to the treaty of peace, the law of nations implied that such agreements carried a general amnesty for injuries incurred in the war, an implication that Congress had accepted and which states were bound to obey. Finally, if the Trespass Act conflicted with either the law of nations or the treaty, state courts were obliged "to construe them so as to make them stand together" (the only reference to judicial review among Hamilton's notes on the case), and because the judges could not presume that the legislature intended that British subjects be denied their rights under the law of nations, the Trespass Act must be set aside.

The court's decision was delivered August 27, 1784. The long opinion, apparently the work of Mayor Duane, was, as one scholar has claimed, "essentially a political one"; it picked its way through the issues presented in a way that gave some comfort to both sides but was satisfactory to neither. First, the court found the Trespass Act to be remedial in nature for the benefit of Mrs. Rutgers and that it did apply to Waddington. Further, for the period when the merchants occupied the property "under the bare unauthoritative permission of the Commissary General" and paid no rent, their use of it had "no relation to the war" and they were liable. Second, as a result of independence, "the law of nations has become an indispensable obligation," of the United States to protect "a member of a foreign nation," the merchants; therefore, "restitution" of rents collected "under

the authority of the British Commander, . . . cannot, *according to the law of nations*, be required." Third, the court sustained Hamilton's contention that states could not "abridge" the treaty of peace, but held that the omission of an "*express* amnesty" in that treaty made it an insufficient defense for the merchants [emphasis added]. Duane did accept Hamilton's point that it could not be presumed that the legislature, in passing the Trespass Act, intended to deprive the defendants of their rights under the law of nations. Finally, although the court felt itself bound to carry out the express terms of statutes, the separation-of-powers principle in the state's constitution required that, where the terms of statutes were general, "interpretation is the province of the court, and, . . . we are bound to perform it."

On September 2, a jury awarded the plaintiff £791.13.4 in rent and 6 pence in costs. Counsel for both sides filed writs of error with the state supreme court, but before that court could act, "a voluntary compromise took place" between the parties by which the defendant paid an unrevealed "sum of money," and the suit was dropped.

Local reaction to the decision was swift and hostile, and the legislature passed resolutions denouncing the court for trying to undermine legislative authority. The atmosphere was so charged that most pending suits under the Trespass Act and other anti-Tory laws were settled before coming to trial. Although Hamilton's brilliant defense was an important milestone in his legal and political career, and the legislature later repealed the Trespass Act's prohibition against pleading military orders as justification, he later admitted that he "was never able to get [his] point established" before the supreme court.

The long-range significance of the Rutgers decision is less clear because of what one scholar has called the "studied ambiguity" of Duane's opinion. The court did not declare the Trespass Act to be void but simply "irrelevant" (for the period when the defendants were authorized by the British commander to use the Rutgers property). Instead, it found that the legislature could not have intended to violate the law of nations recognized in its own constitution. As for the treaty of peace, although Duane held that state law could not violate it, in this case the treaty did not confer on the defendants any rights not already due them under the law of nations.

The power of courts to set aside legislative acts was not directly addressed, but the right of the judiciary to interpret legislative intent in "general" provisions of statutes was asserted, a position denounced by the state legislature. Although *Rutgers v. Waddington* was hardly a ringing declaration of judicial review, one authority finds that the issue was "well aired" in state courts at the time and that it "may have colored" the views of the framers of the U.S. Constitution.

Selected Bibliography

Barck, Oscar Theodore. *New York City during the War for Independence*. Port Washington, NY: Ira J. Friedman, 1966.

Dawson, Henry B. *The Case of Rutgers v. . . . Waddington*. Morrisania, NY: Privately printed, 1866.

Goebel, Julius, Jr., ed. *The Law Practice of Alexander Hamilton: Documents and Commentary*. 5 vols. New York: Columbia University Press, 1964–1981.

Morris, Richard B., ed. *Select Cases of the Mayor's Court of New York City, 1674–1784*, Vol. 2 of *American Legal Records*. Washington, D.C., American Historical Association, 1955.

Syrett, Harold C., et al., eds. *The Papers of Alexander Hamilton*. 26 vols. New York: Columbia University Press, 1961–1979.

The Supreme Court Declares Its Independence: Judicial Review of Federal Statutes

Herbert A. Johnson

School of Law
University of South Carolina

William Marbury v. James Madison, Secretary of State of the United States, 1 Cranch 137 (1803)
[U.S. Supreme Court]

◄◦► THE CASE IN BRIEF ◄◦►

Date
1803

Location
District of Columbia

Court
U.S. Supreme Court

Principal Participants
William Marbury
James Madison, Secretary of State
Chief Justice John Marshall

Significance of the Case
Four proposed district justices and a Supreme Court justice battled in this landmark case—with a unanimous court decision—that established the power of the state and federal judiciary to rule on the constitutionality of legislation.

None of the vast and rapidly growing number of U.S. Supreme Court opinions have occupied such a central place in constitutional law as John Marshall's majority opinion in *Marbury v. Madison*. Correctly identifying *Marbury* as the case that firmly established judicial review in federal law, scholars differ sharply concerning the political motivations underlying the case. They also question the legitimacy of an elite, nonelected body of judges overruling the legislative will of Congress as expressed in federal statutes. On the other hand, the supremacy of constitutional provisions over legislative enactments has never been effectively challenged, nor have critics suggested a practical substitute for the U.S. Supreme Court's judicial review.

Since the American Revolution, and to a degree during the colonial period, government has been viewed as not only derived from the consent of the people, but also as being inherently limited by certain fundamental principles. Those limitations were read into colonial charters and royal or proprietorial concessions; they were incorporated into state constitutions;

and with the ratification of the U.S. Constitution in 1788 and its Bill of Rights in 1791, they became a vital part of federal law. Indeed, the Constitution establishes a government limited to specifically identified powers. All other political authority is by express constitutional mandate reserved to the states or to the people.

In No. 78 of *The Federalist*, Alexander Hamilton pointed to judicial action as the instrument whereby the legislative and executive branches of government would be restricted to the powers granted to them by the federal constitution. However, the concept of judicial review was not novel. Sixteenth- and seventeenth-century English precedents carried an inference of judicial review, most conspicuously set forth by Sir Edward Coke in 1610 in *Dr. Bonham's Case*. Coke's doctrine—that reason and custom limited the effectiveness of legislative enactments—was brought into American colonial law through James Otis's famous 1761 speech vainly opposing the issuance of writs of assistance in Massachusetts Bay. By 1788, American constitutional thought linked judicial review to limited government and was the basis upon which several state legislative programs had been declared unconstitutional by state judges. For the most part, these state statutes involved efforts to seize property without following proper legal procedures or to do so without compensation. In 1796, in *Hylton v. United States,* a federal tax upon carriages was challenged before the Supreme Court, and the Court gave tacit approval to judicial review by considering the case even though it upheld the constitutionality of the statute. However, it was not until *Marbury* that a congressional statute was declared void on constitutional grounds. Such an exercise of judicial review would not recur until the 1857 Dred Scott case in which the Court nullified the federal statute that embodied the Missouri Compromise of 1820.

In American constitutional law, there are two forms of judicial review. The first involves the review of state statutes and court decisions based upon the supremacy of the U.S. Constitution and statutes and treaties made pursuant to it. This type of judicial review is essential to the federal union, and it was in fact inherited from similar control exercised by the British privy council prior to the Revolution. The second form, with which *Marbury* was concerned, dealt with the power of the state and federal judiciary at all levels, to compare legislation with constitutional foundations of governmental power, and to declare legislative enactments null and void when they conflicted with the law of the land as embodied in the state or federal constitutions. The first form of judicial review is essential to the maintenance of the federal union; the second functions as a constitutional and political governing wheel to control excessive use of legislative and executive power.

The hectic last weeks of the Adams administration form the backdrop against which the *Marbury* case took shape. On February 27, 1801, a statute authorizing the appointment of additional justices of the peace for the District of Columbia was passed by Congress and signed by President John Adams. Between then and March 4, when Adams was to surrender his office to the incoming Republican president, Thomas Jefferson, the federalist appointment apparatus was kept running at high speed, and some forty-two "midnight" justices of the peace were commissioned and placed in office. Assisting President Adams at every step of the process was John Marshall, who continued as secretary of state even after he took office on January 31 as chief justice of the United States. Ironically, it was most likely due to Marshall's administrative oversight that the commission of William Marbury (along with those of Robert Townshend Hooe, Dennis Ramsey, and William Harper) was not delivered. Marshall was not the most orderly of men, and from testimony later presented before the Supreme Court, it appears that these commissions may have been lost when others were hurriedly delivered, enabling their recipients to quiet a preinauguration riot in Alexandria.

However the oversight may have occurred, the four commissions were not delivered before the incoming administration took possession of the secretary of state's office. When they were demanded of Jefferson's acting secretary, Levi Lincoln, delivery was refused; Marbury and the three others brought their demand for a writ of mandamus directly to the Supreme

Court. A *mandamus* is a court order directing that a public official either perform a given act, or refrain from doing so. Few litigants in American history risked as little as did Marbury and his colleagues. All were prosperous merchants. Ramsey and Harper were former public officials in the city of Alexandria, and Hooe and Marbury were heavy speculators in Washington, D.C., realty. Ramsey had been a pallbearer at George Washington's funeral in 1799, and Harper commanded the artillery company in the procession. By way of contrast to the claimants' status and wealth, the office of justice of the peace had little monetary or honorific value. District of Columbia justices were to be supported solely by the fees assessed against litigants. Given the wealth of the disappointed judges and their close federalist connections, it is not surprising that the newly elected administration suspected political motives in their seeking judicial relief.

Receiving Marbury's petition on December 16, 1801, the Supreme Court issued an order (1) directing James Madison, as secretary of state, to show cause why a mandamus should not issue and (2) requiring him to surrender the commissions to their recipients. By this point in the litigation, the appointment papers had doubtless disappeared from the State Department office, and Madison, who did not take up the duties of his office until May 1801, may never have seen them. However, neither he nor any member of the Jefferson administration appeared before the Supreme Court, since that might be viewed as acquiescence in the Supreme Court's authority to issue such an order to an executive officer of the government. On the other hand, the new administration did use its majority in Congress to cancel the summer term of the Supreme Court scheduled for 1802, postponing any action on the petition until the February term in 1803.

On February 9 and 10, 1803, the application was argued before the Supreme Court by Charles Lee of Virginia, appearing for the four petitioners. Two State Department clerks were required to testify, and Levi Lincoln, after preliminary objections to the jurisdiction of the Supreme Court, provided the limited information available concerning the commissions. In addition, an affidavit by James Markham Marshall, the chief justice's brother who was a circuit judge for the District of Columbia, was read concerning his effort to deliver commissions during the Alexandria riots.

On behalf of the Supreme Court, Chief Justice Marshall considered three issues in his opinion: (1) Did Marbury and his associates have a right to their commissions? (2) If such a right existed and it had been violated, did the laws of the United States afford a remedy? (3) If they did offer a remedy, was it in the form of a mandamus issued by the Supreme Court? Marshall began with a painstaking consideration of the appointment process, concluding that there had been a valid nomination by the president and confirmation by the Senate, and that a commission had been issued bearing the signature of the president and the great seal of the United States. All that remained was for the secretary of state to perform the ministerial act of delivering the commission to its recipient. Concerning the second issue, Marshall recognized that while the "very essence of civil liberty" included the right to protection of the laws, there were certain political acts by executive-branch officers that could not be examined by the courts. However, that was not the case where private rights had vested, when the discretion of the executive officer had been exercised, and only a ministerial duty remained in that officer. Observing that the United States was "a government of laws and not of men," Marshall suggested that such a reputation would be undeserved if no remedy was provided for a violation of a vested property right. When an executive officer acts illegally under color of his office, mere possession of the office does not exempt him from legal action or submission to a judgment at law. It was not the office that determined the availability of the mandamus writ, but rather the nature of the thing to be done that determined its propriety. Here the thing requested was merely a ministerial act, not involving the exercise of discretion. Justice and equity demanded that an executive officer could not "at his discretion sport away the vested rights of others."

Having thus established Marbury's entitlement to his commission, his vested right in the office, and the circumstance that ministerial rather than discretionary executive action was requested, the chief justice asked the critical question: did federal law provided Marbury with a remedy through Supreme Court issuance of a mandamus writ? Article III of the U.S. Constitution conferred both original and appellate jurisdiction upon the Supreme Court. The provision concerning original jurisdiction was quite specific in its grant of powers, but omitted from the provision was any mention of a mandamus power. Such authority, if it existed at all, was based upon section 13 of the Judiciary Act of 1789. Marshall noted that the Constitution was a superior law, paramount to the provisions of an ordinary congressional statute. The federal government existed upon the general premise that a statute violative of the provisions of the Constitution was void and should not be obligatory upon judges sworn to uphold the U.S. Constitution. Judicial duty demanded that the statute be ignored and the constitutional provision be upheld. He concluded that "the particular phraseology of the constitution of the United States confirms and strengthens the principle, supposed to be essential to all written constitutions, that a law repugnant to the constitution is void; and that *courts*, as well as other departments, are bound by that instrument." In other words, by adding to the original jurisdiction of the Supreme Court, Marshall—speaking for the unanimous Court—ruled that section 13 of the Judiciary Act of 1789 violated the U.S. Constitution and was thus "unconstitutional."

Public reaction to the Court's opinion in *Marbury* depended upon the political affiliation of the commentator. Republican newspapers attacked Marshall's reasoning, and his approach to the case was deemed to be clear evidence of his intention to use judicial power to undermine the proposed reforms of the Jefferson administration. The president himself was particularly agitated at Marshall's chiding him for trampling upon vested property rights and for overstepping the bounds of his constitutional authority. For President Jefferson and many others, the full significance of judicial review seems to have been obscured by the heat of partisan politics. It was not until subsequent

decisions of the Supreme Court built upon the precedent of *Marbury* that the case's true significance was realized.

The legal profession was not slow to challenge *Marbury* in terms of its logic or its approach to the task of judging a constitutional issue. A close historical analysis of the decision suggests that there were a number of grounds upon which the chief justice might have denied relief to Marbury without dealing with the constitutional issue. Denial of the petition on any basis would have avoided an embarrassing confrontation between the Supreme Court and the other two branches of the federal government. But denying relief through the exercise of judicial review—through an opinion that disallowed an excessive grant of power to the Supreme Court—not only read judicial review into federal case law, but it did so in a manner that parried any effective Jeffersonian attack.

Marbury provides two valuable insights into the legal thinking of Chief Justice Marshall. First, more than any other opinion written by him, it shows the logical evolution of one issue from another to reach what appears to be an inevitable conclusion. Significantly, before launching into his opinion, the chief justice warned his listeners that he would not treat the issues in the order followed by counsel. Through his selection of the sequence in which he discussed the issues, Marshall was able to eliminate all other factors before he focused upon judicial review. Unquestionably, *Marbury* is one of the best organized opinions to issue from his pen, and scholars have doubted that it could have been so well constructed during the two weeks between the closing arguments in the case and Marshall's announcement of his opinion. Whatever the circumstances of its preparation, the *Marbury* opinion deserves careful study as the best guide to the chief justice's decision-making process.

The second insight provided by *Marbury* is the way in which Marshall used jurisdictional and procedural matters to enhance the authority of the Supreme Court. In a very real sense, this petition for a mandamus instituted a technique that would be used extensively in the remaining years of Marshall's chief justiceship. Assertions or denials of jurisdiction, carefully selected to minimize overt conflict either with the other two branches of the federal government, or with the authorities of the various states, were critical to the effective growth of Supreme Court authority and eased political acceptance of the Court as the primary interpreter of the Constitution.

It consolidated much of the received tradition concerning limitation of government through written constitutions, and it initiated the period of Supreme Court growth into the foremost tribunal for constitutional litigation in the United States. It also launched the creative tension between judicial review and legislative supremacy that has remained one of the dominant themes of American constitutional history.

Recent scholarship on *Marbury* has placed the decision within a much wider range of constitutional history and a more extended consideration of the development of political theory. It has been suggested that Chief Justice Marshall's signal contribution was to redirect judicial review away from a fundamental, or natural law, basis and toward a "legalized" view of the Constitution. In other words, Marshall construed the Constitution as if it were a superior form of statute rather than as an abstract statement of political ideals. Arguably, it was not until the Supreme Court's 1958 decision of *Cooper v. Aaron* that natural-law principles again played a role in judicial review. While the theme of a broadening and increasingly more abstract type of judicial review is common to many scholars, some would place the resurgence of natural-law influences in about 1901, as the product of the centennial celebrations of Marshall's appointment to the chief justiceship.

These studies suggest that despite *Marbury's* centrality to the history of judicial review, the case deserves even broader historical treatment against the background of English and American constitutional thought, both before and after 1803. Nevertheless, *Marbury* remains preeminent as the federal Supreme Court decision establishing judicial review.

Selected Bibliography

Beveridge, Albert J. *The Life of John Marshall.* 4 vols. Boston: Houghton, Mifflin, 1916–1919.

Bickel, A. M. *The Least Dangerous Branch: The Supreme Court at the Bar of Politics.* Indianapolis: Bobbs-Merrill, 1962.

Clinton, Robert L. *Marbury v. Madison and Judicial Review.* Lawrence: University Press of Kansas, 1989.

Faulkner, Robert K. *The Jurisprudence of John Marshall.* Princeton: Princeton University Press, 1968.

Haskins, George L., and Herbert A. Johnson. *Foundations of Power, John Marshall, 1801–15*, Vol. 2 of *History of the Supreme Court of the United States.* New York: Macmillan, 1981.

Hobson, C. F. *The Great Chief Justice: John Marshall and the Rule of Law.* Lawrence: University Press of Kansas, 1998.

Johnson, Herbert A. *The Chief Justiceship of John Marshall, 1801–1835.* Columbia: University of South Carolina Press, 1997.

Nelson, William E. *Marbury v. Madison: The Origins of Judicial Review.* Lawrence: University Press of Kansas, 2000.

Snowiss, S. *Judicial Review and the Law of the Constitution.* New Haven: Yale University Press, 1990.

Wolfe, C. *The Rise of Modern Judicial Review: From Constitutional Interpretation to Judge-Made Law.* New York: Basic, 1986.

The High-Water Mark of Presidential Power

—◦—

William Lasser

Department of Political Science
Clemson University

United States v. Curtiss-Wright Export Corp. et al., 299 U.S. 304 (1936)
[U.S. Supreme Court]

◦ THE CASE IN BRIEF ◦

Date
1936

Location
District of Columbia

Court
U.S. Supreme Court

Principal Participants
President Franklin D. Roosevelt
Curtiss-Wright Export Corporation
Justice George Sutherland

Significance of the Case
Arms sales to warring countries spurred the Supreme Court's ruling that extended power to the president to regulate foreign affairs.

The constitutional power of the American presidency has ebbed and flowed over the two centuries of the nation's history. Never has that power been given so expansive an interpretation, however, than in the Supreme Court's *Curtiss-Wright* decision of 1936.

The case grew out of international attempts to stop the Chaco War, fought between Bolivia and Paraguay over a strip of land in the plain known as the Gran Chaco. In 1934, several countries, including the United States, agreed to attempt to halt the flow of arms and ammunition into the two countries. President Franklin D. Roosevelt asked Congress for a joint resolution granting him the authority to ban the sale of "arms and munitions of war . . . in any place in the United States to the countries now engaged in that armed conflict" or to any person, company, or association acting on their behalf.

Congress agreed, delegating to Roosevelt the power to ban all such sales if he found that

164

such action "may contribute to the reestablishment of peace between those countries." On the very same day, Roosevelt exercised his power under the resolution and issued a proclamation outlawing arms sales to Bolivia and Paraguay.

The constitutionality of the joint resolution and of Roosevelt's proclamation came to the Supreme Court in 1936, after the Curtiss-Wright Corp. was charged with selling fifteen machine guns to Bolivia in violation of the president's order. Curtiss-Wright charged that the indictment was invalid for a number of reasons, most importantly because Congress lacked the constitutional authority to delegate to the executive branch the power to make law in such a case. By leaving the decision to ban arms sales to the president's "unfettered discretion . . . controlled by no standard," the company contended, the resolution violated the separation of powers.

Curtiss-Wright thus presented an important test of the "delegation doctrine," as it is known, in the field of foreign affairs. Over the years, the Supreme Court had upheld numerous delegations of legislative power to the executive, dating back to decisions as early as 1813. In 1935, however, just a year before the *Curtiss-Wright* decision, the Court had struck down the National Industrial Recovery Act on the grounds that it authorized an unconstitutional delegation of power to the executive branch. Would the Court continue to narrow Congress's power to delegate, or would it return to its earlier, broader conception?

The Court, in effect, did neither. Justice George Sutherland, writing the majority opinion, held that the delegation of legislative power to the executive in the realm of foreign affairs was constitutional because it was superfluous; the president, as the nation's chief executive, already possessed plenary power in this area. "In this vast external realm," wrote Sutherland, "the President alone has the power to speak or listen as the representative of the nation. . . . [A]s [Chief Justice John] Marshall said . . . in the House of Representatives, 'The President is the sole organ of the nation in its external relations, and its sole representative with foreign nations.'"

There was certainly ample precedent to support a broad view of the delegation doctrine, especially in the area of foreign affairs. As Sutherland put it, "practically every volume of the United States Statutes contains one or more acts or joint resolutions of Congress authorizing action by the President in respect of subjects affecting foreign relations, which either leave the exercise of the power to his unrestricted judgment, or provide a standard far more general than that which has always been considered with regard to domestic affairs." Moreover, a number of such delegations had been explicitly upheld by the Supreme Court. None of these precedents, however, could support Sutherland's sweeping statements pushing Congress into the background in the domain of foreign affairs. These statements are especially curious in light of Sutherland's dim view of executive power in the domestic sphere.

The powers of the federal government in the areas of domestic and foreign affairs, Sutherland began, "are different, both in respect of their origin and their nature." In the domestic sphere, "the primary purpose of the Constitution was to carve from the general mass of legislative powers *then possessed by the states* such portions as it was thought desirable to vest in the federal government." Such powers were largely given over to the legislative branch.

The power to regulate foreign affairs, however, was different. Sutherland contended that the "powers of external sovereignty" were *never* vested in the states, but were instead transmitted from the king of Great Britain directly to the Union—first as represented by the Continental Congress, then to the Union under the Articles of Confederation, and finally to the Union under the Constitution. Thus, "the investment of the federal government with the powers of external sovereignty did not depend upon the affirmative grants of the Constitution. The powers to declare and wage war, to conclude peace, to make treaties, to maintain diplomatic relations with other sovereignties, if they had never been mentioned in the Constitution, would have vested in the federal government as necessary concomitants of nationality."

If the foreign-affairs power was different in origin from that over domestic affairs, it was also different in nature. "In the vast external realm," Sutherland concluded, "with its important, complicated, delicate and manifold problems, the President alone has the power to speak or listen as a representative of the nation." To avoid any misunderstanding of his position, Sutherland later repeated himself: "We are here dealing . . . [with] the very delicate, plenary, and exclusive power of the President as the sole organ of the federal government in the field of international relations—a power which does not require as a basis for its exercise an act of Congress."

Sutherland's argument is subject to a number of logical, historical, and theoretical criticisms. For one thing, his claim that the foreign-affairs power of the British crown devolved directly on the United States without passing through the states would have shocked the members of the Continental Congress. For another, his argument that the president's power in foreign affairs is plenary flies in the face of the Constitution itself, which clearly grants to Congress the power to declare war, define and punish piracies on the high seas and offenses against the law of nations, and ratify treaties. Furthermore, his entire argument ignores the commonplace view—in the eighteenth century, as today—that the powers of the U.S. government were delegated to it by the American people. His argument that the foreign-affairs power could not be delegated to the United States because it was never possessed by the states is specious, because in conventional American political theory all the powers of government were reclaimed by the people (both in 1776 and in 1787–1788) and then redistributed as the people saw fit. Finally, whatever the origins of the foreign-affairs power, it is fallacious to argue that such powers automatically devolved onto the executive. Why, it may be asked, did they not descend to the legislative branch? In fact, whatever its origin, the power over foreign affairs was clearly divided by the Constitution among both the legislative and executive branches.

The logical deficiencies of Sutherland's opinion notwithstanding, the case remains a favorite of those who would expand presidential power in the realm of foreign affairs. It has been cited with approval by countless presidents and presidential subordinates: in the arguments over the constitutionality of the Destroyers-for-Bases Agreement before World War II, during the Vietnam War, and by Colonel Oliver North and his associates in the Iran-Contra affair. Perhaps because of its sweeping character, Sutherland's argument has stood for over fifty years as the theoretical high-water mark of presidential power, though it has never been accepted literally in practice, not even by the most expansive advocates of executive power. Although used to great effect in the tug-of-war between the legislative and executive branches, Curtiss-Wright has never been used by presidents in an effort to ignore Congress altogether.

Of course, lawyers and legal scholars have engaged in endless debates over the precise meaning of Curtiss-Wright, and it is possible to read the decision more or less narrowly. Some have argued that the decision speaks only to the question of who executes foreign policy, and says nothing about who is to make foreign policy in the first place. Others have pointed out that the bulk of Sutherland's argument is mere obiter dicta, superfluous commentary that does not carry with it the force of law. Still others have tried to read Curtiss-Wright as merely permitting a looser delegation of power to the executive in foreign affairs than in the domestic sphere, rather than making an absolute claim of executive supremacy. And commentators have pointed out that later decisions of the Supreme Court—in particular the steel-seizure case of Youngstown Sheet and Tube Co. v. Sawyer (1952)—have effectively superseded Curtiss-Wright, or at least cast doubt on its authoritativeness.

It remains unclear just why the conservative Justice Sutherland, who vehemently opposed Roosevelt and the New Deal, wrote such a sweeping decision in support of presidential power. Some have argued that Curtiss-Wright simply shows consistency; they note that the views expressed by Sutherland in 1936 were views he had long held and expressed, and they dated back to well before his appointment to the Supreme Court in 1922. In a 1909 article, for example, Sutherland, then a senator, contended that "national sovereignty inhered in the United States from the beginning. Neither the Colonies nor the States which succeeded them ever separately exercised authority over foreign affairs." This argument was repeated at length in Sutherland's 1919 book, *Constitutional Power and World Affairs.*

Sutherland's early writings may explain his views on the origins of the foreign-affairs power, but they cannot explain his sudden conversion to executive supremacy. Both his 1909 and 1919 writings stand for the principle that the federal government—Congress and the president together—have plenary power in the field of foreign relations, and that constitutional grants of power must be interpreted as broadly as possible. In effect, Sutherland's early arguments are arguments for national, rather than presidential, supremacy. As he put it in 1909, "Over *external* matters . . . no residuary powers do or can exist in the several States, and from the necessity of the case all necessary authority must be found in the National Government, such authority being expressly conferred or implied from one or more of the express powers, or from all of them combined, or resulting from the very fact of nationality as inherently inseparable therefrom." Neither the 1909 article nor the 1919 book contain anything like the sort of executive aggrandizement found in *Curtiss-Wright.*

Sutherland's conversion to the theory of executive domination in the area of foreign affairs thus remains something of an enigma, as does the *Curtiss-Wright* decision itself. On the one hand, it is easy to criticize Sutherland's gran-

diose claims concerning the origin and nature of the foreign-affairs power and to disparage his inflated views of presidential power. On the other, one cannot help but be impressed by Sutherland's prescience—as early as 1909—about the nation's future role in foreign affairs and the necessity for an expansive interpretation of the powers of the national government. Furthermore, while *Curtiss-Wright* has been abused by presidents and presidential advisers who have sought extraordinary powers, its influence is mitigated by the existence of other Supreme Court decisions—such as the steel-seizure decision in 1952—which take a diametrically opposite view of presidential power. As Justice Jackson put it in the steel-seizure case, "Presidential powers are not fixed but fluctuate, depending upon their disjunction or conjunction with those of Congress." In the never-ending debate between the two branches, *Curtiss-Wright* provides a clear, albeit dubious, point of reference.

Selected Bibliography

Levitan, David M. "The Foreign Relations Power: An Analysis of Mr. Justice Sutherland's Theory." *Yale Law Journal* 55 (1946): 467–497.

Lofgren, Charles A. "*United States v. Curtiss-Wright Export Corporation*: An Historical Reassessment." *Yale Law Journal* 83 (1973): 1–32.

Sutherland, George. *Constitutional Power and World Affairs.* New York: Columbia University Press, 1919.

How One Immigrant Shook the U.S. Government to Its Very Core

—◄o►—

Barbara Hinkson Craig

Department of Government
Wesleyan University

Immigration and Naturalization Service v. Chadha, 462 U.S. 919 (1983)
[U.S. Supreme Court]

◄o► THE CASE IN BRIEF ◄o►

Date
1983

Location
California

Court
U.S. Supreme Court

Principal Participants
Jagdish Rai Khiali Ram Nathod Ram
  Chadha
U.S. Immigration and Naturalization
  Service
U.S. Congressman Joshua Eilberg
Chief Justice Warren Burger

Significance of the Case
An immigrant's fight for freedom brought the constitutionality of the legislative veto into question. The Supreme Court upheld the initial ruling that the legislative veto in the immigration act was unconstitutional.

There is no doubt that *INS v. Chadha* is what we call a landmark decision. As one congressional scholar has noted, *Chadha* "will profoundly affect how power is exercised and policy made in America for decades to come." When the Supreme Court handed down its decision in *Chadha* on June 23, 1983, it was front-page news around the country. "Government Power Poised for a Grand Realignment" read headlines in the *New York Times*, and "Decision Alters Balance of Power in Government" appeared in the *Washington Post*. In one fell swoop, the Court had overturned provisions in nearly two hundred different statutes, more than it had struck down in its entire previous history. The decision affected issues ranging from war powers and arms sales to budget impoundments and government salaries. It also touched regulations concerning the environment, consumer protection, worker health and safety, and a whole host of pork-barrel and special-interest programs.

The *Chadha* case is the extraordinary story of how one insignificant immigrant, in his fight to stay in the United States, stumbled into the midst of a battle between titans. Ultimately, it led to a power struggle that pitted the U.S. Congress in all its might against an equally impressive and formidable foe—the president and the entire executive branch. The issue involved was the question of the constitutionality of the legislative veto, a procedural device invented by Congress to constrain the exercise of power delegated by law to the president, executive branch, or independent agencies. It is a case that will be remembered more for the power struggle between the branches that it represented, but it begins with Chadha's own story.

Jagdish Rai Khiali Ram Nathod Ram Chadha is an Indian who was born and raised in Kenya. When Kenya became independent from Great Britain in 1963, individuals born in Kenya prior to that date were automatically made citizens—everyone, that is, except those whose parents had not been born in Kenya. Chadha's father had been born in South Africa, his mother in India. Thus, he had to apply in order to become a citizen in the country of his birth. His application, like those of many others similarly situated, was lost in a sea of red tape. The new Kenyan government also passed a number of restrictions on place and type of employment for noncitizens. It was a catch-22: citizenship was not forthcoming, and employment was restricted without it.

At the encouragement of a number of young Peace Corps volunteers who had befriended him, Chadha decided to pursue a college education in the United States. In 1966, traveling on a British nationality certificate and a British passport, Chadha came to the United States and entered Bowling Green State University. By December 1971, he had earned a B.A. in business administration and an M.A. in political science and economics. His student visa was due to expire in June 1972. Chadha wrote to the Kenyan and British embassies to inquire about how he could return home. Kenya said, in effect, "You're not one of ours anymore." The British said, "It could take years to clear you for a Quota Voucher for employment in England. Why don't you get the U.S. to regularize your immigration status and stay there?"

The quota voucher was Great Britain's response to the flood of Ugandan Indians who

held British colonial passports and were fleeing Idi Amin's regime in the wake of his 1972 order for the immediate expulsion of all Asians. It was a time of worldwide recession, and the indigenous peoples employed in Britain had risen up to protect themselves against cheaper labor competition.

Chadha was truly a man without a country. He tried to get a job in the United States, but employers wanted to see his "green card," that prized piece of paper providing aliens with resident status and the right to work. By the summer of 1973, Chadha was desperate, and he went to the U.S. Immigration Office in Los Angeles to see if he could get a letter or other document that would allow him to work. He was arrested, fingerprinted, photographed, and held well into the evening. Then he was presented with an order to appear before an immigration judge on November 1, 1973, to show cause why he should not be deported.

Chadha was by this time well into the American administrative process, a process that can seem confusing even to Americans who remember their civics-course descriptions of their national government's three separate branches—executive, legislative, and judicial. What Chadha was about to experience was a quasi-judicial proceeding that looked very much like (and had powers very much like) a court of law. But it was not a court of law. It was a regional office of an executive-branch agency, the Immigration and Naturalization Service within the U.S. Justice Department, and the immigration judge was an employee of the executive branch, not a member of the judicial branch.

After a frenetic search for a lawyer he could afford, Chadha found a young, fresh-from-law-school practitioner who had not even had a course in immigration law. There ensued a series of blunders and misunderstandings of the law by his greenhorn counsel. Finally, though, due in no small part to the conscientious actions of an elderly civil servant—an immigration hearing judge—Chadha was granted a "suspension of deportation." The immigration judge's decision and the case information were then sent to the attorney general.

The power to suspend deportations in cases where an alien would suffer "extreme hardship" if deported had been given to the attorney general by Congress in the 1940s and had been regularly renewed since. There was a hitch, however. After determining that the extreme-hardship standard was met, the attorney general was required to send the names of individuals granted suspensions and the case information to Congress to remain before it for two years. During that time, if either house voted by majority vote to veto an individual's suspension, out he or she would go. This congressional veto procedure is called "a one-house legislative veto."

On December 12, 1975, Democratic congressman Joshua Eilberg of Pennsylvania introduced a one-house resolution (a legislative veto resolution) to disapprove Chadha's deportation suspension and that of five others. Without a printed bill, with no hearings, no debate, and no explanation, with no recorded vote and under suspension of the rules (a time when few members are typically on the floor), the resolution was passed. Chadha once again faced being deported.

Chadha did not believe this sort of action could possibly be constitutional, based on what he had learned about American law. He had had a hearing, the government had had a lawyer, he had had a lawyer, and a "judge" in black robes had decided his case. How could one house of Congress overturn his hard-won right to stay? It wasn't fair, and it wasn't equitable. And what of due process?

Again, Chadha needed counsel. Again, he had almost no money. His efforts finally led him to a young immigration attorney, John Pohlmann, who took on his case pro bono. At last, he had someone who really knew immigration law. Unfortunately, that knowledge was not very helpful. The only thing that held any promise—and it was not much—was a constitutional challenge.

The constitutional challenge to the legislative veto that Congress had used against Chadha is based on the principle of the separation of powers. In fashioning a government intended to preserve and protect the liberty of its citizens, the founding fathers relied on the principle of separation of powers and the countervailing principle of checks and balances. Power

was to be divided among three branches: (1) the legislative power was vested in a Congress made up of two houses; (2) the power to execute the laws passed by Congress was given to the executive; and (3) the power to interpret the laws was assigned to the judicial branch. As a check against the possible misuse of power by any one of the branches, each branch was given some power over the others. The Constitution, for example, gives the legislative power to Congress, but it also subjects the exercise of that power to the restraint of a presidential veto—a power that is, in turn, restrained by allowing for two-thirds of both houses of Congress to override a presidential veto.

One could argue that the action of the House of Representatives in vetoing Chadha's suspension of deportation and thereby changing a decision made by the attorney general was an unconstitutional intrusion into the domain of the executive branch. In retort, Congress could argue that it was simply trying to correct a mistake made by the executive branch in its interpretation of the intent of the law. In response to this explanation, though, opponents of the legislative veto would argue that the power to determine whether the executive branch has correctly applied a law passed by Congress belongs to the judicial branch, not to the legislature. Separation-of-powers questions are raised by either effort to explain the legislative veto's function. To determine the constitutionality of the legislative veto in these terms would require a court to balance the core purpose of the separation-of-powers design against the equally important function of the checks-and-balances provisions and then to decide whether the intrusion was significant enough to threaten the independence of either the judicial or executive branches.

Another approach to challenging the legislative veto is to question its constitutionality based on the presentment clause, Article I, Section 7 of the U.S. Constitution, or the incompatibility clause, Article I, Section 6 of the Constitution, or the constitutional requirement of bicameralism. The presentment clause spells out the process for passage of a law: "Every Bill which shall have passed the House of Representatives and the Senate, shall, before it becomes Law, be presented to the President of the United States. . . ." In the event that the president does not sign the bill, of course, Congress can by two-thirds vote in both houses make it law. The framers included the every-order clause to ensure that Congress could not avoid the president's check on the legislative power by calling a bill by another name: "Every Order, Resolution, or Vote to which the Concurrence of the Senate and House of Representatives may be necessary . . . shall be presented to the President of the United States; and before the Same shall take Effect, shall be approved by him, or being disapproved by him, shall be repassed by two thirds of the Senate and House of Representatives. . . ." If the resolution passed by the House of Representatives to veto Chadha's suspension of deportation was in effect a law, it was not passed according to the clear constitutional requirements for passage of a law. Opponents of the legislative veto would extend the logic of this analysis to "prove" the veto's unconstitutionality under a separation-of-powers analysis as well: if it was not a law, then it must be either an effort to execute the law or to interpret it, and these functions belong to the other branches.

Could the House of Representative's actions, without the Senate or the president's involvement, have the constitutional force of law on Chadha? Did not even this lowly immigrant have the right to this most basic of constitutional protections that, as John Adams pointed out, insures that we are "a government of laws, and not of men"? Chadha and his attorney believed that the veto process was wrong and unconstitutional, and they prepared to fight.

Throughout 1976 and early 1977, Chadha's attorney appealed through the administrative process and then to the U.S. Court of Appeals for the Ninth Circuit in San Francisco. By April 1977, though, Pohlmann was forced to tell Chadha that he simply could not go on with the case much longer. The date for filing the written brief was rapidly approaching, and the complexity of the issues involved required an enormous amount of research time. As a single practitioner with a family to support, Pohlmann could no longer afford to spend so much time working for free. If this case were about

the plight of one small alien, it is safe to say that here is where it most likely would have ended. Chadha would have been just one more of the many aliens deported each year. However, the importance of timing should never be underestimated: what was going on in Washington, D.C., during the mid-1970s would work to Chadha's benefit.

In the wake of the Watergate and Vietnam debacles, Congress with an ever-increasing frequency, had attached legislative vetoes to grants of power to the president. In the War Powers Act, Congress had granted to the president the right to use the troops in hostile situations for sixty days. However, if during that period the two houses of Congress, by majority vote, ordered him to bring the men home, he would have to do so. Congress had delegated to the president the power to decide to sell arms to foreign nations, but if both houses voted against the sale, there could be no sale. The president was given the power to impound funds for one year, but if either house passed a legislative veto resolution, he had to spend the funds. There were dozens of other such laws. The president liked the power to act but not the strings of the legislative veto.

The Justice Department under the Ford, Carter, and Reagan administrations was vehemently opposed to the legislative veto as an unconstitutional intrusion on presidential power to execute the law. If Congress wanted to direct the president, it had to do so through a law and over a presidential veto if he objected. One or two houses, acting without the president's involvement, had no constitutional power except to impeach, try impeachments, ratify treaties, and advise and consent on appointees. The Constitution, the Justice Department argued, makes this clear.

But there was a problem. How to get a case? The president could not just bring a case to court against Congress, because the Court would surely call any such attempt a blatant example of a political question. What was needed was a private litigant to bring a case that the Justice Department could join. Again, though, there was a problem. What private litigant could pass the court's standing and political-question tests when foreign policy and presidential power were the issues? Fate was with the executive—and with Chadha.

Elected to the House of Representatives in the post-Watergate class of 1974 was one Elliot Levitas (Democrat, Georgia). Like so many of the "Young Turks," as the freshmen legislators of that year were called by the media, Levitas came to Washington to fight Washington. He was out to get those pointy-headed, overzealous bureaucrats who were the perpetrators of fraud, waste, abuse, and red tape.

To a large extent, his frustration, and that voiced by his constituents, was a response to the flood of regulations that were beginning to hit the business and work world by the mid to late 1970s. These were the regulations that were putting into operation the liberal social policies embraced by Congress. They included dozens of laws that were passed throughout the late 1960s and early 1970s calling for clean air, clean water, safer workplaces, safer products, equal opportunities, and fair advertisement practices. The courts had allowed the broad and often vague delegations of power to the executive branch included in these laws, even though Congress was, in effect, giving away its own lawmaking power. To overcome separation-of-powers concerns about these delegations, the courts rationalized that once the power to make regulations was delegated to the executive branch, it became executive power—even though those regulations were created like laws and looked like laws, and citizens had to obey them like laws.

As the government agencies attempted to implement these congressional goals, the costs of achieving them became very clear to folks who now had to pay. And they screamed loudly to their representatives and senators. But what could members do? Surely, they did not want to go on record as opposed to admirable goals such as clean air.

Throughout the 1970s, the Court, as well as Congress, had forced the rule-making process to be more fair and open, more judicial-like. In so doing, Congress had been effectively shut out of influencing the regulatory outcome. No longer could the committee or subcommittee chair just call up the agency head and hint that any action on X ought to take into considera-

tion the effect on Y Company that just happened to be in the chair's district. The agency head, in most cases, was compelled to keep a full record for possible Court review and was likely to be forced to provide a rational connection between evidence gathered during the rule-making process and his or her final published regulation. It became harder and harder for individual members of Congress to get agencies to respond to their suggestions. If members wanted exemptions or had clear ideas of what they wanted that were not put in the law, they had to go about putting them in another law. But that is not so easy to do. A majority in both houses had to support the exemption. The difficulty of accomplishing that task is one of the major reasons why Congress writes vague and ambiguous laws in the first place: it endeavors, often successfully, to paper over conflict.

To make a long story short, Levitas found the tool to get Congress back in on the regulation process: the legislative veto. If Congress were to adopt a legislative veto over all government regulations, then overly burdensome, counterproductive, or downright crazy regulations could be stopped before they went into effect.

Washington insiders (members and executive-branch actors and the more astute interest groups) quickly saw the legislative veto's real potential: it could be used to stop any regulation for any reason. The legislative veto would allow Congress to narrow the review to a particular regulation, and the broad question of whether consumers or the environment should be protected could be avoided. Powerful organized interests, with compelling economic incentives, would be able to gear up lobbying efforts fast, putting them at a distinct advantage. The amorphous "public interest," even when organized, would be at a distinct disadvantage. Spread thinly trying to cover hundreds of potential regulations, with much less financial backing, they would have a much harder time mobilizing within the thirty to sixty days typically allowed for veto reviews. They would win occasionally with the aid of their major ally, the media, but the balance of power would be tipped against them.

Congress took to the legislative veto like a duck to water. This little procedural device of a few sentences at the end of a statute enabled members to continue to delegate broad, vague power to the executive branch, proving to the electorate their concern for the pressing problems of the moment. Congress could come to closure on controversial issues without the necessity of coming to decisions. Majorities could be gathered to support general principles with the promise held out that, if anyone was really disturbed with the particulars, then the veto would be available. When the agency proposed a rule, and those who would have to pay (the businesses who had to convert equipment to make it safe or nonpolluting, for example) complained, Congress would be able to threaten to veto the rule. Members would be able to say, "Look, I'm for clean air, but this rule is too costly. Do a better job, Mr. and Ms. Bureaucrat, or we will veto your final regulation." And Congress would be under no obligation to say what that better job might be. More importantly, wise executive actors would soon realize the importance of communicating with members (especially members of their oversight committees) during the process of designing their regulations. Many of the troublesome regulations might be altered or stopped before they got to the formal administrative rule-making process and without Congress having even to vote on a legislative veto resolution.

Levitas was quite successful in selling his magic cure-all. In 1976, he came within three votes of getting his legislative veto bill through the House. He lost that year on his across-the-board legislative veto proposal, but managed to get numerous veto provisions into individual statutes over the next few years—for example, NHTSA safety rules, health and environment regulations, and consumer regulations. And all the while he continued his fight on behalf of what he called his "generic veto" with a crusader's zeal.

Consumers, environmental protection groups, labor, and minorities who had fought long and hard to get legislation to accomplish their goals were faced with the prospect of losing regulation by regulation, and Congress could claim to be squeaky clean. Not many saw the danger of this eventuality, but one attorney in a position to do something about it did. He was Alan Morrison, chief litigator for Ralph Nader's legal arm, the Public Citizen Litigation Group.

In 1977, just as Chadha's own attorney was ready to give up, Morrison took over Chadha's case. He did so not so much to fight for the right of a single immigrant but to strive for the consumer protection that had been promised in laws passed by Congress. The Justice Department joined in the case on behalf of the immigration service, arguing along with Chadha and Morrison that the veto was unconstitutional. Left with no one to defend the veto, and with no case or controversy unless a defender could be found, the appeals court asked Congress to submit amici curiae briefs in support of the veto's constitutionality. Before long, the two houses of Congress were forced to intervene formally as parties to the case. The real litigants were now clear. The private litigant, Mr. Chadha, was much beside the point. This was a case of Congress versus the president.

Chadha v. INS was argued before a panel of three judges of the U.S. Court of Appeals for the Ninth Circuit in San Francisco on April 10, 1978. More than two and a half years passed before a decision from the appeals court was announced. During that time, both Morrison and the Justice Department were constantly on the lookout for other cases that they might bring (or join) to challenge the legislative veto's constitutionality. Eventually, at least two other cases (both involving challenges to consumer regulations vetoed by Congress) were found, but it was to be Chadha's case that would decide the veto's constitutionality.

On December 23, 1980, the appeals court announced its decision: it found the legislative veto in the immigration act unconstitutional. The opinion, written by Judge Anthony Kennedy (who later became an associate justice of the U.S. Supreme Court), ruled the legislative veto unconstitutional because "it violates the constitutional doctrine of separation of powers because it is [a] prohibited legislative intrusion upon the Executive and Judicial branches." There was a twofold purpose in the framers' adoption of the separation-of-powers principle. The first, according to the court, was to "prevent an unnecessary and therefore dangerous concentration of power in one branch"; the second was "to facilitate administration of a large nation by the assignment of numerous labors to designated authorities." The Court then proceeded to balance the utility of the legislative veto against its potential for intrusion into another branch's rightful domain, finding the veto to be "an interference with a central function of the Judiciary, and . . . an interference which is both disruptive and unnecessary."

The appeals court's decision showed considerable judicial restraint, carefully confining its analysis to the situation presented by the immigration law. In that form, however, it was not very useful to either Morrison's effort to rid the regulatory process of legislative vetoes or to the Justice Department's goal of eliminating the bothersome presidential-level vetoes in the budget and foreign affairs acts. In another way, though, the appeals court behaved with considerable judicial activism by stretching far beyond what was necessary to deal with the case at hand. In the summer of 1980, Chadha had married an American woman. As the spouse of a U.S. citizen, he easily could have obtained U.S. citizenship. This should have made the case moot, because Chadha no longer stood to lose anything by an adverse ruling. However, the Court's willingness to finesse the question of mootness makes it seem obvious that it wanted to reach the question of the legislative veto's constitutionality.

For Morrison and the Justice Department to achieve the results they wanted, they had to appeal the decision to the Supreme Court and hope for a broader ruling. They had a problem, though. Chadha and the INS had both already won. How could they appeal a win? In the months following the appeals court decision, there were convoluted legal attempts by the Justice Department to enable an appeal. However, in the end, both the Senate and the House of Representatives saved the day by intervening and appealing in their own attempt to get a favorable court ruling on the legislative veto's constitutionality.

INS v. Chadha was argued twice before the Supreme Court—on February 22 and December 7, 1982. The decision was announced on June 23, 1983. The Court was split 7-2. The split was not a conservative versus liberal one. The majority included Justices Warren Burger and Sandra Day O'Connor, Thurgood Marshall and William Brennan, John Paul Stevens and Harry Blackman—not typically allies. Justice Lewis Powell wrote a concurrence, and Justices Byron White and William Rehnquist wrote separate dissents.

In what a *New York Times* editorial called a "supremely simple" decision, Chief Justice Burger, "writing like a patient schoolmaster," explained the Court's reasoning in "familiar and basic terms. "Remember what we all learned in social studies about how laws are made? Well," the editorial continued, "that's just how it should still work." As Burger had pointed out, the Constitution provides "a single, finely wrought and exhaustively considered procedure" for exercise of the legislative power of the federal government. "Explicit and unambiguous provisions of the Constitution," he went on, "prescribe and define the respective functions of the Congress and of the Executive in the legislative process." Any actions taken by either house if "they contain matter which is properly to be regarded as legislative in character and effect" must conform with the constitutionality designed legislative process that includes bicameral passage and presentment to the president.

Burger went on to spell out precisely what the Court would consider to be "legislative in nature." Legislative action is any action that has the "purpose and effect of altering the legal rights, duties, and relations of persons outside the legislative branch." So broad a definition would encompass all the legislative veto provisions on the statute books—from the budget act, to the arms sales, to all the regulatory acts. The first few lines of Justice Powell's concurrence tells it all: "The Court's decision based on the Presentment Clauses . . . apparently will invalidate every use of the legislative veto. The breadth of this holding gives one pause." Justice Powell's opinion presented a far more narrow analysis, akin to Judge Kennedy's appeals court decision.

In a vehement dissent, Justice White defended the legislative veto as "an important if not indispensable political invention that allows the president and Congress to resolve major constitutional policy differences, assures the accountability of independent regulatory agencies, and preserves Congress's control over lawmaking." White attacked the majority decision for its lack of judicial restraint. "[T]he apparent sweep of the Court's decision today is regrettable. . . . To strike an entire class of statutes based on consideration of a somewhat atypical and more readily indictable exemplar of the class is irresponsible."

There was no other law with a legislative veto anything like the immigration law veto that gave Congress the power to overturn a quasi-judicial decision of an agency. Nonetheless, the Supreme Court chose *Chadha* as the case in which it would rid the world of the legislative veto. Why? Why did the Court pick so narrow a case to rule so broadly?

Of course, the Supreme Court does not explain why it rules, but a fair guess is that it was out of fear of the success of Levitas's campaign. Review of administrative rule making and order making (what Chadha was involved with) is one of the Court's prime functions today. Two decades of slow progress toward judicializing (i.e., formalizing) the rule-making process to make it more reviewable by courts was threatened with undoing by behind the door, off-the-record negotiations. What would the Court do if faced with a challenge to a rule that had not been vetoed by Congress? Would Congress's failure to veto mean endorsement? Where would that leave the Court in its role to interpret the meaning of laws, as surely most regulations would not be vetoed? Had Congress used its legislative veto powers with more restraint, perhaps the Court would have exercised more restraint as well. As long as legislative vetoes were applied sparingly and were confined to foreign affairs or special domestic problems like budget impoundments, courts were unlikely to become involved in the interbranch struggle, even though the constitutionality of the legislative-veto device had long been open to question.

A narrow ruling like Judge Kennedy's or Justice Powell's, balancing the due process protections of the individual against Congress's power over lawmaking and oversight of the executive, would not knock out the troublesome

vetoes over regulations. The Court would have been inundated with case-by-case challenges. It was easier to get it over quickly. Still, there were two other cases before the Supreme Court by the 1983 term—a challenge to a congressional veto of a used-car rule intended to protect consumers from devious used-car dealers (*Consumer Union of United States, Inc., v. Federal Trade Commission*) and a challenge to a one-house veto of an incremental gas-pricing rule that had been intended to protect homeowners against the increases in gas prices brought about by natural-gas deregulation (*Consumer Energy Council of America et al. v. Federal Energy Regulatory Commission*). The only answer to why the Court did not chose one of these more appropriate cases seems to be that neither had yet been argued, and the Court wanted to be done with the matter. Two weeks after the *Chadha* decision, the Court ruled without argument and without further comment that the legislative vetoes in both the other 1983 cases were unconstitutional.

In the years since the decisions invalidating the legislative veto, the debate over the implications and effects of the loss of the veto have continued. So, too, has the debate over the prudence of the Court's involvement in the dispute and the wisdom of the majority's opinion. There is no doubt, though, that the *Chadha* case has had, and will continue to have, an effect on constitutional law. Dozens of cases have been brought relying on the strict construction of the nature of the legislative power as interpreted by the majority in *Chadha*. *Bowsher v. Synar*, the challenge to the constitutionality of the Budget Deficit Reduction Act (otherwise known as the Gramm-Rudman-Hollings Act), and *Lowry v. Reagan*, a challenge to the president's use of American troops to protect shipping in the Persian Gulf, are only two examples among many. *Chadha* may have eliminated the legislative veto as a constitutional tool of congressional control over the executive branch, but the incentives for involvement in the regulatory process and the desires to find ways to influence presidential decisions have not disappeared. Congress has been and will continue to be inventive as it searches for constitutional alternatives to the veto. No doubt challenges to the new inventions will one day find their way into the courts as well.

Selected Bibliography

Bruff, Harold H., and Ernest Gelhorn. "Congressional Control of Administrative Regulations: A Study of Legislative Vetoes." *Harvard Law Review* 90 (1977): 1369–1440.

Craig, Barbara Hinkson. *Chadha: The Story of an Epic Constitutional Struggle.* New York: Oxford University Press, 1988.

Fisher, Louis. "A Political Context for Legislative Vetoes." *Political Science Quarterly* 93 (1978): 241–254.

Contemporary Lessons in the Separation of Powers: Congressional Standing and the Line-Item Veto

—◄○►—

Thomas E. Baker

School of Law
Drake University

Raines v. Byrd, 521 U.S. 811 (1997) and *Clinton v. New York*, 524 U.S. 417 (1998)
[U.S. Supreme Court]

◄○► THE CASE IN BRIEF ◄○►

Date
1997, 1998

Location
District of Columbia

Court
U.S. Supreme Court

Principal Participants
Six members of the 104th Congress
Chief Justice William Rehnquist
Associate Justice John Paul Stevens
President Bill Clinton

Significance of the Case
Putting pork-barrel politics aside, the Supreme Court ruled on two cases that examined the constitutionality of the Line Item Veto Act of 1996. The majority ruled that the act was unconstitutional.

Some of the Supreme Court's most important decisions during the tenure of Chief Justice Warren Burger focused on separation of powers, especially the interrelationship between the Congress and the executive branch. Among the notable decisions were *INS v. Chadha* (1983), which struck down the legislative veto, and *Bowsher v. Synar* (1986), which struck down a balanced-budget and deficit-control statute). The successor court, led by Chief Justice William Rehnquist, has followed the lead of the Burger court in taking a highly formalistic and even heroic approach to the separation of powers.

Raines v. Byrd (1997) and *Clinton v. New York* (1998) are similar decisions in that each insists on the punctilios of the separation of powers. They both arise from the same statute, the Line Item Veto Act of 1996. The act permitted the president to cancel specific items contained in spending bills approved by the Congress. According to the terms of the act as passed, the president could cancel: (1) a specific dollar amount of discretionary budget authority; (2) an item of new direct spending; or (3) a limited tax benefit that affected a small number of tax-payers. The president had to determine that a particular cancellation would reduce the federal deficit, would not impair any essential government function, and would not harm the national interest. The act also instructed the president to take into account the bill's legislative history and purpose, any particular information that might be referenced in the bill, and any other available relevant information.

The act required the president to submit a special cancellation message to Congress within five days after enactment of a spending bill, stating particular reasons for the cancellation. The cancellation, however, took effect immediately. The act also provided for expedited consideration by Congress of a disapproval bill that, if enacted, would reinstate the canceled item. Disapproval bills were not themselves subject to presidential cancellation.

The act took effect on January 1, 1997. Six members of the 104th Congress who had voted against the act—four Senators and two members of the House of Representatives—immediately filed a lawsuit contesting its constitutionality. They initiated their lawsuit before any presidential cancellations had taken place under the act. Pursuant to the judicial review section of the act, the six members of Congress filed their suit in the U.S. District Court for the District of Columbia. That court held the act unconstitutional. The government took an appeal directly to the Supreme Court under another provision of the act.

In *Raines v. Byrd* (1997), the Supreme Court ruled that the six members of Congress lacked "standing" to bring the lawsuit. That is, the Court concluded that the members of Congress were not the appropriate persons to bring a constitutional challenge. Standing is a requirement of Article III of the U.S. Constitution, which empowers federal courts to hear and decide only "cases or controversies." That every plaintiff have standing is an essential element of a case or controversy. Specifically, the plaintiff in a federal lawsuit must be the right person to bring the suit according to three criteria. First, the individual plaintiff must have suffered some injury in fact; an abstract or generalized complaint that everyone has in common

is not enough. Second, the plaintiff's injury must be fairly traceable to the action being challenged; the harm must have been caused by what the government did or did not do in this case. Third, the injury must be one that can be redressed by a favorable court decision; that is, it must be possible that a court order against the federal government will make things right. If the parties have a personal stake in the outcome, they will have every incentive to present fully their side of the dispute, and the court's decision making will benefit from their advocacy. Furthermore, the court will be assured that it is acting as a court to decide a real live dispute, rather than as a legislature proclaiming some abstract or general issue of public policy. The Supreme Court is very strict about standing in constitutional cases such as this one.

Chief Justice Rehnquist wrote for a five-member majority holding that the case had to be dismissed because the six members of Congress who were plaintiffs could not allege any direct injury to themselves as individuals other than general allegations of an abstract and widely dispersed institutional harm to the legislative power of the Congress. They had not suffered the required kind of personal, individual injury that would allow them to bring a lawsuit to challenge the constitutionality of the act.

Justice David Souter wrote a separate concurring opinion, joined by Justice Ruth Bader Ginsburg, hedging somewhat on the abstract issue of whether the six members of Congress had standing to bring such a lawsuit. The Souter opinion maintained that it was more appropriate to decide such an important constitutional issue in a suit brought by someone who had been deprived of a benefit after an actual presidential cancellation had taken place under the act.

Justice John Paul Stevens dissented. Insisting that the six members of Congress who sued had standing, he went on to conclude that the act was unconstitutional as a violation of the separation of powers. Justice Stephen Breyer also dissented. Like Justice Stevens, he argued that the six members of Congress who brought the lawsuit had standing, but he did not give his views on the act's constitutionality.

One year later, *Clinton v. New York* (1998) reached the Supreme Court by the same jurisdictional route written into the act. The dispute arose from two different presidential cancellations, affecting two different sets of plaintiffs, and combined in a single case. The first set of plaintiffs included New York City, two hospital associations, a hospital, and two unions of health-care employees. They sued President Clinton to contest his cancellation of a congressional spending provision that would have relieved the state of New York of having to return approximately $2.6 billion that the federal government had already paid to the state under Medicaid to provide health care for the poor. The second set of plaintiffs was an Idaho cooperative of approximately thirty potato growers, calling itself Snake River Potato Growers, Inc. They sued to challenge President Clinton's cancellation of a limited capital-gains, tax-benefit provision for processors of agricultural products. They alleged that the cancellation would cost them $155 million in taxes over the next ten years.

This time around, the Supreme Court reached the constitutional merits and squarely held that the Line Item Veto Act was unconstitutional. Justice Stevens, who had tipped his hand in his dissent in *Raines v. Byrd*, wrote for a solid six-member majority. Whether the line-item veto was a wise measure and whether the president and Congress were wisely exercising their authority under the Line Item Veto Act were political issues that the Supreme Court explicitly refused to consider. The justices dealt only with the legal question of the act's constitutionality.

Without having to rely on more general principles of separation of powers, however, the majority zeroed in on the textual provisions in the Constitution that describe how a bill becomes a law. On the textual level, the Court read the bicameralism and presentment clauses in Articles I and VII of the U.S. Constitution narrowly, literally, and exclusively. The majority insisted that the Constitution, in a few straightforward sentences, required that every bill must be passed by both houses of Congress and then presented to the president before it can become a law. The president can veto a measure, but Congress can override the veto with a two-thirds vote in each house. This remarkably simple yet elegant model of lawmak-

ing was a centerpiece of the debates at the Constitutional Convention of 1787. The Line Item Veto Act violated the plain meaning of the Constitution insofar as it authorized the president to repeal parts of laws that had been duly enacted in accordance with Articles I and VII. That Congress reserved a power to disapprove the president's cancellation did not save the act, for the majority insisted that Congress cannot alter the procedures laid down in Articles I and VII without amending the Constitution.

Justice Anthony Kennedy concurred separately because, as he said, he wanted to emphasize that individual liberty is at risk whenever the federal branches disobey the separation of powers. Kennedy believed that the act attempted to enhance the president's powers beyond what the framers prescribed, and it simply did not matter to him that Congress surrendered the power to him or that he welcomed it.

Three justices dissented. Justices Antonin Scalia, Sandra Day O'Connor, and Stephen Breyer would have upheld the act based on the legal fiction that, constitutionally speaking, the act was not really a line-item veto at all. They argued that every spending and tax statute enacted after the Line Item Veto Act, in effect, incorporated the cancellation procedures of the act. So they deemed that the presentment clause was satisfied under the act's procedures. Furthermore, they viewed the act within the context of the history of the separation of powers to be a politically expedient delegation of power from the legislative branch to the executive. They insisted that "there was not a dime's worth of difference" between the act's authorization of the president to cancel a measure and the two-hundred-plus years of routinely enacted statutes that have given the president discretion whether or not to spend the particular appropriated funds.

The majority had the better of the argument. The Line Item Veto Act fundamentally confused the legislative function of deciding what the law should be with the executive function of implementing the law duly enacted. Those separate and distinct powers belong in the separate and distinct hands of the Congress and the president. The constitutional bottom line, then, is that if the president is ever to have the power of the line-item veto, it cannot come by mere ordinary legislation. Rather, the respective roles of the Congress and the president under our system of separated and blended powers can be adjusted and redrawn only through a constitutional amendment under Article 5, proposed by a two-thirds vote in each house of the Congress and ratified by three-fourths of the legislatures of the fifty states.

In both these cases, then, the Supreme Court held fast to the eighteenth-century parchment of the Constitution against the pull of late twentieth-century bipartisan political expediencies. The justices, in other words, adhered to the wisdom of Justice Robert H. Jackson's prescient observation in *The Steel Seizure Case* (1952): "With all its defects, delays and inconveniences, men have discovered no technique for long preserving free government except that the Executive be under the law, and that the law be made by parliamentary delibera-

tions. Such institutions may be destined to pass away. But it is the duty of the Court to be the last, not first, to give them up."

Selected Bibliography

Antieau, Chester James. *The Executive Veto.* Dobbs Ferry: Oceana, 1987.

Byrd, Robert C. "The Control of the Purse and the Line Item Veto Act." *Harvard Journal on Legislation* 35 (1998): 297–333.

Lessig, Lawrence. "Lessons from a Line Item Veto Law." *Case Western Law Review* 47 (1997): 1659–1670.

Noah, Lars. "The Executive Line Item Veto and the Judicial Power to Sever: What's the Difference?" *Washington and Lee Law Review* 56 (1999): 235–246.

Powell, H. Jefferson, and Jed Rubenfeld. "Laying It on the Line: A Dialogue on Line Item Vetoes and Separation of Powers." *Duke Law Journal* 47 (1998): 1171–1211.

Federalism

Judicial Review of State Court Decisions

———◄◌►———

Richard E. Ellis

Department of History
State University of New York at Buffalo

Martin v. Hunter's Lessee, 1 Wheaton 304 (1816) [U.S. Supreme Court]

◄◌► THE CASE IN BRIEF ◄◌►
Date 　1816
Location 　Virginia 　District of Columbia
Court 　U.S. Supreme Court
Principal Participants 　Patrick Henry 　Spencer Roane 　Chief Justice John Marshall
Significance of the Case 　A delayed 1794 Virginia case seeking 　title to land examined the authority of 　the Supreme Court and the power 　of the Constitution over state laws.

Between the American Revolution and the Civil War, the central constitutional issue in American history was the question of how to distribute power between the federal government and the states. Although the adoption of the U.S. Constitution greatly increased the power of the national government, it did not explicitly provide a clear-cut solution to the problem. During the 1780s, under the Articles of Confederation, various states had adopted laws that circumvented the authority of the federal government. To deal with this threat, James Madison, at the constitutional convention in the summer of 1787, had urged that the central government explicitly be given the power to review and negate state laws. But no such provision was included in the final draft of the Constitution. The closest the Constitution came to dealing with the issue was the second paragraph of Article VI, the so-called supremacy clause, which provides: "This Constitution and the Laws of the United States which shall be made in Pursuance thereof, and all Treaties made, or which shall be made, under the Authority of the United States, shall be the Supreme Law of the Land; and the Judges in every State shall be bound thereby, any thing in the Constitution or Laws of any State to the Contrary notwithstanding."

This language, however, did not totally settle the matter, for it only indicated that federal law should be supreme over state law. It did not clearly indicate what legally constituted body or tribunal should determine when state actions subverted the authority of the federal government. To clarify matters, when the first Congress of the United States adopted the Judiciary Act of 1789, which implemented the judiciary provisions of the Constitution, it included a provision, known as Section 25, that gave the U.S. Supreme Court the power to review all state laws and state court decisions that involved the Constitution, federal laws, and treaties. Making the Supreme Court the final arbiter in disputes between the federal government and the states proved to be highly controversial. Debate over the constitutionality of Section 25 raged for nearly a century after its adoption. *Martin v. Hunter's Lessee* (1816) is the most important Supreme Court decision to deal with this problem, and is particularly significant because in the Court's decision is to be found the view that eventually was to prevail about the nature of the federal union and the authority of the Supreme Court.

Martin v. Hunter's Lessee had deep and complicated roots that went back to the Revolution. Involved was the estate of Thomas, Sixth Lord Fairfax, consisting of over five million acres of extremely valuable lands that had been a kind of proprietary colony in the Northern Neck district between the Potomac and Rappahannock Rivers in the western part of Virginia. Fairfax was a citizen of Virginia, but when he died in 1781 he bequeathed his property to his nephew Denny Martin, a British subject who had never taken up residence in the Old Dominion. When this occurred, Virginia, under the leadership of Patrick Henry, denied the right of an alien to inherit property and passed legislation that removed other special privileges, such as various tax exemptions, that were attached to the land. The state also moved to assume ownership of the unappropriated lands of the estate and, by

1786, had even begun to sell them. Martin challenged these developments in a number of different lawsuits, arguing the validity of his uncle's will. He also pointed out that the peace treaty of 1783 contained a clause prohibiting the confiscation of loyalist estates.

The state essentially ignored these developments, and in 1789 it proceeded to sell some of the lands it had confiscated from the Fairfax estate to David Hunter, a speculator. Martin, however, denied Hunter's title to the land, and a lawsuit followed. The state district court at Winchester in 1794 found for Martin, and Hunter appealed the decision to the state's highest court, the court of appeals in Richmond. But, before a decision was reached, Martin sold a sizable portion of his claim to a syndicate of speculators that included John Marshall and his brother James. Shortly after this, in 1796, the state legislature offered a compromise that had been engineered by John Marshall: Martin and the syndicate that purchased the land from him would relinquish title to the undeveloped lands in the Northern Neck in return for clear title to the manor lands that Lord Fairfax had developed for his own personal use. This apparently was acceptable to both sides, and the compromise was enacted into law. In all probability, this is the way the lands were finally allocated.

This, however, did not end the dispute. The case was never dropped from the docket of the Virginia Court of Appeals, and it was eventually revived by Spencer Roane, Patrick Henry's son-in-law, who in his own right had become a prominent political figure and a member of the Virginia Court of Appeals. He was determined to see the fundamental constitutional issues raised by the case resolved in Virginia's favor. Therefore, after a long delay, in *Hunter v. Fairfax* (1810), the Virginia Court of Appeals reversed the lower court's decision and found for Hunter, who had purchased his land from the state. The Martin-Marshall group responded by appealing the decision to the U.S. Supreme Court on a writ of error, probably signed by Marshall himself, under Section 25 of the Judiciary Act of 1789.

Because of his involvement in the case, John Marshall removed himself. The decision in

Fairfax Devisee v. Hunter's Lessee (1813) was written by Joseph Story, an extreme nationalist, who spoke for a three-member majority with only one justice dissenting. Story reversed the decision of the Virginia Court of Appeals. He rejected the legitimacy of the various statutes under which Virginia had taken custody of the Fairfax lands and argued that Martin's inheritance was protected not only by the common law of descent but also by the anticonfiscation clause of the peace treaty that had been recently reinforced by a similar provision in the Jay Treaty of 1794. He made no mention of the legislative Act of Compromise of 1796. Story then "commanded" the Virginia Court of Appeals to adopt such proceedings as were necessary to implement the mandate of the U.S. Supreme Court.

This was the moment for which Roane had been waiting. Under his leadership, the Virginia Court of Appeals decided to respond to what it called "the mandate" handed down by the Supreme Court. To help it deal with the matter, the Virginia court "invited the members of the bar to investigate it," and it was discussed "in a full and able manner." Following this, "it received the long and deliberate consideration of the Court" itself.

The Court's decision in *Hunter v. Martin, Devisees of Fairfax* (1815) was handed down shortly after the end of the War of 1812 and was unanimous: Section 25 of the Judiciary Act of 1798, allowing appeals from state courts to the Supreme Court in matters dealing with the Constitution, federal laws, or treaties, was unconstitutional. The four judges delivered their opinions seriatim (i.e., in sequence), with no clear "opinion of the Court," but they said much the same thing. They reiterated the position the state had taken on the origins and the nature of the Union in the Virginia resolutions of 1798 and the Report of the Virginia Legislature in 1799. The Constitution, they argued, was the product of a compact made between the different states in 1787–1788. They denied that the U.S. Supreme Court was either the exclusive or final arbiter of constitutional questions, and they argued instead that the states should act as sentinels upon the activities of the federal government. They believed these prin-

ciples had been validated by Jefferson's election in 1800. They further argued that sovereignty was divided between the states and the national government, and that the latter was one of limited and specifically delegated powers. Since the U.S. Constitution had provided no final umpire on constitutional questions or specifically granted Congress the power to bestow such a role on the Supreme Court, the federal and state courts had the right to rule on such questions for themselves, and neither could bind the other on matters before it. In no other way could the states be protected from encroachments by the central government. "No calamity," it was asserted, "would be more to be deplored by the American people than a vortex in the general government, which should engulf and sweep away, every vestige of the state constitutions." In entering judgment, the Virginia Court of Appeals ruled that the U.S. Supreme Court did not have jurisdiction in the case or authority over "this court, and that obedience to its mandate be declined by the Court."

The Supreme Court responded the next year in *Martin v. Hunter's Lessee* (1816). Once again, Marshall did not sit, although Story, who wrote the majority opinion, later indicated he "concurred in every word." The decision itself was carefully crafted, strenuously argued, and incisive. At the outset, Story noted: "The questions involved in the judgment are of great importance and delicacy. Perhaps it is not too much to affirm that, upon their right decision, rest some of the most solid principles which have hitherto been supposed to sustain and protect the Constitution itself." He then proceeded to a nationalist theory about the origins and nature of the Union diametrically opposed to the compact theory offered by the Virginia Court of Appeals: "The Constitution of the United States was ordained and established, not by the states in their sovereign capacities, but emphatically, as the preamble of the Constitution declares, by 'the people of the United States.'"

Story vigorously defended the constitutionality of Section 25 of the Judiciary Act of 1789 and the right of the Supreme Court to review the final judgments of state courts in cases dealing with federal questions. He argued the need for a broad construction of the Constitution that "unavoidably deals in general language," because it was expected "to endure through a long lapse of ages, the events of which were locked up in the inscrutable purpose of Providence." Because of this, Story asserted, the powers of the federal government had been expressed in "general terms, leaving to the legislature, from time to time to adopt its own means to effectuate legitimate objects."

Story further argued that "the Constitution has presumed . . . that state jealousies and state interests, might sometimes obstruct, or control . . . the regular administration of justice." To prevent this, Article II of the U.S. Constitution had given the Supreme Court appellant jurisdiction in all cases involving the Constitution, federal laws, and treaties. Contrary to what the Virginia Court of Appeals asserted, the jurisdiction of the Supreme Court was not limited to cases that came from the lower federal courts but extended to all cases involving federal questions. In other words, it was the issues of the case, not the court from which it came that gave the Supreme Court its appellant jurisdiction. Story believed this point of view was reinforced by the supremacy clause in Article VI.

According to Story, state prejudice had undermined the central government under the Articles of Confederation, and the state courts could not be allowed to be the final interpreters of the Constitution, for it would lead to different judgments in different states and "these jarring and discordant judgments" would inevitably destroy the Union. Uniformity, Story was convinced, was absolutely essential for the future well-being of the nation, and this could only be assured through federal judicial review

of state actions. Not everyone accepted Story's arguments. Thomas Jefferson and Andrew Jackson, who viewed the Supreme Court as the branch of the federal government least responsive to the wishes of the people, for example, agreed with the position taken by the Virginia Court of Appeals, a position most deftly put by Justice Joseph Cabell who remarked in *Hunter v. Martin*: "It must have been foreseen that controversies would sometimes arise as to the boundaries of the two jurisdictions. Yet the Constitution has provided no umpire, has erected no tribunal by which they shall be settled. The omission proceeded, probably from the belief that such a tribunal would produce evils greater than those of the occasional collisions which it would be designed to remedy." As a consequence, the issue was to be a source of constant controversy until the Civil War settled it in the nationalists' favor.

Selected Bibliography

Beveridge, Albert J. *The Life of John Marshall.* 4 vols. Boston: Houghton Mifflin, 1916–1919.

Cullen, Charles, et al., eds. *The Papers of John Marshall.* 5 vols. to date. Chapel Hill: University of North Carolina Press, 1974–.

Miller, F. Thornton. "John Marshall versus Spencer Roane: A Reevaluation of *Martin v. Hunter's Lessee.*" *Virginia Magazine of History and Biography* 96 (1988): 297–314.

Newmyer, R. Kent. *Supreme Court Justice Joseph Story: Statesman of the Old Republic.* Chapel Hill: University of North Carolina Press, 1985.

Warren, Charles. "Legislative and Judicial Attacks on the Supreme Court of the United States: A History of the Twenty-Fifth Section of the Judiciary Act." *American Law Review* 47 (1913): 1–34, 161–189.

Implied Federal Powers:
Pandora's Box?

—◁◦▷—

Maxwell Bloomfield
Columbus School of Law
Catholic University of America

McCulloch v. Maryland, 4 Wheaton 316 (1819) [U.S. Supreme Court]

◀◦▶ THE CASE IN BRIEF ◀◦▶

Date
1819

Location
Maryland
District of Columbia

Court
Maryland Court of Appeals
U.S. Supreme Court

Principal Participants
Chief Justice John Marshall
James W. McCulloch
Daniel Webster

Significance of the Case
Citing the necessary-and-proper clause, the Supreme Court ruled that the federal government could institute a national bank and that the national bank could not be taxed.

Many Americans in the early nineteenth century hated banks. To some, they represented privileged corporations of the sort that had historically oppressed the common folk in England. Others, of a more pragmatic disposition, conceded the utility of a few small banks, but fiercely opposed the creation of large ones. The unsavory practices of one giant institution—the second Bank of the United States (BUS)—caused widespread public anger and demands for political retaliation. In the landmark case of *McCulloch v. Maryland*, the U.S. Supreme Court had to determine not only the legality of a national bank, but also the appropriate test to be applied to any federal power not specifically mentioned in the Constitution. Americans are still experiencing the fallout from this decision today.

The roots of the bank controversy stretched back to the founding period. Alexander Hamilton, the first secretary of the treasury, urged the creation of a national bank as part of a comprehensive program to stabilize the nation's economy. As Hamilton envisaged it, such a bank would be modeled in many ways on the Bank of England and would function as an arm of the federal government. It would receive and hold all federal revenue, facilitate foreign-exchange transactions, regulate the practices of state banks through its discount policy, and provide a uniform currency for the entire country. Like other Hamiltonian proposals, the bank bill aroused strong opposition in Congress, where James Madison and others charged that Congress had no constitutional authority to establish such an agency.

When the bill eventually passed by a sharply divided vote, the debate over its constitutionality shifted to the executive branch. President George Washington, uncertain whether to veto the measure, sought written opinions from Hamilton and from his secretary of state, Thomas Jefferson. The arguments of these men—classic examples of "liberal" versus "strict" constitutional construction—reappeared as major factors in the *McCulloch* case more than a quarter-century later. Persuaded by Hamilton's reasoning, Washington signed the bill, and the first BUS came into existence in 1791.

During its twenty-year life, the bank performed much as Hamilton had predicted. Under conservative management, it assisted the federal government in its fiscal operations and helped to create a favorable environment for domestic and foreign investment. It was part of the Federalist party program, however, and when the Jeffersonian Republicans came to power after 1800, the bank's days were numbered. When its charter expired in 1811, a Republican Congress declined to renew it. Thus, the nation confronted the severe economic dislocations caused by the War of 1812 with no help from a central bank.

The fiscal confusion of the war years led many to reconsider the advantages of such an institution and strengthened the entrepreneurial wing of the Republican party. With the return of peace came a renewed spirit of nationalism that encouraged the bank's advocates to press for new legislation. This time they were successful. In 1816, Congress chartered a second BUS for another term of twenty years.

Like its predecessor, the new bank was an immense undertaking. With a capitalization of $35 million, it was by far the largest corpora-

tion in the country. In addition to its home office in Philadelphia, the bank soon boasted eighteen branches in other cities, from Boston and Savannah on the East Coast to New Orleans, Louisville, and Cincinnati. As before, the federal government owned one-fifth of the bank's stock and named five of its twenty-five directors. But the president of the United States no longer appointed the head of the bank. This officer was now chosen by the stockholders. The change reflected the increased influence of private banking lobbyists who wanted to minimize federal involvement in the bank's affairs. Although the second BUS still performed some valuable services for the government without charge and remained subject (at least in theory) to department of Treasury supervision, it operated in most respects like any private corporation. And under the presidency of William Jones, a bankrupt Philadelphia merchant, it engaged in a frantic quest for profits at the expense of the public interest.

Jones encouraged wild speculation in bank stock and made no effort to curb the inflationary practices of many state banks. In the Baltimore branch of the BUS, a group of insiders—including the president, a director, and the cashier, James W. McCulloch—loaned large sums of money to themselves and their friends without adequate security, and plundered the bank's assets in other ways that reportedly cost Maryland investors between $1.7 million and $3 million. By the fall of 1818, as the country headed toward the worst depression it had yet known, Congress ordered an investigation of the bank's affairs.

Several states, responding to popular suspicion and outrage, had already moved against the local branches of the bank. In February 1818, the Maryland legislature passed a law that required all foreign banks or branches in the state to issue their notes henceforth on stamped paper supplied by the state. The cost of the stamps varied with the size of the notes, and ranged from ten cents to twenty dollars. Alternatively, a bank might make a single payment of $15,000 each year to the state, or it could go out of business. Noncompliance was costly: $500 for each note issued on unstamped paper, the money to be divided equally between the state and whoever provided the authorities with information against an offending institution. The measure went into effect on May 1, 1818.

A few days later, an informer named John James visited cashier McCulloch at his office to inquire about some recent unstamped notes that were circulating around Baltimore. McCulloch admitted that he had issued the notes in defiance of the new law. The state promptly brought suit against him in the Baltimore County Court to recover the prescribed penalties. McCulloch was found guilty and fined, and the case was appealed to Maryland's highest court, the court of appeals, on an agreed statement of facts. The pleadings raised two key questions: (1) Did Congress have the constitutional power to incorporate a bank? (2) Even if it did, was the Maryland tax law nevertheless constitutional? When the court of appeals predictably upheld the state's taxing power, the case was forwarded to the U.S. Supreme Court on a writ of error.

Oral arguments before the Marshall court began on February 22, 1819, and lasted for nine days. Aware of the importance of the case and of the intense public interest it generated, the Court waived its general rule permitting only two counsel to appear on either side. Instead, three prominent lawyers represented each party. Arguing for the bank were Daniel Webster, the magnetic orator and statesman; William Pinkney, widely regarded as the dean of the American bar; and William Wirt, the genial and erudite attorney general of the United States. The state of Maryland retained equally impressive advocates: the scholarly and incisive Joseph Hopkinson; the brilliant Walter Jones, reputed to be a legal genius; and Luther Martin, the aging but still formidable attorney general of Maryland. Throughout the arguments, spectators crowded into the small courtroom in the basement of the Capitol. "The hall was full almost to suffocation," noted Associate Justice Joseph Story, "and many went away for want of room."

On March 6, 1819, only three days after the arguments had concluded, Chief Justice John Marshall delivered the unanimous opinion of the Court. Marshall emphasized at the outset the significance of the case for future federal-state relations, and the feeling of "awful responsibility" with which the justices approached their task. He then turned to the constitutionality of the BUS, noting that its long prior history of public acceptance could not be "lightly disregarded."

Counsel for Maryland had themselves been somewhat apologetic about reopening the question, but pointed out that it had never been judicially determined. Moreover, they urged, the "necessity" that might have justified the creation of a national bank in 1791 no longer existed in 1816 because state banks were by then capable of providing the same range of fiscal services as a national bank. Since the Constitution did not expressly authorize Congress to create corporations, the only basis for the exercise of that power had to be found in the necessary-and-proper clause of Article I, Section 8. Following a long list of enumerated congressional powers, that clause declares that Congress may make "all laws which shall be necessary and proper for carrying into execution the foregoing powers." Defenders of state rights and advocates of an expansive nationalism differed vehemently over the meaning of those words.

To the Maryland lawyers, as to Jefferson back in 1791, the necessary-and-proper clause was restrictive in its effects. Although many means might be appropriate or convenient for carrying out an enumerated power of the federal government, Congress could employ only those means that were indispensably necessary to the execution of a granted power. By the Tenth Amendment, the states retained all sovereign powers that they had not expressly conferred upon the federal government in the Constitution. The power to incorporate was one such reserved power, since Congress could implement any of its enumerated powers without the help of federal corporations. As Walter Jones argued for the state of Maryland, "The power of laying and collecting taxes implies the power of regulating the mode of assessment and collection, and of appointing revenue officers but it does not imply the power of establishing a great banking corporation, branching out into every district of the country, and inundating it with a flood of paper money. To derive such a tremendous authority from implication, would be to change the subordinate into fundamental powers; to make the implied powers greater than those which are expressly granted; and to change the whole scheme and theory of the government."

Even if the necessity for a national bank were conceded, there remained the question of the branches. They, too, would have to pass the test of indispensability, and their justification was even more doubtful than that of the parent bank. The charter, it is true, authorized the federal government to establish branches, but Congress had wrongfully delegated this vital legislative power to a small group of private individuals, the directors of the bank. "Such an exercise of sovereign power should, at least, have the sanction of the sovereign legislature to vouch that the good of the whole requires it, that the necessity exists which justifies it," contended Joseph Hopkinson. "But will it be tolerated, that twenty directors of a trading corporation, having no object but profit, shall, in the pursuit of it, tread upon the sovereignty of the State; enter it without condescending to ask its leave; disregard, perhaps, the whole system of its policy; overthrow its institutions, and sacrifice its interests?"

Marshall rejected all of the state's arguments in his decision, relying instead on Hamilton's famous defense of the first BUS and on additional points raised by the bank's lawyers. To counter the compact theory of the Union advanced by the Maryland advocates of state sovereignty, Marshall briefly traced the history of the founding from a Federalist perspective. The American people, not the states, had created the Constitution, he affirmed. The old Confederation had been a mere "league" or "alliance" of sovereign states, without whose cooperation the central government could not act. But the people, wishing to form "a more perfect Union," had established a new frame of government that effectively divided sovereign power between the nation and the states. The Constitution had come into existence through the action of popular ratifying conventions that functioned independently of the state governments. "The government of the Union, then," Marshall reiterated, "is emphatically, and truly, a government of the people. In form and substance it emanates from them. Its powers are granted by them, and are to be exercised directly on them, and for their benefit."

Although the federal government was limited in its powers to those enumerated in the Constitution, its authority was supreme within its allotted sphere of action. Article VI specifically declared that the Constitution and laws of the United States were "the supreme law of the land," and must prevail over conflicting state legislation. And in carrying out its prescribed sovereign powers, Congress was entitled to employ any appropriate auxiliary powers that accompanied them by implication. The power to coin money thus carried with it the implied power to establish a mint. Such implied powers of execution always resulted from express grants of authority, Marshall suggested, and required no special constitutional justification.

Why, then, did the framers of the Constitution include the necessary-and-proper clause? Did they intend to limit Congress in the choice of means that would otherwise have been available to it for carrying out its functions? Quite the contrary, Marshall asserted. The clause represented an affirmative grant of power, an addition to the list of broad enumerated powers that preceded it in the same section. Had the framers intended it to be restrictive, they would either have placed it in a different section or phrased it in negative terms. They may well have inserted it, Marshall observed, to "remove all doubts respecting the right to legislate on that vast mass of incidental powers which must be involved in the constitution, if that instrument be not a splendid bauble."

Congress could not use its implied powers to legislate on subjects not entrusted to it by the Constitution, of course. There had to be more than a tenuous or doubtful relationship between a proposed measure and an enumerated power to satisfy constitutional criteria; otherwise, the entire federal system would be subverted, and a limited government would be transformed into an all-powerful leviathan state. The necessary-and-proper clause established the essential guidelines for responsible congressional action.

Marshall denied that the word *necessary* meant "indispensable." In common usage, it had many other meanings, he noted, including "needful," "essential," and "conducive to." The framers understood these nuances, for in Article I, Section 10, they prohibited states from levying duties on imports and exports, except those that were "absolutely necessary" for implementing state inspection laws. By omitting the qualifying term *absolutely* in the necessary-and-proper clause, the framers left Congress free to select any reasonable and plainly appropriate means for carrying out its enumerated powers. Such deference to legislative discretion insured constitutional flexibility, Marshall argued in a famous passage: "This provision is made in a constitution intended to endure for ages to come, and, consequently, to be adapted to the various *crises* of human affairs. To have prescribed the means by which government should, in all future time, execute its powers, would have been to change, entirely, the character of the instrument, and give it the properties of a legal code. It would have been an unwise attempt to provide, by immutable rules, for exigencies which, if foreseen at all, must have been seen dimly, and which can be best provided for as they occur."

In the case of the BUS, Congress had chosen to create a corporation to assist the federal government in carrying out its economic powers. The Maryland lawyers strenuously maintained that the power to incorporate was an essential element of sovereignty, a major substantive power that had been retained by the states. Marshall disagreed. There was nothing special about such a power, he insisted; every legislative act represented an exercise of sovereignty. Nor was a corporation ever created as an end in itself; it was simply a means for effecting some other object. While the framers had not directly empowered Congress to erect corporations, they had not forbidden the use of these valuable instruments when appropriate for the execution of some enumerated power. Thus, under its power to "make all needful rules and regulations" concerning the territory of the United States, Congress had established territorial governments, which were corporate bodies.

But was a national bank truly "necessary" for effectuating the fiscal operations of the federal government? Marshall made no effort to demonstrate that it was. He referred at one point to the major economic powers of Congress—to lay and collect taxes, borrow money, regulate interstate commerce, and raise and support armies and navies—but he did not relate these powers to any specific functions of the BUS. "The time has passed away when it can be necessary to enter into any discussion in order to prove the importance of this instrument, as a means to effect the legitimate objects of the government," he blandly asserted. None could deny the appropriateness of the bank at any rate, and the degree of its necessity was a matter exclusively for congressional determination. By the same reasoning, the branches, too, were constitutional, because Congress had decided they were needed for the fulfillment of the bank's "great duties." Their location was a subordinate matter that Congress had properly left in the hands of the directors.

While upholding the bank's constitutionality, Marshall made it clear that the Court would strike down any future law that attempted through the necessary-and-proper clause to deal with a subject not entrusted to the federal government. The guidelines he proposed were carefully drafted and struck an admirable balance between the extremes of states' rights and centralization: "Let the end be legitimate, let it be within the scope of the constitution, and all means which are appropriate, which are plainly adapted to that end, which are not prohibited, but consist with the letter and spirit of the constitution, are constitutional."

The Court's ruling on this phase of the case, although unacceptable to the Maryland attorneys, could scarcely have surprised them, given the prior record of legislative and popular acceptance of a national bank. Of more pressing concern was the issue of the state's taxing power, which the advocates of state sovereignty considered fundamental to the maintenance of the federal system, as they understood it. "This is the highest attribute of sovereignty, the right to raise revenue, . . . without which no other right can be held or enjoyed," argued Joseph Hopkinson. The Constitution expressly prohibited the states from taxing imports and exports, or levying tonnage duties. Otherwise, their taxing power was unlimited and coextensive with that of the federal government. In practice, both Congress and the state legislatures had long exercised a concurrent power to tax such subjects as liquor licenses and land. The bank claimed immunity from the state's general taxing power on the ground that it was a federal agency; however, the Maryland attorneys vigorously denied its public character.

"Strip it of its name," declared Hopkinson, "and we find it to be a mere association of individuals, putting their money into a common stock, to be loaned for profit, and to divide the gains. The government is a partner in the firm, for gain also; for, except a participation of the profits of the business, the government could have every other use of the bank without owning a dollar in it. It is not, then, a bank of the United States, if by that we mean an institution belonging to the government, directed by it, or in which it has a permanent indissoluble interest." Like any other private corporation, then, the bank was subject to state taxation, just as state banks had to pay a federal tax on the notes they discounted.

Marshall's reply to these contentions evaded troublesome facts through appeals to reason and "principle." The states certainly retained a general taxing power, he agreed, but only with respect to property under their jurisdiction. Federal instrumentalities were created by Congress for the benefit of all the American people, and no state could constitutionally interfere with their operations. In support of this argument, Marshall pointed to a core "principle" that permeated the entire constitutional structure: "This great principle is, that the constitution and the laws made in pursuance thereof are supreme; that they control the constitution and laws of the respective States, and cannot be controlled by them. From this, which may be almost termed an axiom, other propositions are deduced as corollaries, on the truth or error of which, and on their application to this case, the cause has been supposed to depend. These are, 1st. That a power to create implies a power to preserve. 2nd. That a power to destroy, if

wielded by a different hand, is hostile to, and incompatible with these powers to create and preserve. 3d. That where this repugnancy exists, that authority which is supreme must control, not yield to that over which it is supreme."

The Maryland tax on the notes of the BUS, thus, could not stand because it conflicted with the bank's congressional charter, the "supreme law of the land." Marshall did not examine the specific provisions of the tax measure; he did not strike it down because it was overtly confiscatory or discriminatory (although, in fact, the BUS was the only "foreign" bank doing business in Maryland). Instead, he argued that *any* state interference with the functioning of a federal agency was a usurpation of power that could eventually destroy the Union. "The power to tax involves the power to destroy," he intoned, echoing a phrase from Webster's brief. Once admit the principle of unlimited concurrent taxation, and the states would be encouraged to carry it to its logical conclusion: "If the States may tax one instrument, employed by the government in the execution of its powers, they may tax any and every other instrument. They may tax the mail; they may tax the mint; they may tax patent rights; they may tax the papers of the custom-house; they may tax judicial process; they may tax all the means employed by the government, to an excess which would defeat all the end of government. This was not intended by the American people."

Once again, Marshall ignored the evidence presented by the Maryland lawyers to show that the BUS was essentially a private profit-making corporation rather than a genuine instrument of the federal government. As he had done in the first part of his opinion, he assumed the legitimacy of the bank's public status without scrutinizing the terms of its charter. He did concede, in a somewhat curious afterthought, that the states might tax the property of the BUS in ways that did not impinge upon its daily operations. Thus, a state might impose a nondiscriminatory tax affecting the real property of the bank, along with all other land located in the state; or it might tax all corporate stock, including shares in the bank, owned by Maryland citizens. The first example is compatible with the rest of the opinion, since land is a state resource that Congress did not create. But it is difficult to see why the bank's stock, authorized by an act of Congress, would not also be considered a means of carrying out a federal power and hence entitled to the same implied immunity from any state tax. In fact, Marshall disregarded his dictum in *Weston v. City Council* (1829), in which he struck down a state tax on the holders of federal securities without inquiring whether it was discriminatory.

If the states could not tax the operations of a federal agency, how could Congress claim to tax state banks? The issue had been raised by the Maryland attorneys, and Marshall discussed it at some length, despite its irrelevance. The two situations were not analogous, he maintained. When Congress taxed state banks, it acted with the consent of the representatives of those states, and its taxes had to be uniform throughout the country. But when a state attempted to tax a federal instrumentality, no such political safeguards existed. "The difference," Marshall urged, "is that which always exists, and always must exist, between the action of the whole on a part, and the action of a part on the whole—between the laws of a government declared to be supreme, and those of a government which, when in opposition to those laws, is not supreme."

By the time the *McCulloch* decision was announced, the bank was under new management, and the worst abuses had been corrected. The congressional investigating committee had uncovered evidence of much wrongdoing and issued a report that was sharply critical of the bank's policies. It did not, however, recommend the revocation of its charter. In January 1819, a few weeks before the Supreme Court began its hearing of the *McCulloch* case, William Jones stepped down from the presidency of the BUS. His successor, Langdon Cheves, was a competent and conservative lawyer from South Carolina, who pressed for immediate reform and a thorough internal housecleaning. A flurry of resignations by bank officials ensued. According to one estimate, half of the branch-office directors resigned, and some found themselves facing charges of criminal misconduct.

In Baltimore, McCulloch, the compliant cashier, was fired and his cronies—branch

president James Buchanan and director George Williams—resigned in disgrace. The bank subsequently prosecuted them in the Maryland courts for conspiring to defraud its shareholders. William Pinkney, who had so eloquently represented the bank in the *McCulloch* case, now defended its former employees with equal success. They had merely displayed "the almost universal ambition to get forward," Pinkney explained; and the failure of their speculations had been due to external factors, such as declining foreign investment, which they could not anticipate. Had their bank stock risen in value, they "would have been looked upon as nobles, as the architects of their fortunes." Such appeals to the cult of the self-made man, combined with the legal technicalities associated with the common-law crime of conspiracy, won acquittal for Pinkney's clients on two separate occasions. Only one dissenting judge reminded the public that the defendants had in fact "taken from the funds of the office a large sum of money, which they converted to their own use," and had "failed to return to the Bank a cent of their spoil."

Ironically, the bank's cleanup efforts made matters only worse in the eyes of some states. By tightening credit and requiring specie payments from state banks, the BUS contributed to a rash of bankruptcies and mortgage foreclosures, especially in the South and West. As an immense amount of property in Cincinnati fell into the Bank's hands, the Ohio legislature moved to rid the state of the hated institution forever. In February 1819, the legislature imposed a prohibitory tax of $50,000 on each of the bank's two branches in the state, and directed the state auditor to compel payment by seizing the funds in the branch vaults, if necessary. Ignoring the *McCulloch* decision, state officials ransacked the Chillicothe branch office seven months later and carried off $100,000 in specie for deposit in the state treasury at Columbus. In *Osborn v. Bank of the United States* (1824), Marshall reaffirmed his holding in *McCulloch,* and the bank controversy died with the return of prosperity. The BUS continued under capable management until 1836, when President Andrew Jackson's bitter hostility led to the nonrenewal of its charter. Thereafter, the nation did without any national banking system until the Civil War era.

The advocates of state sovereignty correctly perceived that Marshall's expansive reading of the necessary-and-proper clause could legitimize extraordinary assertions of federal power in the future. Although *McCulloch* had little impact before the Civil War, it later played an essential role in redefining the scope of national power and justifying the emergence of the modern welfare state. In the late 1930s, the Supreme Court invoked *McCulloch* to sustain the regulatory programs of the New Deal. Three decades later, excerpts from Marshall's opinion appeared in decisions validating the Voting Rights Act of 1965 and the public accommodations provisions of the 1964 Civil Rights Act. The extreme centralization feared by advocates of states' rights has not occurred, however. Perhaps the two-party system, with its built-in bias toward conservatism and compromise, has done more than any verbal formula to preserve the spirit of moderation advocated by *McCulloch*.

In the area of intergovernmental tax immunity, the *McCulloch* legacy has been less positive. Impressed by Marshall's sweeping dictum concerning the destructive power of taxation, later Supreme Courts expanded the principle of implied immunity to encompass a bewildering variety of federal and state activities and personnel. Until the late 1930s, for example, states could not tax the salaries of federal officials; conversely, Congress could not tax the income of state authorities. Since *Graves v. New York ex rel. O'Keefe* (1939), however, the Supreme Court has promoted a more "cooperative federalism" by striking down such restrictive precedents, and judges now scrutinize carefully all new claims of immunity. Associate Justice Oliver Wendell Holmes Jr. anticipated the departure from Marshall's absolutist approach to the immunity question as early as 1928, when he observed in a dissenting opinion: "In those days it was not recognized as it is today that most of the distinctions of the law are distinctions of degree. If the States had any power it was assumed that they had all power, and that the necessary alternative was to deny it altogether. . . . The power to tax is not the power to destroy while this Court sits."

Selected Bibliography

Beveridge, Albert J. *The Life of John Marshall.* 4 vols. Boston: Houghton Mifflin, 1916–1919.

Currie, David P. *The Constitution in the Supreme Court: The First Hundred Years, 1789–1888.* Chicago: University of Chicago Press, 1985.

Franz, Patricia L. "Ohio v. The Bank: An Historical Examination of *Osborn v. The Bank of the United States.*" *Journal of Supreme Court History* 23 (1999): 112–137.

Gunther, Gerald, ed. *John Marshall's Defense of McCulloch v. Maryland.* Stanford, CA: Stanford University Press, 1969.

Hammond, Bray. *Banks and Politics in America from the Revolution to the Civil War.* Princeton, NJ: Princeton University Press, 1957.

Hobson, Charles F., ed. *The Papers of John Marshall.* Vol. 8. Chapel Hill: University of North Carolina Press, 1995.

Johnson, Herbert A. *The Chief Justiceship of John Marshall, 1801–1835.* Columbia: University of South Carolina Press, 1997.

Pious, Harold J., and Gordon E. Baker. "*McCulloch v. Maryland*: Right Principle, Wrong Case." *Stanford Law Review* 9 (July 1957): 710–730.

Smith, Walter B. *Economic Aspects of the Second Bank of the United States.* Cambridge, MA: Harvard University Press, 1953.

White, G. Edward. *The Marshall Court and Cultural Change, 1815–35.* New York: Macmillan, 1988.

Judicial Review of State Court Decisions: Yet Another Round

—◁◦▷—

Richard E. Ellis

Department of History
State University of New York at Buffalo

Cohens v. Virginia, 6 Wheaton 264 (1821) [U.S. Supreme Court]

◁◦▷ THE CASE IN BRIEF ◁◦▷

Date
  1821

Location
  Virginia
  District of Columbia

Court
  U.S. Supreme Court

Principal Participants
  Philip I. and Mendes Cohen
  Chief Justice John Marshall
  Virginia Gov. Thomas Mann Randolph

Significance of the Case
  The sale of Washington, D.C.-based lottery tickets in Virginia raised a Supreme Court review of states' decisions, and held that the court is the final arbiter in conflicts between states and the federal government.

The constitutionality of Section 25 of the Judiciary Act of 1789 and the right of the U.S. Supreme Court to act as the final arbiter in disputes between the federal and state governments was the source of constant controversy in the years between the adoption of the Constitution and the Civil War. Although the Supreme Court had forcefully dealt with these questions in *Martin v. Hunter's Lessee* (1816) and *McCulloch v. Maryland* (1819), several states rejected these decisions as dangerously nationalist in their implications, and the matter remained unsettled for many years. Despite this opposition, Chief Justice Marshall refused to back down. When the important case of *Cohens v. Virginia* (1821) arose, he took the opportunity to restate in very strong terms the High Court's claim to have jurisdiction and to be the ultimate court of appeals in controversies between the central government and the states that involved the powers of the federal government.

The case began when Philip I. and Mendes Cohen were tried, convicted, and fined a hundred dollars by the quarter sessions court of the borough of Norfolk for selling lottery tickets in violation of a Virginia law prohibiting the sale of any such tickets not authorized by the state. The Cohen brothers appealed the decision to the U.S. Supreme Court under Section 25 of the Judiciary of 1789. They argued that their lottery had been incorporated in Washington, D.C., under an act of Congress, which made it a national lottery not bound by state laws. The case immediately took on national significance when a number of prominent attorneys issued a public statement in support of the Cohens' claim that national corporations were exempt from state restrictions. Their argument had profound nationalist implications: "It would indeed, be a strange anomaly, if what Congress had created, or authorized to be created, in a valid manner, . . . could be considered and treated by a state as the subject of a criminal traffic; . . . The power of the union, constitutionally executed, knows no locality within the boundaries of the union, and can encounter no geographical impediments; its march is through the union, or it is nothing but a name. The states have no existence relative to the effect of the powers delegated to congress save only where their assent or instrumentality is required, or permitted, by the constitution itself."

The case raised, once again, the contentious question of the right of the U.S. Supreme Court to review acts of state legislatures and the decisions of state courts. Responding to a summons by John Marshall that "cited and admonished" the state to appear before the Supreme Court in the case of *Cohens v. Virginia*, the governor of Virginia, Thomas Mann Randolph, raised the matter in his annual address to the legislature in late 1820. The legislature proceeded to issue a special report and a series of resolutions that denied the authority of the Supreme Court to hear the case. The report restated the principles laid down in the Kentucky and Virginia resolutions: the Constitution was the product of a compact made by the states in 1787–1788. It denied that the Supreme Court was either the exclusive or final arbiter of constitutional disputes. It reiterated the belief, particularly prevalent in the Old Dominion, that the federal and state governments represented distinct and completely separate sovereignties. It argued the position taken by the Virginia Court

of Appeals in *Hunter v. Martin, Devisees of Fairfax* (1815) that the Supreme Court did not have the power to abrogate the judgments of state tribunals: "The word "*supreme*" is descriptive of the federal tribunal, is relative, not absolute; and evidently implies that the supremacy bestowed upon the supreme court is *over the inferior courts to be ordained and established by congress*; and not *over the state courts*."

The case was heard in February 1821. The lawyers for Virginia were instructed by the legislature to confine their arguments exclusively to the jurisdictional question. They asserted Virginia's sovereignty and denied the authority of the Supreme Court to hear the case. They also claimed that the Eleventh Amendment prohibited the federal courts from taking jurisdiction in a case without the state's explicit permission. The attorneys for the Cohen brothers, on the other hand, stressed the precedent established in *Martin v. Hunter's Lessee*. They argued that the people, not the states, had created the Constitution, and that federal judicial control over state encroachments was absolutely necessary if the Union were to be maintained.

Two weeks later, on March 3, 1821, Marshall handed down his decision for a unanimous Court. It was a particularly eloquent restatement and elaboration of the basic principles of constitutional nationalism that had been enunciated in *Martin v. Hunter's Lessee*:

> The American States as well as the American people, have believed a close and firm Union to be essential to their liberty and to their happiness. They have been taught by experience, that the Union cannot exist without a government for the whole; and they have been taught by the same experience that this government would be a mere shadow, that must disappoint all their hopes, unless invested with large portions of that sovereignty which belongs to independent states. Under the influence of this opinion and thus instructed by experience, the American people, in the conventions of their respective states, adopted the present constitution. . . .
>
> This is the authoritative language of the American people, and, if gentlemen please, of the American States. It marks, with lines too strong to be mistaken, the characteristic distinction between the government of the Union

and those of the states. The general government, though limited as to its objects, is supreme with respect to those objects. This principle is a part of the constitution; and if there be any who deny its necessity, none can deny its authority.

Marshall argued that the jurisdiction of the Supreme Court depended on the nature of the cause and not upon the particular forum in which it was heard on the lower level. This included all cases in law and equity, under the Constitution, laws of the federal government, and treaties of the United States. "America," he pointed out, "has chosen to be, in many respects, and to many purposes, a nation; and for all these purposes, her government is complete; to all these objects it is competent. The people have declared, that in the exercise of all powers given for these objects it is supreme. It can, then, in effecting these objects legitimately control all individuals or governments within the American territory."

Marshall took explicit issue with Virginia's argument that the federal and state courts were distinct and that no appeal existed from state court decisions to the U.S. Supreme Court. Marshall responded that this would lead to chaos. He argued "the necessity of uniformity, as well as correctness in expounding the constitution and laws of the United States, would itself suggest the propriety of vesting in some single tribunal the power of deciding, in the last resort, all cases in which they are involved." Finally, Marshall dismissed Virginia's claim that the Eleventh Amendment exempted the state from federal jurisdiction in this case. The chief justice pointed out that the present action had been initiated by the state against individuals, not the other way around, and that therefore Virginia could not claim immunity under the Eleventh Amendment.

Having used broad nationalist principles to sustain the jurisdiction of the Supreme Court in *Cohens v. Virginia*, the Court proceeded to hear the case on its merits. The central question was whether the act of Congress authorizing a lottery in the District of Columbia had created a truly national corporation with the power to operate within individual states without their permission. Marshall argued that this raised two basic questions: what was the intent of Congress when it passed the law, and was it constitutional? Marshall, again for a unanimous court, ruled that no evidence existed to indicate that Congress intended to create a national lottery or to authorize the sale of lottery tickets in states where they had been declared illegal. This was an important sop to Virginia, but it was not entirely satisfactory to the proponents of states' rights. For Marshall had only ruled that the particular act under question had not created a national lottery. He did not confront the more fundamental issue of whether Congress had the constitutional right to use its powers to legislate for the District of Columbia to create national corporations, immune from state regulations, because at this point it was "merely speculative." But the implication was clear: carefully constructed legislation for the District of Columbia could be used to create national corporations. As Marshall observed, "The act incorporating the city of Washington is unquestionably, of universal obligation; but the extent of the corporate powers conferred by that act, is to be determined by those considerations which belong to the case."

The decision was denounced in Virginia. Spencer Roane took the lead. He believed the Cohens decision "negatives the idea that the American states have a real existence, or are to be considered in any sense, as sovereign and independent states." He attacked federal judicial review of state decisions and the doctrine of implied powers as undermining the concept of true federalism through the idea that the states were subordinate to the national government. He argued "if this power of decision is once conceded to either party, the equilibrium established by the Constitution is destroyed, and the compact exists thereafter but in name." Strong support for this point of view came from John Taylor whose book *Tyranny Unmasked* (1822) denounced the Supreme Court because its decisions consolidated power in the hands of the national government, and because it had become a spokesman for a moneyed aristocracy by defending corporations and special privileges. Thomas Jefferson privately encouraged Roane and Taylor to keep up their assault on the Court and excoriated the *Cohens* decision for being mainly "extra-judicial" in its nationalist pronouncements. The Court, he claimed, could have simply decided the case on its merits and refrained from engaging in its exposition of the origins and nature of the Union. He believed the Court had acted as "an irresponsible body," in order to usurp power from the states and to create a "consolidated government." James Madison, on the other hand, was more restrained. Although he recognized that "the Court had a definite disposition to amplify the authorities of the Union at the expense of the states," he indicated that in matters of conflict between the states and the federal government, the Supreme Court should be the final arbiter, and he declined to get involved in the conflict.

Reacting to these criticisms, Marshall observed, "In Virginia the tendency of things verges rapidly to the destruction of the government." This was an overreaction by the chief justice. Although Virginia's denunciation of the various nationalist decisions handed down by the Supreme Court in the second decade of the nineteenth century, and especially in *Cohens v. Virginia*, was strident and aggressive, it never threatened to get beyond the level of sharp intellectual debate. It was never suggested that the authority of the federal government should be obstructed or forcibly resisted. Roane, at the beginning of his "Algernon Sydney" essays, which spearheaded the attack on the Court's decision in *Cohens v. Virginia*, stated, "I ask from you no revolutions, but what consists in the preservation of an excellent Constitution. I require from you no insurrection, but that of a frequent recurrence to fundamental principles."

The most basic issue raised in the debate between the proponents of states' rights in the Old Dominion and the Supreme Court was the nationalist claim that the Court should be the final arbiter in conflicts between the federal government and the states. In denying this authority to the Court, Roane, Taylor, Jefferson, and others raised a number of extremely important questions that even today are not amenable to easy answers. Because this power was not explicitly provided for in the Constitution, where did it come from? Should the Su-

preme Court be allowed to arrogate this power to itself? What exactly was the relationship of the Court to the will of the people, especially since its members were appointed for life tenure during good behavior and were removable only by resignation, death, or impeachment? Was it proper for the Court to hold its discussions in secret and to hide internal dissent by handing down unanimous decisions? Most important of all, states' rights advocates doubted the Supreme Court could be an impartial arbiter in disputes between the federal government and the states. Because the Court was a creature of the Constitution and a part of the federal government itself, they believed that by increasing the powers of the central government, the Court would be increasing its own powers.

The controversy over Section 25 of the Judiciary Act of 1789 and the Supreme Court's claim to be the final arbiter in federal-state disputes was not settled by *Cohens v. Virginia*. The dispute raged throughout the first half of the nineteenth century, and the matter was finally resolved only when the proponents of states' rights, as well as the South, was vanquished in the Civil War. At this point, Marshall's decision in *Cohens v. Virginia* provided not only a significant precedent but also some very important arguments that were used to undergird a nationalist interpretation of the nature of the Union.

Selected Bibliography

Beveridge, Albert J. *The Life of John Marshall*. 4 vols. Boston: Houghton Mifflin, 1916–1919.

Haines, Charles Grove. *The Role of the Supreme Court in American Government and Politics, 1789–1835*. Berkeley: University of California Press, 1944.

Luce, W. Ray. "The Cohen Brothers of Baltimore: From Lotteries to Banking." *Maryland Historical Magazine* 68 (Fall 1973): 288–308.

Warren, Charles. "Legislative and Judicial Attacks on the Supreme Court of the United States: A History of the Twenty-Fifth Section of the Judiciary Act." *American Law Review* 47 (1913): 1–34, 161–89.

White, G. Edward. *The Marshall Court and Cultural Change, 1815–1835*. New York: Macmillan, 1988.

Federalism Writ Large:
The Eleventh Amendment and
State Sovereign Immunity

Thomas E. Baker

School of Law
Drake University

Alden v. Maine, 527 U.S. 706 (1999) [U.S. Supreme Court]

◄○► THE CASE IN BRIEF ◄○►

Date
  1999

Location
  Florida
  Maine
  District of Columbia

Court
  U.S. Supreme Court

Principal Participants
  Probation Officers
  Justice Anthony Kennedy

Significance of the Case
  Sovereign immunity was upheld by the
  Supreme Court in three 1999 cases that
  argued the implications of federalism and
  the Eleventh Amendment.

The leitmotif of the Rehnquist court has been an emphasis on constitutional separation of powers and federalism. It appears to be part of the Rehnquist court's interpretative enterprise to return to the original understanding of the framers, designers of a complicated and nuanced system of checks and balances to limit government powers in order to protect individual rights.

Two examples illustrate the depth and breadth of this development. In *New York v. United States* (1992), the Court held that Congress did not have the constitutional power to compel the states to pass laws to dispose of radioactive waste generated within their borders. In *Printz v. United States* (1997), the Court held that Congress did not have the constitutional power to require local law-enforcement officers to perform background checks on prospective purchasers of handguns. These decisions stand for the rather unremarkable principle that Congress cannot commandeer a state's legislative or executive branch to enact or administer federal regulations. This principle has been extended by analogy to a favorite technique of legislative indirection often practiced by Congress—that is, to pass a federal statute authorizing private individuals to sue states to enforce federal mandates through private lawsuits.

Some of the most important federalism decisions have involved the Eleventh Amendment to the U.S. Constitution and state sovereign immunity from lawsuits. *Sovereign immunity* is the modern legal understanding that a government may not be sued without its consent; it derives from the medieval idea that the king ruled by divine right and, therefore, could do no wrong and was unanswerable to his subjects for anything he did as king. In *Seminole Tribe v. Florida* (1996), the Court ruled that a state's sovereign immunity provided a complete defense against a federal action, brought by an Indian tribe asserting federal claims, because Congress cannot subject the states to a private suit in federal court when it passes laws under Article I of the Constitution. In *Kimel v. Florida Board of Regents* (2000), the Court held that states are immune and cannot be sued under the federal Age Discrimination in Employment Act. Although Congress has the power to abrogate state immunity for violations of the Fourteenth Amendment, the Court ruled in *Kimel* that the Age Discrimination Act was not a proper exercise of that congressional power.

In a series of three conceptually related cases announced the final day of the 1998 term—each decided by the same 5-4 lineup of justices—the Court revisited the issue of state sovereign immunity under the Eleventh Amendment. In the first case, *College Savings Bank v. Florida Prepaid Postsecondary Education Expense Board* (1999), the Court ruled that a state had not constructively waived its sovereign immunity by simply engaging in for-profit competitive practices that allegedly violated a federal regulatory statute. In the second case, *Florida Prepaid Postsecondary Education Expense Board v. College Savings Bank* (1999), the Court reasoned that the state's sovereign immunity provided a complete defense to a patent infringement suit for private money damages in federal court, and it went on to conclude that Congress had

exceeded its constitutional powers to attempt by statute to authorize such suits.

The third and the most far-reaching of the three cases was *Alden v. Maine* (1999), which extended the concept of constitutional sovereign immunity to a suit brought in state court. The case involved Maine's alleged failure to comply with the federal Fair Labor Standards Act. State probation officers sued in state court for overtime pay and damages under the federal statute. The state trial court dismissed the suit, and the Maine Supreme Judicial Court affirmed. The majority of the U.S. Supreme Court affirmed the dismissal of the suit on the ground of sovereign immunity. This was a matter of first impression, the first time the issue had been squarely presented to the High Court.

Justice Anthony Kennedy's majority opinion was joined by Chief Justice William Rehnquist and Justices Sandra Day O'Connor, Antonin Scalia, and Clarence Thomas. Kennedy returned to the writings of Alexander Hamilton, James Madison, and John Marshall to determine that immunity from private lawsuits was understood by the founding generation to be a fundamental attribute of state sovereignty that predated the Constitution; moreover, the preservation of that immunity was a basic assumption of those who ratified the Constitution. In *Chisholm v. Georgia* (1793), decided just five years after ratification, the Supreme Court ruled that Article III of the Constitution authorized a private citizen of one state to sue another state in federal court. The Eleventh Amendment was immediately proposed and promptly ratified to overrule this unpopular decision. The Eleventh Amendment prohibits federal courts from hearing "any suit in law or equity, commenced or prosecuted against one of the Untied States by Citizens of another State." In *Hans v. Louisiana* (1890), the Supreme Court held that a suit by a citizen of a state against his own state would likewise be prohibited in federal court, even though the express language of the amendment does not say so. The *Alden* majority reasoned that this longstanding precedent evidenced an extra-textual quality to sovereign immunity—that is, the constitutional concept went beyond the specific wording of the Eleventh Amendment.

The majority interpreted the Eleventh Amendment's text and history to have the purpose of fully restoring the original constitutional design. Furthermore, the *Alden* majority read long-standing Supreme Court precedents as establishing that sovereign immunity derives not from the Eleventh Amendment, but is part of the structure of the original Constitution. Consequently, the states' immunity from private lawsuits in their own state courts cannot be abrogated by the exercise of any congressional power in Article I.

Justice Kennedy's opinion in *Alden* drew from history, practice, precedent, and the Constitution's organization and structure. It concluded that Congress does not have the power to abrogate a state's immunity in the state's own courts. Such, Kennedy submitted, was the original understanding. This historical analysis is supported by early congressional practice and the theory and reasoning of nineteenth-century Supreme Court cases. A review of the essential principles of federalism and the essential role the states play in the constitutional design persuaded the majority that such a congressional power would be inconsistent with our constitutional system. The Eleventh Amendment thus serves to reinforce the Tenth Amendment's reservation of state sovereign powers. Otherwise, lawsuits could transform the states into debtors and subject the state treasury to the power of private citizens. That could threaten the financial integrity of state governments and undo the political accountability of state officials.

The *Alden* majority went on to explain that sovereign immunity did not confer on the states a power to disregard the Constitution or evade otherwise valid federal laws. The proper balance between the supremacy of federal law and the separate sovereignty of the states, however, is struck in the doctrine of sovereign immunity itself. For example, a state may consent to be sued. In fact, many states have consented to be sued under state statutes. Furthermore, sovereign immunity bars suits for money damages against the states but not against lesser entities such as cities. Nor does it bar suits against state officers for injunctive and declaratory relief in their capacities as individual persons. Finally, the Eleventh Amendment does not bar a suit brought by the government of the United States against a state.

Because the plaintiffs were private individuals seeking damages from the state of Maine and because Maine had not waived its sovereign immunity, the majority held that, under the U.S. Constitution, the lawsuit against the state could not go forward. The state probation officers could not sue Maine under the federal statute, not even in state courts. This holding seems to be complete and absolute: under the Constitution, a state may never be sued in state court without its consent.

Justice David Souter, joined by Justices John Paul Stevens, Ruth Bader Ginsburg, and Stephen Breyer, dissented in *Alden.* At the outset of his opinion, Souter put forward the dissenters' position in stark terms: "[o]n each point the Court has raised it is mistaken." Souter sought to cast doubt on the zeal with which the majority had invoked principles of federalism in this and other recent cases. Indeed, he insisted that the very concept of sovereign immunity is a constitutional anachronism: it should be considered anathema to American constitutionalism, which is based on the idea of limited government and federal supremacy. He referred to prior dissenting opinions (some of which he had written), suggesting that he and his like-minded Supreme Court brethren would not yield to the majority in this or in future cases. His canvass of the historical record persuaded him that the framers were suspicious and downright hostile to the idea of sovereign immunity. Souter's dissent predicted that *Alden* and other controverted, recent separation-of-powers decisions will be abandoned in future cases.

The upshot of these federalism cases seems to be that Congress cannot simply legislate individual federal entitlements against the states and turn lose private plaintiffs to enforce them by bringing suits against the states in federal or state court. Rather, Congress will be obliged to commit federal resources to prosecuting cases against the states in the name of the United States and on behalf of individuals whose rights are being enforced.

Federalism may mean all things to all people, but to the Rehnquist Court it is an essential principle of American constitutionalism. The justices do have strong disagreements, however, about what federalism implies for the states and nation in particular cases. In their sovereign immunity decisions, the majority believe the Court's role is to maintain the eighteenth-century balance between federal and state power, not merely for the sake of balance or form and not to protect the states against the Congress, but rather for the sake of individual freedom and liberty. In their dissents, the minority justices are equally adamant that the majority has ahistorically and injudiciously miscalibrated the federal-state balance to the profound detriment of individual suitors and congressional powers.

The Rehnquist court's recent federalism decisions call into question a host of federal statutes and regulations currently on the books that affect the states. As a result, we can reasonably expect that, over the next several terms, the docket of the Supreme Court will serve as a forum for litigants, lawyers, and lower court judges to test the justices' structural resolve about federalism. One thing is certain: the larger debate over the relations between the federal government and the states and the proper role of the Supreme Court will go on, as it has throughout American constitutional history.

A decision in February 2001 bore out the prediction regarding the Rehnquist Court's treatment of federalism advanced in the previous paragraph. In *University of Alabama v. Garrett* (2001), with the same 5-4 alignment as in *Alden v. Maine*, the majority held that the Eleventh Amendment prevents suits by state employees, brought pursuant to the 1990 Americans with Disabilities Act (ADA), against agencies of their own state government. The majority opinion, not surprisingly written by Chief Justice Rehnquist, found that the legislative history of the ADA did not present evidence that state agencies had engaged in sufficiently demonstrable patterns of discrimination against persons with disabilities to overcome the state immunity from lawsuits by citizens normally protected by the Eleventh Amendment. By contrast, the dissent by Justice Breyer in *Garrett* raised many of the same complaints about the Court's reading of the Eleventh Amendment that had been enunciated in Justice Souter's dissent in *Alden v. Maine*. Thus, as the Court entered the new century, a small but clear majority maintained a view of federalism that it believed to be consistent with the original understanding of the Eleventh Amendment.

Selected Bibliography

Jacobs, Clyde, *The Eleventh Amendment and Sovereign Immunity.* Westport: Greenwood, 1972.

Orth, John V., *The Judicial Power of the United States: The Eleventh Amendment in American History.* New York: Oxford University Press, 1986.

Rappaport, Michael B. "Reconciling Textualism and Federalism: The Proper Textual Basis of the Supreme Court's Tenth and Eleventh Amendment Decisions." *Northwestern University Law Review* 93 (1999): 819–875.

"Federalism: State Sovereign Immunity in State Court." *Harvard Law Review* 113 (1999): 200–213.

Judicial Procedure

A Rebuke to the Court

Robert S. Lambert

Emeritus Professor of History
Clemson University

Chisholm v. Georgia, 1 Dallas, 419 (1793)
[U.S. Supreme Court]

⟨o⟩ THE CASE IN BRIEF ⟨o⟩

Date
1793, 1798

Location
Georgia
District of Columbia

Court
U.S. Supreme Court

Principal Participants
Alexander Chisholm
U.S. Attorney General Edmund Randolf
Chief Justice John Jay

Significance of the Case
A South Carolina lawyer's attempt to collect a war debt from Georgia won in an appeal to the Supreme Court, spurring an immediate action by Congress to enact the Eleventh Amendment to the Constitution.

Chisholm v. Georgia was the first important decision handed down by the U.S. Supreme Court under the newly adopted Constitution. Reaction to the decision was unfavorable and led almost immediately to the adoption of a constitutional amendment to set aside the Court's interpretation of a portion of the federal judicial power granted by the Constitution.

During the American Revolution, agents of the state of Georgia had purchased clothing, blankets, and other items from Robert Farquhar, a merchant of Charleston, South Carolina. Farquhar delivered the merchandise but did not receive payment for the goods. After Farquhar's death in 1784, his executor, Alexander Chisholm of Charleston, acting for a minor heir, sought payment from the Georgia legislature. That body rejected Chisholm's claim because the state had already paid its agents for the goods. Unable to collect from the agents, who were dead or bankrupt, Chisholm then sought redress in the newly established federal courts.

The Constitutional Convention of 1787 had conferred upon the federal courts jurisdiction over "Controversies . . . between a State and Citizens of another State; . . . and between a State, or the Citizens thereof, and foreign States, Citizens or Subjects." Inserted by its committee of detail in its report to the full convention, that body approved, with little debate, the specific provision for jurisdiction between states and citizens of other states.

In contrast, the laws of the states generally followed the long-established principle in English law of "sovereign immunity," which held that the ruler could not be sued without his consent. Despite their claims of popular sovereignty, and the absence of a king, the American states had adopted this doctrine for themselves after independence. While the states rarely permitted suits against themselves, suits against individual officials were usually accepted by state courts.

Nevertheless, proposals to change the jurisdiction of the federal courts were not among the constitutional amendments that the First Congress approved and sent to the states for ratification.

In February 1791, Alexander Chisholm sued Georgia (*Farquhar's Executor v. Georgia*) in the U.S. Circuit Court for the District of Georgia to recover the debt, the equivalent of $169,633.33 in greatly inflated Continental currency, and damages. The court, consisting of Justice James Iredell of the Supreme Court and a district judge, rejected the suit on grounds that a state could not be sued by a citizen of another state.

Chisholm then turned to the U.S. Supreme Court, filing an action in assumpsit, a contractual remedy, to recover $500,000 from Georgia. When Georgia was ordered to appear at the August 1792 term, it refused to attend, and the Court postponed action until its next term. In February 1793, *Chisholm v. Georgia* was argued before the Court. Although Georgia again refused to appear, the Court handed down its decision two weeks later.

Edmund Randolph, Attorney General of the United States, presented the case for the plaintiff. He argued that under the Constitution and the Judiciary Act of 1789, the Court had jurisdiction over suits by a citizen of one state against another state. The Court apparently accepted this argument, because by a 4-1 margin,

in separate written opinions, it found for Chisholm, and ordered the state to show cause at the next term why the judgment should not be carried out.

The members of the Supreme Court, all appointed by President George Washington, had supported the adoption of the Constitution and were adherents of the emerging Federalist party. Chief Justice John Jay of New York was a strong nationalist and critic of state sovereignty; James Wilson, as a member of the Constitutional Convention and its committee of detail that framed the judicial article, had advocated greatly increased powers for the central government; and former state judges John Blair of Virginia and William Cushing of Massachusetts were consistent, if less conspicuous, nationalists. Justice James Iredell, a moderate Federalist from North Carolina who had participated in the judgment against Chisholm in the circuit court, was the dissenter.

For Jay, the language of the preamble to the Constitution was sufficient. In "We the people of the United States," he found clear evidence that the United States was a nation of individuals and not a group of sovereign states. In addition, the provision that the new government was to "establish justice" marked clearly for Jay the path of duty for the federal judiciary. It was Wilson's view that after independence was declared, the sovereignty of the Crown had passed directly to the people of the whole country; since the adoption of the Constitution, the states existed merely for certain limited and local purposes. The concurring opinions of Blair and Cushing, while less philosophical and sweeping, also found ample constitutional justification for federal jurisdiction over the *Chisholm* suit.

Justice Iredell's dissent was important because of the subsequent action by Congress to negate the effect of the majority opinion. Although a member of the Constitutional Convention and a supporter of ratification, Iredell certainly was aware that his own North Carolina had only belatedly ratified the Constitution and that state rights' sentiment remained strong there. His opinion took the ground that it was up to Congress to implement the powers granted by the Constitution. But, because Congress had failed to give specific authority for the federal judiciary to hear cases against states by outside individuals, the states retained jurisdiction over such suits.

When the *Chisholm* decision was rendered, Georgia was ordered to appear or be judged in default. Counsel for the state did appear in February 1794, but the Court ruled unanimously, Iredell absent, that judgment be entered and a jury be impaneled at the next term to assess damages. Because the issue had entered the political arena, however, the execution of the judgment was postponed each term until cleared from the Court's docket in 1798.

Congress reacted quickly to the *Chisholm* decision. A constitutional amendment to void it was actually introduced in the Senate two days after the judgment was delivered, but it was not acted upon in the closing days of the Second Congress. In the nine months that passed before the Third Congress convened, a number of state legislatures passed resolutions urging their members of Congress to seek a constitutional amendment to negate the decision. Displaying remarkable unity in a period of intense and rising partisanship, the Senate, by a vote of 23-2, and the House of Representatives, by a vote of 81-9, agreed on a proposed amendment and sent it to the states for ratification. Its language was unequivocal: "The judicial power of the United States shall not be construed to extend to any suit in law or equity, commenced or prosecuted against one of the United States by Citizens of another State, or by Citizens or Subjects of a Foreign State," and was a clear rebuke to the majority in the *Chisholm* decision. Despite the very slow communications of that time, within less than a year the legislatures of twelve of the existing fifteen states ratified what became the Eleventh Amendment. Some states were slow to certify their action on the amendment, and it did not go into effect until 1798.

This quick overturning of the Court's position showed that the *Chisholm* decision had violated the generally understood place of the states in the federal system created by the Constitution. Ten members of Congress who had been delegates to the Constitutional Convention voted for the Eleventh Amendment. The overwhelming vote against the Court's interpretation demonstrated more than mere sympathy for Georgia; suits by outsiders and foreigners against six other states were awaiting adjudication before the Supreme Court when it handed down the *Chisholm* decision.

The adoption of the Eleventh Amendment had the immediate effect of removing the pending suits against states from the Court's docket. The prestige of the Court was not enhanced by its obvious inability to enforce its own decisions, although its ruling in the *Chisholm* case may have energized some states to seek settlements with claimants. The assumption of most state debts by Congress in the early 1790s and agreements made with Great Britain under the Jay Treaty had already sharply reduced the likelihood that further suits would be brought by outside claimants against states in the federal courts.

Nevertheless, the long-run effect of the Eleventh Amendment was less restrictive than might be supposed. In the first place, Iredell's opinion in the *Chisholm* case merely stated that Congress had failed to authorize the specific contractual remedy sought. More importantly, under the leadership of John Marshall in the early nineteenth century, the Supreme Court rendered several decisions that narrowed the scope of the Eleventh Amendment. In *Cohens v. Virginia* (1821), it held that an individual convicted in a state court did not violate the Eleventh Amendment by removing his or her case to the Supreme Court in order to challenge the constitutionality of the state law in question. In particular, cases involving state laws adversely affecting private property rights, such as *Fletcher v. Peck* (1810), might be heard in federal courts if such laws violated the constitutional restriction that "no State shall pass any . . . Law impairing the Obligation of Contracts." And a suit against a state official was allowed in *Osborn v. Bank of the United States* (1824) because, on the record, the state of Ohio was not an actual party in the case.

As for the effort to recover what Robert Farquhar was owed, his son-in-law, Daniel Trezevant, accepted Georgia securities in 1794 as a settlement in full of the claim. However, Trezevant failed to cash all the securities in the time permitted by law, and it was not until 1847 that the Georgia legislature finally redeemed the remainder.

Selected Bibliography

Jacobs, Clyde E. "Prelude to Amendment: The States before the Court." *American Journal of Legal History* 12 (1968): 19–40.

Mathis, Doyle. "*Chisholm v. Georgia*: Background and Settlement." *Journal of American History* 54 (1967): 19–29.

Mathis, Doyle. "The Eleventh Amendment: Adoption and Interpretation." *Georgia Law Review* 2 (1968): 207–245.

Morris, Richard B. *John Jay, the Nation, and the Court.* Boston: Boston University Press, 1967.

California Rejects the Mandatory Conciliation Formerly Required under Mexican Law

David J. Langum

Cumberland School of Law
Samford University

Von Schmidt v. Huntington, 1 Cal. 55 (1850) [California Supreme Court]

—◦— THE CASE IN BRIEF —◦—

Date
  1850

Location
  California

Court
  California Supreme Court

Principal Participants
  Employees of a California mining
    company
  Finance committee of the same
    company

Significance of the Case
  A California court overruled the Mexican
  legal practice of conciliation in Mexican
  land incorporated into the United States
  after the Mexican War. This effectively
  halted alternative dispute resolution in the
  mid-nineteenth century.

Currently, there is a national effort to seek methods of dispute resolution that are alternative to the traditional adversarial trial before judge and jury. This is an attempt, first, to relieve overcrowded court dockets and, second, to find less socially costly ways to resolve disagreements and compensate injuries. But there is also the belief that a technique that permits direct input of the disputants themselves, without the direction and control of attorneys, will result in a more psychologically satisfying resolution of disputes. This, in turn, will result in greater compliance with the resolution than happens in the case of a court-ordered judgment.

One of the alternative dispute-resolution techniques being considered in the United States is mandatory conciliation. In fact, in some jurisdictions and under certain conditions, it has been imposed on litigants. It is ironic in light of this current interest that over one hundred and fifty years ago a region of the country, which was then generally regarded as backward, required formal conciliation before litigation could be commenced. That region was the Mexican borderlands, which were incorporated into the United States through the Treaty of Guadalupe Hidalgo that followed the Mexican War.

Conciliation is a process that is often confused with arbitration, but which has its own procedures and history. *Arbitration* is a referral by disputants to some persons or agency, other than a court, to decide a dispute. The full power of the courts, including the processes of execution and garnishment, stand behind an arbitrator's decision.

Arbitrations are sometimes the result of a contractual agreement made before the particular dispute arose. At other times, they are the result of a submission made by the parties after they find themselves in conflict. Sometimes parties empower arbitrators to make whatever orders seem just and fair to resolve a particular dispute, and at other times the arbitral submission limits the arbitrators to issue only such orders as a judge would compose acting solely under statutes and legal precedent. Although styles and procedures of arbitration vary, the gist of the process is the voluntary submission of a dispute, by the disputants, to an agency or persons other than courts for a final, binding, and enforceable solution to their disagreement.

Conciliation, on the other hand, attempts to avoid litigation by a process designed to induce the disputants to settle their differences voluntarily. As such, submitting to conciliation, as opposed to arbitration, is never final and is never binding or enforceable, unless, as a distinct and further voluntary step, the parties agree to adopt a conciliation suggestion as their own settlement. Conciliation submissions may be made to agencies selected by a court or to persons selected by the disputants. Even ordinary judges can act as conciliators. If they do, however, it is understood that their suggestions for settlement are recommendations only, because the gist of conciliation is that no forthcoming recommendation for settlement, regardless of who makes it, is binding or forced on the parties until and unless they voluntarily agree to accept the recommendation.

Because the basis of conciliation is voluntary agreement, at first glance the idea of mandatory conciliation may seem like an oxymoron. But it is not. Mandatory conciliation refers to a legally imposed procedure whereby conciliation is attempted. Under a system of mandatory conciliation, the disputants may be required, under threat of various sanctions, to participate in a nonjudicial hearing where third persons listen to the facts of the dispute and then make recommendations for settlement. But if it is to be a true conciliation process and not arbitration, either of the disputants may refuse the suggestion and demand a formal judicial hearing. When a required conciliation process proves unsuccessful, any party—usually the plaintiff—may then file a formal lawsuit.

Mandatory conciliation was practiced widely in the nineteenth century throughout the Mexican borderlands. It disposed of a large majority of all litigation, perhaps as high as 85 percent. Conciliation had entered the Hispanic world through a statute of the Spanish Cortes in 1812, which was influenced by similar legislation in revolutionary France. When Mexico became independent, its constitution required conciliation as a necessary step before filing a lawsuit. No detailed procedures were spelled out in this 1824 constitution, but a statute of 1837 provided for the steps to be followed. Although very few persons in the borderlands had formally studied law, the lay judges did follow these procedures reasonably well.

When a person had a dispute with another, he or she would first go to the local town judge, called at different times the *alcalde* or the *juez de paz* (justice of the peace). The *juez* would summon the other party and order both plaintiff and defendant to appear at a specified time, under penalty of a fine for nonappearance. The judge would further order each party to select and bring an *hombre bueno*, or good man, to serve as a conciliator. These *hombres buenos* were not advocates, and their function was to provide a community input into the dispute-resolution process, not to advance the interest of the party who had selected him.

The two parties, the two *hombres buenos,* and the *juez* would gather together and informally discuss the problem. Witnesses could be called into the meeting, but usually it involved only a simple explanation by the plaintiff and defendant of their dispute. After each had spoken, the *juez* would make a settlement suggestion. If it were not accepted by both of the parties, then the plaintiff and defendant were asked to leave the room, and the judge would discuss the case with the *hombres buenos*.

The two *hombres buenos* were charged with making a recommendation for settlement to the judge. The statute then required the judge to render a settlement recommendation within eight days that would be most likely, in the words of the statute, "to avoid a lawsuit and obtain the agreement of the parties." Almost always, this recommendation was forthcoming immediately, and in the overwhelming majority of conciliations, perhaps as many as 90 percent, the two *hombres buenos* and the *juez* were unanimous in their recommendation.

The conciliation recommendation was not binding on the parties. Even though they were free to reject it, it was written in the form of a court judgment, so that if the parties agreed to the recommendation, it immediately became a court order. In the event either plaintiff or defendant disagreed, the judge gave the plaintiff a certificate stating that conciliation had been unsuccessfully attempted. With that certificate in hand, the plaintiff could then go on to a different judge and file his complaint in a formal lawsuit.

Von Schmidt v. Huntington involved a mining company. The plaintiffs were operating or working members of the company, and the defendants comprised the finance committee. The plaintiffs had been expelled from the company, and this action was brought to compel the company to reinstate them and for other orders related to the dissolution of the firm. The defendants pled that the plaintiffs had not produced any conciliation certificate, since none had been held, and that, therefore, the trial could not proceed. The trial judge overruled this plea, and after trial he found for the plaintiffs. Defendants appealed to the California Supreme Court on many grounds, including the absence of a conciliation certificate.

International law provides for the continuation of general private law in an area that has been ceded by one nation to another until such time as the new sovereign alters the law. In *Von Schmidt*, the lawsuit was filed in November

1849, after the Treaty of Guadalupe Hidalgo had transferred California to the United States. But Congress had not passed any controlling legislation regarding private law for California, nor had the California legislature yet met. Therefore, the case proceeded on the understanding that Mexican law applied as of the date of the initiation of the lawsuit, November 1849.

The California Supreme Court carefully examined the Mexican statute and found that this case was not within the specifically drawn exemptions from conciliation. However, since the time of filing (November 1849) and the date of deciding the appeal (March 1850), the first California legislature had convened. A month earlier (February 1850), the legislature had passed a statute authorizing the state supreme court to reverse or affirm trial court decisions as "substantial justice" required and to disregard "formal or technical defects, errors, or imperfections, not affecting the very right and justice of the case."

The California court seized upon this statute and declared that the failure to pursue conciliation before the lawsuit was commenced was a technical defect only and could therefore be ignored. The court noted that Hispanic legal scholars placed great importance on conciliation and conceded that it might be beneficial for the Mexicans, but insisted that "amongst the American people it can be looked upon in no other light than as a useless and dilatory formality, unattended by a single profitable result." The court stated that it went into such an extended discussion so that "the objection for the want of conciliatory measures is, so far as the Court is concerned, disposed of now, and, as we sincerely hope, forever." So much for alternative dispute resolution, circa mid-nineteenth century.

Conciliation was likely given such an offhand dismissal because it ran against a then-prevailing tradition in American jurisprudence. The Mexican requirement of conciliation was an effort to *avoid* litigation, to reconcile all persons aggrieved, and to heal the tear in the fabric of society caused by the dispute. It operated well within the homogeneous, preindustrial Mexican borderlands. On the other hand,

American law in this period had a tone of rugged individualism, more fitting the convulsions of a commercial and industrial revolution. Americans thought disputes should be brought to trial and should be resolved in a clear clash, with the jury declaring a winner and a loser. There is an abundance and wide variety of evidence supporting these contrary traditions of jurisprudence, but the evidence that is most pertinent here is how other American jurisdictions treated conciliation.

By 1850, New York and a few other states had provisions in their constitutions authorizing their legislatures to form conciliation courts. But such experiments were never successful. At the New York Constitutional Convention of 1846, one opponent of conciliation argued that such procedures "belonged only to a despotic government, where the people were ignorant, and had a superior class over them, and not for our free Yankee population; who consider they are competent to judge for themselves in such matters."

This individualistic spirit was reflected in a law journal article in 1866 that suggested conciliation would work only where the litigants "look up to the opinion and advice of the judge as only an ignorant and dependent people can look up." The procedure would never suit the sturdy spirit of even "the least elevated and educated Yankee." These words sound so strange today in the midst of the search for nonlitigious methods of dispute resolution, such as the call in 1985 by the chief justice of the United States that American lawyers should become peacemakers and conciliators.

There were several substantive legal concepts that entered American law through contact with Mexican law in the borderlands. The two most important are community property and the exemption from levy and seizure of the family homestead, livestock, and tools of the debtor's trade. There were also some Hispanic procedural ideas that made their way into American law, but not conciliation. Reception of law from one nation to another is almost always very selective. Yet, there is irony in the fact that Americans had the opportunity to embrace, but rejected, a concept for which there is now, a century and a half later, a pressing search.

Selected Bibliography

Hansen, Woodrow J. *The Search for Authority in California*. Oakland: Biobooks, 1960.

Kirkwood, M. R. "Historical Background and Objectives of the Law of Community Property in the Pacific Coast States." *Washington Law Review* 11 (January 1936): 1–11.

Langum, David J. *Law and Community on the Mexican California Frontier: Anglo-American Expatriates and the Clash of Legal Traditions, 1821–1846*. Norman: University of Oklahoma Press, 1987.

———. "The Introduction of Conciliation into Modern Spanish Law and Its Practice in the Spanish-American Borderlands." In *Studies in Roman Law & Legal History*, ed. Manuel J. Peláez, 325–341. Málaga, Spain: Universidad de Málaga, 1989.

McGinty, Brian. "Common Law and Community Property: Origins of the California System." *California State Bar Journal* 51 (July/August 1976): 370–373, 419–421 and (September/October 1976): 478–482, 532–538.

McKnight, Joseph W. "The Spanish Influence on the Texas Law of Civil Procedure." *Texas Law Review* 38 (November 1959): 24–54.

———. "The Spanish Legacy to Texas Law." *American Journal of Legal History* 3 (July 1959): 222–241 and (October 1959): 299–323.

McMurray, Orrin K. "The Beginnings of the Community Property System in California and the Adoption of the Common Law." *California Law Review* 3 (July 1915): 359–380.

Congress Should First Define the Offenses and Apportion the Punishment: Federal Common-Law Crimes

—◄o►—

Yasuhide Kawashima

Department of History
University of Texas at El Paso

United States v. Robert Worrall, 2 Dallas 384 (1798) [U.S. Circuit Court of Appeals]

◄o► THE CASE IN BRIEF ◄o►

Date
1798

Location
Pennsylvania

Court
U.S. Circuit Court of Appeals

Principal Participants
Robert Worrall
Tenche Coxe, U.S. Commissioner of the Revenue
Supreme Court Justice Samuel Chase

Significance of the Case
Stemming from a bribe offered to build a lighthouse, the case was the first involving the issue of whether or not a federal common law of crimes existed.

After the American Revolution, there was a growing sentiment against things English in the United States. The decline in the authority of the common law (i.e., judges' written opinions) was part of this postrevolutionary change in the attitude of the Americans. More specifically, the conviction among Americans that the common law was both uncertain and unpredictable grew stronger, and an attack on common-law crimes became widespread during the 1790s.

The opposition to the common law of crimes, however, was directed not only at the federal level but also at the state level. Vermont chief justice Nathaniel Chipman, in his 1793 essay "Dissertation on the Act Adopting the Common and Statute Laws of England," insisted that "no Court, in this State, ought ever to pronounce sentence of death upon the authority of a common law precedent, without authority of a statute." Two years later, Zepheniah Swift, future chief justice of Connecticut, expressed a similar view and challenged the doctrine that "every crime committed against the law of nature may be punished at the discretion of the judge, where the legislature has not appointed a particular punishment." He argued that "no man should be exposed to the danger of incurring a penalty without knowing it."

The common law of crimes on the federal level generated more heated debates. The common law had always been considered as operating on the local level, "the separate law of each colony within its respective limits" and not "a law pervading and operating through the whole, as one society." The possible establishment of the national government brought the issue into a new dimension. In the Constitutional Convention, George Mason offered a suggestion by advocating that the common law prevail on the federal level and by proposing the Constitution enact the common law. But the common law, he admitted, "stands here upon no other foundation than its having been adopted by the respective acts forming the constitution of the several States."

The formation of the federal government under the Constitution in 1789 turned this issue into a real constitutional question at the national level. *United States v. Worrall* (1798) was the first case involving the issue of whether a federal common law of crimes existed. The defendant, Robert Worrall, was charged with an attempt to bribe Tench Coxe, the U.S. commissioner of the revenue, who had been authorized to receive proposals and to enter into a contract for building a lighthouse on Cape Hatteras in North Carolina. After he submitted his proposal to Coxe, Worrall wrote him a letter, stating that he, "as having always been brought up in a life of industry, should be happy in serving you in the executing of this job" and upgraded his estimate of profit at £1,400. He further wrote that he had been "always content with a reasonable profit" and that, if he should be so happy in Coxe's recommendation of the work, he should think himself very ungrateful if he would not offer Coxe "one-half of the profit" (£350 on receiving the first payment and £350 on the last payment when the work was completed). The sum of £700 (Pennsylvania currency) that he proposed to offer Coxe was valued at $1,866.67.

Worrall's letter, dated September 28, 1797, at Philadelphia, was received by Coxe on the same day in Burlington, New Jersey, where he had moved his office due to an outbreak of yellow fever in Philadelphia. On receipt of the letter, Coxe immediately consulted the Pennsylvania attorney general and then invited the defendant for a conference at Burlington, thus entrapping him into a situation that provided him with further opportunity to bribe the commissioner. At this conference, Worrall acknowledged that he had written and sent the letter, declared that no one else knew its contents, and repeated the offer. When he demanded an answer, the commissioner suggested that Worrall come to his Philadelphia office when it opened again. Accordingly, the defendant called on him when the office was reopened and repeated what he had said previously, that he would give £700 as consideration for Coxe's procuring him the contract.

Worrall was indicted on two counts: (1) offering the bribe in the letter and (2) repeating the offer orally. District Judge Richard Peters and Supreme Court Justice Samuel Chase, sitting together as members of the U.S. Circuit Court for the Third Circuit, tried the case.

Counsel for the defendant argued that it was not sufficient for conviction to prove that the defendant was guilty of an offense. The offense had to be legally defined and had to have been committed within the jurisdiction of the court trying the defendant. Because there was no proof that the letter had been written in Pennsylvania, Worrall's counsel insisted, the first count of the indictment must fail. The proof, instead, was that publication and delivery were at Burlington, New Jersey. Nor could the defendant be convicted, the counsel argued, on the second count, "which is attempted to be supported merely by evidence of recognizing in Philadelphia, a corrupt offer previously made in another place, out of the jurisdiction of the court."

The attorney of the district retorted that the letter being dated at Philadelphia and being mailed in a Pennsylvania post office was sufficient proof that it had been written within the jurisdiction of the court. Accepting the prosecution's argument, the court found that the first count was sufficiently supported and that "no possible doubt" existed about the second count. The jury accordingly returned a guilty verdict on both counts.

One of the defense lawyers then moved in arrest of judgment, alleging that the circuit court could not have jurisdiction over the crime charged in the indictment. He argued that all the judicial authority of the federal courts should be derived either from the U.S. Constitution or from the acts of Congress made in pursuance of the Constitution, but an offer to bribe the commissioner of the revenue was never mentioned as a violation of any Constitution or legislative prohibition.

Nor did Dallas tolerate the argument that it was a common-law offense. He pointed out that the Twelfth Amendment stipulated that "the powers not delegated to the U.S. by the Constitution, nor prohibited by it to the states, are reserved to the states respectively, or to the people." In relation to crime and punishment, the objects of the delegated power of the U.S. are enumerated and fixed. Congress, on the other hand, could make all laws that should be necessary and proper for carrying into execution the powers of the general government, but no reference was made to a common-law authority. Congress undoubtedly had power to pass a law making it criminal to offer a bribe to the commissioner of the revenue, he argued, but not having made the law, the crime was not recognized by the federal code, constitutional or legislative.

The prosecuting attorney responded that it was unreasonable to insist that merely because a law had not prescribed an express and appropriate punishment for the offense, the offense, when committed, should not be punished by the circuit court, upon the principles of common-law punishment. Coxe, if he had accepted the bribe and betrayed his trust, would certainly have been indictable in the federal court. If he would have been so indictable, the offense of the person who tempted him must be equally indictable before the same judicial authority. The prosecution insisted that this indictment could be supported solely at common law.

The court was divided in opinion. Justice Chase maintained that there was no federal common law of crimes. Although he recog-

nized that the indictment was for an offense "highly injurious to morals and deserving the severest punishment," he insisted that the Constitution was the source of all federal jurisdiction, and the department of the government could never assume any power that was not expressly granted by that instrument, nor exercise a power in any other manner than was there prescribed. Besides, Article I, Section 8, granted power to Congress to create, define, and punish crimes and offenses, whenever it shall deem it necessary and proper by law to do so. Although bribery was not among the crimes specifically mentioned, Justice Chase thought it certainly was included in the provision. For him, the question at issue, however, arose about the exercise of the power, not about the power itself. The question was whether the federal courts could punish a man for an act before it was declared by a statute to be criminal. He insisted that it was "essential that congress should define the offences to be tried, and apportion the punishments to be inflicted, as that they should erect courts to try the criminal, or to pronounce a sentence on conviction." "It would be improper," he continued, "for a judge to exercise discretion in prescribing punishments."

Chase believed that the United States, as a federal government, had no common law and therefore, no indictment could be maintained in its courts for offenses merely at the common law. Reviewing the history of the American colonies, Justice Chase stated that when the colonies were first settled, the English settlers brought with them as much of the common law as was applicable to their local situation and change of circumstances. But each colony judged for itself what parts of the common law were applicable to its new conditions and adopted some parts and rejected others. He pointed out that the whole of the common law of England had been nowhere introduced because some states had rejected what others had adopted. The common law of one state was, therefore, not the common law of another, but the common law of England was the law of each state as long as each state had adopted it.

If the courts of the United States acquired a common-law jurisdiction in criminal cases, they must have received it from the United States. How then, Chase asked, did the United States come to possess the common law itself, before the government could communicate it to their judicial agents? The U.S. government did not bring it from England, the Constitution did not create it, and no act of Congress had assumed it. Moreover, what is the scope of the common law the United States might possess? It might be a defect and an inconvenience that the common-law authority dealing with crimes and punishments had not been conferred upon the federal government, but judges could not remedy political imperfection nor correct any legislative omission.

Judge Peters, on the other hand, argued that a federal common law of crimes existed. He maintained that whenever a government had been established, power to preserve itself was a necessary and an inseparable concomitant. The existence of the federal government would be precarious, if—for the punishment of offenses of this nature, tending to obstruct and pervert the administration of its affairs—an appeal had to be made to the state tribunals or the offenders escape with absolute impunity.

Peters insisted that the United States constitutionally possessed the power to punish misdemeanors, which was originally and strictly a common-law power. It could not only be exercised by Congress in the form of a legislative act, but it could also be enforced in the course of a judicial proceeding. Whenever an offense was aimed at subverting any federal institution or corrupting its public officers, Peters concluded, it was an offense against the well-being of the United States. It was cognizable, from its very nature, under the authority of the United States and, consequently, was within the jurisdiction of this court, by virtue of section 11 of the Judiciary Act of 1789.

As Chase and Peters disagreed, it became doubtful whether sentence could be pronounced upon the defendant. The judges and the prosecution wished to put the case into such a form as to be able to obtain the ultimate decision of the Supreme Court, but the defense counsel objected to such a compromise.

The court, therefore, after a short consultation, proceeded to pronounce the sentence, which was declared to have been mitigated in consideration of the defendant's circumstances. The defendant was sentenced to a three-month imprisonment and a fine of two hundred dollars and was ordered to stand committed until the sentence be complied with and the costs of prosecution paid.

Francis Wharton, a compiler of early federal criminal cases, suggested that Chase's opinion, which "greatly surprised not only the bar but the community," must have been influenced by the "persuasions" of the "metaphysical" Virginia lawyers, who led Chase into the belief that the United States had no common law. The oddest part of the case was that Chase, who had expressly denied that there was jurisdiction, "after a short consultation," agreed to impose a sentence of "unequivocally common law stamp." His sudden change of mind is understood to have been the result of his getting the views of his Supreme Court colleagues, who, as it turned out, favored a federal common law of crimes.

The dispute about the federal common law of crimes illuminates early assumptions about the general common law. The question was whether the United States could prosecute crimes under the general common law of crimes, or whether a federal statute declaring the conduct criminal was necessary for such prosecutions. On the other hand, it became increasingly clear about the existence of a general noncriminal common law or the ability of the federal courts to apply it. Shortly after they decided on the *Worrall* case, Justice Chase and Judge Peters heard a case involving a negotiable instrument in which they were in perfect agreement on the existence of a general, noncriminal common law. They decided the case on general principles of law, and neither man questioned the propriety of deciding on that basis.

United States v. Worrall was the first federal case involving a federal common law of crimes. Despite Chase's assertion, the case was finally decided in favor of the federal common law of crimes, confirming the early sentiment of the Supreme Court. The dispute continued, however, and in 1812 the issue was eventually settled the other way in *U.S. v. Hudson & Goodwin,* based upon the doctrine set forth by Justice Chase in the *Worrall* case.

Selected Bibliography

Beale, F. H., Jr. "Criminal Attempts." *Harvard Law Review* 16 (May 1903): 491–507.

Caplan, Russell L. "The History and Meaning of the Ninth Amendment." *Virginia Law Review* 69 (March 1983): 223–268.

Cooper, Edward H. "Attempts and Monopolization: A Mildly Explansionary Answer to the Prophylactic Riddle of Section Two." *Michigan Law Review* 72 (January 1974): 373–462.

Fletcher, William A. "The General Common Law and Section 34 of the Judiciary Act of 1789: The Example of Marine Insurance." *Harvard Law Review* 97 (May 1984): 1513–1577.

Horwitz, Morton J. *The Transformation of American Law, 1780–1860.* Cambridge, MA: Harvard University Press, 1977.

Palmer, Robert C. "The Federal Court Law of Crime." *Law and History Review* 4 (Fall 1986): 267–323.

Presser, Stephen B. "A Tale of Two Judges: Richard Peters, Samuel Chase, and the Broken Promise of Federalist Jurisprudence." *Northwestern University Law Review* 73 (March 1978): 26–111.

Federal Common Law of Crimes

———◦———

James W. Ely Jr.

School of Law
Vanderbilt University

United States v. Hudson & Goodwin, 7 Cranch 32 (1812) [U.S. Supreme Court]

┌─────────────────────────────────┐

◦ THE CASE IN BRIEF ◦

Date
1812

Location
Connecticut
District of Columbia

Court
U.S. Supreme Court

Principal Participants
Editors of the *Connecticut Courant*
President Thomas Jefferson
Associate Justice William Johnson

Significance of the Case
The Supreme Court ruled that criminal
jurisdiction in cases of common law was
not within the power of the federal courts.

└─────────────────────────────────┘

The heated debate over the prosecution of common-law crimes in federal courts was one of the most divisive legal issues in the early Republic. The controversy over common-law crimes raised questions about federalism, separation of powers, the role of the judiciary, and the reception (i.e., acceptance) of English law. Analysis of this issue is hampered by the intensively partisan atmosphere in which prosecution at common law was attempted. Federal jurisdiction over common-law crimes was one of the major issues that divided the Federalists and the Jeffersonians, with the latter opposing such jurisdiction. After decades of public debate, the U.S. Supreme Court in *Hudson & Goodwin* finally ruled that criminal jurisdiction in cases at common law was not within the power of the federal courts.

In England, judges heard the prosecution of offenses recognized by common law in the absence of statutes defining the activity as criminal. Many observers reasoned that the newly created federal courts could likewise try persons for common-law offenses. Under Article III of the Constitution, federal judicial power extended to all cases arising under "the Laws of the United States." Similarly, the Judiciary Act of 1789 gave circuit courts jurisdiction over "all crimes and offenses cognizable under the authority of the United States." The dispute over common-law crimes in federal court turned upon the meaning of this language.

In 1790, Congress enacted the first federal criminal statute, punishing a limited range of offenses such as treason, counterfeiting, and perjury in federal court. Nonetheless, federal judges began to instruct grand juries that indictments could be based on common law without any statutory foundation. Although relatively few cases before the federal courts during the 1790s raised the issue of common-law offenses, a majority of the judges who considered this question believed in the existence of a jurisdiction over nonstatutory crimes. Initially, there appears to have been little public opposition to prosecutions without a statutory basis. Several of the indictments obtained at common law, however, arose from a highly charged political context. For instance, there were several attempts to punish American citizens for breaches of neutrality as the result of activities that aided revolutionary France. As a consequence, many began to question the legitimacy of common-law prosecutions.

The debate over common-law crimes was soon intertwined with emerging political divisions. Anxious to strengthen federal sovereignty, the Federalists argued that the government had inherent powers of self-defense and could punish offenses without criminal statutes. Jeffersonians, on the other hand, saw the doctrine of common-law crime as a political weapon in the hands of federal judges and as a usurpation of power. Aside from partisan struggles, there was sharp division over whether judges or legislators should make law in a republican society. Acceptance of a common-law criminal jurisdiction would have strengthened the federal courts, a result that was not congenial to states' rights adherents.

Following the election of Thomas Jefferson as president in 1800, prosecutions for common-

law crimes largely ceased in federal court. Nonetheless, in 1806, the federal district judge in Connecticut invited the federal grand jury to review certain Federalist newspapers in that state. He directed the jurors to consider prosecution for seditious libel as a common-law offense. The grand jury returned indictments in 1807 against several editors, including Barzillai Hudson and George Goodwin of the *Connecticut Courant,* for libelous attacks on President Jefferson. Specifically, Hudson and Goodwin were accused of publishing allegations that President Jefferson and Congress had made secret payments to Napoleon as a bribe in order to obtain a treaty with Spain. The indictments were ironic because the Jeffersonians had vigorously opposed both the notion of federal common-law crimes and the trial of seditious libel in federal courts. In fact, the prosecution of Hudson and Goodwin prompted debate in Congress, with both Jeffersonians and Federalists criticizing the doctrine of common-law crime.

There is no evidence that President Jefferson instigated the Connecticut indictments, and indeed he directed the prosecutor to dismiss the charges. But the case of *Hudson & Goodwin* was brought to trial before receipt of Jefferson's instructions. The defendants submitted a demurrer (i.e. an assertion that the complaint does not set forth a cause of action upon which relief can be granted) to the jurisdiction of the court. After some delays, the two federal judges conducting the trial divided in opinion concerning the validity of a federal jurisdiction over common-law crimes. Consequently, late in 1808, the matter was certified to the U.S. Supreme Court.

The case came before the Court in March 1812, the first term in which there was a Jeffersonian majority on the bench. Consistent with the Jeffersonian position, Attorney General William Pinckney declined to argue the case on behalf of the government. No counsel appeared for the defendants. Thus, the justices did not have the benefit of a careful argument on this complicated and important question.

The Supreme Court, in a cursory opinion by Justice William Johnson, flatly rejected the doctrine of common-law crimes. Although the case before the court concerned a prosecution of seditious libel, Johnson addressed the broader issue of whether the federal courts could exercise any nonstatutory criminal jurisdictions. Political considerations bulked large for Johnson. Significantly, he emphasized that in the court's mind this matter had "been long since settled in public opinion. . . . [A]nd the general acquiescence of legal men shows the prevalence of opinion in favor of the negative of the proposition."

Johnson's opinion was grounded upon federalism and strict construction of legislation. Stressing the limited nature of the federal government, Johnson declared that federal power was "made up of concessions from the several States" and that the states reserved all powers not expressly delegated. In his view, lower federal courts could exercise only jurisdiction conferred by statute, and Congress had not granted common-law criminal jurisdiction. Johnson refused to decide whether Congress might confer such a jurisdiction upon the courts. Conceding that a sovereign nation might possess certain implied powers to safeguard its existence, Johnson nonetheless insisted that the federal courts could not punish acts until Congress declared the behavior criminal and fixed a punishment. He did recognize one exception to this general rule: the implied power of federal courts to punish contempt and enforce their orders.

No justice filed a written dissent, but scholars are agreed that the opinion was not unanimous. Justices Joseph Story and Bushrod Washington were likely dissenters, and the position of Chief Justice John Marshall cannot be ascertained with certainty.

Story was particularly upset, believing that *Hudson & Goodwin* was poorly reasoned, was inconsistent with past practice, and left the federal government in a weakened position to protect itself against criminal activity. Hence, Story moved on two fronts to limit the impact of *Hudson & Goodwin*. He unsuccessfully urged Congress to enact a statute recognizing common-law crimes as federal offenses. Moreover, Story sought to compel a reconsideration of the issue by the Supreme Court. In *United States v.*

Coolidge, Story, while on circuit, raised the question of common-law crime in the context of maritime jurisdiction, a subject clearly within the power of the federal courts under Article III of the Constitution. Seeking to distinguish *Hudson & Goodwin*, he argued that the common law merely defined the extent of maritime authority granted by the Constitution. The majority of the Supreme Court, however, was in no mood to reopen the explosive debate over common-law crimes. The Supreme Court abruptly reversed Story, relying on *Hudson & Goodwin*.

Thus, decades of acrimonious debate concerning the prosecution of nonstatutory crimes in the federal courts came to an anticlimactic end. Although the Supreme Court could be faulted for deciding *Hudson & Goodwin* in an offhand manner, the outcome was certainly consistent with democratic notions about a popular voice in the definition of criminal behavior.

Selected Bibliography

Bridwell, Randall, and Ralph U. Whitten. *The Constitution and the Common Law.* Lexington, MA: Lexington Books, 1977.

Haskins, George Lee, and Herbert A. Johnson. *History of the Supreme Court of the United States: Volume II Foundations of Power: John Marshall, 1801–15.* New York: Macmillan, Inc., 1981.

Levy, Leonard W. *The Emergence of a Free Press.* New York: Oxford University Press, 1985.

Newmyer, R. Kent. *Supreme Court Justice Joseph Story: Statesman of the Old Republic.* Chapel Hill: University of North Carolina Press, 1985.

Palmer, Robert C. "The Federal Court Law of Crime." *Law and History Review* 4 (Fall 1986): 267–323.

Presser, Stephen B. "A Tale of Two Judges: Richard Peters, Samuel Chase, and the Broken Promise of Federalist Jurisprudence." *Northwestern University Law Review* 73 (March–April 1978): 26–111.

Preyer, Kathryn. "Jurisdiction to Punish: Federal Authority, Federalism and the Common Law of Crimes in the Early Republic." *Law and History Review* 4 (Fall 1986): 223–265.

Warren, Charles. *The Supreme Court in United States History, I, 1789–1835,* rev. ed. Boston: Little, Brown, 1926.

Federal Common Law?

———<o>———

F. Thornton Miller
Department of History
Southwest Missouri State University

Swift v. Tyson, 16 Peters 1 (1842), and *Erie Railroad Co. v. Tompkins*, 304 U. S. 65 (1938)
[U.S. Supreme Court]

-<o>- THE CASE IN BRIEF -<o>-

Date
1842, 1938

Location
New York; Pennsylvania; District of
Columbia

Court
U.S. Supreme Court

Principal Participants
Joseph Swift; George W. Tyson; Erie
Railroad Company; James Tompkins;
Daniel Webster; Justice Joseph Story;
Justice Louis Brandeis

Significance of the Case
An investment company and land
speculator vying over a debt prompted
the Supreme Court to establish a federal
common law from commercial law. But a
1938 railroad case had the Court overturn
the decision.

A federal or national common law was not expressly established by the Constitution. Yet, in 1938, in the case of *Erie Railroad Co. v. Tompkins*, it was necessary for the Supreme Court to strike down a common law that had been developing in the federal courts for the previous one hundred years.

In 1798, the Jeffersonian Republicans criticized the Federalists for claiming that the Sedition Acts were an improvement on the English common law. Did that mean there was a federal common law? The Republicans vehemently denied there was. They contended that the common law had been brought from England and had been modified by the statutes of the colonial legislatures and by the colonial court's constructions of the law. There was a common law for each colony and, after 1776, for each state. There was no general common law that existed separate from the state governments. The lack of a federal common law was not altered by the Constitution or by the First Congress in the Judiciary Act of 1789. All federal law was derived from the Constitution, treaties, and the statutes of Congress. In *United States v. Hudson &*

Goodwin, the Marshall court declared as much. At least on this issue, the Court calmed the Republican states' rights concerns. If there was a national common law, separate from any grant by the Constitution or acts of Congress, then the Jeffersonians were afraid that, first, the federal courts could lay claim to a vast jurisdiction, like the English courts, and second, this law would be supreme over state common law in the federal courts in each state.

If there appeared to be agreement on the limits of federal law and courts, a potential ambiguity arose in a relatively new field of the law, which Daniel Webster described as "a system of most admirable utility, certain, complete, and uniform, to a degree of perfection, approaching the end of all that human wisdom may be expected to reach." Based not on statute but practice, precedent, and construction, it had begun only recently, "at the time of what may be called the commencement of the commercial era of the common law." Webster was referring to the customary commercial law, the rules of which were generally followed by all nations engaged in commerce. In England, and the American states, it had become a new and growing part of the common law. Could it be applied in the federal courts?

Section 34 of the Judiciary Act of 1789, which governed common-law trials in the federal courts, stated that "the laws of the several states, except where the constitution, treaties, or statutes of the United States shall otherwise require or provide, shall be regarded as rules of decision in trials of common law in the courts of the United States in cases where they apply." In most legal areas, where the common law varied from state to state, there was no question about how the federal courts were to proceed. But, in deciding a question in commercial law, where federal and state judges drew upon the same principles, were federal judges to be bound by the decisions of state judges? On a case-by-case basis, the Marshall Court had relied upon the generally accepted rules of commercial law, without declaring there was a general or federal common law separate from state law. Justice Joseph Story, believing it would provide a necessary uniformity, was ready to make commercial law the exception.

Swift v. Tyson began as a dispute involving an investment company in New York and land speculators in Maine. Joseph Swift sued George W. Tyson, based on diversity of citizenship, in the Federal Court for the Southern District of New York. At issue was whether a bill of exchange could satisfy a preexisting debt. There was no New York statute relating to the subject. But, by the state's common law, there were grounds for restricting payment of a bill of exchange if elements of fraud were involved. The federal district court followed New York law and ruled against Swift. Swift then appealed to the Federal Circuit Court for the Southern District of New York. Again, the court followed New York law. Losing once again, Swift now appealed to the U.S. Supreme Court.

Swift's lawyers, including Daniel Webster at one point, argued that where there were no relevant state statutes, on cases to be determined by the generally accepted rules of commercial law, federal judges were not bound by state common law. The word *law* in Section 34 of the Judiciary Act of 1789 was to be interpreted as referring only to state statutes and state judicial construction of statutes, and not to common-law rules laid down by a state court. Story, in giving the opinion of the Court, agreed that federal judges were not bound by state law where the general principles of commercial law were used by federal and state judges alike, and where a state had not passed statutes on the subject. He stated that with "contracts and other instruments of a commercial nature, the true interpretation and effect whereof are to be sought, not in the decisions of the local tribunals, but in the general principles and doctrines of commercial jurisprudence. . . . The law respecting negotiable instruments may be truly declared . . . to be in great measure, not the law of a single country only, but of the commercial world." *Swift* established a federal common law specifically in commercial law.

There was no states' rights opposition to *Swift*. It was not unlike many of the Taney court cases that attempted to strike a balance between the federal and state governments. The Court did not declare a general, federal common law. Indeed, states could pass statutes modifying the commercial law to restrict the actions of federal judges in federal district courts in their state. But, it would not be in the interest of a state to have its commercial law different from that of most other states and foreign countries engaged in commerce. To do so could seriously discourage commercial activity with the state. The general acceptance of *Swift* shows that Story was probably correct that a federal, commercial common law well served most state and business interests.

The existence of federal common law did not appear to offend states' rights advocates through the 1840s and 1850s. There was, however, a problem that would develop into a long-running controversy. If a general law existed separate from the statutes of Congress and the statutory and common law of the states, then would the federal judges be able to show restraint in using it? The Taney court's attempts to base the new law on the Constitution—so that it would not be a general, unchecked usurpation of power—only created another problem. Because the Constitution was superior to all state constitutions and law, the new common law could be interpreted as also being superior to state law. The road was thus paved for the Court to move beyond the bounds of state statute. Also, what could prohibit the federal courts from moving beyond commercial law? Story had not intended to create a general, federal common law. But, a nationalist Court and Congress during the Civil War and Reconstruction period, and pressure from the rising national corporations, would press this development toward its logical conclusion.

Congress expanded diversity jurisdiction to include cases where local prejudice might work against a plaintiff. Creditors and corporations established businesses in far-flung states to secure diversity jurisdiction. Businesspeople and their lawyers favored the *Swift* transformation, and the new doctrine was officially endorsed by the American Bar Association. Its development, through several decades of court cases, was completed by 1887 in *Bucher v. Cheshire Railroad Co.* The Court, viewing the common law as a general law that existed separate from territorial sovereigns, asserted that there was a single American common law. This increased the extent of the jurisdiction of the federal

courts in two ways. First, if the general common law was used in both the state and federal courts, because the federal government was superior to the state governments, federal courts were not bound by state statute. The states were only creating problems by maintaining a law different from that of the federal courts. Second, the common law that began as an exception—a commercial law—had now become general. Far from being the rule of how to construe commercial contracts and negotiable paper, this common law encompassed torts, bonds, and over twenty other doctrines.

Because the kinds of law included in the general common-law jurisdiction expanded, and because states enacted statutes to regulate corporations, there was a growing divergence between federal and state common laws. The phenomenon of two common laws in each state allowed for "forum shopping" (searching for the most favorable courts). Through diversity jurisdiction, corporations could bypass state law. Compared to the states, the federal judiciary tended to support creditors against debtors, and to support corporations against regulation, labor, and liability claims. The conservative Court was thus criticized in the late nineteenth century for political reasons by various groups from Populists to Progressives.

The Court and its now full-embraced *Swift* doctrine were also criticized for legal and constitutional reasons from within the legal profession. For example, Justice Oliver Wendell Holmes, in one of his classic dissents, contended that each state had drawn upon and modified the English common law and had developed its own law through statute and court opinions. He maintained that there had been no law separate from and transcendent to the particular states. Indeed, there was no law in the abstract that existed separate from sovereign governments. Federal judges could not exclusively divine the law from some mystical realm. There was a common law in each state, because it had been established by the legislatures and judiciaries of each state. Holmes argued that neither the U.S. Constitution nor congressional statutes had established a general common law or authorized the Supreme Court to assume that it existed. Thus, this assumption in the *Swift* doctrine was, in Holmes's view, fallacious.

Most of the criticism waged against the *Swift* doctrine was for its use by corporations to circumvent state law. But *Erie Railroad Co. v. Tompkins* began when an individual used diversity jurisdiction to sue a corporation for a liability claim. In Hughestown, Pennsylvania, Harry James Tompkins was walking on a path alongside a track of the Erie Railroad Co. when, he claimed, something extending from a passing train, probably an open door, struck him. By Pennsylvania common law, he was a trespasser on the railroad company's property, and the company was not liable for his injury. Because the company's headquarters were in New York, Tompkins could enter his suit in the U.S. District Court for the Southern District of New York. His lawyers argued that the court should not use Pennsylvania law but the *Swift* doctrine's general common law. The court gave judgment in accord with the latter, and the company appealed to the U.S. Circuit Court for the Second Circuit. Tompkins again won, and the company appealed to the U.S. Supreme Court.

In the *Erie* case, the Court did something it had seldom done before: it declared one of its own decisions unconstitutional. The Court not only ruled against Tompkins, using Pennsylvania common law, but struck down Story's *Swift* opinion, which had established a federal common law. Justice Louis Brandeis wrote the majority opinion. Much of it, of course, had little to do with Story's original opinion. But the *Swift* doctrine was a logical extension of Story's claim that there was a common law separate from the law of particular governments. Bran-

deis believed that it was necessary to throw out the opinion to be rid of the doctrine. To have narrowed the doctrine back to Story's specific, commercial common law would have left open the chance of a later Court restoring the *Swift* doctrine. To make the rule clear, Brandeis could not allow Story's exception to stand. There was no federal common law, and that included commercial law.

It is, perhaps, ironic that Brandeis did not realize that the explosion of federal statutes, beginning with the New Deal, would allow the federal courts, through their constructions, to build a common law anew. But, it is based upon statute, and it is not a general and universal law that transcends all government and has no limits other than those of reason. Brandeis put the constitutionalism back into the jurisdictional boundaries of the federal courts, which, of course, it had never been Story's intention to remove.

Selected Bibliography

Bridwell, Randall, and Ralph U. Whitten. *The Constitution and the Common Law: The Decline of the Doctrines of Separation of Powers and Federalism.* Lexington, MA: Heath, 1977.

Freyer, Tony. *Harmony & Dissonance: The Swift & Erie Cases in American Federalism.* New York: New York University Press, 1981.

Newmyer, R. Kent. *Supreme Court Justice Joseph Story: Statesman of the Old Republic.* Chapel Hill: University of North Carolina Press, 1985.

Purcell, Edward A., Jr. *Brandeis and the Progressive Constitution: Erie, the Judicial Power, and the Politics of the Federal Courts in Twentieth-Century America.* New Haven, CT: Yale University Press, 2000.

A Leg to Stand On: Taxpayer Lawsuits Against the U.S. Government

Roger D. Hardaway

Department of History
Northwestern Oklahoma State University

Flast v. Cohen, 392 U.S. 83 (1968) [U.S. Supreme Court]

⏤⟨◇⟩⏤ THE CASE IN BRIEF ⏤⟨◇⟩⏤

Date
1968

Location
New York
District of Columbia

Court
U.S. Supreme Court

Principal Participants
Florence Flast
John W. Gardner
Chief Justice Earl Warren

Significance of the Case
The right of a citizen to sue the federal government to prevent it from spending taxes for unconstitutional purposes was derived from this case about funding religiously affiliated schools.

Under the U.S. Constitution, the federal government has the power to tax the American people and to spend the money collected through taxation "to pay the Debts and provide for the common Defence and general Welfare of the United States." In 1968, the Supreme Court ruled that taxpayers have a right, under certain circumstances, to sue the federal government to prevent it from spending tax money for unconstitutional purposes.

In the mid-1960s, the Congress passed several laws appropriating money to provide educational materials, guidance services, and instructional assistance to children attending private schools, many of which were religiously affiliated. One such law was the Elementary and Secondary Education Act of 1965. Florence Flast and six other taxpayers sued the Secretary of Health, Education, and Welfare, John W. Gardner, and the U.S. Commissioner of Education to halt the expenditure of the law's funds to religious schools. The plaintiffs based their claim upon the First Amendment, which prohibits Congress from passing any law "respecting an establishment of religion, or prohibiting the free exercise thereof."

A three-judge district court panel in New York City ruled 2-1 in *Flast v. Gardner* that Flast and her fellow taxpayers had no "standing" to sue the U.S. government. Before any plaintiff is allowed to sue any defendant in the United States, the plaintiff must show that he or she has suffered or will suffer an injury because of the defendant's actions or proposed actions. If the plaintiff cannot prove this injury, the lawsuit is dismissed because the plaintiff is not a proper party to file suit. The plaintiff is said to have no standing, because there is no controversy between the parties for the court to resolve.

Judge Paul R. Hays of the Second U.S. Circuit Court of Appeals wrote the district court's decision in *Flast v. Gardner*. Hays reasoned that Flast's lawsuit was barred by the landmark U.S. Supreme Court case of *Frothingham v. Mellon* decided in 1923. In that case, Frothingham had charged that such expenditures could be made, under the Tenth Amendment, only by state governments and not by the U.S. government. Thus, in her opinion, the U.S. government was exceeding its constitutional power to spend taxpayer money.

The Supreme Court had ruled that Frothingham did not have standing to sue the U.S. government. While admitting that courts had generally allowed taxpayers to sue state and local governments, the Supreme Court decided to draw the line at suits against the U.S. government. The interest any taxpayer had "in the moneys of the [U.S.] Treasury . . . is shared with millions of others; is comparatively minute and indeterminable," the Court said. Thus, the injury endured by Frothingham as a result of the government's expenditure of funds for health care was not a "direct" one but rather a minor one she suffered "in common with people generally." Whether the expenditure was, in fact, unconstitutional as Frothingham alleged was not decided.

As for Flast, Judge Hays wrote that she had sustained no "direct dollars-and-cents injury." Like Frothingham, Flast did not possess "the requisite financial interest" in the expenditure of federal funds to allow her standing to sue.

The plaintiffs appealed the district court's decision to the U.S. Supreme Court. By the time the Court issued its opinion in June 1968, Wilbur J. Cohen had replaced Gardner as HEW secretary, changing the name of the case to *Flast v. Cohen*. In an 8-1 decision, the Court distinguished the Flast lawsuit from the Frothingham complaint and reversed the district court's decision. The Supreme Court's opinion, written by Chief Justice Earl Warren, gave federal taxpayers the right to sue the U.S. government to halt allegedly unconstitutional expenditures under certain narrowly defined circumstances.

Before taxpayers would be granted standing to sue the U.S. government, they would have to meet a two-part test. The first part required the plaintiffs to attack only statutes that created direct spending programs. A suit challenging an "incidental expenditure of tax funds in the administration of an essentially regulatory statute" would not be allowed. Both Flast and Frothingham, the Court said, satisfied the first part of this test.

The second part of the test required the federal spending to violate "a specific [constitutional] limitation upon [Congress's] taxing and spending power." Here, Warren reasoned that the establishment clause of the First Amendment specifically prohibited Congress from spending money for religious purposes. This, he said, was a "specific limitation" upon the U.S. government's spending power. Thus, Flast had met the second part of the standard, and she therefore had standing to sue the government. Conversely, Frothingham had challenged a law, because, in her opinion, it exceeded the U.S. government's general powers to spend; she had shown no specific constitutional prohibition upon the spending involved. Warren concluded by asserting that future taxpayers, in order to have standing to sue the U.S. government, would have to allege that their "tax money is being extracted and spent in violation of specific constitutional protections against such abuse of legislative power."

The Court's decision in *Flast v. Cohen* has been criticized by many commentators. Some, like Justice John M. Harlan in his dissenting opinion, prefer *Frothingham*, which would effectively bar taxpayer lawsuits altogether. Other legal experts agree with Justice William O. Douglas, who filed a concurring opinion in *Flast*. Douglas wanted the Court to overrule *Frothingham* and allow most taxpayer lawsuits to be heard as an effective check upon the actions of Congress. Still other critics have noted that the establishment clause may be the only "specific limitation" on Congressional spending in the Constitution.

Certainly, the distinction the Court drew between Frothingham's challenge to governmental spending and Flast's is a legalistic one that some might find illogical. The *Flast* decision, however, gives the American people the right, in some instances, to watch over the actions of the U.S. government and challenge unconstitu-tional expenditures. For this reason, it is an improvement over *Frothingham*.

Selected Bibliography

Kahan, Robert L. "Federal Taxpayers and Standing: *Flast v. Cohen*." *UCLA Law Review* 16 (February 1969): 444–455.

Karabus, Alan. "The *Flast* Decision on Standing of Federal Taxpayers to Challenge Governmental Action: Mirage or Breach in the Dike?" *North Dakota Law Review* 45 (Spring 1969): 353–362.

Tietz, Gerald F. "Standing: Taxpayers Allowed to Challenge Federal Expenditures." *Temple Law Quarterly* 42 (Fall 1968): 70–81.

A Nicaraguan Feast:
Having the Jurisdictional Cake
and Eating It Too

Christopher Rossi

Humanities Iowa
Iowa City, IA

*Case Concerning Military and Paramilitary Activities in
and Against Nicaragua, I.C.J. Reports 169 (1984)*
[International Court of Justice, United Nations]

-◦- THE CASE IN BRIEF -◦-

Date
1984

Location
Nicaragua

Court
United Nations International Court of
Justice

Principal Participants
Nicaragua
United States government

Significance of the Case
The Sandanista government of Nicaragua,
by bringing a suit against the United States
government before the United Nations
International Court of Justice, brought into
question the court's jurisdiction in regard
to the United States and Central and Latin
American relations.

In important ways, the procedural disputes that erupted between Nicaragua and the United States in the *Case Concerning Military and Paramilitary Activities in and Against Nicaragua* in the 1980s underscored problems experienced by the United Nations' International Court of Justice in exercising its power to hear and decide cases. But in a fundamental way, these disputes go far beyond concerns about jurisdiction and procedural propriety. They give rise to questions about the integrity and relevance of the International Court of Justice and the willingness of countries, particularly powerful countries, to seek its services when elliptical and capricious applications of justice conflict with a world disposed toward order, hierarchy, and power. It is by no means clear, particularly when viewing the preliminary stages of this case, that an effective international order can be based on the dictates of justice, even when determined by a court of law.

In 1946, the United States, as a charter member of the United Nations and a permanent member of the U.N. Security Council, had enthusiastically embraced the notion of third-party dispute settlement. Designed as the judicial organ of the United Nations, the International Court of Justice was created to provide its members with a mechanism for peacefully resolving international conflicts. Hopeful of the possibility of establishing a new international legal order, the United States agreed to abide by the decisions of the International Court on disputes involving international law.

However, the American acceptance of the International Court's so-called compulsory theoretical jurisdiction came with certain "reservations"—generally relating to issues concerning the vast area of national security. Effectively, the United States was saying that it would not accept the authority of an international judicial body in connection with any matters touching U.S. national security. Thus, the reservations underscore the inherently political nature of the international legal system and the extent to which powerful states seek to keep control over matters relating to their national interests.

In 1979, after forty years of authoritarian rule, the rebel opposition in Nicaragua succeeded in driving the dictator Luis Somoza from power. After five years of civil war, the popular and socialist Sandinista Party, led by Daniel Ortega, finally took power. This shift toward the left in Nicaraguan politics, however, proved ominous. Suddenly, one of the United States' most reliable "Good Neighbor" allies initiated domestic reforms that reversed its free-market policies and placed into question its previous support for international investment. From the U.S. perspective, Nicaragua's rapport with the Soviet client state Cuba and its ideological embrace of Marxism were even more provocative. While the late seventies' administration of President Jimmy Carter countenanced the Nicaraguan revolution, the election of Ronald Reagan in 1980 brought a renewed focus on America's anticommunism policy of containment. The United States suspended aid to Nicaragua in 1981 and, by 1985, imposed an embargo on trade with Nicaragua.

Faced with what it believed was the beginning of a "second Cuba," the Reagan administration initiated a series of covert paramilitary activities intended to topple the Sandinista government. Operating without congressional consent and allegedly financed with money acquired from a variety of illegal activities, the CIA armed and trained a ten thousand-soldier mercenary army in the neighboring states of El Salvador and Honduras. In 1983, the U.S.-supported Contras, or so-called freedom fighters, began a series of military sorties into Nicaragua against civil targets and economic production centers. Despite the notoriety that accompanied these activities, the Contras continued their hostilities, culminated in 1984 in the mining of Nicaraguan harbors and aerial bombardments.

Convinced that the United States was directing an illegal guerrilla war, Nicaragua filed a complaint with the International Court of Justice in April 1984. It charged the United States with mass violations of international law, including infringements of the U.N. Charter, international treaties, customary international law, regional agreements, and bilateral agreements relating to friendship, commerce, and navigation. In its complaint, Nicaragua demanded that the United States desist from all future acts of aggression and that it pay monetary damages.

In bringing this action before the International Court, Nicaragua relied heavily on Article 36 of the Statute of the International Court (the so-called Optional Clause), arguing that the International Court held compulsory jurisdiction over the matter. According to Nicaragua, the United States was necessarily bound to appear before the court and obey the court's judgment.

Anticipating a verdict against it on the substantive merits, the United States undertook to have the claim dismissed for a variety of procedural reasons. As a matter of basic due process, a standard as exacting in international law as in domestic legal systems, procedural questions are always settled first before moving on to substantive matters. In employing this strategy, the U.S. criticisms depended mainly on the inadmissibility and nonjusticiability of the Nicaraguan claims.

To thwart Nicaragua's attempt to haul the United States into international court, State Department lawyers sought to excuse the United States from the jurisdiction of the court under the optional clause of Article 36. More than any other argument, this was the claim on which the U.S. legal defense depended. To support dismissal on procedural grounds, the United States relied on the well-established international legal principle of reciprocity, which has its grounding in the idea that states are sovereign and equal. Reciprocity grants the plaintiff (Nicaragua) and the defendant (the United States) the right to appear before the International Court on common ground. Each litigant may take advantage of any reservation or weakness in the other state's declaration of adherence to the jurisdiction of the court. In other words, in the unique world of international adjudications before the International Court, compulsory jurisdiction under the optional clause is secured by finding the lowest jurisdictional common denominator. And in this case, the United States sought to rely on Nicaragua's pledge of adherence to the jurisdiction of the court, arguing that a flaw in that pledge deprived the Court of the power for it to hear and decide the case.

The weakness spotted by State Department lawyers traced to the fact that Nicaragua never filed properly the piece of paper—called a signature of protocol—informing the international community that it officially was agreeing, whether unconditionally or otherwise, to the compulsory jurisdiction of the court. Apparently, when Nicaragua signed its signature of protocol—way back in 1929—it never "perfected" the relevant piece of paper by depositing it with the proper authorities, who at that time were associated with the United Nations' predecessor, the League of Nations. How then, argued U.S. attorneys, could Nicaragua claim to have consented to the compulsory jurisdiction of the International Court of Justice, when in fact its original declaration never went into force? Because international proceedings depend on the consent of states to be bound, how may consent be determined when there is no express indication that Nicaragua ever formally agreed to the procedures?

Nicaragua attempted to argue that its consent to be bound was implied by the very fact that it submitted the suit. It also argued that U.S. attorneys were quibbling over a technical-

ity that amounted to no more than a harmless bookkeeping error (committed not by the Sandinista regime itself but by a previous and most certainly defunct government) than to any affront to the notion of procedural due process.

Evidence presented during the case, however, showed that Nicaragua (although not the Sandinista regime) had been reminded on several occasions to ratify its signature of protocol. But Nicaragua never completed that process and, in one instance, actually relied on this imperfection to excuse itself from the compulsory jurisdiction of the court. Could, then, Nicaragua eat its jurisdictional cake and have it too? Yes, according to the International Court.

The court majority ruled that Nicaragua should be treated as having met the jurisdictional requirements under the optional clause, notwithstanding its admission that it had never deposited the signature of protocol, and despite the court's finding that "Nicaragua, having failed to deposit its instrument of ratification . . . was not a party to that treaty." Curiously, the court held that the declaration was binding, notwithstanding Nicaragua's long-standing recognition that the protocol had, at least until that moment, not been in force.

Such a circumlocution of reasoning did not go unnoticed, and it contributed mightily to the U.S. claim that the court was fundamentally predisposed to accommodating Nicaragua's substantive complaints by overriding any questionable procedural weaknesses in its case. With notorious fanfare, the United States walked out of the proceedings and boycotted the remaining stages of the trial.

Reliance on the asserted flaw in the Nicaraguan signature of protocol was only one of several means employed by the United States to excuse itself from the jurisdiction of the court. Shortly before Nicaragua filed suit against the United States, the Americans caught wind of the impending case. Three days before Nicaragua instituted proceedings, U.S. Secretary of State George Schultz deposited a letter with the secretary-general of the United Nations. The so-called Schultz letter of April 6, 1984, informed the international community of a new basis under which the United States would excuse itself from the jurisdiction of the International Court under the optional clause. Exempted immediately from the court's jurisdiction were disputes involving the United States and any Central American or Latin American states. The court properly rejected the legal significance of this feeble and hurriedly produced modification to the U.S. acceptance of the court's compulsory jurisdiction due to the fact that, when the United States originally deposited its declaration and reservations in 1946, it had promised not to modify the term of its declaration without first providing six months' notice. With tables turned, it was now the United States that wanted to eat its jurisdictional cake and have it, too.

More interesting than the convoluted procedural issues, at least from practical and political standpoints, was whether the International Court, in the exercise of its discretion, should have determined that the claims were inadmissible even though it determined it had the power to hear them.

Some of the U.S.' objections to Nicaragua's complaint attempted to appeal to the court's institutional concerns about venturing too far into political, rather than legal, questions. In defining the paramilitary and arguably terrorist activities conducted by the Contras as a "ongoing military conflict," and by emphasizing the multilateral dynamic underwriting this dispute, the United States hoped to contain this issue within a localized and, hence, more tractable decision-making arena: the so-called Contradora process.

Another argument developed by the United States in favor of inadmissibility focused on the context of the case. The strategy here was to redefine this issue in terms less amenable to the International Court's judicial purposes. In adopting this approach, the United States tried to dramatize the dispute as essentially a political disagreement. Thus, according to the Americans, the military underpinnings of this political dispute, especially as they involved guerrilla tactics, were unsuited for judicial settlement because the facts surrounding this conflict were inherently fluid and indeterminate. Conflicts of this nature thus required a political and not a judicial resolution.

In addition, the United States claimed that any bilateral judgment of this case necessarily imposed upon the autonomy of all parties not present. As the current dispute involved the vital interests of El Salvador and Honduras, any decision, and particularly one against the United States, would inflict an injustice on the interests of Nicaragua's two neighboring countries. The court's refusal to entertain a collateral claim by El Salvador against Nicaragua underscored this criticism. Finally, the United States noted its long-standing commitment toward multilateral diplomacy that preceded its membership in the court. Therefore, after invoking the good faith efforts of the Contradora participants, the United States countered that any decision by the court would adversely affect the success of these regional negotiations. Composed of nine Central American countries, the Contradora negotiations attempted to end the violence that affected Central America through the implementation of broader social, economic, and political policies. As the Security Council had already endorsed these talks, the court, in hearing Nicaragua's complaint, was in effect reversing its own executive agency. Thus, while the United States clearly endorsed the wisdom of these talks, its support of the Contradora process can also be seen as an attempt to evade the judgment of the court, all the while endeavoring to influence the outcome of this dispute through the backdoor of regional negotiations.

Should, then, the court have been disposed toward a more circumscribed treatment of the discretionary inadmissibility claims, regardless of its power to hear the case? Certainly, the United States bluntly argued that it should. Nicaragua was alleging a wrongdoing of the highest order against a permanent member of the Security Council. It instituted proceedings in the court while another organ of the United Nations, the Security Council, was moving—albeit at the behest of the United States through use of its veto power—in a nonresolutive direction. The subliminal question the United States sought to have the International Court answer was simple: Was the court actually set up to adjudicate this type of complaint? Or, to express the query in the relevant present tense: Is the international legal system, devoid as it is of a truly compulsory jurisdiction or an effective means of enforcing its judgments, mature enough to withstand attacks against its integrity by the hegemonic power that gave rise to its creation?

In November 1984, the International Court rejected U.S. arguments against admissibility and heard Nicaragua's claim. As a matter of law, the court recognized the consent of Nicaragua as a judicant under its jurisdiction. It also rejected the so-called Schultz Doctrine and held the United States liable for its actions. In a trial on the merits, the court ruled that the United States should respect the sovereignty of Nicaragua and refrain from supporting any further attacks on that country.

When the United States responded with a trade embargo against Nicaragua in 1985, the court unanimously adopted a resolution asking that the United States desist from interfering in Nicaraguan affairs. It also called on both parties to resume a dialogue through the Contradora process. The United States, however, did not appear before the International Court in any of these cases. In 1986, the International Court condemned the United States for extending aid to the Contras and for its embargo against Nicaragua. A year later the court awarded Nicaragua reparations. The United States again did not participate in the proceedings.

The election of the National Opposition Union Party leader, Violeta Barrios de Chamorro, as president in 1993, however, saw a re-versal in U.S.-Nicaraguan relations. After taking office, the pro-U.S. Chamorro government withdrew the case from the docket of the Court of Justice before the court had the opportunity to assess a penalty. This mooted Nicaragua's claim and released the United States from liability, thereby closing the book on this ill-starred quest for international justice in an imperfect and politically perilous world.

Selected Bibliography

Boyle, Francis A. "Determining U.S. Responsibility for Contra Operations under International law." *American Journal of International Law* 81 (1987): 86–93.

Leigh, Monroe. *"Case Concerning Military and Paramilitary Activities in and Against Nicaragua."* *American Journal of International Law* 78 (1984): 894–97.

———. "Jurisdiction—U.S. Nicaragua FCN Treaty—Article 36 of the ICJ Statute-Nature and Effect of Reservations." *American Journal of International Law* 78 (1985): 442–46.

O'Meara, Richard L. "Applying the Critical Jurisprudence of International Law to the Case Concerning Military and Paramilitary Activities in and Against Nicaragua." *Virginia Law Review* 71 (1985): 1183–1210.

Scheffer, David J. "Non-Judicial State Remedies and the Jurisdiction of the International Court of Justice." *Stanford Journal of International Law* 27 (1990): 83–154.

Wagner, Megan L. "Jurisdiction by Estoppel in the International Court of Justice." *California Law Review* 74 (1986): 1777–1804.

From Court Side to Courtroom

—◦—

Charles E. Quirk

Department of History
University of Northern Iowa

NCAA v. Tarkanian, 488 U.S. 179 (1988) [U.S. Supreme Court]

◦ THE CASE IN BRIEF ◦

Date
  1988

Location
  Nevada; District of Columbia

Court
  U.S. Supreme Court

Principal Participants
  Jerry Tarkanian
  National Collegiate Athletic Association
  Justice John Paul Stevens

Significance of the Case
  After the NCAA won a lawsuit against a
  popular college basketball coach in the
  Supreme Court, the coach was then able
  to get the NCAA to surrender in local
  courts. The result was swayed, at least
  partially, by local support for the
  university basketball program and the
  coach in particular.

"It's not over till it's over."

This sports adage applies to the lengthy legal battle between Jerry Tarkanian, the highly successful basketball coach at the University of Nevada at Las Vegas (UNLV) from 1973 to 1992, and the powerful National Collegiate Athletic Association (NCAA).

Since the mid-1970s, the NCAA had hounded Tarkanian and UNLV over alleged recruiting violations and academic irregularities. Coach Tarkanian contended that the NCAA was out to get him for a variety of reasons, including his public statements criticizing NCAA procedures and the organization's perception that he exploited black athletes. The NCAA denied any vendetta against Tarkanian and asserted that it was merely doing its job.

On his home basketball court, the 18,500-seat Thomas & Mack Center, the colorful Tarkanian was almost impossible to beat. His Runnin' Rebels were regularly ranked in the nation's top ten, featuring Tarkanian's characteristic wide-open offense and a full-court pressure defense. In the 1989–1990 season, UNLV won the

233

national championship. Tarkanian's teams relied upon junior-college transfer students, some of whom displayed remarkable basketball skills but questionable academic abilities. Each year, Tarkanian's program garnered several million dollars, a figure that included proceeds from the sale of eighteen-hundred-dollar-seats for the rich and famous UNLV basketball devotees.

In the courtrooms of Nevada, Tarkanian's record was equally impressive. In August 1977, the NCAA found UNLV guilty of thirty-eight violations, ten of which involved Tarkanian. According to NCAA investigators, Tarkanian improperly provided potential recruits with extra benefits such as free airfare. Whereas the basketball program received a probation sentence, the governing body of collegiate athletics ordered UNLV to suspend the popular coach for two years. The institution reluctantly followed the demand rather than encounter additional penalties. Adept at the transition game, Tarkanian went on the offensive with a lawsuit contending that his due process rights had been violated. Eventually, he won a permanent injunction in Nevada district court. In May 1979, the Nevada Supreme Court reversed the decision and ordered the case sent back to lower court for another trial. This time, the NCAA, as well as UNLV, became a party in the case.

In a legal game that attracted the attention of lawyers and fiercely dedicated UNLV basketball supporters, Tarkanian emerged victorious again in the district court in June 1984. At this juncture, UNLV, an unenthusiastic partner at best, dropped out of the case. The court contended that the NCAA was a "state actor" under the Fourteenth Amendment to the U.S. Constitution and, as such, had deprived the coach of his right to due process. District Judge Paul S. Goldman chastised the NCAA for uncritically accepting the word of its investigators and ignoring sworn statements and physical evidence that supported Tarkanian.

As expected, the NCAA appealed to the Nevada Supreme Court. Three years later, the Nevada high court upheld the judgment of the lower court: the NCAA was a state actor when, in concert with UNLV, it sough to disci-

pline a public employee. Record another win for Tarkanian on his legal home court.

In response to the appeal from the NCAA, the U.S. Supreme Court agreed to review the case. Hearing arguments from the two sides in October 1988, the High Court rendered a 5-4 split decision in favor of the NCAA in December 1988.

Was the NCAA acting as a governmental body in pressuring UNLV to suspend Tarkanian? Lawyers for the coach argued in the affirmative because the NCAA acted in conjunction with UNLV. Speaking for the majority, Justice John Paul Stevens concluded that, as a private organization, the NCAA was not bound to follow Fourteenth Amendment provisions. Stevens noted that the NCAA is a private body and members join voluntarily. He also stressed that UNLV had a variety of options, including dropping out of the NCAA. He rejected the contention that the university and association acted together inasmuch as UNLV made every effort to retain Tarkanian.

Justice Byron R. White wrote a brief dissenting opinion, contending that the NCAA acted together with UNLV, thereby becoming a state actor. In the dissent, Justice White stressed that the university suspended Tarkanian because it accepted NCAA rules and had agreed to adopt the findings of the hearings conducted by the association. The big legal game was close, but the NCAA appeared to emerge with the trophy.

But the association found that Tarkanian's legal offense could still generate points. In May 1989, the voluntary, nonprofit organization composed of over nine hundred colleges, universities, and conferences asked the Nevada Supreme Court to dissolve the injunction barring Tarkanian's suspension. Soon thereafter, UNLV admitted that NCAA investigators were examining possible recruiting violations that occurred in 1985 and 1986. On September 28, the Nevada Supreme Court lifted the injunction barring NCAA sanctions against UNLV. But it allowed a lower court to rule on the other injunction preventing UNLV from suspending Tarkanian.

Developments in 1990 seemed almost appropriate for a soap opera. Early in the year, widely publicized reports of a compromise between the NCAA and Tarkanian proved inaccurate. In July, the NCAA banned UNLV from defending its title in the 1991 tournament. Then UNLV requested and, surprisingly, received a reconsideration. The university and the coach offered four mutually exclusive penalties in exchange for which Tarkanian promised not to launch additional litigation against the NCAA. In response, the NCAA offered two options. UNLV selected the one banning the squad from the 1992 tournament and forgoing television appearances in 1991–1992.

The reprieve evoked groans from some basketball precincts and a battery of defensive statements from the NCAA. Athletic officials and coaches at universities where teams had received severe penalties for infractions condemned the compromise. Some expressed surprise that it apparently was possible to negotiate with the NCAA; others indicated their desire for a "multiple-choice" penalty system; and one claimed that it was a total farce. Under siege, NCAA officials stressed the uniqueness of the case and denied setting a precedent for future appeals.

An assessment of the compromise requires attention to several complicating issues. One is the pressure placed on the NCAA by legislation introduced in Congress during 1990, which would require the NCAA to give due process during investigations. Another constraint was the availability of the friendly courts of Nevada for Tarkanian and his players to ensure the opportunity to defend their cherished championship. Also, it is true that UNLV served a two-year probation in the late 1970s. In addition, the coach possessed a permanent injunction preventing suspension by his university. Finally, the UNLV basketball program still faced threats from two sources. At the request of the Nevada Board of Regents, the state attorney general launched an investigation into charges of possible fraud related to compli-

mentary tickets to UNLV basketball games. And then there was the ever-vigilant NCAA. In December 1990, the NCAA released a list of almost thirty alleged UNLV infractions that occurred during the mid-1980s.

Tarkanian resigned from UNLV following the 1991–1992 season. After a brief fling as the coach of the San Antonio Spurs of the National Basketball Association, he returned to the collegiate ranks at Fresno State. Off the basketball court, Tarkanian launched two lawsuits. First, he charged UNLV officials with efforts to ruin his career. In the courtroom, Tarkanian emerged victorious with a lucrative financial settlement from UNLV. Second, in a far more significant case, he sued the NCAA for unfairly conspiring to remove him from coaching at the college level.

Unexpectedly, the NCAA surrendered. The association expressed regret over the lengthy dispute and agreed to compensate Tarkanian in the amount of $2.5 million. Why did the NCAA throw in the towel? It had tried unsuccessfully to move the case out of the Nevada courts. Also, reportedly the NCAA lost several mock trials in the Tarkanian-friendly Las Vegas courts. After almost three decades of conflict between a powerful national organization and a highly controversial coach, the home-court advantage helped immensely in Tarkanian's victory.

Selected Bibliography

Bender, Lee Stewart. "State Action and the NCAA: Will 'Tarkanian" Sport the Old Look?" *Entertainment and Sports Law Journal* 4 (Fall, 1987): 385–409.
Conrad, Mike. "Latest Jury Award Slam-Dunks the NCAA." *New York Law Journal* (1999): 5.
Schwartz, Martin A. "The NCAA State Action Decision." *Public Interest Law* 201 (January, 1989): 3.
Tarkanian, Jerry, and Terry Pluto. *Tark: College Basketball's Winningest Coach.* New York: McGraw-Hill, 1988.

Political Questions

The *Right* of Revolution
v. the Right of *Revolution*

◄○►

Harry W. Fritz

Department of History
University of Montana

Luther v. Borden, 7 Howard 1 (1849) [U.S. Supreme Court]

┌─────────────────────────────────┐

◄○► THE CASE IN BRIEF ◄○►

Date
  1849

Location
  Rhode Island

Court
  U.S. Supreme Court

Principal Participants
  Benjamin F. Hallett; Associate Justice
  Joseph Story; Chief Justice Roger B. Taney;
  Luther M. Borden; Martin Luther; Thomas
  Wilson Dorr; Governor Samuel Ward King

Significance of the Case
  As a response to a rebellion martial law
  was exercised in place of civil government. The Supreme Court ruled that a
  people's constitution was invalid. This
  ruling later aided President Lincoln in
  gaining jurisdiction in the Reconstruction
  of the Southern states after the Civil War.

└─────────────────────────────────┘

In 1849, the U.S. Supreme Court declared the American Revolution unconstitutional! Change in the structure and composition of government, the Court insisted, could occur only with the approval of the existing polity. Since Great Britain clearly did not sanction American independence in 1776, the colonists were forced to secure their goals militarily. They had no *right* of revolution; therefore, they asserted the right of *revolution.* And they won. Might made right.

The case of *Luther v. Borden* did not turn on the American Revolution; indeed, the Court might well have been embarrassed to reflect on the circumstances of the nation's founding. Rather, it arose from a bitter political and constitutional struggle in tiny Rhode Island. There, in the nation's smallest state, a peaceable revolution based on popular sovereignty failed. A tragicomic effort to impose the revolution by force also fizzled. For the presumptive revolutionaries, both right and might fell short. This was the Dorr War, the Dorr Rebellion of 1842.

The Dorrites—as the followers of the rebellion's leader, Thomas Wilson Dorr, were called—

had more than legitimate causes for complaint. The Rhode Island government against which they struggled had no demonstrated popular legitimacy. It had not been properly constituted by accepted revolutionary procedures, either in 1776 or in the aftermath of the federal Constitution of 1787. Instead, its origins stretched back to the seventeenth century, to the original Rhode Island Charter issued by Charles II in 1663. Barely adequate at the time of the Revolution, the charter government was hopelessly out of date fifty years later. Four major deficiencies—representation, the suffrage, a bill of rights, and judicial independence—defined it as a curious colonial anachronism in Jacksonian America. Moreover, the charter of 1663 contained no amendatory procedures. And, by the 1840s, it was a bit late to petition the Crown. Several reform efforts, the last spearheaded by Dorr and the Rhode Island Constitutional Party in the 1830s, proved futile. But the Rhode Island Suffrage Association, founded in 1840, made up for lost time.

In rapid succession, the suffragists called an extralegal constitutional convention, elected delegates, and met in Providence in October 1841. There they drafted an up-to-date document, with expanded suffrage, a reapportioned legislature, an independent judiciary, and a declaration of rights. After setting up their own election procedures, the new People's Constitution was ratified in early 1842 by the astonishing vote of 13,947 to 52. The majority amounted to 60 percent of Rhode Island's adult white males, and even included a clear majority of freemen eligible to vote under the charter government. Buoyed by the apparent success of their peaceable revolution, the suffragists abandoned reform for ideological purity. They turned down a palatable constitutional alternative offered by a freeholders' convention and approved by the incumbent government. The vote in March 1842 was 8,689 to 8,013 against, with the suffragists incongruously allied with diehard charter supporters in the majority. Both sides geared for a showdown, but the loss of over five thousand votes was not auspicious for the Dorrites.

Most charter defenders recognized the need for democratic reform, but they were unwilling

to acquiesce in unauthorized, out-of-doors procedures. When their legitimate constitution was rejected by a threatening if declining popular majority, the general assembly of the standing government got tough. It passed an act—dubbed by both sides the "Algerine Law" for its severity—proclaiming all participants in the proposed new people's government to be traitors. Governor Samuel Ward King sent a delegation to Washington and called on President John Tyler to defend Rhode Island against domestic violence. An aroused law-and-order coalition contested the gubernatorial elections of April 1842. In the official canvas, King won reelection with 4,781 votes; unofficially, Thomas Wilson Dorr became "people's governor" of Rhode Island. His 6,604 votes represented a further decline in suffragist strength. Undaunted, a people's government convened in Providence in May, and piously awaited formal recognition. Soon, the pretenders turned from peaceable to physical revolution. They assembled a ragtag militia and trained two cannons on the state arsenal in Providence. The cannon misfired, the militia disbanded, and the charter authorities remained in power. This was the climax of the Dorr Rebellion.

In the aftermath, the charter government responded with both the carrot and the stick. On the one hand, the general assembly called for a new constitutional convention, extending the vote for delegates to all adult males. Drafted in the fall and ratified in November 1842, the new constitution brought Rhode Island into the modern age. The Dorrites had lost the battle but won the war, even though unscrupulous political practices continued to prevail. On the other hand, the Charterites, terrified by a gathering of diehard Dorrites at Chapachet, Rhode Island, imposed martial law upon the state. In the long run, this declaration was even more revolutionary than suffragist agitation. Never before in American history had a standing civil government suspended operations in favor of military rule.

Acting under the new dispensation, a military contingent headed by one Luther M. Borden entered the residence of a Dorrite shoemaker named Martin Luther in Warren, Rhode Island, on June 29, 1942. Martin Luther was not at home; already threatened by the Algerine Law, he had moved across the border to Swansea, Massachusetts. Luther Borden's armed militia found only Martin's mother, Rachel, her companion, and two hired hands. None suffered physical injury, although Borden sustained a profane tongue-lashing administered by Mrs. Luther, a fervent Methodist. Ultimately, Martin Luther sued Luther Borden in federal court under the common-law action of trespass *quare clausum fregit*. Mrs. Luther also sued to test the constitutionality of martial law; the allegations, evidence, and arguments were the same in both cases. They were brought before Associate Justice Joseph Story of the U.S. Supreme Court and District Court Judge John Pitman, two ardent charter supporters, in October 1842, argued in November, and decided a year later.

The outcome was foreordained. At no time did the Dorrites enjoy the support of any significant segment of the American legal or judicial establishment. Although "Nine Lawyers" had backed the People's Constitution early on, many of them subsequently recanted. In an ex cathedra opinion, the three judges of the Rhode Island Supreme Court warned in March 1842 that further agitation might be treasonous. Both Dorr and Luther were convicted of treason in Rhode Island. Story and Pitman engaged in a collusive private correspondence in defense of the status quo. The Luthers' arguments, presented by Benjamin F. Hallett, a Massachusetts Democrat, fell on decidedly unreceptive ears.

Hallett rested his case on a spread-eagled defense of popular sovereignty. The people of Rhode Island "had the right to reassume the powers of government, and establish a written constitution and frame of a republican form of government." Lawyers for the defendants, John Whipple and Richard Ward Greene, asserted the integrity of the state's long-existing institutions. Predictably, the court, speaking in the name of Joseph Story, refused to admit plaintiff's evidence; the jury held for the defendants, and the cases—one on a writ of error and the other by an artificial division of opinion—went up to the U.S. Supreme Court.

The *Luther* cases were not argued until 1848, nor decided until 1849. The long delay, due to political considerations and an understaffed

Court, rendered the issues in question moot. The Dorrites agreed to demand neither the overthrow of the Rhode Island government nor the installation of the People's Constitution. The arguments took on an ethereal tone—an intellectual contest over the meaning of America's abstract, self-evident truths.

Once again, Benjamin F. Hallett held forth for the plaintiffs; his rhetorical assault lasted for three days. Because "the People's Constitution was in force in Rhode Island as the fundamental law of the State," the issue was "whether the theory of American free government for the States of this Union is available to the people in practice, that is, whether the basis of popular sovereignty is a living principle, or a theory, always restrained in practice by the will of the law-making power." For Hallett, the "right to establish a written constitution" was "independent of the will or sanction of the Legislature, and can be exercised by the right of eminent sovereignty in the people, without the form of a precedent statute law." Anything else was divine right—"the dogma of *despotism!*" If the people have a right of revolution, "they must also have a right to exercise it peaceably."

The lawyers for the defendants, John Whipple and Daniel Webster, were up to the effort. "All changes must originate with the legislature," Whipple stated flatly. Webster agreed: "When it is necessary to ascertain the will of the people, the legislature must provide the means of ascertaining it." "The Constitution does not proceed on the *ground* of revolution," he added; "it does not proceed on any *right* of revolution; but it does go on the idea, that, within and under the Constitution, no new form of government can be established in any State, without the authority of the existing government." Webster added that any effort to supersede the charter government was illegal; besides, the whole matter was "not of judicial cognizance."

Chief Justice Roger B. Taney agreed with Webster. He affirmed the judgment of the circuit court by denying the validity of the People's Constitution. Taney simply refused to consider the arguments of the plaintiffs. Because the Charter government never recognized its adversary, neither did he. The case turned on the proper exercise of judicial power. Because the job of recognizing constitutions was the business of "the political department," the Court was "bound to follow the decisions of the State tribunals." Moreover, under Article IV, Section 4 of the U.S. Constitution, "it rests with Congress to decide what government is the established one in a State." Congress, by admitting its senators and representatives, had decided for the charter. Taney summed up: "No one, we believe, has ever doubted the proposition, that, according to the institutions of the country, the sovereignty in every State resides in the people of the State, and that they may alter and change their form of government at their own pleasure. But whether they have changed it or not by abolishing an old government, and establishing a new one in its place, is a question to be settled by the political power."

Associate Justice Levi Woodbury appended a long dissent. He agreed with his chief that the main question was "not properly of judicial cognizance." But he came down hard on martial law, arguing that it could be proclaimed only by armies in actual conflict. Rhode Island had no business suspending civil law over the entire state. Unfortunately, Rhode Island had done just that, and Taney had approved. In "a state of war . . . the established government resorted to the rights and usages of war to maintain itself, and to overcome the unlawful opposition." The decision broadened the American law of emergency powers, allowing states to suppress dissent whenever they defined it as war.

Enhancing governmental power by adding military to civil sanctions was just one outcome of *Luther v. Borden*. The case long provided the classic expression of the distinction between political and justiciable questions. Taney not only refused jurisdiction but also provided job descriptions for the "political department"—Congress and the president. The chief justice rested his arguments on the guarantee clause of the Constitution, Article IV, Section 4: "The United States shall guarantee to every State in this Union a Republican Form of Government, and shall protect each of them against Invasion; and on Application of the Legislature, or of the Executive (when the Legislature cannot be convened) against domestic Violence." Although

Taney confused the separate clauses of this section, *Luther v. Borden* was "the first great turning point in the history of the guarantee clause." Taney's reading divorced the Court from judicial management of domestic issues for over a century. Not until the Court mandated legislative reapportionment in *Baker v. Carr* (1962) did it at last enforce the guarantee.

Luther v. Borden also marked what one historian called the "triumph of institutionalism"—of the sovereignty of government over that of the people. Established political institutions "divested" sovereignty, nullifying the right of the citizenry to exercise power directly. No less "republican" or even "popular," institutionalism recorded American satisfaction with both past and present, even as the determinants of society shifted from voluntarism to coercion.

In bits and pieces, *Luther v. Borden* added up not just to the denial of the Dorrites' version of popular sovereignty but to the absolute victory of juristic nationalism. When Abraham Lincoln proclaimed martial law in 1861, his attorney general cited Roger Taney's precedent of 1849. In denying his court's jurisdiction, Taney asserted the sovereign authority of the national legislature; he enhanced federal not local power. His *Luther* dicta allowed Congress to reconstruct the Southern states after the Civil War. Six hundred thousand had died to institutionalize the national republic. Like the Dorrites, the Confederates lacked the might to insure their right of revolution.

Selected Bibliography

Conron, Michael A. "Law, Politics, and Chief Justice Taney: A Reconsideration of the *Luther v. Borden* Decision." *American Journal of Legal History* 11 (October 1967): 377–388.

Dennison, George M. *The Dorr War: Republicanism on Trial, 1831–1861.* Lexington: University of Kentucky Press, 1976.

Gettleman, Marvin E. *The Dorr Rebellion: A Study in American Radicalism, 1833–1849.* New York: Random House, 1973.

Wiecek, William M. *The Guarantee Clause of the U.S. Constitution.* Ithaca, NY: Cornell University Press, 1972.

When Was a War a War, and What If It Was?

Thomas D. Morris
Emeritus Professor of History
Portland State University

Prize Cases, 2 Black 635 (1863) [U.S. Supreme Court]

‹o› THE CASE IN BRIEF ‹o›

Date
1863

Location
District of Columbia

Court
U.S. Supreme Court

Principal Participants
President Abraham Lincoln
William Henry Dana Jr.
James M. Carlisle

Significance of the Case
After President Lincoln declared a
blockade of southern ports and seized
ships during the Civil War, his actions
were determined lawful under the precept
that a leader possessed the power to bring
war to an end by any means necessary.

Shortly after the shells exploded over Fort
Sumter, President Abraham Lincoln issued a
series of executive proclamations. On April 19,
1861, Lincoln declared a blockade of the ports
of several of the seceded Southern states, and
on April 27 he extended the blockade to Virginia and North Carolina. He claimed he acted
under the laws of the United States, and "of the
law of nations."

Not long after, a number of ships were seized
and condemned as lawful prize under this
blockade. Among others, two ships claimed by
John and David Currie, Richmond merchants,
were seized. These were the *Crenshaw* and
the *Amy Warwick.* The *Crenshaw,* with tobacco
aboard, was captured off Newport News on
May 17, 1861, and the *Amy Warwick,* loaded
with coffee from Rio di Janeiro, was captured
on the high seas headed for Hampton Roads.
Several others were taken as well, including the
Hiawatha, on May 20 in Hampton Roads, and
the *Brilliante,* captured in Biloxi Bay, June 23,
1861. The *Hiawatha* was a British ship that had
taken on a cargo of tobacco and cotton. The
Brilliante, owned by a Mexican mercantile firm,

was loaded with flour it had taken on in New Orleans and was bound for Mexican ports. To successfully wage war the Confederacy needed trade. It was not even self-sufficient in food. "We cannot eat cotton, nor dine off tobacco and sugar," one Southerner ruefully observed in 1862. If the Union could successfully blockade the South, it would be a tremendous blow to the Confederacy.

But were the seizures and condemnations made under Lincoln's proclamations lawful? That would depend upon the legal definition of the Civil War, and it would depend upon the nature of the war powers, especially the powers claimed by the president. Lincoln consistently said that the states could not withdraw from the Union. Although he was confronted with a "combination of persons engaged in . . . insurrection," critics of Lincoln's proclamations insisted that the war powers did not cover internal uprisings, but that they related only to foreign enemies. There was nothing in the Constitution about a civil war. The dilemma for Lincoln was that if he accepted the argument, he would be forced to do one of two things. To claim the broad range of war powers allowed by international law (the imposition of a blockade that neutrals were obliged to respect being one), he would have to recognize the Confederacy as a foreign state. That would admit the constitutional validity of secession. The Confederate States of America would then be a lawful nation-state, and that would carry with it a range of "rights" to the insurrectionists. It would also constitute an acceptance of the pro-slavery view of the Constitution that Lincoln, as a nationalist, had firmly rejected. Lincoln's alternative would be to try to put down the rebellion without all the powers that would exist if the war was against a foreign nation.

There was, thus, a great deal at stake in the decision of the *Prize Cases* when the U.S. Supreme Court heard the arguments in February 1863 and rendered a divided judgment on March 10, 1863. Eminent counsel appeared for the United States: Richard Henry Dana Jr., author of *Two Years Before the Mast*, and an expert on maritime law, and William M. Evarts, a leading conservative member of the New York Bar. The principal attorney for the shipowners

was a prominent Washington lawyer, James M. Carlisle.

Carlisle argued that only "the sovereign power of the United States" could declare or recognize a state of war and thereby bring into existence "belligerent rights." The "Sovereign power" was Congress, and Congress had not declared war. He was particularly appalled at a new constitutional view: it was the notion that the president was the "embodiment of the Nation, and vested in that behalf with a species of natural right." He possessed, so the argument went, "implied powers." The only limit upon his powers was "necessity." This was a frightening prospect wholly contrary to American constitutionalism. It would make the president a dictator, it would be to make *him* the *sovereign*, as Richard Nixon was latter to claim. The president, Carlisle conceded, did have the power to see that the laws were faithfully executed, but he did not have the right to change the law. The fact was that there was no war in a legal sense under the Constitution, and the federal government could not then claim belligerent rights under international law against the Southern people, or against neutrals.

The most expansive argument for the government was that of Evarts. War, he noted, was a "question of actualities," and a civil war brought with it to the sovereign the rights of war against neutrals, and full power or dominion over the rebels. "The form and spirit of the political institutions of a people, the frame of its very Constitution, do not measure or shape the power or duties of a government, so defended against foreign or civil war. The warlike strength of the nation, and the warlike power brought against it, furnish the only measure and method of the conflict."

Dana's argument had a different tone. He hit at Carlisle's position on a declaration of war. A sovereign, he argued, "never, in form, declares war against a rebellion," and it may exercise belligerent powers against rebels. Lincoln had done so, and Congress had validated his action in July 1861. Since both Congress and the president had acted, Dana claimed, the issue was a political question, and the judgment of the political branches was conclusive. Before the decision of the Court was handed down, Dana wrote to Charles Francis Adams with some concern. It was alarming that the war had been going on for months and only now was the Court going to decide whether the government could use the war powers. If it decided against the blockade, he feared the war would end unfavorably for the Union and leave the country in an awful situation regarding neutrals.

Although the Court divided 5-4, Dana could put his deepest fears to rest. Justice Robert C. Grier took the view that war, which is not declared against rebels, was nonetheless "a fact in our domestic history." Congress could not constitutionally declare war against a state. The majority seemed determined to avoid a highly legalistic approach. The queen of England had, through a proclamation of neutrality, recognized the hostilities. Neutrals then could not ask a court of law to "affect a technical ignorance of the existence of a war," which all knew to be the worst civil war in history, and thereby "paralyze" the government "by subtle definitions and ingenious sophisms." The "President was bound to meet it in the shape it presented itself, without waiting for Congress to baptize it with a name." Moreover, the president, who possessed the whole executive power under Article II as commander in chief, had the duty to suppress the insurrection. It was in his political discretion to determine whether the insurrectionists should be given the status of belligerents, such as by treating captured Confederate soldiers as lawful prisoners of war rather than as traitors. The government, Grier concluded, possessed belligerent rights toward neutrals, and the seizure of the foreign-owned vessels under the blockade order was legal. The seizure of the property of people like the Curries was also legal. Such persons had thrown off their allegiance to the government and were, therefore, no less "enemies because they are traitors." The property of enemies was lawful prize.

Justice Samuel Nelson wrote for the four dissenters, who, including Chief Justice Roger B. Taney, wished to restrain the executive power. Nelson claimed that, until Congress acted, there was no lawful war and no lawful exercise of belligerent rights under international law. The so-called war that existed in the Southern states was a "personal war, until Congress . . . acted." He admitted that war could exist, and be extremely threatening. However, that amounted only to an admission that it existed in a "material sense," but that was of no moment when the question was what was a war "in a legal sense." He did admit that constitutionally Congress had acted to recognize the existence of a civil war "between the government and the Confederate States, and made it territorial." This was on July 13, 1861, when it authorized the president to interdict trade with the South. But that congressional act could not validate the president's earlier proclamations.

What the Court did not decide, of course, was anything whatsoever about the ordinances of secession or of the relation of the Southern states to the Union, a point Dana was careful to make later in a letter to a newspaper. The Court did accept the notion that there was an insurrection going on, one of the greatest civil wars in history, and it did not require a legal declaration to authorize the use of the war powers to put an end to it.

There was some controversy latter about precisely what this might imply. William Beach Lawrence, an expert on international law, claimed that the Court had stripped Southerners of their civil rights, and that a prime example was the Emancipation Proclamation, another presidential proclamation issued under a claimed executive war power. Dana sharply disputed this conclusion, but George S. Boutwell, a prominent Republican, suggested to him that it was reasonable to conclude that the government could use the war powers as a conqueror when the South collapsed. That implied that it was lawful to alter the institutions of the region, such as slavery.

Whatever the full implications, the critical point, as of March 1863, was that a war was a war, even though an insurrection, when it existed, when hostile armies were in the field, and when people were killed in battle. A sovereign possessed a lawful power, under the law of nations, to do what was necessary to bring it to an end. War, at least a civil war, was largely a political and not a legal issue under the Constitution. American courts have always been loath to challenge the legality of any war, or of acts done by executives to win a war. A sad example is the Japanese Internment Cases of World War II, or one might consider the futile efforts to raise the issue of the constitutionality of the Vietnam War. They are within the constitutional tradition of which the *Prize Cases* are an important landmark.

Selected Bibliography

Dowd, Morgan D. "Lincoln, the Rule of Law and Crisis Government: A Study of His Constitutional Law Theories." *University of Detroit Law Journal* 39 (1962): 633–649.

Hyman, Harold M. *A More Perfect Union: The Impact of the Civil War and Reconstruction on the Constitution.* Boston: Houghton Mifflin, 1975.

Randall, James G. *Constitutional Problems Under Lincoln.* Revised Edition. Urbana: University of Illinois Press, 1951.

Swisher, Carl B. *History of the Supreme Court of the United States: The Taney Period, 1836–64.* [Volume 5 in the Holmes Devise History of the Supreme Court]. New York: Macmillan, 1974.

More Than a Trojan Horse:
The Test Oath Cases

——◄○►——

John Walker Mauer
Clemson, South Carolina

Ex parte Garland, 4 Wallace 33 (1867) and *Cummings v. Missouri,* 4 Wallace 277 (1867)
[U.S. Supreme Court]

◄○► THE CASE IN BRIEF ◄○►

Date
 1867

Location
 Missouri
 District of Columbia

Court
 U.S. Supreme Court

Principal Participants
 Augustus Garland
 Father John Cummings
 Justice Stephen Field

Significance of the Case
 In the throes of Reconstruction, the court
 decided two cases on the same day,
 ruling that federal and state governments
 could not require loyalty oaths of their
 citizens. It also marked the first time the
 court overturned a part of any state
 constitution.

Decided on the same day by identical 5-4 votes, *Ex parte Garland* and *Cummings v. Missouri* are jointly known as the "Test Oath Cases." In them, the U.S. Supreme Court ruled that federal and state governments could not require loyalty oaths of their citizens. The Court divided over the question of what was more compelling, the protection of individual property rights from legislative intrusion or the tradition of judicial restraint regarding the legislative lawmaking authority. While the rulings in the Test Oath Cases appeared to reflect straightforward legal reasoning, the cases were actually far more complex. They involved divisive political issues, a shift toward legal formalism, and an expanded vision of civil liberties.

Congress initiated the use of test oaths in 1862 with the so-called Ironclad Oath. By 1865 the use of oaths attesting to past loyalty had greatly proliferated. *Ex parte Garland* involved a challenge to a January 1865 law that extended the Ironclad Oath to anyone seeking to practice law in a federal court. Augustus Garland clearly fell under the provisions of the test oath: before the war he had practiced law in federal courts and had been a U.S. senator, and during the war he had served in the Confederate military and Congress. On receiving a presidential pardon in July 1865, however, Garland petitioned to resume practicing law before federal courts.

Cummings v. Missouri developed from a distinctly different set of circumstances. The Missouri Constitution of 1865 instituted a loyalty oath that, while typical in testing specified past actions, was unusually sweeping in the activities proscribed and categories of people affected. Among the groups covered by the constitutional oath, the clergy, in particular, resisted taking the oath on principle. Most religious groups had individuals who resisted, but one cleric, a Roman Catholic priest named Father John Cummings, forced a legal confrontation by refusing to post bail and insisting on being tried. Cummings lost in both his trial and the resulting appeal to the Missouri Supreme Court.

The Test Oath Cases had a political significance that interested several of the nation's leading Democratic attorneys, including David Dudley Field, the brother of Justice Stephen Field. Opponents of Reconstruction saw the Test Oath Cases having several potential benefits. First, there was the potential, never realized, that the Court might strike down most, or even all, of Reconstruction. Second, even in their specific goals, litigation such as the Test Oath Cases had the potential to constrain Reconstruction and boost its opponents' morale. For example, if these cases resulted in eliminating loyalty oaths, they would enhance the political strength of Missouri Democrats, and they would negatively affect federal programs such as the Freedman's Bureau.

Although politically motivated themselves, counsel for Garland and Cummings used legal arguments not directly connected with Reconstruction. These arguments employed a formalist contention that the practicing of a profession was a property right, in which the loss of that right due to a test oath constituted a punishment. In an opinion written by Justice Stephen Field, a bare majority of the Court accepted this reasoning. The majority further agreed with counsel's reasoning that these oaths consti-

tuted both ex post facto laws because they involved deeds committed before legislative approval and bills of attainder because they were a "legislative act which inflicts punishment without judicial trial."

As with the majority, the Court's minority also avoided political issues and limited its analysis to the legal formalist arguments made to the Court. With Justice Samuel Miller writing the opinion, the minority asserted that these oaths were simply a professional qualification. In making this argument, the minority noted that the diverse use of qualifications for jobs and professions included the Constitution's requirements of oaths for president and vice president. Thus, to the minority, test oaths were not a punishment and could not be ex post facto laws and bills of attainder. The minority also stressed the importance of judicial restraint, because to declare a law unconstitutional "is at all times the exercise of an extremely delicate power." The emphasis on judicial restraint appears all the stronger because the minority disliked what Miller later talked of as Reconstruction's "strain on constitutional government" and, as Chief Justice Salmon Chase put it, the "detestable" test oaths.

The reasoning in the Test Oath Cases was, thus, abstract and nonpolitical. But such reasoning had the effect of diminishing Reconstruction without attacking the broader political concepts upon which the federal Union rested. A few months after these cases, the Court again demonstrated its willingness to limit Reconstruction when presented with economic arguments. In the 1868 decisions of *Georgia v. Stanton* and *Mississippi v. Stanton*, the Court unanimously refused to accept jurisdiction because, as one authority explained, "the rights alleged to be in danger were rights of sovereignty, not of person or property, and that the issue was political and beyond judicial cognizance." Seeing the Court's reference to property rights as an opportunity, Mississippi's counsel sought to amend his client's bill by claiming such rights. The Court came close to accepting the challenge to Reconstruction in this renewed appeal of the Mississippi case, refusing consideration on a 4-4 split. The uses of the property argument rationale in the Mississippi and Test Oath Cases was not simply a Trojan Horse hiding political goals; its validity to contemporaries is underscored by the fact that such reasoning proved persuasive to some staunch Reconstruction advocates, including Republican congressman Thaddeus Stevens. Yet, it did serve political ends by offering a less threatening means to curb Reconstruction than legal arguments pertaining to the nation's basic political fabric.

The Test Oath Cases have continued to have meaning to the generations that followed Reconstruction. The judicial activism in the 1860s was a precursor to and a support for the Court's laissez-faire activism of the late nineteenth century. *Cummings v. Missouri* has a unique legacy as the first case in which the Court overturned a part of any state constitution. Finally and importantly, however, are the lasting effects of the Test Oath Cases in expanding civil liberties on both the federal and the state levels even before the ratification of the Fourteenth Amendment.

Selected Bibliography

Fairman, Charles. *Mr. Justice Miller and the Supreme Court 1862–1890.* New York: Russell & Russell, 1939.

Hyman, Harold M., and William M. Wiecek. *Equal Justice Under Law: Constitutional Development 1835–1875.* New York: Harper & Row, 1982.

Swisher, Carl Brent. *Stephen J. Field: Craftsman of the Law.* Washington, D.C.: Brookings Institution, 1930.

Indestructible Union,
Indestructible States

—◦—

Thomas D. Morris
Emeritus Professor of History
Portland State University

Texas v. White, 7 Wallace 700 (1869) [U.S. Supreme Court]

◦ THE CASE IN BRIEF ◦

Date
1869

Location
Texas
District of Columbia

Court
U.S. Supreme Court

Principal Participants
George White
John Chiles
Chief Justice Salmon Chase

Significance of the Case
A dispute over pre–Civil War bonds in
Texas allowed the Court to reinforce
Republican Reconstruction in the South
and to define what a "state" was in
relation to the Union.

When Texas rebelled from Mexico in 1836, there was no reason to foresee that its conduct as an independent republic, as well as its later rebellion from the United States in 1861, would become elements in the thorny problem of reconstructing the Union.

While it was the Independent Republic of Texas, the government of Texas accumulated substantial obligations, at the same time that it made very expansive territorial claims to land west of the present boundaries of the state, including much of present New Mexico. As the Union slipped into a deep crisis in 1849–50, these two facts crossed each other in such a way as to become part of the effort to hold the Union together. One feature of the Compromise of 1850 was that Texas's debt of ten million dollars would be assumed by the federal government in exchange for giving up its bloated territorial claims. That indemnification, in turn, became part of the complex factual background to the case of *Texas v. White*. One-half of the U.S. bonds, payable to the state or to the bearer and redeemable after December 31, 1864, were delivered to Texas during 1851. Before the bonds could be available to any bondholder, they had to be endorsed by the governor of Texas by virtue of a state law of December 1851.

At the outset of the Civil War there were fewer than 1,000 bonds left in the state treasury, and by a law of 1862 these were made available to the state Military Board, composed of the governor and certain other state officers, to help "provide the defence of the State." U.S. bonds were to be used in aid of the rebellion. As the Confederacy neared its collapse, the Miliary Board, by a contract of January 12, 1865, sold a number of the bonds to George White and John Chiles, among other purchasers. There was good reason to believe that the contracts were corrupt. If White and Chiles failed to perform their part of the contract, which was to deliver cards used in cotton production and certain medicines, they would be forced to pay the Military Board for the gold U.S. bonds they had received. The rate, however, was to be in Texas bonds or treasury warrants. The provisional governor after the war, A. J. Hamilton, noted that this meant they would exchange about eight cents for one U.S. dollar.

At the end of the war Texas tried to stop the federal government from releasing the bonds, while White and others were in Washington trying to cash in. The provisional Reconstruction government of Texas filed an original suit in the U.S. Supreme Court at the outset of 1867 to enjoin White, Chiles, and others from receiving any of the U.S. bonds and to compel the delivery of the bonds to Texas. It was not until early 1869, however, that the Court heard the arguments. It delivered its judgment in December of that year.

The most critical issue in *Texas v. White* concerned jurisdiction. The substantive conclusions on the merits were not fully resolved in this case. Stated simply, the question was whether or not Texas was a state that could bring an original action in the Supreme Court of the United States. The answer, in turn, depended upon the effect of secession in 1861, and upon the Reconstruction policies of Congress. But like *Ableman v. Booth*, not to mention *Dred Scott*, beneath a technical jurisdictional question lay a profound social question involv-

ing the rights of African Americans within the American polity. Moreover, despite the less than thoughtful effort of Chief Justice Salmon Portland Chase, the arguments on the jurisdictional question involved some profound issues of American constitutionalism.

Counsel for White and Chiles, of course, tried to establish the position that Texas was not a state in the Union and, therefore, that it could not bring suit to enjoin the grant of the bonds to their clients. One possible ground for that position would be that Texas had seceded from the Union in 1861 and that this act lawfully took it out of the Union. Another was that if the right of secession were not allowed, then the fact was that Texas still was not in the Union because it had no representation in Congress at the time of the filing of the suit.

One of the routes to affirm the validity of secession was developed by the cantankerous Albert Pike in a rambling brief that touched upon various revolutionary movements throughout history, from Spartacus and Cataline to the Irish Fenians. He concluded that the "United States are estopped to assert principles contrary to the Declaration of Independence." In other words, the federal government was obliged to acknowledge the right of revolution. In a sense Chase did, but not as Pike might have wished.

Chase noted that, after the formation of the American Union, there was "no place for reconsideration, or revocation, except through revolution." The problem was that Chase was not granting a *constitutional* right of revolution, a right that some had tried earlier to ground in the notion that all power derives from the people and that the people have the right to alter and abolish their government at will. This idea indeed appeared in state constitutions from the late eighteenth century down to the years just before the Civil War. It was an idea that the Dorrites built upon in Rhode Island in the 1840s as well, as did some Southerners during the secession crisis. "Revolutionary constitutionalism," it might be called. However, the teeth had already been pulled from the tiger. The guarantee clause (Article IV, Section 4) of the U.S. Constitution had delegitimized violent revolution, and this clause would figure prominently in another part of *Texas v. White*. Moreover, Chief Justice Roger B. Taney had done much to give it less weight in his decision in *Luther v. Borden*, the case that grew out of the Dorr War and the case that Chase would rely upon. Taney conceded that power derived from the people and that they possessed the right to alter or abolish a government. But, he had added, whether they had done so or not was a political decision. Chase did not confront the notion of a right of revolution in the people, a right that could be used to legitimize the secession of the Southern states. He merely referred to revolution in a way that suggested that it would destroy the indestructible Union, and latter, citing the *Luther* decision, he referred to a state "deprived of all rightful government, by revolutionary violence." Southerners might have been engaged in a revolution, but they had lost and there remained no legal or constitutional claim that secession had taken the state out of the union. To put it simply, the Civil War finally buried one significant strand of early American constitutionalism, the revolutionary dimension that granted to the people a constitutional right to alter or abolish the government. Common enough in constitutional discourse before the war, it disappeared soon after. And so did the "revolutionary" clauses in the state constitutions. Government was now more "sovereign," while the "people" were less so. In *Texas v. White* Chase put to rest revolutionary constitutionalism, albeit *sub silentio* (quietly).

The other route to validate secession was in John C. Calhoun's axiom of state sovereignty, the notion that the sovereign states had entered into a contract among themselves to create a union, but a contract that, if altered or broken, would release a state from any contractual obligation. The state, thus, possessed the right to withdraw (to secede) from the violated compact or contract. Chase avoided any full-scale discussion of this claim. He rather relied upon the idea of a more perfect Union, more perfect than the Articles that were declared to be "perpetual." "It is difficult to convey the idea of indissoluble unity more clearly than by these words. What can be indissoluble if a perpetual Union, made more perfect, is not?" But ours

was a Union made up of states, states that had an individual existence, and the right of self-government. These ideas joined led Chase to his famous conclusion, the words most often quoted from the case: "The Constitution, in all its provisions, looks to an indestructible Union, composed of indestructible States." Texas therefore was a state in the American Union, despite the acts of rebellion. It could enter a suit in the federal courts.

But the problem of Reconstruction remained. If Texas was a state, with the right of self-government, what would happen to congressional Reconstruction, especially to the right of suffrage of black people, an aspect of Reconstruction policy central in Chase's thought? He also had to confront some salient points in the dissent written by Justice Robert C. Grier, and supported by Justices Noah H. Swayne and Samuel F. Miller. The fact was that Texas was not politically in the Union, whatever legal theories one might use. It had no representation in Congress, and it was declared a "rebel state" by the Reconstruction act of March 1867, which provided a government for Texas until a legal and republican government could be lawfully created. Moreover, Texas was under military rule at the time the suit was filed. Justice Grier claimed that all he was doing was deferring to the political judgment of Congress. Counsel for White and Chiles prudently had mentioned the *Prize Cases* in which the Court, in an opinion by Grier, held it was bound by the decisions of the political branches of the government. The *Prize Cases*, like the dissent in *Texas v. White*, rested heavily upon the idea that these were extraordinary circumstances, and the Court was presented with facts for which there was no law. These were political, not legal, issues. Constitutional theory was of little moment here. The case, Grier noted, should be dealt with as "political fact, not as a legal fiction." The truth of the matter was that the Constitution contained no provisions to deal with the crisis of these years, any more than it did with the Civil War itself.

But Chase was determined to provide a constitutional foundation for congressional Reconstruction, yet in doing so he had to note that Texas, while a state, was not quite like Massachusetts or his home state of Ohio. The problem was to define what a *state* might be in the American constitutional scheme. The Constitution, Chase maintained, considered states in different ways. For some purposes the word meant the people of an area; for some, it meant the territorial region; and for others, the government. Often it meant the "combined idea of people, territory, and government." Chase then embraced the Reconstruction theory of Representative Samuel Shellabarger of Ohio, viz. that the rights of the state, and the people of the state, were "suspended" during the civil war. The problem, following the suppression of the insurrection, was to restore the proper relations between the state and the Union, of "reestablishing the broken relations of the State with the Union."

The key constitutional provision to fulfill that duty was the guarantee clause, which imposed an obligation upon the federal government of guaranteeing a "republican form of government." The duty to do this was legislative, Chase argued, relying upon Taney's opinion in *Luther*. The real matter of moment was to give some meaning to the phrase "republican form of government." It was here that Chase turned to his deep concern: the validation of black suffrage in the Reconstruction acts of Congress, which he had helped draft. The abolition of slavery was a "great social change," to say the least. Once the slaves became freemen they became part of the "people," and the "people" constituted the state, as they always had. It was the state "thus constituted, which was now entitled to the benefit of the constitutional guaranty." Chase had moved a long way beyond the classical republicanism of the eighteenth century that had rested upon the notion that rule should be in the hands of a propertied, educated class. He also had provided the constitutional theory to uphold the military reconstruction acts of 1867, even though those laws were not before the Court. The "forfeited-rights" theory, however, was in another sense profoundly conservative. Thaddeus Stevens, for instance, had argued that the Southern communities were conquered provinces, and

Charles Sumner maintained that they had committed political suicide. Territorialization of the South of this magnitude was intended, by some at least, as a constitutional foundation for major land reform in the region.

But endangering the property rights of people, other than property rights in man, was seen as much too radical by most. It was enough for nineteenth-century liberalism to allow blacks to become part of the "people." Some, indeed, would have been quite content to have stopped short of the grant of political rights and left those rights secured in the Civil Rights Act of 1866 as the outer boundary. All this was part of the profound political conflict that made up early Reconstruction policy disputes. Chase's opinion in *Texas v. White* embraced a more moderate form of Reconstruction, but even that rested upon the extension of rights to black people. All this lay just beneath the surface of the jurisdictional judgment in the case. Republican Reconstruction had its theoretical base reinforced by Chase.

Following the chief justice's reasoning in *Texas v. White*, secession was legally or constitutionally void, and Republican congressional Reconstruction was valid. Moreover, blacks, now freed of bondage, were part of the "people" who made up the state, and Texas, through the guarantee clause, was a *state* transformed. It might have been "indestructible," but it was not beyond transformation even while part of an "indestructible" union.

Selected Bibliography

Fairman, Charles. *History of the Supreme Court of the United States: Reconstruction and Reunion 1864–88 Part One.* [Volume 6 in the Holmes Devise History of the Supreme Court]. New York: Macmillan, 1971.

Hyman, Harold M. *The Reconstruction Justice of Salmon P. Chase: In Re Turner and Texas v. White.* Lawrence: University Press of Kansas, 1997.

Hyman, Harold M., and William M. Wiecek. *Equal Justice Under Law: Constitutional Development, 1835–1875.* New York: Harper & Row, 1982.

McKitrick, Eric L. *Andrew Johnson and Reconstruction.* Chicago: University of Chicago Press, 1960.

The White Primary

Tinsley E. Yarbrough
Department of Political Science
East Carolina University

Smith v. Allwright, Election Judge, et al., 321 U. S. 649 (1944) [U.S. Supreme Court]

◄◦► THE CASE IN BRIEF ◄◦►

Date
1944

Location
Texas

Court
U.S. Supreme Court

Principal Participants
Democratic Party of Texas
Lonnie E. Smith
S.S. Allwright
Justice Stanley Reed

Significance of the Case
A Texas election judge denied blacks the right to vote in a primary election. An ensuing suit reversed an earlier decision (*Grovey v. Townsend*), forcing an abrupt end to racial discrimination in elections.

Of all the post-Reconstruction stratagems employed to limit black voting, the white primary was undoubtedly the most effective. By the end of the first decade of the twentieth century, the direct primary had become the most common method by which political parties nominated candidates for public office. In the South, where the Republican party—the party of Lincoln and abolition—rarely even fielded candidates, much less won elections, victory in the Democratic primary was tantamount to election. Thus, exclusion of blacks from the primary effectively excluded them from meaningful participation in the electoral process.

The Fifteenth Amendment, of course, forbids racial discrimination at the polls. The white primary's defenders contended, however, that party primaries were not elections in the constitutional sense. Instead, they were simply the private activities of a nongovernmental entity. In support of that position, moreover, they could draw some comfort from *Newberry v. United States,* a 1921 Supreme Court case holding the campaign finance regulations of the

1910 federal Corrupt Practices Act inapplicable to primaries. While the major opinion in the *Newberry* case included the assertion that primaries were "in no sense elections for an office," only four members of the five-man majority accepted that contention. Nevertheless, in the ensuing years, *Newberry* was widely construed to support the view that primaries were private affairs not subject to federal constitutional or statutory restrictions on the conduct of elections.

Although a common feature of southern politics, the white primary was not used in every section of the South. In Texas, it was required by the rules of the state Democratic party, but in a few areas white factions relied on the black vote in the party's primaries. The San Antonio party faction, which did not benefit from that black vote, lobbied for a state law limiting participation in the primary to white voters only. Bolstered by the *Newberry* decision, the Texas legislature yielded to the pressure, and in 1923, it enacted a white primary statute. Its action precipitated over thirty years of litigation, including the Supreme Court's landmark ruling in *Smith v. Allwright*.

Following enactment of the 1923 law, an election judge denied a ballot to Dr. L. A. Nixon, an El Paso black. Nixon filed a suit for damages. When the case reached the Supreme Court in *Nixon v. Herndon* (1927), the Court avoided deciding whether primaries were elections covered by the Fifteenth Amendment's ban on racial discrimination in voting, holding instead that the Texas law was a "direct and obvious infringement" on the Fourteenth Amendment's guarantee to equal protection of the laws. In an effort to circumvent the Court's decision, the Texas legislature then repealed the 1923 law and enacted a new one authorizing the executive committee of each party in the state to "prescribe the qualifications of its own members." When the state executive committee of the Democratic Party promptly voted to exclude blacks from the party's membership and participation in its primaries, the Supreme Court, in *Nixon v. Condon* (1932), again reversed. It termed the executive committee a delegate of the state under the challenged law and thus subject to the requirements of equal

protection. The Court refused to decide, however, whether the party itself could exclude blacks. Instead, it merely noted that "Whatever inherent power a state political party has to determine the content of its membership resides in the state convention." At this point, the Texas legislature took no further action. But the state convention of the Democratic Party enacted a white primary rule; and in *Grovey v. Townsend* (1935), the Supreme Court unanimously upheld the convention, drawing on the findings of Texas's highest court to conclude that the state's political parties were "voluntary associations," not "creatures of the state." As a private entity, the Court ruled, the Democratic Party could exclude blacks from its primaries without violating the equal protection clause, which applied only to state action.

The *Grovey* decision was to be short-lived, however. By 1940, the Supreme Court's membership had changed considerably. Moreover, its 1941 decision in *United States v. Classic*, a federal prosecution for ballot-box stuffing and other notorious incidents of fraud in the conduct of primaries in New Orleans, gave opponents of the white primary a potentially devastating weapon. Rejecting contentions to the contrary, the *Classic* court concluded that a primary is an election and subject to federal constitutional and statutory commands whenever it is "an integral part of the procedure of choice" or "in fact . . . effectively controls the choice."

The primary was clearly an integral part of Texas's election machinery. State law, for example, required that major party candidates be selected by primary, set the date for the conduct of primaries, required a runoff primary in close races, imposed a poll tax for primaries as well as general elections, and provided for the adjudication of contested primaries in the state courts. Therefore, when poll officials persisted in denying blacks the right to vote in the primary even after *Classic*, a would-be black voter sued Allwright, an election judge, and his assistants. The U.S. District Court for the Southern District of Texas dismissed the case; and the Court of Appeals for the Fifth Circuit, citing the *Grovey* decision, affirmed. But on April 3, 1944, more than twenty years after Texas had first enacted a white primary law, the Supreme Court reversed the lower courts and overturned *Grovey*.

Speaking for the majority, Justice Stanley Reed relied heavily on the *Classic* decision and the significant place of the primary in Texas's election machinery. "When primaries become a part of the machinery for choosing officials, state and national, as they have here," asserted Reed, "the same tests to determine the character of discrimination or abridgement should be applied to the primary as are applied to the general election." Measured by that standard, the Texas scheme was clearly forbidden state action, though accomplished through an ostensibly private institution. Justice Reed concluded: "The United States is a constitutional democracy. Its organic law grants to all citizens a right to participate in the choice of elected officials without restriction by any State because of race. This grant to the people of the opportunity for choice is not to be nullified by a State through casting its electoral process in a form which permits a private organization to practice racial discrimination in the election. Constitutional rights would be of little value if they could be thus indirectly denied."

Justice Owen Roberts was the lone dissenter. In his majority opinion, Justice Reed had attempted to justify the Court's overturning of *Grovey*, a comparatively recent precedent. "[W]hen convinced of former error," he contended, "this Court has never felt constrained to follow precedent. . . . This is particularly true when the decision believed erroneous is the application of a constitutional principle rather than an interpretation of the Constitution to extract the principle itself." Justice Roberts was hardly persuaded. Charging his colleagues with assuming a "knowledge and wisdom . . . denied to our predecessors," Roberts attacked their willingness to overturn a unanimous precedent less than a decade old. Such an approach, he complained, brought "adjudications of this tribunal into the same class as a restricted railroad ticket, good for this day and train only." And if *Grovey* had been overruled *sub silento* (silently) in *Classic*, "the situation" was, to Roberts, "even worse than that exhibited by the outright repudiation of an earlier

decision." For no party in *Classic* had suggested that *Grovey* had been wrongly decided, *Grovey* was not mentioned in the opinions filed for *Classic*, and *Classic* involved no question of a voter's eligibility to participate in a primary. Roberts submitted: "It is regrettable that in an era marked by doubt and confusion, an era whose greatest need is steadfastness of thought and purpose, this court, which has been looked to as exhibiting consistency in adjudication, and a steadiness which would hold the balance even in the face of temporary ebbs and flows of opinion, should now itself become the breeder of fresh doubt and confusion in the public mind as to the stability of our institutions."

Justice Roberts's concerns not withstanding, the Court's decision in *Smith v. Allwright* was a clear-cut repudiation of the Texas scheme. Even so, campaigns were mounted in several Deep South states, most notably South Carolina, to circumvent the Court's mandate. Under the *Classic* decision, primaries were held to constitute elections for constitutional purposes if they were integral parts of a state's procedure for choosing government officials *or* if they effectively controlled that choice. Because the Texas white primary was heavily regulated by state law, however, the Supreme Court has based its *Allwright* decision solely on the first prong of the *Classic* rationale, holding the Texas scheme invalid because it was an integral part of the state's election machinery. Seizing on that basis for the Supreme Court's decision, South Carolina governor Olin S. Johnston convened a special session of the state legislature and proposed that all references to the primary be removed from the state's statute books. "White Supremacy will be maintained in our primaries," Johnston exclaimed. "Let the chips fall where they may!" Although a number of South Carolina politicians and newspapers urged caution, warning that the governor's ploy would leave the conduct of primaries in the state vulnerable to all manner of fraud, Johnston's strategy was quickly adopted. Almost as promptly, however, U.S. District Judge J. Waties Waring, an eighth-generation Charlestonian with impeccable social credentials, voided the scheme in a 1947 ruling. Since 1910, Waring reminded his fellow citizens, every governor, state legislator, and member of South Carolina's congressional delegation had been a nominee of the Democratic Party. The Democratic primary thus effectively controlled the election choice and, under *Classic*, was subject to the Constitution's ban on racial discrimination in the electoral process. "It is time for South Carolina to rejoin the union," scolded Waring. "It is time to fall in step with the other states and adopt the American way of conducting elections."

South Carolina politicians were not yet ready to "rejoin the union." After Judge Waring's decision was affirmed by the Court of Appeals for the Fourth Circuit and the Supreme Court declined to review the case, the state Democratic Party enacted new rules requiring blacks who wished to participate in the party's primaries to take an offensive oath of support for "states' rights" and racial segregation and opposition to a proposed federal ban on employment discrimination. In 1948, however, Judge Waring struck down that ploy, too. Proposals to follow the South Carolina approach in Florida failed in 1945 and 1947. In Alabama, voters adopted a state constitutional amendment establishing discriminatory voter-registration requirements. But a three-judge federal district court, composed entirely of native Alabamians, struck down that scheme. And in Virginia, years earlier, lower federal courts had invalidated the Old Dominion's white primary.

Fittingly, however, the final judicial blow to the white primary was to be delivered in a 1953 Texas case, *Terry v. Adams*, decided by the U.S. Supreme Court. The Jaybird Association had been formed in Fort Bend County, Texas, in 1889. All whites on the county voting rolls were automatically listed as association members. Prior to each Democratic primary in the county, the association held its own primary, conducted under the same regulations that governed the party's primary. With few exceptions, winners in the all-white Jaybird primary went on to enter and win without opposition the

Democratic primary and the general election as well. In *Terry*, the Supreme Court rejected contentions that the association was a "mere private group" whose discriminatory policies were beyond the reach of the Fifteenth Amendment. "The only election that has counted in this Texas county for more than fifty years," Justice Hugo L. Black asserted in an opinion announcing the Court's judgment—an opinion capturing the essence of *Classic* and *Smith v. Allwright*

has been that held by the Jaybirds from which Negroes were excluded. The Democratic primary and the general election have become no more than the perfunctory ratifiers of the choice that has already been made in Jaybird elections from which Negroes have been excluded. It is immaterial that the state does not control that part of this elective process which it leaves for the Jaybirds to manage. The Jaybird primary has become an integral part, indeed the only effective part, of the elective process that determines who shall rule and govern in the county. The effect of the whole procedure, Jaybird primary plus Democratic primary plus general election, is to do precisely that which the Fifteenth Amendment forbids—strip Negroes of every vestige of influence in selecting the officials who control the local county matters that intimately touch the daily lives of citizens.

Selected Bibliography

Hamilton, Charles V. *The Bench and the Ballot*. New York: Oxford University Press, 1973.

Key, V. O., Jr. *Southern Politics in State and Nation*. New York: Knopf, 1949.

Strong, Donald S. "The Rise of Negro Voting in Texas." *American Political Science Review* 42 (1948): 510–522.

Weeks, O. Douglas. "The White Primary: 1944–1948." *American Political Science Review* 42 (1948): 500–510.

Yarbrough, Tinsley E. *A Passion for Justice: J. Waties Waring and Civil Rights*. New York: Oxford University Press, 1987.

From the "Political Thicket" to "One Man, One Vote"

―◄○►―

Stephen H. Wainscott

Department of Political Science
Clemson University

Baker v. Carr, 369 U.S. 186 (1962) and *Reynolds v. Sims,* 377 U.S. 533 (1964)
[U.S. Supreme Court]

◄○► THE CASE IN BRIEF ◄○►

Dates
1962, 1964

Location
Tennessee; Alabama; District of Columbia

Court
U.S. Supreme Court

Principal Participants
Chief Justice Earl Warren; Associate Justice William Brennan; Charles Baker; Joe Carr, for the state

Significance of the Case
The Court's ruling on reapportionment showed its willingness to enter an area that was once considered strictly political. The decision represented a consitutional milestone that is often considered the most important decision of the Warren Court.

In the two-hundred-year history of the U.S. Supreme Court, numerous cases stand out as milestones in the evolution of American constitutional law. Far fewer cases deserve to be described as revolutionary. In the 1960s, a revolution occurred, but, unlike the war for independence from Britain, no blood was shed; indeed, not one shot was fired. Yet, in certain respects, the "reapportionment revolution" was as significant for the development of representative democracy in the United States as were the conflicts at Saratoga and Valley Forge. The Supreme Court's decision in 1962 to enter the political thicket of legislative apportionment and districting was nothing less than the judicial equivalent of a declaration of independence. In fact, upon his retirement in 1969, Earl Warren described the reapportionment cases as the most important judgments of his sixteen-year tenure as chief justice.

Like many dramatic court rulings, the reapportionment decisions were rooted in the social and economic developments of previous decades. More specifically, twentieth-century political change in the United States has been largely a by-product of population growth and shift. For example, rapid urbanization helped spawn many demands for political reform during the Progressive Era. As early as the 1910 census, rural America was becoming a thing of the past; for the first time in history, a majority of Americans were reported living in areas classified as "urban." It would not be long before these recently transplanted city dwellers, eager to have a patch of land of their own, would precipitate the creation of a new demographic category, "suburban." By the 1970 census—the first to follow the reapportionment decisions of 1962 and 1964—seventy percent of the nation's population occupied two percent of the nation's land.

As late as World War II, few Americans fully comprehended the problems and dislocations that would result from these vast shifts from the countryside to the city and from farm to factory. Also, few were able to contemplate the enormous new demands that would be placed on government at all levels for services ranging from pollution control to mass transit systems.

Urban America inherited its share of problems and tensions, yet when city folk brought their claims to the public arena, they discovered that population shifts had not been accompanied by a migration in political power. Across the country, halls of government, especially legislatures, had a distinctly rural tilt. Congressional malapportionment was particularly evident in Georgia, where, as of 1950, there was a population disparity of more than half a million between the largest and smallest districts.

However, rural domination was especially flagrant in state legislatures, with Florida's lawmakers providing an excellent case study in malapportionment. From 1950 to 1960, Florida's population grew by nearly eighty percent; most of the growth occurred in the southeastern coastal counties and in the retirement communities of the southwestern Gulf region. Even so, the state legislature was dominated by a coterie of lawmakers, known as the "Pork Chop Gang," who represented the rural counties of the northern part of the state. In fact, a majority of the seats were held by members whose districts accounted for less than fifteen percent of

the state's population. An example of the policy effects of Florida's malapportionment can be seen in the disbursement of revenue from state-operated racetracks. The Pork Chop Gang saw to it that the receipts were equally distributed to the state's sixty-seven counties. As a result, Dade County (Miami) got twenty cents per person, while tiny Liberty County received more than sixty-one dollars per person.

In many respects, malapportionment had a characteristically, though not exclusively, southern flavor. Georgia demagogue Eugene Talmadge, in bragging that he never campaigned in a town large enough to have a streetcar, seemed to echo a widely shared feeling that cities breed sin and that country people have a superior talent for public service. Also, it was part of the southern antiurban prejudice that big cities had ample sums of cash stashed away in secret accounts and, thus, did not deserve the financial largesse of state government.

During the 1920s, Illinois became the setting for the first significant challenges to state and federal apportionment arrangements. With a 1920 population more than eighty percent urban, Illinois was a hotbed of constant conflict between rural downstate interests and the political empires of Cook County (Chicago). For years, the state legislature, a bastion of downstate power, had rejected demands for reapportionment. In 1925, the Cook County Board of Commissioners voted to withhold state taxes collected and even threatened to secede from the state if the lawmakers in Springfield continued to ignore the matter of reapportionment.

In 1930, a Chicago businessman named John Keogh, on trial for federal income-tax evasion, contended that Illinois's failure to reapportion the state legislature had deprived the state of its constitutional guarantee of a republican form of government, thereby absolving Keogh of any obligation to pay taxes. Later, during a foreclosure suit involving one of his businesses, Keogh claimed that the state courts had no legal standing in view of legislative malapportionment. When the court ruled against his motion for dismissal of the case, Keogh shot and killed the prosecuting attorney and fired errant shots at the judge. Upon his arrest for the shootings, Keogh stated that the death of the prosecutor was an unfortunate but necessary sacrifice in the crusade for reapportionment.

In the mid-1940s, the issue of apportionment resurfaced, this time centering on the matter of Illinois's congressional districts. Kenneth Colegrove, a political science professor at Northwestern University, on behalf of several other academicians and Chicago lawyers, filed a suit in federal district court. Colegrove challenged the validity of the state's congressional districts, which ranged in population from 112,000 to 914,000. Colegrove, a resident of the largest district, sought a court order enjoining the state from conducting the 1946 congressional elections under the existing districting arrangement. He further requested an order for the election of U.S. representatives-at-large.

The plaintiffs contended that the enormous disparity in the populations of the state's congressional districts conflicted with certain requirements of the Federal Reapportionment Act of 1911 and with the Fourteenth Amendment's guarantee of equal protection. The suit also argued that the existing apportionment violated the provision of Article I that U.S. representatives be allocated to the states "according to their respective numbers" and that they be elected "by the people of the several States."

The case of *Colegrove v. Green* was argued before the U.S. Supreme Court in March 1946. On its face, the case appeared to turn on the question of whether Colegrove and other residents of more populous districts had been discriminated against. However, before the Court could consider the case on its merits, it had to wrestle with the more vexing questions of jurisdiction and other procedural matters.

From one perspective, the Court could have taken the position that it lacked jurisdiction entirely, as Article I, Section 4, permits states to determine the manner of electing congressional representatives. On the other hand, some justices, including William O. Douglas, believed that the case presented questions of equal protection and due process of law over which the Court could legitimately exercise jurisdiction. A third alternative was that while the Court possessed jurisdiction, it could decline to exercise it. Supporting the latter approach was a long-standing notion of jurisprudence that held

that the Court should refuse to hear cases deemed to be inherently political. Viewed by some as a dodge, the "political questions" concept, properly understood, is intended to extricate courts from controversies in which judicial authority lacks guidance or is incapable of fashioning reasonable and appropriate solutions.

During the time that *Colegrove* was docketed in the Supreme Court, Justice Robert Jackson was serving as prosecutor at the Nuremburg war-crime trials. And, less than a month after the Court heard oral arguments in the case, Chief Justice Harlan Stone suddenly died of a heart attack. Thus, it was a seven-member court that split 4-3 in rejecting Colegove's suit seeking the invalidation of Illinois's congressional districts. Relying heavily on his interpretation of Article I, Section 4, Justice Felix Frankfurter's majority opinion summarily dismissed the suit for lack of jurisdiction. But he went a step further. Deciding *Colegrove* on its merits, he said, would require the Court to embroil itself in "party contests." "It is hostile to a democratic system to involve the judiciary in the politics of the people," he wrote. The courts "ought not enter this political thicket."

Although the ruling in *Colegrove v. Green* legally applied only to congressional districting, the case sent a loud and clear message throughout the American judicial system that reapportionment was a matter for legislatures, not courts, to decide. The posture of judicial nonintervention was especially evident in state courts. In the rare instances in which they claimed jurisdiction, state courts seldom ruled in favor of plaintiffs, and when they did, rulings merely invalidated existing arrangements without providing remedies.

In 1960, Dr. C. G. Gomillion, dean of Tuskegee Institute in Alabama, filed suit challenging the validity of the city's elections. At the time, nearly eighty percent of Tuskegee's population was black. The all-white state legislature, fearful that blacks might soon enjoy a majority of the city's registered voters, passed legislation transforming city boundaries into the shape of a sea horse. The effect of the gerrymander was the exclusion from municipal elections of all but five of the city's black voters. Ruling in Gomillion's favor, but determined not to disturb the precedent of *Colegrove*, the Court ducked the Fourteenth Amendment issue of equal protection. Instead, it declared that the racial gerrymander violated the voting rights guaranteed by the Fifteenth Amendment. Although the issues presented in *Gomillion v. Lightfoot* were only tangentially related to reapportionment, the case nonetheless led the Court back to the edge of the political thicket.

Despite the Court's ruling in *Gomillion* and other foreshadowings of shifting judicial opinion, successful challenges to apportionment schemes were virtually impossible throughout the 1950s. Adding to the frustration of plaintiffs was that few state constitutions required legislative apportionment on an equal population basis. Tennessee was different. The state's constitution, drafted in 1870, called for both houses of the legislature to be apportioned among districts "according to the number of qualified electors in each." Under this seemingly clear directive, the legislature was reapportioned in 1881, 1891, and 1901. Six decades would pass before reapportionment would occur again. The existence of a clear legal mandate for reapportionment and the state's persistent refusal to do so made Tennessee a logical setting for an assault on *Colegrove*.

In many ways, Tennessee was typical of twentieth-century growth trends across the nation. In 1960, only 11 percent of the state's workforce was employed in agriculture, compared to 33 percent in 1940. Between 1950 and 1960, the four principal cities (Knoxville, Memphis, Nashville, and Chattanooga) experienced a population gain of 30 percent. The so-called urban fringe bordering these metropolises grew 135 percent during the same period.

The forces of industrialization and urbanization had clearly put Tennessee in the forefront of the New South, but politically the grip of Old South tradition remained strong. By unspoken custom, the governor almost always hailed from a small town, and the state legislature was an antediluvian assembly of rural potentates. State senate district populations ranged from 25,000 to 132,000. Twenty of the thirty-three senate members were from counties that accounted for barely one-third of the state's population. Had legislative apportionment been

based on population, Shelby County (Memphis) would have been allotted twenty members of the general assembly; instead, it had only nine. Inequalities in the legislative halls of Nashville led to disparities in Washington as well. As of 1960, the congressman from the ninth district (Memphis) represented 170,000 more constituents than did the legislators from two neighboring districts combined.

Breaking the stranglehold of rural power seemed virtually impossible. Tennessee, like most other southern states, had witnessed occasional skirmishing between progressive-minded governors and recalcitrant state legislatures, but few state executives had dared to make reapportionment a top priority. Compounding the frustrations of reapportionment advocates was the fact that the Tennessee constitution—which, until 1953 was the oldest unamended state constitution in the nation—contained no provision for popular initiative or referendum. With legislative pathways effectively blocked, complainants would be forced to go to court, an unappealing alternative in view of the long shadow of *Colegrove*.

Charles Baker was mayor of Millington, Tennessee, a burgeoning suburb of Memphis. From the end of World War II, the greater Memphis area felt the impact of two migration flows: blacks from the cotton fields of western Tennessee and northern Mississippi, and white professionals transferred by their companies from places farther north. As chairman of the Shelby County Quarterly Court, a legislative entity that sliced the financial pie of the state's fastest-growing metropolis, Baker experienced firsthand the pressures of new people and new demands. In trying to cope with the problems of urban growth, Baker got little help from Nashville, where the legislative mindset reflected the sentiments of house floor leader Jim Cummings: "I believe in collecting the taxes where the money is—in the cities—and spending it where it's needed—in the country." Baker believed that until the legislature was forced to reapportion, the Cummings brand of populism would continue to rob his county of its just financial due. So he decided to sue.

The case of *Baker v. Carr* was argued before the Supreme Court in April 1961 and again in

October. Baker and his co-plaintiffs contended that the Tennessee legislature had violated the state constitution by its unwillingness to reapportion. Voters in overpopulated areas, Baker's brief asserted, were deprived of meaningful representation and, therefore, were denied their fair share of state revenues. Entitlement to due process and to equal protection of the laws under the Fourteenth Amendment required that legislative districts be of equal population. The appellants sought invalidation of the state constitution's antiquated apportionment provisions and substantive relief in the form of a court order requiring at-large elections until such time as the general assembly acted to equalize state legislative districts.

As in *Colegrove*, procedural rather than substantive issues dominated the Court's attention in *Baker v. Carr*. At the outset, the Court was concerned with whether the federal courts possessed the jurisdiction to hear claims of Fourteenth Amendment violations stemming from state legislative apportionment. The Court also sought to determine whether Baker and the other appellants were individually affected by an alleged wrongdoing and, therefore, had standing to bring suit. Finally, the Court's decision had to clarify the question of justiciability—that is, whether there existed, regardless of the merits of the complaint, a "judicially discoverable and administrable remedy."

The decision of the Supreme Court in *Baker v. Carr* was announced on March 26, 1962. Justice William Brennan, writing for a six-member majority, declared that the Court would confine its ruling to the matters of jurisdiction, standing, and justiciability. The Court would not pass judgment on the merits of the complaint of malrepresentation. A leading critic of Warren Court activism in the area of reapportionment observed that the Court's approach in *Baker* can be likened to a "three-legged stool with a crucial fourth leg left for future construction."

Somewhat cavalierly, the Court settled the question of jurisdiction. Unless the complaint were so frivolous as to be devoid of merit, the fact that the case presented a Fourteenth Amendment claim was sufficient to convince Brennan that the Court had jurisdiction.

With similar ease, the Court established consensus on the question of standing. The only justice to demur was Felix Frankfurter, who reminded his colleagues that the *Colegrove* case involved not a private wrong but an incidence of alleged public malfeasance. Dismissing this objection, Brennan's opinion stated that, as registered voters in overpopulated legislative districts, the plaintiffs were entitled to claim that they had been personally as well as collectively disadvantaged. Furthermore, they had standing to sue regardless of the merits of their allegations.

As expected, the question of justiciability proved to be much thornier, for it required a reexamination of the doctrine of political questions. Brennan held that several criteria were essential to a finding of a nonjusticiable political question. Among these criteria were (1) a "textually demonstrable constitutional commitment of the issue to a coordinate political department," or (2) "a lack of judicially discoverable and manageable standards for resolving it." Cases involving foreign relations, time limits for ratifying constitutional amendments, and guarantees to states under Article IV (e.g., a "republican form of government") are examples of political questions imposing reasonable constraints on the federal judiciary, Brennan stated.

At considerable length, Brennan's opinion attempted to differentiate between *Baker* and past cases the court had judged to be inherently political and, therefore, nonjusticiable. In *Baker*, "[W]e have no question decided, or to be decided, by a political branch of government coequal with this court," he claimed. Then, in a brash assertion of judicial power, Brennan held that judicial standards necessary for resolving the dispute "are well developed and familiar" and indeed had been available since the ratification of the Fourteenth Amendment. Perhaps sensing his colleagues' unease with such a broad claim, Brennan used the Court's decision in *Gomillion* to show that challenges to certain state governmental arrangements could be construed as justiciable under the Fifteenth Amendment.

The majority opinion was greeted by Frankfurter's stirring dissent. He contended that, except in matters of racial discrimination, mandates under the equal protection clause for judicial intrusion into "matters of state government" were not as self-evident as Brennan seemed to imply. Frankfurter rejected the appellants' contention that their individual votes had been "diluted" as a result of alleged malapportionment. Such a claim, Frankfurter argued, was "circular talk," since the value of a vote was indeterminate. He noted that representation based solely on population was not universally practiced by the states at the time the Fourteenth Amendment was ratified. He summarized his objections by stating that the Court was being asked "to choose among competing bases of representation—ultimately, really, among competing theories of political philosophy" in an ill-advised and misguided effort to devise a preferred system of state elections. In presuming to prescribe an apportionment system suitable for Tennessee or any other state, the Court's majority, in Frankfurter's view, had not only entered the political thicket; it was wallowing in it.

Frankfurter's dissent was somewhat overwrought, for the Court's decision avoided establishing a standard for state legislative apportionment. Instead, the case was remanded to the federal district court in Nashville for trial on its merits.

Reaction to the Court's decision in *Baker v. Carr* was swift. Editorial support came forth from most of the major metropolitan newspapers. The American Municipal Association, the U.S. Conference of Mayors, and major labor unions also expressed approval. Attorney General Robert Kennedy, who would soon represent the government in a Georgia reapportionment case, called *Baker* "a landmark in the development of representative government." And, in sharp contrast to President Dwight Eisenhower's posture of detachment from the Court's school desegregation decision in 1954, President John Kennedy professed unqualified approval of the *Baker* ruling.

However, the decision was not without its critics, especially in the South. In Tennessee, a state representative drew a parallel between the Court's desegregation rulings and the recent reapportionment decision: "Apparently

[the Court's] formula is more Negroes and less money for rural areas." Senator Richard Russell of Georgia accused the Court of setting out to destroy the American system of checks and balances.

Although the Supreme Court itself did not specify precise standards for reapportionment, the practical implication was that at least one house of a state's legislature had to be apportioned on the basis of equal population districts. In the flood of state and federal court litigation that ensued, the mere demonstration of population inequalities was sufficient in most instances for plaintiffs to win decisions invalidating existing apportionment systems.

As an example of Warren court activism, it is tempting to compare the historic *Baker v. Carr* decision to the Court's decree in *Brown v. Board of Education* (1954). Although similarities exist, the differences are more striking. First, unlike *Brown*, which was the capstone of the Court's increasing willingness to strike down racial barriers in public accommodations, *Baker v. Carr* was a dramatic reversal of two decades of precedent. More important, in contrast to the desegregation decision, which met with considerable resistance and noncompliance, the impact of the reapportionment decision was immediate. Within a year of the ruling, thirty-six states were involved in litigation. By the end of 1963, at least one house of each of twenty-four state legislatures had been ruled unconstitutional by either a federal or state court.

Round two of the reapportionment revolution began in March 1963 when the Supreme Court took up arguments in *Gray v. Sanders*. At issue was the validity of Georgia's "county-unit" system for nominating the governor, U.S. senators, and other statewide officers. Under this method, each of Georgia's 159 counties was assigned six, four, or two units, awarded on a winner-take-all basis to the candidate receiving a plurality of the county popular vote. Defenders argued that the procedure was equivalent to the electoral college system. However, unlike the electoral college, in which the allocation of electors to states is adjusted every ten years according to population changes, the allotment of units to Georgia's counties had remained static since 1917. To illustrate the inequity implicit in this method, Fulton County (Atlanta), with a 1960 population of half a million, had six units, while to Echols County's, with a population of 1,800, had two units. Thus, to offset a single popular vote in Echols, a candidate would have needed to receive ninety-nine in Fulton.

In *Gray v. Sanders*, the justices ordered that simple-majority, at-large nomination be substituted for the county-unit system, which was held to be unconstitutional under the equal protection clause of the Fourteenth Amendment. Writing for the majority, Justice William O. Douglas declared that the "conception of political equality . . . can mean only one thing—one person, one vote." Although the decision did not involve questions of legislative apportionment or districting, the catchphrase "one person, one vote" became the guiding force in future reapportionment cases.

In February 1964, the Court handed down another sweeping decision involving the state of Georgia. At issue in *Wesberry v. Sanders* was the apportionment of the state's congressional districts. As of 1960, one of every five Georgians lived in the district encompassing Atlanta. Yet, with a population three times that of the state's smallest district, Atlanta had only one of Georgia's representatives. This time, the Court's majority opinion was written by Justice Hugo Black, who stated that "as nearly as is practicable, one man's vote in a congressional election is to be worth as much as another's."

Having mandated equal population districts for purposes of congressional representation, it was but a matter of time before the federal courts would apply the same principle to state legislatures. In *Reynolds v. Sims* (1964), a case in which challenges to legislatures in six states (Alabama, Colorado, Delaware, Maryland, New York, and Virginia) were joined, the reapportionment revolution finally unfolded.

Few were surprised that the Alabama case would provide the framework for the principal arguments in *Reynolds v. Sims*. Like many of its neighbors, the state was a classic case study in southern political pathology, the dominant symptom of which was the suppression and disfranchisement of Alabama's black population.

The origins of Alabama's reapportionment wars date back to 1901, when, after considerable factional infighting, the all-Democratic legislature adopted a new state constitution. Largely conceived as an instrument for eliminating blacks from the political process, the constitution was an unqualified triumph for the conservative alliance of industrial "Big Mules" and "Black Belt" planters. Over the objections of north Alabama lawmakers who, true to their Populist heritage, advocated state spending policies favorable to their have-not constituencies, the reapportionment plan, while ostensibly based on population, guaranteed each of the state's sixty-seven counties at least one seat in the House of Representatives. Respecting the integrity of county boundaries, single-member Senate districts comprised one or more whole counties.

The constitution of 1901 required reapportionment every ten years according to census enumerations, but this mandate was regularly ignored. In the 1940s and 1950s, Governor James "Kissin' Jim" Folsom, a populist hillbilly with a sympathy for blacks that eventually led to his political demise, tried unsuccessfully to circumvent the legislature's inaction by assembling a constitutional convention. The apportionment formula devised in 1901 remained unchanged until the 1960s, when the first volleys were fired in the case of *Reynolds v. Sims*. Consistent with the provisions of the antiquated constitution, population variances among the state's single-member Senate districts were as great as forty to one. In the House of Representatives, Bullock County—located in the heart of the Black Belt (where blacks were counted for census purposes despite being denied voting rights)—had one representative for its population of 13,000. Jefferson County (Birmingham), with a 1960 population of 600,000, had just seven representatives and, like Bullock, a single senator.

On August 12, 1961, Charles Morgan, a young Birmingham attorney, filed suit in federal district court alleging that he and his five co-plaintiffs were deprived of free and equal elections guaranteed by the Fourteenth Amendment. Noting the failure of the legislature to reapportion for sixty years, the suit claimed that fewer than twenty-three percent of Alabama's voters elected more than half of the state legislators. Personally motivating Morgan, a white liberal with ties to the national Democratic Party leadership, was a belief that racial justice would not come to Alabama until power were wrested from the Black Belt.

A month later, the Fifth U.S. Circuit Court of Appeals, headquartered in New Orleans, assigned the case to a three-member panel chaired by Alabama federal judge Frank M. Johnson. Appointed by President Eisenhower, Johnson was one of the "fifty-eight lonely men"—federal judges cross-pressured between their southern loyalties and their sworn duty to carry out the civil-rights decisions and orders of the Supreme Court. In 1965, Johnson, a law-school classmate of George Wallace, locked horns with the governor when the judge dissolved Wallace's order banning the Selma-to-Montgomery voting-rights march.

After considering two alternative reapportionment schemes, both of which had received the tentative acceptance of the state legislature, the Johnson panel fashioned a compromise calling for a 106-member house of representatives, apportioned according to population provided that each county be guaranteed at least one seat. And, in a plan that differed only slightly from the existing arrangement, thirty-five single-member state senate districts were proposed. Finally, the panel made it clear that its order was temporary pending enactment by the state legislature of a judicially acceptable apportionment system.

The appeal of the Johnson ruling to the U.S. Supreme Court was a most curious one. The state probate judges who were originally named as defendants in the suit presented predictable arguments laced with states' rights rhetoric, and they asked the Court simply to acknowledge its error in *Baker v. Carr* and to reinstate the *Colegrove* rule of nonjusticiability. Charles Morgan's brief, a short one, applauded Johnson's compromise and requested that the final details of reapportionment be remanded to the district court. However, a group of three of the victorious plaintiffs presented a separate brief contending that the Johnson ruling did not go far enough because it guaranteed every county, regardless of population, one house member.

Oral arguments in *Reynolds v. Sims* were held intermittently from November 1963 to April 1964. In his presentation before the justices, Alabama attorney general Richmond Flowers, nominally a defendant in the case, conceded that state legislative apportionment under the 1901 constitution was grossly inequitable. Realizing the unlikelihood that the Court would turn back the clock to the pre-*Baker* era, Flowers argued that "to some extent" population-based apportionment would be essential for both houses of the state legislature.

On June 15, 1964, the Court announced its decision in *Reynolds v. Sims* and the five companion cases. In an opinion remarkable for its simplicity—though critics have called it politically naive—Chief Justice Earl Warren spoke for a six-member majority in establishing population as the only legitimate and constitutionally defensible basis of apportionment. "Legislators represent people, not trees or acres," nor economic interests, he pronounced. Warren rejected the defendants' claim that inexactness among Alabama's state legislative districts was no different from the equal representation of states in the U.S. Senate. At the federal level, the chief justice responded, representation was the result of historical necessities and was forged by "compromise and concession indispensable to the establishment of our republic." Dismissing the federal analogy as specious and unparallel, Warren concluded that the Fourteenth Amendment "requires both houses of a bicameral state legislature to be apportioned on a population basis."

Though the Court's decision was couched principally in equal protection reasoning, Warren could not resist drawing on two decades of precedent setting in the Fifteenth Amendment area of voting rights. Surely, if the Court could void a law permitting some citizens to cast ten votes, it could bar antiquated state legislative apportionment systems that produced the same effect.

Justice John Harlan, the lone dissenter in all six cases, echoed the sentiments of his former colleague Felix Frankfurter in characterizing the decision as an exercise in "venturesome constitutionalism." Acting as an instrument for political reform, the Court had taken it upon itself to amend the Constitution, Harlan said.

Political reaction to the Court's decision was mixed. As expected, southern legislators vilified the decision as yet another judicial intrusion into the affairs of the states. Arizona senator Barry Goldwater, eager to win southern support for his presidential candidacy, denounced *Reynolds v. Sims* as a prime example of the Court's disrespect for limited government. Predictably, liberal Democrats praised the decision as the capstone of recent civil- and voting-rights rulings. However, many moderate Democrats, including President Johnson, who had generally approved of the Court's ruling in *Baker*, wondered if the justices had gone too far in *Reynolds*.

Regardless of one's appraisal of the Court's wisdom, there was universal agreement that a constitutional milestone had been reached. The *New York Times* commented that the reapportionment decisions of 1964 easily surpassed the 1954 desegregation ruling as the most sweeping judgment of the Warren court. Indeed, there was considerable truth in the editorial assessment of *Reynolds* as the most momentous decision since 1803, when, in *Marbury v. Madison*, the Court established the power of judicial review. One legal expert, while regarding the Court's reasoning as constitutionally untidy, nonetheless proclaimed the reapportionment decisions, especially those of 1964, to be as significant for the "theory and practice of representative democracy as the equally bloodless Glorious Revolution of 1688." In *Baker v. Carr,* the Supreme Court took a bold step in indicating its willingness to enter Justice Frankfurter's political thicket. In *Reynolds v. Sims,* the thicket was cleared.

Selected Bibliography

Cortner, Richard C. *The Apportionment Cases.* Knoxville: University of Tennessee Press, 1970.

Dixon, Robert G., Jr. *Democratic Representation: Reapportionment in Law and Politics.* New York: Oxford University Press, 1968.

Graham, Gene. *One Man, One Vote: Baker v. Carr and the American Levellers.* Boston: Little, Brown, 1972.

Hanson, Royce. *The Political Thicket.* Englewood Cliffs: Prentice-Hall, 1966.

Hardy, Leroy, Alan Helsop, and Stuart Anderson, eds. *Reapportionment Politics: The History of Redistricting in the 50 States.* Beverly Hills: Sage, 1981.

Jewell, Malcolm. *The Politics of Reapportionment.* New York: Atherton, 1962.

Key, V. O., Jr. *Southern Politics in State and Nation.* Knoxville: University of Tennessee Press, 1971.

Polsby, Nelson W., ed. *Reapportionment in the 1970s.* Berkeley: University of California Press, 1971.

Rigdon, Louis. *Georgia's County Unit System.* Decatur, Georgia: Selective, 1961.

Taper, Bernard. *Gomillion versus Lightfoot: The Tuskegee Gerrymander Case.* New York: McGraw-Hill, 1961.

The 2000 Florida Election Cases:
Politics over Principles

———⚬———

Christine L. Nemacheck

Department of Political Science
Iowa State University

Bush v. Gore, 531 U.S. ___ (2000); *Bush v. Palm Beach County Canvassing Board,*
531 U.S. ___ (2000) [U.S. Supreme Court]

⚬ THE CASE IN BRIEF ⚬

Date
2000

Location
Florida
District of Columbia

Court
Florida Supreme Court
U.S. Supreme Court

Principal Participants
Governor George W. Bush
Vice President Al Gore

Significance of the Case
The U.S. Supreme Court ruled on the outcome of a disputed presidential election in the state of Florida, thereby determining who became the 43rd president of the United States.

In a 1993 book, political scientists Jeffrey Segal and Harold Spaeth wrote: "If a case on the outcome of a presidential election should reach the Supreme Court, . . . the Court's decision might well turn on the personal preferences of the justices." The 2000 presidential election demonstrated the prescience of this observation.

After an election night (November 7) in which Florida's 25 electoral college votes were first awarded by the major television networks to Vice President Al Gore, then to Governor George W. Bush, and then determined to be too close to call, the court system was left to untangle complex state and federal election law, eventually determining who would be president. The Supreme Court's involvement in the election battle began November 24, when it granted *certiorari* to hear Governor Bush's appeal of a decision allowing hand recounts in Palm Beach County, *Bush v. Palm Beach County Canvassing Board et al.,* and ended December 12 with its decision in *Bush v. Gore,* essentially deciding the election in favor of George W. Bush.

In U.S. presidential elections, the plurality winner of the popular vote in each state is granted all of that state's "electoral college votes." Each state's representation in the electoral college is based on the combined total of its congressional representatives and its U.S. senators. To win the election, a candidate must gain a majority (270) of the electoral college votes. Under this system, states with a large population, such as Florida, are essential in the candidates' campaign strategies. In the weeks before November 7, the two presidential candidates focused heavily on Florida in what was shaping up to be an extremely tight presidential race. Many political pundits gave Governor Bush the advantage in Florida since his brother, Jeb Bush, was the state's governor. However, Vice President Gore also campaigned heavily in Florida, believing he could win the state by drawing a majority of the state's population of senior citizens.

On election night 2000, one of the feared scenarios of a close election came to pass. One candidate, Al Gore, won the popular vote, but the other candidate, George W. Bush, appeared to have a chance to capture a majority of the electoral college. Thus, for the first time since the Cleveland-Harrison election of 1888, it appeared possible that the winner of the popular vote might not win the presidency. These unusual circumstances thrust the U.S. Supreme Court into a politically explosive controversy.

According to Florida election law, if the margin of victory in the presidential election is less than or equal to 0.5 percent, there must be a machine recount of the state's popular vote. When the November 7 votes were counted (with the exception of absentee ballots) Bush had 2,909,135 and Gore had 2,907,351. Thus, a mandatory machine recount was conducted, and, as a result, Bush's lead was further reduced to a mere 327 votes. This was, however, only the beginning of the controversy.

In following weeks, further recounts were begun at the behest of the Gore campaign and then, for one reason or another, halted. Hundreds of lawyers employed by the two parties descended on the Sunshine State. Stories of voting problems throughout Florida were reported in the media. In addition to the automatic recount, the Gore campaign requested hand recounts in four Florida counties—Broward, Miami-Dade, Volusia, and Palm Beach—where election results in Bush's favor seemed to belie the registered voting preferences (Democratic) of a majority of the voters.

The candidates filed numerous lawsuits on a variety of legal grounds. The most important decisions were two by the U.S. Supreme Court that turned on questions of federalism and equal protection. While the Florida Supreme Court reached decisions generally favoring Vice President Gore, the U.S. Supreme Court came to conclusions favoring Governor Bush. As a result, many speculated that the state court, to which former Democratic governor Lawton Chiles had appointed all but one of the members, reached conclusions favoring the Democratic candidate, and the U.S. Supreme Court, to which Democratic presidents appointed only two of the nine justices, leaned to the Republican aspirant.

In response to the Florida Supreme Court's ruling allowing manual recounts and including recounted votes in the state's certified total, Governor Bush petitioned the U.S. Supreme Court for a writ of *certiorari* on November 22. In its December 4 *per curiam* opinion on this matter, the U.S. Supreme Court vacated the Florida Supreme Court's decision and remanded the case for further clarification. In particular, the U.S. Supreme Court was unclear as to what extent the Florida court considered federal statutes, which required that laws governing the electors' appointment, be enacted before the election, and whether its interpretation of Florida election law circumscribed legislative authority, violating Article II, Section 1, of the U.S. Constitution providing for the appointment of electors appointed from each state "in such Manner as the Legislature thereof may direct." The Supreme Court found it was uncertain "as to the precise grounds for the decision" of the Florida court and declined to review the federal questions presented.

The U.S. Supreme Court's decision essentially voided the Florida high court's ruling. In layman's terms, the Court "punted." The decision did not settle the disputed election and left the door open for future Supreme Court involvement in the heated election debate. Many close watchers of the Court were surprised it granted *certiorari* in the case at all, given its normal proclivity to refrain from intruding into state political matters. That the U.S. Supreme Court would agree to review the state court's decision on this question seemed contrary to numerous recent Court rulings favoring states' rights over federal powers.

The second landmark U.S. Supreme Court case addressed votes certified by Florida secretary of state Katherine Harris on November 26. Vice President Gore contested these certified results because they did not include manual recounts. Based on Florida statutory provisions dealing with election contests, a 4-3 majority opinion of the state Supreme Court reasoned there was potential for the election results to be in doubt and it was within the court's authority to provide relief. It thus ordered recounts in all counties with large numbers of ballots not recording a vote for president. The chief justice of the state court strongly dissented, arguing that the lack of uniform county standards in recounting would lead to further disputes and possible congressional action.

Governor Bush filed an application for a stay of this decision. The U.S. Supreme Court granted the stay on December 9 along with a writ of *certiorari* to hear the case. The political fault lines present on the bench were evident in the stay. Justice John Paul Stevens, joined by Justices David H. Souter, Ruth Bader Ginsburg, and Stephen Breyer, issued a strong dissent to the Court's decision to grant the stay. Stevens urged, in language more commonly used by the conservative members of the Court, that the stay violated the norm of judicial restraint absent evidence of irreparable harm to the applicant. In a rare concurring opinion, Justice Antonin Scalia argued that the issue was not about counting "legally cast vote[s]" but whether the recounted votes were legal at all.

The Supreme Court's final decision in *Bush v. Gore* was even more controversial than its prior ruling and again revealed the ideological division of the Court. In a 5-4 *per curiam* opinion, issued on December 12, 2000, the Court reversed the Florida Supreme Court's ruling that manual recounts should take place and remanded the case for further state court attention. The

U.S. Supreme Court's decision effectively ended the presidential election contest as the candidate with the most "official" votes at the time, George Bush, received Florida's 25 electoral votes. Vice President Gore conceded the election the following evening.

The Court's *per curiam* opinion addressed only the question of whether the conflicting county recount standards violated the equal protection and due process clauses of the Fourteenth Amendment. The majority argued that the issue in the recounting process was not determining the "intent of the voter," but rather the absence of uniform standards for counting votes in the first place. It reasoned that, since a recount could not be "conducted in compliance with the requirements of equal protection and due process" by the December 12 deadline for "safe harbor" of the Florida electors, the decision of the Florida Supreme Court should be reversed.

Chief Justice William Rehnquist, along with Justices Scalia and Clarence Thomas, detailed further problems with the Florida Supreme Court's decision. They argued that, while federalism would "compel us to defer to the decisions of state courts on issues of state law," in this case concerning the presidential election it did not. They contended that the question of power between the state's supreme court and legislature pertained to federal constitutional and statutory law, specifically Article II, Section 1, Clause 2 of the Constitution and Title 3 of the U.S. Code.

While the majority argued in favor of the U.S. Supreme Court involvement in counting the disputed votes, the dissenting opinions vigorously maintained that the Court had no place interfering with the state supreme court's interpretation of state law. In her strong dissent, Justice Ginsburg appealed for greater judicial restraint, arguing that the Court should hold to its standard of "deferring to state courts on matters of state law." Justice Breyer also expressed his disagreement with the Court's decision. "The Court was wrong to take this case," he wrote. "It was wrong to grant a stay. It should now vacate that stay and permit the Florida Supreme Court to decide whether the recount should resume."

Bush and Gore demonstrators swap words outside the U.S. Supreme Court in Washington, D.C., as they await the outcome of the historic case involving the disputed vote in Florida in the 2000 presidential election. *Corbis.*

Justice Stevens's dissent, joined by Justices Ginsburg and Breyer, was perhaps the most critical. "When questions arise about the meaning of state laws," Justice Stevens wrote, "including election laws, it is our settled practice to accept the opinions of the highest courts of the States as providing the final answers." Stevens maintained that, if there was an equal protection concern, the appropriate action was to remand the case to the state court for the development of uniform standards. By not following this course of action, he contended, the Court's decision resulted in the "disenfranchisement of an unknown number of voters whose ballots reveal their intent—and are therefore legal votes under state law—but were for some reason rejected by ballot-counting machines."

In the immediate aftermath of the decision, constitutional scholars and political pundits labeled the ruling partisan and feared it would harm the Court's prestige. Highlighting the importance of judicial preferences, several commentators pointed to the ironic nature of the justices' rationale in the cases. Justices noted for their reluctance to become involved in "state" legal issues, constitutional scholars pointed out, reasoned that the federal courts were right to step in and "correct" the decision of the highest state court. By contrast, these scholars observed that justices typically less prone to judicial restraint maintained in this case that the Supreme Court was overly active and wrong to rule on an issue reserved to the states.

Most political scientists contend that there is more to the process of judicial decision making than the neutral application of controlling legal precedent to a particular set of facts. Indeed, these scholars maintain that decision making on the Court ought to be viewed through a framework that encompasses the justices' own attitudes and preferences. This is not to say that the legal basis for justices' decisions is irrelevant. Rather, they maintain that justices use legal precedent to reach decisions consistent with their preferences.

In the wake of the Supreme Court's two 2000 Florida election decisions, discussions of justices' likely biases flooded the popular media. Analysis centered not only on the political preferences of the justices but also on some of their likely career aspirations. Commentators noted that Chief Justice Rehnquist might wish to step down from the bench during the following four years and could do so more comfortably with a Republican president to name his successor. With that in mind, others speculated that Justice Scalia might be angling for appointment as the new chief. When the network news prematurely called the state of Florida for Vice President Gore, Justice Sandra Day O'Connor, at an election night party, reportedly declared, "This is terrible." *Newsweek* reported that Justice O'Connor's husband explained her comment by saying she "was upset because they wanted to retire to Arizona, and a Gore win meant they'd have to wait another four years."

The decision of the Supreme Court in *Bush v. Gore* will be studied for years to come. When internal memoranda and deliberations of the justices are made public, the case will likely provide further evidence for the importance of preferences and strategic behavior in the decision making process. On the day after the Court's opinion was handed down, Justice Clarence Thomas spoke before an audience of high school students. In response to a question about the role of politics on the Court, Justice Thomas declared that he had not heard any "partisan politics" discussed among the justices during his time on the highest bench and implored the students not "to apply the rules of the political world to this institution."

Though many on the bench will continue to assert, as did Justice Thomas, that the Supreme Court is apolitical, the controversy over the 2000 Florida election cases suggests otherwise. The vast majority of American legal scholars accept, almost as a commonplace, that judges and justices act strategically to assert their political preferences. Converting the public to a similar skepticism may be the most important legacy of these two decisions. As Justice Stevens lamented in dissent in *Bush v. Gore,* "Although we may never know with complete certainty the identity of the winner of this year's Presidential election, the identity of the loser is perfectly clear. It is the Nation's confidence in the judge as an impartial guardian of the rule of law."

Selected Bibliography

Epstein, Lee, and Jack Knight. *The Choices Justices Make.* Washington, D.C.: CQ Press, 1998.

Maltzman, Forrest, James F. Spriggs, II, and Paul J. Wahlbeck. *Crafting Law on the Supreme Court: The Collegial Game.* Cambridge: Cambridge University Press, 2000.

Segal, Jeffrey A., and Harold J. Spaeth. *Supreme Court and the Attitudinal Model.* Cambridge: Cambridge University Press, 1993.

Wahlbeck, Paul J., James F. Spriggs, Forrest Maltzman. "Marshalling the Court: Bargaining and Accommodation on the United States Supreme Court," *American Journal of Political Science.* 42 (1998): 294–315.

Wroth, L. Kinvin. "Election Contests and the Electoral Vote," *Dickinson Law Review* 65 (1961): 321–353.

Governmental Scandals

Can Intemperate Behavior
Be a "High Crime or Misdemeanor"?

———◄◦►———

Can Intemperate Behavior Be a "High Crime or Misdemeanor"?

———◄◦►———

Richard E. Ellis

Department of History
State University of New York at Buffalo

The Impeachment Trial of Samuel Chase, (1805) [U.S. Congress]

◄◦► THE CASE IN BRIEF ◄◦►

Date
1805

Location
District of Columbia

Court
U.S. Senate, sitting as a court of impeachment

Principal Participants
Justice Samuel Chase
John Randolph

Significance of the Case
The first impeachment case brought before the Congress raised a fundamental question of whether the Congress could remove a Supreme Court justice for less than "a high crime or misdeameanor."

The trial of Samuel Chase in 1805 was one of the earliest and most dramatic examples of the implementation of the impeachment clause of the U.S. Constitution. The framers of the Constitution had provided for the removal of federal judges who held their offices for "life tenure during good behavior." If a judge committed "treason, bribery, or other high crimes and misdemeanors," the House of Representatives, by means of a majority vote, could impeach the judge and require him or her to stand trial before the U.S. Senate, where a two-thirds majority vote was necessary for conviction and removal. Chase's trial was the first *cause célèbre* involving this mode of removal, and it raised fundamental questions about what constituted "good behavior" for judges and how far Congress could go to make members of the federal judiciary amenable to popular opinion, as well as what meaning a change of administrations had for how the Constitution was to operate.

Samuel Chase, the central figure in the case, was an extremely bright, aggressive, and difficult person. During the 1760s and 1770s, he played an important role in the revolutionary movement in Maryland. He also signed the Declaration of Independence and served as a member of the Continental Congress from 1775 to 1778, but he left in disgrace when Alexander Hamilton denounced him for using privileged information in order to speculate in commodities. Returning to Baltimore, Chase pursued a variety of business interests, practiced law, and reentered politics. He was an important antifederalist leader in the struggle over the ratification of the Constitution in 1787 and 1780, but once it was adopted, for reasons that remain a mystery, he became an ardent nationalist and supporter of the Federalist Party.

During this time, Chase was appointed to several important political posts in Maryland. His career as a state judge was fraught with controversy. He developed a reputation for being partisan, combative, and insensitive to other people's feelings, but also for being extremely energetic and knowledgeable about the law. In 1975, he was nominated to the U.S. Supreme Court. President George Washington was at first reluctant to appoint him, but when he had trouble filling the post, he finally offered it to Chase.

Chase proved to be an important and enthusiastic member of the Supreme Court during the pre-Marshall period. His decisions in *Ware v. Hylton* (1796), *Hylton v. United States,* (1796) and *Calder v. Bull* (1798) are able and learned. At the same time, however, he became increasingly committed to the Federalist cause. He used his charges to grand juries to make political speeches, taking sides in electoral contests and commenting on controversial issues.

Like many of his contemporaries, Chase refused to recognize the legitimacy of the Jeffersonian opposition, viewing them as subversives who intended to overthrow the government created by the Constitution. While it is clear, in retrospect, that Thomas Jefferson and James Madison did not intend this, the Federalist point of view had a certain logic to it, because its adherents had participated in or observed the overthrow of English rule and the discarding of the Articles of Confederation. Their view was further strengthened by the fact that the overwhelming majority of anti-federalists had joined the Jeffersonian opposition.

Federalist concern led in 1798 to the adoption of the Sedition Act, which made it a crime, punishable by fine and imprisonment, to obstruct the execution of a federal law, or to prevent an official of the national government from performing his duties, and to aid or participate in "any insurrection, riot, unlawful assembly, or combination." It also made it a crime to "write, print, utter, or publish . . . any false, scandalous, and malicious writing" against the government or its officers "with intent to defame . . . or to bring them . . . into contempt or disrepute; or to excite against them . . . the hatred of the . . . people . . . or to stir up sedition."

Incensed by the various Jeffersonian attacks upon John Adams and the Federalist-dominated Congress between 1798 and 1800, and lacking a judicial temperament, Chase decided when he covered the middle circuit from April through June 1800 to enforce the Sedition Act with a vengeance. The initial trial came in the case of an English immigrant editor, Thomas Cooper. Indicted under the Sedition Act for attacking Adams and his supporters, Chase, on the whole, conducted the trial fairly, but when he charged the jury he made clear his belief that Cooper was guilty. Chase asserted, in no uncertain terms, that what Cooper had published was untrue. Moreover, it was seditious. He concluded his charge by observing that "this publication in all its parts . . . is the boldest attempt I have known to poison the minds of the people. . . . This publication is evidently intended to mislead the ignorant, and inflame their minds against the president." A short time later, the jury brought in a guilty verdict.

Chase next proceeded to Philadelphia, where he presided over the trial of John Fries, a minor militia officer who had led a group of Pennsylvania Germans in a rebellion against the federal tax collector. Fries had previously been tried, convicted, and sentenced to death, but the discovery that one of the jurors had expressed a bias had resulted in a new trial. The political implications of the trial became clear when two leading Jeffersonian attorneys who were already members of the Philadelphia bar, William Lewis and Alexander Dallas, volunteered their services for Fries's defense. Willing to concede the facts of the case, Lewis and Dallas's strategy was to argue that they did not fit the legal definition of treason. After the jury had been impaneled, Chase, faced with a full docket and eager to expedite the trial, precipitously handed down a ruling confining the defense to the facts. Angered by this development, Lewis and Dallas denounced the ruling as politically motivated and withdrew from the case. Recognizing that he had acted impetuously and had made a mistake, Chase offered to withdraw his ruling. But Lewis and Dallas insisted on withdrawing. This left Fries without counsel, and he was again convicted and sentenced to death, although he was eventually pardoned by President Adams.

Most spectacular of all was Chase's action in the sedition trial of James T. Callender, a particularly scurrilous newspaperman. Chase had been openly critical of Callender and frequently expressed his desire to see him convicted. Moreover, since the trial was being held in Richmond, Virginia, where almost all the leading members of the bar believed the Sedition Act to be unconstitutional, Chase considered the trial a personal test of strength. He was determined to teach the Jeffersonian lawyers who had rallied to Callender's defense a lesson. Before a packed courtroom, Chase began by refusing to grant a continuance of the case and denouncing the defense for requesting it. The confrontation continued with a struggle over how prospective jurors were to be examined and what kind of questions were to be directed to them. Chase also required a juror, allegedly hostile to Callender, to serve, and he required the defense to reduce to writing the questions they intended to ask of their key witness, John Taylor of Carolina. After studying these questions, Chase refused to allow Taylor to testify. He also interrupted, attacked, and embarrassed the defense counsel so often that they finally abandoned the case. Convicted, Callender was sentenced to pay a fine of two hundred dollars and serve nine months in prison.

Next stop on the circuit was Newcastle, Delaware. When Chase learned that the grand jury there planned no indictments under the Sedition Act, he used his address to warn that a treasonable newspaper was being published in Wilmington and ordered the U.S. Attorney to search its files. He also refused a request from the jurors to be discharged, but he was forced to relent the next day when the federal prosecutor indicated that his investigation had revealed nothing seditious. By this time, Chase's activities were receiving considerable public attention, and this episode was carefully noted by his rapidly growing list of enemies, many of whom were on the road to victory in the election of 1800.

Thomas Jefferson's assumption of the presidency in 1801 and his party's capture of both houses of Congress raised a number of important and complex constitutional and ideological questions. It was the first time that an opposition party had come to power under the U.S. Constitution. Would it involve a change only in the personnel and policies of the new government, or would it lead to actual changes in the government itself? To what extent was the Jeffersonian victory a popular mandate for the new administration to do whatever it wanted? Would it be wiser for the new administration, after an especially bitter campaign, to try to accommodate the interests of the defeated minority? Not all Republicans agreed on how to answer these questions. Some, led by John Randolph, viewed Jefferson's victory as only a means to an end, and favored fundamental alterations of the Constitution. Others, led by James Madison, who more than anyone else had created the Constitution, were opposed to these kinds of changes.

Although Jefferson sympathized with the concerns of those who wanted basic changes made, he nonetheless opted for a policy of reconciliation and moderation. He indicated this in his inaugural address when he observed, "We are all Republicans; we are all Federalists." Jefferson simply refused to go along with a direct assault on the Constitution itself. To be sure, he introduced a number of reforms. He reduced the size of the army and the navy, repealed all internal taxes, established a program to pay off the national debt completely, reduced government spending, and introduced policies to encourage settlement of the national domain. But it was all done within the framework of the Constitution.

Nonetheless, Jefferson had a difficult time dealing with the national judiciary. It had been totally dominated by the Federalists in the 1790s. Because its members held their office for life tenure during good behavior, the federal judiciary was not subject to popular control, and it emerged from the "revolution of 1800" without a single Republican member. Even more infuriating to Republicans was that after the election results were known, the Federalist-dominated, lame-duck Congress passed the Judiciary Act of 1801, further expanding the power of the national courts and increasing their personnel by creating a system of circuit courts. Moreover, before he relinquished his office to Jefferson, John Adams made sure that all the appointments under the new law went to Federalists. He also, at the same time, appointed John Marshall, whom Jefferson did not like, as chief justice of the Supreme Court.

Republicans favoring changes in the Constitution argued that these developments justified a thorough overhauling of the national judiciary. But Jefferson pursued a more moderate course. He simply brought about in 1802 a repeal of the Judiciary Act of 1801, returning the national court system with minor modifications, to the way it had existed throughout the 1790s under the Judiciary Act of 1789. Many Federalists denounced these proceedings. They argued that the repeal was unconstitutional because federal judges could be removed from office only when found guilty of high crimes and misdemeanors. They took the matter to the Supreme Court, but that Federalist-dominated body, wary of further provoking the Jeffersonians, refused to declare the repeal of the Judiciary Act of 1801 unconstitutional. At the same time, under the leadership of John Marshall, the High Court handed down its famous decision in *Marbury v. Madison* (1803), declaring a part of the newly revived Judiciary Act of 1789 to be unconstitutional. But *Marbury* was in many ways an extremely ambiguous decision. While the Court claimed for itself the right to oversee the Constitution, it did not claim that its power to do so was either exclusive or final. Moreover, the actual holding of the case

worked to the advantage of Jefferson's administration, for the Court turned down the request of disappointed Federalist appointees for a writ of mandamus ordering the secretary of state to hand over to them their commissions as justices of the peace. The decision in *Marbury v. Madison* was later to take on enormous significance. It was the first example of the Supreme Court declaring a part of an Act of Congress unconstitutional, but at the time it was handed down it was considered, if anything, a defeat for the more belligerent members of the Federalist Party and a conciliatory gesture on the part of the Supreme Court toward the Jefferson administration.

It is clear that in early 1803 both Jefferson and Marshall hoped that the controversy over the national judiciary would abate. Chase, however, was unhappy with these developments. He had vigorously, if unsuccessfully, campaigned behind the scenes for the Supreme Court to declare the repeal law unconstitutional, and he remained adamant in his opposition to the Jeffersonians. "Things," he believed, "must take their natural course, from *bad* to *worse*." Refusing to alter his partisan behavior, Chase continued to attack the Republican Party and its principles.

At this point, certain developments revived and further polarized the question of continued Federalist control of the national judiciary. Jefferson received word of the activities of a Federalist district court judge in New Hampshire named John Pickering, who was engaging in bizarre and partisan activities on the bench. Closer examination revealed that Pickering was both insane and an alcoholic. Jefferson, at first, tried to persuade prominent New Hampshire Federalists to pressure Pickering into resigning. But they refused to do this unless Jefferson guaranteed that he would be replaced by someone of their own choosing. Jefferson reluctantly decided to ask for Pickering's impeachment.

The trial that followed was a mess. Impeachment required a conviction for "high crimes and misdemeanors," but if evidence indicating Pickering's insanity were admitted, it would not be possible to find the demented judge guilty on these grounds. As required by the

Constitution, the case was tried before the Senate with the vice president as presiding officer. Members loyal to the administration, with Jefferson's support, conspired to prevent any discussion of the judge's mental condition. Although Pickering was convicted, it was an unpleasant and partisan business, and a number of the more moderate Jeffersonian senators absented themselves from the final balloting. The outcome of the case, however, did represent a victory for the more extreme Jeffersonians, because the impeachment clause of the Constitution had been successfully used to remove a federal judge from office.

Pickering was the first federal judge to be removed under the impeachment clause of the Constitution. Because of the special circumstances under which he had violated the trust of his office, because the Federalists would not cooperate in obtaining his resignation, and because neither the Constitution nor the existing laws provided an adequate remedy, the Jefferson administration was forced into the uncomfortable position of giving a very liberal definition to the clause in the Constitution defining impeachable offenses. As one observer noted, "the process of impeachment is to be considered in effect as *a mode of removal,* and not as a charge and conviction of high crimes and misdemeanors." Support for this interpretation came from a number of eighteenth-century English and American colonial precedents, where impeachment had indeed been used as a way of removing one's political opponents from office. Nonetheless, it went counter to (1) the Jefferson administration's earnest desire to reduce partisan tensions and (2) to the feelings among many of the president's closest political supporters, feelings that had found muted expression during the Pickering trial, that impeachment should be narrowly defined and likened to a criminal prosecution.

The implications were fully understood by those Republicans who wanted to cleanse the Supreme Court of Federalist influence. William Branch Giles, a U.S. senator from Virginia, argued that "Removal by impeachment was nothing more than a declaration by Congress to this effect: you hold dangerous opinions and if you are suffered to carry them into effect, you will work the destruction of the Union. We want your offices for the purpose of giving them to men who will fill them better." John Randolph went even further, implying alterations to the Constitution by arguing that the constitutional provision that the judges shall hold their offices *during good behavior* was intended to guard them against *the executive* alone, and not by any means to control the power of Congress, on whose representation against the judges the president could remove them.

What this all meant became clear on the very day the Senate convicted Pickering, when Randolph moved and the House passed a resolution to impeach Chase. At first, Jefferson appeared to sympathize with this development. He was furious over a recent charge Chase had delivered to the federal grand jury in Baltimore in 1803. In it, he denounced the repeal of the Judiciary Act of 1801 as unconstitutional, and he attacked Jeffersonian activities on both the national and state level. To a Maryland congressman, Jefferson wrote, "ought the seditious and official attack on the principles of our Constitution . . . go unpunished?" Because most conversations about Chase invariably turned to the issue of impeachment, and because this Maryland congressman was a close ally of Randolph and one of the prosecutors for the House in the proceedings against Pickering in the Senate, the president seemed to be giving his consent to having Chase removed. Despite this, it is a mistake to think of the Chase impeachment as an administration-sponsored measure. In fact, when it became clear that Randolph and his allies intended to redefine the impeachment process so that it would be a way of removing political opponents from office as opposed to a means of removing public officials who had engaged in criminal activities, Jefferson began to back away from the issue and quietly withdrew his support. Chase's impeachment was a direct assault on the independence of the federal judiciary as provided for in the Constitution. For if Chase were convicted, it is highly likely that other members of the Supreme Court would have been similarly removed from office.

The driving force behind Chase's impeachment was John Randolph, who, from the beginning of Jefferson's administration, had been openly critical of its moderate course. Because of this, Randolph was never on close terms with the president. Moreover, Randolph had an abrasive personality and an acid tongue, which made him unpopular with many of his colleagues. "His insolent, haughty, overbearing disposition know[s] no bounds," commented one observer. As a consequence, the administration and many Republican congressmen not only wished to see Randolph's influence curbed, but were actually taking steps to have this done. There are strong indications that this attack upon his influence, combined with a desire on Randolph's part to force the administration to adopt a more aggressive attitude toward the Federalist-controlled judiciary, spurred Randolph to take the initiative and move the impeachment proceedings against Chase. It is doubtful that Randolph made his motion either at the request or with the consent of the president. Still, although there was some opposition in the House from moderate Jeffersonians as well as from Federalists, Jeffersonian antagonism toward Chase was greater in the spring of 1804 than toward Randolph, and so the motion passed.

Jeffersonian divisions deepened in the months between Chase's impeachment and the beginning of his trial. By far, the most important battle took place on the Yazoo compromise. The problem had its origins in 1795, when a corrupt Georgia legislature had been bribed by land speculators to sell, for a penny and a half an acre, over thirty-five million acres of Indian land in the Yazoo territory, located in what are today parts of Alabama and Mississippi. The next year, an irate citizenry elected a reform-minded legislature that rescinded the sale. But in the intervening time, much of the land had been sold to out-of-state speculators who had no knowledge of the fraud involved; many of them had resold it to parties even further removed from the original contract. The federal government became involved in 1802, when Georgia relinquished all claims to the land west of it with the proviso that the national government was to assume responsibility for satisfying the claims of various second-, third-, and fourth-party purchasers of Yazoo land. To

this end, Jefferson appointed a special commission that included the leading members of his administration. Although the commission found against the claimants, it strongly urged—for reasons of "tranquility" and because of "equitable considerations"—a compromise whereby five million acres of land would be set aside to satisfy the claimants.

When the matter came before the House of Representatives, Randolph launched a bitter attack on the commission's report. He argued that the original act was so evil that any compromise with it should be out of the question. In this fashion, Randolph succeeded in preventing Congress from legislating on a matter that the administration considered of great significance. It was a major setback for both the administration and the moderate Jeffersonians. Equally important, it went a long way toward convincing them that Randolph was a more formidable and dangerous opponent than Chase, whose influence on the Supreme Court had been circumscribed by John Marshall.

Randolph had crossed the Rubicon. Up to this point, most Republican members of the House, while quietly expressing their dislike of him, had generally accepted his leadership. Now they were openly critical of him. One Federalist noted that Randolph had "resigned his office of ruling the majority of Congress, for the substantial reason that he finds they will no longer be ruled by him. . . . One thing is certain the party at present seem broken and divided, and do not act with their usual concert." The significance of this was clearly recognized by a member of the House of Representatives, who observed: "The unanimity of the majority is broken. . . . The Samson Randolph is shorn of his locks, and as to any . . . influence . . . is become as weak as another man. Indeed, I believe for him to be very zealous in support of a question, would be a very ready way to lose it if the decision was confined exclusively to the Democratic party."

During all this, Chase quietly contrived to prepare his defense. His trial began on February 4, 1805, a particularly cold and unpleasant day. Aaron Burr, as vice president, was the presiding officer at the trial and had made the necessary preparations. He looked to England for precedents and was particularly influenced by the recent proceedings against Warren Hastings. As a result, the Senate chamber looked as much like a theater as a courtroom. Burr had his own chair placed in the center against a wall. Benches covered in crimson cloth were extended along each side for the senators. Directly in front of them were two enclosed areas. The House managers, led by Randolph, occupied one; Chase and his lawyers, the other. Behind the senators, in three tiers of benches draped with green cloth, sat members of the House of Representatives. Above, in specially built, semicircular galleries, also covered with green cloth, sat the rest of officialdom. Further back and open to the public was the permanent gallery, where over a thousand people were present. The Senate, one of its members commented, was "now fitted up in a style beyond anything which has ever appeared in this country."

The trial began with Chase's response to the charges against him. He extensively analyzed the eight articles of impeachment. In less capable hands, the reply could have been extremely tedious, but it had been prepared by some of the best lawyers in the country; moreover, most of the senators were themselves lawyers, perfectly capable of appreciating the technical arguments involved. Chase's response revealed that the defense's strategy was to deny that any of his actions were indictable offenses under either statute or common law. Chase challenged the legal appropriateness of those articles of impeachment that accused him of misconduct in the trial of Fries and Callender by raising a number of complicated, subtle, and even moot legal questions. They included the binding quality of local customs in federal courtrooms; the reciprocal rights and duties of the judge, jury and defense counsel; the legality of bad manners in a courtroom; the rules for submission of evidence; and the problems involved in proving criminal intent. Chase denied outright that whatever mistakes he may have made in procedure at the Fries and Callender trials were impeachable offenses as defined by the Constitution. To those articles that accused him of misconduct in charging a grand jury and refusing to release it at Newcastle, Delaware, in June

1800, Chase replied that he had only done his duty by directing that body to investigate an alleged offense, and that he had dismissed its members when they refused to make any presentments or indictments. Finally, in response to the article that accused him of misconduct in charging a grand jury in Baltimore in 1803, he denied making any seditious statements. He then gave a brief history of jury charges to demonstrate that he had acted according to custom. Chase concluded by defending his right as a citizen to speak on political topics. Throughout, he referred to the unwillingness of the prosecution to seek impeachment of the district judges who had presided with him at the different trials and who had concurred in his actions. The implication was clear: Chase was being tried for his political convictions.

Randolph did not reply effectively to Chase's carefully crafted defense. Because he was the author of the articles of impeachment, it was only natural for him to try to refute the arguments the defense had raised against them. Randolph could, under the right circumstances, be an effective and moving speaker, but against the intricate legal arguments of Chase's response, his primarily moral and emotional appeal was not persuasive. In the days that followed, Randolph's lack of legal training quickly became apparent as he failed to substantiate the charges against Chase. It also soon became clear that, in a legal sense, the articles of impeachment had been poorly constructed.

Randolph concluded for the prosecution on February 27. It was an embarrassing performance. He began by announcing that he had lost his notes. Then, instead of refuting the defense's interpretation of impeachment, he denounced it. Instead of using logic, he damned his opponents. A member of the House of Representatives described Randolph's performance in these terms: "He began a speech of about two hours and a half, with as little relation to the subject matter as possible—without order, connections or argument; consisting altogether of the most hackneyed commonplaces of popular declamation, mingled up with panegyrics and invectives upon person, with a few well-expressed ideas, a few striking figures, much distortion of face and contortion of body, tears, groans, and sobs, with occasional pauses for recollection, and continual complaints of having lost his notes."

The Senate met shortly after noon on March 1, 1805, to vote on the articles of impeachment. Each article was read in its entirety, and the question was put to each senator whether Chase was guilty or not guilty, as charged, of a high crime or misdemeanor. This took two hours, and throughout that period the chamber, filled with spectators, remained hushed. After the last senator voted and the votes were tabulated, Burr announced that there had not been a constitutional majority (a two-thirds vote) against Chase on any count, and therefore he was acquitted. The vice president then permanently adjourned the court.

All nine Federalists in the Senate voted not guilty on every article of impeachment. Six Jeffersonians joined them. The highest vote for conviction was nineteen on the article accusing Chase of misconduct for delivering a partisan charge to the grand jury in Baltimore. Not a single vote was cast against him on one of the articles alleging procedural mistakes at the Callender trial, and only four votes were cast against him on another article. This was a clear repudiation of Randolph's attempt to broaden the interpretation of what the Constitution intended to be impeachable offenses. Fewer than half the senators voted guilty more than four times. Even the meaning of those guilty votes is not altogether obvious. For example, a Tennessee senator who voted against Chase seven times privately admitted that he was glad the judge had been acquitted because it "would have a tendency to mitigate the imitation of party spirit." Thus, Jeffersonians as well as Federalists were responsible for Chase's acquittal.

Any explanation of Chase's acquittal must place considerable stress on the fact that Randolph did not make an effective case against the judge. Despite this, some scholars have argued that (1) Chase's behavior was not simply reprehensible, but also illegal and therefore impeachable, and (2) that he *deserved* to be convicted, and he would have been convicted if the prosecution had been placed in more capable hands. There is some evidence for this point of view. At least two important members of the

federal judiciary were critical of Chase's blatant political behavior and his often arbitrary rulings. Richard Peters, a particularly able district court judge in Pennsylvania, who often sat with Chase in the circuit courts, noted he never did so without some embarrassment. Chase, "was forever getting into some intemperate and unnecessary squabble." Moreover, Chief Justice Marshall, testifying during the impeachment trial, questioned the judge's conduct in a number of matters.

But it is also clear that Chase's actions were by no means unique. Several important Jeffersonians realized this. For example, the speaker of the House, Nathaniel Macon, a political ally and friend of Randolph, had been unenthusiastic about Chase's impeachment because he knew that other judges, including many Jeffersonians on the state level, had used their positions for partisan purposes. He warned, "It deserves the most serious consideration before a single step can be taken. Change the scene and suppose Chase had stretched as far on the other side, and had praised where no praise was deserving, would it be proper to impeach, because by such conduct he might lull the people to sleep while their interest was destroyed?" And George Clinton, vice president–elect at the time of Chase's trial, a leading anti-federalist, and no friend of either a strong or active central government or a Federalist-controlled national judiciary, explained Chase's acquittal in the following way: "The members who voted for his acquittal had no doubt but that the charges against him were substantial and of course that his conduct was improper and reprehensible, but considering that many parts of it were sanctioned by the practice of the other judges ever since the commencement of the present Judiciary systems and that the act with which he was charged was not prohibited by any express and positive law they could not consistently with their ideas of justice find him guilty of high crimes and misdemeanors. It was to such refined reasoning of some honest men that he owed his acquittal." Another Jeffersonian senator, noting that he and a colleague had voted with the Federalists for Chase's acquittal, observed "we did so on full conviction that the evidence, our oaths, the Constitution, and our consciences required us to act as we have done."

For the highly politicized generation of revolutionary Americans, no clear-cut definition of proper judicial behavior, especially in political trials, existed. Like the contemporary debate over the proper construction of the constitutional impeachment process, where competing definitions clamored for attention, so too the role of the early-nineteenth-century judiciary in cases involving political and partisan questions was by no means a settled matter. It therefore cannot be said that Chase had clearly violated established judicial procedures, or that what he did was singular, especially in a period of American history when lawbooks, treatises, and judicial codes generally did not have wide circulation. In other words, what was considered proper in legal theory often did not have any relationship to what was going on in the courtroom. The significance of the Chase trial seems to be that its results supported the views of those who argued that impeachment should be a criminal process and that judges should refrain from political activities. Since the Chase trial, impeachment for political purposes has been eschewed, at least where federal judges have been concerned. Notwithstanding his acquittal, from the time of his trial until his death in 1811, Chase refrained from engaging in political controversies. And since his impeachment, members of the federal judiciary have come to be thought of as having ideological philosophies (states' rights or nationalist before the Civil War, liberal or conservative after 1865), but not as being spokespersons for particular political parties.

Beyond this, any meaningful explanation of Chase's exoneration must also take into account the struggle within the Republican Party. Randolph recognized this when, after the trial, he complained, "The 'whimsicals' advocated the leading measures of their party until they were nearly ripe for execution, when they hung back. Condemned the step *after* it was taken, and, on most occasions, affected a *glorious neutrality*." President Jefferson was the most important member of the group who "affected a glorious neutrality." In the year preceding Chase's trial, he neither commented upon the impeachment proceedings nor discussed

them in his private letters. When the subject was raised at the numerous dinner parties to which he invited congressmen, the president remained silent. Had he not vigorously favored Pickering's removal, the insane judge probably would also have been acquitted. Jefferson's unwillingness to enforce party regularity on the Chase impeachment must be included as an important factor contributing to the final verdict.

Chase's acquittal delivered so serious a blow to Randolph's prestige and influence among Jeffersonians that he never recovered from it. His lack of preparation and inept handling of the trial put him in an especially bad light, since he "had boasted with great exaltation that this was *his* impeachment—that every article was drawn by *his* hand, and *he* was to have the whole merit of it." Even his friends were disgusted with him. Randolph's loss of influence was made clear the same day Chase was acquitted. Angered by the verdict, he delivered "a violent phillipic" that afternoon in the House, denouncing both Chase and the Senate. Randolph concluded by proposing an amendment to the Constitution giving the president the authority to remove any federal judge at the request of a majority of both houses of Congress. If it had been made before Chase's trial, the proposed amendment might have received considerable support and serious attention. Precedents for it existed in several of the state constitutions. But, coming as it did at the culmination of the intense struggle that had taken place within the Republican Party over the judiciary and constitutional reform, it simply gave Randolph's opponents another opportunity to embarrass him. The administration, it was noted, "disapproved of this extreme measure. By a large majority, the House referred the resolution to a committee and postponed its consideration. Observing these proceedings, Chase wrote, "I have always said that my enemies are as great fools as knaves."

Chase's impeachment trial represented the culmination of four years of struggle between Jeffersonians over the meaning of the "revolution of 1800." Viewed in this light, the acquittal was more a vote against Randolph and what he represented than one for Chase. In many ways, the outcome of the impeachment trial constituted not so much a defeat for the Jeffersonians, as it has so often been portrayed, but a victory for the policy of moderation and conciliation which the administration wanted to see implemented. At the end of Jefferson's presidency, the Constitution remained unimpaired. Perhaps the most important result of Chase's acquittal was the enormously significant legacy of constitutional stability that has marked American history.

Selected Bibliography

Berger, Raoul. *Impeachment: The Constitutional Problems.* Cambridge, MA: Harvard University Press, 1973.

Ellis, Richard E. *The Jeffersonian Crisis: Court and Politics in the Young Republic.* New York: Oxford University Press, 1971.

Haw, James, et al. *Stormy Patriot: The Life of Samuel Chase.* Baltimore, MD: Johns Hopkins University Press, 1981.

Hoffer, Peter C., and N. E. H. Hull. *Impeachment in America, 1635–1805.* New Haven, CT: Yale University Press, 1984.

Presser, Stephen B. "A Tale of Two Judges: Richard Peters, Samuel Chase and the Broken Promise of Federalist Jurisprudence." *Northwestern Law Review* 73 (March-April 1978): 26–111.

Turner, Lynn. "The Impeachment of John Pickering." *American Historical Review* 54 (April 1949): 485–507.

The Right to Remove a President from Office Is Tested

—◄o►—

Wallace Hettle

Department of History
University of Northern Iowa

The Impeachment and Trial of Andrew Johnson, (1868) [U.S. Congress]

◄o► THE CASE IN BRIEF ◄o►

Date
1868

Location
District of Columbia

Court
U.S. Senate, sitting as a court of
impeachment

Principal Participants
President Andrew Johnson
The U.S. Senate

Significance of the Case
Johnson became the first U.S. President
to be impeached by the House of
Representatives, only to be acquitted by
a single vote in the Senate.

In February 1868, Tennessee Democrat Andrew Johnson became the first U.S. president to be impeached by the House of Representatives. Three months later, Republicans, who viewed Johnson as an obstacle to the reconstruction of the Union after the Civil War, failed by one vote to convict him in a Senate trial. While legal arguments over the legitimacy and applicability of the Tenure of Office Act drove discussion of whether Johnson had committed constitutionally impeachable "high crimes or misdemeanors," the impeachment and trial also reflected fierce disagreement between Congress and the president over the future of the post–Civil War South.

Johnson had been elected vice president in 1864 as Abraham Lincoln's running mate. As a Democrat and a southerner, Johnson seemed an ideal choice to balance the ticket. He exemplified Southern unionism, because despite his ownership of slaves, the former Tennessee senator had denounced secession as treason and had criticized pro-slavery politicians. A self-educated former tailor, Johnson fashioned himself as a spokesman for non-slaveholding, white Southerners and as a critic of the planter class.

Upon assuming office after Lincoln's assassination in April 1865, Johnson surprised the country by taking a conciliatory course toward the rebellious planter class. He quickly alienated congressional Republicans. Driven by a deeply held belief in the inferiority of African Americans, he turned his back on Republican hopes for black suffrage and pursued a liberal policy toward former Confederates. Johnson did demand that former Confederate states wishing to reenter the Union abolish slavery, repudiate Confederate debts, and nullify their secession ordinances. But, because the president readily pardoned Confederate leaders and failed to insist on suffrage or civil rights for African Americans, his actions seemed to preclude the radical reorganization of southern society hoped for by most congressional Republicans. By late 1865, Johnson's lenient policies ensured that former Confederates largely controlled the state governments in the South.

In December 1865, when Congress convened for the first time after Johnson had taken office, the president probably believed that the process of restoring the states to the Union was nearly over. Yet, Johnson soon found himself at loggerheads with Republicans. Conflict emerged between congressional Republicans and the president in early 1866 when he vetoed the Freedman's Bureau Bill, an ambitious edifice designed to manage the South's transition from slavery to free labor. Republican outrage increased when Johnson vetoed the Civil Rights Bill, a legislative measure intended to extend federal protection of rights to southern blacks.

Johnson denounced both the bills and Congress in vitriolic terms. He called his former Republican allies, among other things, "a common gang of . . . blood-suckers." He hinted that his enemies in Congress were planning a military coup. Johnson's words and actions provoked a public backlash in the North that carried congressional Republicans to a two-thirds majority in the fall elections of 1866. The large Republican majority, combined with the seem-

ingly irreconcilable differences between Johnson and Congress, put the two parties on a collision course.

Despite their veto-proof majority in Congress, Johnson presented a significant problem for Republicans. They relied on the army to enforce the 1867 Reconstruction Act, which organized the southern states into five military districts and set stringent conditions for their readmission to the Union. By relying on the military, Congress ensured that Johnson, in his role as commander in chief, still played a crucial role in Reconstruction. However, the very act of leaving him with some authority had the unintended consequence of increasing the urgency with which congressional radicals would push for impeachment.

Radical Republicans quickly worked to limit Johnson's power as commander in chief. They feared that Secretary of War Edwin Stanton, who was a holdover from the Lincoln cabinet, would be removed from office if he enforced the Reconstruction acts too vigorously for Johnson's taste. Congress therefore passed the Tenure of Office Act in February 1867. It forbade the removal of appointed officers subject to confirmation of the Senate when the Senate was in session. Removal of officers could only occur after the Senate had confirmed the appointment of replacements. When the Senate was not in session, the law required the president to justify the removal of an appointee and to appoint an interim replacement, who would become permanent if the Senate agreed to the change. If the Senate rejected the president's action in regard to an appointee when it reconvened, the suspended officer would resume his position. Unfortunately, the bill was ambiguous on the crucial point of whether it applied to cabinet officers. Senate Democrats and moderate Senate Republicans insisted that cabinet officers be exempted from the bill, while House Republicans assumed that it applied to cabinet officers. The uncertainty over whether the Tenure of Office Act protected cabinet officers would prove crucial to the outcome of Johnson's impeachment trial.

In early attempts at impeachment, some Republicans argued that the "high crimes and misdemeanors" specified by the Constitution as grounds for impeachment included misfeasance and malfeasance in office, as well as indictable criminal offences. Such an expansive constitutional interpretation by pro-impeachment House members failed to convince their more cautious colleagues.

The impeachment movement had nearly died when Johnson gave it new life by apparently violating the Tenure of Office Act in December 1867. Initially, in compliance with the law, Johnson sent the Senate a message giving his rationale for suspending Secretary of War Stanton. Not questioning the Senate's right to restore Stanton to office, Johnson instead contended that the secretary should have resigned because of his irreconcilable political differences with the administration. At first, Johnson had followed the law in seeking the advice and consent of the Senate, but when the Senate refused, the president forced the issue. He appointed General Lorenzo Thomas as the interim secretary of war even though the Senate was in session, an apparent violation of the Tenure of Office Act. Moreover, critics charged, Johnson had circumvented constitutional procedure for installing cabinet officers because he had appointed Thomas without seeking Senate confirmation. When his actions were questioned, Johnson claimed that he merely had intended to test the constitutionality of the Tenure of Office Act. Republicans rejected his explanation, charging that he primarily sought to remove Stanton and curtail the enforcement of the Reconstruction Acts.

Johnson's actions united a Republican party that had nearly given up on impeachment. The House passed eleven articles of impeachment in late February 1868. The articles overlapped, but ultimately rested on four major charges. The strongest was that the president had violated the Tenure of Office Act by replacing Stanton with Thomas after the Senate failed to consent to Stanton's removal. Second, if that law was not applicable, the president had no constitutional authority to replace a cabinet officer while the Senate was in session without its consultation. Third, and less convincingly, the impeachment managers charged that the president had committed a high crime or misdemeanor in preventing the execution of the Re-construction laws. Finally, a very weak article of impeachment claimed that the president had attempted to bring the Congress into ridicule and disrepute. Discussion in the Senate trial would hinge primarily on Johnson's alleged violation of the Tenure of Office Act.

Johnson's actions had united conservative and radical House Republicans behind impeachment. Yet Johnson, who had a history of rash action and reckless speech, surprised his enemies by putting up a formidable and shrewd defense against the charges. He hired a team of respected, politically moderate lawyers to manage his defense. These men demonstrated that the case was scarcely as clear-cut as House Republicans believed. Johnson's lawyers argued that, assuming he violated the Tenure of Office Act to test its constitutionality, his actions did not merit removal from office. If a president could be impeached for such a cause, then Congress could pass any patently unconstitutional law and impeach the president prudent enough to test that law's constitutionality. Johnson's lawyers also provided two arguments that cast doubt on whether the Tenure of Office Act protected Stanton. First, they argued that the Senate had not intended the law to apply to cabinet members. Second, they declared that, because the law only protected appointees for a single presidential term, it did not apply to Johnson's cabinet. Consequently, Johnson's lawyers argued that Stanton was protected only during the term of President Lincoln, who had appointed him, and that Lincoln's term ended with his death in 1865. Republican managers insisted that the Tenure of Office Act applied to Johnson, and they denied his right to disobey a law because he wanted to test its constitutionality in the courts. They argued that Johnson had implicitly acknowledged its applicability in initially sending word of his suspension of Stanton under the terms of the act. One House manager, Republican James F. Wilson of Iowa, argued that an officeholder could not break a law to test its constitutionality; instead, he should resign if he could not in good faith execute the law. Otherwise, Wilson reasoned, a president would have absolute power to decide which laws to execute and which to ignore.

House managers argued further that Johnson's laxity in enforcing the Reconstruction acts was a high crime or misdemeanor, but support for this proposition was weak. They scarcely mentioned the dubious article that alleged Johnson had brought Congress into disrepute. The case thus hung on the articles related to Stanton's removal.

Political considerations played a crucial role in the outcome of the trial. The president's friends quietly assured conservative Republicans that he would take no rash actions if the Senate acquitted him. Johnson's lawyers delayed the culmination of the process until mid-May 1868, undermining the credibility of the impeachment managers who now appeared vindictive in seeking to remove a lame-duck president. The fact that the man in line to succeed Johnson was Senate president pro tempore Benjamin Wade, a radical Republican and soft-money exponent, stood as an obstacle to impeachment. Conservative Republicans disliked the prospect of giving Wade high office.

Ultimately, seven Senate Republicans broke with their party, and by a single vote, Johnson was acquitted and thus allowed to finish his term. Six of the seven dissenters filed formal written opinions. All agreed that impeachment required commission of a crime. Their opinions either accepted the argument that the Tenure of Office Act did not apply to Stanton, or argued that its provisions with regard to cabinet officers were too opaque to sustain the contention that Johnson had violated the law. Iowa senator James Grimes questioned the constitutionality of the Tenure of Office Act, noting the understanding established by the Congress of 1789 that removal of high officers in the executive branch should be the prerogative of the president.

Appealing for the conviction of Johnson, longtime abolitionist and senator Charles Sumner unabashedly emphasized the political character of the impeachment, denouncing "pettifogging" lawyers for splitting hairs over the Tenure of Office Act while the administration endangered Reconstruction. The Massachusetts senator hoped to make impeachment something akin to a parliamentary vote of no confidence. However, the majority of Republicans disagreed with Sumner's interpretation of the impeachment power. Because they believed that impeachment could take place only for a violation of the law, they found themselves resting their case on the flawed Tenure of Office Act. When seven Republican senators found no violation of that law, they produced an acquittal that affirmed the independence of the executive branch.

In 1887, as an anticlimax to Johnson's impeachment and trial, Congress—responding to repeated appeals from President Grover Cleveland—repealed the Tenure of Office Act. Also, in *Myers v. United States* (1926), the Supreme Court, in an opinion written by Chief Justice William Howard Taft, upheld the presidential-removal power in exceedingly broad terms. The *Myers* decision had the effect, many years after the Johnson impeachment and trial, of indicating to students of constitutional history that the Tenure of Office Act had been unconstitutional. Thus, the attempt to oust a president from office for violating such a defective law, although it might have been politically popular, was constitutionally unjustifiable.

Selected Bibliography

Benedict, Michael Les. "From Our Archives: A New Look at the Impeachment of Andrew Johnson." *Political Science Quarterly* 113 (1998): 493–511.

———. *The Impeachment and Trial of Andrew Johnson.* New York: Norton, 1973.

Bowman, Frank O., III, and Sepunick, Stephen. "High Crimes and Misdemeanors: Defining the Constitutional Limits on Presidential Impeachment." Southern California Law Review 72 (1999): 1517–1562.

Dewitt, David Miller. *The Impeachment and Trial of Andrew Johnson.* New York: Macmillan, 1903.

Rehnquist, William. *Grand Inquests: The Historic Impeachments of Justice Samuel Chase and President Andrew Johnson.* New York: Morrow, 1992.

The Court Topples a Presidency

———<o>———

Richard R. Broadie

History Department
University of Northern Iowa

United States v. Nixon, 418 U.S. 683 (1974) [U.S. Supreme Court]

-<o>- THE CASE IN BRIEF -<o>-

Date
1974

Location
District of Columbia

Court
U.S. Supreme Court

Principal Participants
President Richard M. Nixon
Chief Justice Warren Burger

Significance of the Case
With undeniable evidence pointing to Nixon's participation in the Watergate break-in, the Supreme Court unanimously ruled that the president must submit subpoenaed material to the special prosecutor investigating the affair. This led to Nixon's resignation in August 1974.

Few would disagree with the proposition that, without the discovery of the White House tapes, the case against President Richard M. Nixon would not have resulted in his resignation from the presidency on August 9, 1974. Without this revelation, the Nixon presidency, although noticeably weakened by the allegations against it, would probably have survived to limp across the finish line at the scheduled end of its second term in January 1977. The tapes, key segments of which were obtained after more than one year of prodding and litigation, provided investigators with the so-called smoking gun, irrefutable evidence that Nixon had participated in the cover-up of the Watergate break-in of June 17, 1972. The culmination of the legal effort to obtain the tapes was the unanimous Supreme Court decision of *United States v. Nixon*.

Richard Nixon was not the first American president to tape White House conversations. Historians and political scientists have learned much about high-level decision making during the Kennedy presidency by listening to actual conversations of John and Robert Kennedy responding to various crises. And in proceedings reminiscent of the Watergate hearings, Congress sought to obtain various personal documents—notes, journal entries, even presidential scribblings—from President Ronald Reagan to assess his role in the Iran-contra matter. But never has this type of information been as crucial to an ongoing criminal investigation involving a sitting president as it was in the year prior to the Nixon resignation.

The Watergate investigation went on for some time before the existence of the tapes was discovered. The burglars, arrested at the time of the break-in, were indicted in September 1972 and went to trial in January 1973. Soon after they pled guilty, and after former CIA agent E. Howard Hunt and one-time FBI agent and White House "plumber" G. Gordon Liddy were found guilty, a Senate Select Committee under the chairmanship of Democratic senator Sam Ervin of North Carolina was established to investigate the Watergate affair and to recommend a new set of campaign regulations.

Despite promising to cooperate with the investigation, President Nixon insisted that as a matter of executive privilege neither he nor members of his staff would be willing to testify. Accounts detailing the involvement of White House staffers continued to surface, however, and by April 1973 federal prosecutors became convinced that the administration was involved in a cover-up. Presidential counsel John Dean's testimony late that spring strongly supported this view, but without further documentation it remained Dean's word against Nixon's that the president had been involved.

By their own account, *Washington Post* investigative reporters Bob Woodward and Carl Bernstein—who originally helped to break the Watergate story—"had gotten lazy" by the time the Senate Watergate hearings began in May 1973. Instead of vigorously pursuing their own leads, they began to rely on the information coming out of the committee for their stories. There was one "unchecked entry" on both their lists, however, and sometime that month Woodward asked a committee staff member if Alexander Butterfield, listed as a deputy assistant to the president and an aide to chief of staff H. R. Haldeman, had been interviewed. Early

on in the investigation, they had discovered that Butterfield "supervised internal security and the paper flow to the president," and both were curious about what this meant. After Woodward pursued this with another staff member, it was agreed that the committee's chief counsel, Sam Dash, would be asked to interview Butterfield.

Dash put off the interview on at least one occasion, but on July 13, 1973, he had a lengthy discussion with Butterfield. The next day, Woodward and Bernstein learned that Nixon had "bugged himself"—that is, he had recorded all presidential conversations since February 1971. After some initial concern that the tapes might be a set-up, recorded after-the-fact by Nixon to clear himself, it was soon concluded that the tapes were legitimate and offered the best hope of finding the smoking gun for which they had been looking.

Events of the next thirteen months centered around the efforts of the Ervin committee, the special prosecutor, and the House Judiciary Committee to obtain these tapes. When the committee voted unanimously in April 1974 to subpoena forty-two additional tapes, including a key July 23, 1972, conversation between Nixon and Haldeman, it set in motion a chain of events that led to the president's resignation. Within two weeks, the Nixon White House released edited transcripts of forty-three conversations, including portions of twenty of the conversations that were subject to subpoena. In a speech the next day, Nixon told the American people that "these materials will tell all." Public reaction to the speech—not the first in which the president was less than truthful—was decidedly negative. About the same time, the House Judiciary Committee discovered that key transcripts differed significantly from the original tapes in the committee's possession. Therefore, Special Prosecutor Leon Jaworski continued to press for the tapes and in time demanded several more. Nixon responded by moving to quash the subpoena accompanied by a formal claim of privilege.

The district court that ruled on the case concluded that the special prosecutor had made a sufficient showing to rebut the presumption that the tapes were privileged and satisfied the

President Richard Nixon with transcripts of the White House tapes that he released to the House impeachment investigation in April 1974. The transcripts were heavily edited and did not satisfy the committee or the Watergate special prosecutor, who continued their quest for evidence. *Associated Press AP.*

requirements of Rule 17 (c) of Federal Rules of Criminal Procedure under which the subpoena was issued. The court thereafter denied the president's motion to quash and ordered delivery for *in camera* (i.e., private) inspection the "originals of all subpoenaed items along with an index of these items and tape copies of those parts of the subpoenaed recordings for which transcripts had already been released to the public."

The president promptly appealed this ruling to the Court of Appeals for the D.C. Circuit, and the district court stayed its order pending appellate review. Sensing that the legal process might serve as an effective means of presidential stonewalling, delaying a final resolution for months or even years, the special prosecutor filed in the Supreme Court a petition for a writ of certiorari before judgment. "Because of the public importance of the issues presented and the need for their prompt resolution," the Court granted the special prosecutor's petition and agreed to an expedited briefing schedule. The case was heard on July 8, and the decision handed down on July 24. The Court ruled 8-0 (with Justice William Rehnquist recusing himself due to his prior service in the Nixon administration) that Richard Nixon had to surrender the subpoenaed material. It rejected all the president's assertions, including his most significant, the claim of executive privilege.

The Court, in its opinion written by Chief Justice Warren Burger, first disposed of jurisdictional issues and considered whether the special prosecutor had satisfied the requirements of Rule 17 (c) of Federal Rules of Criminal Procedure. On the former, the Court held that the "order of the District Court was an appealable order" and "the appeal from that order was therefore properly 'in' the Court of Appeals, and the case is now properly before this court." On the latter, it was decided that the production of the tapes would not be "unreasonable or oppressive" and the special prosecutor had shown the tapes to be relevant, admissible, and specific. Thus, the Court refused to say that the district court had "erred in authorizing the issuance of the subpoena."

Tougher issues for the Court to resolve—indeed, those most crucial to understanding what was significant about the ruling—were Nixon's claims about justiciability and executive privilege. The administration took the position that the matter was an intrabranch dispute between the president and the special prosecutor and thus not subject to judicial resolution. According to this view, the dispute did not present a "case" or "controversy" that could be adjudicated in the federal courts. Instead, they argued that it was a jurisdictional dispute within the executive branch between a subordinate and a superior officer. Turning the matter over to the courts would, therefore, be an improper intrusion of one branch into the affairs of another, based on the doctrine of separation of powers. Nixon's lawyers conceded that the president had delegated certain powers to the special prosecutor, but they insisted that this did not include the final authority over what evidence could be used in a criminal trial.

The Court ruled that "Congress has vested in the attorney general the power to conduct the criminal litigation of the United States government." In turn, the attorney general delegated authority to represent the United States to a special prosecutor, who subpoenaed the tapes while operating within the scope of his authority. While the Court agreed that it is possible for the attorney general to "amend or revoke the regulation defining the special prosecutor's authority," it pointed out that he had not done so. The Court ruled that the regulation remained in force and that the president was bound by it. The Court also found that "the demands of and resistance to the subpoena" was indeed a "controversy" in the constitutional sense, which "means the kind of controversy the courts traditionally resolve." It was, therefore, justiciable.

The final point made by Nixon's lawyers was the claim of executive privilege, defined by one legal scholar as "the president's claim of constitutional authority to withhold information from Congress." According to this scholar, the concept of executive privilege as used by Nixon went back no further than the 1950s, when the Eisenhower administration staked out a claim of "uncontrolled discretion" to withhold information from Congress in response to the "bullying tactics" of Senator Joseph McCarthy. But during the Nixon administration, executive privilege had "become a shield for executive unaccountability . . . an iron curtain which shut off critical information from Congress and the people."

The bulk of the opinion is devoted to an analysis of the concept of executive privilege as it is relevant to this case. The president, for example, had contended that it was inconsistent with the public interest to produce confidential conversations between a chief executive and his close advisers. While accepting that "human experience teaches that those who expect public dissemination of their remarks may well temper candor with a concern for appearances and for their own interests . . . ," the Court concluded that "neither the doctrine of separation of powers nor the generalized need for confidentiality . . . can sustain an absolute, unqualified, Presidential privilege of immunity from judicial process under all circumstances. Absent a claim of need to protect . . . [national] . . . secrets, the confidentiality of Presidential communications is not significantly diminished by producing material for a criminal trial under the protected conditions of *in camera* inspection."

Chief Justice Burger, the author of the opinion in *United States v. Nixon*, was willing to concede a presumptive privilege for presidential communications. But he insisted that this privilege could not become absolute because the

need to "develop all relevant facts in an adversary system [of criminal justice] is both fundamental and comprehensive." To deny the courts full access to relevant matters in a criminal investigation under anything less than extraordinary circumstances would "cut deeply into the guarantee of due process of law and gravely impair the basic function of the courts."

While the subpoena was ruled appropriate, Burger was adamant in insisting that "the public interest requires that Presidential confidentiality be afforded the greatest protection consistent with fair administration of justice." In fact, the court ruled that any conversation found to be irrelevant or inadmissible in the criminal prosecution be returned under seal to its lawful custodian.

The tapes, released after *United States v. Nixon* was handed down, did indeed contain the smoking gun that doomed the Nixon presidency. In a conversation between Nixon and H. R. Haldeman held on June 23, 1972, six days after the break-in, Nixon can clearly be heard ordering Haldeman to tell the CIA to fabricate a national security operation to keep the FBI off the case. This was proof that the president had conspired to obstruct justice and lied about his Watergate involvement.

While Richard Nixon lost what he valued most—his presidency—it is not clear at all that the ruling in *United States v. Nixon* is a complete victory for those who forced him from office. Nixon opponents and those like Raoul Berger who claimed that executive privilege is a myth must surely be disappointed that the Supreme Court accepted the notion of the existence of an executive privilege not to divulge certain confidential communications and that "an absolute instead of a qualified privilege may exist where there is 'a claim of need to protect . . . national security secrets'."

In fact, in one view, *United States v. Nixon* is "a quite limited precedent without great doctrinal importance." It raised as many questions as it answered and was decisive only in the sense that it compelled the president to turn over the tapes. Indeed, recent events seem to support this notion. To defend Bill Clinton against obstruction-of-justice charges in the Monica Lewinsky matter, the president's defense team sought unsuccessfully to use the doctrine of executive privilege to protect the confidentiality of conversations with the Secret Service and White House attorneys (i.e., those on the public payroll) regarding matters clearly not involving national security. While strongly rejecting the president's arguments, the courts did little to clarify the Nixon decision.

Given the likelihood of continued conflict between the executive and legislative branches—exacerbated by the United States' recent history of divided government—the issues raised in *United States v. Nixon* are certain to surface again.

Selected Bibliography

Berger, Raoul. *Executive Privilege: A Constitutional Myth.* Cambridge, MA: Harvard University Press, 1974.

Bernstein, Carl, and Bob Woodward. *All the President's Men.* New York: Simon and Schuster, 1974.

Cox, Archibald. "Executive Privilege." *University of Pennsylvania Law Review* 122 (June 1974): 1383–1438.

Kutler, Stanley I. *The Wars of Watergate: The Last Crisis of Richard Nixon.* New York: Knopf, 1990.

Credibility and Crisis
in California's High Court

———◄o►———

Brenda Farrington Myers
Fullerton, California

People v. Tanner, 23 Cal 3d 16 (1978) and 24 Cal 3d 514 (1979)
[California Supreme Court]

◄o► THE CASE IN BRIEF ◄o►

Dates
1978, 1979

Location
California

Court
California Supreme Court

Principal Participants
California Chief Justice Rose E. Bird
California Justice William Clark

Significance of the Case
The appointment of a state chief justice provided a politically charged forum that resulted in such a high degree of distrust and disillusionment that substitute justices were named to decide the case before the court.

In February 1977, California governor Jerry Brown shook up the "good old boys" club by nominating Rose Elizabeth Bird for chief justice of the California Supreme Court. Simultaneously, Brown nominated Wiley Manuel, the first African American ever proposed for membership on the state's highest court. Manuel was confirmed by the Commission on Judicial Appointments without difficulty; Bird was not. Bird was only forty years old and had no prior judicial experience or law-practice experience beyond being a public defender. She had served in Brown's cabinet for two years as secretary of the Department of Agriculture and Services, outraging the agribusiness lobby with pro-farmworker actions. Despite this record, however, Bird gained confirmation.

The controversy did not end when Bird took office. Contrary to tradition, she appointed several of her own associates, changed the locks on her office doors, assigned municipal and superior court justices to sit pro tem (i.e., temporarily), scheduled judicial council meetings in state buildings rather than resort settings, and sold the court's limousine. Bird hoped that these changes would result in a more efficient judiciary; instead, they were perceived as arrogant, abrasive, and excessively expeditious. According to Bird, she moved quickly to implement change because she feared that cancer would prematurely end her judicial career.

The campaign to remove her from office began almost immediately. Under California law, supreme court justices appointed by the governor must be approved by the majority of the electorate at the next gubernatorial election. In Bird's case, this was in November 1978. The opposition, funded by wealthy agricultural interests, was led by Republican state senator Hubert L. Richardson's Law and Order Campaign Committee and the Vote No on Rose Bird Committee. The *Los Angeles Times*, probably Bird's most influential supporter, condemned the malicious attempt to unseat the chief justice. But on election day, the *Times* ran a carelessly researched, front-page story that stated that the Bird court had reached a 4-3 decision to "overturn a 1975 law that requires prison terms for persons who use a gun during a violent crime but has not made the decision public." The story inferred that Associate Justice Mathew Tobriner, a distinguished fifteen-year veteran of the court, was delaying announcement of a controversial decision, *People v. Tanner*, to help Bird win voter approval.

The chief justice won reconfirmation by a narrow margin of 51.7 percent of voters, but the *Times* story was so damaging that Bird called for an investigation by the Commission on Judicial Appointments. The purpose of the hearings was to determine (1) whether *Tanner* or any other politically sensitive case was improperly delayed and (2) if any justice compromised the confidentiality of court deliberations by making improper statements to the press.

The *Tanner* case was as bizarre as the appellate decision's course. Around 3 A.M. on January 9, 1976, Harold Tanner staged a "mock armed robbery" of a 7-Eleven convenience store in order to convince the owner to resubscribe to the security service provided by Tanner's employer. Despite Tanner's testimony, the jury found the defendant guilty of first-degree rob-

bery and the use of a firearm during the commission of a crime. After reading the lengthy probation report and listening to arguments from the parties involved, the trial judge found Tanner's crime to be one of extraordinary circumstances. The court entered an order striking the firearms-use finding, and committed the defendant to the Department of Corrections for the term prescribed by law. However, the court then suspended the sentence and placed Tanner on five years' probation on condition that he serve one year in county jail and undertake a program of psychiatric treatment. The prosecution appealed, and the case was argued before the California Supreme Court.

On December 22, 1978, the state high court announced its decision in *People v. Tanner* (*Tanner I*). The court ruled against the mandatory prison sentence by a vote of 4-3, consistent with the *Times* election-day article. The decision outraged the governor, the legislature, and the public. In an unusual move, the court yielded to public pressure and granted a rehearing. The court announced its decision in *People v. Tanner* (*Tanner II*) on June 14, 1979. Again, the vote was 4-3; however, this time the Court upheld the "use a gun, go to prison" statute. Justice Stanley Mosk was responsible for the reversal. Without offering any explanation, he merely signed the majority opinion instead of writing a separate concurring opinion.

In *Tanner II*, Justice William Clark, writing for the majority, rejected "any contention that courts were inherently or constitutionally vested with ultimate authority in fixing sentences or imposing penalty-enhancing factors for conduct made criminal by legislative enactment." He stated that the issue had to be determined by statutory purpose. Applying the rule of statutory construction that a "specific provision concerning a particular subject must govern a general provision to the contrary whenever both provisions apply," the majority held that the specific provision relating to the limited power of dismissal for probation purposes prevailed over a general power of dismissal.

Despite its substantive holding, however, the court ruled the uncertainty of the law had placed such an unusual burden on the defendant that a second incarceration for Tanner would be unjust. At the time of his rehearing, Tanner had met the conditions of his probation, including a one-year internment at county jail. Bird, Tobriner, and Justice Frank Newman concurred with the majority that Tanner should be placed on probation rather than be sent to prison a second time. However, each filed a separate dissent from the majority's ruling that the trial court did not have the power to strike the gun-use finding. As in *Tanner I*, Bird presented the issue as one of constitutional separation of powers. In *Tanner II*, she criticized the new majority for its "attempt to carve a compromise of expediency" by making the "defendant a pawn" and exempting him "from the very standard that will be applied to all other defendants."

Meanwhile, Bird hoped that the commission's hearings on *Tanner* would "clear the air" and "restore confidence in the Court." Instead, the testimony revealed the lack of collegiality between the justices, particularly Bird and Clark. One focus of the "delay allegation" became Clark's *Tanner I* dissent, which included a footnote citing Bird's separate concurring opinion in *People v. Caudillo*, another 1978 California State Supreme Court decision.

In *Caudillo*, Bird found that the legislature could provide that rape per se did not always involve "great bodily injury." By law, a finding of great bodily injury provided for an enhanced penalty. During the summer preceding the election, the Law and Order Campaign Committee seized upon Bird's *Caudillo* opinion as evidence that she was "soft on crime," and it made *Caudillo* the centerpiece of its campaign to oust the chief justice. When questioned by the commission as to why he had emphasized the politically charged *Caudillo* citation in his footnote, Clark insisted that he was merely trying to persuade Bird that she was inconsistent.

Bird charged that the *Caudillo* footnote was "politically motivated . . . meant to demean her in the eyes of the public." She thereafter treated Clark and his staff in a "cool, but correct" manner. Clark testified that Bird's "chill" continued for weeks, despite his attempts to exchange simple pleasantries. Rather than delete the *Caudillo* reference, Clark elevated the footnote into the body of his opinion, thereby escalating the tension between Bird and himself.

On December 20, 1978, just two days before the *Tanner I* decision was announced, Clark composed a memorandum to the chief justice stating: "In conscience, it must be clear to all on the Court that the *Tanner* case was signed up and ready for filing well in advance of November." Outraged, Bird replied that same day: "It is untrue . . . an affront to your colleagues and to the truth." In his testimony, Clark confirmed that he had written this memo; however, he was unable to produce any evidence to substantiate his claim that *Tanner* "could and should" have been filed. He suspected *Tanner* had been improperly handled, but told the commission that he knew of no impropriety by any of his colleagues in the handling of the case. In fact, the only real evidence of judicial misbehavior was Clark's own admission that he was one of two justices used to confirm the *Times* election-day article.

The other confirming justice, Stanley Mosk, filed a lawsuit to bar his public testimony, on the grounds that an open investigation was unconstitutional. The court of appeal in Los Angeles ruled in Mosk's favor. Ironically, the commission was forced to bring suit against Mosk in the California Supreme Court! Since the justices were subjects of the commission's investigation, they were disqualified, and seven substitute justices were chosen by lot. This ad hoc supreme court upheld the court of appeal's ruling and required closed hearings. On November 5, 1979, the commission tersely announced that no formal charges would be filed against any justice. Gagged by the Mosk suit, the commission could not disclose the reasoning behind its decision.

The *Tanner* case effectively illustrates that the judiciary is not an independent part of the political process. Government—be it the judicial, the executive, or the legislative branch—derives its power from the governed. When the court's constitutional instincts failed to present the prevailing public perception of what the rule of law should be, the court lost credibility. Political prudence dictated that a rehearing of *Tanner* was necessary, but again judicial credibility was lost because Mosk switched his vote without a word of explanation. Rather than for its substantive holding that the legislature could in fact curtail judicial discretion in sentencing, the *Tanner* case will be remembered for the unprecedented political turmoil surrounding an unpopular decision.

What happened to the California Supreme Court in the late 1970s was not so surprising when evaluated in the larger context of the nation's experience in the Watergate crisis. In both Watergate and *Tanner*, investigative reporting played a crucial role. The *Washington Post*'s effort, however, was a journalistic triumph, because it painstakingly exposed the president's connection to the Watergate imbroglio. In contrast, the *Los Angeles Times* ran an erroneous story that directly resulted in a full-blown public investigation of nonexistent wrongdoing. Although painful, the Watergate hearings were an affirmation that the American people could rid themselves of a dishonest leader: Richard Nixon resigned, rather than face certain impeachment and conviction. The *Tanner* hearings, on the other hand, exonerated the justices but failed to put an end to the controversy. Yet, in both instances, the result was the same: distrust and disillusionment were extended not only to those under investigation, but also to the high offices they represented.

In December 1999, the cancer that had caused Judge Bird to move quickly to implement changes in the operation of California's highest court did finally claim her life. Sidney Feinberg, a former appellate judge and long-time friend, eulogized Bird as "a tough lady, and a good lady."

Selected Bibliography

Kang, K. Connie. "The Decline of California's Vendetta-Ridden Supreme Court." *California Journal* 10 (October 1979): 343–347.

Kleven, Paul. "*People v. Barraza*: California's Latest Attempt to Accommodate an Objective Theory of Entrapment." *California Law Review* 68 (July 1980): 776–779.

Medsger, Betty. *Framed: The New Right Attack on Chief Justice Rose Bird and the Courts.* New York: Pilgrim, 1983.

Schrag, Peter. "The Bird Controversy: California's High Court on Trial." *Nation* 229 (December 1979): 582–584.

Stoltz, Preble. *Judging Judges.* New York: Free Press, 1981.

Turner, William Bennett. "From the Tanner Hearings to the Brethren and Beyond: Judicial Accountability and Judicial Independence." *California State Bar Journal* 55 (July 1980): 292–297.

Justice Delayed Is Justice Denied

———◄○►———

Richard R. Broadie

Department of History
University of Northern Iowa

Clinton v. Jones, 520 U.S. 681 (1997) [U.S. Supreme Court]

◄○► THE CASE IN BRIEF ◄○►

Date
  1997

Location
  Arkansas
  District of Columbia

Court
  Eighth Circuit Court of Appeals
  U.S. Supreme Court

Principal Participants
  President Bill Clinton
  Paula C. Jones
  Justice John Paul Stevens

Significance of the Case
  After allegations about the president's personal misconduct led to a civil case against him, the Supreme Court ruled that a sitting president could indeed be forced to give testimony in court while still in office.

If, as Hillary Rodham Clinton once suggested, her husband was the victim of a "vast right-wing conspiracy" aiming to bring down his presidency, then the conspirators surely struck gold with a January 1994 article in the *American Spectator.* Written by David Brock, the article alleged that Bill Clinton, while governor of Arkansas, had made use of state troopers to "approach women and to solicit their telephone numbers . . . ; to drive him in state vehicles to rendezvous points and guard him during sexual encounters . . . and [to keep] tabs on Hillary's whereabouts and [lie to her] about her husband's whereabouts."

One such incident, in 1991, was recounted this way by Brock: "One of the troopers told the story of how Clinton had eyed a woman at a reception at the Excelsior Hotel in downtown Little Rock. According to the trooper . . . Clinton asked him to approach the woman, whom the trooper remembered only as Paula, tell her how attractive the governor thought she was, and take her to a room in the hotel where Clinton would be waiting. . . . On this particular evening . . . the trooper said Paula told him she was available to be Clinton's regular girlfriend if he so desired." After the publication of Brock's piece, Paula Corbin Jones, a twenty-seven-year-old Arkansas state employee, suspected that she was the "Paula" mentioned in the article. Humiliated and angry, she contacted Little Rock attorney Daniel Taylor, who later referred her to Cliff Jackson, a longtime Clinton political opponent. Jackson suggested that Jones tell her story at a public forum on February 11, 1994, that featured several of the troopers Brock had interviewed. Her performance was characterized in one account as being a "fiasco," with Jones, who was apolitical, described as looking like a "right-wing tool."

Perhaps, in part, because of this initial press conference, much of the media was skeptical of Jones's version of events. Eventually, more sympathetic accounts emerged. *Washington Post* reporter Michael Isikoff found a number of friends and family members who indicated that Jones had given contemporaneous accounts about her relations with Bill Clinton that were similar to the ones she had offered to Isikoff. Based upon his own research, Isikoff was able to verify that Governor Clinton was registered at the Excelsior Hotel at the time he allegedly sent the trooper after Jones. Isikoff concluded that while no one except the two principals knew what happened in the hotel room on May 8, 1991, he had been unable to catch Jones in an obvious lie. Later, Stuart Taylor, a journalist specializing in legal matters, wrote a piece in the *American Lawyer* in which he argued that Jones had a pretty good case and was a victim of hypocrisy and class bias in the media.

By the time Isikoff's article appeared on May 3, 1994, Jones had retained the services of two Washington-based lawyers, Gilbert Davis and Joseph Cammarata. President Clinton had sought the help of Bob Bennett, a Washington "superlawyer," who had previously defended Republican officials during the Iran-Contra scandal. Frantic negotiations ensued, aimed at settling the case before the statute of limitations on the alleged crimes ran out. At one point, Bennett implied that Clinton was willing to issue a statement indicating that Jones "did not engage in any improper or sexual conduct. I re-

gret any untrue assertions that may have been made about her." It seemed quite possible that Jones, who at that point wanted only an apology, would have accepted this language and settled. She agreed to delay filing her suit for one day to consider the proposal. Almost immediately, someone in the White House indicated that the delay was because "Jones had no case and her family was opposed." Reportedly furious at the White House's attempt to spin the talks, Jones and her lawyers broke off negotiations, and on May 6, 1994, she filed a lawsuit against William Jefferson Clinton for defaming her and violating her civil rights. In the complaint, she alleged that Clinton had made "abhorrent" sexual advances, and that the rejection of those advances had led to punishment by her supervisors.

The Clinton defense team immediately filed a petition in federal district court, asserting presidential immunity and requesting that pleadings and motions be deferred until after the immunity issue was resolved. The district court rejected the claim of immunity, but ruled that, while discovery could proceed, a trial should be delayed until the end of the Clinton presidency. Jones appealed this decision to the Eighth Circuit Court of Appeals, which affirmed the dismissal denial but overturned the delay of trial as the "functional equivalent of a grant of temporary immunity" to which the president was not entitled. The court concluded that the president is subject to the same laws as all Americans and should not be permitted to escape the consequences of his unofficial acts. The president filed a petition for review by the U.S. Supreme Court. The solicitor general, representing the United States, asserted that the circuit court was "fundamentally mistaken" and had created "serious risk for the institution of the presidency." The Supreme Court granted the petition for review, not because of any judgment on the merits of Jones's suit, but because of what it saw as the importance of the separation of powers and procedural issues raised in the document.

The Supreme Court heard arguments on January 13, 1997, and on May 27, it issued a unanimous ruling that affirmed the decision of the court of appeals allowing the Jones case to proceed. In his opinion, Justice John Paul Stevens expressed the High Court's view that the district court had the requisite jurisdiction to decide the case and that Ms. Jones, "like any other citizen . . . has a right to an orderly disposition of her claims." Stevens addressed the contentions of the president's attorneys and gave little ground in rejecting them. On the issue of presidential immunity, he agreed with the conclusions of the district judge that *Nixon v. Fitzgerald* (1982) had established that "the President has absolute immunity from civil damage actions arising out of the execution of official duties of office." But Stevens cited past decisions establishing that "immunities are grounded in the nature of the function performed, not the identity of the actor who performed it." Thus, presidents do not have immunity for nonofficial acts performed before entering office.

The Court conceded that the presidency is an office "so vast and important that the public interest demands that [the president] devote his undivided time and attention to his public duties." However, Stevens maintained that it does not follow from this that the separation of powers limits the authority of the judicial branch to interfere with the executive branch: "The doctrine of separation of powers is concerned with the allocation of official power among the three branches of government. . . . Whatever the outcome of this case, there is no possibility that the decision will curtail the scope of the official powers of the executive branch." Again, it is clear that the Court drew a distinction between the acts of a private citizen before entering office and the duties of a public official.

The Court rejected two additional contentions of Clinton's defense team. The first was the assertion that national security would be imperiled if the president is subject to "politically motivated harassing and frivolous lawsuits." Stevens dismissed this argument by noting that most frivolous suits are terminated at the pleadings stage or on summary judgment. Furthermore, he submitted, sanctions are available to deter litigation that might be used to harass a president. Previous presidents, as well as President Clinton himself, Stevens pointed out, "have given testimony without jeopardizing the nation's security."

The final point made by Stevens proved to be the most controversial. The Supreme Court concluded that to let the case proceed while Bill Clinton was serving as president would not "impose an unacceptable burden on the president's time and energy, and thereby impair the effective performance of his job." The district court, Stevens maintained, would be aware of the considerable demands on a president's time and be prepared to accommodate its proceedings to his schedule.

After the rulings in *Clinton v. Jones*, discovery in the district court proceeded in Jones's civil suit against the president. One product of the discovery was the identification of Kathleen Willey, a woman who proceeded to accuse the president of making unwanted sexual advances against her in the White House. Discovery also produced another woman, designated as Jane Doe 5 (later identified as Juanita Broaddrick), who accused Clinton of raping her sometime in the 1970s. A key witness in the Willey matter was Linda Tripp, who, after being accused of lying about Willey by Bob Bennett, began taping her telephone conversations with a White House intern, Monica Lewinsky, who claimed to have had sexual relations with Bill Clinton. In denying that he had a sexual relationship with Lewinsky, President Clinton arguably lied under oath. This complicated Clinton's personal legal problems and figured prominently in the two counts of impeachment against him as president, passed by the House of Representatives in 1998 and voted upon by the Senate in 1999.

The Supreme Court decision in *Clinton v. Jones* presented the country with an important but troubling legacy for future presidencies. In retrospect, we know that the Jones case occupied a huge chunk of President Clinton's time after the Lewinsky story broke, if not before. Was Clinton's performance as president impaired by the amount of time he had to devote to the Jones litigation? The president's supporters and opponents alike now believe that it was. If the country had faced a crisis during 1998, would Clinton, given the distractions of the Lewinsky *and* Jones revelations, have been able to act prudently and with dispatch?

Selected Bibliography

Brock, David. "Living with the Clintons," *American Spectator*. (January 1994).

Bugliosi, Vincent. *No Island of Sanity, Paula Jones v. Bill Clinton: The Supreme Court on Trial*. New York: Ballantine, 1998.

Heinrich, Alan. "Clinton's Little White Lies: The Materiality Requirement for Perjury in Civil Discovery." *Loyola of Los Angeles Law Review* 32 (June 1999): 1303–1356.

The Travails of
William Jefferson Clinton

—◄o►—

James D. King
Department of Political Science
University of Wyoming

The Impeachment and Trial of William Jefferson Clinton, (1998–1999)
[U.S. Congress]

◄o► THE CASE IN BRIEF ◄o►

Dates
1998, 1999

Location
District of Columbia

Court
U.S. Senate, sitting as a court of
impeachment

Principal Participants
President Bill Clinton
Kenneth Starr
Monica Lewinsky

Significance of the Case
The Whitewater investigation, the Jones
case, and an affair with a White House
intern aside, alleged perjury in testimony
led to Clinton's impeachment.

Regardless of any policy achievements of his administration, William Jefferson Clinton will forever be remembered as the second American president impeached by the House of Representatives. Like Andrew Johnson 131 years earlier, Clinton escaped conviction and removal from office, but his presidency was nonetheless tarnished. The personal scandal and various investigations of his activities prior to his election and his conduct in office are the principal likely legacies of Clinton's presidency.

Bill Clinton in many ways personifies the career politician who had so often been the target of public scorn in the 1980s and 1990s. Raised in a small Arkansas town, Clinton attended some of the world's most prestigious institutions of higher learning: Georgetown University, Oxford University (as a Rhodes scholar), and Yale Law School. Most people with such educational credentials secure positions with elite law firms and major corporations, but Clinton chose another path. Always intrigued by the political arena, after graduating from Yale he returned to Arkansas in 1974 and launched his political career by seeking election to the U.S. House of Representatives. Ironically, while Clinton was preparing for this first campaign, his Yale classmate and future wife, Hillary Rodham, was a member of the House Judiciary Committee staff investigating President Nixon's alleged crimes and possible impeachment.

Although unsuccessful in his first bid for elective office, Clinton quickly established himself within the Arkansas political community, and in 1976, he was elected state attorney general. Two years later, he won the state's highest office and, at age thirty-two, became the nation's youngest governor. Defeated for reelection in 1980, Clinton reclaimed the office in 1982 and held it until his election as president a decade later. On January 20, 1993, Clinton was inaugurated as president, the third youngest to hold the office.

A combination of fortuitous circumstances led to Clinton's successful presidential campaign. Twenty months before the votes were cast, President George Bush's reelection appeared certain. His leadership during the Persian Gulf War sent his approval ratings in public opinion polls skyrocketing. So popular was Bush that no prominent Democrats were willing to challenge him. But presidential elections hinge more on economics than foreign policy, and a downturn in the economy quickly cut into Bush's popularity. Even more devastating for the president was a perception that he was insensitive to the financial problems of average citizens. This Clinton exploited masterfully in a debate with Bush. With voters rather than representatives of the news media posing questions, Clinton demonstrated a knowledge of the prices of goods regularly purchased by most people. Bush appeared bored by the whole affair and seemed to have difficulty understanding the questions put to him.

A key factor in Bush's lackluster 1992 campaign was his belief that the American people would not elect a man of questionable character as president. Various accusations had kept the Clinton campaign on the defensive for much of the election year. The candidate was forced to confront charges that he tried to

evade military service during the Vietnam War, questions about his involvement in antiwar demonstrations while a student at Oxford, questions about experimentation with marijuana, and allegations of marital infidelity. The last charge came from a former television reporter in Little Rock and posed the most serious threat to Clinton's candidacy. Gennifer Flowers's claim of a twelve-year relationship with Clinton was neutralized only after an appearance by Governor and Mrs. Clinton on the highly rated network television show, *60 Minutes*, and an aggressive defense of the candidate by campaign surrogates. In the end, the outcome of the 1992 election hinged on the economy rather than on personal factors. Clinton's election was more of a rejection of Bush by the voters than an acceptance of the Democratic nominee.

The first two years of the Clinton presidency saw a mixture of successes and failures, with more of the latter than the former. The president created a firestorm during his first days in office when he announced a policy permitting homosexuals to serve in the armed forces. Although most presidential appointments receive prompt approval from the Senate, several of Clinton's nominations to the Justice Department encountered Senate opposition and were withdrawn. Congress became impatient waiting for the president to develop legislative proposals for stimulating the economy, but it approved a somewhat diluted version of the administration's package by very narrow majorities in both houses. A comprehensive health-reform proposal, produced by a committee chaired by First Lady Hillary Rodham Clinton, met substantial resistance on Capitol Hill and failed to pass either chamber. The president's greatest accomplishment was undoubtedly securing bipartisan support for the North American Free Trade Agreement, which altered economic relations among the United States, Canada, and Mexico.

Scandal also reached the White House during Clinton's first year in office. In May 1993, the seven staff members of the White House travel office were abruptly dismissed. Because these staff members served at the pleasure of the president, their removal was clearly within his power. Questions of impropriety arose about the firings, however, when a request that the FBI review travel office records was made outside normal procedures, and when friends of the president with financial interests in airplane charter companies were involved in the staff changes. In October, questions of President and Mrs. Clinton's involvement in a failed Arkansas real-estate development, known as Whitewater, arose in the course of a federal investigation of Madison Guaranty, a failed savings and loan run by James and Susan McDougal, friends of the Clintons. Vincent Foster, a former Little Rock law partner of Hillary Clinton and the deputy White House counsel who had worked on Whitewater-related issues, committed suicide in July. Finally, in January 1994, *American Spectator,* drawing mainly from the statements of former Arkansas state troopers, published a lengthy story on Clinton's alleged extramarital affairs during his time as governor.

The public's generally unfavorable reaction to the events of Clinton's first two years in office set the stage for the pivotal event of Clinton's presidency: the 1994 midterm congressional elections. Democrats were expected to lose seats in the House, as the party controlling the White House had in all but two midterm elections dating back to the Civil War. The Republicans, however, surpassed even the most optimistic projections, gaining fifty-four seats in the House of Representatives and eight in the Senate. For the first time in forty years, Capitol Hill was under Republican control.

The Republican takeover of Congress was crucial to the Clinton presidency in two respects. First and most obvious, it is unlikely that a House of Representatives controlled by Democrats would have impeached the president. A Democratic majority, while not approving of the president's conduct, would have crushed an impeachment movement. A resolution of impeachment would have died, probably of neglect, had the Democrats taken the House in 1994. Second, Clinton was able to run for reelection, not on his record as president, but against the policies of the Republican Congress. The 1996 presidential election bore strong resemblance to that of 1948, when President Truman campaigned effectively against the Republican Congress elected in 1946.

Confident following their success in 1994, Republicans pressed forward with a number of proposals, some popular and some not, during the 104th Congress. Their Waterloo came, however, in fall 1995 during a standoff with the president over the budget. Despite warnings from Clinton that he would veto reductions in appropriations for various federal agencies, the Republican leadership forged ahead with its Draconian cost-cutting proposals. The result was a prolonged government shutdown as several government agencies closed temporarily when Republicans could not muster the votes to override presidential vetoes. The standoff ended when the Republicans blinked and passed appropriations bills more in line with the president's original budget requests. More important, Clinton gave his reelection campaign a substantial boost by casting the Republicans as the opponents of popular programs. Cooperation and compromise replaced conflict and rigidity in executive-legislative relations during 1996, but the advantage Clinton gained during the budget battle could not be overcome by Senator Robert Dole, the Republican nominee. The GOP retained control of both the House and Senate, thus setting up the impeachment battle two years hence. Had the Democrats maintained control of Congress in 1994, Clinton would have been forced to campaign for reelection on the basis of the accomplishments of his administration and may have failed in his bid for reelection, as Jimmy Carter and George Bush had. In that case, Clinton would have been known only as another one-term president, not as an impeached president.

Clinton's impeachment resulted from the convergence of twin legal problems that haunted his presidency almost from the start: a sexual harassment suit filed by Paula Corbin Jones and the investigation of the failed Whitewater real-estate development by an independent counsel. Neither of these alone would likely have yielded an impeachment: the Jones suit was eventually dismissed by the federal district court, and no credible evidence of wrongdoing by Clinton related to Whitewater was uncovered. Instead, it was the independent counsel's investigation of testimony in the Jones case—specifically, that Clinton committed perjury and acted in other ways to mislead the court—that brought the president to impeachment.

Jones's charge of sexual harassment by Clinton stemmed from reports in the 1994 *American Spectator* article that an Arkansas state trooper had escorted a state employee named "Paula" to the governor's suite during a 1991 state government conference at the Little Rock Excelsior Hotel and that Clinton had made lewd advances toward the woman. Jones acknowledged in February 1994 that she was the "Paula" identified in the article, and she filed her lawsuit in federal district court in May. The president denied Jones's allegations and filed a claim of immunity from civil suits while in office. Federal Judge Susan Webber Wright denied the president's motion, allowing discovery in the case to proceed, but she ordered a delay in any trial until the conclusion of Clinton's presidency. The court of appeals upheld the denial of the president's motion for dismissal but overruled the decision to delay any trial.

In a unanimous decision, the U.S. Supreme Court affirmed the judgment of the court of appeals. The justices held in *Clinton v. Jones* (1997) that while the chief executive cannot be the target of a civil suit pertaining to his constitutional duties, the presidency does not convey "an immunity that extends beyond the scope of any action taken in an official capacity." Claims by the president that the doctrine of separation of powers shielded him from judicial scrutiny during his term of office were rejected as inapplicable to a civil suit. "Whatever the outcome of this case," Justice John Paul Stevens wrote for the Court, "there is no possibility that the decision will curtail the scope of the official powers of the Executive Branch." An argument that involvement in a civil suit would consume too much of the president's time at the expense of his official duties was also rejected by the justices, who stated that "if properly managed by the District Court, it appears to us highly unlikely to occupy any substantial amount of [the president's] time."

On April 1, 1998, the Jones sexual harassment suit was dismissed by Judge Wright as

lacking merit, but not before embroiling the president in another controversy. Attorneys for Jones sought to establish a pattern of sexual advances toward women by Clinton to bolster Jones's claim of harassment. In a deposition taken on January 17, 1998, Clinton acknowledged a single liaison with Gennifer Flowers, but he denied having sexual relationships with other women named by the lawyers. Among the other women Clinton was asked about in his deposition was Monica Lewinsky. Although Lewinsky also denied a sexual relationship with Clinton in an affidavit prepared for the Jones lawsuit, she had told friends, including fellow Pentagon employee Linda Tripp, of an affair with the president. Tripp presented this information, along with tape recordings of telephone conversations with Lewinsky, to Kenneth Starr, the independent counsel probing the Whitewater real-estate development. Tripp was later indicted (although never prosecuted) for recording telephone conversations in violation of Maryland state law. Starr's staff arranged to record a luncheon conversation between Tripp and Lewinsky, during which Lewinsky said Vernon Jordan, a prominent attorney and close friend of the president, had asked her to give false testimony in the Paula Jones case. Starr then sought and received permission from Attorney General Janet Reno and the panel of federal judges to expand his jurisdiction to include investigating possibly perjury and obstruction of justice in the Jones case.

Starr was the second special prosecutor to delve into the Whitewater morass. The independent-counsel statute had expired in 1993, but the question of whether the Justice Department could conduct a truly independent investigation of Whitewater prompted the president to request that Attorney General Reno appoint a special counsel. Reno selected Robert B. Fiske Jr., a Republican and former federal prosecutor. After five months of inquiries, Fiske reported finding no improper contacts between the White House and the Treasury Department regarding the latter's handling of the Madison Guaranty savings and loan. And, despite the allegations of some of the president's harshest critics that Vincent Foster was murdered to conceal Whitewater-related crimes, Fiske found no evidence of foul play in Foster's death. On the day of Fiske's report, Clinton signed into law the reauthorization of the Independent Counsel Act. Five weeks later, a panel of three federal judges, empowered under the act to appoint independent counsels, replaced Fiske with Starr. In its order, the panel stated, "It is not our intent to impugn the integrity of the attorney general's appointee, but rather to reflect the intent of the Act that the actor be protected against perceptions of conflict."

A former Justice Department official during the Reagan presidency and a Reagan appointee to the federal court of appeals, Starr was in private practice when he was named independent counsel. His appointment was viewed by some Clinton supporters as a highly partisan move, but the White House adopted a more neutral stance. There can be little doubt, however, that Starr was controversial. Questions were raised during the independent counsel's investigation concerning conflicts of interest, because Starr remained involved in his private practice with conservative political groups and tobacco companies. In addition, a law partner of Starr's had provided legal advice to Paula Jones's attorneys.

Rather than building upon Fiske's work, Starr began the Whitewater–Madison Guaranty investigations anew, eventually securing convictions of James McDougal, Susan McDougal, Arkansas governor Jim Guy Tucker, and Webster Hubbell, a former law partner of Hillary Clinton and a former assistant attorney general. Attracting more attention were aspects of the inquiry that involved the president and first lady. Mrs. Clinton was called to testify before a Little Rock grand jury about her legal work for Madison Guaranty, and a minor scandal emerged when Rose Law Firm billing records—which had been subpoenaed months earlier by the independent counsel—were found in the White House private residence after being reported lost. Despite the extensive investigation, no Whitewater-related charges were filed against the Clintons.

The focus of attention, within Starr's office and among the public, shifted in 1998 to the president's relationship with Lewinsky, the possibility that the president committed perjury in his Jones deposition, and allegations of obstruction of justice. Sexual activity between the president and Lewinsky, which first occurred in November 1995, involved her performing oral sex on Clinton but did not include sexual intercourse. This was an important distinction, as the definition of *sexual relationship* prepared by Jones's attorneys was confusing, allowing Clinton to argue later that oral sex did not constitute sexual relations under that definition. Allegations of obstruction of justice were related to (1) efforts by Vernon Jordan to assist Lewinsky in finding a job in New York (a task he undertook when asked to do so by Clinton), (2) Clinton's request that Lewinsky return gifts he had given her, and (3) discussions Clinton had with various aides that Starr believed were attempts to influence their testimony.

Under an agreement providing immunity from prosecution in exchange for her testimony, Lewinsky admitted lying about her relationship with Clinton in the affidavit submitted for the Jones case, but she denied that Clinton or Jordan attempted to influence her testimony. Tests linked a semen stain on a dress of Lewinsky's to Clinton's DNA, providing physical evidence of the affair. Jordan and several Clinton aides also denied any obstruction of justice when called before the grand jury. Finally, on August 17, 1998, the president gave testimony to the grand jury from the White House in which he admitted having "inappropriate intimate contact" with Lewinsky, but he denied a "sexual relationship" or that he had tried to influence anyone's testimony. That evening, Clinton told a national television audience that his relationship with Lewinsky was "wrong," but he asserted that his answers in the Jones deposition were "legally accurate." He acknowledged misleading his wife and others, and he attacked the independent counsel for prying into his private life.

Serious talk of impeachment had commenced in January 1998, when Clinton's relationship with Lewinsky and the possibility of perjured testimony became public, but the House took no action as Starr's inquiry proceeded. That changed, however, on September

President Bill Clinton gives testimony to the independent counsel, Kenneth Starr, at the White House on August 17, 1998. This testimony as well as earlier depositions given under oath in the Paula Jones sexual harassment suit against him led to Clinton's impeachment by the House in December 1998. *Associated Press AP.*

9, 1998, when Starr delivered to Capitol Hill a four-hundred-page investigative report detailing information relating to the possible impeachment of the president. This "referral" was pursuant to the Ethics in Government Act, which required the independent counsel to "advise the House of Representatives of any substantial and credible information . . . that may constitute grounds for impeachment." The report was controversial, as it presented a detailed case for impeaching Clinton. Many individuals, both within the independent counsel's office and in the public at large, believed Starr's obligation was to make available only to the House the evidence gathered during the course of his inquiry. But, with his referral, the independent counsel had instead become an advocate for impeachment.

Before reviewing the material (although warned of its content), the House of Representatives voted to release Starr's referral to the public. The report was posted on the Internet, and various news organizations soon published excerpts. The explicit details of Clinton's relationship with Lewinsky brought condemnation to both the president for his behavior

and to the independent counsel for producing a report that some considered pornographic. Starr maintained that both Congress and the public had the right to have full knowledge of the matter. It was now up to the House of Representatives to determine if impeachment was justified.

Article II, Section 4, of the Constitution defines the conditions of a president's removal from office: "The President, Vice President, and all civil Officers of the United States, shall be removed from Office on Impeachment for, and Conviction of, Treason, Bribery, or other high Crimes and Misdemeanors." As with so many provisions of the Constitution, the impeachment clause leaves much to interpretation. Specifically, what constitutes an "impeachable offense"? The uncertainty regarding an impeachable offense relates to the last of the three transgressions presented in the Constitution. The definition of "treason" in Article III is presumably applicable to impeachments. The framers did not define "bribery" but few would doubt that they meant offering, giving, or receiving monetary compensation in exchange for special favors. But what are "high Crimes and Misdemeanors"?

Three perspectives, ranging greatly in their breadth, have been offered in response to this question. The narrowest view takes the words *crimes and misdemeanors* literally. Impeachable offenses (other than treason and bribery) are restricted to acts for which an accused can be indicted in a court of law. Only a demonstrable violation of a statute warrants impeachment and removal. The broadest view was given voice by then Congressman Gerald R. Ford in 1970, when he proposed the impeachment of Supreme Court Justice William O. Douglas. An impeachable offense, Ford told his colleagues, "is whatever a majority of the House [considers it] to be at a given moment in history; conviction results from whatever offense or offenses two-thirds of the other body considers to be sufficiently serious to require the removal of the accused from office." This perspective offers Congress an invitation to impeach and remove for any reason. Many constitutional scholars consider Ford's claim incompatible with the intentions of the framers. As evidence, they cite the fate of George Mason's proposal at the Constitutional Convention to include "mal-administration" among impeachable offenses. After James Madison argued that this would amount to the president serving at the pleasure of Congress, Mason withdrew his initial proposal and offered as a substitute the "high Crimes and Misdemeanors" phrase.

Although extreme, Ford's definition reflects the understanding that impeachment is not limited to statutory infractions. According to Alexander Hamilton, writing in *The Federalist* (No. 65), impeachment involves "those offenses which proceed from the misconduct of public men, or, in other words, from the abuse or violation of some public trust. They are of a nature which may with peculiar propriety be denominated POLITICAL, as they related chiefly to injuries done immediately to the society itself." This supports a third perspective—that is, that the framers of the Constitution understood that impeachable offenses are not limited to transgressions of law. A government official can violate public trust without violating a specific statute. "Impeachment is a political act, not a judicial one," according to constitutional scholar Louis Fisher. "The purpose is to remove someone from office, not to punish for a crime." By this perspective, conduct leading to impeachment need not involve criminal activity, but removal of the president cannot rest on minor disagreements between the legislative and executive branches.

Apparently believing that criminal acts produce the strongest arguments for impeachment, the articles of impeachment against Clinton considered by the House of Representatives emphasized alleged violations of law. In this respect, the Clinton impeachment inquiry paralleled those of Andrew Johnson and Richard Nixon. The political nature of impeachment cast a shadow over the proceedings, however. The 1998 congressional elections took place between the release of Starr's report and the opening of committee hearings on impeachment. The Democrats gained five seats in the House of Representatives, the first gains by the president's party in a midterm election in sixty-four years. Efforts by the Republicans to cast the election as a referendum

on Clinton's impeachment had clearly backfired. In the wake of the Republican losses, Speaker Newt Gingrich accepted responsibility and announced his resignation. Supporters of the president argued that the House should delay its impeachment inquiry until the new Congress opened in January 1999, but the Republican leadership pressed ahead.

The House Judiciary Committee heard testimony from a variety of witnesses, but only independent counsel Kenneth Starr spoke directly to the allegations against the president. Other witnesses appearing before the committee—including lawyers, judges, academics, military officers, and private citizens—addressed issues such as the president not being "above the law," the likelihood of a similar perjury offense being prosecuted in the courts, the effect of the president's actions on the military, and whether the offenses committed justified impeachment. None of the principals of the case—Clinton, Lewinsky, Jordan, or various White House aides—were called before the committee, although the president responded in writing to eighty-one questions put to him by Judiciary Committee Chairman Henry Hyde. Audiotape and videotape recordings of Lewinsky's conversations with Tripp and the president's grand jury testimony were played by the majority and minority party counsel to bolster their cases.

In the end, the Judiciary Committee recommended four articles of impeachment, charging the president with:

1. perjury in his August 17, 1998, testimony before the grand jury concerning his relationship with Lewinsky, his testimony in the Jones case, false statements he allowed his attorney to make on his behalf, and his efforts to influence the testimony of others;
2. perjury in his January 17, 1998, deposition in the Jones case;
3. obstruction of justice for concealing evidence in the Jones case by encouraging others to provide false or misleading testimony;
4. failing to respond to and making false and misleading statements in the course of the Judiciary Committee's impeachment inquiry.

The committee votes on the articles followed political party lines with only one defection; one Republican joined the Democrats in dissenting on the second article.

On December 19, 1998, the House of Representatives concluded two days of debate on impeachment by voting on the articles. The principal themes were expressed by Judiciary Committee chairman Hyde and by John Conyers, ranking Democrat on the Judiciary Committee. In his opening remarks, Hyde stated:

> The question before this House is rather simple. It is not a question of sex. Sexual misconduct and adultery are private acts and are none of Congress's business. It is not even a question of lying about sex. The matter before the House is a question of lying under oath. This is a public act, not a private act. This is called perjury. . . . [W]e must decide if a president, the chief law-enforcement officer of the land, the person who appoints the attorney general, the person who nominates every federal judge, the person who nominates to the Supreme Court and the only person with a constitutional obligation to take care that the laws be faithfully executed, can lie under oath repeatedly and maintain it is not a breach of trust sufficient for impeachment.

By contrast, Representative Conyers echoed the opinions of several witnesses before the Judiciary Committee that the president's offenses were minor: "Impeachment was designed to rid this nation of traitors and tyrants, not attempts to cover up extramarital affairs. This resolution trivializes our most important tool to maintain democracy. It downgrades the impeachment power into a partisan weapon that can used with future presidents."

Several Democrats noted that public opinion supported the president on the impeachment issue, while others accused Republicans of trying to overturn the results of the 1996 election through the impeachment process. A Democratic proposal to censure, rather than impeach, the president was mentioned frequently, but the Republican leadership refused to bring a censure motion to the floor.

Voting primarily along party lines, the House of Representatives approved by slim margins the first and third articles of impeachment, charging the president with perjury in his grand jury testimony and obstruction of justice. Three Republicans opposed all four articles, while a single Democrat approved all four. Eight representatives—four Republicans and four Democrats—broke ranks on three of the four articles. The fourth article—charging that the president failed to respond appropriately to the Judiciary Committee—was opposed by more than a third of the Republicans. The partisan nature of the House deliberations was underscored when no Democratic representative agreed to serve as a "manager" and participate in the presentation of the articles of impeachment to the Senate.

The focus then shifted to the other side of the Capitol, where Chief Justice William Rehnquist presided over the Senate trial of President Clinton. Thirteen House managers began a three-day presentation of their case on January 12, 1999. Each laid before the Senate a different segment of the evidence believed to support impeachment on perjury or obstruction of justice. Representative Hyde closed the prosecution's case by reiterating the basic theme of House Republicans: "The matter before this body is a question of lying under oath. . . . That none of us is above the law is a bedrock principal of democracy. To erode that bedrock is to risk even further injustice. To erode that bedrock is to subscribe to a 'divine right of kings' theory of governance, in which those who govern are absolved from adhering to the basic moral standards to which the governed are accountable. . . . Let us be clear: The vote that you are asked to cast is, in the final analysis, a vote about the rule of law." On several occasions, Hyde invoked the memory of members of the armed forces who had defended the United States through its history.

From the start, Clinton's defenders directed their arguments toward Senate Democrats. The Constitution requires a two-thirds majority to remove the president. This suggested a strategy of holding the support of the Democrats rather than winning Republican votes. In a worst-case scenario, 22 of the 45 Democrats would have to align with all 55 Republicans to remove Clinton from office. This was the simple arithmetic that led Senate Majority Leader

Trent Lott to endorse a bipartisan plan—eventually blocked by the president's opponents—for a preliminary vote to test the size of the majority favoring Clinton's removal.

White House counsel Charles Ruff opened the three-day defense with an unambiguous statement on behalf of the president: "He did not commit perjury; he did not obstruct justice; he must not be removed from office." Ruff and other members of the president's defense challenged the evidence presented by House managers, drawing attention to what they believed were inconsistencies in the evidence and, in some instances, evidence that contradicted the arguments of the prosecution. An important component of the defense before the Senate, as in the House, was the gravity of the offenses with which the president was charged relative to the penalty of removal from office. In making this argument, Ruff recalled the words of ten Republican members on the House Judiciary Committee who had deliberated on the impeachment of Richard Nixon and who had written that the framers intended removal from office as appropriate "only for serious misconduct, dangerous to the system of government established by the Constitution."

Perhaps the sharpest disagreement between the prosecutors and president's defense team came over the question of witnesses. The House managers urged the Senate to take direct testimony from Lewinsky, Jordan, and others. The defenders argued in response that if hearing testimony from the principals of the saga was so crucial to a fair resolution of the issue, those witnesses should have been called before the House Judiciary Committee. To call them now, Clinton attorney David Kendall contended, was an act of desperation. Ultimately, the Senate voted along party lines, with only one Democrat, Russell Feingold of Wisconsin, siding with the Republicans, to take depositions from Lewinsky, Jordan, and White House aide Sidney Blumenthal. Thus, no witnesses were called to appear on the Senate floor.

A significant test vote occurred when Senator Robert Byrd of West Virginia, among the chamber's most respected members and considered by many to be a barometer of Democratic opinion, offered a motion to dismiss the charges against the president. Hyde characterized the motion as an "exit strategy" and with other House managers urged its rejection. After debating the motion in closed session, the Senate voted 56-44 to defeat Byrd's motion; Feingold was again alone in breaking party ranks. The real message of the vote was unmistakable: a sufficient number of Democrats opposed conviction. Unless sentiments shifted significantly in the next few days, Clinton would be acquitted and remain in office.

The formality of closing arguments by both sides was observed before the Senate closed its doors to debate the issue in private. On February 12, 1999, the Senate voted on the two articles of impeachment. Forty-five senators voted guilty on the charge of perjury; fifty senators voted guilty on the obstruction-of-justice charge. Five Republicans voted not guilty to both charges; another five acquitted the president on the perjury charge. Democrats were unanimous in voting not guilty on both charges. The constitutionally required two-thirds vote to convict had not been reached on either article. Clinton would serve the final two years of his term.

Why did Bill Clinton escape conviction in the Senate when, by most accounts, Richard Nixon would have been removed from office had he not resigned? Some suggest that Clinton escaped removal because the Democrats were more partisan in 1999 than the Republicans were in 1974. Only five Democrats broke ranks to support Clinton's impeachment in the House of Representatives, while no Democrat voted for conviction in the Senate. Nixon resigned, according to the partisan explanation for Clinton's acquittal, because Republican representatives opposed the president on the impeachment issue.

This explanation fails on two grounds. First, it assumes that senators' votes are dictated by party labels. This is patently false. Men and women join one party or the other because they share its values and perspectives. Two interpretations of the evidence and perspectives on the gravity of the offenses were reflected in coalitions that also reflected party affiliations. Second, although Nixon capitulated after Republican leaders informed him that he faced overwhelming bipartisan majorities for impeachment and removal, a majority of Republicans were nevertheless prepared to vote against impeachment until release of the transcript of Nixon's June 23, 1972, conversation with White House chief of staff H. R. Haldeman. This transcript revealed that the president authorized using the Central Intelligence Agency to block the FBI's probe into the break-in at Democratic Party headquarters at the Watergate office complex. It provided incontrovertible evidence that Nixon was involved in efforts to interfere with the criminal investigation during the week following the crime and therefore had been deceiving the public and his congressional backers for more than two years. The obstruction of justice and Nixon's complicity were clear. Several of Nixon's staunchest defenders announced that they would support the article of impeachment charging obstruction of justice. In forty-eight hours, the makeup of the pro-impeachment coalition changed from being mostly Democrats to a majority of representatives of both political parties.

An alternative explanation for Clinton's acquittal rests with a fundamental principle of democracy. The effort to impeach and remove Clinton from office failed because it lacked public support. From August 1998 to January 1999, public opinion surveys consistently showed slightly more than 60 percent of Americans opposed to the impeachment of President Clinton. By comparison, a Gallup poll conducted the first week of August 1974 showed 57 percent of the public favoring Nixon's removal from office. "Politicians live and die by the polls," Representative Hyde is reported to have remarked privately during Senate deliberations. The American public simply wanted Clinton to continue as president.

The difference in public opinion regarding the impeachments of Nixon and Clinton is due to the nature of the acts of which the presidents were accused—one's offenses were *public* acts; the other's were *private*. The impeachable offenses with which Nixon was charged involved using the machinery of government for political gain. More specifically, Nixon agreed to his chief of staff's proposal to use the CIA to conceal deeds of his campaign committee, and he authorized actions that were illegal (burglary, wiretapping, providing hush money to defendants) or unethical (sabotaging opponents' campaigns). Americans are often cynical about politics, but they expect fairness in the electoral arena. The "win by any means possible" attitude reflected by Nixon and the Committee to Reelect the President, referred to informally as CREEP, was counter to most definitions of "fairness." The revelations concerning CREEP were viewed as undermining the basic democratic process. To make matters worse, the allegations of inappropriate campaign tactics were accompanied by reports that the White House had tried to use the Internal Revenue Service to harass people perceived to be adversaries of the Nixon administration, and it had used unwarranted wiretaps and other extralegal means to try to stop leaks of information to the news media. All of these actions were outside the bounds of acceptable government conduct.

In contrast, some of the events that drove Clinton's impeachment happened before he took office as president, and all these events involved private acts. The Whitewater land deals and the alleged sexual harassment of Paula Corbin Jones occurred while Clinton was governor of Arkansas. Granted, efforts to conceal his relationship with Monica Lewinsky took place during Clinton's presidency, and the articles of impeachment charged that Clinton abused his office by using members of the White House staff to present his false story to the public. In this regard, Clinton's case bears a resemblance to Nixon's. Yet, the perjury was designed to conceal a private, sexual matter. The affair was morally wrong and impossible to condone, but most Americans understood why Clinton had lied when asked about his relationship with Lewinsky. People approved of neither the affair nor the perjured testimony, but they themselves would not have liked being asked the questions put to Clinton, and they recognized that they might have responded similarly. In short, the public agreed with Charles Ruff, who declared in his opening statement before the Senate, "Impeachment is not a remedy for private wrongs." The question of marital infidelity was viewed as a matter between the president and his wife rather than a political issue. An act of perjury in a civil lawsuit on a question of private sexual behavior was not deemed as threatening to the governmental system as was an attempt to retain office by corrupting the electoral process.

Support for this interpretation appeared in the Gallup Poll taken in October 1998 while the House of Representatives was preparing to debate the impeachment of the president. When asked which impeachment charges were more serious, those surveyed indicated the Nixon charges by a ratio of six to one. Nearly two-thirds (64 percent) thought the charges against Nixon were more serious, while only 10 percent gave that response concerning the Clinton charges. Twenty-three percent said the charges were "equally serious." In the public's mind, the crimes of the thirty-seventh president outweighed the sins of the forty-second.

The Clinton impeachment produced two important results for the American governmental process, one short-term and one long-term. The immediate effect was the demise of the independent-counsel statute. Democrats in Congress were unhappy with the way Kenneth Starr conducted the investigation of Clinton and with the methods employed by other special prosecutors who examined the activities of former agriculture secretary Mike Epsy, Interior Secretary Bruce Babbitt, and other administration officials. They were joined by Republicans, displeased with the independent counsels who probed members of the Reagan and Bush administrations, in permitting the statute to expire on June 30, 1999. The question of whether the Justice Department can fairly investigate the president or other high-level administration officials will undoubtedly arise in the future, but for now, Congress was willing to give careful thought before enacting another independent-counsel law.

The long-term impact of the Clinton impeachment has been to establish the precedent that a violation of law is not necessarily an offense worthy of removing a president from office. Constitutional scholars have debated whether impeachment is limited to violations of law or if political acts that undermine the governmental process can be grounds for impeaching and removing the president or other governmental officials. Clinton's impeachment indicates that the severity of the offense is also a factor. Articles I and II of the impeachment resolution, and the accompanying arguments presented to the Senate by the House managers, stressed the crimes of perjury and obstruction of justice. In weighing these charges, senators considered the seriousness of the offenses as well as their nature. Yes, perjury and obstruction of justice are crimes, but *in this instance* the offenses did not pass the critical threshold necessary for removal. There are no guarantees that an act of perjury committed by another president under different circumstances will also result in acquittal. The Senate demonstrated that impeachment is, as Alexander Hamilton noted, a political process. As with any political process in a democratic system, popular support is necessary to carry impeachment to the ultimate conclusion of removing a president from office.

In a denouement to the 1990s impeachment scandal, President Clinton finally admitted to the American people on January 19, 2001, that he had lied about sex. In the waning hours of his embattled administration, Clinton accepted a deal to avoid post-presidential legal prosecution for his statements under oath about his relations with Monica Lewinsky. Robert Ray, the Independent Counsel looking into various irregularities in Clinton's activities as president, succeeded where his predecessor, Kenneth Starr, had failed. The deal that Ray presented and Clinton accepted called for Clinton to pay a fine of $25,000, surrender his license to practice law for five years and, most importantly, to acknowledge publically that he had given false testimony under oath. In exchange, Clinton was spared prosecution for the matters that led to his impeachment. Leaders of both parties were quick to proclaim that this "accommodation" offered a fair and reasonable end to the $55 million investigation into the sex life and questionable financial dealings of the former president.

Selected Bibliography

Berger, R. *Impeachment: The Constitutional Problems.* Cambridge, MA: Harvard University Press, 1974.

Gerhardt, M. *The Federal Impeachment Process: A Constitutional and Historical Analysis.* Princeton, NJ: Princeton University Press, 1996.

McLoughlin, M., ed. *The Impeachment and Trial of President Clinton: The Official Transcripts, from the* *House Judiciary Committee Hearings to the Senate Trial.* New York: Times Books, 1999.

Woodward, B. *Shadow: Five Presidents and the Legacy of Watergate.* New York: Simon and Schuster, 1999.

PART III

ECONOMICS AND ECONOMIC REGULATION

- Contracts

- Commerce

- Labor

- Miscellaneous Governmental
  Regulation

- Substantive Due Process

- Negligence and Tort Law

- Natural Resources, Technology,
  and the Environment

Every day courts are called upon to resolve disputes that involve money or other financial concerns. It should come as no surprise, therefore, that a substantial portion of this volume surveys cases concerning economics and law. Since 1950, the leading scholarly orientation in American legal history has been the so-called "Wisconsin School," identified with James Willard Hurst and his many former students. The focus that Hurst and his disciples placed upon the intersection of economics and law is reflected in most of the fifty-three essays in this section.

Contracts

Article I of the U.S. Constitution contains a "contract clause" that prohibits states from "impairing the obligation of contracts." Given the importance of contracts in commercial transactions, particularly in a rapidly expanding national economy, it was reasonable to expect the contract clause of the Constitution to be tested by litigation in the early national period. One of the first contract clause cases to come before the Supreme Court involved an attempt by Virginia to reserve the power to amend a state charter. Whether this was permitted is discussed in "The Power to Amend Corporate Charters." Two of Chief Justice John Marshall's greatest decisions involved what might be termed "loose interpretations" of the contract clause: These are examined in "When a Contract Obtained by Fraud Is Still a Contract" and "Balancing Private Good and Public Good." The relationship of bankruptcy to contracts is considered in "Justice Story, Bankruptcy, and the Supreme Court."

Perhaps the greatest of the Supreme Court's contract clause decisions involved a dispute between two Massachusetts bridges; this case is examined in "Abridging Vested Interests: The Battle of the Massachusetts Bridges." The last contract selection in this section, "An Innocent Sort of a Duck: Iron Range Pioneers Challenge John D. Rockefeller," involved a dispute on the Minnesota iron range in the waning years of the nineteenth century.

Commerce

Paralleling the stark language of the contract clause in the Constitution is the equally blunt commerce clause in Article I that bestows upon Congress the power "to regulate Commerce . . . among the several States." The first commerce clause case, another one of Marshall's great decisions, is featured in "A More Perfect Union: The Steamboat Case." The steamboat case appeared to extend to Congress plenary power to regulate commerce. But opinions of the Supreme Court headed by Marshall's successor, Chief Justice Roger B. Taney—such as the one discussed in "An Omen of Change: State Power to Regulate Commerce"— seemed to reserve considerable power to the states.

Late in the nineteenth century, as discussed in "When Monopoly Mattered," the Supreme Court held that manufacturing was not commerce. However, two years later, as examined in "Regulation in the Public Interest," the Court discussed how two recently passed federal laws, the Interstate Commerce Act and Sherman Antitrust Act, impinged on the commerce clause.

In the twentieth century, federal courts have generally interpreted the commerce clause broadly. For example, as discussed in "Commerce and National Police Powers," lottery tickets were deemed to fall under purview of the federal commerce power. Two of the great trust-busting cases of the Theodore Roosevelt years are examined in "Busting Trusts with More Backbone than a Banana."

The Great Depression of the 1930s witnessed further expansive interpretations of the commerce clause. "The Wagner Act and the Constitutional Crisis of 1937" probes the U.S. Supreme Court decision to employ the commerce clause to uphold the constitutionality of federal legislation permitting labor unions to organize in the steel industry. By contrast, in "The 'Indigent' Migrant," the Court used the commerce clause to strike down California's attempt to close its borders to indigents. Perhaps the case best illustrating the Court's expansive use of the commerce clause to uphold legislative measures enacted to deal with the bleak economic conditions of the Depression was the 1942 case of *Wickard v. Filburn*, discussed in "Two Hundred and Thirty-Nine Bushels of Wheat." In this instance, the Court upheld a federal law setting the price of wheat, notwithstanding that the wheat at issue in the case was consumed on the farm and never entered the stream of national commerce.

Even the civil rights legislation of the 1960s, as examined in "Of Barbecue and Commerce," has been ruled constitutional pursuant to the commerce power of the federal government. Finally, perhaps the leading antitrust case of the second half of the twentieth century, reviewed in "A Popular Monopoly: *U.S. v. Microsoft*," saw the commerce clause wielded as a weapon against a computer software giant.

Labor

Trade unions have been an important feature of American life since the middle of the nineteenth century. Three selections in this section examine disputes involving labor unions. "The Legitimacy of Labor Organization" discusses two of the earliest cases involving organized labor in American history. "An Injury to One Is an Injury to All" scrutinizes the role of the famous labor leader Eugene Debs in the Pullman Strike. And "Can Children under 14 Legally Hold Full-time Jobs?" examines the constitutionality of an early twentieth-century congressional attempt to do away with child labor.

Miscellaneous Governmental Regulation

The nine essays in this section probe a miscellaneous series of historically interesting legal disputes concerning state and federal economic regulations. "Copyright Law: Limiting Literary Monopolies" reviews one of the earliest copyright cases in American law; ironically this decision involved the literary rights to Supreme Court opinions. "Corporate Growth v. States' Rights" deals with an important banking case of the Jacksonian Era. "The Scope of Admiralty Jurisdiction" treats one of the U.S. Supreme Court's most important opinions on the law of the seas. "'A Sore Grievance' to the Traveler" concerns the legal power of eminent domain. "Destructive Creation" offers an examination of a California case that involved a number of interrelated economic issues. "Minor Case, Major Decision" discusses a seemingly trivial case in which the U.S. Supreme Court, nonetheless, made a momentous ruling: that corporations would henceforth be considered as "persons" under the Fourteenth Amendment and would, thus, be protected by such weighty guarantees as the due process clause of that amendment. "Politics v. Precedents: The Income Tax Cases" provides an account of the great income tax cases of the late nineteenth century. "National Police Powers: The Oleomargarine Case" offers an example of a legal situation in which national regulatory powers were upheld by the High Court. And "State Legislature Power and Municipal Trusts" offers an example of where state power over municipal trusts was upheld by a state court.

Substantive Due Process

The seven cases in this section confront an issue in American law that occupied hundreds of thousands of hours of judicial time and took almost a century to resolve. The question was whether a court could employ its own standards of "reasonableness" in determining whether particular economic legislation violated the due process of an individual or group, even though the law was not prohibited by explicit constitutional language. An early presentation of this matter is discussed in "Prohibition and the Due Process Clause."

Most of the leading cases in the line of substantive due process were based on the due process clause of the Fourteenth Amendment, ratified in 1868. "The Fourteenth Amendment Receives Its First Judicial Construction" concerns the complicated *Slaughterhouse Cases* from Louisiana, cases that would also be important in the sphere of race relations. For the late nineteenth century, two selections probe the spread of economic substantive due process: "The Court Enters the Age of Reform" and "A 'Right' to Make Cigars." The temporary conversion of the Supreme Court to the conservative doctrine of substantive due process came in the case of *Lochner v. New York* (1905) and is discussed in " 'Mere Meddlesome Interferences': The Apogee of Substantive Due Process."

Between 1900 and the mid-1930s, the Supreme Court gave voice to substantive due process on numerous occasions. One such instance is considered in "The Iceman and the Public," where a majority of the justices voted to strike down a remedial state statute and refused to take judicial notice of the traumatic economic facts of the Great Depression. "The Chambermaid's Revenge" profiles the 1937 case which finally buried economic substantive due process.

Negligence and Tort Law

A tort is defined as a private or civil wrong or injury, other than breach of contract. The usual remedy for a decision in tort law is a monetary award. The apportionment of damages through tort litigation can have significant economic implications, particularly in large industries where thousands of individuals are affected potentially by legal precedents.

Many industrial tort actions of the nineteenth century involved the engine of economic development, the railroad. "Fellow Servants Beware," "Contributory Negligence as a 'Brake' on Suits Against Railroads," and "Railroad Development and Nuisance Law" deal with three such cases. One of the great tort law cases of the nineteenth century, however, involved an unfortunate attempt of two men to come between their fighting dogs. This dispute, which proved to be a breakthrough case in the development of negligence, is profiled in "The Great Dog Fight Case."

In the twentieth century, some of the leading tort decisions came from the pen of New York Court of Appeals Judge Benjamin Cardozo. Two of Cardozo's greatest decisions are discussed in "The Origins of Consumer Rights in Tort Law" and "Negligence Theory at Its Zenith." Another important step in the development of tort law was spearheaded by Roger Traynor, Chief Judge of the Supreme Court of California, in 1944; it is discussed in "When 'The Thing Speaks for Itself': *res ipsa loquitur* and the Proof of Negligence." The penultimate selection in this section, "The 'Nuking' of American Civilians" deals with a modern class action suit involving the untoward consequences of atomic testing. The final selection, "You Deserve a Brick Today: Products Liability Law and McDonald's Coffee," examines the much discussed (and much misunderstood) hot coffee cases of the 1990s.

Natural Resources, Technology, and the Environment

Court decisions involving the natural resources or the environment can also have substantial economic consequences. The cases in this section illustrate this economic reality.

The first five essays examine the controversial area of water law, which had distinctly different doctrinal histories in the eastern and western sections of the U.S. "Riparian Doctrine: A Short Case History for the Eastern United States" and "Conflict over Water Power in Massachusetts" discuss leading nineteenth-century cases in the Northeast and the South. "A Law for Water in the West," "Dividing the Rivers: Rule of Law in an Arid State," and "The Hydraulic Society of the Colorado River" examine nineteenth- and twentieth-century cases that arose out of western water litigation.

The final three selections in this section present cases that concern the country's most exotic and expensive modern technology, nuclear energy. "Controversy over a Fast-Breeder," "The Atomic Energy Commission and the Environment," and "Insuring Against Nuclear Plant Accidents" examine cases dealing with the legal, environmental, and economic impact of the commercial atom.

Contracts

The Power to Amend Corporate Charters

Yasuhide Kawashima

Department of History
The University of Texas at El Paso

Currie's Administrators v. The Mutual Assurance Society, 4 Va. 315 (1809) [Virginia Supreme Court]

◄o► THE CASE IN BRIEF ◄o►

Date
1809

Location
Virginia

Court
Virginia Supreme Court

Principal Participants
Estate of Dr. James Currie
Mutual Assurance Society

Significance of the Case
The Virginia state legislature asserted
the power to annul or alter acts of
incorporation. The court also ruled that
such changes are binding even if a
member of the Society was not present at
a meeting that adopted the changes.

In 1819, the Supreme Court held as an unconstitutional impairment of contracts New Hampshire's action in terminating the powers of the trustees of Dartmouth College under a royal charter. The New Hampshire act would have changed the fundamental nature of the college and appropriated its control to the political decision of the state, but the Supreme Court said such is not the American scheme. If, however, a power was reserved for the purpose of subsequently amending the charter, it would be quite another matter. Virginia was one of the states that already had enacted such reservations. *Currie's Administrators v. The Mutual Assurance Society* involved the first Virginia law with the reserved right of amendment.

In 1794, the Virginia legislature passed an act authorizing the establishment of an insurance corporation, the Mutual Assurance Society, to protect buildings against fire. The benefits of the institution were confined clearly and expressly to citizens of the state. Houses situated in the country and in towns were mutually assured: every member of the society, whether residing in town or country, became an insurer for every other member.

Under this act of incorporation, the society was authorized to adopt rules and regulations for its government. It further provided that the society should be at liberty, from time to time, to alter and amend such rules and regulations as it may judge necessary and that the society agree upon the premiums to be paid. Dr. James Currie subscribed to and became one of the initial members of the Society.

Within a few years, experience revealed that the losses in the country bore no relationship to those in towns. Thus the legislature, on January 29, 1805, at the insistence of a majority of the members of the society either personally present or represented by members of the General Assembly, passed another act. This act separated the interests and risks of the inhabitants of the country from those of the towns so that the countryman was no longer liable for losses by fire occurring in towns, nor the townsman for losses occurring in the country. It also declared that there "shall be in future only three directors, out of whom a president shall be chosen," providing that the society should not be prevented from "appointing more than three directors," if necessary.

Shortly thereafter, Alexander McRae was elected president of the board of directors, and on the same day three other persons were appointed directors. The president previously had not been chosen one of the directors, out of whom he was to be chosen but was elected by the same electoral body who chose the directors.

After the election of the president and directors, a resolution was adopted on February 25, 1805, at the meeting of the society's board of directors, calling on the town members, but not on the country members, for half a "quota" (i.e., a premium). Dr. Currie, one of the persons holding a building in a town insured by the society, refused to pay his required quota of $291.73 on two grounds. First, the requisition was made not under the original charter but under a subsequent act that attempted to increase his risk without his consent. Second, the

president of the board of directors was not chosen out of the directors, as the law of 1805 required, and consequently there could be no legal call of a quota.

The district court gave judgment in favor of the Mutual Assurance Society, and Currie appealed to the Supreme Court of Appeals of Virginia. Since he died pending the appeal, the case came to be reviewed in the name of his administrators. The Court that reviewed the case consisted of two judges, the third having declined to sit in the case.

The Virginia Supreme Court rejected the appellants' contention that the legislature could not lawfully increase Currie's risk without his consent because the demand for a quota was not made to the whole society but only to a part of it, thus impairing the obligation of the contract set forth in the original act of 1795. The Court maintained that Dr. Currie had been apprised fully of the power of the society when he became a member of the society, the power to alter and amend "the rules and regulations as they may judge necessary," and, therefore, had no just ground of complaint. The society soon came to realize that the risk was unequal between the town and country subscribers, in favor of the former, and felt it necessary to separate their interests. This change, the Court stated, was a measure essential to the equalization of the risks. A majority of the society, on a representation to the legislature, procured an act of Assembly, passed in 1795, separating these two interests. Furthermore, the Court pointed out, the appellants' principal had less reason to complain because any member had the right to withdraw from the society. It is better for an inconvenient member to be lopped off than for the whole corporate body to perish.

With regard to the election of McRae as president, the Court upheld its validity by accepting the argument of the counsel for the society. The clause, "there shall be in future only three directors, out of whom a president shall be chosen," the Court insisted, should be construed as "there shall be in future only three directors, one of whom shall be president." Here the Court failed to recognize the possibility for a different composition of the board and a different president that a different order of election might produce. The Court instead simply concluded that there would be no utility in requiring an unnecessary circuity of proceeding. Since a previous election as director was not required by the act, there was no objection to the society husbanding its time by appointing a president and director at one ballot.

The Court, thus, affirmed the judgment of the district court and established an important three-part precedent. First, the General Assembly has power, from time to time, to annul or alter acts of incorporation. Second, a member of the Mutual Assurance Society against fire loss is bound by an act of the Assembly varying the terms of the original act of incorporation passed at a legally constituted meeting of the society even though that individual member was not present at the meeting. And third, when an act provides that there shall be "three directors, out of whom a president shall be chosen," it is sufficient if the president be elected by a legally constituted meeting, and at the same time with the other directors, without having been previously appointed a director.

Selected Bibliography

Gibson, George D. "The Virginia Corporation Law of 1956." *Virginia Law Review* 42 (May and June 1956): 445–487, 603–626.

Vagts, Dethev F. "Reforming the 'Modern' Corporation: Perspectives from the German." *Harvard Law Review* 80 (November 1966): 23–89.

When a Contract Obtained by Fraud Is Still a Contract

Harry Fritz
Department of History
University of Montana

Fletcher v. Peck, 6 Cranch 87 (1810) [U.S. Supreme Court]

◄◦► THE CASE IN BRIEF ◄◦►

Date
1810

Location
Massachusetts
New Hampshire
Georgia

Court
U.S. Supreme Court

Principal Participants
Robert Fletcher
John Peck
Chief Justice John Marshall

Significance of the Case
Chief Justice John Marshall ruled that a state grant is a contact and that a state's attempt to repeal such a grant is an unconstitutional impairment of contract. It was the first time a state law was invalidated by the U.S. Supreme Court.

In 1803, one John Peck of Newton, Massachusetts, sold 15,000 acres of land in Mississippi Territory to Robert Fletcher of Amherst, New Hampshire. In a feigned or collusive case, deliberately designed under the diversity of citizenship rule to bypass the Eleventh Amendment, to bring the case in federal courts, and to test a number of disputed issues, Fletcher sued Peck in the U.S. Circuit Court of Massachusetts. The land in question, he claimed, was not Peck's to sell. Seven years later, in an opinion of the U.S. Supreme Court, Chief Justice John Marshall decided for the defendant. The land sale was legal. Therein lies a story.

The case of *Fletcher v. Peck* arose from the tangled state of Georgia land claims—as had *Chisholm v. Georgia* (1793). In 1795 the sovereign state of Georgia sold 35 million acres of its western lands to four land companies for $500,000—about 1.4 cents per acre. Sixteen of the seventeen-member legislative majority that participated in the sale received either cash or shares for their votes. In the following year, on February 13, 1796, Georgia repealed the sale act. Its citizens either rose in righteous indignation against the suborned legislature, or they had received a better offer. These two Georgia measures—the land sale of 1795 and its recission in 1796—are the chief ingredients of *Fletcher v. Peck.*

The Yazoo Land Fraud (Georgia's western lands were collectively named after the Yazoo River, a tributary of the Mississippi) quickly became one of the epic domestic battles of early American history. Three factors fueled the explosion. First, on precisely the same day as the Georgia repeal act, 11 million acres of the Yazoo claims were sold to the New England Mississippi Land Company, a third or "innocent" party, for $1,138,000, for 10.3 cents per acre. Land speculation was profitable. Second, in 1798 Georgia ceded its western lands to the federal government, and Congress created the vast Mississippi Territory. The Yazoo issue went national. Third, most of the investors in the newly-formed New England Mississippi Land Company were northern Federalists, who sought a national verification of their claims, while supporters of the Georgia repeal were states-rights Republicans. Yazoo became a sectional and a partisan issue.

Under President Thomas Jefferson, who assumed office in 1801, the Republicans backed a compromise solution. Negotiated by three administration heavyweights—Secretary of State James Madison, Secretary of the Treasury Albert Gallatin, and Attorney General Levi Lincoln—the deal seemingly satisfied everyone. It paid off Georgia to the tune of $1.25 million thus quieting the state's shrill insistence on the legality of its 1796 repeal. It set aside 5 million acres to satisfy the claims of innocent purchasers, now expanded in number and increasingly bipartisan. It allowed these claimants, the "New Yazooists," to take either land or money. All that remained to close the deal was a congressional appropriation of $5 million to compensate the money claimants. A bill to this effect was introduced in Congress in 1804.

The bill failed. It failed again in 1805, 1806, and 1807. It failed due largely to the inveterate opposition of Congressman John Randolph of Virginia, the self-styled defender of "old republican" principles of 1798. Randolph's magnetic oratory rallied the South, the state's righters,

and the Georgia repealers against the North, the Federalists, and the moderate Republicans in his own party. Though the votes were close, Randolph and his quondam allies continued to deny a powerful array of investors their legislative right to federal largesse. Increasingly, the Yazoo claimants leaned toward a judicial solution.

The case of *Fletcher v. Peck* was held in abeyance in the Massachusetts Circuit Court for three years. These were the years when the entire federal judiciary reeled under the onslaught of the Jeffersonian attack. The case was finally tried before a jury in late 1806. The jury's verdict on the legality of the original sale was noncommittal, but the two federal judges who constituted the court, Supreme Court Justice William Cushing and District Judge John Davis, rewrote the history of Georgia: The Yazoo land sale of 1795 was binding and had not been undone in 1796. Robert Fletcher, the putative loser, asked the U.S. Supreme Court for a writ of error; it was granted and the case was argued before the Court early in 1809. John Quincy Adams and Robert Goodloe Harper, no mean talent, appeared for the defendant, Peck; Fletcher was represented by the volatile Luther Martin of Maryland. Reversed on a technicality, *Fletcher v. Peck* was not remanded to the Massachusetts Circuit Court but continued for another term and was reargued in 1810. Joseph Story, a Massachusetts congressman and Yazoo lobbyist, replaced John Quincy Adams as counsel for Peck. The deck was now carefully stacked.

Rarely in American constitutional history has a decision of the Supreme Court been so foreordained. Every legal and constitutional precedent, every personal and political prejudice, every national and ideological tendency pointed to the reasoning and decision found in John Marshall's opinion of March 16, 1810. *Fletcher v. Peck* was not only managed litigation, carefully crafted to raise every pertinent issue, but it was also deliberately designed to ensure favorable rulings on every disputed point.

Article I, Section 10 of the U.S. Constitution states: "No state shall . . . pass any bill of attainder, *ex post facto* law, or law impairing the obligation of contracts." This is the "contract clause," the key to Marshall's decision. Prior to 1810 it had not been interpreted broadly; it protected, the founders agreed, only private business transactions from state intervention. But there were early signs of its broader potential significance. The U.S. Circuit Court for Rhode Island voided a state debtor-relief law in 1792, citing the constitutional prohibition against impairment of contract. In 1795 the Circuit Court for Pennsylvania, Justice William Paterson presiding, invalidated a state law fixing the ownership of property. The act was unconstitutional, Paterson declared in *Vanhorne's Lessee v. Dorrance*, because it impaired the obligation of a contract and was, thus, contrary to Article I, Section 10 of the Constitution.

More to the Yazoo point were specific legal opinions. As early as 1796, the Federalist congressman from South Carolina and ardent Yazooist Robert Goodloe Harper had argued that the 1795 Georgia sale constituted a contract that could not be broken by one of the parties. Harper's opinions were echoed by Alexander Hamilton, who cited the U.S. Constitution against the Georgia repeal and maintained that "the revocation of the grant by the act of the legislature of Georgia, may justly be considered as contrary to the constitution of the United States, and, therefore null." These views found their way into *Derby v. Blake*, a 1799 decision by the Supreme Judicial Court of Massachusetts which, in the first instance of a state court holding another state's laws unconstitutional, declared the Georgia repeal of 1796 void.

The rigged case of *Fletcher v. Peck* raised each of these issues. Georgia owned the land it legally sold in 1795, and the sale had not been "constitutionally or legally impaired" by the repeal act of 1796. Chief Justice Marshall took up these points in prescribed order.

Marshall quickly disposed of the legal niceties. Georgia possessed title to the Yazoo lands, and nothing in its constitution of 1789 restricted the legislature's power to dispose of them. But since the legislators were "unduly influenced" by shares and promises, was the sale act "a nullity?" He wrote: "That corruption should find its way into the governments of our infant republics, and contaminate the very

source of legislation, or that impure motives should contribute to the passage of a law, or the formation of a legislative contract, are circumstances most deeply to be deplored."

On the other hand, he submitted: "If the title be plainly deduced from a legislative act, which the legislature might constitutionally pass, if the act be clothed with all the requisite forms of a law, a court, sitting as a court of law, cannot sustain a suit brought by one individual against another founded on the allegation that the act is a nullity, in consequence of the impure motives which influenced certain members of the legislature which passed the law."

Marshall, thus, abandoned the ancient common law theory of contract, which held that courts might pry into the circumstances of a bargain. Instead, he articulated the modern "will theory": a deal was a deal, despite the conditions under which it was struck. But he was not through reinterpreting the nature of a contract. Was Peck's title "constitutionally and legally impaired, and rendered null and void," in consequence of the Georgia recission act of 1796? No, for three reasons. First, subsequent purchasers of the Yazoo lands did not participate in the original transaction, however fraudulent. "They were innocent." They "were not stained by that guilt which infected the original transaction." Second, no conceivable legal reasoning could justify the Georgia legislature's pronouncing its own deed invalid. It was "a mere act of power." Courts of equity, not legislative parties, are the proper tribunals; even they cannot set aside "the rights of third persons." Third, "if an act be done under a law, a succeeding legislature cannot undo it. The past cannot be recalled by the most absolute power."

Here Marshall reached the nub of the matter. A law conveying property "is in its nature a contract," and "when absolute rights have vested under that contract, a repeal of the law cannot devest those rights." "[I]f the property of an individual, fairly and honestly acquired, may be seized without compensation," there are no limits to legislative power. But the Georgia legislature is constrained by two bounds. First, it merely prescribes the rules; "the application of those rules to individuals" is "the duty of other departments." Second, Georgia cannot act alone. She is not "a single sovereign power." "She is a part of a large empire; she is a member of the American Union; and that union has a constitution the supremacy of which all acknowledge, and which imposes limits to the legislatures of the several States."

What constitutional limits does the Yazoo repeal transcend? "In considering this very interesting question, we immediately ask ourselves what is a contract? Is a grant a contract?" Marshall defined a contract as "a compact between two or more parties," either "executory" or "executed." Georgia sold the Yazoo lands under an executory contract, which, when the sale was made, became executed. An executed contract is a grant. A grant contains binding obligations and implies a contract. By this somewhat circular reasoning, Marshall, with the aid of the English treatise writer William Blackstone, was able to declare that "a grant is a contract executed." Its obligations continue. The Constitution does not distinguish between executory and executed contracts. Therefore the Georgia recission, "annulling conveyances between individuals" despite their grant/contract, is "repugnant to the Constitution."

One final hurdle remained. Are state grants, that is, state contracts, excluded? Does the Constitution prohibit the impairment only of private, not public contracts? Marshall answered in the negative, "The words themselves contain no such distinction. They are general, and are applicable to contracts of every distinction."

John Marshall thus formulated, in *Fletcher v. Peck*, three fundamental constitutional doctrines: a state grant is a contract, public contracts are no different from private, and a state-attempted repeal of a grant constituted an unconstitutional impairment of contract. *Fletcher v. Peck* both broadened the meaning of contract and, for the first time, invalidated a state law under the Constitution. The case is the federal equivalent of *Marbury v. Madison* (1803), in which Marshall declared a national law unconstitutional. As if that were not enough, Marshall added that the repeal was a bill of attainder, an *ex post facto* law, and contrary to "the general principles of our political institutions." He summed up: "It is, then, the unanimous opinion

of the court, that, in this case, the estate having passed into the hands of a purchaser for a valuable consideration, without notice, the State of Georgia was restrained, either by general principles which are common to our free institutions, or by the particular provisions of the Constitution of the United States, from passing a law whereby the estate of the plaintiff in the premises so purchased could be constitutionally and legally impaired and rendered null and void."

It was a unanimous opinion, but Associate Justice William Johnson appended a concurring statement. Johnson was not quite sure that all Indian title to the Yazoo lands had been quieted—a point passed over by Marshall. He was no advocate of unlimited private property rights, for the state must retain the power of repossession "when necessary for public uses." He stopped short of Marshall's unequivocal defense of "executed" contracts. But he supported the decision on a "general principle" that differentiated between "the right of jurisdiction and the right of soil." The "national sovereignty" could in no way part with the right of jurisdiction, but the rights of soil are unnecessary to political existence and may always be conveyed. And "When the legislature have once conveyed their interest or property in any subject to the individual, they have lost all control over it."

In the short run, *Fletcher v. Peck* greased the wheels for the passage, in 1814, of the long-sought $5 million compensation bill. John Randolph's absence from Congress helped; the opposition, now led by Georgia Representative George M. Troup, could not carry the day. Passage was also aided by the desire of Mississippi for statehood and the need to secure land claims there, as well as a strong political sentiment to placate New England Republicans.

In the long run, *Fletcher v. Peck* elevated the contract clause of the Constitution, and the private property rights it protected, into a strong national mechanism for promoting economic development and restraining state regulation. Marshall's definition of contract reduced the state to the status of a private party and allowed freely contracting agents to set the rules for entrepreneurial activity in a market economy. Courts interpreted contracts strictly, to protect business interests against what Marshall called the "violent acts," and the "sudden and strong passions" of the people. For the rest of the nineteenth century the contract clause was a frequent roadblock to state interference with business and to public regulation of enterprise.

Marshall made quick use of his new contract doctrine. In *New Jersey v. Wilson* (1812) he overturned a state law repealing a tax exemption attached to a land grant. In *Dartmouth College v. Woodward* (1819) he ruled that a colonial charter constituted a contract and was thus immune for state regulation. In *Sturgis v. Crowninshield* (1819) he protected creditors in bankruptcy proceedings, and in *Green v. Biddle* (1823) the Court upheld private land titles in Kentucky. "Contract" assumed a dimension beyond the intent of the framers but conducive to order, speculation, growth, and national power.

Beyond constitutional doctrine, property rights, and economic advancement lay an even higher value enshrined by *Fletcher v. Peck*: individual liberty. The natural law doctrine of vested rights began with the individual. Contractarian ideology reduced each participating agent to a private citizen, the ultimate republican. The free, autonomous individual—free to acquire and use property, to enter into agreements with others, to participate in business and society—represented the highest ideal in early America. *Fletcher v. Peck* swept aside the sordid tangle of Yazoo land claims, interested speculators, and political bargaining, and enshrined that ideal in the United States Constitution.

Selected Bibliography

Margrath, C. Peter. *Yazoo: Law and Politics in the New Republic: The Case of Fletcher v. Peck.* Providence, RI: Brown University Press, 1966.

Wright, Benjamin F., Jr. *The Contract Clause of the Constitution.* Cambridge, MA: Harvard University Press, 1938.

Balancing Private Good and Public Good

Francis N. Stites
Department of History
San Diego State University

Trustees of Dartmouth College v. William H. Woodward, 4 Wheaton 518 (1819) [U.S. Supreme Court]

THE CASE IN BRIEF

Date
1819

Location
New Hampshire

Court
U.S. Supreme Court

Principal Participants
Trustees of Dartmouth College
William H. Woodward
Chief Justice John Marshall

Significance of the Case
Ruling attempted to balance individual rights and public welfare, and it turned the contract clause of the Constitution into an instrument for protection of private property.

In 1819 the Supreme Court met for the first time in its new basement room in the Capitol building. The surroundings, dark and inconvenient, offered no hint that this was the nation's most important tribunal. At eleven o'clock in the morning on February 2, Chief Justice John Marshall and his associates entered, donned their black robes, and took their seats behind the raised bench while the marshal announced the opening of the Court. Then the chief justice, with three associates sitting on each side, began to read the Court's opinion in *Dartmouth College v. Woodward.*

Few decisions have been as important as a precedent. Here the Court was wrestling with some of the early republic's most vexing uncertainties about the implications of the Revolution, the meaning of the Constitution, and the manner of balancing private and public interests. Yet, because we attribute too much to Supreme Court decisions and read them backwards from the present, we know more about the case as precedent than as product of real controversy.

The roots of the case trace to the eighteenth century when one of the Great Awakening's prominent preachers, Eleazar Wheelock, established a pastorate and a school in Lebanon, Connecticut, to teach Indians and English youth dedicated to working as Indian missionaries. Chronic money problems led Wheelock to seek incorporation under a college charter. Colonial colleges were intimate parts of their communities, and their charters generally placed college government in the hands of independent and self-perpetuating board of trustees that included prominent community persons and government officials who would, hopefully, preserve the colleges against factional influence on the legislatures and would protect the donors by giving the trustees the supervisory power to prevent the misuse of funds.

In 1769 the governor of New Hampshire issued a royal charter incorporating the Trustees of Dartmouth College—the namesake was Lord Dartmouth, secretary of state for the colonies and a prominent English donor to Wheelock's school. The charter named Wheelock founder and president and gave him the right to appoint his successor in his will, subject to approval by the trustees. Like most colonial college trustees, those at Dartmouth had the legal right but not the energy to govern, and so they acquiesced in old Wheelock's enlightened if despotic management of the small college on the Connecticut River at Hanover, New Hampshire. They could replace him; they could not displace him.

The republican enthusiasm unleashed by the Revolution helped shape the background to the decision in 1819. Few things were as important to the revolutionary generation as the shaping of future citizens. Americans wanted, paradoxically, freedom, competition, and a uniformly republican government with complementary institutions like colleges. These goals required political leaders to respond to rapidly changing circumstances by balancing government power and individual liberty. Only an educated citizenry could sustain self-government, civic virtue, and the generation of wealth in response to the opportunities the government created. For these reasons Americans prized voluntary associations and lavished attention on problems like the relation of the state to ed-

ucation, how much to spend on education, and what to teach that would secure the blessings of liberty. "The business of education," said Benjamin Rush, "has acquired a new complexion by the independence of our country. The form of government we have assumed has created a new class of duties to every American." With an intimate connection existing between education and the other facets of society, political differences usually reflected policy disagreement over means to consensual ends.

This was the context at Wheelock's death in 1779 when his son, John, assumed the presidency of the college with trustee approval. Although the new president had an imperious manner, his devotion to the college and hard work managing its always precarious finances brought trustee cooperation. Gradually, however, the board began to change as new, less tractable members replaced old ones. Wheelock began both to suspect a conspiracy to deprive him of control and to notice the real power that the board always had but had not exercised. These suspicions provided Wheelock's angle of vision on everything as he finagled for control. By 1810, when the trustees refused to appoint one of his friends to a language professorship, things looked bleak.

In 1811 a quarrel between Wheelock and the local church in Hanover brought an open break at the college. Dartmouth's classics professor and a supine Wheelock friend had been the pastor of the church since 1787. In 1804 the trustees had appointed a new divinity professor—part of whose job was the pastorate at the Hanover church—who necessarily displaced Wheelock's friend. Wheelock insisted that his friend stay in the pastorate; the congregation resisted; and, when Wheelock appealed to the trustees for support, they determined to remain neutral. Wheelock saw this as further evidence of a conspiracy. Repeated efforts at compromise failed, and in 1811 the congregation finally split with Wheelock and his friend and adopted Congregationalism. Wheelock and a small band of followers in Vermont remained Presbyterian. The trustees refused to sanction a church dependent on the college and insisted that their authority as trustees gave them no power over matters of conscience. The long-smoldering feud between president and trustees was now in the open. The board was opposed formally to Wheelock. Over the next several years trustees began eliminating some of his duties and prerogatives. Wheelock was determined to fight, and he petitioned the legislature. He wanted the state to intervene to strengthen his position.

This quarrel, given college-community ties, was essentially a small civil war. Wheelock initiated a pamphlet assault as a prelude to his request for legislative assistance. After arousing public interest with an anonymous eighty-page polemic portraying the trustees as a Federalist-Congregationalist conspiracy dangerous to the public welfare, he joined forces with New Hampshire Republicans. These partisans joined the fray eagerly because they had long been concerned with education. The trouble at Dartmouth was, they said, a matter for public concern because the state liberally had supported the institution and because education ought to be every citizen's concern.

Republicans exploited Wheelock's allegations during the state elections of 1816. When the trustees ultimately fired Wheelock, the Republicans traced the animus to the college's royal charter provision that the trustees be self-perpetuating. The absence of accountability was, they said, more congenial to monarchy than to the spirit of free government. They warned that the future of popular government in New Hampshire demanded state control of Dartmouth. After capturing the legislature and the governorship in 1816, the Republicans converted the college into a state university by changing the corporation's name to Dartmouth University, enlarging the number of its trustees, and adding a board of overseers. Old Wheelock got lost in the enthusiasm.

Stunned, eight of the twelve trustees (known ever after as the Octagon) quickly rallied and resolved not to accept the legislative changes they interpreted as confiscation. Two of the lawyers on the board (there were five lawyers among the eight) drafted a careful pamphlet response to Wheelock's anonymous charges. They argued that a corporate charter was a grant of private property rights, that the state constitution prohibited the legislature from deprivation of property without judicial trial, and, because grants were contracts, that the 1816 legislation violated Article I, Section 10 of the national Constitution, the contract clause.

The 1816 legislation reverberated beyond New Hampshire. Colleges had grown with the nation, and there had been a movement since the 1740s to make them more responsive to public needs by bringing them under government control. The widespread concern generated only a confusion of voices. Everyone apparently wanted colleges to ensure the promise of the Revolution, but uncertainty about the nature, rights, and obligations of the colleges brought only fumbling legislative creations or remakes of colonial colleges. The struggle at Dartmouth was but the latest in this long series. With the legal status of educational corporations still uncertain, the 1816 legislation looked ominous. The 1780 Massachusetts constitution contained a provision reaffirming the traditional legislative power to change government at Harvard, and demands there for change in college government had been continuous since 1800. There were rumors that New Hampshire's success was stimulating Kentucky Republicans to challenge Presbyterian domination of Transylvania College. Those anxious to prevent such changes urged the Dartmouth trustees to "Hold on till the last finger is cut off, and to protest the legality of the measure and if necessary carry that protest to the Supreme Court of the United States." That is what they did!

Wanting the fullest judicial examination as rapidly as possible, the trustees sought tactical advice. Lawyers, including members of the Octagon, urged them to begin their action in the state court. Even so, because the 1816 elections had also placed Republican justices on the New Hampshire superior court, the advisers told the Octagon not to expect final resolution until they had appealed the contract question to the United States Supreme Court. The trustees also engaged the services of Jeremiah Mason and Jeremiah Smith—two of the legal giants of the early nineteenth century—and Daniel Webster, junior counsel and Dartmouth alumnus. In 1817 they sued the former college treasurer who had deserted to the university,

William H. Woodward, for the college records and the college seal.

In the New Hampshire Superior Court, college counsel emphasized the private nature of the corporation, its property, privileges, and rights, and raised an argument based on separation of powers. They used English precedents to show that there were two classes of corporations: civil and eleemosynary. Civil corporations were for purposes of government, trade, or commerce; they might be called public, and the legislature could control them to a certain extent. Eleemosynary or charitable corporations were private and immune from interference. Originating in private gifts, they shared nothing with civil corporations. Hospitals, colleges, and schools had at English common law always been private eleemosynary ones.

Mason turned to the state constitution and asked whether the legislature's power resembled Parliament's before the Revolution. Parliament, he noted, could have abolished the corporation because it was omnipotent, but the king could not do so until he determined it had "become forfeit." For corporations, at least, Mason said, the legislature was the successor to the king. So, there were general limitations on the legislature's power and specific ones (notably Article XV of the New Hampshire bill of rights that provided that no one should be "deprived of his property, immunities, or privileges" without due process of law). One held the right of property, then, under the constitution and not at the will of the legislature. This was not a denial of state power over private corporations, only legislative power. Mason believed it was a settled principle that it was the judiciary's responsibility to protect the rights and enforce the duties of these private eleemosynary corporations. What was true for the state was also true for the national constitutions where Mason found protection in the contract clause.

The 1816 legislation was a "bold experiment" that, unless checked, would set a precedent that would stifle freedom by keeping colleges subservient to state legislatures. Smith said that political men were unfit to manage an "academical institution." He likened the alliance of politics with education to that of state and church and insisted that he preferred in either case for the government to "stand neuter." Who better to enforce such a stance than the judiciary?

New Hampshire's attorney general, George Sullivan, and Ichabod Bartlett, attorneys for the university, tried to show that Dartmouth had always been a civil or public corporation by pointing to its object of serving the public and to the state's contributions since 1769. Because legislatures granted corporate charters only when there was an expectation of public good resulting, they argued that it was a reasonable inference that every charter—even one for a private corporation—contained an implicit agreement that the state might alter the charter for the public good. The college charter, they insisted, was not the sort of contract the framers of the 1787 Constitution had had in mind when they drafted the contract clause.

In November 1817 the New Hampshire court unanimously upheld the legislation. Chief Justice William M. Richardson's able opinion addressed the future of the college and the burning policy question of state control of corporations. Corporations, he said, were of two classes. Private corporations—banks, insurance, and manufacturing companies—were created by individuals for their private benefit. Their property stood on the same legal ground as the property of individuals; their charters were contracts protected by the Constitution. Public corporations were those the state created for public purposes. The legislature had the power to regulate them, Richardson argued, without limitation by the contract clause. Because the education of future generations was a matter of the highest public concern, Dartmouth College was a public corporation and subject to the kinds of alteration the state had undertaken in 1816. That Richardson mentioned business corporations separately from educational ones shows that he was concerned primarily with the relation between education and the state. The Octagon used Section 25 of the 1789 Judiciary Act and appealed to the United States Supreme Court on a writ of error.

The Court at Washington heard three days of argument in the case near the end of the 1818 term. Opening for the college on March 10 and repeating the points of Mason and Smith, Daniel Webster gave one of the most famous performances in the Court's history. For four hours, he asserted the inviolability of private corporate rights under general principles, English common law, and the state constitution. Turning, at last, to the contract clause, he cited the Court's 1810 opinion in *Fletcher v. Peck* to contend that a grant of corporate rights was as much a contract as a grant of land. Like his colleagues in the New Hampshire court, Webster stressed that the Court's ruling would affect "all the literary institutions of the country" and the future of the nation. Everything about him—the flashing eyes, resonant voice, and dramatic gestures—held spellbound the small audience as he paused, then turned to the chief justice and delivered an emotional summation. "Sir, I know not how others may feel, but, for myself, when I see my alma mater surrounded like Caesar in the senate-house, by those who are reiterating stab upon stab, I would not, . . . have her turn to me, and say, . . . And thou too, my son!"

John Holmes, the university counsel, and William Wirt, United States attorney general, could match neither Webster's forensic skill nor his points. Feebly, they rehashed Judge Richardson's argument that the contract clause did not restrain the states in the government of their internal affairs, including public corporations. Joseph Hopkinson, Webster's associate, presented a closing statement for the college with a persuasive argument against state monopolies over education.

Marshall informed counsel that the Court would give the matter all the consideration due an act of a state legislature but warned that an immediate decision was unlikely. Next morning he announced that because the justices were divided the Court would continue the case to 1819.

The continuance gave both sides time to strengthen their causes. The trustees arranged three additional cases in the federal circuit court to bring before the Supreme Court a more complete review of the 1816 legislation. The *Woodward* case had presented only the contract clause question. The larger issue the Octagon wanted to raise through the cognate cases was

whether the "general principles of our governments" restrained the states "from divesting vested rights"—that is, the due process question. To bring cases in circuit court it was necessary that the parties be from different states. So, college counsel and the trustees made arrangements to lease some college lands in New Hampshire to citizens of Vermont and then, in the spring of 1818, to bring three actions in ejectment—an old form of trying land title. In ejectment cases the plaintiff was always a lessee seeking damages resulting from an ouster; recovery involved establishing the lessor's title to the property. This established method of suit regularly involved fictitious lessors and lessees and offered the surest and most convenient way to bring the college questions into circuit court on diversity of state citizenship grounds.

The Octagon hoped the circuit court would act quickly to get these cases before the Supreme Court by the 1819 term. Supreme Court justice Joseph Story, from Massachusetts, had long been hoping to hear these cases because he did not think the *Woodward* case presented all the important contract clause questions. That the cases would come on his circuit aided and encouraged the trustees.

Both the college and the university hurried to gather whatever ammunition they could to persuade the Court at Washington of the correctness of their respective positions on the validity of the New Hampshire legislation. Webster circulated printed copies of his argument. The university retained the redoubtable William Pinkney, flamboyant leader of the federal bar, to reargue the main case during the 1819 term and get some new information before the Court. The university proved inadequately prepared. Cyrus Perkins, a university adviser, approached the 1819 term believing that if the institution could not persuade the Court that Dartmouth was a public institution it would lose the case.

When the Court reconvened in 1819, the chief justice pulled an eighteen-page opinion from his sleeve and shattered the university's hopes. Dartmouth College, he said, was "an eleemosynary, and [as] far as respects its funds, a private corporation." Private corporations could acquire property as could natural persons. The charter was a vested right of the trustees of Dartmouth College, and the corporation was to be governed by them and their successors forever. Its charter as a private eleemosynary corporation was a contract within the meaning of the Constitution; the New Hampshire legislation was unconstitutional. Justices Story and Bushrod Washington filed concurring opinions. William Johnson concurred in Marshall's opinion; Henry Brockholst Livingston concurred in the opinions of Marshall, Story, and Washington. Thomas Todd was absent, and Gabriel Duvall dissented without giving an opinion.

The *Dartmouth College* case climaxed Marshall's expansion of the contract clause into a mighty instrument for the protection of the private property right—understood as the dynamic right to acquire goods. In *Fletcher v. Peck* he had invalidated a Georgia repeal act on both natural law and constitutional grounds. That ambiguity was gone in 1819. Charters of incorporation, he proclaimed unequivocally, were contracts, "the obligation of which cannot be impaired, without violating the Constitution of the United States." The contract clause extended to "contracts respecting property under which some individual could claim a right to something beneficial to himself," and a private corporation was one "endowed with a capacity to take property, for objects unconnected with government, whose funds are bestowed by individuals on the faith of the charter." No stronger judicial defense of property was put forth in the early nineteenth century. Chancellor James Kent, the eminent New York jurist, called the decision the most important step in securing rights derived from a government grant. He believed it made inviolable the "literary, charitable, religious and commercial institutions of our country."

Marshall had immunized private education against state legislative tinkering. Although he believed education a fit subject for government attention, he could not accept Richardson's view that education should be "altogether in the hands of government" because experience had educated him that American education had suffered from the fluctuating policy and repeated interferences of state legislatures. "Does every teacher of youth become a public

officer, and do donations for the purpose of education necessarily become public property?" Marshall thought "the interest which this case has excited" proved that these questions were of "serious moment to society." For him, sound policy to preclude sectarian battles for legislative power required that "private" institutions, especially denominational colleges, have "security and permanence" through federal constitutional protection.

There was a sizeable body of judicial experience with colleges by 1819 that supported Marshall's conclusion. The chief justice had been a lawyer for Virginia in *Bracken v. Visitors of William and Mary College* in 1790 and 1797, and Harvard had made Story a member of its board of overseers in 1818. Justice Livingston's experience with problems between college and state was the most extensive. He had been working for decades to keep Columbia out of the hands of the New York legislature. In 1810 this contest had prompted Chancellor Kent's comment in an opinion for the New York Council of Revision that it was "a sound principle in free governments that charters of incorporation, whether for private or local, or charitable, or literary or religious purposes, were not to be affected without due process of law, or without the consent of the parties concerned." In 1795, during a contest at Yale, Zepheniah Swift, Connecticut's future chief justice, first articulated the distinction between private and public corporations that proved decisive in the *Dartmouth* case. The North Carolina legislature had funded a state university in 1789 and granted it property. In 1800 the legislature repealed the grants, and in 1805 the North Carolina court declared the repeal unconstitutional, in part because it violated the due process clause of the state constitution.

Marshall's 1819 opinion revealed not only his familiarity with the history of English common law governing private colleges' relation to the state but also revealed a talent that had contributed to his success as an appellate lawyer in Virginia, namely the ability to sort through precedents and pick from them the points necessary to win. He did not parade this knowledge in citations to English and state precedents because this was a constitutional opinion, and he was aware of their shortcomings and limited applicability under the Constitution. He relied on the general principles of the common law but preferred to ground these constitutional opinions solely on the Constitution. As he said in *McCulloch v. Maryland*, the other great case of 1819: "We must never forget it is *a constitution* we are expounding."

The Court had clarified the meaning of the phrase "business of education" that percolated through the early republic. Colleges, some called them "nurseries of power and influence," were to be as important as business to American development. Although business and commercial corporations were not Marshall's principal focus, his sweeping statement covered the growing number of business corporations even if he simply assumed that the contract clause covered them. Personal and professional connections with the development of business corporations in Virginia had made Marshall a keen observer of their nominal and actual relation to the state. "Banks, canal companies, and numerous associations of similar description, are formed on the principle of voluntary subscription," he had said in his 1796 argument in *Ware v. Hylton*. "The nation is desirous that such institutions should exist." Ultimately, the *Dartmouth College* rule became one of the principal weights in the balancing of government and the economy in the nineteenth century.

In 1819, however, Marshall considered corporations important only as a species of private property. He noted early in the opinion that the parties in this case differed less on general principles than on the application of them to this case. Even Richardson for the New Hampshire court had admitted that *Fletcher v. Peck* left little room to doubt that some corporate charters were protected constitutional contracts. But Marshall rejected Richardson's standard that a public interest in the objects, that is, the uses, of private property was sufficient to justify state regulation. Such a standard, he believed, would generate blanket state meddling with private rights. Only by protecting the property, either of individuals or groups of individuals, could the government encourage the productive labor necessary to open the continent and develop the national economy. Such a change as the New Hampshire

legislature had made, he said, "may be for the advantage of this college in particular, and may be for the advantage of literature in general; but it is not according to the will of the donors, and is subversive of the contract on the faith of which their property was given."

The question of what individual rights were involved in this case caused Marshall "real difficulty." That was because what he had to demonstrate was that the contract clause protected the charters of privately founded charitable institutions. His answer was another impressive example of his pragmatic, undoctrinaire approach to the Constitution's fundamental principles. Although "an artificial being, invisible, intangible, and existing only in contemplation of law," the corporation was the instrument for perpetuating the design of the original donors. It stood in their place. Corporate rights, then, were equivalent to private individual rights. As in *Fletcher*, the chief justice conceded that the framers did not have such contracts as these in mind when in 1787 they had drafted the Constitution's contract clause. But, he asserted, the framers were also not so imprudent as to attempt to provide specific rules for problems they could not have foreseen. A constitution had to be flexible and adaptable to circumstances. The language of the Constitution did not exclude this particular interpretation, and the "case being within the words of the rule, must be within its operation likewise."

Story attempted to bring business corporations within the embrace of the decision. His lengthy concurring opinion noted, among other things, that the contract clause should protect all state grants of funds to hospitals and colleges, whether the grants were for "special or general purposes, for public charity or particular beneficence." He then said that the clause reached all contracts concerning immunities, dignities, offices or franchises, or other rights deemed valuable in law, including contracts for the exercise of mere authority. "Each trustee has a vested right, and a legal interest, in his office, and it cannot be divested but by due process of law." And he would have found such rights protected both by the general principles of free government and the specific contract clause of the Constitution. Clearly, he wanted to broaden that clause into a general due process clause to protect both public and private institutions.

This broad application prompted Bushrod Washington to write a separate opinion limiting the ruling to corporations similar to Dartmouth College. Washington, like Marshall, was primarily concerned with the immediate issue of education and what it suggested about the balancing of private and public good.

There remained the cognate cases. Discussions between lawyers for both sides and the Court produced an agreement that the Supreme Court should remand the cases to the circuit for more discussion on the facts. There was more maneuvering, but Story's concurring opinion in *Woodward* covered all the points the cognate cases would have raised and so accomplished what college planners had been hoping for all along. When the cases were at length heard at Boston in May 1819, Story delivered another learned opinion covering all the questions again and ruling for the college. Counsel for both sides agreed to let this opinion stand unless the university could produce some decisive new information by June 10. On May 27 the university presented the new facts, but Story did not find them persuasive, and the Court gave its final judgment in the college controversy on June 10 as both parties had agreed.

Isaac Hill, editor of the New Hampshire *Patriot* and a determined Wheelock partisan and ferocious Republican, commented when he learned that the new information would not alter the Court's judgment: "Thus ends the third act of the drama." The first had been the Octagon's firing of Wheelock; the second had been the action by New Hampshire's legislature and court (the "people"). In the third act, Hill said, a "foreign power," the federal courts, had supported the few, the trustees, as opposed to the people. "The fourth act," he concluded, "is yet to come—*the drama is not* ended." But it was. The college had already dispossessed the university. This, plus a burdensome debt and the improbability of state assistance, prompted it to acquiesce. Thus ended not only its existence but the "drama" of the college controversy.

The *Dartmouth College* decision, however, did not end argument about the relation between corporations and the state, between private rights and public needs. Educational corporations appear to have benefitted. Private denomination colleges proliferated throughout the mid–nineteenth century using the decision as their legal base, and the Court's separation of school and state had guaranteed the academic freedom of trustees, faculty, and students. Business corporations prospered, and, by the late nineteenth century, burgeoning corporate power had become the central political-economic issue. Then commentators began reading backwards to the 1819 case to discover there, rather than in subsequent judicial balancings and circumstances, the source of corporate invincibility. This, however, yanked the case out of context and substituted notoriety for significance.

The Court in 1819 had only balanced these competing interests. Only state legislatures could grant corporate charters, and at the moment of the grant the states were free to set whatever limits they deemed appropriate. Marshall's prohibition on subsequent alteration without consent was an admonition to the states to exercise more caution in their grants. Moreover, he suggested the idea later known as the state police power when he said that the framers of the Constitution did not intend to restrain the states in the regulation of civil institutions adopted for internal government. Story observed that a state could amend corporate charters by reserving the authority to do so in the original grant. Reservation clauses had already become common in college charters by the 1790s and by the late 1820s were common in business corporation charters. Improvident legislative grants, more than the *Dartmouth College* rule that corporate charters were contracts protected by the Constitution, robbed states of regulatory power. As in *Fletcher v. Peck*, Marshall insisted that the wisdom of legislative action was beyond the Court's purview. In a 1934 opinion, reminiscent of Marshall and Story in 1819, Chief Justice Charles Evans Hughes noted that the history of the Court's contract decisions showed a "growing appreciation of public needs and of the necessity of finding ground for rational compromise between individual rights and public welfare."

Selected Bibliography

Baxter, Maurice G. *Daniel Webster and the Supreme Court*. Amherst: University of Massachusetts Press, 1966.

Beveridge, Albert J. *The Life of John Marshall*. 4 vols. New York: Houghton Mifflin Company, 1916–1919.

Campbell, Richard A. "*Dartmouth College* as a Civil Liberties Case: The Formation of Constitutional Policy." *Kentucky Law Review* 70 (1981–1982): 643–706.

Herbst, Jurgen. *From Crisis to Crisis: American College Government, 1636–1819*. Cambridge, MA: Harvard University Press, 1982.

Newmyer, R. Kent. *Supreme Court Justice Joseph Story: Statesman of the Old Republic*. Chapel Hill: The University of North Carolina Press, 1985.

Richardson, Leon Burr. *History of Dartmouth College*. 2 vols. Hanover, NH: Dartmouth College Publications, 1932.

Shirley, John M. *The Dartmouth College Causes and the Supreme Court of the United States*. St. Louis: G. I. Jones and Company, 1879.

Stites, Francis N. *Private Interest and Public Gain: The Dartmouth College Case, 1819*. Amherst: University of Massachusetts Press, 1972.

White, G. Edward. *The Marshall Court and Cultural Change, 1815–1835*. New York: Macmillan, 1988.

Justice Story, Bankruptcy, and the Supreme Court

—◄◦►—

Craig T. Friend

Department of History
University of Central Florida, Orlando

Sturges v. Crowninshield, 4 Wheaton 122 (1819) [U.S. Supreme Court]

◄◦► THE CASE IN BRIEF ◄◦►

Date
1819

Location
New York

Court
U.S. Supreme Court

Principal Participants
Josiah Sturges
Richard Crowninshield
Associate Justice Joseph Story

Significance of the Case
Ruling gave states a method to deal with bankruptcy and invalidated retroactivity of portions of New York state's bankruptcy law.

Occasionally, Supreme Court justices abstain from ruling on cases in which they have personal interest. During the Marshall years, such a precedent had not been established, however, and justices participated fully, even when they had much to gain (or lose) from the result. Such a decision to participate was made by Justice Joseph Story when *Sturges v. Crowninshield* came before the Supreme Court in 1819.

In 1811, the state of New York passed a bankruptcy law that freed debtors from obligation upon relinquishing property and listing creditors. Richard Crowninshield used the law to escape his business debts, but Josiah Sturges, who had loaned Crowninshield over £1,000 less than a week before the law's passage, refused to accept the minimal compensation. In October 1817, he filed an action of assumpsit in the federal circuit courts.

Sturges had sufficient reason to believe he could regain his money. In 1814, Justice Bushrod

Washington had decided on his circuit that bankruptcy laws could not be retroactive. Earlier in 1817, Justice Brockholst Livingston confused the issue. On circuit court in New York, he dissented from Washington's opinion and, in a separate case, ruled that such laws could be retroactive. During the October term of the Massachusetts circuit court when Sturges's case was to be heard, Justice Joseph Story was on the bench.

Story's interest in economics was well known. His political reputation had been built on his understanding of economic issues. In 1802, President Jefferson had offered Story a position as commissioner of bankruptcy in Massachusetts. The national Bankruptcy Act of 1801 was repealed before Story could accept the offer, however, and the position was eliminated. Even though President Madison nominated him to the court in 1811, Story remained interested in the national economy.

Even though Sturges may have hoped for Story to rule against the state law, he also had reason to worry. Story had close political ties with the Crowninshield family. In 1808, the Crowninshields had assisted him in gaining one of Massachusetts's seats in the House of Representatives and as a result, Story had chosen alliance with the Crowninshield family over several old friendships. His dedication to the Crowninshields appeared unquestionable.

On circuit court in 1817, Story realized the implications of Sturges's suit, especially if it were decided by the U.S. Supreme Court. Story was convinced that bankruptcy legislation was a power reserved to the federal government, and a favorable decision by the Marshall Supreme Court would establish that power. Story had begun work on a national bankruptcy bill and wanted the path to be cleared for its passage.

Story and the district judge disagreed on the decision, largely due to Story's manipulation to have the case decided by the Supreme Court. Crediting the case to the Marshall Court enabled Story to avoid an official decision on the circuit; the circuit court's decision would be made after the justices collective opinion was heard. Thus, in 1818, when *Sturges v. Crowninshield* came to the Supreme Court, Sturges was certain that Justice Washington would decide for him, Justice Livingston would decide against him, and Justice Story could be the deciding factor.

By February 1819, Chief Justice John Marshall had brought the justices together and had written a unanimous opinion. Marshall united his court through a two-fold examination of the case. The first issue was the Constitution's grant for Congress "to establish . . . uniform laws on the subject of bankruptcies throughout the United States" (Article I, Section 8). Justices Washington and Story argued that only the federal government could legislate on bankruptcy. Justices Livingston, William Johnson, and Gabriel Duvall, however, debated that states could pass bankruptcy laws if the federal government had not done so. Marshall persuaded Story and Washington that the latter interpretation still recognized federal authority.

Overcoming division on the first issue, Marshall turned to the second issue of *Sturges v. Crowninshield*. The constitutionality of New York's law was resolved, but its retroactive nature was not. Marshall, applying the contract clause that he had firmly established in *Fletcher v. Peck* (1810), reasoned that the retroactive law impaired Crowninshield's obligation to Sturges and was, therefore, unconstitutional.

The decision in *Sturges v. Crowninshield* satisfied Story. Even though his national bankruptcy bill was not accepted, the justice remained involved in economic legislation, helping Daniel Webster draft the Bankruptcy Act of 1841. The decision also provided the states with a method to deal with bankruptcy following the Panic of 1819. Yet, the laws that were passed did not provide for retroactive insolvency.

Marshall, however, had not been clear in his written opinion. Many individuals inferred from Marshall's words that states were prohibited from passing bankruptcy laws. His eagerness to resolve the division within the Court had left his resolution of the first issue ambiguous. Others interpreted the decision as allowing bankruptcy laws that could impair subsequent contracts. Eight years later, Marshall would have the opportunity to clarify his words in *Ogden v. Saunders* (1827).

Selected Bibliography

Newmyer, R. Kent. *Supreme Court Justice Joseph Story: Statesman of the Old Republic.* Chapel Hill: University of North Carolina Press, 1985.

Newmyer, R. Kent. *The Supreme Court under Marshall and Taney.* Arlington Heights, IL: Harlan Davidson, Inc., 1968.

White, G. Edward. *The Marshall Court and Cultural Change, 1815–35.* New York: Macmillan Publishing Co., 1988.

Abridging Vested Interests:
The Battle of the Massachusetts Bridges

——◄◦►——

Elizabeth B. Monroe
Department of History
Indiana University-
Purdue University at Indianapolis

The Proprietors of the Charles River Bridge v. the Proprietors of the Warren Bridge,
11 Peters 420 (1837) [U.S. Supreme Court]

◄◦► THE CASE IN BRIEF ◄◦►

Date
1837

Location
Massachusetts

Court
U.S. Supreme Court

Principal Participants
Proprietors of the Charles River Bridge
Proprietors of the Warren Bridge
Massachusetts legislature

Significance of the Case
The case dealt with the issue of the community's overall good versus private vested interests, especially the role the state should play in encouraging private initiative for public benefit.

This "Tale of Two Bridges" shows how increasing demands on legislatures to grant charters to banking, transport, and manufacturing endeavors raised the issue of whether the public interest was better served by fostering new opportunities in the marketplace or by securing existing ones. The two bridges and their corporations represented technologically identical improvements, over the same line of travel, designed to benefit the community by providing ready access between Boston and Charlestown and, of course, to secure a financial return on private investment. The proprietors of the bridges clashed over whether priority was to be given to community rather than private vested interests.

In the early nineteenth century public demands for transportation facilities forced national and state legislatures to consider government support for roads, bridges, canals, and river improvements. Legislative decisions hinged on whether government could intervene, and, if so, to what extent. Congress limited fed-

eral intervention to construction of a few projects of national scope, such as the Cumberland
Road and improvements of the Ohio and Mississippi rivers. Most government provision for
transportation development in the first half of
the nineteenth century took place at the state
and local levels. Support took two forms: direct aid, by which government built the improvement and maintained it; and indirect aid,
by which government provided positive legal
and economic mechanisms (such as corporation
charters and public subsidies) for entrepreneurs
who built and maintained improvements for the
benefit of the community.

By the mid-1820s the phenomenal success of
the state-built Erie Canal and the increasing
prosperity of New York City forced competing
Atlantic seaports and the states of which they
were a part to challenge New York's superior
transportation facilities. Boston merchants and
investors compelled the Massachusetts legislature to consider the improvement of local
transportation in the immediate Boston area
and the development of a major line of travel
from Boston to the eastern terminus of the Erie
Canal at Albany, New York. How the Massachusetts legislature acted on these proposals
raised important legal questions about the ability of the state to promote public benefit by
means of grants to corporations.

With regard to the demand for better transportation facilities between the increasingly
interdependent suburbs and the Boston penin-
sula, the legislature considered chartering a
second company to build a bridge connecting Charlestown and Boston. Proponents of
the new bridge charged that the proprietors of
the existing Charles River Bridge had grown
wealthy at the expense of the public. Tolls collected over its forty-year history far exceeded
construction costs and maintenance. Promoters of the new bridge couched their scheme
in terms of the development of Boston's suburbs and offered to donate their bridge to
the state after they had recovered their initial
investment.

After weighing the investors' risks to provide this public service against the extent of
their rewards, the Massachusetts legislature
chartered the Proprietors of the Warren Bridge.

But the indirect costs of this action met with
marked resistance outside the legislature. The
Proprietors of the Charles River Bridge believed that the corporate charter for a new
Warren Bridge would infringe directly on their
earlier corporate grant by creating a competing bridge along the same line of travel and
in-directly by destroying their property in tolls.
Investors in other corporate improvements
shared the Charles River Bridge proprietors'
concerns. Claims of infringement of one bridge
charter by another immediately led to litigation
and threatened the favorable legal and economic climate that the legislature had created
to lure scarce capital to needed projects.

The Charles River Bridge suit underscored
the inadequacies of surviving colonial solutions when applied to public transportation
problems. Yet the successors of the almost two
hundred-year-old franchise looked to the state
to maintain their exclusive commitment until
its expiration in 1855. The initial grant to provide public transport at the site of the Charles
River Bridge dated from 1640 when the colonial legislature had authorized the newly established Harvard College to operate a ferry
between Boston and Charlestown. For the remainder of the seventeenth century the college
had provided public transportation between
these two villages on the banks of the Charles
River. In 1701 the college began to lease its
ferry rights to concessionaires. By the end of
the revolutionary era, the college found it
necessary to complete extensive repairs to its
boats and ways in anticipation of increased
postwar traffic and resulting rent increases.
But complaints about ferry service continually
reached the legislature. Responding to pleas for
better service from communities north of the
river and to proposals to build toll bridges,
the Massachusetts legislature in March 1785
granted a charter to Charlestown and Boston
bridge promoters.

The Proprietors of the Charles River Bridge
were incorporated to build a bridge in place of
the ferry, to collect tolls for its use, and to indemnify the college for its lost revenue at the rate of
£200 per year. At the end of forty years the bridge
was to revert to the state. By 1792 the success of
the Charles River Bridge had encouraged other

promoters to request charters for similar projects and led the Proprietors of the Charles River Bridge to protest that the proposed bridges would capture some of the Boston-Charlestown traffic and, therefore, reduce their expected revenues. As a result of this protest, the new charter for the West Boston Bridge (connecting Boston to Cambridge) compensated the proprietors of the earlier bridge by extending their charter an additional thirty years.

In the first two decades of the new century the Massachusetts legislature chartered four more bridge companies in the Boston area without providing additional concessions to the Charles River Bridge proprietors. General prosperity and rapid population growth greatly increased the use and therefore the revenue of Boston's oldest bridge. By the 1820s its proprietors could claim a steady income of $20,000 per year on property valued at $280,000. The value of stock had risen over three hundred percent since the original charter was granted. But such success led inevitably to direct challenge; beginning in 1823 Charlestown merchants proposed a new free bridge between Charlestown and Boston that would provide additional access between the two points and break the Charles River Bridge monopoly. The legislative contest between the sponsors of the competing bridges lasted for the next five years.

Legislative issues included the necessity of a competing bridge, the legislature's ability to authorize one, and its potential effect on future investments in the state. The promoters of the new Warren Bridge claimed that public necessity and convenience could not be accommodated by the old bridge and its approaches. The Charles River Bridge proprietors countered that the proposed charter included a clause to the effect that if the Charles River Bridge was surrendered to the state, a new bridge would not be built. Such a surrender clause, they pointed out, demonstrated the specious character of arguments based on increased traffic.

The second issue related to the state's ability to charter a new bridge that would directly compete with the older one. The Warren Bridge developers avowed that the legislature had an "equitable right" to intervene in the public interest to eliminate the burdensome tolls of the

Charles River Bridge and remedy a "public injustice." The Charles River Bridge proprietors felt otherwise, and they cited specific constitutional provisions to back their viewpoint.

Invoking the Massachusetts Bill of Rights, the proprietors pointed to the clause that guaranteed enjoyment of "life, liberty and property." Authorization of the Warren Bridge meant effective destruction of the Charles River Bridge toll receipts, since traffic would divert to the free bridge. According to the proprietors, destroying their property in tolls by the indirect means of chartering a free bridge company violated the Massachusetts constitutional guarantee just as surely as physically destroying the bridge. Even if public interest required the expropriation of the Charles River Bridge, its proprietors believed the state had to comply with the Massachusetts Constitution by offering reasonable compensation. Further, the contract clause of the U.S. Constitution prevented state impairment of contracts, and a legislative charter was recognized as a form of contract. The proposed Warren Bridge, by competing with the Charles River Bridge's monopoly along a line of travel, would violate the U.S. Constitution as well as the state's constitution.

The bridge controversy also underscored the policy clash between those who wanted to provide immediate public benefits and stimulate growth with new corporate grants and those who wanted to protect already ventured capital and maintain a predictable investment environment by denying new competing grants. Differences between the two groups involved attitudes toward the state's role in encouraging private initiative for public benefit, as well as the relative importance of the rights of the community and private property rights.

"An Act To Establish the Warren Bridge Corporation" passed the Massachusetts legislature and was signed by the governor in March 1828. It authorized the new proprietors to build a bridge between Boston and Charlestown and to collect tolls for its use until they had been reimbursed for the cost of construction plus 5 percent interest, so long as the term of toll collection did not exceed six years. The Warren Bridge would then revert to the state and become free. Until reversion the Warren Bridge proprietors were required to pay one-half of the Charles River Bridge's annuity to Harvard College.

The Proprietors of the Warren Bridge immediately began purchase of the site, and in June the Proprietors of the Charles River Bridge filed for an injunction to halt construction of the new bridge. The preliminary request was denied, construction continued, and the Warren Bridge opened to public traffic on Christmas Day. Both bridge companies filed supplemental bills and spent much of following year taking depositions, gathering evidence, and preparing arguments. In October 1829 the Supreme Judicial Court of Massachusetts heard arguments on the merits of the case.

The arguments of counsel for each bridge interest raised similar points to those raised during the prolonged legislative controversy, although the major conflict before the court centered on the terms of the 1785 charter to the Proprietors of the Charles River Bridge. The Charles River Bridge lawyers argued that Harvard College's exclusive ferry privileges over the line of travel had been transferred implicitly to the bridge company, and therefore the Warren Bridge grant impaired the contract between the Massachusetts legislature and their clients. Such an impairment violated both the Massachusetts Constitution and the U.S. Constitution. The Warren Bridge lawyers contended that there had been no explicit grant to the Charles River Bridge and, therefore, the legislature had acted within its rights in authorizing the new bridge.

Both sides placed their arguments within the context of public policy. According to the Charles River Bridge attorneys, an adverse decision would halt public improvements because private capital would be unable to trust the government to honor its contracts. The Warren Bridge counsel argued that public interest demanded an end to monopoly grants that retarded the legislature's ability to meet public needs for improved transportation. A decision adverse to their clients would inhibit the "free course of legislation" and free competition in the marketplace.

In January 1830 the Supreme Judicial Court of Massachusetts dismissed the complaint so

that the Charles River Bridge proprietors could appeal to the U.S. Supreme Court (the Supreme Court could hear appeals only if the state courts sustained state laws challenged as violating the U.S. Constitution). In their opinions, the four Massachusetts justices split evenly over the validity of the 1828 legislative grant to the Warren Bridge. Justices Marcus Morton and Samuel Wilde rejected the claims of the Charles River Bridge proprietors; Justice Samuel Putnam and Chief Justice Isaac Parker upheld them. Justice Morton's opinion emphasized the community's needs for material improvements and accepted the defendant's argument that the 1785 charter to the Charles River Bridge proprietors had not been exclusive. While the new bridge admittedly diverted tolls from the old one, the damages to the old bridge were merely consequential. In Morton's opinion public grants were to be strictly construed. Broad construction and recognition of implied rights and privileges would impede business and community interests; better transportation would be blocked because all such improvements potentially diminished earlier grants. Justice Wilde agreed with Morton.

On the other hand, Justice Putnam's decision found for the complainants by resorting to the "spirit" and "substance" of their charter. According to Putnam, the spirit of the legislature's contract with the Charles River Bridge proprietors was the grant of exclusive privileges and its substance the right to collect tolls. The subsequent charter of the Warren Bridge effectively had destroyed the Charles River Bridge's property in tolls, thereby impairing the earlier contract. The latter grant was therefore unconstitutional. Chief Justice Parker agreed with Morton that the college's exclusive right to the line of travel had not been transferred to the Charles River Bridge proprietors, and, like Morton, he indicated his concerns about technological progress. But he found for the Charles River Bridge proprietors because the state had destroyed their property by enfranchising another bridge in the immediate area. Therefore the first proprietors were entitled to compensation from the state. Since the 1828 law creating the Warren Bridge did not provide such an indemnity, it was unconstitutional. Immediately following the Massachusetts decision the Proprietors of the Charles River Bridge applied to the U.S. Supreme Court for a Writ of Error, and the case was placed on the Court's calendar.

The Supreme Court in January 1831 was composed of seven justices, a majority of whom had served together for twenty years and had acted in concert on many of the important constitutional controversies of the period. Chief Justice John Marshall, the dominant figure of the Court, exerted enormous influence over his colleagues. In his thirty-year tenure Marshall had written almost half of the Court's decisions and had rarely dissented from a majority opinion. In 1831 new appointments to the bench were only beginning to affect the consolidated views of the Marshall era court. Six of the justices heard the arguments of the *Charles River Bridge Case*, and five days later announced their inability to reach a decision.

Failure to reach a decision depended as much on shifting views of public contracts and public policy as on personnel. While the earlier decisions of the Marshall Court had invariably interpreted the contract clause to give primacy to property interests, in the last decade of the Marshall era decisions broadened the scope of state powers at the expense of consistent protection of property rights. In two cases decided the year before the Charles River Bridge arguments were heard, the Marshall court restricted corporate charter rights to those powers specifically conferred, and protected government taxation power from implied immunities in corporate charters.

The Court had become increasingly aware that corporations initially designed to serve the public interest could threaten the state's subsequent ability to supply community needs. Yet, in many instances, protection of vested property interests remained the most efficient means to secure public goals. The justices' divergent views on these issues, together with illnesses and vacancies on the bench, led to delay in resolving the Charles River Bridge dispute. Finally, in 1837 the case was reargued before a transformed Court.

Arguments commenced January 19 and continued for six days. Daniel Webster and Warren Dutton, both of whom had appeared in 1831,

again represented the Proprietors of the Charles River Bridge. The Proprietors of the Warren Bridge had new counsel, John Davis and Simon Greenleaf. All four attorneys were prominent members of the Massachusetts bar: Davis and Webster were U.S. senators, and Greenleaf was Royall Professor of Law at Harvard. Public comment acknowledged the learning and skill of their arguments, while, according to Justice Joseph Story, "it was a glorious exhibition for old Massachusetts."

Webster and Dutton reiterated their presentations to the state court and to the Supreme Court of six years before: The Charles River Bridge had succeeded to the ferry rights held by Harvard College; the ferry had exclusive rights to the line of travel; the bridge assumed the same rights; and the subsequent grant to the Warren Bridge violated the state's contract obligation when the free bridge destroyed the proprietors' property in tolls that was the essence of their original grant.

Resorting to familiar vested rights and contract clause arguments, the Charles River Bridge counsel insisted that in order to protect property interests from capricious actions of legislatures, public charters should be liberally construed. According to Dutton and Webster, the interests of the public demanded security of title and full enjoyment of property rights, for "[n]othing is reasonable but the fulfillment of the contract."

Davis and Greenleaf refuted their adversaries by a different line of reasoning: The ferry had always been subject to the state; the ferry rights had never passed to the bridge, but had been resumed by the state after compensating the college; and neither ferry nor bridge had exclusive rights to the line of travel. When the Charles River Bridge proprietors accepted the extension of their charter in 1792, they acknowledged the state's authority to make competing grants. Therefore, the subsequent grant to the Warren Bridge was within the legislature's authority.

The Warren Bridge attorneys argued that liberal construction of the Charles River Bridge charter would impede government provision for the needs of the community, particularly in the area of transportation. In the case before the Court, the legislature, as the representative of the people, had assessed their needs and granted the Warren Bridge charter. According to Davis and Greenleaf the public interest had been served by curtailing private rights that threatened future economic growth.

The Court that heard arguments in 1837 had been transformed during the intervening six years by the deaths of the chief justice and one associate justice and the resignation of another associate justice. These vacancies on the bench had provided President Andrew Jackson with the opportunity to make the Court more "democratick." Diverging judicial views on protection of vested property rights, which had been discernible at the first Charles River Bridge hearing, became more marked with the new appointments. In 1837 three justices heard the case for the first time; given the deadlock after the previous hearing, the new justices' opinions would be decisive.

The justices' attitudes toward the state's role in the economy reflected the fundamental partisan differences of the period. Jacksonian Democrats encouraged new entrepreneurs' attacks on older capital privilege. Since the legislative and executive branches responded most readily to public demands, they should determine the role of government in the economy. Jackson's opponents, soon to coalesce as the Whigs, believed that private capital could only be coaxed into public action when vested rights were protected from the potentially capricious legislature and the potentially despotic executive. Consistent interpretation of charters based on precedent and determined by the courts should determine the role of the government in the economy.

The arguments of counsel in the *Charles River Bridge Case* also reflected partisan positions. Legislative battles over both the bridge controversy and the proposal to build the east-west railroad had served as catalysts for the resurgence of political parties in Massachusetts in the 1820s. At that time, the promoters of the Warren Bridge had resorted to popular rhetoric, insisting that the Charles River Bridge "monopolists" had received "exorbitant compensation" from "heavy tolls." They consistently portrayed the struggle over whether to charter the Warren Bridge as one between the workers and trades-

men of Charlestown and the rich proprietors of the Charles River Bridge. While counsel for the opposing interests for the most part eschewed the political rhetoric and bombast of the legislative debates, their arguments had appealed to the political attitudes of the time.

Less than three weeks after hearing the arguments, the Court announced its decision. Chief Justice Roger B. Taney and three other Jackson appointees to the bench confirmed the decision of the Massachusetts Supreme Judicial Court and upheld the Warren Bridge charter. The other Jackson appointee voted for dismissal for lack of jurisdiction, while the two pre-Jackson members of the Court dissented from the majority opinion.

Taney's majority opinion and Justice Joseph Story's dissent presented contrasting views of legal principles, government responsibility, and economic progress. The two justices disagreed on matters of judicial interpretation of charters and contracts, the powers of the states, and the relative importance of the rights of the community and the rights of the individual. Their opinions placed the local dispute between two bridge companies in the broader arena of the power and purpose of government.

The new chief justice agreed with the Warren Bridge attorneys that the ferry's franchise had ended with the legislature's charter for the Charles River Bridge. Comparing the legislature's action to a royal grant, Taney found authority for construction in the grantor's favor. The legislature, representing the sovereign power of the people, had granted the privilege to build a bridge and collect tolls to the Charles River Bridge proprietors. Taney reasoned that, like royal bounties, the grant of legislative largess should be construed narrowly to protect the benefactor. In the present case such narrow construction in the public interest disposed of any implied exclusive rights to the line of travel. Therefore, the legislature's later authorization of a competing grant did not amount to destruction of the proprietors' property in tolls. Since the state had not taken private property, compensation by eminent domain proceedings was not required.

The Charles River Bridge proprietors had presumed too generous a legislative grant. While the chief justice declared that the "rights of private property must be sacredly guarded," nonetheless in his eyes the rights of the community were paramount. According to Taney "the object and end of all government is to promote the happiness and prosperity of the community by which it is established; and it can never be assumed, that the government intended to diminish its power of accomplishing the end for which it was created." In order for private property in the form of legislatively granted privilege to be protected, it would have to be conferred explicitly.

Justice Story's dissent followed a different line of reasoning. Instead of viewing the Charles River Bridge charter as analogous to a royal grant, Story insisted that it was a form of contract for valuable consideration. The proprietors had offered to build the bridge at their own expense to further the public good. In return they had received from the legislature the right to collect tolls. Where valuable consideration was received, public contracts were construed in favor of the grantee. Story's broad construction of the bridge charter inferred an exclusive grant to collect tolls along the line of travel. The subsequent legislative charter to the Warren Bridge, by indirectly destroying property in tolls, impaired the earlier contract.

According to Story it was "to the dishonour of the government that it should pocket a fair consideration, and then quibble as to the obscurities and implications of its own contract." Taney was mistaken, Story maintained, in defining the Charles River Bridge charter as a bounty and in justifying the legislature's action as in the public interest. "If the government means to invite its citizens to enlarge the public comforts and conveniences, . . . there must be some pledge that the property will be safe; . . . and that success will not be the signal of a general combination to overthrow its rights, and to take away its profits." Justice demanded that the legislature abide by the consequences of the earlier agreement.

Both Taney and Story favored public policies that encouraged investment and fostered economic progress. Both recognized that if states chose not to build transportation facilities at their own expense, then private capital must be tempted to supply community needs. Taney emphasized broadened entrepreneurial opportunity; Story relied on security of title and the full enjoyment of its benefits.

Their opinions in *Charles River Bridge* also point out their differing attitudes toward the roles of the state and national governments in the American federal system. Taney's opinion shied away from federal involvement in what he saw as a state matter. His reliance on strict construction endorsed the charter to the Warren Bridge proprietors and, therefore, the Massachusetts legislature's determination of the public interest. For Taney, strict construction served the two-fold purpose of limiting judicial interpretation and avoiding federal encroachment on state powers. On the other hand, Story, as an avid supporter of the constitutional nationalism of the Marshall era, used the more conservative doctrine of contract to maintain both judicial interpretation of state contracts and a superior role for the federal government.

Two other important Supreme Court decisions in 1837 complemented the *Charles River Bridge* case. Story dissented in these as well. In *New York v. Miln*, the Court qualified Marshall's broad hints at an exclusive national power over commerce by acknowledging that a state law affecting incoming passengers was not a regulation of commerce but an exercise of state police power. And in *Briscoe v. Bank of Kentucky*, the new Court tempered Marshall's denial of state power to emit bills of credit by accepting that currency issued by a corporation of the state did not violate the Constitution. Taken together, the three decisions broadened areas of state action and narrowed the nationalism of the Marshall Court.

For all Story's despair at the end of the Marshall era, the Court's decision in *Charles River Bridge* did not overturn Marshall's authoritative statement in *Dartmouth College v. Woodward* (1819) on the nature of state charters of incorporation. The 1837 opinion merely held that such a charter would be construed strictly. While this decision represented a departure from Story's concept of contract law, it followed Marshall's own reasoning in *Providence Bank v. Billings* (1830) in which he refused to let exemption from state taxation pass by way of implication. In the *Charles River Bridge* decision, Taney extended Marshall's narrow construction of the Providence Bank charter to the Charles River Bridge charter without damaging the earlier definition of contract contained in *Dartmouth College*.

Corporations had not been slow to grasp the implications of the *Charles River Bridge* litigation. As early as 1831, the promoters of the east-west railroad in Massachusetts had demanded not only an explicit monopoly along the line of travel, but also the ability to set rates (previously established by charter), and eminent domain powers. Concessions to the Boston and Worcester Railroad's investors reflected the extent to which railroads had captured the public imagination and the legislative concern that the pending *Charles River Bridge* suit threatened to discourage investment in state-chartered enterprises. The already volatile climate of railroad promotion was further agitated by the Supreme Court's decision. In order to coax private investment into railroad ventures, state legislatures expanded charter privileges by expressly granting route monopoly, ratemaking, eminent domain, and, in some cases, tax exemption provisions.

The doctrinal impact of the *Charles River Bridge* decision was felt almost immediately. Within a few months a New York court endorsed the decision when it refused to halt construction of a railroad bridge adjacent to a chartered toll bridge. The doctrine of strict construction achieved particularly telling results in state courts in disputes between different transportation technologies since earlier charters had not barred later railroad development. But the Supreme Court restricted its use of the doctrine because strict construction supporting expressly granted corporate privileges might be turned against the public interest. Strict construction of legislatures' reserved powers of charter amendment might also be adverse to the interest of the community. Ambiguity in these cases would be construed in favor of the corporation. While the courts generally used the doctrine to strike down outmoded and obstructionist interests in order to sustain new interests that benefited the community, strict construction was a two-edged sword.

In the *Charles River Bridge* decision that sword had been used in the interest of progress. Although the two bridges were virtually identical and technological development was not at issue in the case, Taney's opinion and the earlier opinions of Massachusetts justices Morton and Parker recognized that the search for speed, dependability, and economy would lead to increased demand for and rapid adoption of new technologies. All three judges were concerned with the potential obstruction of new transportation improvements by older ones. Taney envisioned older corporations "awakening from their sleep and calling upon this court to put down the improvements which have taken their place." Fearing this threat to the millions of dollars already invested in new enterprises, and recognizing the magnitude of the problem which a decision in favor of the older interests would create, Taney fashioned his opinion to justify creative destruction.

Creative destruction of one form of property in order that another might prosper placed a higher social value on new uses of capital than on maintenance of old uses. The Court's decision in *Charles River Bridge*, like legislative action to subsidize improvement corporations, served as an instrumental alliance of law with anticipated technological advances. The decision allowed residents of Massachusetts "to avail themselves of the lights of modern science, . . . which are now adding to the wealth and prosperity, and the convenience and comfort of every other part of the civilized world."

Selected Bibliography

Binford, Henry C. *The First Suburbs: Residential Communities on the Boston Periphery, 1815–1860.* Chicago: University of Chicago Press, 1985.

Horwitz, Morton J. *The Transformation of American Law, 1780 1860.* Cambridge, MA: Harvard University Press, 1977.

Kutler, Stanley I. *Privilege and Creative Destruction: The Charles River Bridge Case.* Philadelphia: J. B. Lippincott Co., 1971.

Newmyer, R. Kent. *Supreme Court Justice Story: Statesman of the Old Republic.* Chapel Hill: University of North Carolina Press, 1985.

Salsbury, Stephen. *The State, the Investor, and the Railroad: The Boston and Albany, 1825–1867.* Cambridge, MA: Harvard University Press, 1967.

Warren, Charles. *History of the Harvard Law School and of Early Legal Conditions in America.* New York: Lewis Publishing Co., 1908.

"An Innocent Sort of a Duck!": Iron Range Pioneers Challenge John D. Rockefeller

——◄o►——

David A. Walker
Department of History
University of Northern Iowa

Rockefeller v. Merritt, 76 F. 909 (1896) [U.S. Circuit Court of Appeals]

◄o► THE CASE IN BRIEF ◄o►

Date
1896

Location
Minnesota

Court
U.S. Circuit Court of Appeals

Principal Participants
Merritt family of Duluth
John D. Rockefeller

Significance of the Case
Rockefeller was able to gain control of extensive iron ore deposits and a rail link to Lake Superior, both of which later became major parts of his Standard Oil Company.

The Mesabi Range in northeastern Minnesota once contained America's richest iron ore deposit. Its initial development in the early 1890s was the result of the efforts of a remarkable group of pioneer residents—the Merritt family of Duluth. Following the initial discovery of high grade ore, the Merritts assumed tremendous financial obligations in order to construct a railroad from the mining range to ore docks on Lake Superior.

Led by brothers Alfred and Leonidas, the Merritts left the comfort of local banking circles and entered the realm of high stakes, eastern financiers. They contacted officials of the American Steel Barge Company, a New York corporation engaged in shipbuilding and transportation on the Great Lakes. John D. Rockefeller had invested substantially in the barge company, thus forming the first, indirect link between the head of Standard Oil and the Duluth family.

The Merritts seemed poised for spectacular growth. Then the nationwide panic of 1893 struck, and the ensuing severe depression years accelerated the replacement of the individual entrepreneur with the merged corporation. Burdened by mounting debt, the Merritts secured a $1 million loan from Rockefeller. But even that sum failed to relieve their deteriorating financial condition. Reopened negotiations with the head of Standard Oil resulted in the formation of Lake Superior Consolidated Iron Mines, a large scale combination of iron mining interests. The two sides later presented conflicting views of the nature of this alliance. Rockefeller claimed that the Consolidated preserved and allowed for the completion of the Merritt railroad, opened the mines, and carried the brothers successfully through the panic. Members of the family portrayed a well planned conspiracy to wrest control of their Mesabi enterprises.

Unfortunately, the country's depressed economy forced the Merritts to sell their Consolidated stock, but they were unable to do so at even 10 percent of its par value. Desperately seeking to regain the family's financial standing, Alfred Merritt filed suit against Rockefeller in the local District Court, attempting to recover $1,226,400 in damages. By the time the jury trial opened on June 5, 1895, both sides had agreed to transfer the proceedings to the United States District Court in Duluth.

Alfred alleged that Rockefeller knowingly inflated the value of the stocks and bonds he contributed to the Consolidated and falsely assured the Merritts that the companies were solvent and prosperous and that their presence in the merger would enhance its value. In response, Rockefeller spokesmen denied that any deception or fraud had been perpetrated. One of the eastern financier's strongest lines of defense was the fact that the Merritts had approached him to purchase their railroad and mining stock, thus initiating the financial relationship. The Merritts had access to the appropriate financial records, and there was nothing to prevent their representatives from examining these documents.

On June 13, after more than five hours of deliberation, the twelve-man jury drawn from throughout Minnesota awarded Alfred Merritt $940,000. Reacting quickly, the Rockefeller forces noted that regional sentiment favored the Mer-

American industrialist and philanthropist John D. Rockefeller, Sr. *AP Photo.*

ritts, pointing out that the family owed substantial sums of money to many Duluth residents and, according to one spokesman, "public sentiment was not averse to the circulation of some Rockefeller money." A local newspaper editor counterattacked, writing that "the Standard Oil octopus . . . would be able to swallow and digest the Merritts. . . . Rockefeller is a financial cannibal who eats men every day." For their part, the Merritts alleged that important documents had been stolen that prevented them from presenting an even stronger case. Their most virulent attacks were aimed directly at Rockefeller, proclaiming that his absence from the Duluth courtroom was indicative of his disdain for the proceedings.

· After weighing several alternatives suggested by counsel and wanting to avoid a new trial in Duluth, Rockefeller took the dispute to the United States Eighth Circuit Court of Appeals. This three-judge tribunal accepted the case on a writ of error that the lower court had "refused to permit" him to show the actual value of the Consolidated stock, and that the presiding judge had improperly instructed the jury on how to determine the amount of Alfred Merritt's loss.

Meeting in St. Louis on November 9, 1896, the appeals court held that "the true measure of the damages suffered by one who is fraudulently induced to make a contract . . . is the . . . loss which he has sustained, and not the profits which he might have made by the transactions." The judges ruled that the damages recovered "far exceeded the just measure of full compensation for this injury. . . . In other words, they were speculative rather than compensatory damages." The appeals court then reversed the lower court's decision, charged Alfred $1,040.35 in costs, and remanded the case back to the district court in Duluth.

The Merritts saw this as the final "staggering blow" in their struggle against eastern financiers. Within a few months, however, the two sides negotiated an out-of-court settlement whereby Rockefeller paid his former business associates a total of $525,000; in turn, twenty members of the Merritt family signed a statement retracting all charges of fraud. Although reluctant to exoner-

ate their combatant, the Merritts accepted the settlement to relieve the family from "their destitution and absolute poverty." More than a decade later, Alfred testified before a congressional committee and admitted, "I was a kind of an innocent sort of a duck."

On the surface it seems puzzling that Rockefeller should have agreed to such a large payment, but past experience had provided him with little faith in local juries. In addition, protracted litigation would be costly in time and money. Rockefeller now controlled an extensive deposit of high grade iron ore and a railroad linking the mines with Lake Superior ore docks. In 1902 this empire formed an essential cornerstone in the creation of the United States Steel Corporation.

Selected Bibliography

Gates, Frederick T. *The Truth About Mr. Rockefeller and the Merritts*. New York: Knickerbocker Press, 1911.

Nevins, Allan. *John D. Rockefeller: The Heroic Age of American Enterprise*. 2 vols. New York: Charles Scribner's Sons, 1940.

Walker, David A. *Iron Frontier: The Discovery and Early Development of Minnesota's Three Ranges*. St. Paul: Minnesota Historical Society Press, 1979.

Commerce

A More Perfect Union: The Steamboat Case

—◄◦►—

Francis N. Stites

Department of History
San Diego State University

Gibbons v. Ogden, 9 Wheaton 1 (1824) [U.S. Supreme Court]

◄◦► THE CASE IN BRIEF ◄◦►

Date
1824

Location
New York
New Jersey

Court
U.S. Supreme Court

Principal Participants
Thomas Gibbons
Aaron Ogden
Chief Justice John Marshall

Significance of the Case
The Supreme Court struck down a monopoly granted by a state and affirmed the supremacy of the federal government to regulate commerce under the U.S. Constitution's commerce clause.

The link between the Constitution and the steamboat began in Philadelphia in the summer of 1787. Delegates to the Constitutional Convention were so alarmed about commercial problems that the commerce clause slipped virtually without discussion or clarity into the Constitution. The interstate tariff war, raging between Connecticut, New Jersey, and New York while they met, was a reminder of the importance of commerce to a more perfect union. It seemed clear that only an energetic national government with power "to regulate commerce with foreign nations, among the several States, and with the Indian tribes" could remove such impediments to the free flow of commerce. The steamboat, the instrument that would revolutionize commerce, also made its first consistent appearance in American waters on the Delaware River out of Philadelphia in August 1787. Some of the framers rode on it, and, its developer John Fitch noted, many more came by to look at it. Fitch's steamboat left in its wake an enlarged possibility both for national commerce and for commercial rivalry between the states. Years later, the promise of the steamboat and the ambiguity of the commerce clause would come together to produce the Supreme Court's first interpretation of the commerce power of the national government in the "Steamboat Case" of *Gibbons v. Ogden* in 1824.

The factual background to the case commenced when Robert R. Livingston and Robert Fulton obtained from the New York legislature in 1807 a steamboat monopoly. It depended upon their success in getting a boat to operate at a stipulated speed within two years. In August 1807 these two men successfully launched their steamboat, known popularly as the *Clermont,* in New York City for its maiden trip up the Hudson River to Albany. New York, then, in 1808 granted a thirty-year monopoly on steam navigation in state waters to Livingston and Fulton or their assignees. In separate legislation the state also empowered the monopoly to seize the boats and equipment of unlicensed operators.

Fulton, unlike Fitch and other early steamboaters, had a talent for duplicating success. So, he shortly had several boats plying New York waters on regularly scheduled runs. Like Fitch, though, Livingston and Fulton envisioned a national network of steamboat lines, moving upstream and downstream and able to carry more goods and passengers farther, faster, and cheaper than other forms of transport, and they would all be under their control. Accordingly, they took the customary step of petitioning state and territorial legislatures (Virginia, Kentucky, Tennessee, Ohio, Indiana, Upper Louisiana, Mississippi, and Orleans) for monopolies like New York's. All but the Orleans Territorial legislature rejected their petitions. Orleans, in April 1811, awarded them an eighteen-year monopoly on the lower Mississippi. By January 1812, one Livingston-Fulton boat, the *New Orleans,* had completed an epic run down the Ohio, over the falls at Louisville and, during the great earthquake at New Madrid in 1811, down the Mississippi to New Orleans. The transportation revolution that would create a national market had begun. So had the reaction against special privilege.

The commercial potential in steam navigation whetted the appetites of speculating entrepreneurs whose boats quickly challenged the monopoly. From the start the monopoly had to contend with arguments that the commerce power of the national government was exclusive and precluded state laws like New York's. That argument came with a major challenge in 1811 when John Van Ingen and other Albany businessmen launched rival boats, *Hope* and *Perseverance,* on the Albany-New York run. The monopolists retaliated by asking the New York Court of Chancery to grant an injunction. When the court ruled against the monopoly, Livingston and Fulton appealed. In 1812 the New York Court of Errors, the highest state court, upheld the monopoly.

In this case, *Livingston v. Van Ingen,* the most important and impressive of the opinions was that of Chancellor James Kent, one of the outstanding jurists in the early nineteenth century. The key question was the relation between the state law and the commerce clause. Was the commerce power exclusive? Could states act if Congress was silent?

Kent reasoned that the power to grant monopolies inhered both in sovereignty and in the English common law. That New York had already granted monopolies to banks, canals, and turnpike companies established an unquestioned legislative power to make grants. The only limits to this power were the state constitution, the fundamental principles of all governments, or the external limit imposed by the national Constitution. Kent ruled that the states' delegation of a commerce power to the national government in 1787 did not preclude the states from exercising the same power. The commerce power, like the taxing power, he asserted, was not exclusive but concurrent. The Constitution did not prohibit it to the states, and the Tenth Amendment proclaimed that powers not delegated still remained.

The "possible contingency of a collision" between state and national laws did not trouble Kent, because the supremacy clause of the U.S. Constitution (Article VI) settled such conflicts conclusively in favor of the United States. There could be no conflict, however, until Congress acted. So long as Congress remained silent, there was room for the states to regulate. His "safe rule of construction" was that "if any given power was originally vested in this State, if it has not been exclusively ceded to Congress, or if the exercise of it has not been prohibited to the States," the state could exercise the power "until it comes practically in collision with the actual exercise of some congressional power." He could find no national law in conflict with New York's laws.

Livingston v. Van Ingen ended only one of many legal challenges to the monopoly. Livingston and Fulton were less successful in Louisiana, where they had to contend with unsympathetic courts, hostile public opinion, and, worse yet, superior competition. Their monopoly there collapsed, and the dissatisfaction became epidemic. New Jersey, Connecticut, and Ohio in 1818 and 1822 banned Livingston-Fulton steamboats from their waterways. Massachusetts, New Hampshire, Vermont, and Georgia retaliated by conferring their own monopolies. The steamboat seemed hopelessly snagged on states' rights, and the promise of free trade in an expanding national market seemed about to dissolve in a commercial civil war.

The monopoly tried co-opting their competition either by purchasing their boats or selling them franchises. One purchaser was Aaron Ogden, a former New Jersey governor, who tried for several years to defy the monopoly by operating a steam ferry from Elizabethtown, New Jersey to New York City. Ogden was aided by friendly legislation from the New Jersey legislature and a federal coasting license. By 1815, however, Ogden had surrendered and purchased a license from the Livingston assignees (both Fulton and Livingston were dead by this time).

Ogden's entrance into a partnership with the cantankerous and independent Georgian, Thomas Gibbons, marked the beginnings of *Gibbons v. Ogden*. The testy partnership collapsed in 1818 when Gibbons used the formidable talents of the unscrupulous young Cornelius Vanderbilt to run an unlicensed steamer on Ogden's route. Ogden sued for an injunction in the New York courts in 1819. Ultimately, the New York Court of Errors upheld Kent's *Van Ingen* opinion and granted a permanent injunction against Gibbons in 1820.

Gibbons appealed to the United States Supreme Court. Using the arguments he had used in the New York courts, he claimed that the New York monopoly, under which Ogden was operating, conflicted with the Federal Coasting Act of 1793, under which he held a license to "navigate the waters of any particular state by steamboat," and with the commerce clause of the U.S. Constitution (Article I, Section 8). There were numerous technical delays, but finally, in 1824, the Court got its first opportunity to discuss and to clarify the meaning of the commerce clause.

Steamboat entrepreneurs and judges were not the only ones debating the meaning of the commerce clause. After 1815, nationalists and states' righters had been at odds over proposals to have the national government pay for internal improvements such as turnpikes and canals. Presidents James Madison and James Monroe had vetoed bills on the strict constructionist grounds that the commerce clause did not authorize a positive federal program of internal improvements.

During the argument in *Gibbons*, Congress was debating a bill to provide a federal survey of road and canal routes. The political and constitutional implications of both the debate and the case troubled southerners who increasingly were aware of their region's minority status and sensitive to any potential threat to the security of their "peculiar institution." The Missouri debates in 1820 brought criticism of broad construction. Senator Philip Barbour of Virginia urged the "necessity of restraining the Federal Government within the prescribed limits, to guard against encroachments on the authority of the States, and thereby prevent a consolidation." A Massachusetts congressman noted that Congress could have no power claimed to restrict slavery in the new states unless it "be constructive." In the General Survey debates, John Randolph warned that if Congress possessed broad power over commerce, "they may *emancipate every slave in the United States.*" Similar southern opposition to the commerce power appeared in the debates on the Tariff of 1824. There was, too, the continual fulmination about repealing Section 25 of the Judiciary Act of 1789, which authorized appeals from the highest state tribunals to the United States Supreme Court. The monopoly's steamboat also carried this load into the Supreme Court.

Chief Justice John Marshall was aware of the cases's political dimensions. After all, he and the Court had been under vigorous attack from Virginia and other states for the ringing endorsements of national power and broad construction in the decisions of 1819–1821. Southerners saw the link between broad construction and commerce in his 1821 *Cohens* statement that in war, peace, in "all commercial relations, . . . [and] in many other respects, the American people are one." Those decisions and criticisms did not mean, however, that the Marshall Court was centralizing.

Regularly, Marshall and his brethren tried to negotiate a path through the divided sovereignty of the American federal system. In the *Dartmouth College Case* (1819), he had said that the framers had not intended "to restrain the states in the regulation of their civil institutions." *McCulloch v. Maryland* (1819) had presented "in truth, a question of supremacy," but Marshall pointed out later in essays answering the trenchant states' rights criticism of Spencer Roane and the Richmond Junto, that "supremacy" did not mean despotism and that "national" was not synonymous with consolidated. In the superheated context of 1824, negotiation was improbable.

The throng of congressmen, reporters, and Washington ladies spilling into the aisles of the Court's chambers in the basement below the Senate reminded all that "the great steamboat question from New York" was no ordinary case. Both sides had retained eminent counsel: Daniel Webster and Attorney General William Wirt, two of the giants of the bar, for Gibbons; Thomas J. Oakley, New York attorney general, and Thomas Addis Emmet, the brilliant Irish expatriate and veteran Livingston-Fulton attorney, for Ogden. Wirt predicted that it would "be a great combat." He was right. After Marshall had sharpened the nib of his quill pen, pulled up the sleeves of his robe, and nodded, counsel began an argument that lasted five days and examined every aspect of the controversy.

Webster probed the commerce clause to decide whether New York had the power to pass the laws. He concluded that, because the commerce power was to a certain extent exclusive to the national government, it could not be a concurrent state power. Webster had the good sense to recognize what Kent had pointed out: that the states had already regulated much interstate commerce with monopolies on banks and turnpikes, and that this regulation could not be undone. He tried to mark out some territory for the states, but he would not do it through the silence of Congress. If Congress did not legislate on a subject, Webster took that as evidence of congressional intent that the subject be left free and unregulated. Existing state regulations of things involved with commerce were not regulations of commerce, Webster said, and hence were not traceable to a commerce power. They were "police power" actions. Webster also saw a conflict between Gibbons's coasting license under the 1793 law and the state law. For him the 1793 law gave Gibbons the right to "navigate freely" all the waters of the United States.

Oakley, who was thoroughly familiar with the arguments in the New York courts, spent over one day arguing for a concurrent state power over commerce that resembled Kent's in *Van Ingen*. The states, ran this argument, had reserved a part of the commerce power and could share it unless there was a conflict between state and national law.

Emmet followed Oakley with a detailed examination of the commerce clause. He stressed the connection between slavery and the commerce to support state concurrent power. States, he noted, had legislated to ban the importation of slaves, and the Constitution treated slaves as articles of commerce. So, a national law of 1803 punishing the importation of slaves into states that had banned their admission was a congressional recognition of a state concurrent power over commerce.

Wirt closed with a powerful argument for Gibbons. Some branches of the "complex, multifarious and indefinite" subject of commerce, he said, "might be given exclusively to Congress; the others may be left open to the states." So, only some national powers over commerce are "exclusive in their nature; and among them, is that power which concerns navigation." Wirt did not think it was necessary in this case to decide the whole commerce power question. The specific issue was navigation. Once Congress "legislated concerning a subject on which it is authorized to act, all State legislation which interferes is absolutely void." The Coasting Act of 1793 was such a congressional action; the New York law was, therefore, invalid.

In an eloquent peroration, Wirt told the Court that it faced a "momentous decision." As in 1787 when the framers were drafting the Constitution, Connecticut, New Jersey, and New York were "almost on the eve of war." If the Court did not mediate and "extirpate the seeds of anarchy which New York has sown, you *will* have civil war. . . . Your republican institutions will perish in the conflict. Your constitution will fall. The last hope of nations will be gone." Justice Joseph Story called it a speech of "great splendour and force."

Three weeks passed before the Court delivered a decision. The reason was that the 69-year-old Marshall had tripped over the cellar door at the justices' Washington boardinghouse, dislocated his shoulder, and bruised his skull.

On March 2, 1824, the chief justice appeared with his arm in a sling and in a feeble voice read his opinion striking down the New York monopoly. He began by expounding the commerce clause with a broad construction in the style of *McCulloch* where he had referred to the "great" power to regulate commerce. Strict construction of this and other enumerated powers would, he said, cripple the national government. The meaning of those powers was intimately connected to the purpose for which they were conferred; the framers of the Constitution "must be understood . . . to have intended what they said." Freedom of commerce among the states was a primary purpose of the Constitution, prerequisite to union and to national economic growth. Marshall asserted that the rule for construing the extent of powers was to take the "language of the instrument" that conferred the powers "in connection with the purposes for which they were conferred."

What meaning would this broad, nationalist interpretation give to the words "regulate," "commerce," and "among the several states?" Commerce, Marshall proclaimed in the classic and still-quoted definition, was more than buying and selling. "Commerce, undoubtedly, is

traffic, but it is something more; it is intercourse. It describes the commercial intercourse between nations, and parts of nations, in all its branches." It embraced, then, navigation, and "every species of commercial intercourse" including steamboats. The power to regulate was the power "to prescribe the rule by which commerce is to be governed" and had no limits other than those "prescribed in the constitution." Commerce that was "among the states" could not stop at the external boundary of each state but might be introduced into the interior.

That meant that Congress could regulate commerce wherever it existed or, by extension, whatever form it might take from pipelines to telecommunications. Marshall based this definition not just on logic but on precedent by analogy. Since 1787, he noted, the United States had experienced exactly what the framers had intended, a broad and flexible interpretation of commerce that extended beyond the commerce clause proper. Moreover, said Marshall turning to the phrase "among the several states," the word "among" meant intermingled with. "A thing which is among others is intermingled with them. Commerce among the states cannot stop at the external boundary line of each state, but may be introduced into the interior." Of course the power to Congress to regulate would accompany the introduction.

It was this sweeping definition of the national commerce power, verging ever so close to exclusive national power, that had alarmed Randolph and the other states' rights critics of broad construction of enumerated powers. So, although his opinion strongly intimated exclusive national power, the chief justice was reluctant to declare it. Sensitive to the practical difficulties of the federal system—what in *Gibbons* he called "genius and character of the whole government," Marshall struggled to negotiate a formula that would accommodate state regulation of local problems and the demands of free trade for an expanding national economy.

Formally repeating the point of his 1819 *McCulloch* opinion, the chief justice emphasized that national power was not plenary. The framers would not have enumerated "foreign nations, among the several States, and the Indian tribes" in the grant of power "had the intention been to extend the power to every description." It did not extend to those concerns "which are completely within a particular state, which do not affect other states, and with which it is not necessary to interfere for the purpose of executing some of the general powers of the government." So, the "completely internal commerce of a state, then, may be considered as reserved for the state itself." He did not, however, say what was "completely" internal commerce that did not "affect other states."

This selective exclusiveness approach enabled the Court to allow states to enact inspection, health, and pilotage laws that might affect interstate commerce. Marshall simply would not admit that such legislation was an exercise of a concurrent commerce power (the word "concurrent" did not appear in the Constitution until the Eighteenth Amendment). He preferred to call it, as had Webster, the state police power. Congress could enter this area, too, if the national interest required it.

And what of Webster's point that the silence of Congress indicated congressional intent that a subject was to be free of regulation? Marshall did not give an explicit answer, but he did say Webster's argument had "great force" and that he was not satisfied "that it has been refuted." By implication, then, the Court would have the responsibility of deciding the extent of permissible state activity in the future on a case-by-case basis.

The one point on which all parties had agreed was that national law took precedence over state law in case of conflict. Marshall used this agreement and the conflict between the 1793 Federal Coasting Act and the New York laws to resolve the steamboat controversy. The 1793 law required only the licensing of vessels engaged in the coastal trade so as to give American vessels an advantage. Marshall turned it into an implicit guarantee of free navigation on the waterways of the United States. He interpreted the Coasting Act to have conferred a license or a "right" to trade. It was, then, a federal regulation of interstate commerce. Because the New York laws impeded free navigation and the right to trade, they conflicted with this national law and were, therefore, unconstitutional.

In the manner of his earlier constitutional decisions, Marshall had again used the case to expound the meaning of the Constitution. This course was "unavoidable," he said, because "powerful and ingenious minds" always used strict construction to "explain away the constitution of our country, and leave it a magnificent structure indeed, to look at, but totally unfit to use." He was as much interested in the health of the Union as in the New York monopoly.

The decision was unanimous. The recently appointed Justice Smith Thompson was absent because of his daughter's death. William Johnson, Jefferson's first Supreme Court appointee who had just determined to speak his own mind in constitutional cases, wrote a powerful concurring opinion asserting what Marshall had not—that congressional power over commerce "must be exclusive" and that the grant of this power carried with it "the whole subject, leaving nothing for the state to act upon."

The explosive issue of slavery was partly responsible for Johnson's vigorous concurrence. In June 1822, Charleston, South Carolina, had learned of a planned slave uprising led by the free black Denmark Vesey. After brutally punishing the alleged conspirators (there is substantial debate among historians as to whether there was an active conspiracy), South Carolina enacted a Negro Seamen law reflecting its belief that free black sailors on ships in Charleston harbor had incited the unrest and requiring that all such sailors be jailed until their ships departed.

A Charlestonian and a strong libertarian, Johnson had publicly attacked the high-handed, summary trial and execution of the conspirators. Then Henry Elkisson, a black sailor and British subject, petitioned Johnson's circuit court for a writ of *habeas corpus*. In *Elkisson v. Deleisseline* (1823), Johnson boldly ruled the Negro Seamen Act unconstitutional because it violated a treaty with Great Britain and the "paramount and exclusive" power of Congress to regulate foreign commerce. Johnson asserted that the grant to Congress had to have "swept away the whole subject" and "left nothing for the states to act upon." Otherwise, the Union would become like the old Confederation—a "mere rope of sand." A wave of indignation swept the South. South Carolina defied this decision using an exclusive national power to threaten the "peculiar institution." More ominous was the threatening talk of states' rights, secession, and forcible resistance.

After reading Johnson's opinion in the *National Intelligencer,* Marshall thought it had unnecessarily fueled the fire at which states' rights extremists would "roast the Judicial Department." The chief justice was more circumspect. He had had a similar case, *The Wilson v. U.S.,* on his Richmond circuit in 1820, but he had more prudently chosen to avoid the commerce question and to avoid being snagged "in a hedge composed entirely of thorny State-Rights." Because it was not "absolutely necessary" to consider the constitutional question of the commerce clause, Marshall, unlike Johnson, "escaped on a construction of the act." He was "not fond," he wrote Justice Story, "of butting against a wall in sport."

Gibbons showed Marshall's talent for avoiding the practical difficulties of constitutional questions and for "escaping" both commerce and slavery by construction. He dismissed the latter in one paragraph by noting that the constitutional ban on slave trade action until 1808 was exceptional because it allowed states some power to act on that subject only during that time. State laws enacted after that would be invalid, he said.

Most of the nation applauded *Gibbons* for hastening the demise of a hated and obnoxious monopoly. Some have called it the first antitrust decision in United States history. Newspapers in New York and elsewhere that had scarcely noticed the *Clermont*'s 1807 voyage, reprinted the full opinion. This "masterpiece of judicial reasoning concerns every citizen," ran a typical comment, because "unlimited scope is now afforded to enterprise and capital in steam navigation." For once, it seemed, a Marshall decision had articulated popular aspirations. A Missouri paper chided New York for its restive reception of the decision. New Yorkers, it continued, "may rest assured that it is a decision approved of in their sister States, who can see no propriety in the claim of New York to domineer over the waters which form the means of intercourse between that State and others, and over that intercourse itself."

Realizing the benefits the success of steamboat operation would bring to transportation and to his personal fortune, Henry Wheaton, Court reporter, published a separate pamphlet report of *The Case of Gibbons against Ogden* in October 1824. Others, like John Randolph, remained unhappy and alarmed. Randolph knew it was fashionable to praise the opinion, but confessed to one correspondent that he was not noted for being a fashionable man. He thought the opinion "unworthy" of Marshall because it contained a "great deal that has no business there, or indeed anywhere."

Gibbons, unfortunately, did leave everything about as unsettled as before. One could read the decision equally as expanding national power in the tradition of *McCulloch* or as admitting limits to the reach of national power. Marshall had used the "sense of the Convention" to reject an exclusive national bankruptcy power in *Sturges v. Crowninshield,* also in 1819. For him a "mere grant of power to Congress did not imply a prohibition on the States to exercise the same Power." In *Gibbons* he said that "the sovereignty of Congress" had always been understood to be "limited to specific objects" though it was "plenary as to those objects." By holding only that an undefined exclusive power existed and had been used in 1793 regarding steamboats, Marshall had invalidated the interstate operation of the New York monopoly. But what of the monopoly within New York?

The opinion in *Gibbons* did not offer much help to New York courts as they wrestled with that question in subsequent litigation. The range of opinions about what Marshall had actually said offers compelling evidence of its ambiguity. Ultimately, the New York courts used *Gibbons* to invalidate the monopoly's intrastate operation.

One result of that contemporary confusion has been a persistent confusion about Marshall's opinion—a tendency to call it a commerce clause decision even though it was a conflict of laws decision. Nevertheless, the expansive interpretation of commerce has become the controlling legacy of the decision. Marshall stands as the progenitor of the flexible and centralized national power that now governs the United States. Congressmen and judges, among others, have sprinkled the magic phrases from *Gibbons v. Ogden* through their justifications for expanding national power. As late as 1942 in *Wickard v. Filburn*, the Supreme Court cited *Gibbons* and the commerce clause as the constitutional foundation for virtually unlimited national power. *Wickard* upheld federal regulation of wheat grown for on-farm consumption. It is doubtful that such regulation was the sort that Marshall had intended as commerce "among the states" in 1824.

Commerce questions were not about to diminish. In 1827 and again in 1829 the Marshall Court had to deal with the questions first raised in *Gibbons*. In *Brown v. Maryland* the Court asserted an exclusive national power to regulate foreign commerce, but on the thorny question of state concurrent power to regulate commerce, Marshall would only grant a state police power as he had in 1824. The same question came up again two years later in *Willson v. Blackbird Creek Marsh Co.*, the last commerce case of the Marshall years. Once more the Chief Justice used selective exclusiveness. This time, however, his pragmatism caused him to rule for the state and to neglect the same 1793 Coasting Law he had used to such good effect to "escape" in *Gibbons*.

Marshall's commerce clause cases showed how carefully he could preserve the principles of a "truly federal" union by both enlarging national power through broad construction and preserving a measure of power for the states. This practice, first used in *Gibbons* represented a shift from states' rights to concurrent power as the basis of state sovereignty. Such a shift preserved the states by recognizing federal supremacy, not challenging it. This negotiation served the Court and the Union well by accommodating the times and winning public acceptance for the decisions. Marshall attempted no more good than the people could bear because he knew full well that the Court could not enforce its opinions and had to rely on persuasion. His comprehensive definition of the national commerce power had made it possible for Congress to act, but it remained to be seen whether and to what extent social, economic, political, and sectional pressures would allow it to do so.

Selected Bibliography

Baxter, Maurice G. *Daniel Webster and the Supreme Court*. Amherst: University of Massachusetts Press, 1966.

Baxter, Maurice G. *The Steamboat Monopoly: Gibbons v. Ogden*. New York: Alfred A. Knopf, 1972.

Beveridge, Albert J. *The Life of John Marshall*. 4 vols. New York: Houghton Mifflin Company, 1916–1919.

Currie, David P. *The Constitution in the Supreme Court: The First Hundred Years, 1789–1888*. Chicago: University of Chicago Press, 1985.

Frankfurter, Felix. *The Commerce Clause under Marshall, Taney and Waite*. Chapel Hill: University of North Carolina Press, 1937.

Newmyer, R. Kent. *Supreme Court Justice Joseph Story: Statesman of the Old Republic*. Chapel Hill: University of North Carolina Press, 1985.

White, G. Edward. *The Marshall Court and Cultural Change, 1815–1835*. New York: Macmillan, 1988.

An Omen of Change:
State Power to Regulate Commerce

—◄◦►—

Craig T. Friend
Department of History
University of Central Florida, Orlando

New York v. Miln, 11 Peters 102 (1837) [U.S. Supreme Court]

◄◦► THE CASE IN BRIEF ◄◦►

Date
1837

Location
New York

Court
U.S. Supreme Court

Principal Participants
William Thompson
George Miln
Associate Justice James Barbour

Significance of the Case
In affirming the constitutionality of a New York state law imposing regulations on the admittance of ship passengers into New York, the Court supported some state power over commerce.

One of the important characteristics of the United States Supreme Court is the adherence to precedent. Sometimes, however, justices find it hard to cling to precedents as social conditions change and new justices come to the bench. The 1837 decision of *New York v. Miln* demonstrated both of these features of Supreme Court decision-making.

In 1824 the Supreme Court had decided *Gibbons v. Ogden*, the first great commerce clause case. Chief Justice John Marshall's nationalistic philosophy prevailed here as it would throughout most of his tenure. Yet, even after Marshall died in 1835, his influence remained in the form of his judicial precedents and his friend, Joseph Story.

Marshall's successor was Roger B. Taney, a man who did not share many of Marshall's legal views. As a Jacksonian Democrat, Taney opposed strong centralization of the federal government. Prior to his appointment as chief justice, Taney served as U.S. attorney general, a position which made him a key figure in Jackson's decision to veto the Bank of the United States. Supporters of Marshall's nationalistic philosophies, therefore, did not greet Taney's appointment to the Court's center seat with much enthusiasm.

One of the earliest decisions by the Taney Court was *New York v. Miln*, a case continued from 1834. The argument concerned a New York statute requiring captains of vessels arriving in New York to submit a list of all passengers within a day after docking. The purpose of the law was the regulation of indigents. This reasoning provided the state with its surest defense—the right to exercise "police power." Even the great nationalist, John Marshall, when he wrote the opinion in *Gibbons v. Ogden*, had referred to the police power as a power through which the welfare of citizens could be protected. The present statute, however, appeared to interfere with interstate commerce. If all the justices had been present in 1834 when the case first came before the Court, Marshall would have probably seen the dispute as an occasion for another nationalistic opinion. As it was, however, several justices missed the session and the decision was postponed. It reappeared on the docket in 1837.

The Court of 1837 faintly resembled that which Marshall had known. The election of Andrew Jackson to the presidency had initiated an evolution of thought within the federal government which reached into the judiciary. The death of Marshall and two other justices provided Jackson the opportunity to mold the Court as he desired. Only Joseph Story and Smith Thompson survived as reminders of the Marshall years. They were joined by five Jacksonian appointees, all Democrats: John McLean, Henry Baldwin, James Moore Wayne, Philip Pendleton Barbour and, of course, Roger Taney. The Court's new composition essentially foretold the demise of Marshall's nationalistic precedents.

Joseph Story had reason to be concerned over the changes on the bench. During his previous twenty-six years as a justice, he had, at times, appeared more of a nationalist than Marshall. Although his role in *Gibbons v. Ogden* is unknown, Story concurred with Marshall's opinion which did not expressly exclude states from exercising power over interstate commerce, but clearly permitted Congress to claim

supremacy through legislation. Indeed, *Gibbons v. Ogden* seemed extremely similar to *New York v. Miln*. Both cases centered around state regulation of shipping; and the state claimed policing rights in both instances. To Story the resolution was clear.

To the other extreme was Justice James Wayne who, as mayor of Savannah, Georgia, had sponsored similar state laws. During his administration, restrictions were placed on immigration, and the purchase of bonds was required to assist the city in providing health measures for sickly passengers. As Story surely noted, Wayne would support New York's claim as a policing agent.

Yet, Story attempted to convince the justices of his interpretation of the law. He believed that case could be resolved in point with Marshall's *Gibbons* opinion. Congress had been regulating passenger ships since 1819, and Story understood a clear conflict between federal and state powers in the New York statute. His fellow justices, however, disregarded Story's plea.

Justice James Barbour produced the written opinion for the majority. Barbour had previously demonstrated his states-rights ideals in 1821. As counsel for the defense in *Cohens v. Virginia*, he argued zealously before the Supreme Court that the federal judiciary had no power to review decisions made in state courts. Barbour's reasoning was lost in the increasingly nationalistic ideology of the Marshall court. His opportunity to reverse that tide came with *New York v. Miln*.

Thus, in his only major Supreme Court opinion, Barbour wrote that "a state has the same undeniable and unlimited jurisdiction over all persons and things, within its territorial limits ... where that jurisdiction is not surrendered or restrained by the Constitution of the United States." Although the statement echoed Marshall's opinion in *Gibbons v. Ogden*, there were two specifics which made Barbour's opinion decisively different. Initially, he emphasized that the justices "shall not enter into an examination of the question whether the power to regular commerce, be or be not exclusive of the states, because ... we are of opinion that the act is not a regulation of commerce, but of police." Second, Barbour supported his first premise by noting that the ships in question were transporting persons, not goods, and that persons were not the subject of commerce. The opinion was read in conference the evening before the term ended and a majority agreed. Only Story dissented, with "the consolation to know that I had the entire concurrence, upon the same grounds, of that great constitutional jurist, the late Mr. Chief Justice John Marshall."

Barbour's logic established an exclusivity for the states which was, to that point in American history, unprecedented. The concept of internal policing powers had been implied in several previous cases, but Barbour's interpretation created a realm of state power beyond the restrictions of the Tenth Amendment of the Constitution. The other justices accepted Barbour's ideas and served notice to supporters of Marshall nationalism. The term ended the following day and *New York v. Miln* appeared to be resolved.

Twelve years later, however, the decision haunted the Taney court when it confronted the *Passenger Cases*. New York and Massachusetts had placed taxes upon immigrants. Once again Taney supported the internal police power of the states, but his opinion was that of the minority. The majority noted that the levies were in conflict with the commerce clause; Justice Wayne concurred in a separate opinion. He stated that persons could be commerce and that the present statutes were unconstitutional. Wayne then proceeded to question whether Barbour's statement in 1837 that persons could not be commerce had actually been presented to the justices when the decision was read. Henry Baldwin agreed with Wayne and recalled that he noticed the sentence after the Court's adjournment, too late for a modification.

Barbour had died in 1841, unable to respond to Wayne's accusation. Taney took up the gauntlet, however, and replied that the statement had been clear and agreed upon. He then expounded on the dangers of dismissing precedent. If one phrase of an opinion could be so easily overlooked, he implored, the public's confidence in the Court itself could be jeopardized. Wayne did not respond to Taney's exhortation and the debate thus ended.

New York v. Miln left the distinction between regulation of commerce and a state's police powers more ambiguous than before. As an early decision of the Taney Court, *New York v. Miln* demonstrated that John Marshall's influence was waning less than two years after his death. Story clung tenaciously to the nationalistic precedents of former Court decisions. But Taney, Barbour and the rest of the Court embraced a new interpretation of the conflict between state and federal governments. Paralleling the change in the Supreme Court was an increasing fragmentation within it. The unity of the Marshall Court that usually produced only one opinion per case, dissolved so that by 1849, when the *Passenger Cases* were decided, several justices offered their own opinions to supplement the majority and minority decisions. The significance of *New York v. Miln*, therefore, was as an omen of change, not only for the Court but for the nation as well.

Selected Bibliography

Frankfurter, Felix. *The Commerce Clause under Marshall, Taney and Waite.* Chicago: Quadrangle Books, 1937.

Newmyer, R. Kent. *Supreme Court Justice Joseph Story: Statesman of the Old Republic.* Chapel Hill: University of North Carolina Press, 1985.

Newmyer, R. Kent. *The Supreme Court under Marshall and Taney.* Arlington Heights, IL: Harlan Davidson, Inc., 1968.

When Monopoly Mattered

——◄◦►——

Robert Stanley
Department of Political Science
California State University, Chico

United States v. E. C. Knight Co., 156 U.S. 1 (1895) [U.S. Supreme Court]

◄◦► THE CASE IN BRIEF ◄◦►

Date
1895

Location
New Jersey
Pennsylvania

Court
U.S. Supreme Court

Principal Participants
United States government
E. C. Knight Company
Chief Justice Melville Fuller

Significance of the Case
The case was decided on a narrow interpretation of the commerce clause of the Constitution, in which manufacturing was ruled outside of the definition of "commerce" and thus could not be regulated by the government.

Business corporations stood at the heart of the process of industrialism that fractured and refashioned American society in the period after the Civil War. Among the first to recognize the social power to be gained from increased size and reduced competition, large corporations began during the 1870s to experiment with several new forms of combination: pools, trusts, and holding companies. At the same time, farmers, workers, merchants, and urban consumers united around an old, radically democratic tradition that called for the removal of barriers, private or governmental, to a more equitable pattern of economic power. Antimonopoly sentiment collided with corporate combination throughout the 1880s, and by the depression of the 1890s social struggle had been channeled into constitutionally charged conflict.

In *United States v. E. C. Knight Co.*, the Supreme Court faced for the first time the broad political question of how to apportion antimonopoly authority within the still-diffuse American state. A specific legal question directly provoked the contenders: Had the widely hated Sugar Trust, through its control of 98 percent of the refining capacity in the United States, run afoul of the newly minted Sherman Antitrust Act of 1890? The Court's emphatically negative answer infuriated antimonopolists, left with the states a legal load they proved unwilling to carry, and generated a formalistic view of interstate commerce that remained influential until the depression crisis of the 1930s. Yet for all its infamy, the *Knight* decision proved to be less determinative of the future paths of combinations and commerce than emblematic of the rapidly fading antebellum economic and legal conceptions on which it relied. Engulfed in an onrushing tide of corporate gigantism and cooperative governmental centrism, *Knight* looked resolutely and hopefully backward.

The key to understanding the evident paradox of *Knight* lies in Gilded Age conceptions of the corporation. Lawmakers viewed the business corporation as a legal creation, dependent for its existence and power upon the state legislative charter that gave it life. From the perspective of any single state, for example Pennsylvania, regulatory problems might arise over domestic corporations (those chartered by the Pennsylvania legislature) or with "foreign" corporations (those chartered by other states and doing business in Pennsylvania).

Through the corporate charter, each state legislature enjoyed power to promote and to regulate business activity. The charter could specify the size and purpose of the corporation, prescribe whether it might combine with others, and guarantee the probity of its activities. When the corporation acted against any limitations established in the charter, court-approved doctrines empowered state officials to invalidate the transactions or dissolve the charters, through what were called *quo warranto* proceedings. Through the charter and its enforcement devices, the state therefore possessed legal power to control corporate pools, trusts, and holding companies at their organizational roots.

Without additional authority to prevent foreign corporations from migrating into states and engaging in activities forbidden to domestic corporations, however, these devices to protect the public interest would have been useless. An effort by Pennsylvania to prohibit the establishment of a domestic holding company in the

sugar refining business, for example, would have been superfluous if a foreign corporation could enter and make just such a move with impunity. But in their early efforts to control foreign corporations within their jurisdictions, the states faced challenges raised by the commerce clause of the federal Constitution.

The Supreme Court chose to allow the freest possible trade among the states without, at the same time, opening the gates so widely that they would be unable to control foreign corporate activity that might undermine their own domestic business policies. Viewing the problem in categorical terms, as it had in labor and taxation cases, the Court developed two distinct lines of doctrine. And, in order to achieve its delicate policy balance, it rigidly policed the frontiers. Whether a state's foreign corporation law violated the commerce clause would depend on the Court's definition of what constituted "commerce" among the states, and here the Court drew a distinction between marketing and non-marketing acts of corporations.

The first line of cases reflected the Court's crusade against state and local trade barriers, which prohibited all measures tending to block the introduction of foreign products on a parity with domestic products. Following the leading case of *Welton v. Missouri* (1876), the Court struck down state laws that laid discriminatory taxes on foreign goods or required licenses of out-of-state salesmen not also required of locals. The Court feared, in such legislation, a reenactment of the interstate tariff wars that had preceded the adoption of the Constitution, and were understood to have led to the drafting of the commerce clause itself.

The second line of cases represented the Court's insistence that the states be empowered to control the non-marketing acts of corporations within their jurisdictions. If the commerce clause protected *only* marketing, juridical room would exist for the states to regulate foreign corporate migration. Here the leading case was *Paul v. Virginia* (1869), which sustained Virginia's foreign corporation law against a challenge by a New York insurance company. Between 1888 and 1903, the Supreme Court approved several state foreign corporation laws prohibiting the local exercise of franchises by foreign corporations. Most significantly, it did so by simply declaring that the processes of manufacturing, mining, and issuing insurance policies did not constitute interstate commerce. Pursuant to this line of cases, state legislatures might exclude, license, or otherwise regulate foreign corporations consistently with their domestic corporate policies. The states, therefore, held formal legal authority under their own charter grants to dictate to domestic corporations what their form of organization would be, and under the Court's *Paul* line, could apply that authority to foreign corporations wishing to do business within their jurisdictions.

Faced with the economic pressures that foreign corporations brought to bear in the late nineteenth century, state officials rarely used their disciplinary power. But, beginning in the late 1880s, prompted by antimonopolist anger at newly forming trusts in oil, whiskey, and sugar, several states brought successful *quo warranto* proceedings challenging the legal power of corporations to reorganize themselves under their charters.

For a brief moment it seemed that the states might combine legal authority and political will to overcome concentrated private economic power. Yet, at virtually the same time, New Jersey in 1889 enacted a law which permitted all of its domestic corporations to acquire control of foreign firms. In 1890 the Sugar Trust took advantage of the law to reorganize itself as a New Jersey corporation. By the end of the century all of the trusts dissolved by the states in their moment of control had done the same, as had some 270 other large combinations. In the wake of this development a political firestorm broke over the administration of Grover Cleveland, forcing Attorney General Richard Olney to bring the first Sherman Antitrust Act prosecution against the Sugar Trust. Drafted with sensitivity to state authority over corporations, adopted in 1890 at the peak of state antimonopoly activity, the Sherman Act made illegal, contracts or combinations "in restraint of trade or commerce among the several States," and monopolies in "the trade or commerce among the several States." The act relied for its authority on the commerce clause of the Constitution.

Given the Court's determination to preserve for state corporate regulatory purposes a categor-

ical conception of interstate commerce, poorer facts for the government's challenge could hardly have been invented than those at issue in *Knight*. The Sugar Trust refineries were all located in the single state of Pennsylvania, its products were distributed by independent wholesalers, and the contracts creating the holding company provided only for the standard transfer of stock. The government argued that the contracts created a combination in restraint of trade and that the company constituted a monopoly. And it sought to break the combination back into its constituent parts—one of which was the Knight Company. The government boldly interpreted the act in economic terms familiar to twentieth-century sensibilities, arguing that control over the manufacture of sugar meant a practical monopoly over a basic necessity for which interstate commerce was required. Control over manufacture yielded, in practical fact, control over interstate commerce.

Chief Justice Melville W. Fuller's opinion for the majority (only Justice John Marshall Harlan dissented) framed the issue as "whether, conceding that the existence of a monopoly in manufacture is established by the evidence, that monopoly can be directly suppressed under the act of congress in the mode attempted by this bill." Fuller relied for his negative answer on the distinction between the state police power, which exclusively governed locally chartered corporate activities, and Congress's equally exclusive power over interstate commerce, which supported the Sherman Act. Since *Gibbons v. Ogden* (1824), Fuller argued, "that which belongs to commerce is within the jurisdiction of the United States, but that which does not belong to commerce is within the police power of the state." The key question raised by the government was whether the control over the manufacture of refined sugar that the contracts gave to the Sugar Trust fell within interstate commerce. Fuller said no. "Commerce succeeds to manufacture," he contended, "and is not a part of it." Thus, the contracts that aimed to control manufacturing remained outside the formal conception of commerce, and therefore beyond the reach of the Sherman Act, despite the acknowledged practical link to eventual interstate sale.

The distinction was "vital" for Fuller. While the commerce power "furnishes the strongest bond of union," the state police power "is essential to the preservation of the autonomy of the states as required by our dual form of government." To call manufacturing a part of commerce would give the Congress "to the exclusion of the states . . . power to regulate not only manufactures, but also agriculture, horticulture, stock-raising, domestic fisheries, mining; in short, every branch of human industry." Such a result would mean that "comparatively little of business operations and affairs would be left for state control."

Fuller understood that to have ruled otherwise would have undermined the *Paul* line of cases and vastly expanded *Welton's* scope, leaving the states unable to prevent foreign manufacturing corporations from exercising franchises within their borders and rendering useless their charter-based control over domestic corporations since they could simply reorganize as newly untouchable New Jersey corporations and avoid *quo warranto* dissolution. To call manufacturing a part of commerce was to deny the states their traditional control over the roots of corporate organization and activity, and to hand to Congress virtually complete authority over the economy.

But the Sugar Trust's escape from the Sherman Act did not mean a free hand for corporate combination, since "the relief of the citizens of each state from the burden of monopoly . . . was left with the states to deal with." Under existing state law, as long as firms chartered outside of New Jersey were denied the power in their charters to become members of larger combinations, then their efforts to do so could be met with state prosecution. Further, under *Knight*, whether or not chartered in New Jersey, foreign corporations could still be met with Court-approved regulation via *Paul*. The relief called for by the government in *Knight* was already available in the Pennsylvania courts, and was a far more direct procedure—prosecution based on a charter violation—than determining under the Sherman Act whether a restraint or monopoly existed.

In the short run, *Knight* shaped the conflict between corporations and their critics, the broad question of authority to regulate combinations, and the meaning of the commerce clause. In the longer term, its power over the trust problem quickly diminished and its influence as a commerce power benchmark slowly disintegrated. As the first symbol of the fitful course of antitrust law it remains both prominent and problematic today.

For antimonopolists the case speedily conjured their worst nightmare: a shadowy and abstraction-fixated Court was in the pocket of big business stripping the national government of the ability to stop the onward rush of dangerous combinations. Subsequent progressive commentators, eager to destroy the last impediments to the New Deal of the 1930s, likewise too quickly assumed that a weakened Sherman Act meant that trusts would escape regulation altogether.

Relying on a long history of state control over the organization of corporations, the decision contemplated state success against the new giants. Yet, while the legal tools existed to do the job, the political will was rapidly routed by their practical economic influence. The states simply found it lucrative in terms of jobs and revenue to permit domestic corporations to join New Jersey combinations and to relax foreign corporation laws.

Fuller's conception of the distinction between manufacturing and commerce, so tenuous in economic and social terms, so removed from the realities of business intentions, was nevertheless critical to his conception of federalism. The formal line had to be drawn to protect state autonomy. Its implications for the commerce clause frustrated those whose vision empirically forecast a future of huge interstate combinations, obsequious state legislatures, and a crippled Congress. From *Knight* until the 1930s, Fuller's contention that commerce was a logical, categorical concept limited the ability of the Congress to regulate certain kinds of economic activity. Notoriously, for example, in *Adair v. United States* (1908), the Court struck down on interstate commerce grounds a congressional attempt to ban yellow-dog labor contracts in railroads, ruling that no "legal or logical connection" existed between membership in a labor union and interstate commerce.

Considered in the longer term, *Knight*'s significance took on a different shape. Its hold on the trust problem was brief, in large part because its facts were so peculiarly narrow. Almost immediately, the same Court began to support the government in its own half-hearted efforts to bring the combinations under some control. The Court soon sustained Sherman Act prosecutions of pools and associations designed to control the pricing of pipe, railroad rates, and beef. It also upheld prosecutions of holding companies engaged in railroading and oil refining.

Knight's influence in the commerce clause context was more pronounced, in large part because Fuller's clearly defined antebellum position permitted the Court to hold important activities beyond the pale of commerce. Yet, within a few years, two alternative styles of analysis linking local business activity to interstate commerce had emerged that took into account the economic realities of the business process and the failure of the states to meet the challenge. In 1905 the Court announced, through Justice Holmes, that local business activity might be reached by the Sherman Act if it occurred in the "current of commerce." In the *Shreveport Rate Case* (1914) the Court held that local activities directly "affecting commerce" could be prosecuted. The spirit of *Knight* flared for the last time in *Schechter Poultry Corp. v. United States* (1935) and *Carter v. Carter Coal Co.* (1936), but was quickly interred as the New Deal triumphed in *NLRB v. Jones & Laughlin Steel Co.* (1937) and *Wickard v. Filburn* (1942). Empirical commerce analysis dramatically expanded congressional power, and Fuller's prediction came true.

By the late 1990s, the top 17 percent of corporations were collecting 95 percent of all corporate receipts. The largest one tenth of one percent of industrial firms accounted for 75 percent of all industrial sales. The wealthiest corporation, Citicorp, and the largest industrial firm, Ford, together controlled as much wealth as all of the nation's thirteen million proprietorships combined. Under these circumstances, it seems at best irrelevant to label as a failure a decision which in retrospect could not have solved the problem of corporate combination had it gone the other way. If the Court's tenacious commitment to a formalistic antebellum resolution of the issue seems at this date mannered and quaintly antique, the confident progressive antitrust program called for by its critics—empirical, brashly functional, statistical, and "modern" to the core—has hardly proven more effective as a public counterweight to private economic concentration. *United States v. E. C. Knight Co.* stands finally as the first dramatic embodiment of the persistent and perplexing failure of the radical democratic tradition to develop juridical concepts and social strength capable of creating the more equitable sharing of economic power demanded by antimonopolists over a century ago.

Selected Bibliography

Arnold, Thurman W. *The Folklore of Capitalism.* New Haven: Yale University Press, 1937.

Freyer, Tony. *Regulating Big Business: Antitrust in Great Britain and America, 1880–1999.* Cambridge: Cambridge University Press, 1992.

Hurst, James Willard. *Law and Markets in United States History: Different Modes of Bargaining Among Interests.* Madison: University of Wisconsin Press, 1982.

Hurst, James Willard. *The Legitimacy of the Business Corporation in the Law of the United States, 1780–1970.* Charlottesville: University Press of Virginia, 1970.

Letwin, William. *Law and Economic Policy in America: The Evolution of the Sherman Antitrust Act.* New York: Random House, 1954.

McCurdy, Charles W. "The Knight Sugar Decision of 1895 and the Modernization of American Corporation Law, 1869–1903." *Business History Review* 53 (autumn 1979): 304–342.

Regulation in the Public Interest

———◁◦▷———

Robert A. Waller

Emeritus Professor of History
Clemson University

U.S. v. Trans-Missouri Freight Association, 166 U.S. 290 (1897) [U.S. Supreme Court]

◀◦▶ THE CASE IN BRIEF ◀◦▶

Date
1897

Location
Midwestern United States

Court
U.S. Supreme Court

Principal Participants
United States government
Trans-Missouri Freight Association
Associate Justice Rufus W. Peekham

Significance of the Case
The Court held that the Sherman Antitrust Act prohibited all restraints of trade in interstate or foreign commerce, without exception, not just those that were thought to be "unreasonable."

During the late nineteenth century, this nation came to grips with the issue of private gain versus national regulation through action of the Congress, the courts, and the new independent regulatory commissions. Through the legislative, judicial, and administrative processes, the relationship between railroad empires and the public interest was established. Among these responses was the decision of the United States Supreme Court regarding the conduct of the Trans-Missouri Freight Association, a voluntary pooling arrangement for rail traffic west of the Missouri River. This case is a subject of great controversy in achieving balance between companies and consumers.

The congressional expression of the relationship between the nation's major businesses and the consumers' needs took a principal form in the Interstate Commerce Act of 1887. In this early legislation, proponents established the need to accomplish three essential goals: (1) to prohibit charging more for the short haul than for the long haul, (2) to publish the interstate commerce carriers' rates and forbid charging more or less than the published schedules, and (3) to prohibit pooling of services by competing railroads. The administration of these principles was placed in the hands of a commission, but enforcement was the province of the courts. It was expected that publicity would deter the transportation giants from practices inimical to the consumer's interest. The five-person commission proceeded to enforce the act vigorously, but soon judicial roadblocks were encountered, for compliance was not always forthcoming without resort to the court procedures provided in the law.

The companion legislation, the Sherman Antitrust Act, was passed by the Congress in 1890. In response to public resistance to monopoly practices, the law forbad businesses, in very general and sweeping terms, from engaging in unfair practices. This legislation prohibited every contract, combination, and conspiracy in restraint of trade in both interstate and foreign commerce. Here again, the provisions were to be enforced by judicial process through the federal courts. Wittingly or unwittingly, the administrative and legislative prerogatives were surrendered to still a third branch of government. Problems were to arise.

The issue became the interpretation of both pieces of legislation. Were these acts intended to prohibit all restraints of trade or only those deemed to be unreasonable? The United States Supreme Court first dealt with these alternatives in the *Trans-Missouri Freight* case in 1897. In a 5-4 decision, the majority held that the Sherman Act prohibited all restraints of trade in interstate or foreign commerce, without exception, not just those that were deemed unreasonable at common law.

The case arose when the federal government brought suit to dissolve an association of midwestern railroads formed for the purpose of fixing rates. For the majority on the Court, Associate Justice Rufus W. Peckham wrote: "A contract . . . that is in restraint of trade or commerce is by the strict language of the act prohibited even though such contract is entered into between competing common carriers by railroad, and only for the purpose of thereby affecting traffic rates for the trans-portation of persons and property." Peckham rejected the contention that rate agreements were authorized by the Interstate Commerce Act. "It may not in terms prohibit [an agreement of this nature], but it is far from conferring either directly or by implication any power to make it." Ostensibly, there was no conflict between the Interstate Commerce Act and the Sherman Act.

Justice Edward D. White and three others dissented. The minority opinion argued that the act prohibited only unreasonable restraints of trade. Utilizing the concept of a "rule of reason," White argued that "The plain intention of the law was to protect the liberty of contract and freedom of trade. Will this intention not be frustrated by a construction, which, if it does not destroy, at least gravely impairs the liberty of the individual to contract and the freedom of trade? If the rule of reason no longer determines the validity of contracts upon which trade depends and results, what became of the liberty of the citizen or of the freedom of trade?" This interpretation became the majority opinion in *Standard Oil of New Jersey v. U.S.* (1911) case and allowed a distinction between "good" and "bad" trusts. For the time, however, the signal being sent by the nation's highest court was unclear if not chaotic in its result.

The definition of "public interest" frequently lies in the eyes of the beholder. In the American experience, a resort to boards or commissions has been a principal vessel to navigate the narrow channel of quasi-administrative, quasi-legislative, and quasi-judicial function. The Interstate Commerce Act was a major national effort to reconcile competing interests using the commission approach as typified by the late nineteenth-century progressive desire for informed, disinterested administration. In the school of trial and error to achieve that balance, *U.S. v. Trans-Missouri Freight* was a temporary setback. Subsequent legislation in the form of the Hepburn Act of 1906 rectified that interruption.

Selected Bibliography

Harbeson, Robert W. "Railroads and Regulation, 1877–1916: Conspiracy or Public Interest?" *Journal of Economic History* 27 (June 1967): 230–242.

Martin, Albro. "The Troubled Subject of Railroad Regulation in the Gilded Age—A Reappraisal." *Journal of American History* 61 (September 1974): 339–371.

McGraw, Thomas K. "Regulation in America: A Review Article." *Business History Review* 49 (summer 1975): 159–183.

Commerce and National Police Powers

—◄o►—

Fred D. Ragan

Emeritus Professor of History
East Carolina University

Charles F. Champion, Appt. v. John C. Ames, 188 U.S. 321 (1903) [U.S. Supreme Court]

◄o► THE CASE IN BRIEF ◄o►

Date
1903

Location
Illinois

Court
U.S. Supreme Court

Principal Participants
Charles Champion
John Ames
Associate Justice John Marshall Harlan

Significance of the Case
The so-called "Lottery Case" gave the federal government broad regulatory discretion under the guise of the tax power and the commerce clause.

Dubbed "the Lottery Case," *Champion v. Ames* reflected the growing willingness of the Court at the beginning of the twentieth century to sustain Congress's use of its delegated powers to remedy social and economic ills. All parties fully realized the significance of the case, and the justices scheduled arguments on no less than five occasions. At issue was an 1895 statute prohibiting interstate transportation of lottery tickets to safeguard public morals. If the Court sustained Congress's power, it would take an important step toward creating federal police powers to protect the health, welfare, safety, and morals of the national community.

The government charged Charles F. Champion and companions with conspiring to ship, by Wells Fargo Express Company, Paraguayan lottery tickets from Texas to California. Arrested in Chicago to assure appearance at trial in Texas, Champion sued for a writ of *habeas corpus*.

The defense, led by the distinguished advocate William D. Guthrie, developed three lines of argument. First, lottery tickets were not commerce within the meaning of the Constitution since they had been used for "worthy" public purposes before drafting the Constitution and since. The Constitution, Guthrie argued, meant today what it did when it was adopted. He also compared lottery tickets to insurance policies because both were essentially tickets of chance. Second, Guthrie asserted that Congress's power to regulate commerce did not include the power to prohibit. For if Congress had such a power, it would convert the "limited power to regulate commerce, [into] the unlimited power to regulate all intercourse, including public morals." Finally, he conceded that the power to prohibit existed but not at the national level. If states desired to exclude "noxious articles," the power was "absolute." This police power knew only two limitations: a state could not prohibit articles of commerce; nor could it prohibit importation of noxious articles when they remained in the "original package." But when the states had not acted, Guthrie recognized no limitation upon the right of his client. Although he won a minority of four justices to his position, Guthrie failed to convince the majority.

Justice John Marshall Harlan delivered the majority opinion. After a review of commerce cases, he embraced John Marshall's sweeping language to define commerce and Congress's power over it. Commerce encompassed "navigation, intercourse, communication, traffic, the transit of persons, and the transmission of messages by telegraphs." Congress's power over commerce "is plenary, complete in itself"; and in determining the nature of regulations, Congress has a "large discretion" which is not limited because the courts, in their opinions, do not think the "best or most effective" method has been employed. Guthrie's comparison of lottery tickets to insurance policies found little sympathy with Harlan. He contended that the "tickets were the subject of traffic; they could have been sold; and the holder was assured that the company would pay to him the amount of the prize drawn." Consequently, the tickets were commerce and "subjects of commerce, and the regulation of the carriage of such tickets . . . by independent carriers is a regulation of commerce among the . . . states."

Next Harlan addressed the argument that Congress could regulate but not prohibit commerce. Drawing upon *McCulloch v. Maryland*, Harlan emphasized that Congress must be allowed a choice of means, especially involving this "particular kind of commerce." If the state governments can take into view the nature of the evil to be suppressed, why could Congress not insure that commerce among the states "shall not be polluted"? Congress "no doubt shared" with the Court the view that the "suppression of nuisances injurious to public health or morality is among the most important duties of government." To the argument that such power denied Champion his Fifth Amendment liberty, Harlan emphasized the limits of such liberty. It meant the right to be free to live and work where one desired, to earn a livelihood by lawful means, and to follow interest by engaging in all contracts which may be proper. Liberty did not include the right to "introduce into commerce . . . an element that will be confessedly injurious to the public morals."

Also, Harlan rejected Tenth Amendment arguments. The issue here, he countered, was the use of a power "expressly delegated to Congress." Congress had not interfered with lotteries conducted "exclusively within the limits of any state. . . ." But as a "state may, for the purpose of guarding the morals of its own people, forbid all sales of lottery tickets . . . , so Congress, for the purpose of guarding the people of the United States against the 'widespread pestilence of lotteries' and to protect the commerce . . . may prohibit" the lottery traffic. Somewhat defensively, Harlan maintained that Congress only "supplemented" the action of states trying to protect public morals. "We should hesitate long before adjudging that an evil of such appalling character, carried on through interstate commerce, cannot be met and crushed by the only power competent to that end." After so sweeping a statement, Harlan hedged. Conceding that Congress could not use its power in an arbitrary manner, he nevertheless refused "to lay down a rule for determining in advance" every case that may arise.

The dissent, written by Chief Justice Melvin Fuller for himself and Justices David Brewer, George Shiras, and Rufus Peckham, drew heavily from defense counsel arguments. Fuller feared for the traditional division of power within the Union. If Congress could prohibit lottery tickets, he asked, what were the limits to its power? Adopting a position "inconsistent with the views of the framers," Fuller asserted that the majority had taken a "long step in the direction of wiping out all traces of state lines, and the creation of a centralized government."

All parties recognized the importance of this case. Fuller, expressing his reverence for the existing federalism, bitterly attacked the decision because it created national police powers. Harlan and the majority seemed to recognize the need for an enlarged role for Congress if problems of an increasingly complex industrial so-

ciety were to be effectively managed. Certainly, these men could not have foreseen that later generations would find in the commerce clause the power to prohibit individuals from growing food crops and discriminating against one another. Coupled with *McCray v. U.S.* (1904), the majority opinion in the Lottery Case gave the national government broad new regulatory police powers under the guise of the tax power and the commerce clause.

Selected Bibliography

Semonche, John E. *Charting the Future: The Supreme Court Responds to a Changing Society, 1890–1920.* Westport, CT: Greenwood Press, 1978.

Busting Trusts with More Backbone Than a Banana

David A. Walker

Department of History
University of Northern Iowa

Northern Securities Company v. United States, 193 U.S. 197 (1904)
Standard Oil Company of New Jersey et al. v. United States, 221 U.S. 1 (1911) [U.S. Supreme Court]

◄०► THE CASE IN BRIEF ◄०►

Dates
   1904, 1911

Location
   Minnesota
   New Jersey

Court
   U.S. Supreme Court

Principal Participants
   United States government
   Northern Securities Company
   Standard Oil of New Jersey
   Justices Oliver Wendell Holmes Jr.
   Justice Edward D. White
   Justice John Marshall Harlan

Significance of the Case
   The Northern Securities and Standard Oil decisions established the constitutionality of the Sherman Antitrust Act of 1890.

Theodore Roosevelt appointed Oliver Wendell Holmes Jr. to the U.S. Supreme Court in August 1902. He did so after being assured by Senator Henry Cabot Lodge that Holmes would support the administration's position on trusts. Roosevelt based his decision on the fact that many of Holmes's Supreme Judicial Court of Massachusetts opinions had been roundly criticized by corporate and railroad executives. But when the new associate justice defied the president in 1904 and offered a vigorous dissent in *Northern Securities Company v. United States*, an outraged Roosevelt reportedly commented, "I could carve out of a banana a judge with more backbone than [Holmes]."

The so-called "trust cases" of the early twentieth century arose in an attempt to define enforcement powers provided by the Sherman Antitrust Act (1890), the oldest and perhaps most important antitrust law in American history. In this legislation, Congress was responding to growing public pressure to control the rapidly expanding power of gigantic corporations that emerged as the American economy assumed world industrial leadership. Legislators sought to protect open competition, economic opportunity, efficiency, and reasonable consumer prices. The near unanimous, bipartisan final vote in July 1890 satisfied public clamor without seriously threatening big business entrepreneurs. In straightforward fashion, the law stated: "Every contract, combination in the form of trust or otherwise, . . . in restraint of trade or commerce among the several States, or with foreign nations, is hereby declared to be illegal. . . ." Enforcement was left to a weak, understaffed, and underfunded Department of Justice.

In the most significant of the few suits brought under the Sherman Act before 1904, the Supreme Court in *United States v. E. C. Knight Co.* (1895) ruled that Congress could regulate commerce but not manufacturing. Since the sugar trust in *Knight* was involved primarily in manufacture, it was exempt from federal prosecution. This decision opened the door to an explosion of corporate mergers.

James J. Hill, J. P. Morgan, and E. H. Harriman represented the cutting edge of powerful economic forces controlling sectors of the American economy at the turn of the new century. Hill had built a transportation empire with his Great Northern Railroad, running from St. Paul to Seattle. His closest competitor, the Northern Pacific Railroad, had been forced into bankruptcy in 1893. Over the next three years the Northern Pacific (NP) reorganized under Morgan as a representative of the bondholders. Morgan turned to Hill, whom he greatly admired, in hopes of turning the Northern Pacific into a profitable venture. In the spirit of a "community of interest," the Great Northern provided collateral for a new issue of Northern Pacific bonds. In return, Hill received half of the NP capital stock and a majority of seats on the board of directors. Minnesota's challenge of the agreement was upheld by the U.S. Supreme Court in March 1896 in *Pearsall v. Great Northern Ry.* on the grounds that a state statute prohibited a Minnesota railroad (Great Northern) to "consolidate with, lease, or purchase, or in any way become owner of, or control any other railroad corporation, . . . which owns or controls a parallel or competing line." Thereupon, as private investors, Hill and his associates purchased ten percent control of the NP and retained their alliance with Morgan.

In 1900, the Hill-Morgan combine sought access to markets east of the Mississippi River by purchasing the Chicago, Burlington, and Quincy line. This brought them into direct competition with E. H. Harriman's Union Pacific Railroad. When Harriman's offer to join in purchase of the Burlington Road was rebuffed, he retaliated by quietly seeking stock control over the Northern Pacific. With Morgan in Europe and Hill in Seattle, the Harriman coup was nearly successful. The bitter and potentially devastating confrontation was resolved when all agreed to give Harriman influential representation on the NP board. Resolution of the Burlington dispute led directly to incorporation of the Northern Securities Company, a holding company organized in New Jersey on November 12, 1901, with an authorized capital of $400 million. Great Northern and Northern Pacific shareholders exchanged their stock for stock in the new firm where Hill controlled 55 percent of the shares.

Almost immediately, Minnesota Governor Samuel R. Van Sant invited the governors of surrounding states to a conference that unanimously condemned the merger as stifling competition. Early in 1902, Minnesota's attorney general filed suit to dissolve Northern Securities. Before the Supreme Court heard oral arguments, however, U.S. attorney general Philander C. Knox announced that the federal government would shortly take Northern Securities to court. President Roosevelt, abandoning his tactic of influencing public opinion against "bad" trusts, had made the decision apparently alone, without seeking advice from his cabinet or his closest advisor Elihu Root. Roosevelt justified his action when he said "large corporations . . . though organized in one state, always do business in many states, often doing very little business in the state where they are incorporated. There is utter lack of uniformity in the state laws about them. . . ."

The legal battle began in March 1902 when a petition was filed in St. Paul before the Eighth Circuit Court against Northern Securities, Great Northern, Northern Pacific, and numerous individuals including Hill and Morgan. The suit alleged that the holding company was not an investment firm but "a mere depository, custodian, holder, and trustee of the stocks" of two railroads. It owned the capital stock of parallel and competing railroads "pursuant to a combination or conspiracy in restraint of trade." The Hill-Morgan counsel centered a defense on the grounds that Northern Securities existed to buy stocks, not to manage railroads. In fact, each railroad operated independently through its own board of directors. The railroad lawyers also argued that the holding company had been established under the protection of New Jersey and hence was beyond the realm of federal control. On April 9, 1903, the four members of the circuit court quickly and without dissent declared Northern Securities an illegal combination, ordering it to cease the following activities: acquiring additional stock, exercising control over either railroad, or paying dividends to stockholders. Finally, the Securities Company was "permitted"—not mandated—to return to former shareholders any of the railroad stocks it had transferred to it.

The case moved quickly to the U.S. Supreme Court under the terms of the 1903 Expediting Act. Oral argument took place in December 1903, and the final judgment was rendered March 14, 1904. Justice John Marshall Harlan spoke for the five-member majority by endorsing the circuit court's conclusions. He made it clear that "restraint of trade" meant direct interference with competition. Harlan felt that the holding company was a transparent sham, violating the Sherman Act by its mere existence. Its "principal, if not the sole, object" was to prevent "all competition between the two lines . . . [and to] see to it that no competition is tolerated." The majority was formed only when Justice David J. Brewer, who disagreed with portions of Harlan's argument, wrote a concurring opinion stressing that the Sherman Act should apply solely to an "unreasonable" restraint of trade such as the Northern Securities Company.

Justice Edward D. White challenged Harlan by concluding that, although freedom to use property was limited and could be restricted by government to preserve competition, there is "no foundation for the proposition that government [has] power to limit the quantity and character of property which may be acquired and owned." This was a stock transfer, not a railroad case. Congressional regulatory power did not include the acquisition and ownership of stock. In concurrence with Brewer, White stated that he believed the Sherman Act applied only to unreasonable restraints of trade but, unlike Brewer, White found nothing "unreasonable" about Northern Securities.

Privately, describing the Sherman Act as "a humbug based on economic ignorance and incompetence," Justice Holmes wrote the case's most important dissent. Grounded in his scholarly knowledge of common law, Holmes saw the formation of Northern Securities as having little impact upon competition. Stock transaction was "an ordinary incident of property and personal freedom." What a merger did and how it acted, not the mere fact of its size, determined legality. "Size in the case of railroads is an inevitable incident . . . every railroad monopolizes in a popular sense the trade of some area." Demonstrating that he completely divorced personal political opinion from judicial responsibility, Holmes penned this often quoted language: "Great cases like hard cases make bad law. For great cases are called great not by reason of their real importance in shaping the law of the future but because of some accident of immediate overwhelming interest which appeals to the feelings and distorts the judgment."

Roosevelt was deeply troubled by Holmes's dissent. He "should have been an ideal man on the bench. . . . As a matter of fact he has been a bitter disappointment." But, overall, Roosevelt portrayed the suit as "one of the greatest achievements of my administration. . . . I look upon it with great pride, for through it we emphasized . . . the fact that the most powerful men in this country were held to accountability before the law." Like the president, the Supreme Court's decision was politically popular, but it did not change railroad dominance in the northern tier of states, nor did it end cooperation among Hill, Morgan, and Harriman.

Roosevelt's antitrust reputation was based as much on force of personality as on legal activity. William H. Taft, the president succeeding Roosevelt, proved to be a more unrelenting crusader against monopolies, filing seventy antitrust suits in four years, compared with Roosevelt's forty suits in seven years. Several important cases were carried over from the Roosevelt to the Taft administrations. In November 1906, the federal government brought suit against the Standard Oil Company of New Jersey, a holding company formed in 1909, together with sixty-five subsidiaries and powerful individuals including John D. and William Rockefeller. Standard Oil's actions were abusive and unfair. The company accepted rebates from shippers, portrayed bogus subsidiaries as independent firms, demanded cutthroat prices, bribed, intimidated, and committed industrial espionage. The circuit court unanimously ruled that the company had violated the Sherman Act in its control of over 75 percent of the petroleum industry and, therefore, should be dissolved. Upon appeal, the case was first argued before the Supreme Court in March 1910. It was reargued in January 1911 because of the death of Justice Brewer and the absence of Justice William H. Moody. A unanimous decision was handed down May 15, 1911.

Speaking for the Court, Edward White, recently elevated to the chief justiceship, sustained the lower court and formalized the "rule of reason" that he and Justice Brewer had introduced in earlier cases. White wrote that the Sherman Act protected freedom of commerce and did not prohibit all contracts and agreements that might appear to restrain trade but were reasonable based upon a common law definition. The Court judged Standard Oil's actions "unreasonable" because its "intent and purpose [was] to maintain dominancy over the oil industry, not as a result of normal methods . . . , but by new means of combination . . . in order that greater power might be added than would otherwise have arisen. . . ." The holding company was ordered to divest itself of the subsidiaries within six months and cease to exercise control over them. Although part of a unanimous Court, Justice Harlan bitterly opposed the new doctrine as "judicial legislation." The majority justices, Harlan intoned, "not only upset the long settled interpretation of the act, but . . . usurped the constitutional functions of the legislative branch. . . ." For Harlan, the clear intention of Congress was to prohibit every restraint of trade; he saw no statutory freedom

for courts to exercise their judgment as to the "reasonableness" of monopolies.

On May 29, 1911, the Court upheld the "rule of reason" in a unanimous decision against American Tobacco Company, a conglomerate formed by James B. Duke in 1904. Within a few weeks the justices found that two of the most powerful commercial enterprises had created a monopoly that amounted to undue and unreasonable restraint of trade.

The *Standard Oil* and *American Tobacco* decisions played an important role in the 1912 presidential campaign and provided the genesis of the Clayton Act and the Federal Trade Commission Act two years later. The rule of reason furnished essential flexibility and remained the basis for future antitrust action for two decades. For a quarter century after passage of the Sherman Act, the Supreme Court had not been called upon to rule directly on its constitutionality. But, following the progression of decisions from *E. C. Knight* (1895) and culminating in *Standard Oil* (1911) and *American Tobacco* (1911), the general constitutionality of the statute was settled beyond a reasonable doubt. The country now had a body of law to maintain reasonable competition among its economic giants. Clearly antitrust activity was pursued with a backbone sturdier than a banana.

Selected Bibliography

Bickel, Alexander M., and Benno C. Schmidt Jr. *The Judiciary and Responsible Government, 1910–21.* New York: Macmillan, 1984.

Chernow, Ron. *Titan: The Life of John D. Rockefeller Sr.* New York: Random House, 1998.

Fiss, Owen M. *Troubled Beginnings of the Modern State, 1888–1910.* New York: Macmillan, 1993.

Letwin, William. *Law and Economic Policy in America: The Evolution of the Sherman Antitrust Act.* New York: Random House, 1965.

Semonche, John E. *Charting the Future: The Supreme Court Responds to a Changing Society, 1890–1920.* Westport, CT: Greenwood Press, 1978.

Strouse, Jean. *Morgan, American Financier.* New York: Random House, 1999.

Thorelli, Hans B. *The Federal Antitrust Policy, Origination of an American Tradition.* Baltimore: Johns Hopkins University Press, 1955.

The Wagner Act and the Constitutional Crisis of 1937

———◁◦▷———

Richard C. Cortner

Department of Political Science
University of Arizona

National Labor Relations Board v. Jones & Laughlin Steel Corporation,
301 U.S. 1 (1937) [U.S. Supreme Court]

◁◦▷ THE CASE IN BRIEF ◁◦▷

Date
1937

Location
Pennsylvania

Court
U.S. Supreme Court

Principal Participants
National Labor Relations Board
Jones & Laughlin Steel Corporation
Chief Justice Charles Evans Hughes

Significance of the Case
In affirming the extension of congressional power in the regulation of local and intrastate activities that affected interstate commerce, the Supreme Court helped abort a plan by the Roosevelt administration to "pack" the Court.

In 1935, the Jones & Laughlin Steel Corporation was the fourth-largest steel producer in the United States, with gross assets of over $181 million, and the corporation employed twenty-two thousand workers at its plants at South Pittsburgh and Aliquippa, Pennsylvania. Beginning in July 1935, Jones & Laughlin systematically began to discharge from its workforce the ten leaders of the Amalgamated Association of Iron, Steel, and Tin Workers who had organized a local of that American Federation of Labor (AFL) union at its Aliquippa plant. Jones & Laughlin justified the discharges on the basis of relatively trivial infractions of company rules by the workers, but the elimination of the local union of the Amalgamated Association was the readily apparent motive for the company's actions. Like the steel industry as a whole, the Jones & Laughlin Steel Corporation was adamantly opposed to the unionization of its employees, and the company had successfully resisted unionization through its tight control of its company town of Aliquippa and the intimidation of union organizers and members by its private police force. Indeed, the company's effectiveness in preventing the unionization of its work force led union organizers to refer to Aliquippa during the 1930s as "Little Siberia."

Prior to the 1930s, the firing of the ten union leaders by Jones & Laughlin would have been a private matter between the company and the discharged men, but the election of Franklin D. Roosevelt as president in 1932 and the initiation of his New Deal programs had resulted by 1935 in revolutionary changes in the law governing labor-management relations. On July 5, 1935, only four days before Jones & Laughlin began firing the union leaders at Aliquippa, President Roosevelt signed into law the National Labor Relations Act (NLRA), which had been approved by Congress at the end of June in the face of intense and bitter opposition by business leaders. Popularly known as the Wagner Act, after its chief sponsor in the Congress, Senator Robert F. Wagner of New York, the NLRA committed the national government to protecting the right of workers to organize unions. Under the act's provisions, it was unlawful for an employer to discharge or otherwise discriminate against an employee because of his or her membership in a labor union. Representational elections were also provided for by the act through which a majority of the workers of an employer could vote in favor of being represented by a union for collective bargaining purposes, and, if unionization was supported by a majority of the employees, the union selected would be certified as the exclusive bargaining agent for those employees.

To enforce these provisions, a new administrative agency was created, the National Labor Relations Board (NLRB). The NLRB was empowered to hold representational elections and to certify unions as collective bargaining agents as well as to order employers to cease and desist discharging or discriminating against workers because of their union membership or activities. The Jones & Laughlin Steel Corporation's discharge of the ten men at its Aliquippa plant for union activities was, thus, no longer a private matter between the company and the discharged men. Rather, it had developed into a crucial test of the constitutional power of the national government to impose upon labor-

management relations the policies embodied in the National Labor Relations Act.

To the nation's business leaders, who opposed the NLRA with virtual unanimity, the policies embodied in the act were regarded as a dangerous assault on fundamental values supposedly safeguarded by the Constitution. Immediately following the passage of the NLRA by Congress, therefore, the act was assailed as being patently unconstitutional by many leading industrial and trade associations. Among the leaders of the assault on the NLRB was the American Liberty League. Financed by Du Pont and General Motors, the Liberty League was founded in 1934 to represent the business community in its struggle against many of the policies of Roosevelt's New Deal. In response to the enactment of the NLRA by Congress, the Liberty League organized a National Lawyers Committee under the chairmanship of Earl F. Reed, a prominent attorney for steel corporations, and the lawyers committee issued a report in September 1935 condemning the NLRA as unconstitutional. Signing the Liberty League report, in addition to Earl Reed, were some of the most prominent conservative leaders of the American bar, including James M. Beck, a former U.S. solicitor general, and John W. Davis, also a former solicitor general and an unsuccessful Democratic presidential candidate in 1924.

The Liberty League report found the NLRA invalid under the Constitution on two principal grounds. First, the report noted, the NLRA was based on the power of Congress to regulate interstate commerce under the commerce clause of the Constitution. The Supreme Court had held in numerous cases, however, that under the commerce clause Congress was limited to regulating interstate commerce itself as well as any activities having a direct effect on interstate commerce. Activities having only indirect effects on interstate commerce, the report argued on the other hand, had always been held by the Court to be beyond the legitimate reach of congressional power under the commerce clause. And manufacturing and production enterprises, along with the labor relations associated with such enterprises, were regarded by the Court to involve local activities, having only indirect effects upon interstate commerce, and were thus beyond the reach of congressional power under the commerce clause. The attempt by Congress to regulate the labor relations of industry generally under the NLRA, the Liberty League concluded, thus constituted an unconstitutional attempt to regulate local activities having, if any, only indirect effects on interstate commerce.

In addition, the Liberty League report found that the NLRA violated the due process clause of the Fifth Amendment of the Bill of Rights. Under the due process clause, it was noted, the Supreme Court had held that a "liberty of contract" was protected between employers and employees. Under the liberty of contract doctrine, the Court had held that the terms and conditions of employment should be the result of free contractual relations between employers and employees unburdened by governmental interference. The provisions of the NLRA prohibiting employers from discharging or otherwise discriminating against employees because of union membership, the Liberty League also argued, constituted an unconstitutional invasion of the right of liberty of contract protected by the Fifth Amendment by interfering with the right of employers and employees to determine for themselves the terms and conditions of employment. Considering the NLRA "in the light of our history, the established form of government, and the decisions of our highest Court," the Liberty League report declared, "we have no hesitancy in concluding that it is unconstitutional and that it constitutes a complete departure from our constitutional and traditional theories of government."

Despite this unequivocal condemnation of the NLRA by the Liberty League, the state of constitutional law in the decisions of the Supreme Court was not as clear-cut as the Liberty League report indicated. During the 1930s, the Court in fact had conflicting lines of precedent both under the commerce clause and regarding the doctrine of liberty of contract, and the fate of government policies was largely determined by which line of precedent the Court opted to follow in judging the constitutional validity of those policies. While the Court had held, as the Liberty League noted, that congres-

sional power under the commerce clause did not extend to the regulation of essentially local activities having only indirect effects upon interstate commerce, in other cases the Court had sustained the broad use of the commerce power to regulate essentially local activities. In a series of cases, the Court had, thus, held that if local activities were related to and affected "a constantly recurring stream or current of interstate commerce," Congress could regulate those local activities if their regulation was necessary to the effective regulation of interstate commerce itself. These "stream of commerce" cases were, therefore, precedent for broad uses of congressional power under the commerce clause, while the cases using the direct-indirect effects test as to whether local activities could be regulated under the commerce power supported a much narrower interpretation of the commerce clause, as the Liberty League report emphasized.

The doctrine of liberty of contract, which the Liberty League also charged was violated by the NLRA, had emerged in the decisions of the Supreme Court during the 1890s as a guarantee of the due process clauses of the Constitution. By the 1930s, however, the Court had also sustained significant governmental encroachments upon the liberty of employers and employees to contract freely regarding the terms and conditions of employment. Labor laws limiting the number of hours employees could be required to work had been upheld by the Court by 1920, despite the clear interference of such laws with liberty of contract between employers and employees. And while the Court had earlier invalidated on liberty of contract grounds governmental attempts to protect the right of workers to belong to labor unions, in *Texas & New Orleans Railroad Co. v. Brotherhood of Railway and Steamship Clerks* (1930) the Court upheld the constitutionality of the Railway Labor Act of 1926. The Railway Labor Act prohibited the railroad carriers from discharging or otherwise discriminating against their employees because of union membership and activities, and, in answering an argument that the act thus abridged liberty of contract, the Court held that its earlier decisions, prohibiting governmental protection of the right of workers to organize and belong to unions, were inapplicable to the provisions in that regard in the Railway Labor Act. Since 1923, on the other hand, the Court had maintained that governmental attempts to set minimum wages did violate liberty of contract and that wages should be determined by bargaining between employers and employees, free of governmental interference. As was the case with its commerce clause decisions, during the 1930s the Supreme Court also had lines of conflicting precedent regarding the doctrine of liberty of contract, and the validity of governmental policies interfering with liberty of contract depended on which competing sets of precedent the Court chose to follow.

When the Supreme Court was confronted with the bold and unprecedented uses of national power by President Roosevelt and Congress in implementing the New Deal, the Liberty League report correctly noted, the Court had from 1933 through 1936 nevertheless demonstrated a decided propensity to choose to follow those precedents that narrowed the scope of governmental power over the national economy. The centerpiece of the New Deal's program to resuscitate the nation's industrial economy from 1933 to 1935 was the National Industrial Recovery Act (NIRA), which imposed production controls on industry as well as regulating minimum wages and maximum hours, and guaranteeing the right of workers to organize unions. In *Schechter Poultry Corp. v. United States*, decided in 1935, however, the Supreme Court unanimously declared the NIRA to be unconstitutional in part because it exceeded the reach of congressional power under the commerce clause. As applied to the Schechter Poultry Corporation, Chief Justice Charles Evans Hughes said for the Court, the NIRA went beyond the scope of the power of Congress under the commerce clause because the act reached and regulated essentially local activities that had only indirect effects on interstate commerce.

In the *Schechter* case, the Court thus opted to use the direct-indirect effects formula as the test of the scope of the commerce power of Congress—a formula that narrowed the scope of that power. And the Court emphasized in the *Schechter* case that the direct-indirect effects

formula reflected a fundamental constitutional value. "In determining how far the federal government may go in controlling intrastate transactions upon the ground that they 'affect' interstate commerce," Chief Justice Hughes said, "there is a necessary and well-established distinction between direct and indirect effects." While the difference between local activities having direct or only indirect effects on interstate commerce could be determined only on a case-by-case basis, the chief justice conceded, nevertheless, that "the distinction between direct and indirect effects of intrastate transactions upon interstate commerce must be recognized as a fundamental one, essential to the maintenance of our constitutional system." Without such a limiting distinction imposed on the commerce power of Congress, the Court appeared to be saying, congressional power under the commerce clause might be exercised so as to swallow the power of the states over essentially local activities and thus destroy the constitutional principle of federalism.

The following year the Court once again emphasized that local activities, such as those involved in manufacturing and production enterprises, had only indirect effects on interstate commerce and were thus beyond the reach of the congressional commerce power. In declaring unconstitutional the Bituminous Coal Conservation Act in *Carter v. Carter Coal Co.* (1936), the Court invalidated the act's provisions that were intended to regulate wages and conditions of work in the coal industry, as well as the protection of the right of miners to organize unions. Speaking for the majority of the Court, Justice George Sutherland reiterated the doctrine that production enterprises, such as coal mining and manufacturing, were local activities beyond the scope of the commerce clause and that the labor provisions of the Bituminous Coal Conservation Act were thus unconstitutional. "The employment of men, the fixing of their wages, hours of labor and working conditions, the bargaining in respect to these things," Sutherland said, "whether carried on separately or collectively—each and all constitute intercourse for the purposes of production not of trade. The latter is a thing apart from the relation of employer and employee, which in all producing occupations is purely local in character." "Everything which moves in interstate commerce has had a local origin. Without local production somewhere, interstate commerce, as now carried on, would practically disappear," Sutherland continued. "Nevertheless, the local character of mining, of manufacturing and of crop growing is a fact, and remains a fact, whatever may be done with the products."

Chief Justice Hughes dissented from the Court's decision to invalidate, in addition to the labor provisions of the act, provisions directed at the control of production and the price of coal, but he concurred in the Court's decision that the labor provisions of the act were unconstitutional, suggesting that those provisions could be sustained only if the Constitution were amended to give Congress the power to enact them. If "the people desire to give Congress the power to regulate industries within the States, and the relations of employers and employees in those industries," Hughes said, "they are at liberty to declare their will in the appropriate manner, but it is not for the Court to amend the Constitution by judicial decree."

In both the *Schechter* and *Carter* cases, the Court rejected arguments that the congressional policies invalidated in those cases could be sustained under the "stream of commerce" precedents justifying broader uses of the commerce power than those allowable under the direct-indirect effects formula. And similarly, in construing the doctrine of liberty of contract, the Court in 1936 also appeared to be opting to rely upon precedents justifying a more strict application of that doctrine than that suggested by other cases. In *Morehead v. New York*, dividing 5-4, the Court thus invalidated a New York minimum wage law for women as violative of liberty of contract. Justice Pierce Butler said for the majority that in "making contracts of employment, generally speaking, the parties have the equal right to obtain from each other the best terms they can by private bargaining. Legislative abridgment of that freedom can only be justified by the existence of exceptional circumstances. Freedom of contract is the general rule and restraint the exception."

In *Morehead* as well as other significant decisions of the Supreme Court during the 1930s, it became apparent that the justices were divided into three factions when confronted by the fundamental constitutional issues posed by the New Deal. Justices George Sutherland, Pierce Butler, Willis Van Devanter, and James McReynolds formed a solid conservative bloc on the Court that was rather consistently anti–New Deal. Justices Louis Brandeis, Harlan Fiske Stone, and Benjamin Cardozo, on the other hand, proved to be on the whole sympathetic to New Deal measures. Holding the balance of power on the Court consequently were Chief Justice Hughes and Justice Owen Roberts, whose votes were crucial in many cases in determining whether New Deal measures would be invalidated or upheld. But unfortunately for many important New Deal measures challenged before the Court from 1933 to 1936, either the chief justice or Justice Roberts or both voted with the conservative, anti–New Deal block of justices. Whether that voting trend would continue was crucial to the constitutional fate of the National Labor Relations Act.

Given the Supreme Court's decisions under both the commerce clause and the doctrine of liberty of contract, the National Labor Relations Board was acutely aware of the necessity of using the utmost care in selecting those cases that would test the constitutionality of the act before the Court. If the Court maintained the position that governmental protection of the right of workers to organize unions was prohibited by the doctrine of liberty of contract, the NLRA was, of course, constitutionally invalid as applied to any industry. If, however, the Court were to follow the *Texas & New Orleans Railroad* decision, it was possible the NLRA might be upheld as applied to businesses clearly operating in interstate commerce in a manner similar to the operations of an interstate railroad. The NLRB's first priority was, therefore, to develop test cases involving the application of the NLRA to businesses whose operations plainly involved interstate commerce, and two such cases were eventually developed by the board—cases involving the Associated Press, which transmitted news in interstate commerce, and the Washington, Virginia and Maryland Coach Company, a bus company engaged in the transportation of passengers across state lines.

Given the Supreme Court's decisions in the *Schechter* case and especially the *Carter* case, the validity of the NLRA was most in doubt when applied to manufacturing and production enterprises, since the Court had held that the activities of such enterprises, as well as the labor relations associated with them, were local in nature, having only indirect effects on interstate commerce that Congress could not legitimately regulate under the commerce clause. The NLRB nevertheless also ultimately developed three test cases by enforcing the NLRA against three manufacturing enterprises. The most important of the board's manufacturing cases was the *Jones & Laughlin* case, which the board initiated on April 9, 1936, by finding after an administrative hearing that the company had discharged its employees for engaging in union activities. The company was ordered to cease and desist interfering with its employees' right to organize a union and to reinstate with back pay the ten workers whom it had discharged for their union activity. The board similarly initiated cases against two other manufacturing companies that had violated the NLRA by discharging workers for engaging in union activities—the Fruehauf Trailer Company of Detroit and the Friedman-Harry Marks Clothing Company, a clothing manufacturer in Richmond, Virginia.

Represented by Earl F. Reed, who had chaired the Liberty League's lawyers committee, the Jones & Laughlin Steel Corporation challenged the NLRB's order requiring it to reinstate its ten former employees with back pay, and the Friedman-Harry Marks Clothing Company and the Fruehauf Trailer Company also contested the NLRB orders directed against them. The U.S. circuit courts of appeals, in which the NLRB's orders were initially reviewable, held in each case that the application of the NLRA to these manufacturing enterprises was unconstitutional. In the *Jones & Laughlin* case, using language typical of the decisions in all these cases, the Court of Appeals for the Fifth Circuit thus held that the NLRB "has no jurisdiction over a labor dispute between employer and employees touching the discharge

of laborers in a steel plant, who were engaged only in manufacture. The Constitution does not vest in the federal government the power to regulate the relations as such of employer and employee in production and manufacture."

While the NLRB uniformly lost the cases involving the application of the NLRA to manufacturing enterprises in the courts of appeals, those courts did uphold the application of the act to the Associated Press and the Washington, Virginia and Maryland Coach Company, since the latter were clearly operating in interstate commerce. The NLRB and the Associated Press and the Washington, Virginia and Maryland Coach Company appealed the cases they had lost in the courts of appeals to the U.S. Supreme Court, with the result that five cases testing the constitutionality of the NLRA were approaching the Court by the fall of 1936. The Court granted the appeals in all the cases, and the cases were scheduled for decision during the spring of 1937.

Franklin D. Roosevelt had in the meantime been overwhelmingly reelected president in the fall of 1936, and immediately following the election, he ordered the consideration of means by which the Supreme Court could be eliminated as a roadblock to the implementation of his New Deal policies. Not only the NLRA but also the Social Security Act of 1935 was facing a crucial constitutional test before the Court, and Roosevelt was apparently convinced the time had come to obtain a Supreme Court that would uphold the kind of national power over the economy deemed necessary by the president and the New Deal Congress. In acting on that conviction, however, Roosevelt precipitated the gravest constitutional crisis witnessed by the nation since the Civil War.

On February 5, 1937, Roosevelt announced that he was forwarding to Congress legislation that would authorize the president to appoint to the Supreme Court an additional justice for each of the incumbent justices who had reached the age of seventy but had failed to retire—up to a maximum of six additional justices. Justifying the "court-packing plan," as the measure was soon called, Roosevelt initially ingenuously suggested that the Court was behind in its work and that new, younger justices would help the Court to keep pace with its workload.

Despite the apparent overwhelming endorsement of the president and the New Deal by the public in the election of 1936, the reception of the court-packing plan by the public and Congress was decidedly unenthusiastic, and a bitter and divisive political battle over the plan was soon underway. The opponents of the measure were aided considerably when Chief Justice Hughes, in a letter to the Senate Judiciary Committee endorsed also by Justices Brandeis and Van Devanter, refuted Roosevelt's initial contention that the Court was behind in its work. Since Congress had given the Court almost total discretionary power in 1925 to decide which cases to accept, Hughes pointed out, the Court had been able to manage its workload. And additional justices, he noted, were unlikely to make the Court more efficient in disposing of cases, since additional justices would require the consultation and exchange of views with more individuals as the Court performed its work.

The Hughes letter appeared to place the Court itself among the ranks of the opponents of the court-packing plan, and it undoubtedly aided the opposition to the plan. The debate over the plan nevertheless continued in Congress and in the country at large during the spring of 1937 as the cases testing the constitutionality of the NLRA were argued before the Court. And Roosevelt's attack on the Court via the court-packing plan made these cases a crucial test of conflicting conceptions of the scope of national power over the economic system and potential turning points of profound importance in American constitutional development.

While Chief Justice Hughes's letter to the Senate Judiciary Committee undoubtedly bolstered opponents of the court-packing plan, the decisions of the Court during the spring of 1937 further diminished support for the plan. On March 29, the Court decided *West Coast Hotel v. Parrish* and, by a 5-4 vote, upheld the validity of a state minimum wage law for women. Since Justice Owen Roberts had voted only a year previously with the majority in the *Morehead* case to invalidate such a law under the doctrine

of liberty of contract and yet joined the majority in the *Parrish* case to uphold such a law, his behavior was soon being humorously referred to as "the switch in time that saved nine." To the public at large, Roberts's change of his position on minimum wages was attributed to the court-packing plan, but in reality he had voted to sustain the minimum wage in the *Parrish* case before President Roosevelt announced the plan in February.

The principal shift of constitutional doctrine in the spring of 1937, however, involved not just Justice Roberts but Chief Justice Hughes as well, and that shift was made apparent when the Court upheld on April 12 the constitutionality of the National Labor Relations Act in all five of the cases pending before it, including the crucial case of *NLRB v. Jones & Laughlin Steel Corporation*. Although both the chief justice and Justice Roberts had joined in the holding in *Carter v. Carter Coal Company* only a year previously that production and manufacturing enterprises, as well as the labor relations associated with those enterprises, were local in nature with only indirect effects upon interstate commerce, both joined Justices Brandeis, Stone, and Cardozo in the *Jones & Laughlin* case in upholding the constitutional validity under the commerce clause of the NLRA's application to just such enterprises.

Speaking for the majority of the Court in the *Jones & Laughlin* case, Chief Justice Hughes noted that the purpose of the NLRA was to guarantee the right of workers to organize into unions and to thereby reduce the number of strikes that disrupted interstate commerce. And if a strike occurred in Jones & Laughlin's Aliquippa steel plant, even though only manufacturing activities were involved, he noted, "it is idle to say that the effect would be indirect or remote. It is obvious that it would be immediate and might be catastrophic." "Because there may be but indirect and remote effects upon interstate commerce in connection with a host of local enterprises throughout the country," Hughes continued, "it does not follow that other industrial activities do not have such a close and intimate relation to interstate commerce as to make the presence of industrial strife a matter of the most urgent national concern. When industries organize themselves on a national scale, making their relation to interstate commerce the dominant factor in their activities, how can it be maintained that their industrial labor relations constitutes a forbidden field into which Congress may not enter when it is necessary to protect interstate commerce from the paralyzing consequences of industrial war? We have often said that interstate commerce itself is a practical conception. It is equally true that interferences with that commerce must be appraised by a judgment that does not ignore experience."

Having sustained the NLRA as a legitimate enactment under the commerce power of Congress, Chief Justice Hughes also rejected the liberty of contract argument against the act's validity. The NLRA did not interfere with an employer's right to hire or discharge employees, Hughes said, but the "employer may not, under the cover of that right, intimidate or coerce its employees with respect to their self-organization and representation."

Following its decisions in the *Jones & Laughlin* and the other NLRA cases, the Court also sustained the validity of the Social Security Act, with the result that the Court had finally conceded that the federal government did in fact possess sufficient national power to regulate effectively the economic system. Having sustained the contentions of President Roosevelt and the New Dealers on this crucial point, the Court's decisions also diminished support for congressional passage of the court-packing plan, which was now increasingly viewed as unnecessary. Further reducing the court-packing plan's chances of passage was the announcement on May 18 of Justice Willis Van Devanter's retirement from the Court. Roosevelt was thus assured of his first appointment to the Court, while the departure of Van Devanter removed from the bench one of the New Deal's most hardline opponents. Although the fight over the court-packing plan continued on into the summer of 1937, the Court's reversal of its position on crucial issues of the constitutional power of the national government regarding the economy and Van Devanter's departure presaged the plan's ultimate demise in the Congress.

While he thus ultimately lost the battle over the court-packing plan in Congress, President

Roosevelt always maintained he had won the larger war over the legitimacy of the regulation of the economy by the national government. And in a real sense he was correct, since the *Jones & Laughlin* decision marked the abandonment by the Supreme Court of its role as censor of socioeconomic policies adopted by the elected branches of the government. Justice Van Devanter's retirement in 1937 was only the beginning of a transformation of the personnel on the Court, and by the early 1940s, a majority of the Court were Roosevelt appointees. And the members of the "Roosevelt Court" made certain through their decisions that henceforth judgments as to the wisdom of governmental regulation of economic affairs would be left to the elected branches of government. Having abandoned that role, however, the Court soon began concentrating on issues related to civil rights and civil liberties, a role that has continued to characterize the Court to the present. The beginning of modern constitutional development with its focus upon civil rights and civil liberties is therefore usually identified with the Court's decision in the *Jones & Laughlin* case in 1937.

While the *Jones & Laughlin* case thus had a profound effect on the reorientation of American constitutional law after 1937, it also had an important effect on labor-management relations in American industry. The upholding of the NLRA by the Supreme Court resulted in a massive unionization of American industry, since the right to organize unions was now effectively protected by the national government. The impact of the decision upon the Jones & Laughlin Steel Corporation was consequently one that the company shared with industry generally. Under the decision of the Court, the ten discharged Jones & Laughlin workers were reinstated with back pay by the company. And shortly after the Court's decision, the Jones & Laughlin Steel Corporation recognized the Steel Workers Organizing Committee, an affiliate of the Congress of Industrial Organizations (CIO), as the exclusive bargaining agent of its employees. "Little Siberia" thus ceased to exist at Aliquippa, Pennsylvania.

Following its decision in the *Jones & Laughlin* case, the Supreme Court repeatedly held that the scope of congressional power under the commerce clause included the regulation of not only interstate transactions but also local or intrastate activities that affected interstate commerce either directly or indirectly. Under its post-1937 commerce clause decisions, the Court thus left any limitation of the commerce power largely to Congress and the electoral process rather than to judicially imposed limitations, as had characterized the pre-1937 era.

In the 1990s, however, the Rehnquist Court again began to impose restrictions on the scope of the commerce power. Under the Tenth Amendment, the court held, the states retained a measure of governmental autonomy that could not be diminished by Congress under the commerce clause. Employing this reasoning in 1997, for example, the Court thus invalidated the requirement that state and local law enforcement officers conduct background checks of prospective handgun purchasers under the Brady Handgun Violence Prevention Act of 1993. The Court has additionally ruled that for local or intrastate activities to be validly regulated by Congress under the commerce clause, the effects of such activities on commerce must be "substantial." And the Court ruled in 1995 that the effects on commerce of the possession of firearms in school zones were insufficiently substantial to sustain the validity under the commerce clause of the Gun Free School Zone Act of 1990.

The Court has therefore again begun displaying a propensity to impose some limitations on the commerce power in contrast to its decisions following the *Jones & Laughlin* case. There has yet appeared, however, no disposition on the part of the Court to impose the kind of substantial limitations on congressional power under the commerce clause to regulate the national economy that prevailed prior to the Court's decision of the *Jones & Laughlin* case in 1937.

Selected Bibliography

Baker, Leonard. *Back to Back: The Duel Between FDR and the Supreme Court.* New York: Macmillan, 1967.

Bernstein, Irving. *The New Deal Collective Bargaining Policy.* Berkeley: University of California Press, 1950.

Cortner, Richard C. *The Wagner Act Cases.* Knoxville: University of Tennessee Press, 1964.

———. *The Jones & Laughlin Case.* New York: Knopf, 1970.

Irons, Peter H. *The New Deal Lawyers.* Princeton, NJ: Princeton University Press, 1982.

Jackson, Robert H. *The Struggle for Judicial Supremacy.* New York: Knopf, 1941.

Mason, Alpheus T. *Harlan Fiske Stone: Pillar of the Law.* New York: Viking, 1956.

The "Indigent" Migrant

—◄◦►—

Joseph Glidewell

Elberton, Georgia

Edwards v. California, 314 U.S. 160 (1941) [U.S. Supreme Court]

◄◦► THE CASE IN BRIEF ◄◦►

Date
1941–1942

Location
California

Court
U.S. Supreme Court

Principal Participants
Fred F. Edwards
State of California
Justice James Byrnes

Significance of the Case
The case established the right of every citizen to move freely within the United States without interference by the states. "Indigence" could not be a source of rights nor a reason for denying them.

The right of Americans to move from state to state when they choose has always been, according to one Supreme Court Justice, "an incident of national citizenship." However, it took an "indigent migrant American citizen" to establish this right for future travelers in the United States.

This case, known as *Edwards v. California,* arose when Fred F. Edwards of Marysville, California, left his home in December 1939 for Spur, Texas, with the intention of bringing back to Marysville his wife's brother, Frank Duncan, a citizen of the United States and a legal resident of Texas. On January 1, 1942, Edwards, along with his brother-in-law and his family, left Texas; they reached Marysville on January 5. Six days after they arrived Duncan applied to the Federal Farm Security Administration for prenatal aid for his wife. However, from the time he entered California for a period of about two weeks, Duncan was unemployed. This put Edwards, the person who had brought Duncan into California, in violation of California Statute 2615, which stated: "Every person, firm, or corporation or officer or agent thereof that brings or assists in bringing into the state any indigent person who is not a resident of the state, knowing him to be an indigent, is guilty of a misdemeanor."

A complaint was filed against Edwards and he was tried, convicted, and received a six-month sentence (suspended) in the county jail. Edwards appealed his sentence to the Superior Court of Yuba County, California, where, after reviewing the case, the court upheld the decision as a valid police power of the state of California, although the Superior Court regarded the validity of the law as "questionable."

At this stage Edwards had no higher state court to which to appeal. Therefore, the appeals process was carried into federal system, where Edwards's lawyers argued that his constitutional rights as a U.S. citizen had been violated. Eventually the case made it to the U.S. Supreme Court, where it was argued in April and October 1941.

In presenting its case, the state of California argued several main points. First, it stated that the basis for the law was the need for some relief from the devastating effects of the Depression on the states during the 1930s. This argument had merit. The Depression was the result of a worldwide phenomenon resulting from industrialization and the chaos that followed World War I. In the United States too much wealth had fallen into too few hands, with the result that consumers were unable to buy all the goods produced. Underconsumption led to mounting inventories, which in turn led manufacturers to close plants and lay off workers. This caused demand to shrink further. Prices dropped sharply, foreign trade fell off, business failures multiplied, banks went under, and unemployment grew from five million in 1930, to nine million in 1931, to thirteen million in 1932. To the average person, the horrors of the troubled times were real. Savings disappeared, homes were lost, soup kitchens opened, breadlines formed, and, under the weight of all this, local relief systems broke down.

As the Depression lingered on into the mid-1930s, the nation was struck by another disaster, this one from Mother Nature. This was the so-called Dust Bowl. The name was coined as the soil of the Great Plains began to blow away. By 1935, in the twelve identified drought areas, more than twelve percent of the farmers were on relief. Many were forced to abandon their lands. And tens of thousands took to the roads and moved westward on the rumors of work in the farm areas of California and the Pacific Northwest.

As the numbers increased, local relief organizations in cities and towns began to run out of money. Most cities had no regular relief organizations, and many of the smaller cities and towns that did have some type of organized public relief programs began to fail. Local taxes and other financial resources were not enough to provide more than a bare subsistence for the many in need.

It was from these conditions that California's Statute 2615 originated. However, the statute was not the first of its kind. Similar statutes had been passed in 1860 and in 1901, all with the purpose of controlling "pauper" immigration into the state. Their passage was designed to provide California some protection from the very problems that had affected so many states during the Depression.

After establishing the need for the law, the state argued it was not the intention of the legislation to exclude "paupers" per se, nor was it the intention to exclude indigent persons or any indigent family. Its purpose was to control the actions of persons who "as volunteers and without any tie of legal support to the indigent, knowingly bring or assist in bringing indigent persons to the State." The state claimed these people led to an alarming increase in taxes, which would be paid by the people of California. The insinuation was clear. This was unfair to the residents of California.

In concluding their argument, the lawyers for the state cited the living and social conditions of those who migrated to California. Describing the nutritional and social diseases that were prevalent among the indigents, as well as the high crime rate found among these travelers, the state claimed that without the protection of Act 2615, other states would "push them from their borders into California because of the immeasurably higher standard of social services" found in California.

The defendant's argument was based on two major points. First, he maintained that the California statute was a violation of the commerce clause of the U.S. Constitution. Second, he argued it was in violation of the Fourteenth Amendment to the U.S. Constitution. In advancing the commerce clause argument, numerous previous court cases were cited. Act 2615 was "a definite, arbitrary interference and burden on interstate commerce, over which Congress has exclusive jurisdiction," Edwards's lawyers claimed.

The second point argued was that the act violated the equal protection clause of the Fourteenth Amendment. The lawyers reasoned that "a person . . . able and willing to work and who can afford to pay for his transportation on a public carrier, is not an indigent; while a person who possesses like qualifications but who can not afford to pay for his transportation, is an indigent." The lawyers added that "Freedom of movement . . . must be a fundamental right in a democratic state." They concluded their case by stating that the Fourteenth Amendment was not a "fair weather protection of the liberties of persons and its operation not limited to time of economic security when there is no pressure upon the states to curtail liberty."

On November 24, 1942, slightly one month after hearing arguments, the U.S. Supreme Court rendered its decision. Newly appointed Justice James Byrnes wrote the majority opinion for the Court. Byrnes began the opinion by summarizing the details of the case. He then raised the fundamental question. Byrnes noted that Act 2615, as well as the similar acts named in the state's argument, were not "accorded an authoritative interpretation by the California Courts." The term "indigent" as written by the California legislature did, according to the appellee's lawyers, include "only those persons who, destitute of property and without resources to obtain the necessities of life, and those who have no relatives or friends able and willing to support them." Byrnes noted that the act gave no limit as to exactly what an "indigent" person was, "therefore the Court accepted the narrow definition given in argument."

Once Byrnes satisfied the definition of the term "indigent," he proceeded to explain his ruling. He acknowledged the immense problems the states faced in dealing with the Depression, but he submitted that this situation did not necessarily create "boundaries to permissible areas of state legislative activity." Byrnes felt that attempts on the part of any single state to "isolate itself from difficulties common to all of them, by restraining the transportation of persons and property across its borders, were prohibited." Quoting former Justice Benjamin Cardozo, Byrnes stated, "The Constitution was . . . framed upon the theory that the peoples of the several states must sink or swim together." He then added, "Interstate trade, the redistribution of population, the right to migrate in pursuit of livelihood, freedom of opportunity, freedom of passage from State to State, the needs of national industry, the requirements of national defense . . . are not merely local internal affairs and matters on which the State may have some power to affect interstate commerce. Whether . . . California seeks to bar the passage of indigents directly or indirectly, her action in either event invades the power of the National Government over interstate commerce." Therefore, Act 2615 was unconstitutional as it violated the commerce clause of the Constitution. Chief Justice Harlan Fiske Stone and Justices Owen Roberts, Stanley Reed, and Felix Frankfurter joined in Byrnes's opinion.

However, Justice William Douglas wrote a separate concurring opinion joined by Justices Black and Murphy stating that the right of a citizen of the United States to move freely was protected by the privileges and immunities clause of the Fourteenth Amendment. Informing Justice Byrnes that "I would stand on my head to join with you . . . but I can not," Douglas based his opinion on the belief that the rights of persons to move freely from state to state "occupied a more protected position in our constitutional system than . . . the movement of cattle, fruit, steel, and coal across state lines." Citing several previous cases that came prior to the addition of the privileges and immunities clause under the Fourteenth Amendment, Justice Douglas believed that the right to move freely was one of "National Citizenship" and, though it was implied in the Constitution, "it did not make it any less 'guaranteed' by the Constitution." Thus by the time the Fourteenth Amendment was adopted in 1868, "the right to move freely had been squarely and authoritatively settled," and it was protected by the privileges and immunities clause of the Fourteenth Amendment against state interference.

The matter of the privileges and immunities clause had caused concern for several of the justices. Justice Byrnes, in writing his opinion, had been urged by both Chief Justice Stone and Justice Frankfurter not to use the clause for several reasons. Chief Justice Stone, in a letter to Byrnes in November as the opinion was being prepared, asked him to consider that "to bring such rights within the protection of the privileges and immunities clause involves a construction of that clause which has been repeatedly rejected for more than a half a century and requires an extension of the clause in a way, in the future, and with a changed complexion of the Court, that might well expose our constitutional system to dangers to which it has been exposed in the last fifty years though overexpansion and refinement of the due process and equal protection clauses."

Justice Frankfurter, in a letter to Byrnes written about the same time as Stone's letter, summed up the feelings of the justices who were not inclined to use the privileges and immunities clause in the case by informing Byrnes that "in previous cases, particularly the *Slaughterhouse Cases*, that to argue such would allow a vast and vague power into the Constitution which would allow the Court to be a perpetual censor upon all legislation of the States, on its civil rights of their own citizens, with authority to nullify such as it did not approve as they existed at the time of the adoption of the Fourteenth Amendment." Clearly, a substantial faction of the Court was apprehensive about bringing the privileges and immunities clause into the case.

However, Justice Robert Jackson, in a separate concurring opinion, entertained no such fear. In agreeing with Justice Douglas, he too believed that the privileges and immunities clause was the appropriate constitutional principle. Whereas Douglas defined the clause as being implied and not an extension of the Fourteenth Amendment, Jackson argued that the Court should use this clause to "hold squarely and unequivocally that it is an indispensable privilege of citizenship of the United States to enter any state of the Union. . . . If citizenship means less than this, it means nothing."

To Jackson, the crux of the case rested on the definition of the term *indigence* as defined by the California statute. He asked if the definition constituted a basis for restricting the freedom of a citizen as crime or contagion warrants its restriction. He then answered his own question: "We should say now and in no uncertain terms, that a man's mere property status, without more, cannot be used to test, qualify, or limit his rights as a citizen of the United States." Jackson went on to state that the California law in question was flawed by its definition of "indigence" and that "indigence in itself is neither a source of rights nor a basis for denying them. The mere state of being without funds is a neutral fact—constitutionally an irrelevance, like race, creed, or color."

Although the reasoning of the nine justices was divided, the opinion was unanimous. The California statute was indeed a violation of the Constitution and therefore invalid. *Edwards v. California* established that the right of all citizens to move freely within the United States was a right that could not be interfered with by the states.

Selected Bibliography

Byrnes, James F. *All in One Lifetime*. New York: Harper & Row, 1958.

Figg, Robert. "James F. Byrnes and the Supreme Court 1941–1942." *South Carolina Law Review* 25 (1973): 543–48.

James F. Byrnes Papers. Special Collections, Clemson University Library, Clemson, SC.

Two Hundred and Thirty-Nine Bushels of Wheat

—◄○►—

C. Herman Pritchett

Deceased Professor of Political Science
University of California, Santa Barbara

Wickard, Secretary of Agriculture, et al. v. Filburn, 317 U.S. 111 (1942) [U.S. Supreme Court]

—◄○► THE CASE IN BRIEF ◄○►—

Date
1942

Location
Ohio

Court
U.S. Supreme Court

Principal Participants
Roscoe C. Filburn
Secretary of Agriculture Claude Wickard
Associate Justice Robert Jackson

Significance of the Case
The Supreme Court upheld the right of Congress to regulate intrastate commerce when the activity could be demonstrated to affect commerce among the states or with foreign countries. The outcome was a return to a broader reading of the commerce clause.

Roscoe C. Filburn was a small farmer in Ohio. He maintained a herd of dairy cattle, raised poultry, and sold milk, poultry, and eggs. It was his practice also to plant a small acreage of winter wheat, the major portion of which he fed to his poultry and livestock or used in grinding flour for home consumption. The rest he retained for seed.

Filburn's legal difficulties began in 1941 when he planted twenty-three acres in wheat, whereas under the Agricultural Adjustment Act of 1938 the Department of Agriculture had given him a wheat acreage allotment of only eleven acres. Filburn's twelve acres of unauthorized planting produced some 239 bushels of wheat, on which the government imposed a penalty of forty-nine cents a bushel. Filburn challenged the action, contending that the congressional power to regulate commerce did not extend to local production and consumption.

The Agricultural Adjustment Act was motivated by congressional concern during the 1930s about low prices for agricultural products. The 1938 statute authorized the secretary of agriculture, in years of excessive supply, to prescribe marketing quotas for various agricultural products. Quotas on tobacco had been upheld by the Supreme Court in *Mulford v. Smith* (1939). In 1941 the secretary established wheat quotas when worldwide overproduction had driven the price of wheat down to forty cents a bushel. By limiting acreage in the United States, the government hoped to raise the price to the level of $1.16, which previous legislation had guaranteed to American farmers.

In legislating for control of wheat production, Congress had a problem. Unlike tobacco, practically all of which was marketed, much of the wheat produced was consumed on the farm and never entered the stream of interstate commerce. Yet, to make the acreage control program effective, Congress amended the statute in 1941 to apply to the entire wheat crop. But this action created a constitutional problem—the one Filburn presented—whether congressional power over commerce extends beyond the portion of a crop actually marketed or sold in commerce.

Article I, Section 8, of the U.S. Constitution authorizes Congress "to regulate commerce . . . among the several States." Beginning with the regulation of railroads in 1887, Congress has enacted hundreds of statutes to promote or regulate the U.S. economy. Any activities crossing state lines are clearly subject to regulation. But manufacturing or processing operations, mining, and lumbering frequently occur within individual states, and the products only subsequently move into the stream of interstate commerce. Is federal regulation of these "local" operations authorized by the commerce clause?

In the famous case of *Hammer v. Dagenhart* (1916), the Supreme Court declared unconstitutional a congressional statute banning the transportation in commerce of goods produced by child labor. Manufacturing was held to be a local activity, preceding interstate commerce. The commerce power, wrote Justice Day, is the power "to control the means by which commerce is carried on," not the right "to forbid commerce from moving."

The unprecedented economic legislation of the New Deal engendered renewed constitutional challenges. The National Industrial Recovery Act, which imposed extensive controls on the nation's most important economic activities, was declared unconstitutional in *Schechter Poultry Corp. v. United States* (1935). The Court held that slaughtering chickens in Brooklyn was a "local" activity, having only an "indirect" effect on commerce. The next year, in *Carter v. Carter Coal Co.*, a divided Court ruled that mining of coal, no matter how large an operation, was a local business having only an "indirect" effect on commerce.

But in 1937 came President Roosevelt's "court-packing plan" and the subsequent "switch in time that saved nine" in *West Coast Hotel Co. v. Parrish*. Shortly thereafter the Court approved the statute promoting and protecting labor organizations in *National Labor Relations Board v. Jones & Laughlin Corp.* (1937), bluntly rejecting the "direct-indirect" constitutional test. Subsequently the Fair Labor Standards Act, fixing maximum hours and minimum wages for employees engaged in commerce or the production of goods for commerce, was upheld in *U.S. v. Darby Lumber Co.* (1941).

While these decisions seemed to clear the way for judicial approval for government control of wheat production on the farms, it was still true that none of the previous decisions involved regulations concerning products intended for interstate commerce or intermingled with such products. *Wickard v. Filburn* presented such a problem. However, Justice Robert Jackson for a unanimous Court had no difficulty in extending the commerce power over the "wheat industry" to cover Filburn's 239 bushels. His justification was that "even if appellee's activity is local and though it may not be regarded as commerce, it may still, whatever its nature, be reached by Congress if it exerts a substantial economic effect on interstate commerce, and this irrespective of whether such effect is what at some earlier time has been defined as 'direct' or 'indirect.'"

Actually, *Wickard* added little to *Darby*, so far as guiding principles are concerned, but it did go considerably further in upholding federal power over products that do not move in commerce at all, and it did clear away some constitutional deadwood. Justice Jackson named the *Hammer*, *Schechter*, and *Carter* decisions as being specifically overruled.

The principle of the *Wickard* decision has been unquestioned. It was cited 61 times by the Supreme Court from 1941 to 1982, and 161 times by the federal courts of appeal. A 1943 *Michigan Law Review* article characterized the ruling as a return to John Marshall's conception of the commerce clause, standing along with *Darby* "for the obliteration of a vast amount of precedent built up during the interim period." The Supreme Court summarized the *Wickard* rule in a 1981 case as follows: "Even activity that is purely intrastate in character may be regulated by Congress where the activity, combined with like conduct by others similarly situated, affects commerce among the States or with foreign nations." In the words of one constitutional scholar, the lesson of *Wickard* was simply that "any attempt in good faith by Congress to cope with a national economic problem will be respected."

Selected Bibliography

Peter, H. Marshall. "Constitutional Law—Interstate Commerce—Agricultural Adjustment Act." *Michigan Law Review* 41 (February 1943): 729–32.
Stern, Robert L. "The Commerce Clause and the National Economy, 1933–1946." *Harvard Law Review* 59 (July 1946): 883–947.

Of Barbecue and Commerce

—◄◦►—

Richard C. Cortner

Department of Political Science
University of Arizona

Katzenbach v. McClung, 379 U.S. 294 (1964) [U.S. Supreme Court]

┌─────────────────────────────────┐

◄◦► THE CASE IN BRIEF ◄◦►

Date
1964

Location
Alabama

Court
U.S. Supreme Court

Principal Participants
Ollie's Barbecue
United States government

Significance of the Case
The case was one of two that tested
the constitutionality of the public
accommodations provision of the Civil
Rights Act of 1964, one aspect of which
banned segregation in restaurants.

Katzenbach v. McClung, along with *Heart of Atlanta Motel v. United States*, tested the constitutional validity of the public accommodations provisions of the Civil Rights Act of 1964 that prohibited discrimination based on race, religion, or national origin in facilities of public accommodation, such as motels, hotels, restaurants, and theaters. The public accommodations provisions of the act were predicated on the commerce clause in Article I of the U.S. Constitution that grants to Congress the power to regulate interstate and foreign commerce. As they applied to restaurants, the public accommodations provisions prohibited discrimination by any restaurant that served or offered to serve interstate travelers or in which a substantial portion of the food or other products sold or served had moved in interstate commerce.

As the Civil Rights Act of 1964 neared final passage by Congress, the Birmingham, Alabama Restaurant Association retained a local law firm to explore the possibility of a constitutional challenge to the validity of the act's public accommodations provisions by the city's restaurants. Attorney Robert McDavid Smith reported to the association that any attack on the public accommodations provisions by restaurants serving or offering to serve interstate travelers would be futile, given the substantial effects the operations of such restaurants had on interstate commerce. Smith further advised the restaurant association that a challenge to the public accommodations provisions might be successful if it were on behalf of a restaurant that served food that was purchased from a local (intrastate) supplier and did not advertize or cater to interstate travelers. It might be possible, Smith felt, to convince the courts that such a restaurant's operation constituted a remote and insubstantial link to, or effect on, interstate commerce so as to be beyond the valid scope of congressional power under the commerce clause.

Ollie's Barbecue in Birmingham, owned by Ollie McClung Sr. and Ollie McClung Jr., appeared to be just such a restaurant: It served a local clientele and engaged in no advertising, and it was remote from interstate highways, airports, and railroad or bus stations. Ollie's Barbecue could not consequently be viewed as a restaurant serving or offering to serve interstate travelers. But it did purchase annually approximately $70,000 worth of meat that had moved in interstate commerce. The Birmingham Restaurant Association therefore urged Robert McDavid Smith to contact the McClungs and inquire if they would volunteer as plaintiffs in a test case challenging the public accommodations provisions of the 1964 Civil Rights Act.

An intensely religious man, Ollie McClung Sr. believed that God was responsible for his restaurant's success and that any change in its operations, including desegregation, would be contrary to God's will. Ollie's Barbecue traditionally had refused to serve blacks in the restaurant, although it did serve blacks on a take-out basis. The restaurant employed thirty-six employees, twenty-six of whom were black, and employees were not paid wages but shared in the profits of the establishment. At a meeting of the employees, McClung explained why be believed the restaurant should continue to operate on a segregated basis and why he wished to allow his restaurant to serve as a vehicle for a test of the constitutionality of the public accommodations provisions of the Civil Rights Act. The employees expressed no objections to Ollie's intentions. Accordingly, Robert McDavid Smith filed suit in the U.S. District Court for the Northern District of Alabama on July 31, 1964, seeking an injunction against the U.S. attorney general to prohibit the enforcement of the act's public accommodations provisions against Ollie's Barbecue. The Birmingham Restaurant Association underwrote the cost of the litigation.

Before the *McClung* case was filed in Birmingham, the public accommodations provisions of the act had also been challenged by the Heart of Atlanta Motel and Lester Maddox's Pickrick Restaurant, both in Atlanta, Georgia. Just over a week prior to the filing of the *McClung* suit, a three-judge district court in Atlanta had sustained the validity of the public accommodations provisions as applied to the Heart of Atlanta Motel and the Pickrick restaurant. Both establishments were enjoined by the court from continuing to operate on a segregated basis. The *Heart of Atlanta Motel* case was immediately appealed to the U.S. Supreme Court, and a notice of an appeal to the Court was also filed in the *Pickrick* case.

At the time of the filing of the *McClung* case in Birmingham, the Department of Justice felt that the public accommodations provisions would be best tested before the Supreme Court in the Atlanta cases because the facts in those cases appeared most favorable to the government. Since the Department of Justice had contemplated no enforcement action under the Civil Rights Act against Ollie's Barbecue, and indeed had never heard of that establishment prior to the filing of its lawsuit, the Department filed a motion to dismiss the *McClung* suit on the ground that no case or controversy existed. Nevertheless, a three-judge U.S. district court in Birmingham overruled the government's motion to dismiss the *McClung* case and further ruled the public accommodations provisions unconstitutional as applied to Ollie's Barbecue. Meanwhile, an appeal to the Supreme Court was never filed in the *Pickrick* restaurant case from Atlanta. As a result, the *McClung* case was linked with *Heart of Atlanta Motel.* Together, these cases became the principal test cases before the U.S. Supreme Court of the public accommodations provisions of the Civil Rights Act of 1964.

The Supreme Court announced its decisions on December 14, 1964, unanimously upholding the validity of the public accommodations provisions in *Heart of Atlanta Motel v. United States* and *Katzenbach v. McClung.* Since the Heart of Atlanta Motel had 216 rooms and was accessible from two interstate and two state highways, since it solicited interstate trade in the national media and through fifty billboards and highway signs throughout Georgia, and since fully 75 percent of its guests were interstate travelers, the Court held that racial discrimination by the motel discouraged and burdened interstate travel by blacks. While the racial discrimination practiced by the motel was admittedly a local activity, the Court held that it nevertheless resulted in adverse effects and burdens on interstate commerce. Congress, the Court further ruled, could, therefore, validly remove these burdens and effects on interstate travel by blacks by prohibiting discrimination by motels and hotels under the commerce clause through the application of the public accommodations provisions upon their operations.

In *Katzenbach v. McClung,* the Court similarly sustained the validity under the commerce clause of the application of the public accommodations provisions to Ollie's Barbecue. Rejecting the argument that the $70,000 worth of food purchases by Ollie's Barbecue constituted an effect on interstate commerce insufficient to justify congressional prohibition of segregation in the restaurant, the Court ruled that segregation in Ollie's Barbecue and all other similarly situated restaurants produced adverse effects and burdens on interstate commerce substantial enough to accord Congress the power to

regulate them under the commerce clause. Segregation in restaurants like Ollie's Barbecue, the Court found, reduced the expenditures by blacks in restaurants and other public accommodations nationally, reduced the flow of products which would otherwise flow in commerce, and aroused protests in the communities where segregation was practiced, resulting in depressing effects on business in such communities. Restaurant segregation, the Court further held, also deterred blacks from interstate travel, "for one can hardly travel without eating," and discouraged individuals and businesses from relocating to communities where segregation was practiced, again with adverse effects on commerce. Although the purchases of interstate food by Ollie's Barbecue, when viewed in isolation, were minimal, if added to the interstate food purchases of all similarly situated establishments, the Court held, the effect of segregation in such restaurants on interstate food sales was far from trivial.

Ollie McClung Sr. had been present during the oral argument of the *McClung* case before the Court. After the argument, Robert McDavid Smith informed McClung that the case was likely lost. Having been prepared for defeat, McClung Sr. peacefully desegregated his restaurant without incident two days after the Supreme Court's decision. Ollie McClung Sr. died in 1989. Ollie's Barbecue, since relocated near an interstate highway, continues to be a thriving business under the management of Ollie McClung Jr. And the Supreme Court's decision in the case involving Ollie's Barbecue remains an important example of the modern scope of congressional power under the commerce clause.

Selected Bibliography

Cortner, Richard C. *Civil Rights and Public Accommodations: The Heart of Atlanta Motel and McClung Cases.* Lawrence: University Press of Kansas, 2001.

A Popular Monopoly: *United States v. Microsoft*

—◄◦►—

David A. Walker

Department of History
University of Northern Iowa

United States v. Microsoft Corporation, 87 F. Supp. 2d 30 (2000) [U.S. District Court]

◄◦► THE CASE IN BRIEF ◄◦►

Date
2000–?

Location
District of Columbia

Court
U.S. District Court

Principal Participants
United States government
Microsoft Corporation
Bill Gates
Judge Thomas Penfield Jackson

Significance of the Case
The most significant antimonopoly case of modern times, the ongoing litigation (as of 2001) would determine if one of the largest companies in the United States had engaged in illegal, monopolistic practices to secure its market dominance.

Arguing before U.S. District Judge Thomas Penfield Jackson, Microsoft Corporation lawyers wrote: "Having an extremely popular product does not make the company a monopolist." Judge Jackson, appointed to the U.S. District Court in Washington, D.C., by President Ronald Reagan, presided over the leading antitrust case of the late twentieth and early twenty-first century against one of the world's most dynamic corporations, Microsoft. The Redmond, Washington–based computer software giant was founded in 1975 by Seattle native Bill Gates, shortly after he dropped out of Harvard University. Ten years later Microsoft began marketing the initial Windows software package, replacing its MS-DOS that had dominated operating systems for Intel-compatible personal computers. By 1990 Microsoft was nearly synonymous with all PC applications; another brand name had become a product.

The Department of Justice, on behalf of the U.S. government, nineteen states, and the District of Columbia, filed suit in May 1998 against Microsoft, charging violation of the Sherman Antitrust Act (1890). The often volatile trial lasted sixteen months, including seventy-eight days of courtroom testimony. David Boies, a private antitrust attorney hired by the Justice Department, referred to Microsoft as an old-fashioned monopolist in high-technology clothing, a reference to Judge Jackson's comment during final oral arguments that "I don't see a distinction" between the current defendant and John D. Rockefeller's Standard Oil Company, which the U.S. Supreme Court had split into several dozen separate companies almost a century earlier. In an interesting legal strategy, John Warden, Microsoft's lead attorney, mounted a vigorous defense by relying on arguments previously ignored by Judge Jackson. Clearly the corporation hoped to minimize its losses and await a more favorable verdict on appeal.

On November 5, 1999, Judge Jackson handed down a blistering and lengthy "findings of fact," concluding "the company harmed consumers in ways immediate and easily discernible." He agreed with the government that Microsoft attempted to crush a threat posed by Web browser pioneer Netscape Corporation's Navigator and by Sun Microsystems Java programming language technology. Two weeks later he appointed Richard Posner, chief judge of the Seventh U.S. Circuit Court of Appeals in Chicago, as mediator. For four months, Posner heard arguments from both sides. The hearing disclosed a split in the antitrust alliance. Several state attorneys general, led by Iowan Tom Miller, favored breaking up Microsoft. The Justice Department seemed willing merely to modify the corporation's conduct. For its part, Microsoft refused to discuss proposals calling for its breakup and limited responses to "conduct remedies." But the Justice Department refused to accept any Microsoft offers as containing too many loopholes with no enforcement mechanisms. Following nearly two dozen proposals and counterproposals, Posner announced that mediation had failed. Two days later, Judge Jackson delivered his legal opinion.

The plaintiffs contended that Microsoft maintained its monopoly power through "exclusionary, anticompetitive, and predatory" action; that the computer giant illegally "bundled" its Internet Explorer browser to the Windows operating system; and that Microsoft attempted to monop-

olize the Web browser market through exclusive agreements with manufacturers. On April 3, 2000, in a long-anticipated verdict, Judge Jackson concluded that Microsoft violated sections one and two of the Sherman Antitrust Act. He ruled on behalf of all plaintiffs that indeed Microsoft held its monopolistic control of computer software operating systems through anticompetitive means, that it attempted to control the browser market, and that it illegally tied its Web browser to its operating system. However, the court did not find that Microsoft practiced unlawful marketing arrangements depriving competitors access to PC users worldwide. The court concluded that Microsoft possessed a "dominant, persistent, and increasing share" of the computer operating system and Web browser markets. It maintained that position through application barriers preventing competitors from entering the market "on the merits of what they offer customers."

In highly inflammatory language, Judge Jackson referred to Microsoft's "predatory behavior," its "oppressive thumb," its campaign to "quash innovation," and actions that "trammeled the competitive process." Through anticompetitive practices, Microsoft maintained monopolistic power crushing potential threats. "In essence, Microsoft mounted a deliberate assault upon entrepreneurial efforts that . . . could well have enabled the introduction of competition into the market . . . , the result of a deliberate and purposeful choice to quell . . . competition."

Fundamental to the issue was court opposition to Microsoft's decision to tie its newly developed Internet Explorer browser to the Windows operating system. Government counsel argued this was not a technical design decision but merely "bolting" together a browser and operating system, thus restricting PC manufactures to accept both products whether they wanted them or not. Gates's lawyers held that this bundling created an "integrated product," not two distinct entities tied together as argued by the government. Microsoft required computer equipment manufacturers to license and install Internet Explorer as a requirement to license Windows 95 on the basis that this created advantages unavailable if the products were

Bill Gates, founder and chairman of Microsoft, testifies on Capitol Hill. *Reuters/Larry Downing/Archive Photos.*

purchased separately and then combined by the customer. Earlier, in June 1998, a three-judge appeals court panel in the District of Columbia had ruled against Judge Jackson's decree enjoining the bundling practice, warning that the court should not get involved in highly technical product design. This provided Microsoft with a powerful defense of its marketing decision. Judge Jackson retaliated by criticizing, even dismissing, the appeals court decision. He concluded that Microsoft "set out to maximize [its browser's] share . . . at Navigator's expense." This "increased the likelihood that preinstallation of Navigator into Windows would cause user confusion and system degradation." This had a "dramatic, negative impact on Navigator's usage share," plummeting from "well above seventy percent" down to forty percent. As a result, "Netscape suffered a severe drop in revenues from lost advertisers, Web traffic and purchases of server products."

As might be expected, Microsoft's corporate spokesmen denied all charges. Counsel launched an appeal on legal, factual, and procedural grounds. Bill Gates's corporation enjoyed high public approval ratings throughout the years of litigation. Opinion polls, often as high as sixty-three percent favorable, revealed that consumers overwhelmingly opposed the Justice Department suit. Even international competitors like Compaq and Apple were reluctant to demand a breakup of the software giant. The world's richest person concluded: "this ruling turns on its head the reality that consumers know—that our software has helped make PC's more accessible and more affordable to millions." "Success of this industry . . . is by common knowledge the engine that has driven the nation's unprecedented economic expansion."

In the most far-reaching antitrust decision in the United States since the court ordered breakup of AT&T in 1984, Judge Jackson ordered the dissolution of Microsoft on June 7, 2000. In a much publicized ruling that granted nearly everything requested by the Justice Department, the district court ordered the division of Microsoft into two business entities— one for the Windows operating system, and the other for "everything else," including the company's Internet browser and its myriad software applications. Under the terms of the order, the separate firms would be barred from reuniting for a decade, and Microsoft would be compelled to share technical information to create a more competitive marketplace. Giving the company four months to devise a plan for the breakup, Judge Jackson concluded that, since Microsoft had shown "no disposition to voluntarily alter its business protocol in any significant respect," the court must "terminate the unlawful conduct, prevent its repetition in the future, . . . and revive competition."

During a torrid week of front page headlines and speculation by business and legal experts that followed the district court decision, Bill Gates announced his company's intent to appeal Judge Jackson's ruling to a higher court. Microsoft initially attempted to bypass the circuit courts of appeal and have the antitrust action heard directly by the U.S. Supreme Court. However, in September 2000, the Supreme Court refused to take the case, sending it instead to the Court of Appeals for the District of Columbia. Throughout the waning months of 2000, Judge Jackson made himself available for comment to journalists and legal experts studying the case; he demonstrated little hesitancy to contain his disdain for Microsoft's business practices. Besides contesting the district court decision on substantive grounds, in their appellate court briefs attorneys for Microsoft cited the many post-decision comments of Judge Jackson as evidence of a bias toward the software giant. In late February 2001, the Court of Appeals heard lengthy oral arguments on Microsoft's appeal. As this volume went to press, a number of judicial resolutions in *U.S. v. Microsoft* remained possible. Regardless of how the case turns out, it is certain that Microsoft products will continue to be popular computer software choices for the indefinite future.

Selected Bibliography

Auletta, Ken. *World War 3.0: Microsoft and Its Enemies.* New York: Random House, 2001.

Brinkley, Joel, and Steve Lohr. *U.S. v. Microsoft.* New York: McGraw-Hill, 2001.

DeVries, Michael W. "United States v. Microsoft." *Berkeley Technology Law Journal* 14 (Winter 1999): 303–346.

Heilermann, John. *Pride Before the Fall: The Trials of Bill Gates and the End of the Microsoft Era.* New York: Harper Collins, 2001.

Manes, Stephen. *Gates: How Microsoft's Mogul Reinvented an Industry—And Made Himself the Richest Man in America.* New York: Doubleday, 1993.

Wallace, James, and Jim Erickson. *Hard Drive: Bill Gates and the Making of the Microsoft Empire.* New York: Wiley, 1992.

Labor

The Legitimacy of Labor Organization

——◀◦▶——

William M. Wiecek

College of Law and Department of History
Syracuse University

People v. Fisher, 14 Wend. 9 (1835) [New York Supreme Court of Judicature]
Commonwealth v. Hunt, 45 Mass. 111 (1842) [Supreme Judicial Court of Massachusetts]

◀◦▶ THE CASE IN BRIEF ◀◦▶

Date
1835, 1842

Location
New York; Massachusetts

Court
New York Supreme Court of Judicature
Supreme Judicial Court of Massachusetts

Principal Participants
Journeyman shoemaker named "Fisher";
Chief Justice John Savage (New York);
Commonwealth of Massachusetts; Chief
Justice Lemuel Shaw (Massachusetts)

Significance of the Case
Fisher ruled that organizing a labor union
was a conspiracy. *Hunt* held that such
activity was not a conspiracy. The two
opinions symbolized the legal conflict
over the rights of labor unions in the
nineteenth century.

Shoemakers pioneered tactics of labor organization in the United States, partly because their trade was one of the first to experience the wrenching differentiation of management from worker and capital from labor. *People v. Fisher* loomed large on the legal landscape as a monument to this separation and to American jurists' determination that workers must not be allowed to explore the possibilities of collective action.

In 1833, a journeyman shoemaker (an employee of a master shoemaker) known to us only as "Fisher" and an unspecified number of his unnamed fellow workers organized what Chief Justice John Savage of the New York Supreme Court of Judicature called a "club"—a proto-union. They drew up by-laws prohibiting members from making men's boots for master shoemakers for less than one dollar a pair. They also agreed that they would not work for any master who employed a journeyman for less than a dollar-a-pair rate. When a master named Lum employed a journeyman at the rate of seventy-five cents a pair, Fisher and others walked off the job. For this, Fisher was indicted for violation of

409

a New York statute making it a criminal conspiracy "to commit any act injurious to . . . trade or commerce."

In his defense, Fisher claimed that, since it was not illegal for him and any of his fellow journeymen to refuse to work for less than a specified rate as individuals, they could not be prosecuted for doing the same thing in concert. To refute this argument, Chief Justice Savage relied on two strands of argument: Anglo-American common-law precedent, and policy.

Drawing on vague and imprecise English precedents, Savage held that concerted labor actions were "against the spirit of the common law." The doctrinal problem confronting Savage was this: At common law, a conspiracy was criminal if organized for an illegal objective or to accomplish a legal objective by illegal means. Savage conceded that, from the viewpoint of the individual worker, the *objective* of higher wages was not illegal. So, if he was to conclude that a conspiracy existed, he was forced to find the *means* illegal. Though he did not cite them directly, two prominent American precedents, the *Philadelphia Cordwainers' Case* of 1806 and the *New York Cordwainers' Case* of 1810, provided the support he needed. Both had upheld conspiracy convictions of shoemakers who had struck for higher wages or a closed shop. Because Fisher was being prosecuted for violation of a statute, not the common law crime of conspiracy, Savage was able to hold that the mere act of conspiring together, even if for a legal end, was indictable, because the means were declared illegal by statute. That is, concerted employee action, including a strike, was "injurious . . . to trade or commerce," in the terms of the statute.

To prove this latter point, Savage turned to policy arguments, demonstrating that union organization interfered with the workings of a laissez-faire market economy. The major portion of his opinion was a tract on the free market. He argued, for example, that "it is important to the best interests of society that the price of labor be left to regulate itself, or rather be limited by the demand for it." Because "competition is the life of trade," he went on, the "officious and improper interference" of the journeymen with the natural workings of the market created "a monopoly of the most odious kind."

Fisher was in the mainstream of American precedent in labor cases; the law stood as a formidable lion in the path of union organization. For that reason, the great case of *Commonwealth v. Hunt* has been called "the Magna Carta of labor" in the United States. Decided by Chief Justice Lemuel Shaw of the Massachusetts Supreme Judicial Court in 1842, the *Hunt* decision held that labor organization is not, of itself, a criminal conspiracy indictable at common law. Shaw acknowledged the considerable precedential weight of *Fisher*, but distinguished it on the grounds that the New York decision turned on the construction of a statute, while the Massachusetts case involved only the common law. Finding that neither the objective nor the means employed by the Massachusetts bootmakers were unlawful, Shaw held that "we cannot perceive, that it is criminal for men to agree together to exercise their own acknowledged rights, in such a manner as best to subserve their own interests." Shaw thus rejected Chief Justice Savage's basic assumption. *Hunt* did not legitimate all union activity, however. It merely removed the stigma of criminality that automatically attached to collective action under the *Fisher* holding.

A change in the law, represented by the shift from the New York to the Massachusetts rule, did not endear labor organization to employers, especially as industrialization drastically altered the terrain of labor-management relations in the later nineteenth century. With conspiracy a dulled and rusting weapon after *Hunt*, corporate employers sought more effective instruments to bludgeon unions. Between 1870 and 1900, they found such weapons in two places, the labor injunction and the antitrust laws. The labor injunction bore no relation to the *Fisher* doctrine; it permitted judges to enjoin some union activity, such as organizing a strike, and then to hold workers disobeying the order in contempt of court, whereupon the judge could impose fines and jail sentences without the inconvenience of having to submit the case to a jury. Prosecutions of unions and labor organizers for violation of the Sherman Antitrust Act (1890), on the other hand, hearkened back to the theory of *Fisher*, for such judicial assaults on labor proceeded on the premise that union organization and strikes were in restraint of trade, the pivotal point of Chief Justice Savage's opinion. This revival of an early nineteenth century assumption proved to be protean and long-lived, being reburied only by the labor policies of the New Deal in the 1930s. *Fisher* thus had a lingering influence long after its specific doctrines had become obsolete.

Selected Bibliography

Forbath, W. E. *Law and the Shaping of the American Labor Movement.* Cambridge, MA: Harvard University Press, 1991.

Levy, L. W. *The Law of the Commonwealth and Chief Justice Shaw: The Evolution of American Law, 1830–1860.* New York: Harper & Row, 1967.

Nelles, Walter. "Commonwealth v. Hunt." *Columbia Law Review* 32 (1932): 1128–1169.

Sayre, Francis B. "Criminal Conspiracy." *Harvard Law Review* 35 (1928): 393–427.

Tomlins, C. L. *Law, Labor, and Ideology in the Early American Republic.* Cambridge, England: Cambridge University Press, 1993.

Witte, Edwin E. "Early American Labor Cases." *Yale Law Journal* 35 (1926): 825–837.

"An Injury to One Is an Injury to All"

———◦———

Wayne K. Hobson

American Studies Department
California State University, Fullerton

In re Debs, 158 U.S. 564 (1895) [U.S. Supreme Court]

◦ THE CASE IN BRIEF ◦

Date
1895

Location
Illinois

Court
U.S. Supreme Court

Principal Participants
Eugene V. Debs
American Railway Union
General Managers Association
Attorney General Richard Olney

Significance of the Case
Although a decision against a labor union, the *Debs* case was one among several cases in which the government began to define the relationship between the forces of labor and those of capital in the United States.

Does a labor union have the right to obstruct interstate commerce while pursuing otherwise legitimate aims? Do federal courts have jurisdiction to issue injunctions against unions in such cases? Is it legitimate for federal officials and officers of struck corporations to coordinate their strategies so that the government acts as an agent of the corporations against the striking union? Does it strain reason to extend the provisions of a law enacted by Congress to restrict monopolistic business practices to labor unions engaged in conflicts against such businesses? Will labor organizing be confined to the "bread and butter" aims of skilled craft workers, or will the labor movement speak for a broader range of workers and seek a more radical restructuring of the American society and economy? If courts and the political system seek to block radical labor, what strategies will labor adopt in reply? How, if at all, should judicial thinking and legal institutions modify their historic individualistic assumptions in the face of new patterns of organized corporate power and new efforts of organized labor to combat that power?

These were major questions in the dramatic Pullman strike and ensuing court battles of 1894–1895, which culminated in a unanimous U.S. Supreme Court decision upholding the contempt convictions of Eugene V. Debs and other American Railway Union (ARU) officers. Debs's union had ignored a federal court injunction ordering it to cease supporting a massive railroad strike. The injunction had been issued by federal judges William A. Woods and Peter S. Grosscup at the request of Attorney General Richard Olney, who was acting in concert with the railroads. The Pullman strike had begun in early May 1894 among workers in the Pullman Company's sleeping-car manufacturing plants. These workers had endured a 33 percent wage cut since the previous summer with no corresponding reduction of food prices, rents, or utilities. Workers in Pullman, a "model" company town, already deeply resented the company's paternalistic and autocratic control of their lives. In late June, as their situation became more desperate, the Pullman strikers appealed to the recently formed ARU, led by Debs. This union represented a major departure for organized labor in the railroad industry. Four railroad brotherhoods organized along craft lines had long dominated labor organizing in the industry. The brotherhoods were cautious, serving their members more by their insurance programs than by advocacy of workers' interests against the railroad companies. The ARU, on the other hand, was an industrial union committed to confronting employers and welcoming as members all white nonmanagement employees who served the railroads in any capacity. Even coal miners, longshoremen, and car builders, if in the employ of a railroad, were invited to join.

ARU leaders recognized a sympathy strike or boycott was very risky. The nation was in the midst of an economic depression. There was good reason to believe either the state or federal government, or both, would intervene on the employers' side, and the railroad companies were powerful and well organized. Twenty-four railroads with terminals in Chicago formed a tightly knit organization, the General Managers Association (GMA), which coordinated the companies' economic and labor practices. The GMA was a formidable opponent for organized labor. It had been organized to counteract labor's impressive organizing successes in the mid-1880s. In turn, Debs's decision to create the ARU was a deliberate response to the organized power demonstrated by the GMA in labor disputes in 1893. Organization, Debs believed, had to be met with counter organization.

Despite their leaders' resolve to be cautious, the ARU's national convention, meeting in nearby Chicago, voted to support the Pullman workers by boycotting trains connected to Pullman cars. Delegates had visited the community of Pullman and were moved by the desperate conditions there. They could also plainly see that without outside support, the strikers' cause was hopeless. ARU delegates had come to Chicago with mounting grievances against the railroad companies, which were systematically reducing wages and using blacklists and other devices to break the new union. The delegates were convinced a crisis was building in their industry as the organized power of the GMA threatened to obliterate workers' power. Unity and solidarity on the one side had to be met with unity and solidarity on the other.

On June 26, ARU members began refusing to handle Pullman cars. When the GMA responded by firing those workers, the boycott against Pullman cars became a strike against the railroads. But the conflict was not destined to be a pure test of power between only the GMA and ARU; the federal government became the third and decisive actor in the drama. On July 2, Attorney General Olney, working in conjunction with railroad lawyers, devised a strategy to crush the strike. Olney, a former Boston railroad lawyer, appointed Edwin Walker, a leading Chicago corporate lawyer, and counsel to the GMA, as a special U.S. attorney. He directed Walker to seek an injunction against any ARU action that would impede interstate commerce or obstruct the passage of the mails. The resulting injunction, which the issuing judges assisted Walker in drafting, was so comprehensive in scope that the *New York Times* called it "a Gatling gun on paper."

ARU leaders decided to ignore the injunction. Even before labor's response was clear, President Grover Cleveland sent 2,000 troops to Chicago to ensure that mail would be transported. This order came over the strong objection of Governor John Altgeld of Illinois and despite the fact that the ARU had deliberately relaxed its boycott so that there would not be any serious obstruction of the mail. Clearly, the administration's aim in calling out troops was to break the strike. These federal troops soon became violent participants in the conflict, escalating the situation well beyond what it had been. Their presence, however, did break the strike. By July 13, all rioting ended and trains were running on schedule. On July 20, the strike formally ended and attention shifted to the courts, where both criminal and civil actions were initiated against Debs and other ARU leaders.

Injunctions are an equitable remedy giving courts the power to diminish a nuisance or to prevent irreparable damage to private property that could not adequately be compensated in an action at law, and they were unusual in labor disputes in 1894. The first major use of this device against organized labor was during the nationwide railway strike of 1886–1887. Several appellate court decisions were rendered shortly thereafter, but the *Debs* case was the first U.S. Supreme Court test.

Debs's lawyers did not dispute that he had defied the injunction. The issue was whether the injunction had been legitimate. Judge Woods, in December 1894, found Debs guilty of contempt. Woods's forty-page decision relied heavily on the Sherman Antitrust Act of 1890, ruling that Section 4, which authorized the government to seek injunctions against conspiracies in restraint of trade, applied to labor unions. Woods sentenced Debs to six months in jail and his fellow national officers to three months.

Meanwhile, Walker secured a criminal conspiracy indictment against ARU leaders, including Debs, and began a federal district court trial. Criminal conspiracy prosecutions were, at the time, a more common legal strategy than injunctions issued in civil courts for employers and government officials who were anxious to end labor actions. However, the new reality and transparency of organized corporate and government power created obstacles in securing criminal convictions against labor leaders. In a master stroke, Debs's lawyer, Clarence Darrow, appearing in his first case as an advocate for labor, subpoenaed the minutes of GMA meetings, which suggested that the railroads and the government were united in a conspiracy to reduce wages, control the union, and prevent the formation of a national labor organization. Troubled by this evidence and impressed by Debs's testimony that he had tried actively to prevent violence, the jury, which contained no workingmen, apparently was leaning strongly toward acquittal. Hence, when one of the jurors became ill and the judge suspended the trial for three months, Olney decided to drop the criminal case entirely.

Debs's fate now rested in the hands of the Supreme Court, to which his contempt conviction was appealed. The ARU lawyers, Darrow, Stephen Gregory, and former senator Lyman Trumbull, made four points in their briefs and oral arguments. They argued, contrary to Woods's reading, that the Sherman Act did not apply to unions. Furthermore, they maintained, the defendants had done nothing unlawful by urging ARU members to quit their employment. In any case, the government had no right to apply for an injunction to restrain interference with the private property of the railroads; the federal government could apply for injunctions only to protect public property. Finally, Debs's attorneys argued that if he had done anything unlawful, he should have been subjected to prosecution in the criminal courts rather than in civil tribunals.

The government's case was argued by Olney, one of only two times he appeared before the Supreme Court during his tenure as attorney general. In his oral argument he declared both the Sherman Act and the federal obligation to protect the mails unessential to the government's case. He did not deny the validity of those arguments, but he invited the Court to issue a far broader ruling than had Woods. Olney insisted the key basis for the federal government's jurisdiction was its general constitutional power to regulate interstate commerce, deriving both from the Constitution and from the Interstate Commerce Act of 1887. This act, Olney asserted, gave Congress full and complete authority over the nation's railroads and denied such power to the states. If the states had no right to interfere with the operation of railroads, how much less right had mere citizens, such as Debs, to interfere with their operation? Olney contended that the federal government had the power to act as a trustee of the railroads. Furthermore, the ARU boycott produced a massive blockage of railroad traffic. The federal government was the only entity with sufficient authority to end that chaos.

Two months later the Supreme Court ruled, in a unanimous vote, to uphold Debs's contempt conviction. Justice David J. Brewer wrote the decision, taking Olney's arguments and making them the opinion of the Court. Brewer agreed the federal government had power to prevent anyone from interfering with interstate commerce. He cited numerous past instances where the federal government had used this constitutional power to deny state government interference with interstate commerce. Echoing Olney, Brewer argued that if it could exercise such power vis-à-vis a state, it could certainly do so vis-à-vis a mere voluntary association of individuals. Brewer ignored Woods's reliance on the Sherman Act as the basis for the federal government's authority until the opinion's final paragraph, in which he stated that he was not necessarily overturning the circuit court and not necessarily affirming it. He preferred, instead, to rest the judgment on a broader ground—the federal government's constitutional right to regulate interstate commerce.

Brewer's opinion, as he acknowledged, extended federal equity jurisdiction substantially. He went well beyond the traditional view of injunctions by sanctioning their use even in the absence of an irreparably threatened property interest and extending their application from the traditional one of protecting the rights of private parties to the novel one of preserving public rights and punishing public wrongs. What remained to be determined were the limits on the use of this new weapon against labor. Brewer's decision, construed narrowly, applied only to federal injunctions against obstructions of interstate commerce.

The next several decades were to see a greatly expanded use of injunctions against labor unions, at least 4,000 by 1930, according to one scholar. The key question became whether a union was engaging in a permissible form of economic pressure. In most jurisdictions it became settled that if a union called a strike to gain higher wages, shorter hours, or improved working conditions for its members, an injunction could not be granted as long as the union was not engaging in criminal activity. However, when the aims of a strike or boycott were less obviously directly beneficial to the members, such as boycotts of nonunion goods and materials, sympathy strikes, or strikes to establish a closed shop, courts were much more willing to sanction injunctions. Brewer's *In re Debs* opinion had implicitly invited this activist state effort to limit the scope of labor union activity. Workers often considered these injunctions illegitimate infringements on their freedom of action, as had Debs. But if they violated the injunctions, usually by engaging in peaceful picketing, they were arrested and branded by judges and an often unsympathetic press as lawless and irresponsible. Ironically, this image seemed confirmed when employers precipitated violence by hiring private police or called on the state militia to enforce the decrees.

The *Debs* decision was one of three major Supreme Court decisions in 1895. The other two were *United States v. E. C. Knight Company*, restricting the Sherman Act's applicability as a weapon against monopolistic practices, and *Pollock v. Farmers' Loan & Trust Company*, invalidating a federal income tax law. These decisions, taken together, decisively marked the emergence of a new era in which the Supreme Court would take a more activist role as one of the shapers of public policy in national affairs. Although the majority of justices from the 1890s to the late 1930s adhered to a laissez-faire ideology hostile to governmental regulation of business, their decisions in most areas are now seen by Court historians as conservative and pragmatic rather than as dogmatically ideological. One major exception is labor law. Here the Supreme Court, until the late 1930s, consistently issued decisions against labor unions and against economic legislation to protect workers. In doing so, it relied not only on a formalistic laissez-faire ideology, but it also evidenced a class-based and often ethnically based hostility toward organized labor. In this sense, it was significant that, whereas the Court was divided in the *Pollock* and *Knight* decisions, Brewer spoke for a unanimous Court in *Debs.*

In the broadest sense, the Pullman strike and *Debs* decision dramatized where the balance of power lay between the forces of labor and capital in the United States in the 1890s. The episode taught Americans on all sides what the underlying social, economic, and political realities of power were. Certainly that was the lesson Eugene Debs drew. His ARU did not survive the strike's failure. Rank-and-file railway workers dropped affiliation with the union, in part from disappointment with its failure to defeat the companies, but also because the railroads established a severe and effective blacklist to deny employment to union supporters and activists. Railway workers, convinced that major obstacles to interstate commerce would be suppressed by the federal government, hesitated for years to engage in strikes or boycotts of any significance. Debs emerged from his six months in jail at Woodstock, Illinois to announce that the combined forces of capital and government were too strong for traditional union activities to prevail. He was abandoning economic struggles, switching from reliance on strikes to reliance on politics and the ballot. Debs also announced his conversion to socialism and soon became the leader and perennial presidential candidate of the Socialist Party of America.

Within the labor movement, the failure of the Pullman strike helped swing the balance toward Samuel Gompers's brand of unionism. Gompers, president of the American Federation of Labor, favored a conservative approach, concentrating on craft unions and "bread and butter" issues of wages, hours, and working conditions. He had seen the ARU as a threat and had discouraged Chicago trade unions from participating in an ARU-sponsored general strike in Chicago called for July 10, 1894, to protest government intervention. The general strike's failure helped seal the fate of the ARU and with it the hopes of those who saw militant industrial unions as the best challenge to capitalist domination of American workers.

Both Debs and Gompers recognized that the Pullman strike marked the emergence of a new

era in labor-capital relations. All elements of the federal government were now clearly aligned on the side of capital and were willing to countenance the use of force to compel an outcome favorable to that side. The two working-class leaders drew different conclusions about how to respond to this situation, but they did agree that industrial unionism was not a viable basis for labor organization until the attitude of the federal government altered. That did not happen until the 1930s.

For outside observers, the meaning of the Pullman strike and its legal aftermath seemed both clear and menacing. If the strike cemented an alliance between government and capital, it also stirred middle-class concerns about the rising power of big business. The U.S. Strike Commission, for example, spoke for many. This three-member body had been appointed by President Cleveland to investigate the broader issues revealed by the Pullman strike. The commission interviewed over 100 witnesses and issued a report condemning all sides in the dispute. Debs and the ARU were criticized for admitting nonrailway workers, such as the Pullman car builders, into their union. They were also criticized for not seeing the inherent futility of their boycott-strike in a time of widespread unemployment. George Pullman was criticized for his stubborn refusal to deal with the union representing his employees and for not arbitrating the issues in the dispute. The GMA was excoriated for its unsavory policies, especially for its arrogance in refusing to deal with the ARU and for its monopolistic control over the industry. Despite the fact that the commission had been appointed by President Cleveland, his Justice Department and attorney general were criticized for their close relationship with the railway companies, especially for permitting loyal railroad employees to be sworn in as deputy U.S. marshals. In essence, these railway workers became federal officers paid for, armed, fed, and housed by the GMA. In private correspondence, Carroll D. Wright, the chair of the commission, called the strike a "pig-headed affair all around."

The commission implicitly rejected the view of labor-capital conflict that the major actors had shared: a battle to the death between rival

Eugene Victor Debs, five-time socialist party candidate for president, addresses a political meeting in New York. *Hulton Getty Collection/Archive.*

conceptions of industrial America. Instead, the commission took the view that industrial disputes were matters that reasonable men could resolve if they would only adopt a conciliatory attitude. The commission's concerns and approach pointed toward new legal and political conceptions recognizing the inevitability of organized power, the need for countervailing powers, and the importance of mechanisms to equitably and peaceably resolve conflicts. These ideas gained increasing acceptance during the next several decades, particularly as labor violence continued and labor leaders disputed the legitimacy of "government by injunction." A new generation of legal writers and a handful of liberal judges, legislators, and other policymakers began to imagine, and attempted to implement, an alternative and more equitable model of labor-capital relationships. In this sense, the commission's report stands alongside Brewer's decision and Debs's and Gompers's reorientations as the major legacies of the Pullman strike of 1894. Nevertheless, until the industrial, political, and constitutional upheavals of the 1930s, capital had the clear upper hand in labor disputes, thanks to its newly won injunction

weapon and its strengthened alliance with the federal government.

Selected Bibliography

Ernst, D. R. *Lawyers Against Labor: From Individual Rights to Corporate Liberalism.* Urbana: University of Illinois Press, 1995.

Forbath, W. E. *Law and the Shaping of the American Labor Movement.* Cambridge, MA: Harvard University Press, 1991.

Lindsey, A. *The Pullman Strike: The Story of a Unique Experiment and of a Great Labor Upheaval.* Chicago: University of Chicago Press, 1942.

Novak, D. "The Pullman Strike Cases: Debs, Darrow, and the Labor Injunction." In *American Political Trials,* ed. M. R. Belknap, 129–151. Westport, CT: Greenwood Press, 1981.

Papke, D. R. *The Pullman Case: The Clash of Labor and Capital in Industrial America.* Lawrence: University Press of Kansas, 1999.

Salvatore, N. *Eugene V. Debs: Citizen and Socialist.* Urbana: University of Illinois Press, 1982.

Schneirov, R., S. Stromquist, and N. Salvatore, eds. *The Pullman Strike and the Crisis of the 1890s: Essays on Labor and Politics.* Urbana: University of Illinois Press, 1999.

Can Children Under 14 Legally Hold Full-Time Jobs?

——◄◦►——

Philippa Strum

Department of Political Science
Brooklyn College—City University of New York

Hammer v. Dagenhart, 247 U.S. 251 (1918) [U.S. Supreme Court]

◄◦► THE CASE IN BRIEF ◄◦►

Date
1918

Location
North Carolina

Court
U.S. Supreme Court

Principal Participants
Roland H. Dagenhart on behalf of
    Reuben and John Dagenhart
William Hammer
Associate Justice William R. Day

Significance of the Case
The Supreme Court struck down a federal law regulating child labor, thus limiting the power of the Congress to use the commerce clause as a means of dealing with social problems ignored by the state.

During the late nineteenth and early twentieth centuries as the United States became industrialized, the country gradually changed from an economy based largely upon family farms and small businesses into one in which many people worked for huge, impersonal corporations. In addition, successive waves of immigrants brought to the country large numbers of people anxious to establish themselves economically and ready to accept whatever jobs were available. With such an extensive labor supply, employers in mills, factories, mines, and other work places were able to set whatever terms they chose regarding wages, hours, and conditions of employment.

The conditions of employment, by today's standards, were appalling. Men, women, and children all worked for as many as twelve hours a day and for as many as seven days a week on premises that were frequently unsafe and unsanitary. Wages were low; and, of course, this was before the days of federal laws that regulated minimum wages, maximum hours, and working conditions, or the provision of unemployment insurance, disability insurance, social

418

security pensions, and medical care for the poor.

The situation produced a labor union movement that was viewed by employers and most politicians as threatening the traditional American way of life—as well as corporate profits. Unions insisted that individuals were no longer in a position to negotiate with prospective employers on a one-to-one basis, as had been possible in the days of small and individually owned businesses, and that the only hope of bettering the working conditions of laborers was to present collective demands made through organizations sufficiently strong to challenge the financial power of employers. The translation of financial power into political power was evident in the treatment of unions by the state and federal governments. In general, government believed that unions threatened the status quo, not only by demanding a more equitable distribution of wealth, but also by asking if the American society really was one in which any individual who worked hard enough could be economically successful.

The union movement was hampered by the existence of the federal system, which left most economic matters in the hands of the states. Thus, if workers became too bothersome in a particular state, employers had the option of moving their businesses to other states that were harsher in their treatment of unions. And states, recognizing that more businesses meant a bigger tax base, additional jobs, and additional revenue from the purchases made by workers (in short, economic prosperity) competed with each other to attract businesses by being increasingly less responsive to the demands of workers.

A reform movement with the purpose of bettering workers' conditions gradually came into existence. It focused not only on how long laborers worked and for how much, but also on who worked, particularly on the situation of women and children in the work force. As a result, by 1916 every state in the Union had established a minimum age for child labor. The regulations varied widely, however, as states attempted to balance the demands of the reform movement with their competition for corporations. Child labor laws were most stringent in

the northern industrial states where labor was most powerful; southern states, by comparison, had relatively weak laws. North Carolina, for example, prohibited only children under 12 from working. The leniency of the southern regulations had the effect of making the northern labor laws milder than they might have been, for the northern states realistically feared the movement of factories—particularly in the textile industry—to the South. Thus, there was a growing sense of frustration not only among unions and within the reform movement but, where such matters as child labor were concerned, among increasingly large numbers of voters.

Clearly, many felt, the only effective remedy would be enactment of federal regulation. Congress, therefore, decided to discourage the hiring of small children by passing a law affecting producers, manufacturers, dealers, mines, mills, canneries, factories, and workshops that employed children younger than 14 or employed children ages 14 through 16 for more than eight hours a day, more than six days a week, or before 6 A.M. or after 7 P.M. The Federal Child Labor Act of 1916 decreed that products from any such workplace could not be shipped in interstate commerce until thirty days after use of such child labor was ended.

In passing the law, Congress relied upon the power given to it in the Constitution, Article I, Section 8, to "regulate commerce among the several states." The Supreme Court had interpreted the commerce clause as meaning that Congress could regulate the movement of goods across state lines. The Court had ruled earlier that interstate commerce involved transportation, but not production of goods. Production, the Court said, could only be regulated by the states.

The Court derived its interpretation from a theory known as "dual federalism," which held that in their respective spheres, Congress and the states were sovereign and their power could not be interfered with by another body. The Constitution gave Congress sovereign power over foreign policy, for example, and the states could not act in that area. Similarly, the Tenth Amendment, which reserved to the states all powers not specifically given to the national government, thereby gave the states sovereign control over the "police power"—the power to regulate health, welfare, safety, and morals—and Congress could not constitutionally act in *that* sphere. That meant that, while Congress could control interstate commerce, it had no right to regulate intrastate commerce (commerce within one state), including the terms for which labor was performed. Thus, the labor leading to production of cotton in a North Carolina mill, which constituted intrastate commerce, could be regulated only by that state.

The Court had, however, made exceptions. In *Champion v. Ames* (1903) it had upheld an 1895 federal act making it unlawful to transport lottery tickets into a state from another state; in *Hipolite Egg Company v. United States* (1913), it upheld the Food and Drug Act of 1906, which excluded impure food and drugs from interstate commerce; in *Hoke v. United States* (1913), it validated the Mann Act of 1910, which forbade the transportation of women in interstate commerce for the purpose of prostitution; and in *Clark Distilling Company v. Western Maryland Railway Company* (1917), it legitimized the Webb-Kenyon Act of 1913, which outlawed interstate commerce in intoxicating liquors. The Court had held that Congress might well consider each of these forms of commerce undesirable, and opponents of child labor hoped the Court would interpret the clause similarly when dealing with the employment of children.

It did not. In fact, it took the occasion to issue the strongest possible statement of dual federalism.

The question reached the Court when the North Carolina child labor law was challenged by Roland H. Dagenhart, father of Reuben and John Dagenhart, all of whom worked in a Charlotte, North Carolina, cotton mill. Reuben was under 14 and John was between 14 and 16; both worked longer work weeks than those permitted by the federal statute. Mr. Dagenhart claimed that the act was not a true regulation of interstate commerce, that it violated the Tenth Amendment, and that it also violated the due process clause of the Fifth Amendment by depriving his sons of their liberty to work. Scholars have suggested that Mr. Dagenhart was induced by his employers to bring the suit as a

way of eliminating the restriction on child labor, since assertions of violations of rights must be made by those possessing them (or, in the case of minors, by their parents) and the employers could not sue on behalf of the children. In any event, after the trial court agreed with Mr. Dagenhart and enjoined the federal government from enforcing the act, the government appealed to the Supreme Court.

Justice William R. Day wrote the opinion for the 5-4 majority (himself, Chief Justice Edward D. White, and Justices Willis Van Devanter, James McReynolds, and Mahlon Pitney), upholding the lower court's ruling. He said that not only was commerce in the articles involved in the earlier cases harmful, but that interstate transportation was necessary to the accomplishment of the harmful results Congress wished to avoid. In this case, however, there was nothing harmful about the goods the cotton mill wished to ship as indicated by the fact that they could move into interstate commerce thirty days after the mill ceased using the proscribed child labor. The law was not a real regulation of commerce, the Court said, but rather an attempt to regulate the employment of children. Justice Day added that child labor had nothing to do with commerce among the states. Regulation of child labor was a matter reserved for the "police power" of the states by the Tenth Amendment.

In so holding, Justice Day said that powers "not expressly delegated to the national government" are reserved to the people and the states. This is a misstatement of the Tenth Amendment, which does not use the word "expressly" but says only that "The powers not delegated to the United States by the Constitution, nor prohibited by it to the States, are reserved to the States respectively, or to the people." In fact, the records of the First Congress, which formulated the Bill of Rights, show that it had specifically rejected inclusion of the word "expressly" in the Tenth Amendment. And Chief Justice John Marshall, in *McCulloch v. Maryland*, had held that omission of the word "expressly" from the Tenth Amendment meant that the question of whether or not a particular power had been delegated by the Constitution to Congress had to be decided by looking at the entire document.

There, one finds that Article I, Section 8, paragraph 3 gives Congress the "Power . . . to regulate Commerce . . . among the several States," and that paragraph 18 gives it the "Power . . . to make all Laws which shall be necessary and proper for carrying into Execution the foregoing Powers." Thus, whether or not exclusion of the products of child labor was within Congress's power depended upon whether one considered such exclusion either necessary or proper, or both, for carrying out the power to regulate interstate commerce. For Justice Day, however, the answer was not given in the Constitution but depended upon a value judgment. His opinion, therefore, indicated his and his four fellow justices' distaste for governmental regulation of child labor rather than an interpretation that was mandated by the Constitution.

Justice Day acknowledged that "all will admit" that "there should be limitations upon the right to employ children in mines and factories" and that North Carolina's prohibition on the employment of children under 12 was an indication that it opposed employment at too early an age. Other states had set the age minimum higher, but it was North Carolina's right to choose the age it considered appropriate. Uniform child labor laws might be desirable public policy but, however noble Congress's purpose, it could not force such laws upon the states. To do so would be to violate the "essential" constitutional principle that gave the states power "over matters purely local."

Addressing the argument that the desire to attract businesses had led some states to pass more "lenient" laws that gave the business establishments in those states an unfair advantage over their competitors in other states, Justice Day replied that Congress had no power to rectify the situation. Some states, he noted, had passed laws limiting the hours that could be worked by women or fixing minimum wages for them, but Congress had no more right to force other states to follow their example than it did to achieve the same result indirectly by keeping goods produced by women out of interstate transportation.

Justice Day was concerned not only about the *Hammer* case but about its wider implications—what he called the "far reaching result of up-

holding the act." Were the Court to do so, he argued, Congress would be able to regulate virtually any local activity simply by prohibiting the movement of goods in interstate commerce. The prospect of such a phenomenon distressed Justice Day. Not only did it imply to him that "all freedom of commerce" would end; worse still, the power of the states over local matters would also be eliminated, "and thus our system of government [would] be practically destroyed."

The Court's decision was in keeping with its general attitude toward laws dealing with governmental control of business. Interpreting the Constitution as giving business as much freedom as possible, the Court tended to read statutes regulating hours of work, minimum wages, and other limitations on employers as unconstitutional. This approach was challenged, however, in the dissenting opinion that Justice Oliver Wendell Holmes Jr., wrote in the case for himself and Justices Joseph McKenna, Louis D. Brandeis, and John H. Clarke. Holmes began by stating that which "no one is likely to dispute—that the statute in question is within the power expressly given to Congress if considered only as to its immediate effects," which is to keep goods out of interstate commerce, and that if it is invalid there must be some reason. But Holmes could find no such reason. Congress's power over interstate commerce is "given . . . in unqualified terms," he stated, and "the power to regulate" includes "the power to prohibit." This was made clear by the decisions listed above, holding it constitutional for Congress to prohibit such things as impure food and drugs from being transported in interstate commerce.

Since Congress had the undoubted right to prohibit products of child labor in interstate commerce, the question then became whether the regulation was unconstitutional because of its effect upon the states. But the Court itself had made clear that a congressional regulation of interstate commerce was not unconstitutional simply because it interfered with the domestic policy of a state. Holmes pointed to Court decisions upholding federal interstate regulations that "interfered" with things that states normally would control. These included the manufacture of oleomargarine, state banking policies, and businesses within a state that happen to have branches in other states as well. Indicating outrage that the Court would uphold Congress's right to prohibit transportation of "strong drink" but not "the product of ruined lives," he reminded the justices that "if there is any matter upon which civilized countries have agreed—far more unanimously than they have with regard to intoxicants . . . it is the evil of premature and excessive child labor." So, even if the Court permitted Congress to prohibit transportation in interstate commerce of some articles but not others (a power Holmes thought the Court had no right to exercise), it could not claim that Congress was acting irrationally in attacking child labor.

As for the argument that the motivation for Congress's action had been a desire to wipe out child labor rather than a concern about interstate transportation as such, Holmes cited earlier decisions in which the Court stated that the purpose of a law forbidding an article in interstate commerce was irrelevant as long as the power exercised was legitimate. "It is enough," he stated, "that in the opinion of Congress the transportation encourages the evil."

The case was a crucial one because it severely limited the ability of the federal government to use the commerce clause as a means of dealing with social problems ignored by the states. The Court would later hold that Congress could not utilize the spending and taxing power clause to regulate child labor. Together, these cases made federal regulation of child labor impossible. Thus, what might appear to be an obscure argument about the interpretation of the commerce clause was actually the reflection of a clash among the justices about the way in which society should be organized and about approaches to constitutional interpretation. Reflecting the dissension within society, members of the Court were divided about which group should be given greater governmental protection: corporations, which benefited from the competition among the states and from an absence of uniform national legislation regulating the workplace; or the workers, whose terms of employment might be bettered if Congress was permitted to legislate. In addition, Justice Day's method of constitutional interpretation was challenged by that of Justice Holmes who

believed that the Constitution had been designed to be adjusted to the "felt necessities" of different historical eras and that the Court should interpret it so as to permit Congress to respond to changing societal conditions unless some provision of the Constitution specifically prohibited it from doing so. The majority of the Court could accept federal regulation when it dealt with morality or health, but not when it affected traditional economic arrangements— and the Court saw no implications for either morality or health in conditions of labor.

Neither disagreement—which economic groups should be given governmental protection, or the method of constitutional interpretation—would be resolved until the 1930s and 1940s when Supreme Court justices appointed by President Franklin D. Roosevelt decided decisively in favor of government protection of labor and a flexible interpretation of the Constitution. Congress passed the Fair Labor Standards Act in 1938, regulating child labor, and in 1941 a unanimous Court said in *United States v. Darby Lumber Company* that it was constitutional and that Justice Day, in *Hammer v. Dagenhart*, had misread the Constitution. The answer to the question of whether children under 14 could be employed became a resounding "No."

The Supreme Court struck down no laws based on Congress's commerce power between 1936 and the mid-1990s. In 1995, in *U.S. v. Lopez*, a closely divided bench declared unconstitutional a statute prohibiting the possession of guns near schools. In that case, five justices thought that Congress had gone too far in its use of the commerce clause to regulate social policy. Justice Day's gloomy prognostication about the effects on government and American life if such regulations as that in issue in *Hammer* were upheld, however, was not entirely wrong. Since the advent of the New Deal, Congress indeed has used the commerce clause, as well as the Taxing and Spending, and the "necessary and proper" clauses, to minimize state control not only of production and labor but also of many other governmental functions supposedly left to it by the Constitution. These include education, police, health, agriculture, and economic welfare. Extensive funding is made available to the states by Congress for such functions, on condition that the states follow specific policies laid down by Congress. This has turned the states into something far more equivalent to administrative agencies for the federal government than the sovereign bodies favored by Justice Day and, perhaps, by the writers of the Constitution. Nonetheless, the decision to do so has been ratified repeatedly by the American people in elections which have returned to office those politicians responsible for creating a welfare capitalist state in which the central government accepts responsibility for a minimum level of individual well-being. It is this system that has replaced a central government practicing laissez-faire policies along the lines favored by Justice Day.

The political system with a relatively weak central government favored by the Founding Fathers towards the end of the eighteenth century has been altered greatly in the last 200 years due to shifts in American values and changing technology. The Court was asked in *Hammer* to help speed along the process of change through constitutional interpretation. It declined to do so, but society ultimately rejected its decision. Mr. Dagenhart won his case, and the view of Justice Day and his supporters on the Supreme Court triumphed temporarily. But it was Justice Holmes's vision of a constitutional system that responded to the changing desires of the electorate in different historical eras that has become the basis for more recent decisions of the Supreme Court and for the constitutional jurisprudence now practiced in the United States.

Selected Bibliography

Forbath, W. E. *Law and the Shaping of the American Labor Movement.* Cambridge: Harvard University Press, 1991.

Pratt, W. F. *The Supreme Court under Edward Douglass White, 1910–1921.* Columbia: University of South Carolina Press, 1999.

Ross, W. G. *A Muted Fury: Populists, Progressives, and Labor Unions Confront the Courts, 1890–1937.* Princeton: Princeton University Press, 1994.

Semonche, John E. *Charting the Future: The Supreme Court Responds to a Changing Society, 1890–1920.* Westport, CT: Greenwood Press, 1978.

Wood, Stephen B. *Constitutional Politics in the Progressive Era: Child Labor and the Law.* Chicago: University of Chicago Press, 1968.

Miscellaneous Governmental Regulations

Copyright Law: Limiting Literary Monopolies

Maxwell Bloomfield

Columbus School of Law
Catholic University of America

Wheaton v. Peters, 8 Peters 591 (1834) [U.S. Supreme Court]

◦► THE CASE IN BRIEF ◄◦

Date
1834

Location
District of Columbia

Court
U.S. Supreme Court

Principal Participants
Henry Wheaton
Richard Peters
Associate Justice John McLean

Significance of the Case
As a result of this case, American authors to this day can claim only the copyright protection that is specifically written into statutory law.

Advocates of republican government in the late eighteenth century always insisted that its survival depended upon a well-informed and responsible citizenry. As one means of public improvement, the framers of the Constitution (in Article I, Section 8) empowered Congress to "promote the progress of science and the useful arts, by securing for limited times to authors and inventors the exclusive right to their respective writings and discoveries." The First Congress acted to protect literary property by passing a copyright law in May 1790; its provisions were supplemented by further legislation in 1802. Pursuant to these statutes, an author who followed certain prescribed notification procedures could enjoy complete control over the publication and sale of a book or map for a period of fourteen years. No writer tested the limit of copyright protection until 1831, when a court reporter sued his successor for copyright infringement. The case established the foundations of modern American copyright law and, incidentally, revealed some major contradictions in the republican value system.

Court reporters were the legal drudges of the early republic. Underpaid and overworked, they found their only real compensation through the sale of their published reports for which they claimed monopoly rights under the copyright laws. Henry Wheaton, who served as the third reporter of the United States Supreme Court from 1816 to 1827, brought out twelve volumes of *Reports* before he resigned to become chargé d'affaires to Denmark. Wheaton planned to renew each copyright as it expired by issuing a new edition; he hoped in this way to secure a steady annual income of $2,000 for many years.

But his successor, Richard Peters, had other plans. Citing the high cost and relative inaccessibility of the previous twenty-five volumes, Peters proposed to publish an inexpensive set of *Condensed Reports* in only six volumes. These would comprise all Supreme Court decisions down to 1827, leaving out the accompanying arguments of counsel and other material supplied by the original reporters. The series would then continue with the publication of Peters's ongoing *Reports* each year, enabling him to profit both from his own labors and from the work of his predecessors. Such a project appealed to the competitive entrepreneurial spirit of the Jacksonian age, and Peters had no difficulty in lining up 900 advance subscribers. Despite Wheaton's outraged protests, the several volumes of *Condensed Reports* appeared as promised between 1830 and 1834, at a total cost to the public of only $25.

As soon as he saw "his" cases back in print, Wheaton sought an injunction to restrain Peters from further publication and to compel him to account for any profits he had already made through copyright violations. Wheaton's attorneys appealed both to the federal statutes and to Anglo-American common law, which in their view gave authors perpetual and exclusive control of their literary works.

In response, Peters's lawyers denied that he had violated any law. Wheaton's rights depended solely upon congressional legislation, they argued, and he had not performed one of the essential conditions prescribed for establishing those rights. Moreover, they argued, no one could obtain a copyright in judicial opinions that were as much the law of the land as legislative acts, and hence fell within the public domain.

Wheaton v. Peters forced the federal judiciary to choose between two basic components of republican ideology: the promotion of competition and democratic access to markets and knowledge, on the one hand; and an equally strong commitment to the sanctity of private property on the other. In the federal circuit court at Philadelphia Judge Joseph Hopkinson ruled against Wheaton. Hopkinson's learned and persuasive opinion was later adopted in large part by a majority of the United States Supreme Court that heard the case on appeal early in 1834.

The arguments and opinions fill 108 pages in Peters's *Reports*. Associate Justice John McLean, speaking for four of the six participating judges, disposed first of Wheaton's common-law claims. There is no common law of the United States, McLean flatly declared. Each colony was settled at different times and under different conditions; and the settlers adopted only those parts of the English common law that were suited to their varying needs. In addition, the English common law of copyright remained undeveloped and confused down to the eve of the American Revolution; it could not have provided a coherent body of principles that the early settlers of Pennsylvania—or, by implication, any other colony—might have brought with them. Wheaton therefore could look only to the federal copyright laws for the protection of his literary rights.

Since those congressional statutes did confer temporary monopolistic privileges, McLean reasoned that their provisions should be strictly construed in the public interest. The record did not provide sufficient proof that Wheaton had deposited one copy of each volume with the secretary of state, as required by the act of 1790. Accordingly, McLean ordered the case remanded to the circuit court so that a jury might determine the facts.

Although Wheaton may have taken some small comfort from this part of McLean's opinion, the faulty state of federal record keeping made it extremely unlikely that he could ever prove to a jury's satisfaction that he had complied with the law. And McLean's final words effectively demolished any lingering dreams of future enrichment he may still have entertained: "It may be proper to remark that the court are unanimously of opinion, that no reporter has or can have any copyright in the written opinions delivered by this court; and that the judges thereof cannot confer on any reporter any such right." In other words, Wheaton's copyright, if it existed at all, extended only to his supplementary notes, not to the decisions themselves.

As a result of *Wheaton v. Peters*, American authors today can claim only the copyright protection afforded them by statute. And judicial opinions continue to belong only to the public. They must always be available "for the free and unrestrained use of the citizens of the United States," one of Peters's lawyers urged, because "knowledge of them is essential to the safety of all."

Selected Bibliography

Baker, Elizabeth Feaster. *Henry Wheaton*. Philadelphia, PA: University of Pennsylvania Press, 1937.

Joyce, Craig. "The Rise of the Supreme Court Reporter: An Institutional Perspective on Marshall Court Ascendancy." *Michigan Law Review* 83 (April 1985): 1291–1391.

Newmyer, R. Kent. *Supreme Court Justice Joseph Story: Statesman of the Old Republic*. Chapel Hill: University of North Carolina Press, 1985.

White, G. Edward. *The Marshall Court and Cultural Change, 1815–35*. New York: Macmillan Publishing Company, 1988.

Corporate Growth v. States' Rights

————◄◦►————

Eric Monkkonen

Department of History
University of California, Los Angeles

Bank of Augusta v. Earle, 13 Peters 519 (1839) [U.S. Supreme Court]

◄◦► **THE CASE IN BRIEF** ◄◦►

Date
 1839

Location
 Alabama; Pennsylvania

Court
 U.S. Supreme Court

Principal Participants
 Joseph Earle
 Bank of Augusta
 Second Bank of the United States
 Daniel Webster
 Charles Jared Ingersoll
 Chief Justice Roger B. Taney

Significance of the Case
 The Court rejected the "extraterritoriality" of a corporation but did not reject the legal theory of comity (respect for the laws of another jurisdiction within one's own territory).

The cases coming together in *Bank of Augusta v. Earle*, known as the Alabama or Comity Cases, have had a continuing, though changing, significance in American constitutional and economic history. The decision handed down by Chief Justice Roger Taney marked the end of a legal conflict that raged during the Panic of 1837; the decision also marked the beginning of the U.S. Supreme Court's stand on foreign corporations, the beginning of economic nationalism, and the beginning of the peculiar American attitude towards control of economic forces.

The case arose out of Joseph Earle's refusal in Mobile to pay a bill of exchange to the Bank of Augusta. Earle contended that out-of-state banking corporations were forbidden by Alabama's constitution that gave the state bank a monopoly. Earle also tried the same trick on the New Orleans and Carollton Railroad Company, a banking corporation. The Bank of Augusta brought suit in circuit court, and newly appointed Justice John McKinley of Huntsville decided in favor of Earle. His decision was based on two points: first, he agreed with Earle that the Alabama Constitution prohibited out-of-state banks from doing business within the state; second, he argued that the international legal theory of comity (respect for the laws of another jurisdiction within one's own territory) did not apply and that corporations cannot operate outside the jurisdiction of the legislative body which created them (the so-called "restrictive theory" of corporations).

Not too surprisingly, given the loophole offered by McKinley's decision, a man named William Primrose refused to honor a bill of exchange on the Bank of the United States, a bank operating under a charter from the state of Pennsylvania. As most banks, including the Bank of Augusta, suspended payment during the Panic of 1837, a legal basis for refusing to pay on bills of exchange would have been a boon to cotton factors and merchants. The Panic ended quickly, however; "flush times" returned, and Earle's device was no longer needed. The case went up to the Supreme Court on a writ of error, with Justice Joseph Story noting that McKinley's decision had "frightened half of the lawyers and all the corporations of the country out of their proprieties."

The Court considered these cases together. Although touching upon McKinley's first point, the language of the Alabama Constitution, the focus of the arguments and of Taney's decision was the question of comity and the related problem of the "restrictive" theory of corporations. This theory holds that the corporation has no extraterritorial existence; it is created as a legal entity and cannot exist beyond the jurisdiction of its creating authority. This theory had evolved in the seventeenth and eighteenth centuries as a corollary to the special, privileged nature of corporations. The competing "liberal" theory of corporations, on the other hand, holds that once chartered, the corporation may move from the area of jurisdiction in which it was created. Proponents of this theory, which is implicitly accepted today, admit its somewhat illogical basis—for it amounts to extraterritorial legislation—but point to its practicality. In 1839, the terms, "liberal" and "restrictive," were not applied this way, but the arguments before the Court accepted and even defined these concepts.

Daniel Webster, arguing for the Second Bank of the United States, took the "liberal" point of view, contending that once created a corporation was free to move about and was, in fact, a citizen under the Constitution. This entitled corporations to the benefits of the privileges and immunities clause, Article IV, Section 2 of the U.S. Constitution: "The Citizens of each State shall be entitled to all Privileges and Immunities of Citizens in the several States." Charles Jared Ingersoll argued, for James Earle, the "restrictive" theory: "Corporations are creations of municipal law, having no existence or power to contract whatever, until enabled so to do by a law, or other legitimate permission of the sovereignty wherever acting. Especially is this conservative principle indispensable as an undelegated right of these United States. Otherwise the smallest member of this Union may legislate for and govern all the rest." The other arguments before the Court ran along the same lines, the major variation being the argument of attorney D. B. Ogden who claimed that comity was an implicit binding principle between states. The principle of comity, though used in conjunction with the "liberal" theory of corporations, was really an independent argument that did not consider corporate law.

In his decision, Taney took advantage of the principle of comity to avoid confronting a choice between the "restrictive" and "liberal" theories. He denied that corporations were citizens and agreed that laws, including corporate charters, did not have extraterritoriality. But he held that comity was implicitly accepted by every state and, unless it was explicitly repudiated, the Court had to assume its existence.

Interpretations of the meaning of his decision have varied greatly due to its avoidance of issues and inherent ambiguity. After all, Taney rejected the "liberal" practice. This has led one recent commentator to plead for a revision of the theory and for an end to the deplorable difference between theory and practice. Other commentators see Taney's decision as a brilliant acceptance of the "liberal" theory of corporations and his conceding to states the right to repudiate comity as a sensible approach to corporate regulation. At the time of his decision, Alabamians saw it as an encroachment upon their rights; Justice McKinley, in his dissenting opinion, saw the Court as imputing national power to the states. The old Federalists saw the decision as a boon to corporations; Justice Story congratulated Taney on the decision and said it did "honor" to Taney and the Court—no doubt thinking of the Federalist Marshall Court. Other recent writers have seen the case as laying the foundations for the non-regulatory state after the Civil War, while some see it as a causal factor in the growth of corporate capitalism. Finally, some see it as a concession to the status quo, neither retarding nor creating institutional, economic, or legal change.

But the most significant impact of the case is in its legitimizing and institutionalizing of the concept of positive regulation. This position was hinted at by McKinley in his dissenting opinion: "[the] Court having . . . conceded that Alabama might make laws to prohibit foreign banks to make contracts, thereby admitted, by implication, that she could make laws to permit such contracts. I think it would have been proper to have left the power there, to be exercised or not, as Alabama, in her sovereign discretion, might judge best for her interest or comity." In other words, McKinley sketched two approaches to regulating corporations: one gave the state the power to forbid, the other gave the state the power to permit. Put another way, one required positive effort on the part of the state to regulate, the other having implied regulation, required positive effort to allow corporate action. The first is the concept of positive regulation, the other, negative regulation. By approving the concept of positive regulation, Taney set the stage for continuing efforts of the state to police corporations, with laxness on the part of the state allowing often dangerous corporate freedom. Had the negative regulation concept been sanctioned, the corporation would be required to ask permission for all actions, a change that would put the state automatically in control of corporate action. Thus, the implications and long-range effects of this case are still being felt, even though these effects change with the economy. And what was once a regulatory and egalitarian point of view has become an anti-regulatory and privileged position.

There are three levels of cultural context within which to view *Bank of Augusta v. Earle*: the integrated commercial-political structure of Alabama as the participants themselves viewed it; the nature of institutional growth and change in the period from our perspective; and, finally, the broader patterns of economic growth and change, again seen from our point of view.

The best, and most entertaining, way to find how the actors perceived their own environment may be to review the writings of the southwestern humorist, lawyer, and legislator, Joseph G. Baldwin. Widely known and appreciated by his fellow Alabamians for his wit and insight, Baldwin saw the economic world as one of "humbug" and deception, with paper money and corporations at its false base. Also, William Garrett, the secretary of state of Alabama, later described the carnival atmosphere connected with bank affairs, thus corroborating Baldwin's views.

More attention has been devoted to the second level of explanation. It describes, from a modern point of view, the institutions of the period, especially those of corporations. It emphasized the lack of banking facilities in Mobile (there were two), and this created difficulties for the merchants and factors in the busy cotton-exporting port. Until 1836, corporations, as government agencies, were chartered mainly for public services, schools, and hospitals, "to facilitate the growth, prosperity, and welfare of the community." The pace of incorporation speeded up in 1836, and a state bank was finally chartered in hopes of stopping currency drain and loss of profits to other states. The bank's key role in public policy indicates its political, economic, and public importance, a role approximated by that of Alabama's state-owned bank. It is small wonder, then, why Alabama felt threatened by out-of-state banks. The Bank of Augusta, with one-sixth of its stock reserved for the state, was a good source of income for Georgia, although even it had to suspend payments in the Panic of 1837.

The third level of explanation provides a description of broad movements in the economy and attempts to measure the effects of government intervention. Quantitatively, little money was spent by government agencies in the nineteenth century (about 2.4 percent of GNP in 1839). This small amount was highly significant in stimulating economic growth because of the way in which it was spent—in specific and direct support to selected industries; in risk taking, innovation, and bottleneck removing; and in creating a favorable economic climate and thereby raising the expectations of the private sector.

Because southern cotton was the major American export, fluctuations in its price caused fluctuations in the American economy and, when the fall of cotton prices in 1837 was joined by the drop in western land sales, a major depression set in. Interregional and international trade depended on money transfer through bills of exchange. Because of these factors, Taney's decision could easily have wrecked the American economy had it been against the plaintiff. We cannot claim Taney's decision caused the corporate and economic growth of the nineteenth century, but certainly it provided the foundation of federal policy and legitimized the basis of the American economy.

We may never know if James Earle was just trying to pull a slippery maneuver during the Panic of 1837 or whether the case represented the result of a long struggle in Alabama. The national importance of the case has obscured its origins and, if it were not for the broader patterns described above, the case would seem almost like a random occurrence. The accounts of Garrett and Baldwin make clear that the Panic of 1837 was perceived as a result of Andrew Jackson's specie circular. Perhaps Earle's maneuver was viewed as another attempt to fight back against the false paper corporations. Clearly, the Panic and the following depression caused some desperate economic behavior in the West, and westerners were not reluctant to try any expedient. Possibly the most important aspect of this case is its relationship to the attempt of Alabama to control corporations in its local economy, from the state bank chartered by the constitution in 1822 to the state's obvious lack of control over various external factors in 1848. If the experience of Pennsylvania is at all typical, most states lost control of

their quasi-public corporations; the image that emerges is of the states holding a tigerish economy by the tail.

Perhaps one of the most significant elements in this case was the newly appointed justice, John McKinley. McKinley, a native of Culpeper County, Virginia, was a Huntsville resident who distinguished himself first in the United States Senate and later in the House. "He was," in the words of his only biographer, "a man of high and noble aims, possessed of remarkable force and energy. In appearance he was tall and commanding, with a countenance that exhibited great strength of character, and wore an habitual benevolent expression. . . ." His dissent in *Bank of Augusta v. Earle*, essentially a recasting of his circuit court opinion, remains a fitting monument to his life. Upholding the restrictive theory of foreign corporations, and the rights of Alabama, McKinley's decision radically ignored the dependence of the national economy on bills of exchange. He perceived a difference between Jacksonian principles and contemporary practice and opted in favor of principles. Like Thoreau or Ann Hutchinson, he did so at a crucial moment, such that his decision threatened society; like Thoreau's or Hutchinson's, his decision could not have been allowed to stand.

All of the lawyers who argued this case before the Court were well known in their day, but, with the exception of Daniel Webster, their significance seems to have faded. The name of Charles Jared Ingersoll, Philadelphia poet, playwright, historian, and lawyer, was once a rallying standard for the enemies of large corporations, money powers, and other unpopular causes. Described to his grandson as "sharp and incisive as a hatchet," he was noted for his enmity toward John Sergeant and his eccentric penchant for wearing costumes of the revolution. Little fame remains of this once controversial and eccentric character.

Daniel Webster was, of course, an archetypal lawyer, and there is more material on him than on anyone else involved in this case. In his published letters, the only reference Webster makes to the Court before which he argued this case is a blasé, "the business before the court is not now great, nor is the court itself what it has been." His main concern is over his upcoming European trip! Yet, one Webster biographer claimed that this case was one of Webster's "most important banking and corporation cases."

Representing the Second Bank along with Webster was John Sergeant, the Second Bank's chief legal political advisor and Charles J. Ingersoll's enemy. Somewhat surprisingly, David B. Ogden, who represented the Bank of Augusta with a state's sovereignty-comity argument, was a well-known Federalist. In a famous argument, he once said, "We deny . . . there is any such thing as a sovereign state." Little is known about William J. Vande Gruff, the lawyer who defended Primrose, except that his last name was likely spelled Vandergraff. Nineteenth-century Supreme Court reporters frequently misspelled the names of litigants.

The composition of the Supreme Court in 1839 was truly Jacksonian: only Story, appointed by Madison, and McKinley, appointed by Van Buren, were not Jackson appointees. The key to understanding the Jackson court is Chief Justice Roger B. Taney. For five generations, the Taney patriarchs had purchased plantations for their sons, but in Roger's generation this was no longer feasible or profitable; thus he went to college and became a lawyer, a sign of changing times and a changing economy. Taney apparently distinguished carefully between "great moneyed corporations," which he hated, and "normal" corporations, if still very large, which he could abide. Remembering that Taney was of the landed gentry and a Federalist bank director whose main legal specialty was business suits should help us keep some perspective. In *Bank of Augusta v. Earle*, Taney steered a middle course between polar positions, denying a corporation's extraterritorial existence, yet circumventing this by implied consent through comity.

The best criticism of Taney's decision came in McKinley's dissenting opinion. Using the restrictive theory of corporations, McKinley claimed that, "This is the first time since the adoption of the Constitution of the United States, that any federal court has, directly or indirectly imputed national power to any of the states of the Union." Governor Bagby of Alabama seconded McKinley's reaction. The Court's decision, he claimed, was a "palpable and direct encroachment upon the sovereignty of Alabama."

Two remarks in letters written by Justice Story stand as evidence of the fear McKinley's decision created and the relief of Taney's decision. Story, in a letter to Charles Sumner, of June 1838, says, "My brother, McKinley, has recently made a most sweeping decision in the Circuit Court of Alabama which has frightened half the lawyers and all the corporations of the country out of their proprieties. . . . What say you to all this? So we go!" In another letter, written to Taney after the case, Story says, "Your opinion in the corporation cases has given very general satisfaction to the public; and I hope you will allow me to say that I think it does great honor to yourself as well as the court." The only personal reaction on the losing side of the case, other than in McKinley's dissenting decision, is a letter written to Ingersoll by a Mr. Gilpin in which Ingersoll "was told in reply that he should not be worried at his inability to defeat a corporation, when the whole country had to bear them, as Sinbad had his burden."

Many scholars see in Taney's decision the foundations of corporate growth in the nineteenth century. In one view, this decision and Taney's other corporate decisions demonstrated how "law lent its weight to the thrust of ambitions" in the nineteenth century. Another author claims that the decision encouraged the "commercial harmony" of the country while the long-range result "was decidedly to encourage corporate expansion." Finally, another scholar of the period claims that *Bank of Augusta v. Earle* laid the "legal foundation" of the "promotional, non-regulatory state of post–Civil War America." On balance, the legacy of Taney's implied comity doctrine, which introduced the concept of positive regulation, has been responsible for the continuing difficulty in governmental control of corporate behavior. Thus, corporate behavior is implicitly sanctioned, while regulation has become, at best, a rear-guard attempt to follow the economy.

Selected Bibliography

Baxter, Maurice. *Daniel Wester and the Supreme Court.* Amherst: University of Massachusetts Press, 1966.

Hurst, J. Willard. *Law and the Conditions of Freedom in the Nineteenth Century United States.* Madison: University of Wisconsin Press, 1967.

Swisher, Carl B. *The Taney Period, 1836–1864.* New York: Macmillan, 1974.

The Scope of Admiralty Jurisdiction

---◄◦►---

James W. Ely Jr.
School of Law
Vanderbilt University

Propeller Genesee Chief v. Fitzhugh, 12 Howard 443 (1851) [U.S. Supreme Court]

◄◦► THE CASE IN BRIEF ◄◦►

Date
1851

Location
Lake Ontario

Court
U.S. Supreme Court

Principal Participants
Owners of the *Genesee Chief*
Owners of the *Cuba*
Chief Justice Roger B. Taney

Significance of the Case
Taney's ruling established the basis for subsequent judicial extension of admiralty jurisdiction to be applicable to all waters determined to be "navigable in fact." The decision encouraged the extension of commerce throughout the United States.

A nighttime collision between two ships on Lake Ontario afforded an opportunity for the United States Supreme Court to reconsider the scope of federal judicial authority under the admiralty clause of the Constitution. The result was a significant extension of admiralty jurisdiction to encompass navigable fresh water lakes and rivers.

Admiralty jurisdiction in England was limited to waters within the ebb and flow of the tide. An acceptance of this doctrine in the United States would have precluded an exercise of federal admiralty power in the Great Lakes and the extensive chain of inland rivers. Dissatisfaction with the traditional rule mounted as the country grew in size, and commerce on western lakes and rivers increased rapidly. Yet shipping on lakes and rivers was governed by a patchwork of often inconsistent state laws and cases were tried in state courts. Anxious to promote trade on the interior waterways, Congress enacted a statute in 1845 extending the jurisdiction of the federal courts to certain cases arising upon the Great Lakes and rivers connecting them. The constitutionality of this measure was soon put to a test.

In May of 1847 the steamboat *Genesee Chief* hit and sank the *Cuba,* a schooner engaged in transporting wheat. The owners of the *Cuba* filed an action for damages in the United States District Court. They alleged that the accident was caused by the negligence of the crew of the *Genesee Chief.* Their lawsuit was instituted under the 1845 act. The owners of the *Genesee Chief* blamed the mishap on the *Cuba.* More important, the owners also argued that the collision occurred within New York waters and, consequently, the federal court had no jurisdiction over the case.

The district court judge ruled in favor of the owners of the *Cuba,* and the owners of the *Genesee Chief* appealed to the circuit court. When the tribunal affirmed the decree, the owners of the *Genesee Chief* carried their case to the Supreme Court. The attorney for the *Genesee Chief* advanced a states' rights position. They argued that the 1845 act was unconstitutional because there was no basis for admiralty jurisdiction. Further, the statute did not purport to regulate commerce between the states and, thus, could not be upheld by virtue of the commerce clause.

Chief Justice Roger B. Taney skillfully led the Supreme Court to sustain the validity of the 1845 act and thereby enlarge federal admiralty jurisdiction. In a bow to states' rights sentiment, Taney first concluded that the statute dealt with the reach of judicial authority and could not be upheld as a regulation of commerce. He then turned to the thorny issue of federal admiralty jurisdiction. The Constitution simply provided that the judicial power should extend "to all cases of admiralty or maritime jurisdiction." The crucial question was the extent of this authority.

The Supreme Court, in an 1825 opinion by Justice Joseph Story, had adopted the traditional English rule restricting admiralty jurisdiction to tidal waters. In order to undercut this precedent, Taney began his analysis by stressing the differences between England and the United States with respect to maritime commerce. In England there were no major rivers or lakes beyond the ebb and flow of the tide, so courts might naturally equate tidewater with navigation. Such a restrictive defi-

nition was entirely unsuitable in the United States with its "thousands of miles of public navigable water, including lakes and rivers in which there is no tide." Taney characterized the Great Lakes as "in truth inland seas." According to the chief justice, admiralty jurisdiction depended upon "the navigable character of the water, and not upon the ebb and flow of the tide."

Taney then explained that the 1825 decision was rendered "when the commerce on the rivers of the west and on the lakes was in its infancy, and of little importance. . . ." The chief justice also stressed that Congress had recognized a broad scope for admiralty jurisdiction by enacting the measure under review. He proceeded to overrule the earlier decision on the ground that it "was founded in error," and he thus upheld the constitutionality of the 1845 act. Turning to the facts of the pending case, Taney found that there was evidence of carelessness on the part of the *Genesee Chief*'s crew. Consequently, the decree of the circuit court was affirmed.

Only Justice Peter V. Daniel dissented. An ardent champion of states' rights, he maintained that the admiralty power of the federal courts was determined by the English practice at the time the Constitution was adopted. Moreover, Daniel expressed sharp disagreement with Taney's method of analysis, declaring that the Constitution could not be enlarged "according to the opinions of the judiciary, entertained upon their views of expediency and necessity."

It is difficult to exaggerate the significance of the *Genesee Chief* decision for American commerce and navigation. Indeed, Charles Warren observed that "few decisions had ever produced so revolutionary a change in Federal jurisdiction. . . ." Technically the Supreme Court only concluded that the 1845 Act was within the constitutional grant of admiralty power, but the rejection of the tidal waters doctrine had wider implications. As a result of *Genesee Chief,* shipping on inland lakes and rivers was regulated by uniform federal admiralty principles. This, in turn, encouraged the extension of commercial activity throughout the country.

The decision in *Genesee Chief* offers valuable insights into the workings of the Supreme Court under Taney's leadership. Although supposedly less nationalistic than his predecessor, John Marshall, Taney was prepared to extend greatly federal power in appropriate circumstances. Moreover, Taney demonstrated that he was no blind adherent to the principle of *stare decisis.* His opinion in *Genesee Chief* was apparently only the second by the Supreme Court that overruled a prior constitutional ruling.

In addition, Taney was willing to accommodate legal doctrine to the emergence of new technology. The invention of the steamboat revolutionized travel on inland waterways and rendered the restrictive tidal rule obsolete. Indeed, Taney observed that, "until the discovery of steamboats, there could be nothing like foreign commerce upon waters with an unchanging current resisting the upward passage." Like Taney's opinion in *Charles River Bridge, Genesee Chief* exemplified the impact of technology on the growth of law.

Selected Bibliography

Conover, Milton. "The Abandonment of the 'Tidewater' Concept of Admiralty Jurisdiction in the United States." *Oregon Law Review* 38 (December 1958): 34–53.

Currie, David P. "The Constitution in the Supreme Court: Article IV and Federal Powers, 1836–1864." *Duke Law Journal* 1983 (September 1983): 695–747.

Lewis, Walker. *Without Fear or Favor: A Biography of Chief Justice Roger Brooke Taney.* Boston: Houghton Mifflin Co., 1965.

Swisher, Carl B. *History of the Supreme Court of the United States.* Vol. 5, *The Taney Period, 1836–64.* New York: Macmillan Publishing Co., Inc., 1974.

Warren, Charles. *The Supreme Court in United States History, II, 1836–1918.* Rev. ed. Boston: Little, Brown and Co., 1926.

Wiecek, William M. *Liberty Under Law: The Supreme Court in American Life.* Baltimore: Johns Hopkins University Press, 1988.

"A Sore Grievance" to the Traveler

—◄○►—

Elizabeth B. Monroe

Department of History
Indiana University-
Purdue University at Indianapolis

The West River Bridge Company v. Joseph Dix and the Towns of Brattleboro and Dummerston,
in the County of Windham, 6 Howard 507 (1848) [U.S. Supreme Court]

◄○► THE CASE IN BRIEF ◄○►

Date
1848

Location
Vermont

Court
U.S. Supreme Court

Principal Participants
West River Bridge Company
Joseph Dix and towns of Brattleboro and
    Dummerston, Vermont
Daniel Webster and Jacob Collamer
Samuel Phelps
Associate Justice Peter V. Daniel

Significance of the Case
The Court found the state power of
eminent domain superior to the
constitutional protection of private
property.

In 1842 Joseph Dix and fifty-four other petitioners of Brattleboro and Dummerston, Vermont, spoke of "a sore grievance" to the traveler to describe the nearby toll bridge over the West River. In their petition, Dix and his fellow citizens requested that the county court follow the procedures of a recent state statute which provided for public takeover of "any real estate, easement, or franchise" when "the public good requires a public highway." According to the statute, courts could take such private property providing the owner was compensated for the loss. In answer to the petition, the Windham County Court appointed a commission to examine the matter. In May 1843 the commissioners reported that the bridge should be taken for public use and that the towns of Brattleboro and Dummerston should pay the West River Bridge Corporation $4,000 for the bridge, toll-house, two acres of land, and the franchise. Both of the towns and the bridge company filed objections to the commissioners' findings. In November the county court heard arguments but accepted the commissioners' report and assessed the two towns for payments to the bridge company.

439

In 1844, the Vermont Supreme Court reviewed the constitutional issues of the case. Attorneys for the bridge company stated that their clients had received their charter from the Vermont legislature in 1795 and that this charter was a contract. Their clients had agreed to build and maintain the bridge at their own expense, and, in exchange, the legislature had granted them the privilege of collecting tolls for 100 years. The bridge company had fulfilled its obligations and conformed to all of the requirements of the charter. The attorneys argued that, according to the Vermont Constitution, revoking their clients' charter required specific action by the legislature or in a jury trial at common law. Since the 1839 statute did not provide for either of these procedures, it appeared to violate the state constitution. Because the statute infringed on the bridge proprietors' charter, it also appeared, on its face, to violate the U.S. Constitution, which proscribed state impairment of contractual obligations. The defendants' attorneys contended that the statute was constitutional and that the county court proceedings had conformed to the statute. The Vermont Supreme Court decided in favor of the defendants: it ruled that the statute was valid for the purpose of revoking the franchise in order to create a free public highway; and it held that the proceedings were a lawful exercise of the eminent domain authority of the state. Therefore, the state supreme court held that the statute did not violate either the Vermont Constitution or U.S. Constitution.

Eminent domain had been used during the colonial period to condemn private property for public highways, ferry-ways and bridges. In the early national period, eminent domain continued to be used for state takings of private property for public use. Public demand for better transportation facilities also compelled state legislatures to grant corporate charters to investors who agreed to meet public transportation needs in exchange for the ability to collect tolls for a period of years. But, by the second quarter of the nineteenth century, many corporations had collected tolls far in excess of their construction and maintenance costs. Other corporations had charters conferring long-term monopolies along important lines of travel. As a result, by the 1830s the public perceived outstanding charters as burdens and impediments to future transportation development, and they demanded the termination of extensive privileges. State legislatures soon invoked their powers of eminent domain to condemn existing charter rights in order to create free access to transportation improvements and to expedite replacement of old technologies with new ones.

The bridge company appealed to the U.S. Supreme Court and retained Daniel Webster and Jacob Collamer as counsel. Samuel S. Phelps represented the defendants. The Court heard the arguments of the two sides in early 1848. Webster and Collamer contended that the power of eminent domain reached only real and personal property. According to these legal luminaries, a corporate franchise was not property, but was "pure franchise." Therefore, it was not available for taking. Even if eminent domain could reach franchises, the contract clause of the U.S. Constitution barred such action. On the other hand, Phelps argued that eminent domain was an indispensable attribute of sovereignty, limited only in its application by "public use" and "just compensation" restrictions. The county court's expropriation of the West River Bridge and the company's charter complied with these restrictions. There only remained the question of the superiority of the contract clause. According to Phelps, every grant from the state was subject to eminent domain. While the contract clause protected the grantee from legislative bad faith, it could not protect private property from the sovereign power to provide for public purposes.

Justice Peter V. Daniel wrote the opinion of the Court. He accepted the view that the charter was a contract, but he declared that it contained implicit as well as explicit terms. Among the former was the state's power of eminent domain, for "it cannot be justly disputed, that in every political sovereign community there inheres necessarily the right and the duty of guarding its own existence, and of protecting and promoting the interest and welfare of the community at large." Eminent domain was "paramount to all private rights vested under the government" and "in no wise interfere[d] with the inviolability of contracts." According to the Court, the internal improvement policy of the country rested on this power that condemned private property for public use. Franchises were merely one form of property, and there was "nothing peculiar to a franchise which can class it higher or render it more sacred than other property." Vermont's exercise of eminent domain to extinguish the West River Bridge franchise did not violate the U.S. Constitution.

Justice Daniel recognized that government must continue to meet changing public needs, even at the expense of private property. In *West River Bridge v. Dix* he found the state power of eminent domain superior to the constitutional protection of private property by the contract clause. By the late nineteenth century, when public concern shifted to the need to regulate private property "affected with a public interest," courts returned to Daniel's reasoning in *West River Bridge* to uphold state exercise of reserved police powers.

Selected Bibliography

Frank, John P. *Justice Daniel Dissenting: A Biography of Peter V. Daniel, 1784–1860.* Cambridge: Harvard University Press, 1964.

Scheiber, Harry N. "The Road to *Munn*: Eminent Domain and the Concept of Public Purpose in the State Courts." *Perspectives in American History* 5 (1971): 329–402.

Destructive Creation

—◄◦►—

Gordon Morris Bakken
Department of History
California State University, Fullerton

People of California v. Gold Run Ditch and Mining Company, 66 Cal. 318 (1884)
[California Supreme Court]

◄◦► THE CASE IN BRIEF ◄◦►

Date
1884

Location
California

Court
California Supreme Court

Principal Participants
State of California
Gold Run Ditch and Mining Company

Significance of the Case
The state government intervened and stopped a large mining company from polluting nearby rivers. In protecting the public interest, the court ruled that private enterprise had no right to destroy the environment.

Gold mining in the American West pushed the creative fervor of technology to ecologically destructive ends. Hydraulic mining quickly developed with a gospel of efficiency to produce more gold more quickly than by other methods. Huge supplies of water were appropriated and channeled a great distance into high pressure nozzles aimed at the gold-bearing hillsides of the motherlode country of California. These monstrous streams of water slashed away dirt, sand, grass, trees, gravel, and a little gold. They also created floods of mud slopping into sluices. Gold was obtained with rapidity and the topography was brutally altered. Profit was obtained, but downstream the mud cascaded into channels of trade and onto fertile agricultural fields.

The hydraulic mining caused the channels of the American and Sacramento rivers to begin to fill. The filth fouled Suisun Bay and swirled into the San Francisco and San Pablo Bays. The bed of the American River oozed up 10 to 12 feet, and the Sacramento ascended by 6 to 12 feet. The river channels widened and the spring floods invaded the rich farm lands of the delta, destroying more acreage every year. Deep draught river steamers could no longer navigate to Sacramento City except during the spring flood season. Commerce and agriculture were clearly impaired, and victims looked to law for recourse. Ultimately, on behalf of many victims, the state sued the mining company.

The California court in the *Gold Run Ditch and Mining Company* case took judicial notice of the navigation of the Sacramento River as "a great public highway." As a public highway, the people had "paramount and controlling rights" including "a right to use the water flowing over it, for the purposes of transportation and commercial intercourse." The law provided that "an unauthorized invasion of the rights of the public to navigate the water fouling over the soil is a public nuisance; and an unauthorized encroachment upon the soil itself is known in law as a purpresture." This law of the case was based on English law (particularly upon Sir Edward Coke's *Institutes of the Laws of England*) and state cases decided in the eastern states.

The court also dispensed with the defendant's argument regarding identifying the company's debris amid the turbid waters. Why should one hydraulic mining operation be stopped when the pollution is the aggregate product of many hydraulic miners and the forces of nature? The court reminded counsel that it had decided recently that in equity proceedings involving an action to abate a public or private nuisance, "all persons engaged in the commission of the wrongful acts which constitute the nuisance may be enjoined, jointly and severally." It was the nuisance that would be enjoined if it were found to be destructive of public or private rights in property.

The mining company also argued that it had gained a right to pollute by custom, by prescription, and by the statute of limitations. The law protected enterprise regardless of the impact of the operations on businesses. It was quite clear that it had been the custom of miners from the earliest days to use water in placer mining and to allow the debris to fall where it may in the process. Based on these customs, many mining corporations had invested heavily in the process of hydraulic mining. They deserved the protec-

tion of the law in the pursuit of profit. The *Gold Run* court clearly rejected the implications of the argument and turned the essence of the common law upon its claimants. "But a legitimate private business," the court wrote, "founded upon a local custom, may grow into a force to threaten the safety of the people, and destruction to public and private rights; and when it develops into that condition, the custom upon which it is founded becomes unreasonable, because it was dangerous to public and private rights, and could not be invoked to justify the continuance of the business in an unlawful manner." An enterprise, creative and positive in inception, thus, could become destructive of economic development after many years of operation.

Further, the government could not absolve itself of its duty to protect a public trust. While government could authorize uses of the waters and regulate them, it could not alienate the right of the people in their public waterways. Even more certainly, an enterprise could not gain the same position by prescription. There was no right to continue a public nuisance acquired by prescription. The court ordered a perpetual injunction.

Although California's Supreme Court helped end one of mining's greatest environmental abuses, the fight continued across the West. Colorado's Supreme Court issued a similar injunction as late as 1935, and the fight with the Homestake Mining Company in South Dakota continued into the 1930s. The balancing of enterprise and environment became the focus of the twentieth century, replacing the contest of enterprises of the nineteenth century. Public nuisance and public trust doctrines developed in prior centuries and became increasingly important as environmental interests attacked the threats to ecology posed by mining. As the environmental awareness of the nation increased, the federal government offered legislation to strengthen the law's hand in keeping the government's promise to protect the public trust.

Selected Bibliography

Bakken, Gordon Morris. "American Mining Law and the Environment: The Western Experience." *Western Legal History* 1 (1988): 211–236.

Kelley, Robert L. *Gold vs. Grain: The Hydraulic Mining Controversy in California's Sacramento Valley.* Glendale, CA: Arthur H. Clark, 1959.

Rosen, C. "Differing Perceptions of the Value of Pollution Abatement Across Time and Place, 1840–1906." *Law and History Review* 11 (fall 1993): 303–381.

Smith, Duane A. *Mining America: The Industry and the Environment, 1800–1980.* Lawrence: University Press of Kansas, 1987.

Minor Case, Major Decision

—◄◦►—

Don L. Hofsommer
Department of History
St. Cloud State University

Santa Clara County v. Southern Pacific Railroad Company, 118 U.S. 394 (1886) [U.S. Supreme Court]

◄◦► THE CASE IN BRIEF ◄◦►

Date
1886

Location
California

Court
U.S. Supreme Court

Principal Participants
Santa Clara County, California
State of California
Southern Pacific Railroad
Associate Justice John Marshall Harlan

Significance of the Case
A seemingly minor jurisdictional dispute in California led to a momentous decision that established the legal precept that corporations were persons within the meaning of the Fourteenth Amendment.

Revolutionary is not too strong a word to employ in describing the impact of the railroad on American society during the nineteenth century and early twentieth century. Indeed, the influence of the railroad was so pervasive, and American adoption of railroad technology so eager, that it produced what justifiably can be called the "steam car civilization" or the "railway age." The industry helped lay the foundation for the modern American economy: it gave birth to advanced methods of finance and management; it produced new styles of labor relations and regulation of competition; and it opened up new fields of opportunity for financiers, bankers, and speculators. The expanding network connected manufacturer and consumer. As service became more dependable, railroads enabled inventory practices to be changed, aided in the rise of the factory system, and offered huge new opportunities for wholesalers. In short, the railroad (and its immediate cousin, the telegraph) were at center stage throughout the years when the United States extended its frontiers to the farthest corners of the West while simultaneously undergoing a profound transformation that would see it become a powerful urban and industrial nation.

During the tumultuous years from 1865 to America's entry in World War I, the country's railroad network increased by a factor of seven (to 253,626 miles), and the industry's gross operating revenues rose thirteen-fold. In fact, by the end of the nineteenth century, American trackage exceeded all the railroad mileage of Europe. The railroad was America's first big business; it spawned the first industrial fortunes; it was the scene of the nation's first massive labor unrest; and it was the country's first industry to feel the heavy hand of government regulation.

The railroad touched every American in one way or another. If one traveled, one took the train. If raw materials and finished goods moved from place to place, they went by rail. An order for merchandise made to Sears, Roebuck & Company from some distant place was delivered by the United States Post Office Department, but only through an agency of the railroad companies which provided postal cars; goods were delivered by one of the express companies (likewise under contract with the railroads) or by rail freight. Telegrams were dispatched from railroad depots, and those same depots, whether splendid urban edifices or homely country structures, set the tempo of each community. For that matter, "standard time" derived from the railroad industry. These monumental changes came with a bewildering rapidity. The world had never seen the power of great industries—railroads, petroleum, steel, copper, and so forth—and the moguls who owned and directed them. How to deal with the new order was a vexing question. How to do it and at the same time maintain integrity with tightly held allegiance to laissez-faire economic traditions and devotion to property rights only added to the difficulty.

Earnest debate accompanied America's transformation from a rural and agrarian society/economy to one that was increasingly urban and industrial. Public policy shifts occasioned new legislation and, eventually, the litigation necessary to interpret the legislation and public policy. Among many cases that served to de-fine the status of business corporations in the new American order was *Santa Clara County v. Southern Pacific Railroad*, argued in January 1886 and decided four months later.

On the face of it, the case was mundane, almost trivial. Set in California, the issue appeared as an intramural squabble between the state's Board of Equalization and Santa Clara County. At issue was the Southern Pacific's right-of-way fences and whether they should be assessed and taxed by the state or by the county. State law provided that the Board of Equalization could assess the "roadway" (ordinarily a 100-foot right-of-way generally understood to include the grade, ties, rails, and fixtures), but the Board interpreted "roadway" to include fences defining land owned by the railroad and land of coterminous proprietors. Santa Clara County disagreed and sought to invoke its own taxing authority on these fences. Ultimately, this local dispute went all the way to the U.S. Supreme Court, with the nation's highest court ruling that the fences were not part of the roadway, but were improvements to property and, thus, assessable and taxable only by the county and not the state.

Southern Pacific, for its part, had declined to pay these taxes—arguing, in part, that it had received its franchise from the federal government, that it was not merely a state corporation, and that as a result it was not subject to state taxation. Moreover, said Southern Pacific, the California Constitution of 1879 and various state laws establishing taxes on the property of railroads operating in more than one county of the state were in violation of the Fourteenth Amendment of the United States Constitution because railroads such as Southern Pacific were denied equal protection of the laws. The immediate issue—whether the state or the county should assess and tax right-of-way fences—was of modest importance. The *Santa Clara* case is remembered, however, because it established the legal precept that corporations were persons within the meaning of the Fourteenth Amendment.

The holding in *Santa Clara* is indicative of a developing judicial principle that a corporation and a sole proprietorship were merely alternative forms of business organization and that owners of property held in the name of a corporation should receive the same constitutional protection as those persons who held property as individuals. In other words, corporations were merely associations of persons united for a particular purpose and permitted to engage in business under a unique name. The interests of a corporation were the same as those of its shareholders. Thus a corporation should enjoy the same protection given any sole proprietorship or partnership.

These ideas, of course, did not emerge full-blown in a single thrust in *Santa Clara*; they evolved over time. John Marshall, for example, in *Providence Bank v. Billings* (1830), wrote that "the great object of a corporation is to bestow the character and properties of individuality on a collective and changing body of men." Even earlier, in *Dartmouth College v. Woodward* (1819), the Marshall Court declared that a corporation was an artificial person. In addition, Chief Justice Roger Taney in *Bank of Augusta v. Earle* (1839) ruled that a corporation of one state could do business in another state, subject to that state's permission and regulations.

In *Santa Clara*, written by Justice John Marshall Harlan I, the Supreme Court unanimously granted corporations a distinct status by deeming them persons under the Fourteenth Amendment. In the process, the Court solved the problem of guaranteeing the rights of shareholders without requiring each shareholder to litigate individually, but it did not establish corporations as entities with rights separate from their shareholders. It also affirmed that corporate property was protected as property of the corporation.

Subsequent decisions built on *Santa Clara*. In *Minneapolis & St. Louis Railway v. Beckwith* (1889), the Court clearly recognized the right of corporations to "involve the benefits of . . . the Constitution and laws which guarantee to persons the enjoyment of property, or afford them the means for its protection, or prohibit legislation injuriously affecting it." This decision had the effect of extending due process guarantees to corporations. Eight years later the Court would rule in *Chicago, Burlington & Quincy Railroad v. Chicago* that taking of property without just compensation violated the company's Fourteenth Amendment right of due process.

Several state courts continued to conclude that liberty of contract was liberty unique to people, *Santa Clara* and the general applicability of the Fourteenth Amendment notwithstanding. They would not ultimately prevail. Indeed, following the lead of *Santa Clara*, most courts by the end of the nineteenth century established that the liberty and property of corporations were protected against unreasonable state laws, and that a corporation was a person and thus entitled to the protections of due process and equal protection.

Critics during the Progressive Era and after looked at *Santa Clara* and its legal offspring as decisions favoring "big business," handed down by reactionary courts. In fact, however, *Santa Clara*'s antecedents were deep and reflected a more Jacksonian flavor in the constitutional merging of the corporation and ordinary enterprise. Among other things, *Santa Clara* granted corporations the same freedom from state regulation that liberty of contract and substantive due process provided unincorporated business firms.

Selected Bibliography

Coates, John C., IV. "State Takeover Statutes and Corporate Theory: The Revival of an Old Debate." *New York University Law Review* 64 (October 1989): 806–876.

Horwitz, Morton J. "*Santa Clara* Revisited: The Development of Corporate Theory." *West Virginia Law Review* 88 (1985).

Hovenkamp, Herbert. "The Classical Corporation in American Legal Thought." *Georgetown Law Journal* 76 (June 1988): 1593–1690.

Hurst, James Willard. *The Legitimacy of the Business Corporation in the Law of the United States: 1780–1970*. Charlottesville: University Press of Virginia, 1989.

Mark, Gregory A. "The Personification of the Business Corporation in American Law." *University of Chicago Law Review* 54 (fall 1987): 1441–1483.

Warren, Elizabeth Salisbury. "The Case for Applying the Eighth Amendment to Corporations." *Vanderbilt Law Review* 49 (October 1996): 1313–1346.

Politics v. Precedents: The Income Tax Cases

—◀◉▶—

Maxwell Bloomfield

Columbus School of Law
Catholic University of America

Pollock v. Farmers' Loan & Trust Co., 157 U.S. 429 and 158 U.S. 601 (1895) [U.S. Supreme Court]

◀◉▶ THE CASE IN BRIEF ◀◉▶

Date
1895

Location
New York
District of Columbia

Court
U.S. Supreme Court

Principal Participants
Chief Justice Melville Fuller
Charles Pollock
Farmers' Loan and Trust Company
Various other litigants grouped under the
Pollock case

Significance of the Case
The Court declared an income tax unconstitutional, imposing the laissez-faire beliefs of the majority and preventing the government from instituting a needed revenue-gathering system.

Judicial decisions seldom pulse with emotion. Especially in the late nineteenth century, when judges professed to be objective scientists, they wrote opinions that aimed at a dry-as-dust technical precision. On occasion, however, cases arose that tore away the judicial mask and revealed the nonrational aspects of decision-making. One such episode occurred in 1894, when Congress passed an income tax law that threatened to redistribute the nation's wealth in a significant way. The resulting litigation raised important, and still unresolved, questions concerning the separation of powers and the limits of judicial review.

Congress imposed the first income tax in 1861, at the start of the Civil War, and followed it with eight other income tax measures within a decade. Graduated rates were in effect during wartime; by 1865 they ranged from 5 percent on incomes of $600 to $5,000 up to 10 percent on incomes above $10,000. Although postwar Congresses lowered the rates and abandoned the graduation principle, they continued to enact new income tax laws down to 1870. Opponents challenged this legislation four times in federal courts; but the United States Supreme Court in each instance upheld congressional power, except for taxes levied on the salaries of state officials.

In 1872 a revenue surplus enabled conservative critics to block further income taxation. Thereafter the federal government relied exclusively upon tariffs and domestic duties on consumer items to meet its financial needs. This regressive tax system severely burdened lower-income groups, and contributed to a climate of continuing economic instability that culminated in the Panic of 1893. The following year, in the wake of massive unemployment and farmer protest, a coalition of Democrats and Populists from the Midwest and South pushed through Congress a new income tax law, as part of a tariff reform package.

The Wilson-Gorman Tariff Act of 1894 proposed to make substantial reductions in existing tariff rates and to compensate for the resulting revenue loss by imposing a tax of 2 percent on all personal income above $4,000. Corporations would be taxed at the same rate on any profits they made beyond operating expenses. Although protectionists in the Senate managed to restore most tariff cuts through multiple amendments, Republicans and conservative Democrats were unable to defeat the income tax provisions of the bill. In this mutilated form, the measure became law on August 28, 1894, without the signature of President Grover Cleveland, who was deeply disappointed at the failure of tariff revision.

Frustrated in their legislative efforts, opponents of the income tax now sought to prevent its collection with the help of the courts. At first, however, their chances of obtaining an early judicial hearing appeared negligible. An 1867 statute prohibited any advance interference with the collection of a federal tax; only after a person had paid such a tax under protest could he challenge its constitutionality in a lawsuit. Despite this prescribed procedure, ex-Senator George F. Edmunds of Vermont launched a test case in the District of Columbia in mid-December. Edmunds's client, taxpayer John G. Moore, sought an injunction from a federal district judge to restrain the collector of internal revenue from collecting an allegedly unconstitutional tax.

Correctly perceiving that Edmunds's frontal assault was unlikely to succeed, a shrewd New York attorney devised a more subtle strategy for striking down the income tax before it could affect any pocketbooks. William D. Guthrie, at thirty-five already a partner in a prestigious Wall Street firm, proposed to evade statutory restrictions by raising the tax issue in a private suit that did not directly involve tax collecting. Guthrie first persuaded the boards of directors of two major New York trust companies to announce that they were setting aside funds to pay the tax. He then found two stockholders willing to pose as plaintiffs in actions to restrain their respective companies from paying an unconstitutional tax. Finally, he arranged with Lawrence Maxwell, the solicitor general of the United States, to expedite the passage of the cases through the federal courts.

The income tax law went into effect on January 1, 1895. Guthrie filed his suits in a New York circuit court on January 19, and Maxwell promptly entered demurrers—formal declarations that the facts as alleged did not create a legal cause of action. On January 24 the court sustained the government's position without opinion, and the cases were ready for appeal to the United States Supreme Court. Four days later Maxwell performed his last friendly service for Guthrie. Without consulting either the president or Attorney General Richard Olney, he induced the Court to revise its calendar so as to hear opening arguments in all three pending tax cases on the first Monday in March. When Olney learned of this arrangement, which left the government with very little time in which to prepare its case, he reacted with a furious outburst that sparked Maxwell's immediate resignation.

Contemporary observers were generally aware of the collusive—some called it "conspiratorial"—nature of these proceedings. Perhaps in order to reassure the public that both sides would be fairly represented, the indefatigable Guthrie persuaded the Continental Trust Company, one of the defendants, to employ James C. Carter as its counsel. Carter, a leading New York practitioner, was a past president of the American Bar Association and an advocate of unquestioned integrity. He joined Attorney

General Olney and Assistant Attorney General Edward B. Whitney, both hardworking and competent lawyers, in defending the constitutionality of the income tax.

To challenge the law, Guthrie assembled an even more impressive team. Besides himself, it included the distinguished head of his law firm, Clarence Seward, George Edmunds, and—at a reportedly extravagant fee—Joseph Hodges Choate, the most famous legal orator and trial lawyer of the time. Popular interest in the fate of the tax insured that the approaching litigation would receive nationwide press coverage.

On March 7 oral arguments began before an eight-man Supreme Court (Associate Justice Howell E. Jackson did not participate because of serious illness) headed by Melville W. Fuller, a former corporation attorney. Spectators, including congressmen, lawyers, and the general public, crowded into the courtroom in the Capitol—once the Senate Chamber—to listen to the debate, which lasted for five days.

At issue was the meaning of several key tax provisions in the Constitution. Article I, Section 8 gave Congress the power "to lay and collect taxes, duties, imposts, and excises, to pay the debts and provide for the common defense and general welfare of the United States." But in exercising this sweeping authority, Congress had to follow certain prescribed procedures. A "capitation, or other direct tax" had to be apportioned among the states on the basis of population, while duties, imposts, and excises had to be "uniform throughout the United States." The briefs raised two questions which dominated the oral arguments: (1) Was an income tax a direct tax? and (2) If not, did the exemptions provided in the Wilson-Gorman Act violate the principle of uniformity?

In response to the first question, the defenders of the income tax could rely on an unbroken chain of supportive judicial precedents and legislative practices that stretched back to the beginnings of the republic. From *Hylton v. United States* (1796) to *Springer v. United States* (1881) the Supreme Court had consistently maintained that the only direct taxes were those levied upon lands or persons-subjects found in every state and capable of assessment according to census figures. The *Springer* precedent was particularly relevant, since in that case a unanimous Court had upheld a similar income tax after hearing exhaustive arguments from counsel. Moreover, Congress had always followed these judicial guidelines. It had imposed direct taxes on three occasions—in 1798, 1812, and 1861—to meet wartime emergencies; and each time it had taxed only land and its fixtures. To overturn a constitutional exposition almost coeval with the Constitution itself, urged Attorney General Olney, would "set a hurtful precedent and go far to prove that government by written constitution is not a thing of stable principles, but of the fluctuating views and wishes of the particular period and the particular judges when and from whom its interpretation happens to be called for."

Since an income tax was not a direct tax, it had only to be assessed in a uniform way to meet constitutional criteria. The term "uniform," argued Olney and his associates, referred to geographical uniformity. Congress could not tax a commodity at one rate on the East Coast and at a different rate in the West. Similarly, Congress had to tax all persons within a particular class of taxpayers at the same rate. In establishing categories of taxpayers, however, or in exempting certain classes from the payment of taxes, Congress could claim broad discretionary power under the Constitution. So long as a legislative classification might be reasonably related to a public purpose, James C. Carter insisted, the legislature's action "cannot be reviewed by the judicial tribunals." Thus, when Congress exempted mutual savings banks and other cooperative institutions from the coverage of the Wilson-Gorman bill, it did not act arbitrarily, since it may have wished to promote habits of thrift and self-reliance among a mass of small investors. The wisdom of such a policy was a matter for Congress alone to determine; and Carter warned the Court not to engage in judicial lawmaking over the income tax: "Nothing could be more unwise and dangerous—nothing more foreign to the spirit of the Constitution—than an attempt to baffle and defeat a popular determination by a judgment in a lawsuit. When the opposing forces of sixty millions of people have become arrayed in hostile political ranks upon a question which all men feel is not a question of law, but of legislation, the only path of safety is to accept the voice of the majority as final."

The opposing lawyers split the issues neatly between them for purposes of argument. Guthrie and Edmunds concentrated on the uniformity question, while Seward and Choate elaborated a new theory of direct taxation that became the controlling element in the Court's decision. In Guthrie's view, a uniform tax had to fall equally upon all persons or types of property. "The requirement of approximate equality inheres in the very nature of the power to tax," he maintained; "and it exists whether declared or not in the written constitution." Since the Wilson-Gorman Act, through its arbitrary exemptions, placed the tax burden on less than 2 percent of the population, it clearly failed the constitutional test. In a more emotional presentation Edmunds appealed to the Court to strike down this monstrous piece of class legislation by applying the equal protection principle found in the Fourteenth Amendment.

The arguments of Seward and Choate invited the Court to engage in more radical judicial revisionism. The time had come, Seward declared, to correct a century of error by reexamining the meaning of direct taxation, as understood by the founding fathers. In a scholarly analysis that drew upon eighteenth-century dictionaries, economic tracts, and state records, as well as the debates in the Federal Convention, he sought to show that the framers had used the term "direct tax" in a precise way that had later been misunderstood by the courts. When asked by one justice how he could advocate overturning so many precedents, Seward replied: "There is a tradition in the legal profession that once when a suggestion was made to Mr. Lincoln that a judicial decision settled a question, he responded with some firmness that in this country nothing was settled until it was settled right."

Choate's presentation, which closed the arguments, did not disappoint his admirers. With ingenuity and verve he linked the tax issue to state rights, past and present. Less than 2 percent of the population paid four-fifths of the income taxes assessed under the 1870 law, he noted; and these wealthy taxpayers all lived in four eastern states—New York, Pennsylvania, Massachusetts, and New Jersey. Using historical sources,

he argued that the framers had inserted the direct tax provisions expressly to prevent the exploitation of property owners in a few states through the combined political power of the rest. In a stirring peroration he called upon the justices to stand firm in the defense of private property and equality before the law: "If it be true, as my learned friend said in closing, that the passions of the people are aroused on this subject, if it be true that a mighty army of 60 million citizens is likely to be incensed by this decision, it is the more vital to the future welfare of this country that this Court again resolutely and courageously declare, as Marshall did, that it *has* the power to set aside an act of Congress violative of the Constitution, and that it will not hesitate in executing that power, no matter what the threatened consequences of popular or populistic wrath may be."

The arguments ended on March 13. During the next three weeks the newspapers speculated at length on the probable outcome of the litigation, analyzing for readers the personal and philosophical backgrounds of the justices. On April 8 Chief Justice Fuller announced the opinion of the Court. Speaking for a six-man majority, Fuller reinterpreted the meaning of "direct taxes" in light of the historical data supplied by Seward and Choate. Taxation and representation were inseparably linked in the minds of the framers, he argued. At the Federal Convention the seaboard states ultimately made enormous tax concessions to the federal government. They gave up their right to tax imports and interstate commerce, and granted Congress concurrent power over all other forms of taxation. In return, however, they sought to safeguard the property of their citizens from despoilment at the hands of political majorities from poorer states. Their chief instrument for this purpose was the direct tax, with its apportionment requirement, which guaranteed that any federal tax on property would fall "upon the immediate constituents of those who imposed it." According to Fuller, the framers anticipated that direct taxes would be imposed only in national emergencies. At all other times, the private property of citizens would fall, as a practical matter, within the exclusive purview of state authority.

But what exactly did the framers mean by a direct tax? Here Fuller read back into the historical record an economic definition that attained popularity only in the nineteenth century. A direct tax, he asserted, was any tax on an individual's property whose burden could not be shifted to a third party; that is, any tax other than a tax on consumption. Such a definition had never been accepted by the federal courts; but Fuller avoided overruling earlier precedents by distinguishing them on narrowly technical grounds, as Choate had suggested. Thus, he pointed out that the Court in the *Springer* case had not considered some of the specific sources of taxable income identified in the Wilson-Gorman Act; hence their constitutionality remained open to question.

Two such undecided issues involved congressional efforts to tax the rents or income from real estate and the income from state or municipal bonds. There was no difference in principle, Fuller maintained, between a tax on land, which everyone agreed was a direct tax, and a tax on the income from land. He ignored the fact that the proposed tax was a general one levied upon a person's net income, which was derived from many different and commingled sources. A tax on the income from municipal bonds was also unconstitutional, though for different reasons. It represented an illegal interference with the borrowing power of states and their instrumentalities. The doctrine of intergovernmental tax immunity was well established in the jurisprudence of the late nineteenth century. Just as the Marshall court had declared in *McCulloch v. Maryland* (1819) that states could not tax the operations of the federal government and its agencies, so the Supreme Court in the decades since the Civil War had applied the same rule to the federal government. Even the dissenting justices in the income tax cases conceded this point. Only recently, in *South Carolina v. James A. Baker, III, Secretary of the Treasury* (1988), has the Rehnquist court overruled this part of the *Pollock* decision by holding that Congress may impose a nondiscriminatory tax on the income from state bonds.

Up to this point in Fuller's opinion it seemed that the Court was going to strike down the entire income tax law in a piecemeal fashion. But suddenly the chief justice revealed that the majority's consensus had shattered over three remaining questions: Did the elimination of the tax on income from land invalidate the rest of the law? Was a tax on the income from personal property also a direct tax? Were other provisions, although not direct taxes, nevertheless invalid for lack of uniformity? On these issues the justices divided 4-4, leaving most of the income tax law still in effect.

Fuller's opinion was studiously dispassionate and "scientific." Crammed with citations to other court decisions, it conveyed none of the intense emotionalism that the income tax proposal aroused in liberals and conservatives alike. Much more revealing in this regard was the concurring opinion of Associate Justice Stephen J. Field, whose individualistic philosophy had been forged in the antebellum years. Field denounced the entire income tax as unconstitutional class legislation, concluding with an apocalyptic vision of America's future that might have been lifted from one of the period's popular dystopian novels: "The present assault upon capital is but the beginning. It will be but the stepping-stone to others, larger and more sweeping, till our political contests will become a war of the poor against the rich; a war constantly growing in intensity and bitterness." Such visceral fears may well have influenced other members of the majority as well, despite the resolutely "objective" tone of Fuller's opinion.

The two dissenting justices, while avoiding strident rhetoric, emphasized their profound disagreement with the majority's position. Edward Douglass White, a moderate traditionalist, provided a thorough and penetrating critique of Fuller's logic and methodology. White particularly condemned the majority for ignoring its own controlling precedents in its dubious pursuit of the original intent of the framers. If such judicial activism were legitimate, he warned, "then every question which has been determined in our past history is now still open for judicial reconstruction." John Marshall Harlan, the Court's leading liberal, argued in a brief concurrence that the Court should have refused to hear all three suits, since they violated the jurisdictional guidelines established by Congress.

The decision in *Pollock v. Farmers' Loan & Trust Co.*, as the income tax cases were collectively designated in the official reports, pleased neither side. Within a week Guthrie petitioned the Court for a rehearing on the remaining issues. In reply, the attorney general requested that, if a rehearing were granted, it should cover all of the legal and constitutional questions previously argued. The government, he explained, had not expected the direct tax to become a major issue, and had not researched the question as carefully as it otherwise would have done. The Court granted both petitions, and set May 6 as the date for reargument. Justice Jackson, although far from well, agreed to participate in the rehearing, to prevent any further tie votes.

This time the arguments were more restrained, as each side sought to buttress its position with copious historical data on the nature of eighteenth-century taxation. Only two lawyers were permitted to represent the respective parties. Guthrie and Choate again appeared for the antitax forces, while Olney and Whitney presented the government's case. The Court's first opinion set the parameters of debate in both the briefs and the oral arguments. Olney labored valiantly to convince the Court that a tax on rents was not a tax on land, and that the inclusion of rents with other sources of income did not convert a general income tax into a direct tax. The realty provisions of the law were essential, he believed, to its effective operation, since without them the government would lose a major share of its anticipated revenue. William Waldorf Astor, the wealthiest New York landlord, would, for example, reportedly save $108,000 in taxes if the Court's original decision concerning landed income were not reversed. "Unless the Court can be induced to reconsider that question," Olney informed a legal associate, "what remains of the law is hardly worth preserving."

Although Olney's presentation was lucid and forceful, it was again eclipsed by the artful pleading of Choate. Treating the Court's first decision as fixed and irrevocable, Choate now invited the justices to take the next logical step by declaring that a tax on the income from personal property, like that on the income from realty, constituted a direct tax on the property itself. Alternatively, he urged that the Court's prior invalidation of the tax on rental income required that the rest of the law should be struck down as well, since Congress had not intended that the remaining taxpayers should bear the full burden of taxation. "The biggest fish," he observed, "have got out through the rent that Your Honors have made in the meshes of the law. Will you allow the little fish to be alone made the victims?"

The arguments went on for three days, ending on May 8. On May 20 the Court handed down its decision before a hushed and expectant audience, many of whom had been waiting for hours for the courtroom doors to open. Once the justices had taken their seats, the chief justice leaned forward and, without any preliminary comment, began to read in a low voice the final majority decision in the *Pollock* case.

"Whenever this Court is required to pass upon the validity of an act of Congress as tested by the fundamental law enacted by the people," he began, "the duty imposed requires in its discharge the utmost deliberation and care, and invokes the deepest sense of responsibility. And this is especially so when the question involves the exercise of a great governmental power." With this perfunctory nod in the direction of judicial self-restraint, Fuller proceeded to reaffirm the questionable revisionism of his first opinion. Again he insisted that direct taxes were those that fell squarely and inescapably upon property; that the states alone had levied such taxes prior to the Federal Convention; and that the founders expected that the states would continue to meet their revenue needs through direct taxes, while the federal government would rely primarily upon tariffs and other indirect taxes on consumption. A land tax was clearly a direct tax, he reiterated; and a tax on the income from land was equally direct, and must be apportioned among the states.

The argument to this point was familiar enough; but Fuller now moved beyond *Pollock I* by ruling that a tax on the income from personal property, including corporate stock, was also a direct tax on the property itself. This conclusion required a leap of creative imagination, since it defied both history and common sense. In the past Congress had levied direct taxes upon land; but it had never attempted to tax personal property directly, even in wartime emergencies. On the other hand, it had passed an early excise tax on carriages, over the strong objections of many who considered it a direct tax requiring apportionment. In *Hylton v. United States* (1796) a unanimous Supreme Court had sustained this carriage tax. Associate Justice William Paterson, who had participated in the Federal Convention, explained in his opinion the origins of the direct tax: "The provision was made in favor of the southern States. They possessed a large number of slaves; they had extensive tracts of territory, thinly settled and not very productive. A majority of the States had but few slaves, and several of them a limited territory, well settled, and in a high state of cultivation. The Southern States, if no provision had been introduced in the Constitution, would have been wholly at the mercy of the other States. Congress in such case, might tax slaves, at discretion or arbitrarily, and land in every part of the Union after the same rate or measure; so much a head in the first instance, and so much an acre in the second. To guard them against imposition, in these particulars, was the reason of introducing the clause in the Constitution, which directs that representatives and direct taxes shall be apportioned among the States according to their respective numbers." Fuller attempted to dismiss the *Hylton* case as involving solely the definition of "excises," but his analysis was as unconvincing as the spurious law-office history concocted by Seward and Choate to explain the "original" meaning of direct taxes.

With the two principal sources of anticipated revenue nevertheless invalidated, the chief justice turned to the remaining tax provisions. While the proposed tax on income from state and municipal bonds could not stand because of intergovernmental tax immunity, taxes on the income from business, professions, or employment were in the nature of excises, and therefore constitutionally permissible. These indirect taxes were minor and dependent parts of a general revenue system, however; without its major

props—the realty and personality provisions—the entire structure must fall. Otherwise, Fuller observed, paraphrasing Choate, "what was intended as a tax on capital would remain in substance a tax on occupations and labor."

As Fuller finished his opinion and looked up from the manuscript, there was perfect stillness in the crowded chamber. Then a few spectators began to clap, until silenced by a gesture from the marshal. Several reporters squeezed out of the room to get the news to the wire services: the income tax was dead, and there was no possibility of any further legislation, since it would be impossible to apportion such a tax equitably among the states. If two states, for example, had approximately equal populations, each would be assessed the same amount of tax. But if a hundred persons with incomes over $4,000 lived in state A, while only ten persons of such wealth lived in state B, the wealthy residents of state B would have to pay ten times more in income taxes than their counterparts in state A. Such pragmatic considerations led the Court in the *Hylton* case to reject the argument that carriage taxes were direct taxes.

The majority in *Pollock II* was even smaller than that in *Pollock I*. Supporting the chief justice were Associate Justices Field, David J. Brewer, George Shiras Jr., and Horace Gray; while Justices Harlan, White, Jackson, and Henry B. Brown dissented. Each of the dissenters read an opinion. Substantively, their analyses added little to the critique made by White in *Pollock I*; but collectively they testified to the deep concern that each man felt over the Court's aggressive activism and its potential consequences for the future.

Harlan's performance was by far the most dramatic. His voice cracking with barely suppressed anger, he assailed the majority for depriving the national government of a vital economic power. What particularly incensed him was that the Court had struck down only the income tax sections of the Tariff Act, although the entire law was intended to form a comprehensive revenue system. As a result, Americans of modest means would continue to pay most of the government's operating expenses through high taxes on consumer goods. "The practical effect of the decision to-day," Harlan concluded, "is to give to certain kinds of property a position of favoritism and advantage inconsistent with the fundamental principles of our social organization, and to invest them with power and influence that may be perilous to the portion of the American people upon whom rests the larger part of the burdens of the government, and who ought not to be subjected to the dominion of aggregated wealth any more than the property of the country should be at the mercy of the lawless." The other three dissenters, although less vehement, were equally outspoken. Brown referred to "the surrender of the taxing power to the moneyed class"; Jackson called the decision "the most disastrous blow ever struck at the constitutional power of Congress"; and White predicted that, if Congress should ever attempt to levy an income tax through apportionment, "the red spectre of revolution would shake our institutions to their foundations."

The amending process proved the only practicable way of overturning *Pollock II*, and it took eighteen years to accomplish that result. Meanwhile the gap between rich and poor steadily widened, and the federal government experienced novel financial needs as it began to construct the institutions of the modern welfare state. The Sixteenth Amendment, which took effect on February 25, 1913, at last authorized Congress "to lay and collect taxes on incomes, from whatever source derived, without apportionment among the several States, and without regard to any census or enumeration."

In broader terms the income tax cases point up the political nature of the Supreme Court's work, and the impossibility of neatly separating "legal issues" from the personalities and ideological presuppositions of the justices. Jackson was supposed to be the swing man in *Pollock II*; but his vote had no effect on the outcome of the case, because one of his associates switched sides during the rehearing. The identity of this "vacillating jurist" remains a mystery, although commentators have expended enormous en-

ergy and ingenuity in efforts to flush him out. What matters, of course, is not the man but his behavior, which seems to have been motivated more by fear than by reason or logic. Indeed, the same charge might be leveled against the other members of the *Pollock* majority, who took it upon themselves to rewrite the law in conformity with their laissez-faire convictions. Judges in any age may sometimes confuse their personal predilections with the mandates of constitutional law. When they do, as *Pollock* demonstrates, no effective institutional remedy exists, apart from the amendment procedure. That procedure Fuller aptly described as "a slow and deliberate process, which gives time for mere hypothesis and opinion to exhaust themselves, and for the sober second thought of every part of the country to be asserted."

Selected Bibliography

Eggert, Gerald G. "Richard Olney and the Income Tax Cases." *Mississippi Valley Historical Review* 48 (June 1961): 24–41.

Ely, James W., Jr. *The Chief Justiceship of Melville W. Fuller, 1888–1910.* Columbia: University of South Carolina Press, 1995.

Farrelly, David G. "Justice Harlan's Dissent in the *Pollock* Case." *Southern California Law Review* 24 (February 1951): 175–182.

Fiss, Owen M. *Troubled Beginnings of the Modern State, 1888–1910.* New York: Macmillan Publishing Co., 1993.

King, Willard L. *Melville Weston Fuller.* New York: Macmillan Publishing Co., 1950.

Paul, Arnold M. *Conservative Crisis and the Rule of Law: Attitudes of Bench and Bar, 1887–1895.* Ithaca, NY: Cornell University Press, 1960.

Ratner, Sidney. *American Taxation: Its History as a Social Force in Democracy.* New York: W. W. Norton & Co., 1942.

Swindler, William F. *Court and Constitution in the Twentieth Century: The Old Legality, 1889–1932.* Indianapolis, IN: Bobbs-Merrill Company, Inc., 1969.

Westin, Alan F. "The Supreme Court, the Populist Movement and the Campaign of 1896." *Journal of Politics* 15 (February 1953): 3–41.

National Police Powers: The Oleomargarine Case

—◄◌►—

Fred D. Ragan

Professor of History, Emeritus
East Carolina University

McCray v. United States, 195 U.S. 27 (1904) [U.S. Supreme Court]

◄◌► THE CASE IN BRIEF ◄◌►

Date
   1904

Location
   Ohio

Court
   U.S. Supreme Court

Principal Participants
   Government of the United States
   Leo W. McCray
   William D. Guthrie
   Associate Justice Edward D. White

Significance of the Case
   In upholding a congressional text on oleomargarine that was designed to help the butter industry, the Court sanctioned the use of the taxing power as a police power.

As the twentieth century began, the U.S. Supreme Court struggled with cases arising from the enlarged role Congress had begun to play over economic and social aspects of national life. Along with *Champion v. Ames*, this decision played a prominent role in recognizing and expanding national police powers. The development came when Congress responded to pressure from dairy interests and in 1902 enacted an excise tax intended to drive a competing product, oleomargarine colored to resemble butter, from the market.

Developed in France during the Napoleonic wars, margarine underwent numerous improvements before being introduced into the United States during the 1870s. Confronted with problems of overproduction and falling commodity prices, agricultural interests fought the unwelcomed competitor. Although an early producer labeled his product "artificial butter," others were less scrupulous and fraud and deception soon plagued the marketplace. New York in 1877 began state regulatory efforts when it passed legislation to protect its farmers from "deception in the sale of butter." Other states followed the example of the Empire State but consumption continued to increase.

Demanding a national solution to their problem, dairy farmers prevailed upon Congress to enact legislation in 1886 designed to control and regulate the oleomargarine industry. The law required a license for manufacturers, wholesalers, and retailers and placed a production tax of two cents per pound. The statute, however, did not address the fundamental reason for oleomargarine's growing popularity, the practice of coloring to imitate butter in appearance.

Beginning in 1888, the Supreme Court produced a series of decisions which arbitrated margarine's destiny. The first decision rejected Pennsylvania's attempt to prohibit the sale of oleomargarine produced in the state; six years later it conceded that, although a legitimate article of commerce, a state could forbid importation of colored oleomargarine, since the intent of coloring was to deceive consumers. Two years later, the Court upheld the 1886 act. Ending its first decade of decisions, the Court concluded that a state could not bar the sale of oleomargarine delivered and sold in its original package nor could a state require that it be colored pink.

Even as Congress responded to dairy interest demands with the 1886 act, New Jersey and New York enacted legislation to ban the sale of colored oleomargarine. After the Court found the approach acceptable in 1894, other states rapidly followed this approach. By 1902 thirty-two states prohibited sale of colored margarine. Others required the product be "branded," while still others insisted that diners in hotels and restaurants be informed when served the product. Production and consumption of oleomargarine increased, nonetheless, setting a record in 1902.

That reality set the stage for Congress to reexamine the 1886 law. By this time, however, agricultural interests had become sharply divided. Preferring to have the product prohibited, the National Dairy Union endorsed a tax increase to ten cents per pound on colored oleomargarine as an acceptable method of limiting consumption. The lard-white appearance of uncolored margarine had no consumer appeal. Defenders included cotton and cattle producers because they had found a new market for their oils. Dairy interests, however, controlled the day and Congress amended the 1886 law to tax colored oleo at ten cents a pound, about half of the retail price, while at the same time, reducing the tax on the uncolored product to ¼ cent a pound. The act also substantially reduced the cost of a license for wholesalers and retailers.

Almost immediately the law was challenged. Leo W. McCray, a retail dealer in Ohio, bought a shipment of colored margarine and paid the ¼ cent rather than the required ten cent tax. The government sued for a penalty and the tax. McCray, represented by noted attorney William D. Guthrie, argued that the margarine color came from "natural" ingredients, since the manufacturer, the Ohio Butterine Company, had used creamery butter to produce the yellow color. Consequently, the margarine was not artificially colored within the meaning of the law. McCray also argued that the tax was repugnant to the Constitution. Since butter was colored by the same process as margarine during all seasons of the year except spring, the tax on margarine constituted discriminatory treatment of an industry in favor of a competitor. Moreover, the tax made it impossible to produce and sell margarine in competition with butter, thereby destroying an otherwise legitimate business. Such action violated McCray's Fifth Amendment rights by depriving him of property without due process of law. Finally, the defense argued that Congress had overstepped its authority and invaded the police powers reserved to the states.

In a 6-3 decision, Justice Edward D. White of Louisiana wrote for the Court upholding Congress's use in this circumstance of the tax power. White found that McCray should have paid the ten cents tax since the oleomargarine he purchased "was not free from artificial coloring," regardless of the fact that its color was derived from butter which had itself been artificially colored. Rejecting Guthrie's argument that a valid tax must be reasonably related to raising revenue, White refused to inquire into Congress's motives and held that its power to impose excise taxes was "completely established." When the power of tax is exercised oppressively, the responsibility is that of Congress and not the courts. If dissatisfied with the exercise of that power, the remedy "lies, not in the abuse by the judicial authority of its functions, but in the people, upon whom . . . reliance must be placed for the correction of abuses . . . of a lawful power." Finally, White dismissed Fifth and Tenth Amendment arguments. Neither of the amendments diminished "the grant of power to tax. . . ." If the tax destroyed the industry, it "cannot be said that such repression destroys rights which no free government could destroy;" and consequently, no ground exists to justify intervention by the judiciary to "save such rights from destruction."

Although the move was a hesitant one, the Court, with *Champion v. Ames,* allowed Congress to expand the means it could employ when responding to national problems tradi-tionally associated with state police powers. When the justices agreed with the ends sought by Congress, they sanctioned the use of the taxing power as a police power. But dual federalism did not quickly fade from the scene. In *Bailey v. Drexel Furniture Company,* the Court rejected the child labor law and held, as it refused to do in *McCray,* that a tax must have a natural and reasonable relation to the raising of revenue.

Selected Bibliography

Cushman, Robert E. "The National Police Power Under the Taxing Clause of the Constitution." *Minnesota Law Review* 4 (March 1920): 247–281.

Riepma, Siert F. *The Story of Margarine.* Washington, DC: Public Affairs Press, 1970.

State Legislature Power and Municipal Trusts

—◄◦►—

Sondra Spencer
Department of History
California State University, Fullerton

City of Monterey v. David Jacks, 203 U.S. 360 (1906) [U.S. Supreme Court]

◄◦► THE CASE IN BRIEF ◄◦►

Date
1906

Location
California

Court
U.S. Supreme Court

Principal Participants
David Jacks
City of Monterey, California
Associate Justice McKenna

Significance of the Case
In a case that extended over many years and involved a complex land dispute over former Mexican pueblo territories, the Court confirmed state authority to rule municipal trusts.

This case pitted David Jacks, a shrewd Scotsman, against the Board of Trustees of the city of Monterey, California. The United States Supreme Court affirmed the judgment by the California State Supreme Court, settling a land grant dispute which began in 1848 with the Treaty of Guadalupe Hidalgo, ending over half a century later. This dispute focused on the authority of Monterey, as the successor of the pueblo of Monterey, to dispose of lands held in trust. The United States Supreme Court held, on December 3, 1906, that pueblo lands were a municipal trust, and not a proprietary trust, and since Monterey was a municipality it was "a creature of the laws of the state and subject to the state." Consequently, this ruling affirmed state control over municipal trusts and has been cited, as recently as 1955, in defense of that control.

The city of Monterey was originally established on June 3, 1770, as the Presidio of Monterey, a Spanish military outpost. On June 23, 1813, under the decree of the Cortes, Monterey was incorporated and became the capital of the Province of Upper California. Although the original land records confirming the Spanish grant of pueblo lands to Monterey were lost, the city was consistently referred to in this case as the former "pueblo of Monterey." But unlike most pueblos, and by special concession from the Spanish crown, Monterey was entitled to more than the four square leagues of land generally allocated to the pueblos. It was this large grant of land which became the focal point for this dispute. After the independence of Mexico, the constituent congress authorized municipal authorities of the towns to retain their pueblo lands for common use or to dispose of them, as long as their actions would benefit the town and the town's inhabitants. Authority over the pueblo lands was transferred to the United States, on July 4, 1848, following ratification of the Treaty of Guadalupe Hidalgo. Provisions in this treaty provided for ceding the territory of California to the United States whereby the United States agreed to honor and ratify all legal Mexican land grants conferred to the ranchos, missions, and pueblos residing within the boundaries of the territory.

However, for most recipients of Mexican land grants, including the town of Monterey, their title was not clear and their boundaries were not certain. In addition, the promise by the United States government to ratify all grants proved to be a difficult task. In order to dispose of fraudulent claims and to quiet title to legitimate grants, the United States Congress passed the Land Act of 1851. This act established definitive guidelines a claimant had to follow to obtain a land patent and authorized the formation of a Board of Land Commissioners to adjudicate these claims.

On March 22, 1853, the city council of Monterey resolved to petition the Board of Land Commissioners for confirmation of the pueblo grant to the pueblo of Monterey. Participating in this resolution were Delos R. Ashley and David Jacks, future owners of the pueblo lands. Ashley was a local attorney who served as a city alderman and as the city attorney. Jacks, a Scotsman who moved to Monterey from San Francisco in 1849, was currently the city treasurer. In this resolution the council directed Ashley, as

attorney for the city of Monterey, to present the pueblo land titles to the commissioners.

Title to the pueblo lands was confirmed to the city of Monterey by the Board of Land Commissioners on January 22, 1856. A subsequent appeal of this confirmation, by the United States Government, was dismissed in 1858. Following the confirmation, and presumably at the request of the Board of Trustees of the city of Monterey (the city council was replaced by trustees in 1853 by state statute), the California legislature authorized the trustees to sue for the recovery of property of the city and, in order to pay for the expenses of prosecuting the title of the city, to sell and transfer any property for such price as they may deem reasonable.

On January 24, 1859, the trustees reconvened for the first time in almost six years. This new board received Ashley's claim of $991.50, for attorney fees and expenses in successfully prosecuting the title of the pueblo lands. The board resolved on the following day that, since the city's treasury was broke, to pay Ashley's claim by auctioning the pueblo lands of Monterey on the 9th day of February 1859.

The auction notice was published in the *Pacific Sentinal* for the next two weeks and on February 9, 1859, one bid was received; a joint bid from David Jacks and Delos R. Ashley for $1002.50. This was the exact amount required to settle the city's debt with Ashley and to pay $11.00 for the public notice in the *Pacific Sentinal*. On February 12, 1859, the city of Monterey conveyed the pueblo lands to Jacks and Ashley with the conveyance being recorded on June 11, 1859.

Immediately following the conveyance, the first of several surveys were initiated to establish the legal description of the pueblo lands. However, because of several serious disputes over the interpretation of the original land grant, the final survey was not recorded until 1890. This long period in establishing the boundaries was an unfortunate delay for Jacks.

A new, hostile, board of trustees were elected on June 5, 1865. Shortly thereafter, this board declared the initial sale unauthorized and illegal. They ordered that notice be served "that the Board is ready to negotiate for the relinquishment, by Jacks and others, of any and all claims that he or they may have to the pueblo lands."

Jacks's first apparent response was, on April 2, 1866, when the California legislature amended the act to incorporate the city of Monterey. This act ratified and confirmed all sales and conveyances made by the board of trustees since February 8, 1859 (one day before the public auction). This act corrected a possible defect in the deeds to Jacks and Ashley, whereby the city may not have been previously authorized to convey the lands. It is this act, and the associated authority assumed by the California legislature to both ratify the conveyance of municipal trust lands and to ratify a possible unlawful transaction, that the city would later question.

On November 19, 1891, with the final survey having been recorded the previous year, the city of Monterey was issued a Patent of the United States to pueblo lands. The lands documented encompassed a region "from the mouth of the River of Monterey in the sea to the Pilarcitos; thence running all along the Canada to the Laguna Seca, which is in the high road to the Presidio; thence running along the highest ridge of the mountains situated towards the Mission of San Carlos unto Point Cypress further to the north and from said point following all the coast unto the said mouth of the River of Monterey." This patent covered a total of four tracts consisting of 29,698.53 acres and was the last step necessary in providing clear title to the pueblo lands. David Jacks was now the legal owner following the ratification of the conveyance by the state legislature in 1866 and with the previous purchase of Ashley's interest in the pueblo lands in 1869.

However, the city maintained the belief that both the purchase and the ratification were illegal. Consequently, the city filed suit against David Jacks in the Superior Court of the County of Monterey on December 19, 1891. In the initial complaint the city of Monterey, as the plaintiff, alleged that it was the owner of Lot No. 2 of the pueblo lands and that the defendants' claim was an estate or interest adverse to the city. A second complaint, filed on November 17, 1896, against Jacks alleged that additional property, consisting of the sum

total of tracts one through four, was owned by the plaintiff.

The court found on September 25, 1899, that the plaintiff, the city of Monterey, was a municipal corporation, that plaintiff was not entitled to any relief, that David Jacks was the owner of the land described in the complaint, and that Jacks was entitled to recover his costs. Subsequently, the city requested and was denied a new trial.

The city of Monterey filed a notice of appeal with the Supreme Court of the state of California on April 3, 1900. The contention was that the former trustees did not have the authority to sell or convey the pueblo lands, the former trustees were never officially trustees for the city, that the act of April 2, 1866, did not ratify the sale, and that the legislature did not have the power to ratify the transaction.

On July 11, 1903, the California State Supreme Court issued its ruling. The court agreed that the question "is not what power the pueblo or the city of itself had over the pueblo lands, but what power or control the legislature had over them." Additionally, the court observed that there is a significant difference "between lands which are held by a municipality in trust for public municipal purposes, such as pueblo lands, and lands acquired by a municipality through purchase or special grant, and held in proprietary right." The court held that the pueblo lands were previously a municipal trust subject to the authority of the Mexican government, that the state of California succeeded to the sovereignty previously exercised by Mexico, and therefore the state had authority both to authorize and confirm the sale of these pueblo lands. In addition, the court ruled that the legislature's power extended over all of the pueblo lands, that the act of April 2, 1866, ratified and confirmed all defects in the sale and cured an alleged defect in the conveyance, and held that the trustees who signed the deed were at least de facto trustees for the city of Monterey.

Following this ruling, the city appealed to the U.S. Supreme Court. The question presented to the Court was whether "the California Legislature could enact the act of April 2, 1866, ratifying conveyances made by the corporate authorities of the city of Monterey of pueblo lands confirmed to that city by the

United States, and afterwards patented to it, its successors and assigns."

David Jacks, however, did not place all his faith in receiving a favorable Supreme Court ruling. Concurrent with the city's appeal, and again presumably through his efforts, Congress passed an act designating the city of Monterey as trustee of the pueblo lands and confirming the land to the city as patented. This act, passed on June 15, 1906, effectively eliminated the city's argument that they did not have legal title to the pueblo lands, and therefore could not legally convey title to said lands.

On December 3, 1906, Justice McKenna delivered the opinion of the U.S. Supreme Court that affirmed the judgment of the lower court. The Court held that "if the United States was, as contended, a paramount sovereign, and, as such, possessed the power to direct the trust to which pueblo lands were subject, it did not do so, but conveyed land to the 'city of Monterey, its successors and assigns.'" Therefore, "the conveyance was made to a municipality of the state of California, a creature of the laws of the state and subject to the state."

This case is significant because of its confirmation of state authority to rule municipal trusts. As late as 1955, this case was cited in support of that position. In *Mallon v. City of Long Beach* the court held, on April 5, 1955, that the city of Long Beach was still subservient to the state when trust property was placed under its management. Justice Roger Traynor, one of California's leading jurists, did not dispute the precedent cited in the *City of Monterey v. David Jacks*. Consequently, the power of the legislature to control municipal trusts was preserved.

This case represents both an affirmation of the authority of the state over municipal corporations and the critical role of legislation in the resolution of land title disputes. Fortunately, David Jacks lived to see the resolution of a dispute that spanned nearly a half century.

Selected Bibliography

Bakken, Gordon Morris. *The Development of Law in Frontier California: Civil Law and Society, 1850–1890.* Westport, CT: Greenwood Press, 1985.

Beck, Warren A., and David A. Williams. *California: A History of the Golden State.* Garden City, NY: Doubleday, 1972.

Bestor, Arthur Eugene, Jr. *David Jacks of Monterey, and Lee L. Jacks His Daughter.* Stanford, CA: Stanford University Press, 1945.

Gates, Paul W. *California Ranchos and Farms, 1842–1862.* Madison: The State Historical Society of Wisconsin, 1967.

Substantive Due Process

Prohibition and the Due Process Clause

———◦———

William M. Wiecek

College of Law and Department of History
Syracuse University

Wynehamer v. The People, 13 N.Y. 378 (1856) [New York Court of Appeals]

◦ THE CASE IN BRIEF ◦

Date
1856

Location
New York

Court
New York Court of Appeals

Principal Participants
James G. Wynehamer
Thomas Toynbee
State of New York
Justice George M. Comstock

Significance of the Case
The case was the first time a court had used the due process clauses of the state or federal constitutions for holding a statute unconstitutional on substantive, instead of procedural, grounds.

Two powerful forces of antebellum America clashed in state courtrooms during the 1850s: the drive to outlaw "demon rum," and the development of higher-law doctrines. Each profoundly impacted on the other when the New York Court of Appeals determined that the 1855 "Act for the Prevention of Intemperance, Pauperism and Crime" violated the New York Constitution's prohibition against taking property without due process of law. This holding anticipated the doctrine of substantive due process that was to dominate the turn-of-the-century American jurisprudence, and it set the stage for the later campaign to secure national Prohibition by constitutional amendment.

The issue in *Wynehamer* and its companion case, *People ex rel. Mathews v. Toynbee,* was straightforward. James G. Wynehamer, a Buffalo barkeep, and Thomas Toynbee, a Brooklyn hotelier, were convicted of selling rum, brandy, gin, wine, whiskey, "strong beer," and champagne to their customers after the state had banned the retail sale of intoxicating beverages. In what amounted to test cases, both men challenged the constitutionality of the recently enacted New York Prohibition law on the grounds that it conflicted with various provisions of the federal and state constitutions. The court of appeals, New York's highest court, focused on the sibling clauses of the New York Constitution providing that "no member of this state shall be disfranchised, or deprived of any of the rights or privileges secured to any citizen thereof, unless by the law of the land or the judgment of his peers" and that "no person shall be . . . deprived of life, liberty, or property without due process of law; nor shall private property be taken for public use without just compensation."

The court thus confronted one of the most determined reform movements of the antebellum years, the crusade to make America alcohol-free. Americans during the first half of the nineteenth century drank more alcohol per capita than at any time before or since. Reformers who were worried about the social and economic costs of alcoholism in the bibulous republic reacted by promoting "temperance" (something quite different from Prohibition). Like its contemporaneous counterpart, the early effort to encourage the manumission of slaves, temperance relied on suasion rather than legal force. Temperance reformers sought to persuade alcohol consumers to reform themselves by drinking only in moderation and by setting a moral example for others. This early phase of the movement was dominated by middle-class leaders, many of them industrial or agricultural employers who wanted a sober work force, and by evangelical Protestant ministers.

The temperance reformers represented a moderate, gradualist phase of the effort, and they became frustrated when confronted with the intransigence of liquor interests and the hostility of the drinking public. The movement responded by turning toward more radical ends and means. Moderate drinking and voluntary abstinence gave way to teetotalism; suasion to political action; and moral example to legal coercion. A Portland, Maine, businessman, Neal Dow, labored uncompromisingly for enactment of a state law that would ban outright the sale of alcohol for beverage purposes. His effort were rewarded in 1851 with the passage of the so-called "Maine Law," a Prohibition statute copied

in the next four years in twelve other states and territories. Prohibition lobbyists touted the Maine Law prototype as a remedy not only for alcoholism but for broader social ills: as the title of New York's statute declared, Prohibition was the solution to vice, poverty, immorality, madness, and deviance.

The New York statute, which Justice George M. Comstock labeled a "fierce and intolerant proscription," banned the sale and possession for sale of alcohol and provided for seizure and destruction of existing liquor stocks—the fatal flaw of the measure, in the eyes of the court. The statute contained exceptions for medicinal, chemical, and sacramental uses.

When the *Wynehamer* and *Toynbee* cases reached the court of appeals, five of the eight judges found the statute unconstitutional. Although Judge Comstock considered a variety of possible grounds for voiding the measure—including natural law and separation of powers—he passed them by in favor of the due process and law-of-the-land clauses. In doing so, he relied on the second great force implicated in *Wynehamer*, the expansion of higher-law jurisprudence in the United States.

In the landmark 1798 case of *Calder v. Bull*, Justice Samuel Chase of the United States Supreme Court acclaimed the natural-law tradition to American jurisprudence, arguing that "there are certain vital principles in our free republican governments which will determine and overrule an apparent and flagrant abuse of legislative power. . . . The legislature cannot . . . violate . . . the right of private property." Chief Justice John Marshall endorsed this approach in the 1810 decision of *Fletcher v. Peck*, and it received the persistent support of Justice Joseph Story throughout his career.

But Marshall and a majority of the justices of the U.S. Supreme Court grew uneasy about the vagueness of formulations like "vital principles of free republican governments," coming to agree with Chase's *Calder* colleague Justice James Iredell that a standard so vacuous can mean nothing more objective than the policy preferences of the individual judge applying it. Accordingly, in *Dartmouth College v. Woodward* (1819), Marshall abandoned the higher-law formula in favor of requiring that a statute be shown to violate some specific provision of the U.S. Constitution (such as, for example, the contract clause of Article I, Section 10) in order for the Court to hold it unconstitutional.

But the higher-law tradition did not disappear; it lingered on in state court jurisprudence, as the highest courts of Maryland, North Carolina, Delaware, Connecticut, Alabama, and New York developed various formulas embodying the idea that state laws might be void for incompatibility with some vague standard of republicanism or natural law. However, the state judges also looked for some textual basis in their state constitutions for voiding a statute, especially as the movement to elect judges attracted popular support. The state judges realized that vague declarations about republican principles provided a flimsy basis for voiding popular laws, and they too turned to the firmer ground of specific provisions in their states' constitutions.

It was because of this search that *Wynehamer* was so significant in its time, for no court had theretofore used the due process clauses of the state or federal constitutions, or their law-of-the-land analogues, as a basis for holding a statute unconstitutional on substantive grounds. Before 1856, the due process clauses had an exclusively procedural connotation, mandating that life, liberty, or property could be taken only in the course of a common-law trial and only by compliance with various traditional safeguards such as jury trial, indictment, and so on. This accounted for the path-breaking quality of Comstock's opinion. He began by demonstrating that extant stocks or liquor were property and thus entitled to whatever protection the law afforded any other sort of property. Judge Comstock insisted that if the legislature's claim that liquor was dangerous to individual health or civic virtue "can be allowed to subvert the fundamental idea of property, then there is no private right entirely safe, because there is no limitation upon the absolute discretion of the legislature, and the guarantees of the constitution are a mere waste of words." He acknowledged that in popular governments, "theories of public good or public necessity may be so plausible, or even so truthful, as to command popular majorities. But," he intoned, "there are some absolute private rights beyond their reach." The

due process clauses thus for the first time took on substantive significance.

Thus, the enduring contribution of Prohibition litigation, especially *Wynehamer*, to constitutional development was the identification of a specific textual touchstone—property as protected in the due process clauses—to replace the nebulous generalities of higher-law doctrine. This extended the life of natural law at a time when it had matured to the point of expiration. Thus reinvigorated, higher-law retained its hold on the judicial imagination for the next two generations. The contribution of substantive due process doctrine to liquor control, by contrast, was to submerge the political development of Prohibition for the time being, and in the long run divert it to constitutionally more drastic channels.

The New York Court of Appeals was not alone in groping toward a substantive concept of due process as a means of protecting property rights. In the same year, Justice Benjamin R. Curtis of the U.S. Supreme Court stated in *Murray's Lessee v. Hoboken Land and Improvement Company* that the due process clause of the Fifth Amendment "is a restraint on the legislative as well as on the executive and judicial powers of the government." In 1854 in *Fisher v. McGirr*, Chief Justice Lemuel Shaw of the Massachusetts Supreme Judicial Court held the Massachusetts version of the Maine Law void on various grounds, among them as a violation of the state constitution's law-of-the-land clause, construed in a procedural sense. And in 1856 in *Beebe v. State*, the Vermont Supreme Court struck down its state's prohibition law on natural-law grounds.

The most extraordinary support for New York's innovative reading of the due process Clause came from United States Supreme Court Chief Justice Roger B. Taney in his 1857 *Dred Scott* opinion. Taney held that a congressional statute excluding slavery from the territories "deprive[d] a citizen of the United States of his liberty or property, without due process of law, merely because he came himself or brought his property into a particular territory of the United States . . . [and] could hardly be dignified with the name of due process of law. . . ." Though the rest of Taney's opinion was repudiated in the course of the Civil War, his suggestive reading of the Fifth Amendment's due process clause attracted little attention. In 1870 in *Hepburn v. Griswold*, his successor, Chief Justice Salmon P. Chase, relied on the clause to hold unconstitutional Congress's declaration that paper money should be legal tender for paying preexisting debts.

As a political matter, *Wynehamer* was a stunning blow to the Maine Law and the Prohibition movement. While Prohibition statutes survived judicial scrutiny in two states—Connecticut, which upheld its statute against a takings-clause challenge, and Vermont, which sustained it against a law-of-the-land clause attack—the Prohibition movement itself collapsed. It had been strikingly sectional, being limited to the northeast United States and to a handful of Midwestern states and territories peopled by migrants from New England and New York, and even there its support dwindled. Elsewhere Prohibition had always been a nonstarter.

But the two great issues implicated in *Wynehamer*, Prohibition and substantive due process, were far from dead. In a different social environment, Prohibition was revived by the Women's Christian Temperance Union and the Anti-Saloon League during the last two decades of the nineteenth century, and grew in appeal until its great but short-lived triumph in the Eigh-

teenth Amendment. Substantive due process fared better. The U.S. Supreme Court, after first rejecting it in the *Slaughterhouse Cases* of 1873, accepted it during the 1890s and exalted it to the status of dogma in such landmark cases as *Lochner v. New York* (1905) and *Adkins v. Children's Hospital* (1923), where it served as a vehicle for the Court's hostility to labor organization and state legislative efforts to ameliorate the conditions of labor. State courts also embraced the innovative doctrine, to the same ends. Historians and other constitutional scholars, seeking to understand the origins and expansion of so potent a doctrine, rediscovered *Wynehamer*, attributing to it and to *Dred Scott* a doctrinal significance little noticed in their own time.

Selected Bibliography

Haines, Charles G. *The Revival of Natural Law Concepts.* Cambridge, MA: Harvard University Press, 1930.

Mott, Rodney L. *Due Process of Law.* New York: Da Capo Press, 1973.

Tyrrell, Ian R. *Sobering Up: From Temperance to Prohibition in Antebellum America, 1800–1860.* Westport, Conn.: Greenwood Press, 1979.

Wiecek, William M. *The Lost World of Classical Legal Thought: Law and Ideology in America, 1886–1937.* New York: Oxford University Press, 1998.

The Fourteenth Amendment Receives Its First Judicial Construction

——◄o►——

Donald G. Nieman

Department of History
Bowling Green State University

Slaughterhouse Cases, 83 U.S. 36 (1873) [U.S. Supreme Court]

◄o► THE CASE IN BRIEF ◄o►

Date
1873

Location
Louisiana

Court
U.S. Supreme Court

Principal Participants
Crescent City Stock Landing and Slaughterhouse Company and competing slaughterhouses; State of Louisiana; Associate Justice Samuel Miller

Significance of the Case
The Court adopted a narrow reading of the Fourteenth Amendment, refusing to see it as a measure to protect private property from state interference. The ruling strengthened a decentralized federal system in which states retained broad authority to define individual rights.

When they reached the Supreme Court in 1870, the *Slaughterhouse Cases* did not seem to be the stuff of which epic constitutional decisions are made. They were brought by disgruntled butchers who challenged a Louisiana law regulating the slaughtering of livestock in the New Orleans metropolitan area. Yet the cases attracted considerable attention because the plaintiffs challenged the statute as a violation of the recently ratified Fourteenth Amendment. Thus, in ruling on the butchers' claim, the nation's highest court would offer its first interpretation of a new constitutional provision that defined citizenship, expanded national protection for individual rights, and promised to make dramatic changes in the balance of power between states and the national government. Moreover, when the Court rendered its decision in 1873, it cast a long shadow into the future, giving the amendment a narrow reading and thus minimizing its effect on the American federal system.

The cases originated in the byzantine world of Reconstruction-era Louisiana politics. In 1869 the Louisiana legislature passed a bill incorporating the Crescent City Stock Landing and Slaughter House Company and authorizing it to build a stockyard and slaughterhouses south of New Orleans. The law gave the company a monopoly: after June 1, 1869, all livestock entering New Orleans and the three surrounding parishes for sale or slaughter were to be sent to the company's stockyards, where they would be examined by state inspectors. Moreover, all slaughtering in the three parishes was to be done in the company's slaughterhouses. Independent butchers might rent space there at reasonable rates, but would have to close their shops in other parts of the city and slaughter and prepare meat for sale in the Crescent City Company's facilities.

In passing this measure, legislators invoked the police power, a venerable constitutional principle which allowed states to restrict individual liberty and property rights in order to promote the public health, safety, and welfare. The law, legislators contended, would make the city more sanitary and protect the public health by requiring inspection of livestock and concentrating slaughtering in one location outside the city. In adopting the slaughterhouse statute, Louisiana was following the lead of several northern states. Concern about urban public health had already prompted legislatures in New York, Massachusetts, Wisconsin, and California to enact similar regulations for rapidly growing cities in their jurisdictions.

More than concern for public health lay behind the Louisiana law, however. The entrepreneurs who formed the Crescent City Company saw substantial profits to be made from controlling the stockyards and slaughterhouses that supplied meat to a bustling city of 200,000. With the vast cattle herds of Texas nearby and the promise of refrigerated ships and railroad cars in the offing, they believed that New Orleans would become a major supplier of fresh meat to the entire nation. And they were confident that the slaughterhouse monopoly would enable them to dominate this lucrative business. Indeed, in 1869, a great fortune (which Chicago packers such as Swift and Armour would soon realize) seemed within the grasp of members of the Crescent City Company. Driven by these visions of grandeur, they turned to politics to secure the legislation that would enable them to

dominate livestock shipping and slaughtering in New Orleans, bribing legislators and other politicians whose support for the measure was critical.

In May 1869, shortly before the statute was to take effect, a series of suits and counter-suits began, as opponents and defenders of the monopoly each looked for protection to state judges who were friendly to their respective causes. A group of some four hundred small, independent butchers, who had formed the Butcher's Benevolent Association two years earlier, struck first. They retained John A. Campbell, who had resigned from the U.S. Supreme Court in 1861 to serve the Confederacy, and J.Q.A. Fellows, a prominent local attorney. Appearing in a state district court, Campbell and Fellows won an injunction blocking the Crescent City Company's monopoly from taking effect. The company launched a counteroffensive, engaging a group of distinguished local attorneys led by Christian Roselius, the head of the University of Louisiana (now Tulane) School of Law. Roselius and his colleagues went before a different state judge and obtained an injunction against the association, barring it from harassing the company with lawsuits aimed at blocking implementation of the law.

While these cases went forward, matters became even more complicated. Substantial livestock dealers, fearing that the monopoly would destroy them, formed the Live Stock Dealers' and Butchers' association. In defiance of the monopoly, the association promptly acquired land south of New Orleans and began constructing stockyards and a slaughterhouse there. This group also retained Campbell, who won an injunction against Crescent City prohibiting it from blocking his client's plans. Louisiana Attorney General Simeon Belden then entered the fray and obtained an injunction against the Live Stock Dealers' Association.

In January 1870, after the lower courts had rendered contradictory decisions in these cases, appeals were taken to the Louisiana Supreme Court. In a 4-1 decision announced in April, the state's high court sustained the law, dissolving the injunctions against the company and sustaining those against the butchers and livestock dealers. But the monopoly's opponents had not exhausted their remedies. In state court they had contended that the monopoly statute violated the Thirteenth and Fourteenth Amendments to the U.S. Constitution. Consequently, Campbell and Fellows employed a provision of federal law permitting appeals from the highest court of any state to the U.S. Supreme Court in cases involving the Constitution, federal laws, or treaties to win a hearing before the nation's highest court.

While the appeals awaited consideration by the U.S. Supreme Court, the Crescent City Company and the state attorney general instituted new suits aimed at breaking opposition to the monopoly. In June 1870, the company obtained an injunction against the sale of meat prepared outside its facilities, and the Metropolitan Police immediately seized $20,000 worth of fresh meat, which quickly spoiled in the early summer heat. At about the same time, Attorney General Belden moved to have his injunction against the Live Stock Dealers' Association enforced.

The butchers and livestock dealers turned to the federal circuit court, then in session in New Orleans, seeking an injunction barring the Crescent City Company and the police from further action against them pending the outcome of the appeal to the U.S. Supreme Court. Their motion was heard by William Woods, the circuit judge, and Supreme Court Justice Joseph P. Bradley, who served as circuit justice for the Deep South. In a lengthy opinion that offered the first extended judicial interpretation of the Fourteenth Amendment, Justice Bradley held that the law establishing the monopoly denied the butchers rights protected by the amendment. However, a 1793 federal statute prohibited federal courts from issuing injunctions to stop proceedings in state courts. Therefore, while Bradley enjoined Crescent City from bringing new suits against the butchers, he declined to bar state courts from acting in suits that had already been instituted.

This proved a hollow victory. Most of the independent butchers, stung by the Metropolitan Police's action and aware that the injunction against the sale of meat prepared in violation of the slaughterhouse statute was still in force, moved into the Crescent City Company's slaughterhouses. However, the appeal pending in the Supreme Court meant that the butchers and the livestock dealers might still prevail. Indeed, at least one member of the Court had unequivocally supported their claims. The situation was thus ripe for a compromise, and in March 1871, members of the Crescent City Company reached an agreement with the leaders of the Live Stock Dealers' Association. The latter promised to drop its appeal, while the Crescent City Company agreed to purchase the association's slaughterhouse, give it a block of shares, and place several of its members on Crescent City's board of directors. Although the parties believed that members of the Butchers' Benevolent Association would follow the lead of the livestock dealers, they refused to compromise the suits to which they were parties and kept the matter before the Supreme Court.

In January 1872, the Court heard two days of arguments in the cases, but failed to render a decision. Justice Samuel Nelson, who was ill, did not participate, and the other eight justices divided evenly. A tie vote would have allowed the holding of the Louisiana Supreme Court to stand, but would have offered no clear resolution of the important constitutional issues involved. Therefore the justices ordered the cases reargued the following term, hoping that a reconsideration before the full Court would produce a clear-cut decision.

The justices were so sharply divided because they confronted a new constitutional provision that had the potential to alter the federal system. Prior to the Civil War, states enjoyed almost complete freedom to define the rights of individuals. In *Barron v. Baltimore* (1833), the U.S. Supreme Court had ruled that the Bill of Rights had been adopted to allay fears of a powerful central government and that its provisions did not apply to the states. Thus neither Congress nor the federal courts could prevent states from denying their citizens rights enumerated in the first eight amendments.

Moreover, the Constitution itself imposed only a few explicit restrictions on the states, prohibiting them from enacting *ex post facto* laws, bills of attainder, and laws impairing the obligation of contract. The privileges and immunities clause of Article IV, Section 2 ("The

Citizens of each State shall be entitled to all Privileges and Immunities of Citizens in the several States") held out the prospect of more meaningful federal protection of individual rights. Some judges, legal writers, and politicians had argued that it guaranteed citizens the rights essential to freedom and barred the states from impairing these rights. However, most observers had contended that it merely guaranteed a citizen of one state who entered another state the rights enjoyed by the citizens of that state, whatever they might be. This left states free to define the rights their citizens possessed, but not to deny these rights to citizens of other states. Since neither Congress nor the Supreme Court had resolved this dispute before the Civil War, the clause's meaning had remained unclear and it had offered little protection for individual rights.

The events of the Civil War and Reconstruction had led Republican Congresses to adopt measures designed to expand federal power to protect individual rights. In order to defend wartime emancipation from constitutional challenge, Congress had adopted the Thirteenth Amendment in 1865. Declaring slavery and involuntary servitude illegal and giving Congress power to enforce the ban, the amendment had destroyed states' authority to sanction slavery and had expanded Congress's authority over individual rights. In the months following the war, presidentially reconstructed state governments in the South had enacted the black codes, imposing harsh restrictions on the freed people and sharply curtailing their freedom. Congressional Republicans believed that the Thirteenth Amendment empowered them to sweep aside such vestiges of slavery and to guarantee blacks the rights essential to freedom. In early 1866, they had enacted the Civil Rights Act, guaranteeing blacks equal rights in state law and imposing penalties on persons who denied blacks equality before the law.

Concerned about potential challenges to the constitutionality of the Civil Rights Act, congressional Republicans had also adopted the Fourteenth Amendment. The first section of this amendment overturned the Supreme Court's holding in *Dred Scott v. Sandford* (1857) that blacks were not entitled to United States citizenship. All persons born in the United States, the amendment declared, were citizens of the United States and of the state in which they resided. Other parts of Section 1, reflecting awareness of the plight of former slaves, provided sweeping guarantees against state denial of individual rights. States were forbidden to abridge the "privileges and immunities" of United States citizens, to deprive any person of life, liberty, or property without due process of law, or to deny any person "equal protection of the laws." Although the courts could protect these rights in the absence of congressional action, the amendment gave Congress authority to enforce them by "appropriate legislation."

How much the amendment increased federal authority to protect individual rights was unclear. After all, what were the privileges and immunities of citizens of the United States, and what did due process of law entail? Debates on the amendment in Congress had not clarified the meaning of these sweeping, but vague, phrases. John A. Bingham, the Ohio Republican who drafted Section 1, had commented that they included "the inborn rights of every free person," but this offered little in the way of specific guidance. Senator Jacob Howard, a leading Republican and a member of the committee that had proposed the amendment, had admitted that these rights could not be defined precisely, but had maintained that they included at the very least the rights enumerated in the Bill of Rights. Yet the debates had not indicated whether most Republicans shared this view. When the amendment was ratified and took effect in 1868, it was left to Congress and the courts to grapple with its meaning and to determine its effect on the federal system.

In his appearances before the U.S. Supreme Court on behalf of the butchers, John A. Campbell exploited this ambiguity, pressing for an interpretation of the amendment that would increase substantially national authority to protect individual rights. He began by emphasizing that the law creating the monopoly was not a legitimate exercise of the state's police power. Protection of the public health might justify confining slaughterhouses to one section of the city, but it did not extend to granting one firm an exclusive right to establish and operate slaughterhouses. According to Campbell, the legislature's real aim had been to confer special privilege on a few, not to promote the public health. Although states might have been free to enact such oppressive legislation prior to the Civil War, Campbell argued, the Fourteenth Amendment had removed individual rights from their previous dependence upon state law. By making national citizenship primary and prohibiting states from denying the privileges and immunities of U.S. citizens, it had created one people who enjoyed fundamental rights guaranteed by the Constitution. He admitted that the amendment did not define these rights precisely, but maintained that the right to pursue a lawful occupation was so essential to personal liberty that it was protected by the privileges and immunities clause.

Campbell also claimed that the slaughterhouse monopoly violated other Fourteenth Amendment guarantees. He asserted that because it unreasonably prohibited the butchers from operating their own shops, it denied them liberty without due process of law. He also contended that the law gave one group a right—to establish and operate slaughterhouses—that others were denied, thus depriving the butchers of equal protection of the laws.

Finally, Campbell asserted that the statute creating the monopoly violated the Thirteenth Amendment. Reminding the Court that the amendment did not mention race and made involuntary servitude as well as slavery illegal, he contended that it went far beyond abolition of Negro slavery. It banned anything that established and maintained personal servitude, including laws that discriminated between classes of persons and compelled one group to serve another. The Louisiana statute, he asserted, gave to a privileged few an exclusive right to own and operate slaughterhouses and compelled the city's butchers to pay them a toll for the privilege of pursuing their craft. Like feudal laws requiring peasants to use the mills, wine presses, and ovens of their lords, Campbell concluded, the slaughterhouse monopoly established a personal servitude in violation of the Thirteenth Amendment.

In the High Court, Campbell was opposed by a new team of lawyers representing the Cres-

cent City Company. Charles Allen, who had distinguished himself as attorney general of Massachusetts, and Thomas Jefferson Durant, a prominent Louisiana Republican and an early advocate of black suffrage, prepared briefs for the company. Senator Matthew Hale Carpenter of Wisconsin, a leading civil rights advocate and one of the most eloquent members of the Supreme Court bar, joined Durant in presenting the company's oral argument.

Crescent City's lawyers emphasized that the law creating the monopoly was a legitimate exercise of the state's police power. By restricting slaughtering to one location and by providing for inspection of livestock, they contended, the law promoted sanitation and helped to prevent the spread of disease. They also defended the Crescent City Company's exclusive right to operate landing and slaughtering facilities. The monopoly did not, they argued, deny the butchers the right to practice their craft: any butcher had the right to rent space from the Crescent City Company at reasonable rates. Moreover, the courts had consistently maintained that legislators, not judges, had the authority to determine the means best calculated to promote the public good. Thus, they concluded, if the Louisiana legislature believed that the most effective way to control disease and odors was to concentrate meat preparation at one great slaughterhouse and preferred to have the facility built with private capital rather than state funds, nothing prevented it from doing so.

Durant, Carpenter, and Allen also maintained that the Thirteenth and Fourteenth Amendments did not affect the police power. They argued that the public debates on these measures demonstrated that they were designed to eradicate Negro slavery and to guarantee former slaves the same rights that whites enjoyed. The framers of the amendments had sought to secure freedom and equal rights for blacks and had no intention of eroding the states' power to promote the public health and welfare. To interpret their work otherwise would undermine states' rights and carry out a constitutional revolution that the amendment's framers had not intended.

The Court heard the reargument February 3–5, 1873, and announced its decision on April 14.

Before the reargument, Justice Nelson, whose absence had left the Court deadlocked 4-4 a year earlier, had resigned and had been replaced by Ward Hunt. A former chief judge of the New York Court of Appeals, Hunt was a firm supporter of the police power. While on the New York court, he had written an opinion upholding a state law requiring New York City butchers to move their slaughterhouses outside the metropolitan district. With the other justices remaining evenly divided, Hunt's support for the police power was decisive, and the Court rejected the butchers' plea, 5-4.

Justice Samuel Miller of Iowa, a conservative Republican who was nonetheless sympathetic to the congressional civil rights program, wrote the opinion for the majority. Miller began by asserting that the Louisiana law was unquestionably a legitimate exercise of the state's police power. By concentrating the obnoxious and potentially hazardous activity of slaughtering livestock in one small area outside the city, it clearly attempted to promote the public good. Miller also found unexceptionable the legislature's decision to give a private corporation exclusive rights to operate a slaughterhouse. Although some might deny the wisdom of this decision, choosing the best means of protecting the public health was a matter of policy that legislators must decide. Moreover, he flatly rejected Campbell's claim that the statute destroyed the butchers' right to pursue a lawful occupation. While it restricted their freedom in order to promote the public good, the law guaranteed the right to practice their occupation in the Crescent City Company's facilities at reasonable rates.

Admitting that the recent amendments might have placed restrictions on the police power, Miller next addressed the butchers' claims under the Thirteenth and Fourteenth Amendments. He began by asserting that the amendments could only be properly understood in light of their historical origins. Congress had passed them in order to bring an end to the conflict over slavery, which had driven the nation into a bloody civil war, and to guarantee substantive freedom to the slaves, who had fought valiantly on behalf of the Union. In enacting the amendments, Miller concluded, Congress had intended to eradicate

Negro slavery, guarantee the freed people equality before the law, and give the national government adequate authority to secure freedom and equality for blacks. However, he argued, Congress had not intended to concentrate in the federal government all power to define and protect individual rights.

After these preliminary remarks, Miller discussed specific provisions of the amendments, devoting most of his attention to the Fourteenth Amendment's privileges and immunities clause. He pointed out that the amendment clearly recognized a dual citizenship, expressly stating that Americans were both citizens of the United States and of the states in which they resided. Consequently, he asserted that they possessed two separate and distinct sets of rights, one deriving from U.S. citizenship and the other from state citizenship. Because the Fourteenth Amendment forbade states to abridge the privileges and immunities of U.S. citizens, he concluded, it only protected those rights that attached to United States citizenship. Rights that derived from state citizenship were not protected by the amendment.

What were the privileges and immunities of United States citizens? According to Miller, they constituted a small group of rights "which owe their existence to the Federal government, its national character, its Constitution, or its laws." These included the right of *habeas corpus,* the right to assemble and petition the government for redress of grievances, the right to protection from the government on the high seas and in foreign lands, the right of access to navigable rivers and ports in the United States, and the right to travel to the nation's capital. Thus, he rejected the notion that the privileges and immunities clause protected all of the fundamental rights necessary to freedom, suggesting instead that it secured a modicum of rights that were of limited importance to Americans in their day-to-day lives.

Miller justified this narrow interpretation by pointing out the revolutionary consequences of Campbell's contention that the privileges and immunities of U.S. citizens included all of the fundamental rights of citizens. Such a ruling would make the Fourteenth Amendment a grab-bag of rights and the federal courts "perpetual censors" of the states, passing judgment on the myriad provisions states established to regulate individual rights. This would not only swamp the federal courts with a caseload they were ill-prepared to handle, but would also deprive the states of the authority they needed to govern themselves.

There was another danger, according to Miller: Congress possessed authority to enforce the Fourteenth Amendment's guarantees by enacting "appropriate legislation." He warned that if the privileges and immunities of U.S. citizens were broadly defined, Congress, under the guise of legislating to protect these rights, might establish a code of laws minutely defining the rights of Americans. This would transfer from the states to the federal government authority to make the laws governing contracts, property, family relations, crime and punishment, and the like.

Speculating on what the framers of the amendment had intended, Miller asserted that Congress would not have taken such revolutionary action by simply declaring that no state shall abridge the privileges and immunities of U.S. citizens. Had it intended to make sweeping changes in the federal system, it would have stated its intention clearly and would not have left the matter in doubt.

Deeply concerned about preserving federalism's delicate balance between state and national power, Miller produced a badly strained argument. The sweeping consequences that he imagined would result from a broad interpretation of the privileges and immunities clause actually shed no light on the question of the framers' intent. Indeed, many of the framers had clearly believed that the amendment substantially increased the power of the federal government to protect individual rights. Moreover, he greatly exaggerated the consequences that would result if the Court accepted a broad interpretation of the privileges and immunities clause. If the privileges and immunities of U.S. citizens included rights that were truly fundamental—such as those enumerated in the Bill of Rights—the results would have been much less disruptive than Miller suggested. States would have continued to regulate individual rights to make contracts, hold property,

conduct business, marry, and the like. However, the federal government would have possessed authority to guarantee that in doing so they did not abridge such rights as freedom of speech or protection against self-incrimination. Finally, the rights that Miller listed as being among the privileges and immunities of citizens of the United States were, for the most part, rights that had been subject to federal protection prior to ratification of the amendment. Thus he came close to arguing that the privileges and immunities clause was meaningless verbiage added to the Constitution.

Miller dispensed with Campbell's other constitutional claims in short order. The context in which the Thirteenth Amendment was adopted, he asserted, suggested that the framers intended it to root out Negro slavery. They had prohibited involuntary servitude as well as slavery in order to destroy any subterfuges—such as peonage or apprenticeship—that states or individuals might use to keep blacks in bondage. However, they had not intended the amendment to prevent the states from imposing such restrictions on liberty as were necessary to protect the public health. He also rejected the butchers' claims under the Fourteenth Amendment's equal protection clause, explaining that it was clearly intended to prohibit laws, like the black codes, which discriminated on the basis of race.

Finally, Miller argued that the concept of due process of law was familiar in American law, but that the courts had never given it the interpretation Campbell had suggested. Although he did not elaborate, his meaning was clear. Campbell had contended that the clause established a right to have the courts determine whether a measure that deprived a person of life, liberty, or property was, in substance, fair and equitable. But due process, as traditionally understood, had a procedural meaning, requiring government to follow certain procedures when it deprived persons of life, liberty, or property. In criminal proceedings, for example, due process guaranteed that the accused was informed of the charges, enjoyed protection against self-incrimination, had the right to counsel, and received a jury trial. Read as a procedural rather than a substantive guarantee, due process offered no basis to challenge the legitimacy of the Louisiana statute.

Miller's opinion was greeted by sharp dissent. Noah Swayne, a staunchly antislavery Republican who had been President Abraham Lincoln's first appointee to the Court, charged that the majority fundamentally misunderstood the Fourteenth Amendment. Its framers, he argued, had been aware of the shortcomings of the antebellum federal system and had intended to make significant changes in it. They had believed that the greatest threat to liberty came from the states and had sought to empower the national government to protect the fundamental rights of its citizens, regardless of race. By assuming that the amendment was limited in its scope, Swayne concluded, the majority established limitations that the framers had not intended and transformed "what was meant for bread into a stone."

Two other dissenting opinions offered more detailed analyses of the amendment. Justice Stephen J. Field, a California Democrat who served on the Court from 1863 to 1897 and became its most vigorous advocate of conservative judicial activism, wrote a passionate dissent that was joined by Chief Justice Salmon P. Chase and Justices Swayne and Bradley. While Miller refused to probe the legislature's motives and judgment, Field subjected them to careful scrutiny. He indicated that the state might legitimately restrict individuals' use of their property, holding that those provisions of the act which limited slaughtering to areas below the city and required inspection of livestock were legitimate exercises of the police power. However, he argued that the slaughterhouse monopoly did not really promote public sanitation, but merely conferred special privileges on the Crescent City Company at the expense of its rivals. In a thinly veiled reference to the political corruption that had produced the slaughterhouse statute, Field concluded, "The pretense of sanitary regulations for the grant of the exclusive privileges is a shallow one."

While Field admitted that the antebellum Constitution had offered no protection against such obnoxious legislation, he contended that the Fourteenth Amendment had supplied a remedy. The amendment made national citizenship primary and, by demanding that states confer citizenship upon all national citizens re-

siding within their borders, made state citizenship derivative and subordinate. According to Field, individuals possessed the fundamental rights of free persons as U.S. citizens, and the Fourteenth Amendment's privileges and immunities clause protected these rights. Nothing was more fundamental, he concluded, than the freedom to pursue a lawful occupation without interference from special-interest legislation. The slaughterhouse monopoly, he asserted, was a "most barefaced and shameless" violation of the Fourteenth Amendment.

Justice Bradley, who had ruled in favor of the butchers while on circuit, issued a third dissent. Clearly appalled by the chicanery by which the monopoly was established and enforced, he penned a sharp denunciation of the law. Much of his opinion followed Field, maintaining that national citizenship was paramount and that the privileges and immunities clause protected fundamental rights, including the right to protection against legislation conferring special privileges. However, Bradley also urged that the slaughterhouse monopoly violated the Fourteenth Amendment's due process clause. Creating a monopoly was not necessary to protect the public health, he argued, and was an "unreasonable, arbitrary, and unjust" measure adopted to promote the interests of "a few scheming individuals." Thus the Louisiana statute deprived New Orleans butchers of their liberty to pursue a lawful occupation and the intangible property that they had in their occupation without due process of law in violation of the Fourteenth Amendment. In making this argument, Bradley moved from a procedural to a substantive definition of due process. Laws must be reasonable and just to pass constitutional muster, he argued, and the courts should decide these very subjective matters.

The opinions in the *Slaughterhouse Cases* were of considerable significance. The Fourteenth Amendment's privileges and immunities clause had the potential to permit the federal government to protect a wide range of fundamental rights—including those enumerated in the Bill of Rights—against infringement by the states. Miller's opinion for the majority, however, held that the privileges and immunities clause protected only a few rights that were not of much consequence to most Americans. Combined with subsequent rulings that interpreted the amendment's due process clause narrowly, it signaled that the Court rejected making major changes in the federal system by expanding significantly national protection for individual rights.

Indeed, the *Slaughterhouse Cases* dealt the privileges and immunities clause a blow from which it never recovered. In the fifty years after *Gitlow v. New York* (1925), the Court decided a series of cases holding that states may not violate selected provisions of the Bill of Rights. And since *Griswold v. Connecticut* (1965), it has held that persons have a right to privacy that states may not violate. In deciding these cases, however, it has relied on the Fourteenth Amendment's due process clause and has not rehabilitated the privileges and immunities clause.

It is easy to exaggerate the role of the case in signaling the Court's retreat from Reconstruction and its abandonment of blacks. To be sure, by limiting the rights protected by the Fourteenth Amendment the case made it more difficult for Congress and the federal courts to check repressive state action against unpopular minorities. However, the main problem confronting blacks in the 1870s was not direct state action denying them rights, but private acts of discrimination and violence. Even if the minority had prevailed in the *Slaughterhouse Cases*, the decision would have been of limited value in protecting blacks from these threats. Moreover, one must remember that Miller insisted that the Reconstruction amendments had been adopted to guarantee full freedom and genuine equality for blacks. His language clearly offered Congress and the federal courts broad authority under the Thirteenth Amendment and the Fourteenth Amendment's equal protection clause to deal with racially motivated discrimination. If in subsequent cases the Court did not fully exploit this analysis, the outcome was not dictated by Miller's *Slaughterhouse* opinion.

The outcome of the cases also indicated that the Court would permit states to engage in economic regulation under the police power. The Court clearly refused to read the Fourteenth Amendment as a measure protecting private property from state interference. It also refused to probe behind the action of legislatures, scrutinize their motives, and determine whether police regulations they enacted were fair and reasonable. Four years later, in the *Munn v. Illinois* (1877), the Supreme Court confirmed this, upholding state legislation setting railroad and warehouse rates. Thus, during the 1870s the Court demonstrated a consistent concern for maintaining a decentralized federal system in which states not only retained broad authority to define individual rights but possessed adequate power to cope with the problems that rapid economic growth presented. It did not, as scholars have sometimes suggested, strip the Fourteenth Amendment of its capacity to protect the rights of blacks and transform it into a bulwark of private property.

The dissents of Field and Bradley also proved influential. They offered to make the amendment a vehicle to protect property and to authorize courts to determine whether restrictions on property rights were equitable and reasonable. This vision of the amendment would ultimately triumph and be used by the Supreme Court to protect capital from legislation aimed at protecting the rights of workers and consumers. However, this did not occur until the early years of the twentieth century, long after the *Slaughterhouse Cases* had been decided.

Selected Bibliography

Connor, Henry G. *John Archibald Campbell, Associate Justice of the United States Supreme Court, 1853–1861.* Boston: Houghton Mifflin, 1920.

Franklin, Mitchell. "The Foundation and Meaning of the Slaughterhouse Cases." *Tulane Law Review* 18 (October-December 1943): 1–88, 218–262.

Hyman, Harold M., and William M. Wiecek. *Equal Justice Under Law: Constitutional Development, 1835–1875.* New York: Harper & Row Publishers, 1982.

Kaczorowski, Robert J. *The Politics of Judicial Interpretation: The Federal Courts, Department of Justice and Civil Rights, 1866–1876.* New York: Oceana Publications, Inc., 1985.

Nelson, William E. *The Fourteenth Amendment: From Political Principle to Judicial Doctrine.* Cambridge, MA: Harvard University Press, 1988.

Palmer, Robert C. "The Parameters of Constitutional Reconstruction: Slaughter-House, Cruickshank, and the Fourteenth Amendment." *University of Illinois Law Journal* (1984): 739–770.

The Court Enters the Age of Reform

Richard R. Broadie

Department of History
University of Northern Iowa

Munn v. Illinois, 94 U.S. 113 (1877) [U.S. Supreme Court]

⊸◦⊱ THE CASE IN BRIEF ⊸◦⊱

Date
1877

Location
Illinois

Court
U.S. Supreme Court

Principal Participants
Ira Y. Munn
State of Illinois
Chief Justice Morrison R. Waite

Significance of the Case
The decision established that a state may regulate any business that is public in nature or that affects the public interest. The case was a small first step toward the use of the state government as an agent of reform.

Prior to the last third of the nineteenth century, reform movements arose, more often than not, in response to moral and social dilemmas. Abolitionists, prohibitionists, feminists and various utopian crusaders all tackled tough problems, but concluded that finding solutions to them did not necessarily require government coercion. Individuals were often encouraged to "take the pledge"—give up strong drink, free their slaves, be born again, and so forth—because most reformers did not expect the state to assume a direct role in remaking the world according to their own image.

Economic problems were thought by many to be caused by forces over which people (and their government) have little control. As economist Lester Thurow has pointed out, preindustrial agricultural economies are often strong or weak depending on the whims of nature: it's too hot or too cold, too wet or too dry. What can the politicians in Washington or the various state capitals do to fine-tune the economy at this level of economic development? And even if government wants to provide direct aid to those battered by the forces of nature—give them welfare, to use twentieth century lingo—from whom can the funds to finance these programs be expropriated? Societies where little surplus wealth is created simply cannot afford compassionate government.

During the first decade after the Civil War it became apparent that the subsistence farmer was no longer the linchpin of the American economy. Industrial growth was far outpacing any increases in wealth derived from land ownership or crop production. Those farmers who were able to hang on were increasingly vulnerable to the fluctuations of the market and what they perceived to be the machinations of various middlemen from whom they bought what they needed and sold what they produced. It is not necessary for one to accept the view held by some historians that farmers felt victimized by villains acting in a conspiratorial manner to acknowledge that they were able to spot those segments of the evolving market economy that did not have their best interests at heart.

As it was clear that government had already taken a hand in promoting economic growth—protecting infant industries, financing railroads and canals, administering western lands, and so on—it was perhaps inevitable that some would conclude that the state should be used to regulate the market economy and aid those considered losers in the new economic arrangement.

According to an early twentieth-century historian, the Granger movement of the 1860s and 1870s was "a movement for agricultural organization for the advancement of farmers in every possible way—socially, intellectually, politically, and economically—by concerted effort." As times on the farm became worse in the 1870s, the emphasis shifted from the social and intellectual to the political and economic. The so-called "Granger laws"—passed mostly in the 1870s in the Midwestern states of Iowa, Wisconsin, Illinois, and Minnesota—were early attempts at economic regulation. It is incorrect to suggest that the Grange itself was behind this legislation—the organization was officially apolitical. It would also be a mistake to believe that the more radical elements of the Grange wrote the Granger laws. Rather, the Granger railroad laws were "prepared by lawyers with the aid of merchants and shippers and sometimes with the aid of railroad officials." Regulations put on the books by the Granger laws often roughly corresponded to the farmers' interests, but it is worth pointing out that they often did not and were routinely criticized for not going far enough by the more vocal members of the Grange.

In Illinois, a bill passed the state house of representatives as early as 1861 (six years before the Grange was formed) which aimed to "prevent and punish any fraudulent discrimination by railroad companies." The Illinois state senate and governor rejected this approach and the bill did not become law. The cause did not die, however, and a bill regulating railroad rates was passed in 1869. The law provided no adequate provision for enforcement and was described by one historian as a "mere encumbrance on the statute books."

Led by a coalition of reformers which included elements of the Grange, the voters of Illinois ratified a new constitution in 1870 that contained provisions granting authority to regulate railroads, public elevators, and warehouses for the storage of grain. The sections relating to railroad and warehouse regulation proved to be extremely popular with voters, which created a strong impetus for reform in the next legislative session. This, coupled with the fact that unusually high numbers of farmers pledged to support regulation were elected to the Illinois legislature that convened in 1871, led to the passage of many of the Granger laws during the year that followed.

While most Granger laws in Illinois and elsewhere attempted to regulate railroads, there were exceptions. Considerable time and effort was also devoted to leashing other middlemen whose practices—in particular, pricing their goods and services—farmers found objectionable. Illinois enacted a statute in April of 1871 that regulated "public warehouses and the public inspection of grain." This law classified public warehouses according to how the grain was stored—mixed together or segregated by farmer—and the size of the city in which the warehouse was located. "Class A warehouses," for example, were defined as "all warehouses, elevators and granaries in which grain is stored in bulk, and in which the grain of different owners is mixed together, or in which grain is stored in such a manner that the identity of different parcels cannot be accurately preserved. . . ." In addition, a Class A warehouse must be located in a city of at least one hundred inhabitants—a requirement that only Chicago met in 1871. And finally, the law required all Class A warehouses to procure a license and set rates based on the length of time the grain had been stored.

Most companies technically complied with the provisions of the railroad and warehouse acts but officially denied the validity of these laws and declared all of their rights to be reserved. Others, such as Munn and Scott of Chicago, "managers and lessees of a public warehouse known as the Northwestern Elevator," defied the statute. In 1872, a suit was instituted against Munn and Scott for failure to take out licenses required by law and charging in excess of the rates established in January 1872 under the provisions of the statute.

After a brief delay caused by the Chicago fire, the defendants were found guilty by the Criminal Court of Cook County and fined $100. This decision was later affirmed by the Illinois Supreme Court but rose on appeal to the U.S. Supreme Court. A decision on *Munn v. Illinois*, and several other Granger cases, was issued on March 1, 1877.

The decision in the *Munn* case was placed first, according to historian George Miller, because Munn and Scott was a partnership rather than a corporation, thus "its suit, free of all complications resulting from corporate charter provisions, permitted a more direct confrontation with the basic issues raised by the plaintiff's counsel." The Court's majority opinion, written by Chief Justice Morrison R. Waite, rejected the arguments of the plaintiff's counsel on all counts, thus upholding the Illinois statute by a 7-2 margin.

The Court in the *Munn* case, and in others such as *Chicago, Burlington and Quincy Railroad Company v. Iowa*, established several propositions that collectively laid the legal foundation on which early reform legislation was based. With them—and several others going back to 1867—the Court entered what political scientist Robert G. McCloskey called the "second

great period of constitutional history" during which the major interest of the Supreme Court became the relationship between government and business.

The *Munn* decision established that a state may, under its police power, regulate, to the extent of determining maximum rates, any business which is public in nature or has been "clothed with a public interest." Warehouses and railroads were considered sufficiently of a public nature as to permit their regulation. And, although a railroad charter is a contract, the Court held that the Constitution does not interfere with the right of a state to regulate charges unless it contains a direct stipulation to that effect.

Waite established two other principles that were later overturned or significantly modified. First, the majority concluded in *Munn* that lacking federal legislation, states were permitted to regulate interstate commerce so far as its citizens are affected by it. In 1886, the Court reversed itself by ruling that "national commerce must be nationally controlled, if it is to be controlled at all."

Perhaps even more crucial for understanding *Munn v. Illinois* was how the court addressed the issue of procedural versus substantive due process—a debate which would reappear in many significant decisions involving the relationship between business and government throughout the remainder of the nineteenth century. The attorneys for Munn and Scott had argued that certain sections of the Illinois statute were repugnant to the first section of the Fourteenth Amendment that ordains that no state shall "deprive any person of life, liberty or property without due process of law, nor deny to any person within its jurisdiction the equal protection of the law." The Court's response to these points, though clearly making the job of the regulators easier, left plenty of room to maneuver.

Waite's majority opinion provided for a narrow procedural construction of the due process clause of the Fourteenth Amendment. According to the Court, the Fourteenth Amendment could not be used to interfere with state regulatory initiatives as long as the property had become "clothed with the public interest." This occurs, according to Waite when it is used in a manner "to make it of public consequence, and affect the community at large." If a business, such as a railroad or a warehouse standing in "the very gateway of commerce," is involved in an activity in which the public has an interest, it "grants to the public an interest in that use, and must submit to [control] . . . for the common good." As long as a business was deemed to be affected with a public interest, the substantive regulations (an example, per *Munn*, would be the storage rates set by the statute) were placed outside the scope of judicial review. If property owners were not given reasonable compensation—the power to regulate could be abused, Waite acknowledged—then the proper recourse was at the polls, not in the courts.

Legal scholars have detected a loophole in Waite's opinion in that he seemed to concede some of what Justice Stephen Field had argued in his minority opinion. Waite was careful to say that "under some circumstances" a statute may deprive an owner of his property without due process of law. Waite, however, did not make clear when and under what circumstances future courts would be justified in handing down rulings limiting government regulation of business. Within roughly ten years, Waite's views were abandoned in favor of Field's substantive due process position that sought to safeguard private property from what conservatives termed "arbitrary and unreasonable" regulatory schemes. In addition, the reach of the Fourteenth Amendment was extended by later Courts, establishing that a corporation is legally a person and cannot be deprived of its property without due process. A far cry, indeed, from the Court's position in *Munn*.

Thus, it can be argued that the *Munn* decision was a false start—favorable to reform but severely gutted in later decisions. To a point, this is a reasonable conclusion to reach. But it would be unfortunate to conclude that *Munn v. Illinois* was of no value to later reformers. In it, the Court established principles, such as the propriety of government regulation under the state's police powers, which were never overturned. The pace of reform was slow during the remainder of the century, but in all probability this was a result of more than simply a recalcitrant Court. When political majorities began to demand reform during the Progressive Era, the politicians found a way to put new regulations on the books.

In spite of what the Court did in the next two decades to back away from *Munn*, the fundamental principles of the Granger cases still stood. In 1913 historian Justus Buck pointed to the "voluminous restrictive railroad legislation of the last 40 years" as the legacy of the Granger cases. The Court, though never wild about the "schemes" of many reformers, had become a willing partner in the age of reform. There was no turning back.

Selected Bibliography

Buck, Justus S. *The Granger Movement: A Study of Agricultural Organization and Its Political, Economic and Social Manifestations, 1870–1880.* Cambridge, MA: Harvard University Press, 1913.

McCloskey, Robert J. *The American Supreme Court.* Chicago: University of Chicago Press, 1960.

Miller, George H. *Railroads and the Granger Laws.* Madison: University of Wisconsin Press, 1971.

A "Right" to Make Cigars

—◄◦►—

Melvin I. Urofsky

Center for Public Policy
Virginia Commonwealth University

In re Jacobs, 98 N.Y. 98 (1885) [New York Court of Appeals]

<table>
<tr><td colspan="2" style="text-align:center">◄◦► THE CASE IN BRIEF ◄◦►</td></tr>
</table>

Date
1885

Location
New York

Court
New York Court of Appeals

Principal Participants
Peter Jacobs
State of New York
Judge Robert Earl

Significance of the Case
The court adopted the doctrine of substantive due process to safeguard property from interference by the state. In doing so, it struck down reform legislation and became a precedent for judicial protection of property rights.

Today's apartment dwellers would properly object if their neighbors ran noisy industrial machines or manufactured noxious products. And they would be able to call upon the law to put an end to the nuisance. Even though we proclaim that a person's home is his/her castle, most of us assume that the power of the state can and should be used to prevent one person's use of property from infringing upon the right of others to enjoy theirs. In fact, one of the most oft-quoted of the old common-law maxims is *sic utero tuo ut alienum non laedas*—use your own property so as not to injure the property of others.

But our sense of how one may properly use his or her property is quite different from that held a century ago, a period when initial efforts of the state to exercise its police powers ran headlong into a prime tenet of prevailing legal thought, the sanctity of property and the right to use it for gain. One can easily see the difference between our views and those of the latter nineteenth century in this famous case of the tenement cigar-maker.

Although industrialization affected nearly every aspect of the American economy after the

482

Civil War, some trades remained labor intensive and immune from the need to cluster workers around machines in giant factories. In many American cities, workers in such trades as garment manufacturing labored in lofts, storefronts and often in their own homes. Individuals contracted with wholesalers to do piecework, and they did the work in the crowded tenements where immigrants who comprised the bulk of these labor forces lived.

One such trade was cigar-making, which remained essentially an individual hand-rolling operation, the worker wrapping tobacco leaves into shape. One needed no special machinery, nor did the laborer have to go to a factory; only a chair and a table were required. In the mid-1880s, the bulk of the nation's cigars were produced in New York tenements, and reformers concerned about the possible health risks involved sought legislation to move the noxious weed out of living quarters and into regular commercial space. In May 1884, the New York legislature passed an act "to improve the public health" by prohibiting cigar-making in tenements in the state's two largest cities, New York and Brooklyn, and imposed criminal penalties of up to $100 and/or six months in jail for violation of the law.

Two days after enactment of the law, the police arrested Peter Jacobs, who with his wife and two children lived in a New York tenement. The Jacobs family enjoyed a relatively spacious seven-room flat, occupying an entire floor of the building. In one room, Jacobs prepared tobacco leaves and made cigars, and according to the police report, there was no smell of tobacco in any room in the flat except that one.

Jacobs had plainly violated the law, and the local magistrate committed him to prison for trial. He appealed to the state supreme sourt (which in New York is the lowest court of record in the state judicial system), which ordered him released and declared the cigar act unconstitutional. The prosecuting attorney then appealed to the state's highest tribunal, the court of appeals, which heard the case on December 17, 1884. A month later, on January 20, 1885, Judge Robert Earl spoke for a unanimous court in declaring the act unconstitutional, since it had deprived Peter Jacobs of his rights to property, in this case the right to labor at a lawful trade, without due process of law.

The case must be seen in the light of a debate going on at the time between defenders of the new industrial system and those who sought through reform to mitigate its more harmful effects. For the latter, the state's nascent police powers could be used to regulate property in order to protect the health and safety of the people. Conservatives admitted that the state had this power, but took a very narrow view of its extent. Influential legal writers, such as Christopher Tiedeman and Thomas M. Cooley, argued that the government should do no more than provide police protection against criminals who would injure life or property.

To erect a legal barrier against the police power, conservative jurists in state and federal courts adopted the doctrine of "substantive due process," which invested property, including the right to pursue any lawful trade, with safeguards against interference by the state. The doctrine did not win the approval of a majority of the U.S. Supreme Court until *Allgeyer v. Louisiana* (1897), but it captured many state courts well before then. The conservative New York Court of Appeals was one of the first to adopt the idea of substantive due process to strike down reform legislation.

The cigar law, according to Judge Earl, bore no relation to health or safety, but interfered "with the profitable and free use of his property by the owner . . . and arbitrarily deprives him of his property and some portion of his personal liberty." This liberty, according to the court, "means the right, not only of freedom from actual servitude, imprisonment or restraint, but the right of one to use his faculties in all lawful ways, to live and work where he will, to earn his livelihood in any lawful calling." Any laws, of whatever type, which restricted this liberty, violated constitutional protection.

While admitting the broad reach of the police power, the court noted that the legislature could not, under the guise of the police power, trammel basic constitutional rights. The courts had the obligation to protect those rights, and, therefore, it would be the final arbiter of whether the statute was a reasonable exercise of the police power. Thus the court arrogated to itself not only the relatively narrow role of determining if a specific power existed, but also the broader authority to pass on the wisdom of the statute.

In re Jacobs quickly became one of the most cited state court decisions of its time, quoted approvingly by both state and federal jurists for its defense of property rights, as well as its expansive view of judicial power.

Selected Bibliography

Corwin, Edward S. *Liberty Against Government.* Baton Rouge: Louisiana State University Press, 1948.

Paul, Arnold M. *Conservative Crisis and the Rule of Law: Attitudes of Bar and Bench, 1887–1895.* Ithaca, NY: Cornell University Press, 1960.

Urofsky, Melvin I. "State Courts and Protective Legislation in the Progressive Era: A Reevaluation." *Journal of American History* 72 (1985): 63–91.

Wiecek, William M. *The Lost World of Classical Legal Thought: Law and Ideology in America, 1886–1937.* New York: Oxford University Press, 1998.

"Mere Meddlesome Interferences": The Apogee of Substantive Due Process

———◁◦▷———

Fred D. Ragan

Emeritus Professor of History
East Carolina University

Lochner v. New York, 198 U.S. 45 (1905) [U.S. Supreme Court]

◄◦► THE CASE IN BRIEF ◄◦►

Date
1905

Location
New York

Court
U.S. Supreme Court

Principal Participants
Joseph Lochner
State of New York
Master Bakers Association
Henry Weismann
Associate Justice Rufus W. Peckham

Significance of the Case
By overturning a New York law limiting the working hours of bakers, the Court created a kind of economic constitutional right, substituting its own view of the proper relation between management and labor for that of the state legislature.

It is rare to have an advocate of legislative reform change his position and call upon the United States Supreme Court to undo his handiwork. When Henry Weismann, former baker and union leader, appeared before the Court in 1905, he insisted in the name of freedom of contract that the Court overturn his work as a union leader.

As the twentieth century dawned, a divided Supreme Court struggled to implement old values amid the new realities of the industrial era. In its desire to protect property from the rising tide of state regulatory legislation, a position often urged upon the Court by some of the most influential members of the bar, the Court developed the due process clause of the Fourteenth Amendment into an instrument, much as the Supreme Court of the early nineteenth century had used the doctrine of vested interest and the contract clause, that would permit it to determine whether states acted in an appropriate, direct, and reasonable manner when regulating business. If the state overstepped its authority, the Court struck down the law as arbitrary and unreasonable. Employing this new weapon of substantive due process, the Court took upon itself the responsibility to balance rights claimed by business against the traditionally recognized right of a state to protect the health, safety, and welfare of its people under the police powers.

The depression of the 1890s inspired and intensified efforts by reformers to improve conditions of employment and the working environment. Although lacking a unity of motives, goals, and methods, the Progressive reformers at the state level tried to humanize industrial plants by limiting child labor, establishing maximum hours and minimum wages, and aiding organized labor. Their efforts ran into judicial opposition. To counter state regulations, especially those of hours of work and wages, courts further developed the doctrine of freedom of contract, which held that government interference with free market forces constituted the exception to the rule of untrammeled liberty of contract. This doctrine, discovered in the liberty protected by the Fourteenth Amendment and a legal extension of laissez faire economic thought, protected a right not enumerated in the Constitution, one created by judicial fiat. Unless convinced of the danger of an occupation, judges struck down state interference with what the courts viewed as a worker's right to contract freely for a work day and wages they thought acceptable. The doctrines of economic substantive due process and freedom of contract, in the eyes of critics, made the Supreme Court into "a superlegislature," writing its own views into law unrestrained by the balancing of power with the other two branches of government.

The judicial opposition to the reformer's efforts, however, was not absolute. The *Lochner* case began in 1901 when a New York court convicted Joseph Lochner of violating a state statute limiting bakers from working more than ten hours a day or sixty hours a week. When the Supreme Court struck down the law four years later, reformers cried foul, painting the Court as a bastion of economic conservatism. Recently writers have revised that long accepted view of the courts, especially the U.S. Supreme Court, as a major obstacle to Progressive Era reforms. If no longer universal, most authorities have continued to question the Court's *Lochner* deci-

sion and its use by the later Courts of the 1920s and 1930s.

The shorter-hour movement for bakers in New York began in earnest after passage in 1868 of federal legislation regulating the hours of labor on public works projects. Two years later, New York adopted a statute modeled after the national act. At the time, bakers, a trade dominated by German immigrants, had not organized themselves into trade unions. According to one source, they earned $5.00 for a 120-hour week, while plasterers in the building trades, who were organized, earned $4.50 for a 48-hour week. Over the next few years, bakers, chiefly those in New York City, began to unionize. Objecting to long hours and especially to Sunday work, a labor paper reported improvements by 1883. It complained, nonetheless, that lack of strong unions meant "eight dollars for ninety hours" of crushing labor which continued to produce "so many coffins. . . ."

The next year the Baker's Progressive Union, a recently organized group trying to promote concerted action among New York City bakers, called for meetings to plan a strategy for achieving shorter work days. Although it insisted that the "yellow-dog contract" (an agreement many workers were forced to sign as a condition of employment, promising that they would not join a union) be outlawed, its principal goal was for the ten-hour day with additional pay for overtime. The union's representative on the Central Labor Union of New York City took the lead in drafting a bill for introduction at the next session of the legislature. Success in that arena did not come quickly, however.

The decade of the 1880s was one of turmoil for organized labor. The eight-hour day became a major long-term goal, and in 1885 labor groups formed the National Eight Hour Association in Chicago. Amid a new sense of enthusiasm and confidence, a reinvigorated trade union movement sponsored demonstrations and adopted resolutions demanding shorter work days. Few tangible improvements grew from the activities, however. The 1886 Chicago Haymarket violence not only added a nail to the coffin of the Knights of Labor but also temporarily stymied the eight-hour movement. Increased agitation did produce, however, new strategies for furthering baker union goals. Adopting the example of the cigar makers union, New York City bakers began using the union label. More effective, however, was their use of the "strike boycott," a device that contributed to significant improvement for members of the baker's union. By the late 1880s, many New York City bakers had won the ten-hour work day for themselves. Those not members of unions, especially the recently arrived Italian and Jewish bakers, continued to work long hours. According to a New York State factory inspector report, the recent immigrants worked "12, 13, or 14 hours a day. . . ."

Other developments during the 1880s also helped to further the interest of labor. The establishment of state and national agencies that gathered information on working conditions represented one important advancement. While not replacing the often vague and generalized humanitarianism upon which many reformers acted, agency reports anchored the impulse upon a more realistic view of industrial life. The reports helped to publicize workers problems and mobilize union members and sympathizers. When presenting their reports or testifying before legislative committees, agency officials also served as an informed lobby against industrial abuses.

Recognizing the necessity of mobilizing their own rank and file and galvanizing public support, labor publications issued calls for action. For bakers, the *Baker's Journal,* first published in 1887 in both English and German, served as a forum for grievances and a vehicle for motivating supporters. Probably the *Journal*'s most important role after Henry Weismann assumed leadership in 1890 became that of advocate for legislation to improve working conditions.

A baker in his native Germany prior to coming to San Francisco, Weismann successfully led California bakers before moving to New York. His leadership seemed to energize the Journeymen Bakers Union, as he agitated for legislation and recruited the support of influential reformers, especially religious leaders who helped lobby the state legislature. An endorsement from the Church Association for the Advancement of Labor gave his cause a significant boost. Only three years after his arrival, Weismann could boast of a measure of success.

In 1893 the legislature made it illegal for bakers to be "required or permitted to work" more than "sixty hours in any week or more than ten hours in any one day," unless to reduce Sunday work. Along with regulation of hours of work, the law, "An Act To Regulate The Manufacture of Flour and Meal Food Products," also established standards for plumbing, construction, storage of flour and meal, hygiene facilities, and sleeping quarters for bakers. Placing enforcement of the statute under the state factory inspector, the 1893 law failed to provide penalties for violation, prompting Morris Hillquit, a leading socialist and labor advocate, to label it as a "purely platonic" exercise.

Having achieved a partial victory, the campaign continued to add penalties to the law. Pointing out the law's deficiencies in the *Journal*'s pages, Weismann also rallied allies. He reported the lack of compliance with sanitation provisions by some establishments while urging local baker's unions, community leaders, and leaders of national labor organizations to renew their efforts to strengthen the law. Yielding to the continuing pressure, the 1895 legislature amended the law and established penalties. For first offenders, fines ranged from $20 to $50; for a second violation, fines could be not less than $50 nor more than $100 and imprisonment could be for no more than ten days; and for a third offense, fines of not less than $250 and jail terms of no more than thirty days could be imposed. When the 1897 legislature reorganized its laws, the baker's law joined other acts regulating employee hours, sanitation, and working conditions in a section entitled "The Labor Law."

The excitement of victory and hope for the dawn of a new day soon turned into frustration. Many bakery shops simply ignored the law. Fear of being fired made employees reluctant to report violations; when an employer was indicted and tried, workers made poor witnesses. Also, since the statute provided no flexibility for emergencies or for workers who desired to work beyond the ten-hour day for additional pay, some in both groups seemed to have resented the law.

To combat the growing influence of the Journeymen Bakers Union, owners organized the

Master Bakers Association when legislation first appeared in the early 1890s. With their ranks composed of middle class entrepreneurs, many of whom had moved from worker to owner, their association prevented the inclusion of penalties in the 1893 legislation. Defeated in 1895, however, master bakers felt trapped between the growing power of labor with its demonstrated ability to influence the legislature on the one side and the new competitive challenge presented by large commercial bakery factories on the other side. To survive in this environment, master bakers simply required more from their workers and often refused to comply with the law's provisions.

As the century drew to an end, bakery workers concluded that the hours law could only be made effective where a strong union existed. The *Baker's Journal* reported a survey that revealed over one-third of bakeries worked their employees either more than the ten-hour day or in excess of the sixty-hour week. A practice thought to be on the decline, work through Saturday night, the *Journal* now found to be a common requirement in at least one-third of the bake shops. Only in bakeries with a strong and effective union did the *Journal* find that the provisions of the law were respected. Drawing a clear message from their findings, the *Journal* acknowledged the law's usefulness but concluded it could not rely upon the state for enforcement. To make the ten-hour day a reality, the union had to organize the nonunion bake shops. If it could do that, the union, not the state, would force compliance with the law using the strike and boycott. With that goal, the union launched a major organizing effort not only in New York City but also in upstate communities.

In a period of general increase in union membership, the Journeymen Bakers Union achieved significant success with its organizing effort. Increasingly New York City bakeries fell in line, recognizing the union and honoring the ten-hour day. Resistance increasingly came from upstate bakers. To combat the unionization effort, the members of the Master Bakers Association developed a two-prong attack. First, they created company unions, retaining for themselves control over the work place and allowing them

to maintain the open shop and reject the union label on their products.

Their second line of attack came in the form of court challenges to the constitutionality of the hours law. To further its organizing campaign, the Journeymen Bakers Union recruited community supporters who informed state authorities when they found noncompliance with the law. In Utica, the state charged that Joseph Lochner, the operator of a nonunion bake shop, "permitted and required" Aman Schmitter to work more than the sixty hours allowed under the statute. This was Lochner's second time before the court, having been convicted in 1899 of the same offense. Refusing to defend himself and raising no arguments against the law, the Oneida County Court convicted him in 1901. After Lochner's conviction, the Master Bakers Association appealed his case on constitutional grounds.

The law failed the test of constitutionality on several grounds, the association argued. Although the state described the act as a health statute, it was not, and for that reason was not a legitimate exercise of the state's police powers. What the law was, the Master Bakers Association argued, was special class legislation that discriminated against all those excluded from its protection. It also violated the liberty guaranteed by the Fourteenth Amendment of the U.S. Constitution. Conceding that liberty was not absolute, it could only be abridged when the state acted upon compelling reasons. In this case, the state had cited no such reasons.

The Appellate Division of the Supreme Court of New York rejected Lochner's arguments by a split vote of 3-2. The Master Bakers Association then appealed to the Court of Appeals, New York's highest court. Again, a divided court, 4-3 this time, ruled against Lochner. For the court's majority early in 1904, Chief Judge Alton B. Parker, later that year the Democratic presidential candidate, conceded the difficulty of defining the extent of the state's police powers. The real test, he maintained, was whether the statute had a "reasonable relation" to public health, welfare, and safety. Although some justified the practice, the courts should not, he argued, "substitute their judgment for that of the Legislature." The health problems of bakery workers, chronic bronchitis, pulmonary diseases, and "dust-laden air," convinced the majority that the "occupation of a baker or confectioner is unhealthy, and tends to result in diseases of the respiratory organs."

The dissenters rejected the majority's judicial restraint. They viewed the law as arbitrarily depriving workers of their liberty, the opportunity to work longer than a ten-hour day. Rejecting the contention that the law was a health measure, Judge Denis O'Brien, employing a bit of judicial logic popular during the period, maintained that a loaf of bread baked by one who worked more than ten hours was no more "unwholesome" than a loaf baked by a person working only ten hours. To the majority view that the court must not substitute its judgment for that of the legislature, the dissenters countered that the courts "must determine for themselves whether in any given case the legislation which is claimed to be an exercise of the police powers is what it is claimed to be."

After defeat in the New York courts, the Master Bakers Association appealed to the U.S. Supreme Court. To present their arguments, they recruited Henry Weismann, the former editor of the *Baker's Journal*, secretary of the journeymen's union, and probably the individual most responsible for enactment of the ten-hour law. Weismann abruptly resigned his union positions in the fall of 1897. Later, other union officials charged that while being paid to represent the union's interest, he fraternized with their enemies! "The truth," Weismann later explained, was that he had "never been in sympathy with the radicals in the labor movement." After his departure from the union, Weismann became a bake-shop owner, but the enterprise soon failed. He later entered politics and became the chief deputy to the clerk of King's County. While in that post, Weismann studied law and passed the New York bar examination as Lochner's case worked its way through the state's court system. His appeal to the Master Bakers Association appears obvious: as a former baker who opposed the law, he would help respond to Justice Henry Brown's sharp rebuff of employers who argued for freedom of contract for their employees. The argument "would certainly come with better grace and greater

cogency," the justice asserted in *Holden v. Hardy*, if it came from the workers. Weismann just might provide that "grace" and "cogency." Also, Weismann had come to "recognize the injustice" the law created. This strongly held conviction, one story has it, prompted him to study law to attack the constitutionality of the hours law. After the Court's decision, however, Weismann acknowledged that he supported the ten-hour law, opposing only the inability of a "man to work an hour or so overtime for extra compensation if necessity arises and he needs the money and is willing to do the work."

The Supreme Court granted Weismann special permission to argue before it since his brief law practice had not made him eligible for membership at the Court's bar. Joined by Frank H. Field, Weismann's brief repeated arguments addressed in the court of appeals. He argued that the law denied "certain persons" in the baking trade the "equal protection of the law" since it limited protection to a special group; for example, it did not cover the housewife, the "real artist in biscuits, cake, and bread, not to mention the American pie." For his main argument, he accepted the validity of police powers but challenged their use in this case. Granted, it was "difficult to define" the extent of those powers, Weismann acknowledged, but that difficulty cannot be used to allow a legislature to "sweep away the most cherished rights" of Americans. When laws interfered with contracts, property, and the "freedom to exercise a trade or calling," the Court should, he emphasized, scrutinize them closely and resolve doubts in favor of individual liberty; for to do otherwise "would lead to absurd conclusions . . . more consistent with autocratic" states than this republic.

Endorsing the Court's decision in *Holden v. Hardy*, which upheld a Utah law limiting miners to an eight-hour day because mining was a "hazardous and unhealthful" occupation, Weismann contended no more danger existed in the bakery trade than a wide range of unprotected employment. This law, which recognized no circumstances where an emergency might legitimately require work beyond the ten hours, in contrast to Utah's act, was "purely a labor law." As such the Court should strike it down because it constituted an unreasonable use of state police powers.

New York's attorney general, Julius M. Mayer, argued the state's case. Questioning whether Lochner should be allowed to raise constitutional issues since he raised none at the initial trial, Mayer defended the act as a reasonable exercise of police powers. Those powers, "necessarily elastic," allowed the state to respond to "new and changing conditions" of industrial life. Determining where to draw the "line" to protect workers and the public, he argued, was "eminently a matter for the Legislature...." Mayer also addressed the controversial wording of the statute, making it illegal for workers to be "required or permitted" to labor in excess of sixty hours a week. The legislature used that language to prevent employers from arguing that they had not "orally or in writing *required*" employees to work additional hours but did so by "inference and acquiescence." Mayer also raised the issue of the state's interest in protecting "certain classes of men" to have them healthy and available "at its command" when a need might arise. For reasons of internal security and national defense, he argued, the state has a "profound interest" in the "vitality" of its citizens.

The appointees of President Benjamin Harrison and President Grover Cleveland dominated the U.S. Supreme Court in 1905. Cleveland appointed three members, two who make up part of the *Lochner* majority—Chief Justice Melvin W. Fuller of Illinois and Associate Justice Rufus W. Peckham from New York, the author of the majority opinion. Peckham's dissent, while a member of the New York Court of Appeals, in *People v. Budd* telegraphed his views on the use of state police powers. Following the lead of the Supreme Court in *Munn v. Illinois*, the state fixed maximum charges for grain elevators, but Peckham saw the law as an invasion of rights of property and liberty of contract that was "not only vicious in its nature, communistic in its tendency ... but illegal." The third Cleveland member of the Court, Edward Douglass White of Louisiana, dissented. Harrison contributed two to the majority, David J. Brewer from Kansas, nephew of Justice Stephen J. Field, and Henry Billings

Brown, author of the 1898 *Holden v. Hardy* decision. William McKinley made one appointment, Joseph McKenna of California, who joined the majority. Theodore Roosevelt added two who dissented, Oliver Wendell Holmes Jr. of Massachusetts and the Ohioan, William R. Day. Rutherford B. Hayes appointed the senior member of the Court in 1877, John Marshall Harlan of Kentucky, a dissenter.

Hearing arguments over a two-day period in late February 1905, a majority of the Court during conference initially agreed to sustain the lower court decision. Justice Harlan accepted the task of writing that opinion. Justice Peckham led four dissenters. In a situation reminiscent of *Pollock v. Farmers' Loan and Trust Co.*, someone abandoned Harlan's majority and joined Peckham, creating a new majority. Since Harlan, White, Day, and Holmes dissented and Peckham, Brewer, and Fuller were the strongest advocates of liberty of contract, either Brown or Mckenna is left as the probable switcher. In the past, both had upheld broad construction of state police powers. Although it is impossible to identify the "vacillating jurist," it is possible that Weismann's role answered the issue raised by Brown in *Holden v. Hardy*. That individual, nonetheless, must bear much of the responsibility for the attacks on the Court that followed.

Writing for a sharply divided Court, Peckham addressed the central question of which should prevail, the power of the state legislature or the "right of the individual to liberty of person and freedom of contract." Court observers that day must have recognized from the outset that the law was in trouble. Noting that the statute lacked provisions for "special emergencies," Peckham reviewed instances when the Court had sanctioned the use of police powers to interfere with the "right of contract" but emphasized the limits to the "valid exercise" of such power. To pass the constitutional test, a law must be "fair, reasonable and appropriate," Peckham contended.

Arguments of internal security and national defense failed to impress Peckham. If the Court sustained this law based upon the need for a "strong and robust" population, almost any interference could be justified. "Not only the hours of employees, but the hours of employers, . . . doctors, lawyers, scientists, all professional men, as well as athletes and artisans, could be forbidden to fatigue their brains and bodies. . . ."

Denying that it was a question of substituting the Court's judgment for that of the legislature, Peckham, nonetheless, argued that the Court must determine for itself not only whether the act fell within the scope of a legislature's powers but also the motives for passing the act. To sustain this act, it must be as a health law. But such a law cannot have only a "remote" relation to the ends of the legislation but must have a "more direct" effect on the public's or the baker's health. If a connection existed, Peckham felt it "too shadowy and thin" to warrant interference with liberty of contract. Acknowledging that bakers faced a greater danger to health than some occupations, the justice concluded, however, that "common understanding" never regarded baking as unhealthy labor. It seemed incredible to Peckham that hours of work could be construed as a public health issue; "wholesome bread does not depend upon whether the baker works but ten hours per day or only sixty hours a week." To be a health measure, the protection must be for the general public and extend beyond the worker in a bakery. The law then raised "at least a suspicion" that factors other than the "public health and welfare" motivated the legislature. The "real object and purpose" he found in the legislature's desire "simply to regulate the hours of labor between the master and his employees (all being men, *sui juris*)" engaged in a business not dangerous to any substantial degree. Such acts, regulating "grown and intelligent men," are "mere meddlesome interferences with the right of the individual. . . ."

Harlan, joined by White and Day, vigorously dissented. Echoing Justice Brown in *Hardy v. Holden*, Harlan emphasized that employees did not stand on an equal footing with their employers and that it lacked realism to argue that employees voluntarily agreed to work for hours the legislature deemed harmful to their health. Unless the legislature's determination clearly went beyond reasonable bounds, the

Court should not interfere. Citing medical evidence used by New York, Harlan agreed that the legislature had a reasonable basis for its judgment, and this use of police powers should be sustained.

If Harlan's dissent read as the reverse side of the judicial standards applied by the majority, Holmes virtually dismissed both Harlan and Peckham for being outside the proper role of the judge. "It does not need research to show," Holmes maintained, that this statute did not "infringe fundamental principles as they have been understood by the traditions of our people and our law." Underlying the majority view, Holmes found "an economic theory which a large part of the country does not entertain." Whether he agreed or disagreed with that theory had "nothing to do with the right of the majority to embody their opinions in law." After listing examples, "ancient" and "more modern" of police powers that had been permitted, he noted that "liberty of the citizen to do as he likes so long as he does not interfere with the liberty of others to do the same" had been a "shibboleth of some well-known writers. . . ." The Fourteenth Amendment had not enacted "Mr. Herbert Spencer's Social Statics." Some Court-approved laws "embody convictions or prejudices which judges are likely to share. Some may not. But a constitution is not intended to embody a particular economic theory. . . . It is made for people of fundamentally differing views. . . ." To Holmes, "liberty in the Fourteenth Amendment" had been "perverted" when "held to prevent the natural outcome of a dominant opinion" unless a "rational and fair man" concluded that the law violated "fundamental principles" of law and tradition. Of course, Peckham's majority thought that was exactly what the New York law did.

Although the press reported a threatened strike immediately after the Court's decision, it never occurred. New York bakers gradually came to question the impact of the ruling. The *Baker's Journal* continued to find that the ten-hour day prevailed where unions were strong. Continuing to attack the Court for its philosophy, labor leaders emphasized anew the need to organize the nonunion bakeries.

If the effect of the ruling was limited among bakeries, it did not affect workers outside that industry, leading one authority to label it as an "aberration." Prior to its ruling in *Lochner*, the Court had upheld state legislation limiting hours for public workers. Nor did the Court reverse *Holden v. Hardy*, limiting hours for occupations considered dangerous. Railroad workers were also accepted as legitimate subjects for protection. After *Muller v. Oregon* (1908), which limited hours of women and children, men constituted the only group not generally protected, unless employed by the state, railroads, or in dangerous work. But even there, protection increased. New Jersey, for example, revised its ten-hour bakery law in 1912, providing that bakers could work overtime for additional pay during emergencies. By 1917 when the Court upheld in *Bunting v. Oregon* a law that limited the work hours of all factory employees, the majority *sub silentio* seemed to overrule *Lochner*. But since it had not done so explicitly, a new Court majority in the 1923 *Adkins v. Children's Hospital* decision prohibited Congress from authorizing a commission to establish minimum wages in the District of Columbia and revealed a majority unmoved by the arguments that a relation existed between "low wages and long hours and low morals...." Not until 1937 in *West Coast Hotel v. Parrish* did the Court finally turn its back on *Lochner* and the impulse to substitute its judgment of the proper relation between management and labor for that of the state legislature.

After the Court's retreat from *Lochner* in 1937, it rejected, as its critics insisted it must, the creation of economic constitutional rights and superimposing its own view of wise social and economic policy for those of the legislature. Justice Hugo Black in the 1963 case of *Ferguson v. Skrupa* summarized the Court's position thusly: "The doctrine that prevailed in *Lochner* . . . and like cases—that due process authorizes courts to hold laws unconstitutional when they believe the legislature has acted unwisely—has long since been discarded. We have returned to the original constitutional proposition that courts do not substitute their social and economic beliefs for the judgment of the legislative bodies, who are elected to pass laws.... We refuse to sit as a superlegislature to weigh the wisdom of legislation...."

Critics of recent Supreme Court decisions have detected, or in some cases desired, a return to *Lochner*. One defender of economic liberties argues that the Court has an obligation to protect those freedoms in order to promote a "free, humane, and plentiful society." The Court's abdication of its role as protector of economic liberties, signaled in Justice Harlan Fiske Stone's famous footnote number four in *Carolene Products*, has failed to produce, he argues, the results critics of economic substantive due process expected. What it has done, one authority maintains, is turn the "economic marketplace" over to regulations and regulators who have "frequently and frivolously" wielded enormous power harmful to the nation's welfare. The regulators, often individuals whose only "expertise" consisted of winning a local election or support of a winning candidate, have "critical power" over the economy. In light of what we presently have, it is "difficult to believe that *Lochner* would have harmed so many so often."

Other critics have struck at the Court for more telling reasons. They have criticized it for creating new "fundamental" rights, like "liberty of contract," regardless of whether they have a connection with any constitutional value marked as "special." In *Griswold v. Connecticut*, decided in 1965, Justice William Douglas held unconstitutional a law prohibiting married couples from using contraceptives because it violated their right to privacy. The Court, in the 1973 *Roe v. Wade* decision, significantly enlarged that right when it applied it to an unmarried pregnant woman who wanted an abortion. Although *Lochner* and *Roe* are "twins," they are "not identical," asserts constitutional scholar John Hart Ely. Finding *Lochner* a "thoroughly disreputable" decision, Ely worries that *Roe* "may turn out to be the more dangerous precedent." While Justice Peckham balanced the state's interest against the liberty of the individual, Justice Blackmun established a "compelling" interest test for the exercise of those state powers. Employing the balance of interest test, *Lochner* sowed the "seeds" of its own destruction because it argued that long working hours are not reasonably related to the promotion of the ends of health and safety. In *Roe*, the

Court made no convincing attempt "to trace its premises to the charter from which it derives its authority." Certainly with *Lochner*, the Court took an issue, raised it to constitutional principle, was overly influenced by counsel, and intruded where it had "no business."

Selected Bibliography

Ely, John Hart. "The Wages of Crying Wolf: A Comment on *Roe v. Wade*." *Yale Law Journal* 82 (June 1973): 920–949.

Fiss, Owen M. *Troubled Beginnings of the Modern State, 1888–1910*. New York: Macmillan, 1993.

Gillman, Howard. *The Constitution Besieged: The Rise and Demise of Lochner Era Police Power Jurisprudence*. Durham, NC: Duke University Press, 1993.

Groat, George Gorham. "The Eight Hour and Prevailing Rate Movement in New York State." *Political Science Quarterly* 21 (1906): 414–433.

Kens, Paul. *Lochner v. New York: Economic Regulation on Trial*. Lawrence: University Press of Kansas, 1998.

Urofsky, Melvin I. "State Courts and Protective Legislation during the Progressive Era: A Reevaluation." *The Journal of American History* 72 (June 1985): 63–91.

The Iceman and the Public

———◄◦►———

Melvin I. Urofsky
Center for Public Policy
Virginia Commonwealth University

New State Ice Company v. Liebmann, 285 U.S. 262 (1932) [U.S. Supreme Court]

◄◦► THE CASE IN BRIEF ◄◦►

Date
1932

Location
Oklahoma

Court
U.S. Supreme Court

Principal Participants
New State Ice Company
Liebmann
Associate Justice George Sutherland

Significance of the Case
The decision was a powerful example of the Court's support of property rights without any recognition of changing economic and social conditions. In a few short years, the Court would defer to legislatures in these matters.

The Depression that began to grip the United States in the winter of 1929 led to vast human suffering and incalculable economic distress. This, in turn, led politicians to rethink the role of the state in economic matters and caused legal scholars to reevaluate the constitutional restraints on legislative action. The traditional view of government had been succinctly summed up by President Grover Cleveland during the Panic of 1893 when he declared that, although the people should cheerfully support the government, it was no business of the government to support the people. In a nation in which one-third of the citizenry was ill-housed, ill-clothed, and ill-fed, people demanded that the government do something to alleviate the widespread distress.

Although the Hoover administration clung to older notions of the limits of governmental powers, a number of states began experimenting with ways either to provide relief or to mitigate the economic suffering. Governor Franklin D. Roosevelt, for example, initiated a "Little New Deal" in New York that anticipated some of his later programs on the national stage. Although providing relief to hungry people raised only a muted protest from conservatives, experimental legislation that affected property rights, such as mortgage moratoria, led to court challenges in a number of states. Depression or not, the defenders of property interests believed that the nation could survive only if it adhered to traditional values. Reformers, on the other hand, believed that the abuse of property rights had been a cause of the Depression, and they insisted that only by controlling private interests could the public good be secured.

Nearly all economists believed that overproduction and the enormous expansion of productive facilities beyond the capacity of the market to absorb goods had been a chief factor in the economic crash. The wild prosperity of the twenties had led many companies to expand their factories, assuming that a growing market would be able to dispose of all they could produce. Now factories stood idle, and some economists argued that productive capacity had to be reduced to bring supply into balance with limited demand; once that balance had been achieved, they believed, the laws of the marketplace would begin to function again in a more normal manner.

In Oklahoma the legislature had passed a law in 1925 declaring that the manufacture, sale, and distribution of ice constituted a "public business," and those who would enter the business first had to secure a license from the State Corporation Commission. In the prosperous twenties anyone could secure a license, but now the Corporation Commission saw the requirement as a means to keep out new manufacturers. As failing ice firms closed up shop, the refusal to grant new licenses meant that fewer firms would be in the business, and supply could be reduced to meet the demand. When that happened, prices would supposedly stabilize and keep the remaining companies operating at a profitable level. Whether the theory would in fact have worked is unknown, because a conservative majority of the U.S. Supreme Court struck down the statute by a 6-2 vote in *New State Ice Company v. Liebmann* (1932). Although the majority's ultraconservative views would lead to a constitutional crisis in 1937, an eloquent dissent by Justice Louis

Brandeis pointed the way to the jurisprudence of the future.

The New State Ice Company, under a license granted by the Corporation Commission, operated an ice business in Oklahoma City, manufacturing as well as selling and distributing ice. Over the years the owners invested some $500,000, a very healthy sum for that time, in their plant and facilities. Liebmann, without securing the required license, purchased land in the city and began constructing an ice plant. The New State Ice Company then sought an injunction to prevent Liebmann from entering the ice business on the grounds that he lacked the license. Both the federal district court and the Circuit Court of Appeals accepted Liebmann's argument that the manufacture and sale of ice did not constitute a public business, and the requirement for a license to engage in that business deprived him of his property without due process of law.

Although the license regulation predated the Depression, *New State Ice Company* was in many ways the first of the Depression-related cases to reach the Supreme Court, and it dealt directly with the key issue that would face the Court for the next several years—to what extent may the state regulate private interests for the public good. Oklahoma defended the statute in part on the grounds that it allowed the state to exercise its police power to protect citizens adversely affected by the economy. Ever since *Munn v. Illinois* (1877), the Court had admitted that businesses affected with a public interest could be regulated by the state, and a series of cases during the Progressive Era had confirmed that the state's police powers could legitimately impinge on property rights when exercised for the public welfare.

But the Court in the 1920s had retreated from this view and had reinforced the older conservative concepts of substantive due process and freedom of contract to restrict the police power. The question now and for the rest of the Depression would be whether the radically changed economic conditions confronting the country would be judicially recognized by the courts. Would state and federal governments be able to respond to the crisis with greater energy and creative programs, or would conservative justices insist that the sanctity of property could not be violated under any conditions? Justice George Sutherland, in writing the majority opinion, took the latter view and denounced the Oklahoma statute as unconstitutional.

Sutherland began by conceding that "all businesses are subject to some measure of public regulation," but restrictions beyond this minimal level could be justified only for those businesses affected with a public interest. Oklahoma had relied in large measure on *Frost v. Corporation Commission* (1929), in which the Court had upheld Oklahoma's regulation of cotton gins. Cotton, Sutherland explained, was the chief crop of the state and, therefore, the state had a legitimate interest in regulating the gins, which had a demonstrable relation to the public interest.

But he could find no justification at all for considering the ice business in a similar manner. "We are dealing with an ordinary business," he wrote, "not with a paramount industry upon which the prosperity of the entire state in large measure depends. It is a business as essentially private in its nature as the business of the grocer." Merely because the state declared the ice business to be of public concern did not make it so; New York had tried a similar stratagem regarding theater ticket brokers, and the Court in 1927 had struck down regulation of ticket prices. The courts, not the legislature, would make the final determination of whether a particular business could be regulated. Efforts to regulate private businesses, Sutherland argued, violated the due process clause of the Fourteenth Amendment.

Lest the ruling be interpreted merely as a blind defense of private property, he also attacked the statute as promoting monopoly. Just as there was nothing in the ice business that could characterize it as a public business, neither was there anything that would justify treating it as a natural monopoly akin to gas, water, or transportation services. In language resounding with phrases from the Progressive Era attack on trusts, Sutherland denounced the law for stifling competition and hamstringing the marketplace.

Although Sutherland did not once mention the Depression, it was obviously on his mind, especially the claim put forward in the dissenting opinion that states had to have some flexi-

bility in order to respond to the economic crisis. "It is not necessary to challenge the authority of the states to indulge in experimental legislation," he concluded, but they may not do so "by enactments which transcend the limitations imposed by the federal Constitution. . . . [T]here are certain essentials of liberty with which the state is not entitled to dispense in the interest of experiments."

Justice Brandeis, writing for himself and Justice Harlan Fiske Stone (Justice Cardozo had only recently joined the Court and did not participate in this case), entered a thirty-one-page dissent in which he explained and defended Oklahoma's decision to regulate the ice business. His dissent is notable for several reasons and is often cited as the epitome of judicial restraint— the idea that judges should stifle their own personal predilections and defer to the judgment of the elected legislatures in fashioning public policy. One might have assumed that, as an inveterate foe of monopoly, Brandeis would have opposed the statute, but whether he personally favored it or not is unknown. As one of his biographers explained, Brandeis recognized that "concepts of liberty and property must be remolded from time to time to meet changed conditions." An open mind, not rigid preconceptions, must guide the judicial process.

In his elaborately documented opinion, Brandeis explained why Oklahoma believed the ice business was affected with a public interest and why it should be subject to regulation. He also confronted the reality of the Depression directly. There had to be "power in the states and the nation to remold, through experimentation, our economic practices and institutions to meet changing social and economic needs." Brandeis did not know if the state's assumptions about the effect of regulation in revitalizing the economy would prove correct, but that did not matter. "It is one of the happy incidents of the federal system that a single courageous State may, if its citizens choose, serve as a laboratory, and try novel social and economic experiments without risk to the rest of the country."

The Court also shared power in the federal system, and Brandeis demanded that it restrict itself to determining the law, and not second-guessing the legislatures on the wisdom of particular policy decisions. In a passionate summation, he appealed to his brethren to allow the federal system to be innovative and adaptive. This Court, he wrote "has the power to prevent an experiment. We may strike down the statute which embodies it on the ground that, in our opinion, the measure is arbitrary, capricious or unreasonable. We have the power to do this, because the due process clause has been held by the Court applicable to matters of substantive law as well as matters of procedure. But in the exercise of this high power, we must be ever on our guard, lest we erect our prejudices into legal principles. If we would guide by the light of reason, we must let our minds be bold."

Newspaper editorials across the nation for the most part criticized the majority ruling and applauded the dissent. Brandeis, according to the New York *World-Telegram*, "has dealt with a major national need in words that should carry far and wide, exerting profound influence upon judges, legislators, industrialists, businessmen, economists—everyone involved in the carrying out of social and economic readjustments that we can only put off at peril."

The Court seemed to respond to Brandeis's plea in the next few cases in which it reviewed state emergency measures. It upheld the 1933 Minnesota Mortgage Moratorium Law in *Home Building & Loan Association v. Blaisdell* (1934), and the New York State Milk Control Act of 1933 in *Nebbia v. New York* (1934). But then the conservatives regained control and proceeded to strike down nearly all state and federal emergency measures until the Court crisis in 1937. Following the resignation of the conservative bloc in the late 1930s, the new members of the Court proved acutely sensitive to the demand by Brandeis that judges show restraint in evaluating economic legislation. The Court adopted what has become known as a rational basis test for such laws: if the legislature can show that it has a rational reason for imposing particular economic regulations, the judiciary will defer to those reasons. The Sutherland opinion marked for many people the worst aspects of judicial conservatism, the idée fixe of property rights without any recognition of changing social and economic conditions. The Brandeis dissent, however, became accepted as the "correct doctrine."

Selected Bibliography

Clark, Jane C. "Emergencies and the Law." *Political Science Review* 39 (1934): 268–283.

Konefsky, Samuel J. *The Legacy of Holmes and Brandeis.* New York: Macmillan, 1956.

Mason, Alpheus T. *Brandeis: A Free Man's Life.* New York: Viking, 1946.

Paschal, Joel F. *Mr. Justice Sutherland: A Man Against the State.* Princeton, NJ: Princeton University Press, 1951.

Strum, Philippa. *Brandeis: Beyond Progressivism.* Lawrence: University Press of Kansas, 1993.

The Chambermaid's Revenge

—◄o►—

C. Herman Pritchett

Deceased Professor of Political Science
University of California, Santa Barbara

West Coast Hotel Co. v. Parrish, 300 U.S. 379 (1937) [U.S. Supreme Court]

◄o► THE CASE IN BRIEF ◄o►

Date
1937

Location
Washington

Court
U.S. Supreme Court

Principal Participants
Elsie Parrish
West Coast Hotel Company
Chief Justice Charles Evans Hughes
Associate Justice Owen J. Roberts

Significance of the Case
The Court supported a minimum wage law, effectively reversing precedents going back to *Lochner* and handing the New deal a major victory just as FDR's "Court-packing" plan was being debated.

Elsie Parrish was employed at the Cascadian Hotel in Wenatchee, Washington, as a chambermaid at $12 for a 48-hour week. Under the state minimum wage law, adopted in 1913, she should have received $14.50. Rejecting the hotel's offer of a $17 settlement, she sued for $216.19. The state supreme court supported her claim, but the hotel appealed. On March 29, 1937, the United States Supreme Court agreed with the state court and upheld the minimum wage law by a vote of 5-4.

There was a distinguished audience in the Court chamber that morning, for it was widely anticipated that the justices might rule on the constitutionality of the National Labor Relations Act, a highly controversial New Deal statute. They did not. But Elsie Parrish's case was a worthy substitute, for it not only resolved the Court's long uncertainty about the constitutional rights of women in industry, but also signaled the surrender of the Court to President Roosevelt's New Deal.

Chafing under a series of rebuffs by the Court during his first term, Roosevelt had sent his so-called "Court-packing" plan to Congress

498

on February 5, 1937. He proposed that the president be authorized to appoint one additional justice to the Court for every sitting justice over the age of 70, up to a limit of six new justices. His argument was that overage justices (five of the nine were 70 or over) had slowed the efficient dispatch of judicial business. The proposal set off an uproarious national debate. Even those who had opposed the Court's conservative course rejected this assault on the judicial tradition. Realizing that his initial approach had been a blunder, on March 4 Roosevelt made a radio address charging that the real problem was the Court's assumption of the powers of a policymaking body. In rebuttal, Chief Justice Charles Evans Hughes on March 20 presented to the Senate Judiciary Committee an effective document arguing that the Court was fully abreast of its work.

The *Parrish* decision, approving in dramatic fashion significant regulatory legislation, came down nine days later, with Hughes writing the opinion. The shock effect of the ruling was heightened because only a year earlier the Court in *Morehead v. Tipaldo*, also by a vote of 5-4, had declared a similar New York minimum wage law unconstitutional. The reversal was due to the change of position by Justice Owen J. Roberts between the two cases, an action promptly characterized in the nation's press as "the switch in time that saved nine."

In fact, it appears that Roberts had not been happy with his vote in *Morehead* and that he had "switched" before Roosevelt's Court-packing message. According to Hughes's biographer, Justice Roberts had disclosed to Hughes in a private conversation his intention to vote to sustain the Washington law. Hughes was delighted with the prospect of a majority to reverse *Morehead*. But when the *Parrish* case was argued, Justice Stone was absent due to illness, and the result was a 4-4 division. If this vote had been allowed to stand, the state law would still have been upheld by reason of the state court's favorable vote. But Hughes held up announcement of the decision until Stone returned (possibly at the urging of Roberts), and a 5-4 vote was assured. In the meantime, however, Roosevelt had proposed his Court-packing plan. So in order not to seem to be acting under pressure from the White House,

Hughes withheld announcement of the Court action until March 29.

By 1937 the Supreme Court had had thirty years of experience with laws protecting women in industry, and its record was mixed. In 1908 the Court had upheld a ten-hour law for women workers in *Muller v. Oregon*. It was in this case that a Boston lawyer, Louis D. Brandeis, so impressed the Court by a brief that contained only two pages of legal arguments and over a hundred pages of extracts from reports of official committees, bureaus of statistics, commissioners of hygiene, and factory inspectors—all of which demonstrated the evil effects of long working hours upon women. In its decision, the Court took "judicial cognizance of factors that make women the weaker sex," and held that "she is properly placed in a class by herself." Legislation "designed for her protection could be sustained even when like legislation is not necessary for men and could not be sustained."

Indeed, the Court in *Lochner v. New York* in 1905 had rejected a New York law limiting bakery employees (presumably all male) to a ten-hour day or a sixty-hour week. This famous case was decided by a vote of 5-4. The law, said Justice Peckham for the majority, could be upheld only as a measure "pertaining to the health of the individuals engaged in the occupation of a baker." Did the health of bakers need protection? Peckham thought not, and he gave two reasons. First, "to the common understanding the trade of a baker has never been regarded as an unhealthy one." Second, statistics regarding trades and occupations show that although "the trade of a baker does not appear to be as healthy as some other trades, [it] is vastly more healthy than still others." In the absence of special health hazards about baking, to permit bakers' hours to be regulated would be to permit general legislative control of hours in industry. This was so unthinkable for Peckham that it clinched his argument. "Statutes of the nature of that under review, limiting the hours in which grown and intelligent men may labor to earn their living, are mere meddlesome interferences with the rights of the individual." Unless the Court called a halt, he asserted, we would all be "at the mercy of legislative majorities."

Justice Holmes dissented from the Peckham opinion with some of his best known rhetoric: "This case is decided upon an economic theory which a large part of the country does not entertain. . . . The Fourteenth Amendment does not enact Mr. Herbert Spencer's Social Statics. . . . I think that the word liberty in the Fourteenth Amendment is perverted when it is held to prevent the natural outcome of a dominant opinion, unless it can be said that a rational and fair man necessarily would admit that the statute proposed would infringe fundamental principles as they have been understood by the traditions of our people and our law."

Did the decision in *Muller* override the *Lochner* doctrine of laissez-faire, or did it merely classify women as exceptions to the *Lochner* rule and so entitled to special treatment? At first it appeared that *Lochner* had been fatally weakened. In *Bunting v. Oregon* (1917) the Court approved a ten-hour law for both men and women in industry without even mentioning the *Lochner* decision. As Chief Justice William Howard Taft said subsequently, he had assumed that *Lochner* had been overruled *sub silentio* by *Bunting*. But in *Adkins v. Children's Hospital* (1923), the *Lochner* ruling was resurrected to strike down a District of Columbia minimum wage law for women.

For the five-judge majority in *Adkins*, Justice George Sutherland's opinion was a paean to freedom of contract in its purest form, with no nonsense about the special needs of women or inequality of bargaining position. The District of Columbia law was "simply and exclusively a price-fixing law, confined to adult women . . . who are legally as capable of contracting for themselves as men." Sutherland considered that the standards set by the statute to guide the administrative board in fixing minimum wages were vague and fatally uncertain. The sum necessary to maintain a woman worker in good health and protect her morals, he submitted, is not precise and unvarying. It will depend upon her temperament, her habits, her moral standards, and her independent resources. It could not be determined "by general formula prescribed by a statutory bureau." Moreover, the law was invalid because it took account of "the necessities of only one party to the contract," compelling the employer to pay the minimum wage whether or not the employee was worth that much to him.

Chief Justice Taft, dissenting, argued that the *Adkins* case was controlled by *Muller*. He could see no difference in principle between regulating maximum hours and minimum wages. Justice Holmes agreed. "The bargain is equally affected whichever half you regulate." He had supposed that *Lochner* "would be allowed a deserved repose." Justice Sanford also dissented, but Justice Brandeis disqualified himself because his daughter worked for the minimum wage board.

Following the *Adkins* decision, many states assumed that a minimum wage law that *did* take into account the value-of-service-rendered principle would be constitutional and, therefore, enacted statutes including such provisions. A New York law of this type came before the Supreme Court in *Morehead v. Tipaldo* (1936), in the midst of the Court's furious battle with the New Deal. But the four surviving members of the *Adkins* majority—George Sutherland, Pierce Butler, Willis Van Devanter, and James McReynolds—joined with Justice Roberts to invalidate the New York law. Justice Butler dogmatically restated the *Adkins* objections in these words: "The State is without power by any form of legislation to prohibit, change, or nullify contracts between employers and adult women workers as to the amount of wages to be paid."

This bland reiteration in 1936 of a position that had had little enough support in 1923 was one of the great mistakes in Supreme Court history, and it did more to destroy the country's confidence in the Court as then constituted than some of its more publicized anti–New Deal decisions. The ruling earned the dissent of as distinguished a foursome as ever sat on the high court—Chief Justice Hughes and Justices Brandeis, Cardozo, and Stone. The chief justice wrote a long opinion that was a devastating refutation of the unreality of the majority's "free bargaining" assumptions.

Morehead v. Tipaldo was all the more surprising in that the Court had already begun to give way on issues of price control. In *Nebbia v. New York* (1934) a 5-4 majority had accepted the validity of a depression-born state law regulating milk prices, with none other than Justice

Roberts writing the opinion. Yet in *Morehead,* Roberts's vote returned the *Nebbia* foursome to a minority position, though—as it turned out— for only a brief period.

It was only ten months after *Morehead* that *Parrish* was decided, with Roberts joining the *Morehead* dissenters to form a 5-4 majority. Chief Justice Hughes wrote the Court's opinion. First, he accepted as valid the stated purposes of the Washington law: prevention of employment of women and minors "under conditions of labor detrimental to their health and morals" or at wages "not adequate for their maintenance." To achieve these purposes the statute had created a commission directed to establish wages and conditions of labor that were reasonable, not detrimental to health and morals, and "sufficient for a decent maintenance of women."

Second, the *Adkins* precedent had to be disposed of or explained. The Washington Supreme Court, Hughes said, had "refused to regard the decision in the *Adkins* case as determinative and has pointed to our decisions both before and since that case as justifying its position.... This ruling of the state court demands on our part a reexamination of the *Adkins* case."

Beginning this process, Hughes stressed the prestige of the *Adkins* dissenters, including Chief Justice Taft. But more important was Hughes's rejection of the *Adkins* conception of liberty of contract: "The Constitution does not speak of freedom of contract. It speaks of liberty and prohibits the deprivation of liberty without due process of law. In prohibiting that deprivation the Constitution does not recognize an absolute and uncontrollable liberty.... The liberty safeguarded is liberty in a social organization which requires the protection of law against the evils which menace the health, safety, morals, and welfare of the people. Liberty under the Constitution is thus necessarily subject to the restraints of due process, and regulation which is adopted in the interests of the community is due process."

Continuing, the chief justice rehearsed all the cases, going back to *Holden v. Hardy* (1898) and *Muller v. Oregon* (1908) where the Court had approved legislative restrictions on freedom of contract. He stated: "This array of precedents and the principles they applied were thought by the dissenting Justices in the *Adkins* case to

demand that the minimum wage statute be sustained.... We think that the views thus expressed are sound and that the decision in the *Adkins* case was a departure from the true application of the principles governing the regulation by the State of the relation of employer and employed.... Our conclusion is that the case of *Adkins v. Children's Hospital* ... should be, and it is, overruled." Nothing was said about *Lochner v. New York,* but we can assume, with Taft, that this time it had been overruled *sub silentio.*

Third, Hughes undertook to explain the Court's apparent reversal of the *Morehead* decision and, incidentally, Justice Roberts's switch between the two cases. The explanation was rather technical. In deciding *Morehead,* Hughes explained, the New York Court of Appeals had concluded that the New York statute was in no material respect different from the District of Columbia statute in *Adkins.* Consequently, the *Adkins* ruling had to be followed by the state court as a matter of respect for the Supreme Court. In turn, Justice Roberts in the *Morehead* appeal to the Supreme Court concluded that the state court's views of the statute had to be respected. On that basis, the only issue for Roberts was whether *Adkins* was distinguishable. But counsel for the state had not raised that issue. Apparently reluctant to ask for the overruling of *Adkins,* they had only contended in state court that the statutes in the two cases were distinguishable and that the state court had held that they were not. Given this ruling, the only way the Supreme Court could have upheld the New York law was to overrule *Adkins.* But counsel for New York had not *asked* the Supreme Court to overrule *Adkins.* In this dilemma, Roberts took the incredible position that the Supreme Court could not overrule its own decision in *Adkins* because counsel had not *asked* the Court to do so.

Whatever one may think of Roberts's reasoning in *Morehead,* his reconsideration and vote in *Parrish* gave the New Deal one of its major constitutional victories. The Washington law had been passed in 1913 and enforced continuously thereafter. Like the District of Columbia statute condemned in *Adkins,* it contained no value-of-service standard and so seemed more in defiance of the *Adkins* ruling that the New York law. But Chief Justice Hughes completely ignored that issue. He constructed his majority opinion out of quotations from Taft and Holmes, asking questions such as: "What can be closer to the public interest that the health of women and their protection from unscrupulous and overreaching employers?" In fact, as a contemporary scholar pointed out, Hughes's opinion "spoke more about the justice of minimum wages than about the right to enact them without judicial interference."

Justice Sutherland wrote for the dissenters. He argued that the *Adkins* and *Morehead* majority opinions were "a sufficient answer" to all that Hughes had said, but nevertheless he thought it well to restate the reasons and conclusions of the minority. His emphasis was on the personal nature of the judicial obligation. He rejected the recent and widely quoted warning by his colleague Justice Stone, who in the case of *United States v. Butler* (1936) had written that "the only check upon our own exercise of power is our own sense of self-restraint." Such a view, Sutherland retorted, was "both ill-considered and mischievous." Sutherland, facing these New Deal statutes, could not "subordinate his convictions . . . and keep faith with his oath or retain his judicial and moral independence." Self-restraint "belongs to the domain of will and not of judgment." The only restraint on the judge should be that "imposed by his oath of office, by the Constitution, and by his own conscientious and informed convictions."

The Supreme Court's blessing on minimum wage legislation provided legal and political support for Congress in adopting the Fair Labor Standards Act in 1938. On the constitutional foundation of the commerce clause, the act provided for a minimum wage of twenty-five cents per hour for employees engaged in interstate commerce or in producing goods for commerce. It also required payment of 50 percent more for overtime for all hours worked over forty-four per week. Generally known as the Wages and Hours Act, it was unanimously upheld in *United States v. Darby Lumber Co.* (1941). Justice Stone wrote: "Since our decision in *West Coast Hotel Co. v. Parrish*, it is no longer open to question that the fixing of a minimum wage is within the

legislative power and that the bare fact of its exercise is not a denial of due process under the Fifth more than under the Fourteenth Amendment. Nor is it any longer open to question that it is within the legislative power to fix maximum hours."

The constitutional support that *Parrish* provided for the Fair Labor Standards Act was its most immediately significant role. However, the decision quickly became a standard citation in all decisions involving freedom of contract, price control, or other statutory ventures in state or federal regulation of the economy. In fact, on the very day that the decision was handed down, Justice Hugo Black invoked it in upholding the Railway Labor Act, saying: "The Fifth Amendment, like the Fourteenth, see *West Coast Hotel Co. v. Parrish*, decided this day . . . is not a guarantee of untrammeled freedom of action and of contract."

From 1937 to 1980, *Parrish* was cited 41 times by the Supreme Court, in 46 rulings of the federal courts of appeals, and in 68 federal district court decisions. Typical is the case of *Bass Plating Co. v. Town of Windsor* (1986), involving a municipal requirement concerning disposal of industrial wastes: "A government regulation that does not impose on fundamental rights, that is adopted in the interests of the community and is not arbitrary or discriminatory does not violate due process so long as there is a reasonable relationship between it and the legitimate end it seeks to further." In *Long Island Lighting Company v. Cuomo* (1987) where the issue was exclusion of the cost of a nuclear power plant from the rate base, a federal judge wrote: "Since the Supreme Court's landmark decision in *West Coast Hotel Company v. Parrish*, the federal courts have consistently refused to limit the scope of the police power of the states in addressing perceived social and economic problems through economic legislation if that legislation does not impinge upon fundamental personal rights, and have been extremely deferential in assessing the reasonableness of actions taken pursuant to that police power."

The authors of a 1984 *Stanford Law Review* article awarded *Parrish* a key position in the development of American legal thought: "Since 1800, America has experienced at least three different phases of legal thought, each of which has responded in some way to [the] need to regard adjudication as a rational process. Up to the mid-nineteenth century, there was wide acceptance of a broadly instrumental approach to law; judges decided cases by overt reference to policy considerations. Around 1860, there began a discernible, if tentative, shift away from this broad conception of the legal process. By the 1890s, this transformation was completed. The legal community had fallen victim to the classical contagion. Judges claimed to resolve disputes by the rigorous application of rules alone. This train of legal thought—commonly known as conceptualism—flourished for a couple of decades or more, reaching its zenith by the mid-1920s. Its subsequent decline was swift and dramatic. If the triumph of conceptualism

was *Lochner v. New York* in 1905, its official death knell was *West Coast Hotel Co. v. Parrish.*"

Selected Bibliography

Baer, Judith A. *The Chains of Protection: The Judicial Response to Women's Labor Legislation.* Westport, CT: Greenwood Press, 1978.

Hutchinson, Allan C., and Patrick J. Monahan. "Law, Politics, and the Critical Legal Scholars." *Stanford Law Review* 36 (January 1984): 199–245.

Leonard, Charles A. *A Search for a Judicial Philosophy: Mr. Justice Roberts and the Constitutional Revolution of 1937.* Port Washington, NY: Kennikat Press, 1971.

Mason, Alpheus T. *Harlan Fiske Stone: Pillar of the Law.* New York: Viking Press, 1956.

Pusey, Merlo J. *Charles Evans Hughes.* New York: Macmillan Company, 1951.

Negligence and Tort Law

Fellow Servants Beware

——◄◦►—

John W. Johnson
Department of History
University of Northern Iowa

Farwell v. The Boston and Worcester Railroad Corporation, 4 Metc. 49 (1842)
[Supreme Judicial Court of Massachusetts]

◄◦► THE CASE IN BRIEF ◄◦►

Date
1842

Location
Massachusetts

Court
Supreme Judicial Court of Massachusetts

Principal Participants
Nicholas Farwell
Boston and Worcester Railroad Co.
Chief Justice Lemuel Shaw

Significance of the Case
The *Farwell* decision extended the fellow-servant rule into the industrial world and became a widely cited precedent. By finding a company not liable for an employee's injury caused by another employee's negligence, the court shifted a potentially heavy economic burden from companies to the working class.

From 1835 to late 1837, Nicholas Farwell worked as an engineer for the Boston and Worcester Railroad Company. He earned two dollars a day, a relatively high industrial wage for the time. In fact, it was substantially more than what Farwell had earned in his previous position as a machinist. On October 30, 1837, while Farwell was operating one of his company's engines, his train barreled through a switch that was "left in a wrong condition" by another employee of the railroad company, a man named Whitcomb. The engine was derailed and the train's wheels crushed Farwell's right hand. He sued the railroad to recover damages for his injury. This is the simple and uncontested set of facts in one of the most famous state court decisions in American legal history: its impact upon American industrialization would be hard to overemphasize.

The Farwell suit presented the first occasion for a Massachusetts appellate court to rule on the question of whether an employer should be held liable for damages stemming from the injury of one of his employees caused by the carelessness of another employee. But it was not the first Anglo-American court ever to confront this issue. There were two other "fellow-servant" cases that attorneys for Farwell and the railroad brought to the attention of the Massachusetts court: *Priestly v. Fowler,* an 1837 case from the British court of the Exchequer, and *Murray v. South Carolina Railroad Co.,* an 1841 decision of the South Carolina Court of Errors. In both of these cases, the courts found that a employer was *not* liable for an injury to an employee caused by the carelessness of another employee. Thus, the "fellow-servant rule" was born.

The *Farwell* opinion was handed down by the Supreme Judicial Court of Massachusetts. In the mid-nineteenth century, this highest appellate court of the Commonwealth of Massachusetts was one of the most prestigious judicial bodies in the United States; some legal historians have even argued that it was of more renown than the U.S. Supreme Court. The Massachusetts court's reputation derived mainly from the legal erudition and powerful writing style of its chief justice, Lemuel Shaw. Shaw was a legal giant in what historians have called "golden age of American law." He was certainly one of the most brilliant and prolific jurists in American history. He served as chief justice of the Supreme Judicial Court from 1830 to 1860. During his long tenure on the bench, Shaw wrote over 2,000 opinions. His opinion for a unanimous court in the *Farwell* case may have been his best-known decision; it was certainly one of his most controversial.

Any decision emanating from the pen of Lemuel Shaw demanded attention from the American legal community. Shaw's reputation and the prestige of his court gave his rulings great persuasive value in other state courts. But this was not just any decision. It was a decision involving industrial accidents at just the time that America was industrializing. Whatever Shaw decided would be studied very closely by judges, lawyers, and corporate leaders across the United States. Shaw, never one to downplay his own significance, knew that he was deciding a case that would alter the course of American industrial and legal history. In a careful and powerfully phrased opinion, Shaw followed and extended the holdings in the English and South Carolina

cases, thus denying recovery to the injured plaintiff.

Shaw began his opinion by discussing a general principle of tort liability known by the Latin phrase, *respondeat superior.* This maxim holds that masters are responsible for the negligent acts of servants causing injuries to clients or strangers so long as the servants are operating within the normal course of their duties for the master. But Shaw declared that a situation involving two persons in the same service or employment is different than one involving a company's agents and the general public. The employer, he said, is liable to the public for the tortious acts of its employees, but he is not liable to one of his employees for the carelessness of another employee. Thus, a case involving fellow servants falls outside of the general principle of *respondeat superior.*

Chief Justice Shaw based his opinion in favor of the railroad upon three grounds. First of all, he concluded that an employee such as Farwell "takes upon himself the natural and ordinary risks and perils" of his employment. If the job is dangerous, Shaw maintained, the employee does not have to accept it or continue in it. But if he takes the job or remains in it, he assumes the risks. Moreover, dangerous jobs usually carry wages commensurate with the danger. After all, Farwell the railroad engineer commanded a higher wage than Farwell the machinist. The "implied contract" between employer and employee compels the employee to accept the risks of his employment or find another job. This became known as the "assumption of risk" doctrine.

The second ground for the decision was what Shaw termed one of "policy." Safety of employees is best promoted, Shaw contended, when they are expected to be responsible for their own conduct *and* that of fellow employees. A single employee can observe the conduct of his fellow workers. If one worker is behaving in such a way as to endanger the safety of others, then an employee should bring this to the attention of the careless worker so that he can take corrective action. If the careless worker fails to respond to constructive suggestions, the employer can then be notified so he can then act accordingly. In this way, employee safety is best encouraged by placing the responsibility upon the workers themselves. By contrast, Shaw pointed out, the best policy to promote the safety of railroad passengers or others not employed by the railroad who might be injured through the carelessness of an employee is to make the company liable.

The final ground for the decision addressed a concern of Farwell's attorney who maintained that the facts in the Massachusetts case were distinguishable from those in the English and South Carolina fellow-servant rule cases. In both the other situations, the injured employee and the employee whose carelessness led to the injury were working in the same contained working place. In the English case both were on a butcher's van, and in the South Carolina case both employees were in the cab of a railroad engine. The attorney for the injured Farwell, a man named Loring, argued that the fact that Whitcomb and Farwell worked in different divisions of the railroad and had no reasonable way of monitoring each other's work made this case legally different from its predecessors.

Shaw acknowledged that Farwell and Whitcomb worked in different divisions of the railroad. But the important factor in their job situations was that they shared a common employer. The chief justice stated that it would be "extremely difficult to establish a practical rule" governing what constitutes a separate division and what does not. Should it depend, Shaw asked rhetorically, on the distance that the employers are apart? Or should there be some other rationale for determining when two employees are sufficiently separated so that they could not be said to be in close enough proximity to monitor each other's carefulness? Shaw could not envision a workable rule. Furthermore, Shaw submitted, the argument of Farwell's attorney presupposes "an assumed principle of responsibility which does not exist." The chief justice maintained that the "implied contract [between the employer and employee] . . . does not extend to indemnify the servant against the negligence of any one but himself." Shaw, therefore, rejected the "different division" argument and found for the defendant railroad corporation, thus extending the fellow-servant rule to apply to complex industrial situations in which an in-

jured worker might have no close contact with another worker whose carelessness might lead to his own injury.

Shaw closed his opinion with a caveat. He admonished lawyers and judges reading his decision not to venture "any hasty conclusion as to the application of this rule to a case not fully within the same principle." He cautioned that his opinion did not say that there were no implied warranties arising out of the relationship between employer and employee. If the engine had been defective, or if the track had been bad, or if the railroad had not employed a switchman who was generally deemed competent, Shaw intimated that the resolution of the case might have been different. But mere employee negligence was not enough to justify an employer's liability.

In the generation following the *Farwell* decision, the fellow-servant rule was adopted by virtually every state court that was called upon to confront the issue. For example, when the highest court of Wisconsin favorably received the fellow-servant rule in 1861, it commented that the doctrine had been "sustained by almost unanimous judgments of all the courts both of England and this country." And the holding in *Farwell v. The Boston and Worcester Railroad* became *the* fellow-servant rule case most prominently cited by jurisdictions faced with suits mounted by employees alleging management liability for injuries caused by worker carelessness.

There were several reasons that the Massachusetts precedent was a stronger one for employers to cite than either *Priestly v. Fowler* or *Murray v. South Carolina Railroad Company* First of all, the English case offered scant quotable language, and the South Carolina opinion came with several dissents that muddled the precedent. Second, the *Farwell* precedent extended the fellow-servant rule into complex industrial situations. By contrast, the English case dealt with a fact situation involving a preindustrial individual proprietorship, and the South Carolina case concerned an engineer and a fireman in the same cab of an engine. What the *Farwell* decision told the industrial community was that the impersonality of the industrial environment did not make an employer any more liable for the consequences of employee negligence than would be the case in a small business where all the employees are regularly in close contact. It was a ready tool to be used by lawyers defending corporations against suits by employees. Finally, the *Farwell* opinion had more precedent value than the previous fellow-servant rule decisions because of the prestige of Lemuel Shaw and the Supreme Judicial Court of Massachusetts.

The decision in the *Farwell* case and the fact that most courts in the country followed in its wake helped to place the unintended but tragic costs of industrialization upon the working poor. As a result, employers did not have to bear the costs of most industrial accidents. If the decision had gone the other way, the costs to businesses might have served as a brake upon economic development in the crucial early stages of America's industrial revolution.

Some legal historians have found Shaw's *Farwell* opinion to be a clear example of the anti–lower-class bias of the nineteenth-century judiciary. In the words of one historian, decisions like this threw "the burden of economic development on the weakest and least active elements in the population." It is clear that the sweat of the working poor helped to fuel the American industrial revolution, and certainly the fact that businesses did not have to absorb the cost of industrial accidents also helped industrialization to gain momentum, but the *Farwell* decision should not be taken as a sign of Shaw's hostility to labor. Only about a week after handing down the *Farwell* decision, Shaw was the author of *Commonwealth v. Hunt*, a decision recognizing the right of a labor union to exist. The *Hunt* decision has been referred to as the "Magna Carta of American trade unionism." Historians who maintain that Shaw was hostile to the working class have a tough time reconciling the *Farwell* and *Hunt* decisions. A more likely philosophical basis for the chief justice's position in *Farwell* is that Shaw had a special place in his legal heart for the railroad. During Shaw's tenure on the Massachusetts high court, scores of railroad cases were decided. Although Shaw generally upheld the state's right to place regulations upon railroads, in disputes between railroads and individuals—passengers, highway

travelers, and railroad employees—the railroads invariably emerged victorious. Shaw was well aware that had he ruled in favor of Farwell, a great burden would have been added to the New England railroads that were, at least in 1842, struggling to survive.

In the sixty years after the *Farwell* decision, industrial accidents in the United States increased in severity and frequency. By 1900 it was estimated that each year 35,000 deaths and 2 million injuries occurred on the job. Sympathy for injured and killed workers led some courts to fashion exceptions to the fellow-servant rule. For example, the "vice principal rule" permitted a worker to recover damages from his employer if his injury was caused by the negligence of another worker who was in a supervisory position and thus could be said to be more than just another fellow servant. Also, some courts fashioned a "safe place rule" that allowed an injured employee to recover damages if he could demonstrate that his injury was the result of a hazardous working environment that might have compounded the negligence of a fellow employee. Furthermore, by the turn of the century a number of lawyers were willing to accept clients upon a contingent-fee basis. This provided many a poor man or woman with the opportunity to retain an attorney and no doubt stimulated thousands of lawsuits in which injured employees attempted to affix their employers with financial responsibility.

In 1885 a Connecticut court commented that the tendency in nearly all jurisdictions was to "limit rather than enlarge" the coverage of the fellow-servant rule. Spurred on by reformers appalled by the untoward consequences of industrialization, the Congress and many state legislatures moved to restrict the ambit of the fellow-servant rule. In 1908 Congress enacted the Federal Employers Liability Act that abolished the fellow-servant rule for interstate railroads. And by 1911, twenty-five states had laws modifying or completely dispensing with the fellow-servant rule for railroads wholly within their state boundaries.

In order to provide compensation for victims of industrial accidents, states in the early twentieth century began to adopt "workmen's compensation statutes." These laws abolished the fellow-servant rule and the assumption of risk doctrine. Furthermore, they established schedules for compensation for injuries and took the responsibility for settling any disputes involving the amounts of employee claims away from courts and placed them in the hands of administrative boards. In 1911 Wisconsin was the first state to have its workmen's compensation survive a constitutional test. Mississippi, in 1948, was the last state in the Union to adopt a compensation law. In addition, in the twentieth century, many labor-management contracts have established compensation schedules for employees in industries affected by collective bargaining.

Payments to injured employees under workmen's compensation were (and are) seldom large enough to indemnify an injured person for the total costs and long-term consequences of industrial accidents. But they do provide a systematic means of recovering some damages and they remove one large class of disputes from the court system. If Nicholas Farwell had sustained his injury today, he would not only have received better medical care and a guar-

anteed amount of compensation, but he would also not have been victimized by the fellow-servant rule.

Selected Bibliography

Friedman, Lawrence M., and Jack Ladinsky. "Social Change and the Law of Industrial Accidents." *Columbia Law Review* 67 (1967): 50–82.

Horwitz, Morton J. *The Transformation of American Law, 1780–1860.* Cambridge, MA: Harvard University Press, 1977.

Hurst, James Willard. *Law and the Conditions of Freedom in the Nineteenth-Century United States.* Madison: University of Wisconsin Press, 1967.

Johnson, John W. "Creativity and Adaptation: A Reassessment of American Jurisprudence, 1801–1857 and 1908–1940." *Rutgers-Camden Law Journal* 7 (summer 1976): 625–647.

Levy, Leonard W. *The Law of the Commonwealth and Chief Justice Shaw: The Evolution of American Law, 1830–1860.* New York: Harper & Row, 1967.

White, G. Edward. *Tort Law in America: An Intellectual History.* New York: Oxford University Press, 1980.

Contributory Negligence as a "Brake" on Suits Against Railroads

—◄◦►—

Paul M. Kurtz

School of Law
University of Georgia

Haring v. New York and Erie Railroad Company, 13 Barb. 9 (1852) [New York Supreme Court]

◄◦► THE CASE IN BRIEF ◄◦►

Date
1852

Location
New York

Court
New York Supreme Court

Principal Participants
Mrs. Haring
New York and Erie Railroad Company

Significance of the Case
Relief was denied to the widow of a man killed in a rail accident because he had contributed to his demise through "gross negligence." The case was notable also because it approved removing the consideration of the case from a jury.

Professor Lawrence Friedman, in his *History of American Law*, states that in the 1800s, almost "every leading case in tort law was connected, mediately or immediately, with [the railroads]." Friedman states that the railroad "was the key to economic development. It cleared an iron path through the wilderness. It bound cities together, and it tied the farms to the city and the seaports. Yet, trains were also wild beasts; they roared through the countryside, killing livestock, setting fire to crops, smashing passengers and freight. Railroad law and tort law grew up, then, together. In a sense, the two were the same."

Several tort doctrines were, therefore, created by the courts that had the effect of protecting the burgeoning industrial mechanism from potentially ruinous lawsuits. Perhaps the most important was the adoption of a negligence standard that required that, before a plaintiff could recover in tort for injuries caused by the defendant, the plaintiff would have to show the defendant's behavior failed to measure up to a standard of reasonableness. Rather than impose absolute liability for "accidents" caused by defendants, the courts denied recovery unless the defendant was acting unreasonably under the circumstances.

A natural concomitant of a rule of law requiring proof of defendant's negligence is a rule disqualifying a culpable plaintiff. This doctrine has come to be known as contributory negligence. Under the doctrine of contributory negligence, no recovery could be obtained if the plaintiff's unreasonable behavior contributed in any way to the injuries he or she had suffered at the defendant's hands. While some cases described this as a defense that could be offered by the defendant, other cases imposed on the plaintiff the affirmative obligation to show that the defendant's behavior was the "sole cause" of the injuries suffered. The doctrine was first enunciated by an English court in 1809, but was rarely used in this country before the 1850s. One of the earliest American cases to utilize contributory negligence to deny a plaintiff recovery was *Haring v. New York and Erie Railroad Company*, an 1852 railroad case arising in New York.

In *Haring*, the plaintiff's husband was riding on a sled across a railroad track and was struck by the engine, thrown from the sled and killed. It is apparent that the railroad was negligent through its failure to abide by a statute that required the use of a bell to warn pedestrians of the train's approach. The plaintiff's wife sued the railroad company in what would be described today as a wrongful death action.

The trial court, however, after hearing the plaintiff's evidence refused to allow the jury even to consider the case and granted the defendant's motion for a nonsuit, which today would be called a directed verdict. The court noted the sled was traveling at 12 to 15 miles per hour at the time of the crash, the decedent knew trains passed the intersection hourly and, because of a high embankment at the side of the track, the decedent was unable to see the oncoming train. The court described the decedent's behavior as gross carelessness and stated that the "law, while it imposes duties upon the railroad companies, also imposes duties upon the citizens. . . ."

The New York Supreme Court upheld the trial court's action. The court wrote that where the plaintiff "has defeated his claim by his own misconduct, there can be no propriety in requiring the jury to pass upon the evidence." The court revealed its fear of allowing suits by citizens against railroads to go to a jury by stating that: "We can not shut our eyes to the fact that in certain controversies between the weak and the strong—between a humble individual and a gigantic corporation, the sympathies of the human mind naturally, honestly and generously, run to the assistance and support of the feeble . . . and that compassion will sometimes exercise over the deliberations of a jury, an influence which, however honorable to them as philanthropists, is wholly inconsistent with the principles of law and the ends of justice." Thus, Mr. Haring's widow was left without relief because of her late husband's negligence.

The opinion in the *Haring* case was particularly striking in that it approved of removing the case from the jury's consideration. It is one thing to allow a jury to consider the possibility that the plaintiff was negligent in deciding a case, it is much more drastic to find contributory negligence as a matter of law and refuse to allow the jury to even consider the case. *Haring* was one of twelve reported appellate cases between 1850 and 1860 to approve of a nonsuit against a plaintiff on grounds of contributory negligence. In the 1860s, thirty-one such cases were reported. In the 1870s, there were fifty-eight such cases. As Friedman has written, "(t)he doctrine of contributory negligence kept pace with crossing accidents."

Selected Bibliography

Friedman, Lawrence M. *A History of American Law.* New York: Simon and Schuster, 1973.

Landsman, Stephan. "The Civil Jury in America: Scenes from an Unappreciated History." *Hastings Law Journal* 44 (March 1993): 579–619.

Malone, Wex S. "The Formative Era of Contributory Negligence." *Illinois Law Review* 41 (July-August 1946): 151–182.

Railroad Development and Nuisance Law

—◄o►—

Paul M. Kurtz

School of Law
University of Georgia

Hentz v. The Long Island Railroad Co., 13 Barbour's Supreme Court Reports 646 (1857)
[New York Supreme Court]

◄o► THE CASE IN BRIEF ◄o►

Date
1857

Location
New York

Court
New York Supreme Court

Principal Participants
Mr. Hentz
Long Island Railroad Company

Significance of the Case
By refusing to allow plaintiff to sue a
railroad that ran near his business as a
nuisance, the Court refashioned the
traditional law of nuisance and revealed
a prodevelopment bias.

The transformation of the United States
from agrarian nation to industrial giant
is an oft-told story. This epic tale, however,
consists of many small chapters, one of the
most interesting of which is a series of cases in
which single landowners challenged the operation of railroads, particularly during the nineteenth century. The main legal weapon that
these landowners attempted to utilize was the
law of nuisance.

The English common law of nuisances,
adopted by the colonies and eventually the
states, was a strict one, imposing absolute liability on those who interfered with another's use of
property. Unlike modern concepts under which
liability depends on a defendant acting in some
culpable or negligent fashion, the common law
was expressed in the stern command of the legal
maxim, *sic utere tuo ut alienum non laedas* ("use
your own so as not to injure others"). The story
of how courts refashioned nuisance law reflects
what some experts call the instrumental use of

law—the use of law to achieve a desired societal goal that, in this case, was an efficient industrial economy.

Hentz v. Long Island Railroad Co. is a paradigmatic case for witnessing a part of this refashioning of the law. The plaintiff was a landowner in the New York village of Hempstead who objected to a railroad track that had been constructed in front of his dwelling house and store on Main Street. He complained that the trains were responsible for obnoxious smoke, odors and noise that constituted a "danger, nuisance and inconvenience." He filed suit against the railroad company, seeking $2,000 in damages and, more broadly, an injunction prohibiting the operation of the railroad in front of his house altogether. The *Hentz* plaintiff had previously obtained an emergency order forbidding the operation of the railroad and the New York State Supreme Court (then as now a *trial* court) was asked to make the order permanent.

The plaintiff offered three different theories to justify the relief he sought: (1) a claim that the defendant had violated the New York legislative authorization for the laying of its tracks; (2) a claim that the railroad had taken his land without just compensation in violation of the state constitution; (3) an assertion that the railroad's operation in front of his house and store constituted a public nuisance, particularly injurious to him. All three claims were rejected by the trial court judge on the basis of an examination of the pleadings and affidavits filed in the case. There apparently was no hearing.

With regard to the first claim, Hentz did not complain about the laying of most of the defendant's tracks but instead asserted that the Hempstead station was in an inappropriate place and, thus, the portion of the track in front of his property leading to that station was also inappropriate. The court, however, pointed out that the legislation permitted the company to establish a branch road *into* the village and to construct the railroad on "the most practicable route." Clearly reflecting its prorailroad bias, the court said that the choice of route would not be disturbed unless the company management had "*clearly* erred. . . . If a mere difference of opinion between [the railroad operators] and those whose immediate interests might be

affected . . . should be allowed to annul their proceedings, but few of them could be sustained. . . ." [emphasis in original].

The court pointed out that wherever the tracks might have been laid there would be the same smoke, danger of fire, "exposure of human life," and obstacles to passage through the streets complained of by the plaintiff. While the court might declare, therefore, that all railroads within villages were nuisances, it felt powerless to do so in light of the "action of both the legislative and judicial departments of this state." What the court was describing here is what has been called the statutory authorization defense for railroad placement; as long as the railroad was complying with the legislative mandate, its very existence could not be found actionable.

To bolster its conclusion of state authorization, the court pointed out that when the track was originally laid fourteen years earlier there had been very little objection, that a number of local property owners (including, incredibly enough, Mr. Hentz) had lent the company money to construct the tracks and that there had been a public meeting that approved of the re-laying of the track just a year before Mr. Hentz brought his action. At this point in the opinion, therefore, the court concluded the railroad was not liable for laying the tracks where it did because it was merely doing something that the state (and the public) had authorized. It reserved until later the question of whether the particular way the railroad was being operated constituted an actionable nuisance.

As for the second theory of recovery, the plaintiff argued that the railroad had taken a portion of his property without paying for it in violation of the state constitution. Interestingly, this assertion was based *not* on the claim that the smoke, noise, risk of fire, etc., interfered with his peaceable enjoyment of his house and store, but on the narrower argument that the railroad tracks in the middle of Main Street were on his property. Hentz said his property extended to the middle of Main Street and that a portion had been taken by the laying of the tracks.

In dealing with this, the court conceded that compliance with the legislative authorization to lay track could not justify an action that otherwise would constitute a taking of plaintiff's land. The court, however, found no such taking for several reasons. First, in a very careful reading of the complaint, the court noted that the plaintiff had alleged he had *possessed* the property, but not that he had *title* to it. Of course, only the owner would be entitled to compensation for a taking and the court was suggesting that the plaintiff might not even be the owner.

Second, the court went on to point out that Hentz had alleged possession of the Main Street land for only the past five years. Thus, said the court, even if he was alleging ownership, he had alleged it for only five years. The track had been originally laid fourteen years earlier. Again, there would be no valid claim by a property owner who had purchased the property nine years after the tracks had been laid. As the court said, "(i)f the land was subsequently conveyed to the plaintiff, as it probably was, he took it . . . with the railroad upon it."

As if these two conclusions were not enough to defeat the plaintiff, the court further observed that even if there had been a taking an injunction would be inappropriate. The court asserted that if there had been a taking without compensation it would be appropriate to seek compensation when the property was first taken, but the court would not be "doing justice to the public to allow him to stop the cars until he might coerce the company to pay him an exorbitant amount. . . ." The court concluded a plaintiff ought not be allowed to wait until an injunction would be "seriously injurious" before seeking relief. Again, the court was showing its bias in favor of allowing industrialization, once begun, to continue.

Hentz's final theory was nuisance. Perhaps the statute authorized the laying of the tracks here, and perhaps his property on Main Street had not been taken, but certainly the operation of the trains with the risk of injury, noise, odors (the court noted that "manure and merchandise" were carried on the trains), and smoke constituted an interference with plaintiff's use of his house and store. Unfortunately for Mr. Hentz, the court did not agree.

The court began its analysis with a listing of other cities in which the legislature had authorized the operation of railroads and other cases that had rejected the claim of nuisance and then posed the question, "[i]s there any thing peculiar to Main-street, or in the management of the defendants, which makes the railroad where it passes the plaintiff's house a nuisance?" The court found the railroad did not constitute an impediment to other travel on the street, the rails were not "badly laid down" and many other residents of the village and the street had sworn in depositions that the street had actually been improved as a "passway" by defendant's "works upon it."

As for the claim that the steam locomotive's operation in front of plaintiff's house was particularly noxious, the court found nothing in the railroad's charter or the statute prohibiting this and decided to "leave the matter to the good sense of the [railroad's management]." The plaintiff had alleged no serious accidents and, as for the smoke, while it must "undoubtedly be annoying to some extent" it was no more "disagreeable or prejudicial than what may proceed from many lawful establishments in the village. . . ."

While the court purported to be simply examining the facts of *Hentz* to determine whether this defendant was operating a nuisance, its language makes clear that it was painting on a much broader canvas. Thus, in minimizing the risks to the plaintiff, the court wrote: "Accidents to children, or to adults who are not grossly careless, from the locomotives when passing through our most populous cities, are very rare. The times of their passage are generally known, and the noise made by the movement over the rails, and the engineer's whistle, give timely notice of the approach of the train. When the usual precautions are practiced the danger is very slight, and when there is any carelessness or mismanagement the company and its officers are very properly held to a rigid accountability."

The court went on to conclude that the "evils of which the plaintiff complains are by no means peculiar to himself. They are the necessary concomitants of this species of locomotion, whether in the city or in the country. They cannot be prevented without an entire suspension of one of the greatest improvements of modern times." In summarizing its rejection of the plaintiff's claim, the court wrote: "There are some useful employments which endanger the lives of human beings which cannot and *ought not* to be prohibited. Lives are sometimes destroyed by an omnibus, a carman's cart, a stage or a steamboat, but so long as they are not imminently dangerous they cannot be prohibited. We cannot enjoy our private rights, nor can we avail ourselves of the many advantages resulting from modern discoveries, without encountering some risk to our lives, or our property, or to some extent endangering the lives or injuring the property of others" [emphasis added].

Interestingly, while the case ostensibly involved only the question of whether an injunction should be issued, the court in passing stated that if the "injury or danger to others" from a legitimate pursuit was "inevitable," there would be "no remedy either by way of *indemnity* or prevention" [emphasis in original]. The court was clearly suggesting that damages would also be inappropriate in this and similar ones.

The *Hentz* court, through its treatment of the plaintiff's claim, was making it clear that the traditional law of nuisance that had been received from a preindustrial England had to make way for the urbanization and industrialization of the United States. Both its attitude and its language revealed a prodevelopment bias. While it did not overtly utilize a balancing approach weighing the advantages to society against the harm to the individual (a test that would become commonplace later in the century), it was obvious that the strict law of nuisance was a matter of legal history by the time this case was decided.

Selected Bibliography

Bone, Robert G. "Normative Theory and Legal Doctrine in American Nuisance Law: 1850 to 1920." *Southern California Law Review* 59 (September 1986): 1101–1226.

Brenner, Joel Franklin. "Nuisance Law and the Industrial Revolution." *Journal of Legal Studies* 3 (June 1974): 403–433.

Coquillette, Daniel R. "Mosses from an Old Manse: Another Look at Some Historic Property Cases about the Environment." *Cornell Law Review* (June 1979): 761–821.

Kurtz, Paul M. "Nineteenth Century Anti-Entrepreneurial Nuisance Injunctions—Avoiding the Chancellor." *William & Mary Law Review* 17 (summer 1976): 621–670.

Scheiber, Harry N. "Public Economic Policy and the American Legal System: Historical Perspectives." *Wisconsin Law Review* (1980): 1159–1189.

Scheiber, Harry N. "State Law and 'Industrial Policy' in American Development, 1790–1987." *California Law Review* 75 (January 1987): 415–444.

The Great Dog Fight Case

—◄○►—

Kermit L. Hall
President and Professor of History
Utah State University

George Brown v. George K. Kendall, 6 Cushing 292 (1850) [Supreme Judicial Court of Massachusetts]

<table>
<tr><td colspan="2">

—◄○►— THE CASE IN BRIEF —◄○►—

Date
1850

Location
Massachusetts

Court
Supreme Judicial Court of Massachusetts

Principal Participants
George Brown
George K. Kendall
Chief Justice Lemuel Shaw

Significance of the Case
Shaw laid the foundation for the modern concept of liability by articulating a theory of liability for unintentionally caused harms and a theory of contributory negligence.

</td></tr>
</table>

Until the middle of the nineteenth century, the term "tort," which has emerged as the most protean legal concept of the twentieth century, had no well-defined legal meaning. Instead, wrongs that are covered by the concept today were treated in this earlier era in a piecemeal fashion. There were such archaic actions as trover, deceit, slander, assault, and the various forms of trespass. The last of these was the most important because it provided the basis upon which most personal injuries were covered.

The various kinds of trespasses were lumped into two separate legal actions: trespass and trespass on the case (or, as it was often simply termed, "case"). Trespass actions were based on direct contact between a plaintiff and defendant. If one person struck another with a stick, for example, the suit would have been for trespass, and all that was necessary as proof to secure damages was to show that the injury was direct. Case, on the other hand, treated indirect contact. Hence, if a person left a stick in the street and someone tripped over it through no

518

negligence of his own, the action that applied was "trespass on the case." Under this theory, an injured party had to prove not only that the stick belonged to the person that left it in the street but that tripping over it was the fault of that same person. Hence, the critical difference between trespass and trespass on the case was proving negligence. In the first instance, the person hit by the stick had only to prove that the other person wielded it. In essence, that person was strictly liable, even it he was not negligent. But with action on the case, the injured person had to prove that the other person had acted negligently in leaving the stick in the street, a difficult matter at best.

While legal historians agree about the broad outline of the distinction between trespass and case, they sharply disagree about how significant the differences were, the contribution of *Brown v. Kendall* to the establishment of modern tort law, and the acclaim to be credited to the author of that opinion, Lemuel Shaw, chief justice of the Supreme Judicial Court of Massachusetts and the most influential state judge of the mid–nineteenth century. On the one side is Charles O. Gregory, whose research and writing in the 1950s stressed the distinction between trespass and case sketched above. Gregory and others have given high marks to Shaw for essentially giving birth to modern tort law through his opinion. On the other side is Morton J. Horwitz, whose revisionist writing departed radically from that of Gregory. Horwitz, for his part, claimed that there is no evidence that American judges ever accepted either the pleading distinction between trespass and case or that trespass was based on strict liability and case on negligence. Horwitz insists that, at the time of *Brown*, the negligence action already had begun to flower and that Shaw merely added the force of his intellect to developments already well underway. That is, even if the distinction had once existed in American law between strict liability for trespass and negligence for case, that distinction was in collapse by the time that Shaw penned his opinion for a unanimous court in *Brown*. The historiographical dispute notwithstanding, *Brown v. Kendall* remains of special importance precisely because a judge of Shaw's reputation lent his prestige to the proposition

that where unintentional acts were involved there could be no liability without fault.

As is so often true in American legal history, the facts surrounding *Brown* were mundane. Kendall and Brown were both residents of Boston, and their dogs fell into fighting on a city street. Kendall attempted to separate them by hitting the animals with a four foot stick, but his efforts proved unavailing and, as the snarling dogs moved closer to him, he continued to retreat toward Brown. As Kendall raised the stick over his back to strike the dogs, he accidentally hit Brown, who was standing behind him, doing serious damage to Brown's eye.

Brown sued Kendall for damages in a Boston trial court. Kendall's attorney asked the judge in the case to instruct the jury to find for his client because Kendall was using "ordinary care" and because Brown had himself contributed to his own injury by failing to get out of the way of Kendall and the fighting dogs. Kendall insisted that the burden of proof was on Brown to prove that he had done wrong; it was not up to Kendall to show that he had *not* done wrong. Brown's attorney pressed an opposite line of argument, one that the trial judge incorporated into his jury charge. Brown's attorney claimed that Kendall was responsible for the injuries, unless Kendall was "doing a necessary act" or was under a "duty" to separate the dogs. Since Kendall could prove neither of these conditions, the jury found against him and awarded damages to Brown.

Kendall then appealed to the Supreme Judicial Court of Massachusetts. In the time between the jury verdict and the argument on appeal, Kendall died. Under the common law his death would have ended the action, but Massachusetts had provided by statute that actions in trespass survived, and Kendall's wife stood in his place during the oral arguments on appeal.

Shaw's opinion began by brushing aside many precedents that would have supported Brown and turned instead to the writing of Simon Greenleaf, a prominent treatise writer whose two-volume work on the law of evidence was widely available to lawyers. Shaw relied on Greenleaf for the rule that a plaintiff must present evidence to show that the defendant was at fault or that the defendant's intentions were unlawful. Shaw, therefore, placed the burden of proof in the case squarely on the plaintiff (Brown) in direct opposition to the action of the trial judge. Since Kendall had acted lawfully, the key question became whether he had exercised "ordinary care" in attempting to separate the fighting animals. Shaw went on to define "ordinary care" as "that kind and degree of care, which prudent and cautious men would use, such as is required by the exigency of the case, and such as is necessary to guard against probable danger." Only a negligent person, therefore, could be held responsible for unintentionally inflicted harm on another. "If, in the prosecution of a lawful act," Shaw concluded, "a casualty purely accidental arises, no action can be supported for an injury arising therefrom."

But Shaw did even more. In addition to spelling out the requirement for the plaintiff to show the defendant's negligence, Shaw also enunciated another doctrine—contributory negligence. Under this theory an injured party cannot recover from a negligent defendant if the injured party was even slightly responsible for the accident. "[I]f the defendant was chargeable with some negligence," Shaw observed, "and if the plaintiff was also chargeable with negligence, we think the plaintiff cannot recover without showing that damage was caused wholly by the act of the defendant, and that the plaintiff's own negligence did not contribute as an efficient cause to produce it."

Whether Shaw intended to do so or not, the upshot of his decision was to provide an indirect stimulus to emerging industries during the last half of the nineteenth century. Well into the twentieth century, courts regularly freed railroads, trolleys, and other forms of transporta-tion from paying damages in accidents because the counsel for them was able to show that the plaintiffs had contributed to the accident. State legislatures, of course, sometimes circumscribed the full impact of this common law doctrine by passing legislation that made railroads and other businesses strictly liable for some facets of their conduct (spewing sparks and such) without regard to the plaintiff's negligence.

Shaw overturned the jury verdict in favor of Brown and ordered a new trial. His opinion articulated a modern theory of liability for unintentionally caused harms and a theory of contributory negligence. While historians disagree about the extent to which Shaw was a legal innovator in this case, there is little doubt that his opinion successfully adapted the common law to the demands of a thriving and expanding society and laid the cornerstone upon which the modern concept of liability rests.

Selected Bibliography

Adlow, Elijah. "Chief Justice Lemuel Shaw and the Law of Negligence." *Massachusetts Law Quarterly* 42 (October 1957): 55–74.

Friedman, Lawrence M., and Jack Ladinsky. "Social Change and the Law of Industrial Accidents." *Columbia Law Review* 67 (1967): 50–82.

Gregory, Charles O. "Trespass to Negligence to Absolute Liability." *Virginia Law Review* 37 (April 1951): 359–397.

Horwitz, Morton J. *The Transformation of American Law, 1780–1860*. Cambridge: Harvard University Press, 1977.

Schwartz, Gary T. "Tort Law and the Economy in Nineteenth-Century America: A Reinterpretation." *The Yale Law Journal* 90 (July 1981): 1717–1775.

The Origins of Consumer Rights in Tort Law

———◄○►———

G. Edward White

Department of History and School of Law
University of Virginia

MacPherson v. Buick Motor Company, 216 N.Y. 382 (1916) [New York Court of Appeals]

◄○► THE CASE IN BRIEF ◄○►

Date
1916

Location
New York

Court
New York Court of Appeals

Principal Participants
Donald C. MacPherson
Buick Motor Company
Judge Benjamin Cardozo

Significance of the Case
The ruling initiated the modern concept of consumer protection by removing product liability from contract law to tort law, thus making it easier for consumers to recover damages for injuries from defective products.

It is not too much to say that the rights of consumers to recover against manufacturers for injuries caused by defective products originated in *MacPherson v. Buick*. The decision, issued by the New York court of appeals (that state's highest court) in 1916, was an example of a prescient judge seizing upon a fortuitous moment in time to recast the legal rights and responsibilities of countless persons. The judge was Benjamin Cardozo, in only his third year on the Court of Appeals. The time was the second decade of the twentieth century, witnessing the rise of the most dramatic and influential symbol of modernized America, the motorcar. The persons affected were all those who purchased products under the emerging system of American merchandising, now taken for granted but then itself a revolutionary development, under which consumers of products did not buy them directly from the persons who made them.

Everything, thus, came together in the *MacPherson* case: the transportation, merchandising, and legal relationships of the future and the legal doctrine of the past. The injury that spawned *MacPherson* had been caused by a wheel that suddenly broke off a Buick Model 10 Runabout. It was the kind of injury that was likely to occur again as more and more Americans turned to the motorcar as a means of transportation. The suit in *MacPherson* was not against the dealer who had sold the car, Close Brothers of Schenectady, New York, but against the Buick Motor Company of Detroit, Michigan, which had assembled the automobile and sold it to Close Brothers. The principal legal issue in the case was not whether Donald C. MacPherson, the driver of the Model 10, could recover against Close Brothers, but whether he could recover against Buick itself, with whom he had no contractual relations. And on this point the New York Court of Appeals' decision in *Torgeson v. Schultz* (1908), handed down eight years before *MacPherson*, seemed clear: persons not in contractual relations with the manufacturers of defective products could not recover in tort against those manufacturers. Yet Donald MacPherson won his case, and a new era in the law of consumer rights came into being.

The *MacPherson* case commenced when Donald MacPherson purchased the Buick with the defective wheel from Close Brothers in 1910. Close Brothers had bought the car from the Buick Motor Company a year earlier. Buick assembled cars from its own parts and parts supplied by other manufacturers: the wheels on the Model 10 had been made by the Imperial Wheel Company of Flint, Michigan. The Model 10 was a two-seater with a rumble seat; its horsepower was twenty-two, and it could go fifty miles per hour. MacPherson used the car in the summer and fall of 1910, put it up on blocks for the winter, and began using it again in May, 1911.

On July 25, 1911, MacPherson, who lived in Galway, New York, was on his way to Saratoga Springs to take John E. Carr, also a resident of Galway, to the Saratoga Springs Hospital. He was driving the car, John Carr was riding in the front passenger seat, and Charles E. Carr, John's brother, was seated in the rumble seat. As the MacPherson car approached Saratoga Springs, one of its hind wheels ran into a rut. Donald MacPherson turned off the engine and twisted the steering wheel to the left so as to stabilize the car. He then turned the engine back on and turned back toward the right-hand side of the road, where he had been traveling. As he turned a cracking sound occurred, and the rear left-hand side of the car began to collapse, eventually resting at a spot six to eight inches off the ground, with the axle scraping on the road. The front end of the car began to swing to the right, approaching a telephone pole, and as MacPherson turned the steering wheel to the left to avoid the pole, the right side of the car's frame caught the pole, twisting the car completely around until it faced in the opposite direction. MacPherson was thrown from his seat and pinned under the hind axle of the car. He suffered injuries in the process.

Testimony in the trial court established that MacPherson was only traveling about fifteen miles an hour at the time of the accident, when the spokes of the left rear wheel had broken out. Testimony also established that many of the spokes were not of first quality wood and that the manufacturer could have performed tests to determine the quality of wood in the wheel. Nevertheless, the trial court found for the Buick Motor Company at the close of MacPherson's presentation. The court believed that the fact that MacPherson had no contractual relations with Buick made it impossible for him to recover.

MacPherson appealed to the appellate division of New York's court system, an intermediate court. That court reversed the judgment of the trial court. Its decision rested on three factors: the fact that Buick Motor Company knew that the automobiles that it sold to Close Brothers in Schenectady might be used in a wide radius around Schenectady, including Galway and Sarasota Springs; the fact that the car was represented as capable of going fifty miles an hour and thus needed wheels to withstand such speed; and the fact that Buick had the ability to submit the wheels of its cars to pressure tests. These factors, in the view of a majority of the judges on the appellate division, made a car with a defective wheel an "inherently dangerous" product, which under a line of New York cases resulted in liability extended from the producer of such products to remote purchasers injured by them. One judge of the appellate division dissented from this characterization of the case, preferring to reverse on the ground that MacPherson had made out a *prima facie* case of negligence against the Buick Motor Company by showing that it had failed to inspect the wheels on Model 10 Runabouts. All of the judges agreed that MacPherson was entitled to a new trial.

Before that trial could take place, however, the Buick Motor Company appealed to the Court of Appeals. The issue in *MacPherson* had always been doctrinal, not factual: Buick conceded that it had not inspected the wheel to determine whether the spokes were in good condition or could withstand the pressure of a 1,800 pound car traveling at up to fifty miles per hour. Buick was likely negligent, then, but negligent to whom? An old English case, *Winterbottom v. Wright,* which had held that a supplier of mail coaches to the English postmaster general was not liable to persons injured while riding in them suggested that "privity of contract" was the controlling doctrinal principle: liability ran only as far as contractual relations. There were policy justifications for this doctrinal proposition as well: to extend liability for injuries for defective products beyond contractual relationships ran the potential risk of very extensive manufacturer liability. In an industrializing society, the ramifications of defects in products used in commerce could be very significant, raising the specter that growing industries might face crippling losses from lawsuits.

On the other side, there were policy justifications for extending liability in the *MacPherson*-type situation. The exception to the "privity" principle for "inherently dangerous" products suggested that there should be disincentives for manufacturers to put products on the market that had the capacity to do severe harm. Poisons, explosives, and products that gave off toxic fumes were examples: public policy suggested that the liability of manufacturers of such products should not be confined to persons in contractual relations with them. While the social utility of such products suggested that they should remain on the market, their capacity to do harm suggested that those who made profits from their manufacture should

be accountable to those injured by them, assuming the injuries could be prevented by ordinary care. *MacPherson v. Buick,* then, resolved itself into an exercise in doctrinal conceptualization. If an automobile were treated as an "inherently dangerous" product, liability beyond privity might ensue; if it were treated like a stagecoach, liability would remain confined to privity.

The genius of Judge Cardozo's opinion for the Court of Appeals extending liability was that he made an automobile seem more like a poison bottle than a stagecoach. In an artful synopsis of the precedents governing "inherently dangerous" products in New York, Cardozo suggested that the "principle" of protection to remote purchasers from injuries caused by dangerous products had long been part of New York law. In actuality the "inherently dangerous" line of cases had been a limited exception to the English rule of *Winterbottom v. Wright.* Cardozo ignored *Winterbottom* throughout most of his opinion, however, concentrating on the evolution of the "inherently dangerous" cases to include products such as coffee urns and scaffolds. That evolution, he suggested, meant that "inherently dangerous" did not simply refer to the product's nature, but to the potential risks created by the product when negligently made. Coffee urns could blow up if placed too near heat; scaffolds could collapse if the wood used to construct them was inferior. In the scaffold example, Cardozo revealed how he was conceptualizing the Model 10 in *MacPherson*: a wheel with spokes made from inferior wood was as "dangerous" as a scaffold. He then dismissed *Winterbottom*: "[p]recedents drawn from the days of travel by stagecoach do not fit the conditions of travel today." Buick was liable to the consumers of its motorcars if it could be shown to have been negligent in their manufacture or their inspection.

So stated, the principle of *MacPherson* was potentially vast: any product could be "dangerous" if manufactured in a way so as to create risks, and any person might come within the ambit of the manufacturer's liability. A manufacturer of a component part might ship a defective batch; the batch might not be discovered by the assembler on inspection; in a subsequent accident caused by the defect an onlooker, not even the purchaser of the product, might be injured. But the *MacPherson* opinion was firmly rooted in negligence theory. The same tests that subjected the manufacturer to potential liability could be used to limit it. Manufacturers were not liable for defects that could not be discovered on reasonable inspection, for products that had been altered in the chain of distribution, or for products not used in a reasonably foreseeable manner. Manufacturers could show that, on balance, it was more expensive for them to prevent injuries than to permit an occasional one. If their cost of prevention exceeded the expected seriousness and frequency of injuries caused by their products, they were not supposed to be held liable.

By the 1960s, the doctrinal structure created by *MacPherson*, came to be thought insufficient to compensate the victims of defective products. Although *MacPherson*-type liability had been expanded in the two decades after its appearance to cover nearly any product, as early as the 1940s an alternative theory of liability had surfaced to afford greater protection to the consumer. Under this theory—typically referred to as "strict" liability—manufacturers of defective products were deemed liable to injured consumers whether or not they could have discovered or prevented the defect through reasonable care. They were liable simply because they had put the product on the market and were in a better position than the consumer to bear the costs of its defectiveness. Among the grounds cited for the installation of strict liability in the defective products area was the tendency of negligence theory to *prevent* recovery by injured consumers.

MacPherson was, thus, revolutionary only in a historical sense. As Cardozo said, the decision wrested products liability from contract and put it "where it belongs"—"in the law," by which he meant tort law. This was a significant achievement, marking a shift in the modern law of products from a regime dominated by contract principles and damages to a regime dominated by the negligence principle. The shift implicitly conceded that in industrialized societies most persons injured by defective products were not likely to have any ongoing relations with the persons that had made the products. The tests and standards of negligence law were those of hypothetical "reasonable" men and women, not the subjective standards of bargained-for transactions. Contract was, in a sense, out of place in the standard modern products liability suit; *MacPherson* recognized this. But negligence has been seen to be inadequate for some consumer injuries, and most jurisdictions have gone beyond *MacPherson*. Nonetheless the modest accident of Donald MacPherson and his companions was a major event in twentieth-century American law.

Selected Bibliography

Kaufman, A. *Cardozo*. Cambridge, MA: Harvard University Press, 1998.

Polenberg, Richard. *The World of Benjamin Cardozo: Personal Values and the Judicial Process*. Cambridge, MA: Harvard University Press, 1997.

Posner, Richard A. *Cardozo: A Study in Reputation*. Chicago: University of Chicago Press, 1990.

Seavey, Warren. "Mr. Justice Cardozo and the Law of Torts." *Harvard Law Review* 52 (1939): 372–404.

White, G. Edward. *Patterns of American Legal Thought*. Indianapolis: Bobbs-Merrill Company, Inc., 1978.

White, G. Edward. *Tort Law in America: An Intellectual History*. New York: Oxford University Press, 1980.

Negligence Theory at Its Zenith

—◄o►—

G. Edward White

Department of History and School of Law
University of Virginia

Palsgraf v. Long Island Railroad Co., 248 N.Y. 339 (1928) [New York Court of Appeals]

◄o► THE CASE IN BRIEF ◄o►

Date
  1928

Location
  New York

Court
  New York Court of Appeals

Principal Participants
  Helen Palsgraf
  Long Island Railroad Company
  Chief Judge Benjamin Cardozo

Significance of the Case
  An accident involving a bizarre chain of events led to a ruling that attempted to end proximate causation as a doctrinal force in tort law, substituting a negligence principle focused on duty and foreseeability.

In law classrooms all over the country countless "hypothetical" cases are posed. The hypothetical cases are designed to show the application of legal doctrines to unusual situations: they demonstrate how the meaning of legal rules can never wholly be separated from the fact situations to which they are thought to be applied. The *Palsgraf* case is an example of a real case that has served professors better than nearly any hypothetical. The wonder of *Palsgraf* is that it not only arose out of a million-to-one series of events, it arose at a time when legal scholars and judges believed that legal doctrine in the law of torts had reached a stage where no set of facts, however bizarre, could remain ungoverned by a legal rule. But the rule chosen to govern *Palsgraf* collapsed on application, and with it a whole structure of tort doctrine. *Palsgraf* was, thus, both the culmination and the end of an era in the intellectual history of American tort law.

The *Palsgraf* case began at 10:00 A.M. on August 24, 1924, when 40-year-old Helen Palsgraf was standing on the platform of the East New York station of the Long Island Railroad. With her were two of her three children, Elizabeth, aged 15, and Lillian, aged 12. August 24 was a Sunday, a very hot day, and Mrs. Palsgraf and her daughters were planning to spend the day at the beach. They bought their tickets to Rockaway Beach and proceeded to the platform to wait for a train. Many other persons had the same idea: the platform was crowded with people carrying bundles. As the Palsgrafs were waiting for their train, Mrs. Palsgraf asked Lillian to buy a Sunday paper, and Lillian went off to a newsstand on the platform.

The next train to come into the East New York station was the "Jamaica Express." A Mr. Herbert Gerhardt, a resident of Brooklyn who was also waiting for the Rockaway Beach train, testified as to what happened as the Jamaica train pulled into the station. "Two Italians came up," he said, "and they wanted to make this here Jamaica express . . . and the two of them come, and one of them had a bundle under his arm . . . and just then the train was starting off and this fellow who had the bundle was last, the other fellow was already on the train and the train was in motion and the guard inside [the Jamaica train] was trying to help the fellow on, and the platform man was trying to help him on from the outside. . . . [The second Italian] had a bundle in his right hand; the platform man pushed his arm and the bundle fell between the platform and the train . . . and about a second later, why, everything went in a black smoke and explosion."

Subsequently Gerhardt revealed that the bundle that "one of the Italians" had been carrying was about 18 inches in diameter, wrapped up in a newspaper. He also indicated that, after the guard had succeeded in assisting "the second Italian" onto the train, he waved the train on, and the train, after a momentary pause, pulled out of the station. As it did the explosion occurred. At trial neither "the Italians" nor the platform guards were present, but it was stipulated that the bundle that had exploded contained fireworks and that the bundle had been dislodged when one of the guards assisted "the second Italian" onto the Jamaica train.

Mrs. Palsgraf then gave an account of what happened next. She and Elizabeth had taken a position on the platform next to a weighing scale that was about as high as her head. The scale had a glass fronting. On the other side of Mrs. Palsgraf was the wall of the station; the spot where the Palsgrafs stood was about 30 feet from the place where the explosion occurred. Lillian was not standing at that spot when the bundle exploded; she was returning from the newsstand. When the explosion occurred Mrs. Palsgraf heard "fireworks shooting," and then "a ball of fire came, and we were choked in smoke." She told Elizabeth to turn her back, and then the glass of the scale broke, sending glass flying through the air, and the scale toppled over on its side. On its way down the scale fell against Mrs. Palsgraf, striking her on her left arm and thigh. She remembered Lillian crying "I want my mama," her holding onto Elizabeth's wrist, and the crowd pushing away from them. Subsequently a police officer arrived and led Mrs. Palsgraf and the children to a bench by the newsstand, and eventually assisted her down to the waiting room, where several ambulances eventually came and an "ambulance man" examined her. About half an hour later she and the girls took a taxi home to 238 Irving Avenue in Ridgewood, Kings County.

Mrs. Palsgraf testified at her trial that, as a result of the accident, she had suffered from nervousness and stammering, which her doctor, Karl A. Parshall, diagnosed as traumatic shock. She had previously worked as a janitor before the accident, making about $420 a year and receiving $10 a month deducted from her rent. After the accident she had been less able to work, and in 1926 had stopped work altogether, being supported by her children. She also testified that she was married, but her husband clearly did not live with her or provide any support.

At the trial the Long Island Railroad put no witnesses on the stand. Its lawyers, Joseph F. Keany and William McNamara, contented themselves with cross-examining Mrs. Palsgraf and the two doctors who testified in her behalf. The trial judge charged the jury that if they found that the railroad's guards acted in a negligent manner in assisting "the second Italian" onto the train, and thereby causing the package to fall, and that their negligence resulted in the injury to Mrs. Palsgraf, they should find the railroad liable to Mrs. Palsgraf. The jury brought in a verdict for Mrs. Palsgraf of $6,000, to which was added $142.45 for court costs.

The railroad appealed, and the jury verdict was sustained by the five-judge appellate division, New York's intermediate appellate court, by a 4-1 margin. Judge Seeger wrote the opinion for the majority. He noted that the jury had found that the railroad's guards had been negligent and that their actions had caused the bundle to explode. He added that Mrs. Palsgraf was a passenger of the railroad and was thus owed "the highest duty of care required of common carriers." The dissenter, President Judge Lazansky, agreed that the guards were negligent but believed that their negligence was not a "proximate cause" of Mrs. Palsgraf's injuries. "Between the negligence of defendant and the injuries," Lazansky argued, "there intervened the negligence of the passenger carrying the package containing an explosive. . . . The explosion was not reasonably probable as a result of defendant's act of negligence." The 4-1 decision of the appellate division meant that the trial court's verdict was upheld, and the railroad appealed once more to the New York Court of Appeals, that state's highest court.

The 1928 *Palsgraf* case in the Court of Appeals, represented a consummate test of two of the leading doctrines of twentieth-century negligence theory, duty and proximate causation. The concept of a "duty" owed by each person to take care not to injure his neighbor was perceived by early twentieth-century scholars to lie at the very core of tort law. Negligence amounted to the breach of such a duty, and before negligence could be found the existence of a duty had to be shown. In many instances, such a showing could easily be inferred from a defendant's conduct, but in the *Palsgraf* case the existence of a duty was more problematic. If the guards owed a duty not to jostle persons in assisting them on trains, or perhaps not to attempt to assist them onto moving trains at all, they most likely were responsible for injuries to those persons or their property. Should "the second Italian" have surfaced and demanded compensation for his damaged fireworks, then, he might have recovered against the railroad,

or at least he would have been able to demonstrate that the guards owed a duty either to refrain from assisting him or to assist him more carefully. But he was not suing the railroad; Mrs. Palsgraf was. Did the guards owe a duty to her?

If the railroad, through its guards, owed a duty of care to all its passengers, perhaps Mrs. Palsgraf could anticipate protection from injury while a passenger. But what did that duty amount to? It certainly included a duty of safe passage on the train and perhaps a duty to maintain train platforms in a safe condition. But did that duty extend to protection against unseen dangerous objects in bundles carried by passengers? If "the second Italian" had dropped the bundles himself, would Mrs. Palsgraf have been able to recover against the railroad? That seemed unlikely. But why did it matter that the guards, and not "the second Italian," had dislodged the package when the guards had no notice that it contained fireworks? How far, in other words, did the duty of the guards extend?

That the concept of duty did not extend to cover all situations where an injury could be factually traced to a careless act on the part of the dutyholder was another central proposition of early twentieth-century tort law. The way in which spatial and temporal limits on the scope of duties was represented was through the concept of proximate causation. The term "proximate" in proximate causation was designed to distinguish those causal connections between breaches of duty that were "too remote" in time and space to permit recovery from those that were close enough to be labeled "proximate." Mrs. Palsgraf's injury was remote in space and, to some extent, in time. She had been injured by a scale felled by the explosion; she was standing about 30 feet from the spot where the bundle exploded. She was on the scene and a passenger of the railroad, to be sure, but she was nowhere near the guards who had assisted "the second Italian" onto the Jamaica Express. It was only because of a freakish connection between the explosion and the scale, and because of her proximity to the scale, that Mrs. Palsgraf was injured more severely than the wife of Mr. Gerhardt, who had been jostled by "the second Italian" just before he attempted to board the

Jamaica Express and who subsequently fainted when she heard the explosion and saw the smoke.

In one sense, then, Mrs. Palsgraf's injuries were a "proximate" result of the guard's having dislodged the bundle, and in another sense they were not. The case was truly a close one in terms of the ordinary language of proximate causation. Perhaps for this reason, and perhaps because he and other jurists had grown increasingly skeptical about the usefulness of the concept of proximate cause, Chief Judge Benjamin Cardozo persuaded the court of appeals to adopt a different approach to the *Palsgraf* case. He grounded the decision on duty, as measured by the foreseeability of a person in the position of the defendant. "The risk to be perceived," he said, "defines the duty to be obeyed." Risk was determined by "relation": it was "risk to others within the range of apprehension." This meant that the conduct of the guard was not a "wrong" to Mrs. Palsgraf, because Mrs. Palsgraf was not in the range of persons whose safety the guard might reasonably fear should he dislodge a bundle carried by someone in his immediate vicinity. "The law of causation," Cardozo concluded, was "foreign" to the *Palsgraf* case. Before inquiries about causation could be made inquiries about negligence needed to be satisfied, and the guard was not negligent with respect to Mrs. Palsgraf.

Cardozo's solution to *Palsgraf* and similar "unforeseeable plaintiff" cases was thus to subsume questions of causation in questions of negligence. Duty, risk, and relation controlled "proximate cause" cases: the reasonable foreseeability of the defendant determined the scope of the defendant's duty. Saying that an injury was the "proximate cause" of a defendant's conduct was just another way of saying that the plaintiff's injury was something that a reasonable person in the position of the defendant should have foreseen. The *Palsgraf* case was, thus, intended to be the end of proximate causation as a doctrinal force in tort law, and the elevation of the negligence principle, with its focus on duty and foreseeability, to an all-encompassing status.

Cardozo's solution, of course, was premature. In the dissent in *Palsgraf*, Judge William S. Andrews brushed aside elevated talk of duty and foreseeability and conceptualized the case as one in which the label "proximate" could be arbitrarily attached in favor of or against liability. Andrews's approach has come to be the way in which the case is presently understood. A universalistic conception of "duty" also guided Andrews's dissent: he spoke of "negligence in the air," such as recklessly driving down a street without yet having injured anyone. Cardozo sought to displace this idea of "duty" in the abstract with the more relational theory of *Palsgraf*, in the hope that foreseeability of risks would become the guiding principle of negligence theory. That hope has not panned out. There still exist cases, like *Palsgraf*, where one could not have imagined the scenario of an accident in one's wildest dreams, and yet one still is confronted with an injured person and some strange causal connection between that injury and a defendant's careless act. The archetypal "proximate cause" case is thus still with us, and no amount of doctrinal rearrangements will make it go away. *Palsgraf* remains a compelling case not for Cardozo's attempted doctrinal solution, but for its strange combination of circumstances. That Cardozo's solution ended up taking away Helen Palsgraf's $6,000 verdict, and imposing court costs of $350 (nearly a year's healthy wages) on her should, at a minimum, make us pause before accepting it.

Selected Bibliography

Kaufman, Andrew L. *Cardozo*. Cambridge, MA: Harvard University Press, 1998.

Noonan, John T., Jr. *Persons and Masks of the Law*. New York: Farror, Straus and Giroux, 1976.

Polenberg, Richard. *The World of Benjamin Cardozo: Personal Values and the Judicial Process*. Cambridge, MA: Harvard University Press, 1997.

Posner, Richard A. *Cardozo: A Study in Reputation*. Chicago: University of Chicago Press, 1990.

White, G. Edward. *Tort Law in America: An Intellectual History*. New York: Oxford University Press, 1980.

When "The Thing Speaks for Itself": *res ipsa loquitur* and the Proof of Negligence

—◄◦►—

H. Daniel Holm Jr.
Ball, Kirk & Holm, P.C.
Waterloo, Iowa

Escola v. Coca-Cola Bottling Company of Fresno, 24 Cal.2d 453 (1944) [California Supreme Court]

◄◦► THE CASE IN BRIEF ◄◦►

Date
  1944

Location
  California

Court
  California Supreme Court

Principal Participants
  Gladys Escola
  Coca-Cola Bottling Company of Fresno
  Members of California Supreme Court

Significance of the Case
  The ruling weakened the rules of negligence and made it easier for plaintiffs to recover damages from companies in injury cases.

Gladys Escola was a waitress in a restaurant. One of the responsibilities of her job was to stock a refrigerator with bottles of carbonated beverages, including the ever-popular Coca-Cola. Regularly, a driver for Coca-Cola Bottling Company of Fresno would deliver cases of Coca-Cola to the restaurant, stacking them one on top of the other behind the counter. Gladys would then individually place the bottles in the refrigerator to chill them for potential customers.

On the day in question, several cases of Coca-Cola were delivered to the restaurant and, as always, placed behind the counter. The cases sat untouched for a period of at least thirty-six hours before Gladys began transferring the individual bottles to the refrigerator. Gladys picked up the top case and placed it upon a nearby ice cream cabinet, about 3 feet from the refrigerator. She then transferred the bottles from the case to the refrigerator, one at a time. She placed three bottles in the refrigerator without incident. She picked up the fourth bottle and moved it about 18 inches. Then it exploded in her hand. Gladys remembered hearing a loud "pop." The contents of the Coca-Cola bottle flew all over Gladys, the walls of the restaurant and her co-worker. The bottle itself broke into two jagged pieces in Gladys's hand. As a result, she suffered a deep 5-inch cut that severed nerves, blood vessels, tendons and muscles of the thumb and palm of the hand.

Gladys Escola had a serious injury, but she and her lawyer had a serious proof problem. They knew that Gladys had done nothing herself to cause the accident. They also knew that, in the general course of things, a carbonated beverage bottle does not explode unless someone, most likely the bottling company, has been negligent. However, they did not know precisely why the bottle had exploded. Had it been overcharged with carbonation? Was the bottle itself in a weakened, defective condition? There was no way to know for sure, since the bottle was completely destroyed in the explosion. Gladys and her lawyer could not prove the precise negligent act or acts that led to the explosion. Their only hope was to rely on the legal doctrine of *res ipsa loquitur*.

The law generally holds that negligence is never presumed. It must be proven with evidence. The mere fact that an accident has occurred does not establish that someone was negligent. To establish negligence, evidence must be produced from which reasonable people could conclude that someone failed to act in a reasonable and prudent manner. The evidence necessary to prove negligence need not be of the direct, "eyewitness" variety. It may be circumstantial. One type of circumstantial evidence is embodied by the theory of *res ipsa loquitur*. In Latin, the phrase literally means "the thing speaks for itself." The theory can be traced to an 1863 English case, *Byrne v. Boadle*. In *Byrne*, a barrel of flour rolled out of a warehouse window and fell upon a passing pedestrian, seriously injuring him. The English court concluded from the unusual facts that the warehouse was probably at fault for the injury, despite a lack of evidence establishing the precise negligent act leading to the incident.

The general outline of the theory in American law has remained constant for a century.

To claim *res ipsa loquitur*, it is necessary for the plaintiff to establish the following: (1) the event must be of a kind that ordinarily does not occur in the absence of someone's negligence; (2) it must be caused by an agency or instrumentality within the exclusive control of the defendant; and (3) it must not have been due to any voluntary action or contribution on the part of the plaintiff. The doctrine has been applied in numerous factual circumstances, including the explosion of boilers or engines under a defendant's control, the collapse of structures, and injuries occurring during surgery while a patient is under general anesthesia.

At the trial court level, Gladys Escola and her lawyer successfully persuaded the trial court to submit the theory of *res ipsa loquitur* to the jury. On the basis of the theory, the jury held that the bottling company was negligent and responsible for Gladys's injuries. The bottling company appealed, contending that the doctrine of *res ipsa loquitur* did not apply in the case, and that the evidence was insufficient to support the judgment.

On appeal, the California Supreme Court began its analysis by pointing out that *res ipsa loquitur* only applies if the defendant had exclusive control of the thing causing injury and the accident is of such a nature that it ordinarily would not occur in the absence of negligence by the defendant. The court observed that the control exercised by the defendant over the instrumentality causing injury does not have to extend to the time of injury. It is enough that the defendant had control at the time of the alleged negligent act, provided that the plaintiff can prove that the condition of the instrumentality had not been changed after it had left the defendant's possession. The court went on to state that Gladys had to prove that she handled the bottle carefully and that no action on her part had contributed to the accident. The court stated that the reason for this rule was to "eliminate the possibility that it was the Plaintiff who was responsible." The court did not require Gladys to eliminate every remote possibility of damage to the bottle after it had left the control of the bottling company. She was only required to produce evidence that permitted a reasonable inference that the bottle was not accessible to extraneous harmful forces and that it was carefully handled by her or any third party who may have moved or touched it.

After setting forth the general principles of *res ipsa loquitur,* the court examined the facts of Gladys's injury. It held that the evidence was sufficient to support a reasonable inference that the bottle was not damaged by any extraneous force after it had been delivered to the restaurant where Gladys worked. According to the court, it therefore followed that the bottle was in some manner defective at the time the bottling company relinquished control, "because sound and properly prepared bottles of carbonated liquid do not ordinarily explode when carefully handled." The court then moved to the question of whether Gladys could rely upon the doctrine of *res ipsa loquitur* to supply an inference that the bottling company's negligence was responsible for the defective condition of the bottle at the time it was delivered to the restaurant. The court began its analysis on this point by observing that the explosion could have been caused either by excessive internal pressure in a "sound" bottle or by a defect in the glass of a bottle containing a "safe" pressure, or by a combination of those two possible causes. If, under the evidence produced in the case, it was probable that the bottling company was negligent in any of those respects, the doctrine of *res ipsa loquitur* would apply.

The court continued its analysis by observing that the evidence established that the bottle was charged with gas pressure, and the charging of the bottle was within the exclusive control of the bottling company. The court reasoned that an overcharge would not ordinarily result without negligence. The court went on to state that, if the explosion had resulted from a defective bottle containing a safe pressure, the defendant would be liable if it negligently failed to discover the flaw. If the defect in the bottle were visible, an inference of negligence would arise from the failure of the defendant to discover it. The court submitted that, where defects are discoverable, it can be assumed that they will not ordinarily escape detection if a reasonable inspection is made, and if such a defect is overlooked an inference arises that a proper inspection was not made. The court found more difficult the question of whether

the bottle possibly contained a flaw that was not detectable by a reasonable visual inspection. However, the court found the evidence sufficient to deal with this contingency as well. Gladys's lawyer had presented the testimony of a chemical engineer for a glass company who explained how glass is manufactured and the methods used in testing and inspecting bottles. He testified that "pressure tests" were routinely employed in the industry that made it nearly impossible for a defective bottle to make its way into public circulation. Therefore, the court found that, even if the defect had been undetectable by visual inspection, reasonable testing probably would have discovered it.

The court concluded its analysis with this statement: "Although it is not clear in this case whether the explosion was caused by an excessive charge or a defect in the glass there is sufficient showing that neither cause would ordinarily have been present if due care had been used." Consequently, the California Supreme Court held that the doctrine of *res ipsa loquitur* was properly presented to the jury in Gladys's case.

Special note should be made of the brilliant concurring opinion of Chief Justice Roger Traynor. In his concurrence, the chief justice voiced his opinion that a manufacturer's negligence need no longer be required as an element of proof for a plaintiff to recover in cases like Gladys's. He stated: "In my opinion, it should now be recognized that a manufacturer incurs an absolute liability when an article that he has placed on the market, knowing that it is to be used without inspection, proves to have a defect that causes injury to human beings." Traynor's opinion relied heavily on public policy considerations and an analysis of who was best able to bear the burden of injury caused by defective products. He observed that public policy demanded "that responsibility be fixed wherever it will most effectively reduce the hazards to life and health inherent in defective products that reach the market." He argued that it is the manufacturer of the product, and not the public, that can anticipate such hazards and guard against them. He reasoned that the cost of an injury sustained due to a defective product, in terms of loss of time or health, can be an overwhelming problem for the person injured, and the loss suffered should be "insured by the manufacturer and distributed among the public as a cost of doing business." Traynor went on to observe that application of the rule of *res ipsa loquitur* actually approached the rule of strict liability and that it was "needlessly circuitous to make negligence the basis of recovery and impose what is in reality liability without negligence."

Traynor cited various legal "fictions" that had been employed to hold manufacturers responsible for injuries caused by their products, and then argued forcefully for a uniform application of principles of strict liability and warranty to the ultimate consumers or users injured by defective products. Traynor concluded that application of these rules of law was necessary because of the rapidly changing relationship between manufacturers and consumers. He observed that there no longer existed a close relationship between the producer and consumer of a product. Manufacturing processes for products were either inaccessible to or beyond the knowledge of the general public. The consumer no longer had the means or skill to investigate for himself whether a product was safe and well

made prior to purchase. The consumer's vigilance had been softened by the advent of mass advertising. These factors had combined to produce a consumer who no longer approached products warily but who accepted them "on faith, relying on the reputation of the manufacturer or the trademark." In such a world, Traynor reasoned, it was necessary that the manufacturer of a defective product be responsible for injuries caused by the product, without regard to proof of negligence. Justice Traynor's opinion lucidly pulled together all of the disparate threads of product liability law and articulated the intellectual basis for the products liability explosion in the 1960s.

Selected Bibliography

Hall, Kermit L. *The Magic Mirror: Law in American History.* New York: Oxford University Press, 1989.

Prosser, William Lloyd, John W. Wade, and Victor E. Stewart. *Cases and Materials on Torts,* 9th ed. St. Paul, MN: Foundation Press, 1994.

White, G. Edward. *Tort Law in America: An Intellectual History.* New York: Oxford University Press, 1985.

The "Nuking" of American Civilians

—◦—

Howard Ball
Department of Political Science
University of Vermont

Allen et al. v. United States, 816 F 2d 1417 (1987) [U.S. Court of Appeals]

◦ THE CASE IN BRIEF ◦

Date
 1987

Location
 Nevada
 Utah

Court
 U.S. Court of Appeals

Principal Participants
 Mr. Allen and other plaintiffs
 Government of the United States
 Judge Bruce S. Jenkins

Significance of the Case
 The court ruled that an agency of the U.S. government was immune from tort liability actions, thus forcing the plaintiffs to seek remedies through legislation passed by Congress.

For over a decade, from 1951 to 1963, the United States detonated atomic weapons on the American continent. In December 1950, President Harry S. Truman approved a proposal, presented to him by the Atomic Energy Commission (AEC), that America develop an atomic testing facility on the continent in order to maintain nuclear superiority over the Soviet Union. The reasons for the AEC's proposal seemed plain enough at the time. First of all, America's military and political leaders had recently been angered and shocked by the exposure of a Russian spy operation that had been passing secrets of the atom bomb to the Soviet Union since 1944.

In the summer of 1950, Julius and Ethel Rosenberg had been arrested by the government and charged with conspiracy to pass secrets to the Russians—a violation of the 1917 Espionage Act. Also, in June 1950, the cold war suddenly turned very hot as Americans became involved in the "police action" in Korea. For the commissioners of the AEC, concerned about the maintenance of security as well as the difficulties in sustaining an operational research and development facility thousands of miles away from our scientific laboratories at their Pacific Ocean test facility site, it was imperative that they locate another atomic test facility in a fairly remote section of the continental United States.

They chose an old World War II gunnery range in the Nevada Desert. The AEC view was that the land, owned by the government, was "virtually uninhabitable" and therefore would not be a threat to the health and safety of significant numbers of Americans. They did take into account the fact that some amounts of radioactive fallout would drift off-site and deposit radioactive particles on the tens of thousands of Americans—all loyal, patriotic citizens—living in small towns in Nevada, Utah, and Arizona—to the east and north of what has been called the Nevada Test Site (NTS) by the government since 1954.

A review of the AEC commissioners' "Top Secret" minutes clearly indicates that these political appointees knew of the human risks of the atomic testing on the continental United States. However, as they all insisted, while the risk to the people of St. George, Utah, for example, existed (St. George "always gets plastered," said one of the commissioners), the much greater risk was allowing the Soviet Union to gain the upper hand in the race for nuclear superiority. Using a benefit-cost analysis, the AEC concluded that the testing had to go on at the NTS. Nothing would stop the testing, said another commissioner in 1957. All told, there were over 120 atomic shots in the desert air north and west of Las Vegas, Nevada. Over eighty of these atmospheric shots deposited radioactive debris off-site, or downwind, of the test site.

There is no question that the pathological and genetic dangers of ionizing radiation were well known to the nuclear scientists working at the NTS as well as to the AEC administrators. The AEC's Division of Biology and Medicine scientists and doctors, responsible for the safety and health of persons coming into contact with the testing program knew of the danger that faced persons exposed to radioactive fallout. Engaged in bureaucratic struggles with the AEC's Division of Military Application scientists and Department of Defense administrators, however, they always seemed to lose out to the men who were responsible for producing the fissionable materials and conducting the research and development of atomic weapons. From the beginning of the AEC's history, in 1946, it was given a contradictory task: develop atomic weapons in order to maintain superiority over the Soviet Union but develop these weapons within a safe environment. When a clash occurred between these two principles, weapons development was always primary. Eugene Zuckert, chairman of the AEC from 1952 to 1954 put it starkly: The atomic weapons testing program was characterized by a "lack of balance between the safety requirements and the requirements of the program.... [When there was a] conflict, the balance was apt to tip on the side of the military programs."

In 1978, reporters used the Freedom of Information Act (FOIA) to uncover documents (held in AEC files since the late 1950s and early 1960s) disclosing that the "downwinders" had been exposed to unsafe levels of radioactivity. Furthermore, the documents indicated that early AEC and the Public Health Service (PHS) medical reports had informed the AEC of the dangers but that the AEC did little to warn the persons who were exposed to the fallout. A deputy director of the AEC justified the lack of data to the downwinders in this way: "Well, look, we've told these people all along that its safe and we can't change our story now, we'll be in trouble." The documents also revealed that the AEC officials were negligent, that is, did not take adequate safety precautions as mandated by the 1946 Atomic Energy Act, when they implemented the program.

After a rebuff from the Department of Energy, a group of petitioners that would number almost 1,200 by 1980, sought remediation in federal court from the government for injuries and deaths—primarily cancers and leukemia—of their children, spouses and/or parents due to exposure to the fallout from the atomic tests over the Nevada desert in the 1950s. Using the 1946 Federal Tort Claims Act (FTCA), legislation passed by Congress that enables citizens to sue the government and government agents under certain circumstances, is difficult enough under ordinary circumstances, that is, when a person suffers a traditional injury such as getting hit by a U.S. mail truck. This was not an ordinary case, however. First of all, *Allen v. U.S.* involved the AEC's implementation of a major governmental policy involving national security (atomic testing), and the FTCA contains an exception (called "discretionary function") that disallows persons from suing the government if the injury occurs as a consequence of a government agent using judgment to implement such a policy. Additionally, the *Allen* litigation charged that the governmental negligence during the testing period led to nontraditional injuries. That is, due to the detonation of the atom bombs in the 1950s, years—even decades—later, biological injuries occurred to plaintiffs and to their progeny.

The lawyers representing the downwinders in the suit against the U.S. government had to meet and overcome two legal burdens: first, they had to convince the federal judge that the actions of the federal agents who implemented the testing policy at the NTS in the 1950s were not immune from a tort liability suit under the FTCA. If they could not persuade the federal judge in the trial court that the "discretionary function" exception did not apply in their case, the case was over before reaching the substantive issue. Second, assuming that they made the case for jurisdiction, the lawyers for the plaintiffs in *Allen* had the very difficult burden of showing that the cancers and leukemias, discovered in the 1960s and 1970s, were "more likely than not" caused by the negligence of the government when it exploded atom bombs over the Nevada desert in the 1950s.

The federal judge who heard the case, Bruce S. Jenkins, grew up in Utah. He was appointed to the federal district court in Utah in 1978 by President Jimmy Carter. A year later he was assigned the *Allen* case. Living in Salt Lake City, he was familiar with the news stories and television specials about the activities of the AEC personnel at the NTS during the 1950s. Jenkins was, from the beginning, leery of the government lawyers' arguments that: (1) there was absolute immunity from any FTCA suit brought by petitioners due to the "discretionary function" exception, (2) there was not a "scintilla" of

evidence that plaintiffs could present at trial to show that the government acted negligently or carelessly when it detonated the atom bombs and that, furthermore, (3) there was no way to prove, scientifically, that the cancers and leukemias contracted by the persons who lived "downwind" of the NTS were caused by the radioactive fallout produced by the atomic testing at the NTS.

Three times between 1979 and 1982, the period of discovery prior to the formal trial, the government lawyers asked Jenkins to dismiss summarily the suit on the grounds of the "discretionary function" exception. Three times he turned aside their request. The last rejection occurred during the trial. Jenkins, in rejecting the government petition, stated that the jurisdiction issue was so important and so intertwined with other issues that he could only rule on it after hearing the evidence presented at trial.

The trial lasted three months. Thousands of documents were introduced into the record. Dozens of witnesses—former AEC employees, Department of Energy bureaucrats, medical epidemiologists, nuclear physicists, oncologists, and the downwinders themselves—testified before Judge Jenkins in his courtroom. In December 1982, Judge Jenkins took the case under advisement and then spent, over the next year and one-half, a great deal of time—with a law clerk who he kept on the payroll for eight months after his clerkship had expired—crafting his opinion. The judge and the clerk, Russell Kearl, toiled away in the document room, the "Theoretical Physics Division, U.S. District Court," as they called it, until the opinion was ready to be handed down. In early May 1984, *Allen* was announced.

On the jurisdictional issue, that is, whether the government was immune from tort litigation, Jenkins ruled that the local agents at the NTS, and the AEC monitors working in the local towns that dotted the deserts and the valleys of the Southwest, were not immune from tort action under the FTCA. They were responsible for carefully administering a discretionary policy. For Jenkins, the manner in which the tests were conducted, carefully or carelessly, was also a matter of choice, but was not a matter of discretion because such operational conduct was subject to a standard of due care. The downwinders were owed a duty by the AEC to act with due care. These government personnel, according to Jenkins's review of the facts, did not provide certain safety activities: they did not provide adequate warnings, adequate measurements of the fallout, adequate educational programs. "Jurisdiction is proper," Jenkins announced in *Allen*, because the carelessness and negligence of the AEC local officials were not immunized by the FTCA. The AEC provided a reasonable standard of care and the AEC personnel in the field could be held accountable if that standard was not met. Furthermore, Jenkins found that the personnel clearly breached their responsibility to act with due care.

Having established jurisdiction and determining that the AEC showed a lack of due care to the downwinders, Jenkins then turned to the very difficult question of causation. Did the AEC's negligence and breach of duty more likely than not cause the petitioners' illnesses and deaths. In any tort action for damages, Jenkins wrote that the plaintiffs had the burden of showing that the injury suffered was "a result of the defendant's conduct, at least in part" and must "demonstrate factually that there is a reason why this particular person is the defendant."

In the downwinders suit, the factual connection was "in genuine dispute" due to the lengthy latency of the diseases—leukemia and cancer—that petitioners claimed were caused by the careless AEC testing of atomic devices. Proving causation-in-fact in this type of "indeterminate causation" litigation was difficult, admitted Jenkins. Therefore, said the federal judge, in a burst of creative adjudication, the "court must use its own best judgments, experience, and common sense in light of all the circumstances." Accordingly, he ruled that the difficulty that the downwinders had in proving that the government caused their cancers did not mean that the government did not, "in fact," cause the damage.

To assist in the search for justice, Jenkins "fashioned" a "remedial framework" to determine the causation question. He held that if the AEC created a radiological hazard for an identifiable group, and members of that group

contract "a biological condition that is consistent with having been caused by the hazard to which [they have] been negligently subjected, then a federal judge "may reasonably conclude that the hazard caused the condition absent persuasive proof to the contrary offered by the defendant."

Jenkins then reviewed each of the twenty-four plaintiffs in the *Allen* litigation in light of the remedial framework: were they exposed to excess amounts of radiation, were they living in the area downwind of the NTS at the time of the above-ground testing program, and did they succumb to a type of cancer or leukemia that was radiogenic, that is, caused by radioactivity. In ten of the cases, he found for the plaintiff: the cancers and leukemias that had killed them were the consequence of AEC "risk-taking conduct" and therefore liability was imposed on the government by the federal judge. The award totaled almost $3 million. The remaining fourteen, Jenkins concluded, did not show that the government was more likely than not the cause of their cancers.

The response to the Jenkins ruling was predictable: the government immediately criticized his judgment as inconsistent with precedent in the area of tort law and filed an appeal in the Tenth Circuit U.S. Court of Appeals in Denver. For the Reagan administration's Justice Department, the Jenkins opinion was an "outrageous new theory of liability [created by an] activist judge engaging in social engineering."

The court of appeals handed down its judgment nearly three years later. On April 20, 1987, a three-judge panel overturned the Jenkins judgment. The panel concluded that the AEC activities were immune from tort liability actions under the FTCA by virtue of the presence of the "discretionary function" exception. All the actions of even the most local of AEC operatives "also fall within the discretionary function exception." The opinion concluded that the government was "immune from liability for the failure of AEC administrators and employees to monitor radioactivity more extensively or to warn the public more fully than they did." If there is any justice to be dispensed in the issue, they said, it is for the Congress and not the federal courts to so apportion. Until Congress acts, said a concurring judge, "we have no choice but to leave them uncompensated."

The downwinders then took the case to the U.S. Supreme Court, hoping that the Court would grant *certiorari* and review the issue on the merits. However, the Court, without a single publicly announced dissent from the denial of *cert*, refused to hear the *Allen* case. The court of appeals's overturning of Judge Jenkins's *Allen* opinion was affirmed. A month after Jenkins handed down his *Allen* opinion, the Supreme Court handed down an opinion that maintained the narrowly drawn scope of the FTCA as developed by the Court as early as a 1953 case. This may explain why the Court did not grant *certiorari* in *Allen*.

The legal remedy is no longer available to the *Allen* plaintiffs. The only remediation for the downwinders was legislation passed by Congress. In 1990, Congress passed and President George Bush signed the Radiation Exposure Compensation Act. It established a trust fund for claims for injuries and deaths due to exposure to radiation from nuclear testing and uranium mining in the Southwest.

Selected Bibliography

Ball, Howard. *Justice Downwind: America's Atomic Testing Program in the 1950's.* New York: Oxford University Press, 1988.

Titus, A. C. *Bombs in the Backyard: Atomic Testing and American Politics.* Reno: University of Nevada Press, 1987.

You Deserve a Brick Today:
Products Liability Law and McDonald's Coffee

—◦—

H. Daniel Holm Jr.

Ball, Kirk & Holm, P.C.
Waterloo, Iowa

Liebeck v. McDonald's Restaurants, No. CV-93–02419 (1994) [New Mexico District Court] and
Holowaty v. McDonald's Corp., 10 F. Supp. 2d 1078 (1998) [U.S. District Court]

◦ THE CASE IN BRIEF ◦

Date
1994, 1998

Location
New Mexico

Court
New Mexico District Court
U.S. District Court

Principal Participants
Stella Liebeck
Rosalind Holowaty
McDonald's Corporation

Significance of the Case
Two courts reached opposite conclusions concerning the liability of McDonald's for injuries suffered by customers who were burned by hot coffee. In one case, the judge handed down a directed verdict and did not let a jury hear the evidence.

In the summer of 1994, 79-year-old Stella Liebeck of New Mexico took McDonald's Corporation to court to recover damages for injuries suffered when she inadvertently spilled a cup of the fast food giant's coffee in her lap. The jury's $2.9 million verdict against McDonald's unleashed a torrent of public outrage against the civil justice system. The criticism, fueled by insurance companies, corporations and other "tort revisionists," never focused on the specific facts of the case. Rather, the strategy was to ridicule the jury system with "sound-bite" attacks, bemoaning how far our country had fallen when an individual could spill coffee on herself and recover millions of dollars from an "out-of-control" jury.

When the specific facts of Ms. Liebeck's case are laid out, however, a strong case can be made that McDonald's Corporation was preparing its coffee for sale in a very dangerous way. Nevertheless, public opinion failed to support the jury's decision in the New Mexico state case of *Liebeck v. McDonald's Restaurants* (1994). The decision in *Holowaty v. McDonald's Corp.* (1998), a federal district court case from Minnesota that held as a matter of law that a plaintiff could not maintain a products liability suit against McDonald's for coffee burn injuries, proves that the judiciary was not immune from the attacks leveled against the civil justice system in the wake of the *Liebeck* verdict.

The starting point in understanding the contradictory rulings in *Liebeck* and *Holowaty* is with American product liability law that seeks to compensate individuals who are injured by products. Numerous legal theories are employed to hold product manufacturers liable for injuries caused by their products. Those theories include negligence, misrepresentation, and breach of express or implied warranty. However, the theory that attracts the most attention and debate is the theory of strict liability. The American Law Institute's *Restatement of the Law, Second, Torts*—a compilation of suggested legal principles intended to simplify and standardize the law of torts—posits that one who sells any product in a defective condition that is unreasonably dangerous to the user or consumer is subject to liability for physical harm caused to the ultimate user or consumer, provided that the seller is engaged in the business of selling the product, and provided that the product reaches the user or consumer without substantial change in condition. The theory behind strict liability with respect to products is simple and just: one who profits from the sale of a defective product should be responsible for the injuries it causes.

It is hard to imagine a factual situation more appropriately within the definition of strict liability as set forth in the *Restatement* than that presented by Stella Liebeck's case. In February 1992, Mrs. Liebeck and her grandson patronized a McDonald's in Albuquerque, New Mexico. They used the drive-through window, and Mrs. Liebeck ordered coffee. That coffee was served in a Styrofoam cup. After receiving the order, Mrs. Liebeck's grandson pulled his car forward and stopped momentarily so that Mrs. Liebeck could add cream and sugar to her coffee. She placed the cup between her knees and attempted to remove the plastic lid, spilling the entire contents of the cup into her lap. The sweat pants she was wearing absorbed the coffee and held it next to her skin,

Stella Liebeck, left, attends a news conference in March 1995 to oppose the Common Sense Reform Acts. Liebeck had previously been awarded $2.7 million by a jury as a result of her highly publicized lawsuit against McDonalds in which she sued for damages after spilling hot coffee on her lap. *AP Photo/Joe Marquette.*

causing extremely serious burns. A surgeon determined that Mrs. Liebeck suffered "full-thickness burns" over 6 percent of her body, including her inner thighs, perineum, buttocks and genital and groin areas. She was hospitalized for eight days, during which time she underwent extensive skin grafting. Mrs. Liebeck offered to settle her claim for $20,000, but McDonald's Corporation refused.

During discovery in the case, McDonald's admitted that it brewed coffee at temperatures higher than 190 degrees Fahrenheit and held coffee at between 180 and 190 degrees Fahrenheit to "maintain optimum taste." Evidence established that most other restaurants served coffee at substantially lower temperatures, and coffee served at home was generally 135 to 140 degrees. Testimony from McDonald's employees demonstrated that they were aware that a burn hazard existed with any food substance served at 140 degrees or higher. They further testified that McDonald's coffee, at the temperature at which it is poured into the styrofoam cups, was not fit for consumption because it would burn the mouth and throat. Additional testimony proved that McDonald's had been aware of more than 700 serious burn complaints involving its coffee in the ten years prior to the *Liebeck* trial. Experts retained by Mrs. Liebeck testified that lowering the serving temperature to about 160 degrees would make a big difference: it takes less than three seconds to produce a third-degree burn at 190 degrees, about twelve to fifteen seconds at 180 degrees, and about twenty seconds at 160 degrees. A McDonald's executive testified at the trial that the corporation knew its coffee sometimes caused serious burns, but that McDonald's had not consulted burn experts about the danger. He also testified that McDonald's had decided not to warn customers about the possibility of severe burns from its coffee. Finally, he testified that McDonald's did not intend to change any of its coffee policies or procedures, saying "there are more serious dangers in restaurants."

Initially, the jurors in the case were skeptical of Mrs. Liebeck's claim. The person eventually chosen to serve as foreman recalled that, at the beginning of the trial, he "wasn't convinced as to why I needed to be there to settle a coffee spill." As testimony in the case developed and jurors became aware of the serious injuries sustained by Mrs. Liebeck, their attitude changed markedly. One juror stated afterward that the evidence "made me come home and tell my wife and daughters 'don't drink coffee in the car, at least not hot.' " By the time all of the evidence had been presented, the jurors were unanimous in their conclusion that the McDonald's coffee was unreasonably dangerous, and that McDonald's Corporation had shown a callous disregard for the safety of its customers by refusing to address the situation. They awarded Mrs. Liebeck $160,000 in compensatory damages and $2.7 million dollars in punitive damages. The $2.7 million dollar punitive damage award was based on testimony that the sum represented two days of McDonald's

Corporation coffee sales. The New Mexico trial judge eventually reduced the jury's punitive damage award to $480,000. In doing so, he did not exonerate the actions of McDonald's. He indicated that he was also outraged by its actions, stating that McDonald's engaged in "wanton conduct" when it served coffee it knew was "too hot for human consumption."

Judge John R. Tunheim in *Holowaty v. McDonald's Corp.* did not voice the same degree of outrage as did the judge in the *Liebeck* case. *Holowaty* was a federal court case brought in Minnesota by Canadian residents. On July 9, 1995, Rosalind Holowaty and her husband were traveling through Rochester, Minnesota, and stopped at a McDonald's restaurant for breakfast. Mr. Holowaty purchased food, juice, and a large cup of coffee. A McDonald's employee placed the drinks in a beverage tray and gave them to Mr. Holowaty. He removed the lift-tab on the lid of the coffee, creating an opening to drink through. After returning to their car, Mrs. Holowaty held the beverage tray in her lap. As her husband drove down a steep decline the coffee spilled, soaking into Mrs. Holowaty's shorts and causing second-degree burns to her upper and inner thighs. The burns took two months to heal and left permanent scars. The manager of the McDonald's restaurant where the coffee was purchased testified that he set the brewing temperature at 190 degrees, producing a holding temperature of approximately 180 degrees. The plaintiffs had enlisted the services of a biomedical and mechanical engineer, who testified that second-degree burns will result in one second if 158-degree coffee comes into contact with bare skin.

The plaintiffs' complaints against McDonald's included design defect, failure to warn, negligence and breach of warranty. Prior to trial, McDonald's Corporation moved for summary judgment, contending that it was entitled to a judgment as a matter of law. Judge Tunheim agreed with this contention and granted the motion. On the design defect claim, the Holowatys had contended that the temperature of the coffee was excessively hot, and thus constituted a "defect" within the meaning of the *Restatement of the Law, Second, Torts.* McDonald's argued that "heat" is an inherent quality of coffee and that the coffee purchased by the Holowatys was no hotter than the coffee it regularly served. The judge agreed with McDonald's. He stated that the issue should not be whether a product can cause an injury, but whether a reasonable manufacturer would have designed the product in a different way to avoid foreseeable risk of injury. Stated another way, the court held that the plaintiffs' evidence did not establish that a reasonable restaurant owner would have sold the coffee at a lower temperature. The court further held that the Holowatys could not prevail against McDonald's Corporation based on a "failure to warn" theory. The Holowatys contended that McDonald's did not adequately warn of the danger attending its coffee because of its high temperature. The court concluded that the risk of burns resulting from spilled coffee was an "obvious" risk that did not require a warning. The judge also rejected the Holowatys' contention that reasonable consumers would not anticipate the severity of the injury caused by McDonald's coffee, and he held that McDonald's had no duty to warn of the severity of injury that could be caused if the coffee came into contact with skin. The court went on to hold as a matter of law that the Holowatys could not prevail on their negligence theory or their implied warranty of merchantability theory. As such, the federal district court dismissed the Holowatys' case in its entirety.

The decision in *Holowaty* is disturbing for at least two reasons. First, the federal district court's decision, though well crafted, usurped the jury's function as fact finder. A summary judgment is only appropriate when, after reviewing the facts, a court concludes that there is "no genuine issue as to any material fact and that the moving party is entitled to a judgment as a matter of law." Although it is impossible to know precisely what facts were presented to the court, even the facts recited by the court in its decision make it clear that there were factual issues that should have been decided by a jury. Second, and perhaps more important, the federal district court in *Holowaty* completely absolved and exonerated McDonald's Corporation for selling a consumer product, without warnings, that could cause a second-degree burn in one second of contact with bare skin. To reach such a conclusion, as a matter of law, defeats the substantial benefits that have been conferred upon society by judicious and sensible application of product liability law.

Selected Bibliography

American Law Institute. *Restatement of the Law, Second, Torts*. Philadelphia: The American Law Institute, 1992.

Gerlin, Andrea. "A Matter of Degree: How a Jury Decided That a Coffee Spill is Worth $2.9 Million." *Wall Street Journal* (September 1, 1994): 1+.

Mead, Susanah. "Punitive Damages and the Spill Felt Round the World: A U.S. Perspective." *Loyola Los Angeles International & Comparative Law Journal* 17 (fall 1995): 829–859.

Natural Resources, Technology, and the Environment

Riparian Doctrine: A Short Case History for the Eastern United States

—◁◦▷—

William F. Steirer Jr.

Department of History
Clemson University

H. & W. Omelvanny v. Elisha Jaggers, 2 Hill 634 (1835) and
White v. Whitney Manufacturing Company, 60 S.C. 254 (1901) [South Carolina Supreme Court]

◁◦▷ THE CASE IN BRIEF ◁◦▷

Date
  1835, 1901

Location
  South Carolina

Court
  South Carolina Supreme Court

Principal Participants
  Elisha Jaggers
  H. & W. Omelvanny
  Mr. White
  Whitney Manufacturing Company

Significance of the Case
  Two South Carolina cases—one in 1835, the other in 1901—dealt with the use of waterways by private individuals. The courts had to balance the rights of the individual to use waterways adjacent to private property with the rights of others to use the same waterways.

East of the thirty-first parallel in the United States, the doctrine governing the uses of surface water is called riparian. Today that doctrine generally holds that owners of land contiguous to watercourses possess the right to use that water provided the use is reasonable and kept within the basin's boundaries. Riparian doctrine developed in Europe and bypassed the normal channels whereby legal doctrines were imported to the United States from England. A 1793 Connecticut decision is apparently the first case decided on riparian principles in the United States, but, gradually during the next four decades, most of the northeastern states embraced riparianism. The rejection of prior-appropriation tenets (the idea that the first proprietor on a stream possessed a superior right) remained incomplete in the East until well into the nineteenth century. As late as 1821, the Massachusetts Supreme Judicial Court still was applying prior-appropriations remedies to water use conflicts.

The 1835 South Carolina case of *Omelvanny v. Jaggers* provided a point of definition for riparianism in the Southeast where, even more than in the northeastern states, the spread of riparian doctrine was both steady during the last half of the nineteenth century and unchallenged in court and custom. *Omelvanny* came at a time when attitudes about property and entrepreneurial opportunities were shifting dramatically toward the individualization of society known to historians as Jacksonian democracy.

Historians, generally, understand Jacksonian democracy to have been the celebration of the individual in society, that individual effort took priority over a sense of collective responsibility and that what an individual wanted was at least equal to the community's wants and needs and that all inhabitants of society deserved equal access to the exploiting of natural resources. *Omelvanny v. Jaggers* reflected the Jacksonian credo in opening the rights to water use to all comers on an equal basis regardless of prior claims. Quoting New York's Chancellor James Kent, the court observed in *Omelvanny* that "Every proprietor of lands in the banks of a river, has naturally an equal right to the use of the water which flows in the stream adjacent to his lands, as it was wont to flow . . . without diminution or alteration. No proprietor has a right to use the water to the prejudice of other proprietors above or below him, unless he has a prior right to divert it, or a title to some exclusive enjoyment. He has no property in the water itself, but a simple use of it while it passes along."

In these words, the South Carolina Supreme Court articulated in 1835 the early version of riparian doctrine known as the natural flow theory. H. & W. Omelvanny erected a mill a short time after Elisha Jaggers built his mill one-half mile downstream on the Rocky Creek. There had been a mill on the Jaggers site from 1794 to 1814, so Jaggers had a prior claim to the water in Rocky Creek. In 1833, it was discovered that the defendant's dam raised the water at the plaintiff's mill by four and one-half feet, sufficient for the wheels not to turn.

The lower court held that Jaggers possessed a prior right to use the water and "to deprive the first occupant of this privilege at the pleasure of the owner above, would be giving one owner an unreasonable advantage over the other, which might be exercised capriciously and unjustly."

Speaking for the South Carolina Supreme Court's majority, Chancellor Harper overturned the lower court's application of prior-appropriation's doctrine. In spite of an unfortunate misquoting of Kent (stating "reasonably" where "unreasonably" appeared), the point was clear. Claims based on prior occupancy or use are "opposed to the weight of reasoning and authority." The natural flow of a watercourse may not be interrupted to the injury of other riparian proprietors in spite of claims to prior occupancy.

With the abundance of surface water available, few conflicts over water rights needed to be resolved in eastern state courts during the nineteenth century. South Carolina saw only three riparian cases reach its supreme court before 1900. Shortly thereafter, the supreme court rendered the definitive decision in *White v. Whitney Mfg. Co.* (1901), rejecting the natural flow theory in the process. Instead, the court held that a riparian proprietor had a right to use the water in a stream in a "reasonable way." In *White*, the defendant's right to use the water even though it interfered with the natural flow of Lawson's Fork Creek was upheld. The court stated: "But as between different proprietors on the same stream, the right of each qualifies that of the other, and the question always is not merely whether the lower proprietor suffers damage by the use of the water above him, nor whether the quantity flowing on is diminished by the use, but whether, under all the circumstances of the case the use of the water by one is reasonable and consistent with a correspondent enjoyment by the other."

The court carefully observed that "Streams of water are intended for the use and comfort of man, and it would be unreasonable and contrary to the universal sense of mankind" to prevent a riparian proprietor from using the water in ways "conformable to the usages and wants to the community, . . . and not inconsistent with a likewise reasonable use by the other proprietors of land on the same stream above and below." Determination of reasonable use, the court said, should be left to the jury in each case.

Flexibility and freedom from administrative strictures and costs continue to be the advantages of maintaining riparian principles in the late twentieth century. Whether those advantages will suffice in the face of perceived shortages of surface water and apparent conflicts in water uses in South Carolina and other eastern states is problematical. Already, Florida, Kentucky, and Mississippi have turned toward administrative solutions for allocating water. Pressures are building everywhere to devise some kind of administrative remedy, but the precedents established in cases like *Omelvanny v. Jaggers* and *White v. Whitney Manufacturing Company* still prevail.

Selected Bibliography

Cox, William E., ed. *Legal and Administrative Systems for Water Allocation and Management.* Blacksburg: Virginia Water Resources Research Center, 1978.

Dewsant, Richard L., and Dallin W. Jensen, eds. *A Summary—Digest of State Water Laws.* Arlington, VA: United States Government Printing Office, 1973.

Conflict over Water Power in Massachusetts

———◄○►———

James W. Ely Jr.
School of Law
Vanderbilt University

Cary v. Daniels, 49 Mass. 466 (1844) [Supreme Judicial Court of Massachusetts]

┌─────────────────────────────────────┐

◄○► THE CASE IN BRIEF ◄○►

Date
1844

Location
Massachusetts

Court
Supreme Judicial Court of Massachusetts

Principal Participants
William H. Carey
Albert Daniels
Chief Justice Lemuel Shaw

Significance of the Case
As a result of this case, courts began to view the use of water for mills and machinery as requiring special consideration. This was an issue of great importance as the nation industrialized.

└─────────────────────────────────────┘

Access to water power was crucial for industrial technology in the nineteenth century. The heavy demand for water power required lawmakers to reconcile the conflicting interests of riparian landowners in the use of rivers and streams. Indeed, litigation over water rights increased rapidly in antebellum America. A dispute between two mill owners on the Charles River raised the difficult question of which operator was entitled to priority in water use, and allowed the Supreme Judicial Court of Massachusetts to reformulate water law.

Before 1833 William H. Cary was one of several tenants in common who owned two mills on the Charles River. While the mills were under common ownership, a practice developed of opening the gate on the lower mill dam to relieve the upper mill from back water. In 1833 the co-tenants conveyed the upper mill and adjacent land to a third party, who in turn transferred the property to Cary in 1837. The lower mill and surrounding land were conveyed several times. Finally, in 1838, Albert Daniels became the sole owner. The lower mill dam was carried away by the river, and so Daniels built a new and larger dam. The new dam raised the water level above its usual height, and caused the river to flow back upon Cary's mill wheel. This hampered Cary in the use of his mill.

Cary then brought a lawsuit against Daniels, alleging two counts of unlawful interference with his rights. First, Cary charged that Daniels had improperly obstructed the use of Cary's mill. Second, Cary asserted that Daniels had interfered with his right to enter the lower mill property and open the gates on the lower dam. The case was tried before a jury and resulted in a verdict for the plaintiff on both counts. Cary was awarded $300 in damages on the first count, and $100 on the second. Thereafter the supreme judicial court heard legal arguments on whether judgment should be entered upon the verdict.

Water law in the United States was in the process of evolution during the antebellum era. Eminent jurists, such as Joseph Story and James Kent, fashioned riparian rights upon their understanding of English common-law principles. They formulated the reasonable use doctrine under which every landowner along a river or stream, by virtue of such ownership, enjoyed a right to use the water in its natural flow. Thus, all riparian owners had equal rights to use the water and none could lawfully cause injury to landowners above or below him.

The reasonable use doctrine posed several problems. One was the obvious difficulty of determining reasonable use under a variety of circumstances. Another was that the reasonable use doctrine tended to inhibit the most productive uses of water by preventing any riparian owner from heavy consumption. Yet to allow one riparian owner to reduce the flow of water for his own benefit could destroy the value of the other mill sites.

In his *Cary* decision, Chief Justice Lemuel Shaw sought to adjust the reasonable use doctrine to the need of mill operators to harness water power. Stressing the commercial value of water power, Shaw declared that in the United States "one of the most important" uses of a watercourse "is its application to the workings of mills and machinery; a use profitable to the owner and beneficial to the public." Qualifying the reasonable use doctrine with novel consider-

ations, Shaw explained that "each proprietor is entitled to such use of the stream so far as it is reasonable, conformable to the usages and wants of the community, and having regard to the progress of improvement in hydraulic works. . . ."

Although in the abstract each riparian owner was allowed reasonable use of streams and rivers, Shaw's analysis moved toward the doctrine of prior appropriation. He asserted that "the proprietor who first erects his dam for such a purpose has a right to maintain it, as against the proprietors above and below; and to this extent, prior occupancy gives a prior title to such use." In short, the first appropriation of a watercourse for mill purposes was a property right. Consequently, the damages caused by back water from a previously established mill dam was a mere inconvenience and did not constitute a legal injury.

Applying these principles to the case before the court, Shaw ruled that Daniels received the lower parcel of land subject to the prior appropriation of the Charles River by plaintiff's upper mill dam. Thus, Daniels had no right to erect a new dam that was higher than his old one. The court, accordingly, upheld the jury verdict for obstruction of plaintiff's mill. However, the court disallowed the second count, holding that once the properties were separated the owner of the upper estate had no right to enter the lower mill parcel.

As a result of *Cary*, courts began to view the use of water for mills and machinery as requiring special considerations. Judicial recognition that the first proprietor who built a mill dam had a right to maintain it facilitated industrial use of waterpower. This desire to encourage efficient use of water undercut the notion of equal distribution that was at the heart of the reasonable use doctrine.

Selected Bibliography

Clark, Robert Emmet, ed. *Waters and Water Rights.* Indianapolis, IN: Allen Smith Company, 1967.

Horwitz, Morton J. *The Transformation of American Law, 1780–1860.* Cambridge, MA: Harvard University Press, 1977.

Lauer, T. E. "The Common Law Background of the Riparian Doctrine." *Missouri Law Review* 28 (1963): 60–107.

A Law for Water in the West

Gordon Morris Bakken

Department of History
California State University, Fullerton

Irwin v. Phillips, 5 Cal. 140 (1855) [California Supreme Court]

```
⤙◇⤚ THE CASE IN BRIEF ⤙◇⤚

Date
  1855

Location
  California

Court
  California Supreme Court

Principal Participants
  Mr. Irwin
  Mr. Phillips
  Justice Solomon Heydenfeldt

Significance of the Case
  The doctrine of prior appropriation of
  water was recognized legally, and it
  became a leading principle of resource
  allocation in water for the West.
```

The flood tide of humanity that followed the lure of gold to California in 1849 brought with it concepts of law that found immediate popular application in the gold fields. People from all walks of life found themselves toiling in the mines of the mother lode country and quickly developed law to regulate their enterprise. Forming local mining districts, the early miners wrote down these rules and regulations, created institutions to enforce the law, and carried these early district regulations from place to place as they searched for gold. All of this activity took place on the public domain without federal legislative direction. Part of these local mining district regulations involved the use of water.

Water was critical to the mining industry. To work a claim successfully, a miner had to have water to wash gravel and sand away to reveal the glitter. First in the humble pan, then in sluice boxes and "long toms," and finally in elaborate timbered edifices, the miners brought the gold laden gravel and sand in contact with water.

Water cleansed metal of its common medium, but water was, itself, too often a scarce commodity. Conflicts over use arose in the mining districts and manifested themselves in lawsuits.

The question before the California Supreme Court in 1855 went beyond mining district regulations because it involved water and the English common law concept of riparian rights. The riparian proprietor gained rights in water by ownership of the stream bank. The rights included the quantity and quality of stream flow along the property abutting the stream. Owners of land on the stream above a riparian owner were "upper riparian proprietors" and those below were "lower riparian proprietors." All had rights to the quantity and quality of water undiminished by reasonable use of the other riparian owners. In *Irwin v. Phillips*, a canal company had diverted water from the natural watercourse for the purpose of supplying water to miners. This diversion took place prior to miners staking claims to the bank of the stream as "lower riparians." The "lower riparians" wanted the diversion stopped to assure their common-law right to a water supply.

Justice Solomon Heydenfeldt, after noting the fact that the parties were on the public domain, looked to the history of mining to find legal authority. He noted that, by 1855, neither the state government nor the federal government had exhibited any intent to regulate the business of mining on the public domain. Rather, a system had "been permitted to grow up by the voluntary action and assent of the population, whose free and unrestrained occupation of the mineral region has been tacitly assented to by the one government, and heartily encouraged by the express legislative policy of the other."

The history of federal land policy had been one of spending land for the public benefit and specifically for mineral lands, encouraging rapid exploitation by private parties. The rough and tumble mining camps had, in turn, written rules and regulations that protected the interests of the first arrivals in the name of entrepreneurial liberty.

Heydenfeldt viewed the mining district regulations as "crude and undigested," yet having legal force. Despite the nature of these regulations, "there are still some [rules] which a universal sense of necessity and propriety have so firmly fixed as that they have come to be looked upon as having the force and effect of *res judicata*" (matters settled by judgment). He found two principles to be clear in the regulations. First, the miners were to be protected in their locations. A miner who staked a claim in accordance with the district regulations had a location at law and that location was to be protected by law. Second, the regulations protected "the rights of those who, by prior appropriation, have taken the waters from their natural beds, and by costly artificial works have conducted them for miles over mountains and ravines, to supply the necessities of gold diggers." This latter right must be accorded legal protection because, without the water companies, "the most important interests of the mineral region would remain without development." Beyond the public policy basis for the encouragement of enterprise, the legislature had more than tacitly recognized the district regulations by reference in statutes. Canals and water races were property subject to taxation. The property of canal companies liable for assessment and taxation included "dams, . . . canals, or other works for mining purposes." Regardless of the fact that the enterprise was on the public domain, it was property and it had received "recognition from the sovereign power."

Miners seeking mineral wealth on the public domain took claims subject to prior interests. The priority principle, devised by miners, known to miners, and recognized by statute, informed any subsequent claimant that if water had "been already diverted, and for as high, and legitimate a purpose as the one he seeks to accomplish, he has no right to complain. . . ." The doctrine of prior appropriation of water had received judicial recognition and would become the leading principle of resource allocation in water for the arid West.

Selected Bibliography

Bakken, Gordon Morris. "American Mining Law and the Environment: The Western Experience." *Western Legal History* 1 (1988): 211–236.

Hundley, N., Jr. *The Great Thirst: Californians and Water, 1770s-1990s.* Berkeley: University of California Press, 1992.

Paul, Rodman W. *Mining Frontiers of the Far West.* New York: Holt, Rinehart, and Winston, 1963.

Pisani, Donald J. *From the Family Farm to Agribusiness: The Irrigation Crusade in California and the West, 1850–1931.* Berkeley: University of California Press, 1984.

Pisani, Donald J. *To Reclaim a Divided West: Water, Law, and Public Policy, 1848–1902.* Albuquerque: University of New Mexico Press, 1992.

Smith, Duane A. *Mining America: The Industry and the Environment, 1800–1980.* Lawrence: University of Kansas Press, 1987.

Dividing the Rivers:
Rule of Law in an Arid State

———◄◦►———

M. Catherine Miller
Department of History
Texas Tech University

Lux v. Haggin, 69 Cal. 255 (1886) [California Supreme Court]

◄◦► THE CASE IN BRIEF ◄◦►

Date
1886

Location
California

Court
California Supreme Court

Principal Participants
Charles Lux and partner
James Ben Ali Haggin and partners
Judge Benjamin Brundage
Members of California Supreme Court

Significance of the Case
Following this case, courts treated water as a part of land, rejecting the notion that water is a separate resource governed by independent principles. The ruling as a defeat for water policy and a victory for the strict rule of law to protect property rights.

L*ux v. Haggin* was one of the most controversial cases to confront the California Supreme Court in the nineteenth century. At issue was the meaning of California's law of waters and, to many, the future of the state's arid lands. In 1850, the California legislature adopted the common law as the rule of decision in the state. Presumably it had received the common law of waters, riparian rights, which viewed water as "part and parcel" of the land through which it flowed. But, as miners transported water away from streams to wash fortunes from the auriferous hills, the doctrine was ignored. Most miners were trespassers on the public lands. With the federal government making no effort to protect its rights as a riparian owner, judges settled rival claims to water as they had those to land: first in time, first in right. While riparian rights were not abrogated, in 1872 the legislature codified rules governing this appropriation of water.

In *Lux v. Haggin* the state supreme court was asked to decide which of these doctrines governed the water rights of privately owned agricultural land. Underlying this request were conflicting views of the role of law and the judiciary. Advocates of riparian rights called on the court to apply traditional principles. The proponents of prior appropriation demanded that it be flexible and democratic, recognizing regional differences, encouraging entrepreneurial activity, and accepting the will of the people as expressed in public opinion and local custom. In 1886, the California court insisted that it must uphold rule of law and declared in favor of riparian rights, a decision that to this day continues to be assailed as inappropriate to the needs of the state.

Lux v. Haggin was a clash between titans. On one side were the cattlemen Henry Miller and Charles Lux. Former rivals, these immigrant butchers had formed a partnership that dominated the San Francisco meat industry. They purchased hundreds of thousands of acres of land in California, Oregon, and Nevada on which they raised cattle, sheep, and hogs. Much of their land was riparian, bordering rivers that could irrigate pastures and water stock. James Ben Ali Haggin and his partners, Lloyd Tevis and William Carr, were likewise wealthy and politically powerful. All had been connected with the Southern Pacific, and Carr was the railroad's political boss in the state legislature. Together and individually they had invested in large-scale financial and mining ventures and owned a million acres of western land.

Both of these groups sought control of the Kern River, located in the county of the same name in the southern end of California's rich Central Valley. Flowing past expanses of high desert, the river ultimately dwindled into Buena Vista Slough and the swamplands it fed before terminating in a shallow inland lake. In the 1850s, federal largesse and the connivance of state land officials attracted speculators to the swamplands at the lower end of the river. Some 90,000 acres of Kern County land were granted to a group proposing to develop irrigation and transportation canals that would link the region with San Francisco and its lucrative markets. When this scheme failed in the 1860s, cattlemen took up the overflowed lands. Miller and Lux acquired 40,000 acres along Buena Vista Slough. They excavated a canal to drain the wetlands and irrigate the reclaimed acres and, with large

herds pastured in the region, began fencing their ranges.

Haggin and his partners arrived in Kern County with the opening of the Southern Pacific line in 1874. Holding options on railroad land, they bought up the numerous canals that small farmers had scratched out further upstream. Haggin also acquired thousands of acres north of the river, much of this through fraudulent use of the Desert Land Act. Promising to expand irrigation systems and to subdivide his holdings, Haggin and his money were welcomed by local boosters as the leavening needed for rapid economic development. In fact, as he achieved control of land and canals, the area under irrigation grew seven-fold.

In 1877 the Central Valley suffered a profound and costly drought. Little water reached Buena Vista Slough, and the cattlemen helplessly watched their pastures wither and their cattle die. Banding together, they blamed Haggin for the severity of their losses. Haggin had recently opened the Calloway Canal that irrigated his desert lands. This diversion, they charged, had stolen water that should have flowed to their fields in even the driest years. After an unsuccessful attempt to negotiate a division of the river, Miller and Lux and their allies filed seventy-eight suits against Haggin and other upstream water users. Asserting that they were riparian owners and thus entitled to use the full flow of the stream, Miller and Lux asked the court to restrain Haggin's interference with their rights and property.

In responding, Haggin denied that Miller and Lux were riparian owners. After the cattlemen established their title to land and the extent of the damages, Haggin countered that possession of these wetlands did not convey water rights. This factual contention occupied the greater portion of the forty-nine-day trial. Parading forth a dreary stream of engineers, surveyors, and friends, he alleged that the slough was not a watercourse as required by law. Lacking defined banks and a steady flow, it was merely part of the swampy morass that Miller and Lux were obliged to reclaim. In addition, having allowed the Kern Valley Water Company to erect a dam at the head of the slough, the cattlemen had cut off both the flow of water and their entitlement. Besides, Haggin pointed out, he had initiated his appropriation of water in 1875, three years before Miller and Lux received the final patents to their land; thus, any water rights they might have were subject to his prior claims.

More important to the history of the case was Haggin's attack on the riparian doctrine itself, both in the arguments of his attorneys and in his funding of a public antiriparian campaign. Citing decisions recognizing prior appropriation in the mining districts, Haggin's forces insisted that riparian rights had been abolished. To bolster this reasoning, they appealed to public policy: the common-law doctrine should not (and could not) be accepted in California because it did not serve the needs of arid regions. By binding water to the land through which it flowed, riparianism gave a monopoly to cattlemen like Miller and Lux who contributed little to the development of the state. Vast stretches of land that when irrigated would support thousands of families would lie in waste and be held hostage to this few. In contrast, under the doctrine of appropriation these lands could produce the bountiful harvests that would secure the state's future.

William Stewart, former senator from Nevada, author of the federal mining code of 1866 that recognized prior appropriation on the public domain, and friend of Haggin, marshaled a kind of popular sovereignty to resolve the seeming conflict of law inherent in California's recognition of two water doctrines. Geography and climate dictated which doctrine suited, he argued, riparianism for humid parts of the state, appropriation for the arid; and local judges and juries with their knowledge of the community should decide which applied in a given case. The usages and customs of reasonable men, not precedent or statute, must determine law, which if it reflected local standards would set the stage for rapid economic growth and development.

Benjamin Brundage, the land agent and recently elected Kern County judge who tried the case, accepted this reasoning when he ruled against Miller and Lux. During the hearing he had denied the cattlemen's request to enter additional evidence rebutting Haggin's assertions that there was no watercourse through

the swamplands and that the diversion into the Calloway Canal antedated their acquisition of land. He then decreed that the swamplands possessed no riparian rights and were subject to Haggin's appropriation. Behind this law was a belief that only such a ruling protected the future of the community. Irrigation was a natural want, and the opening of Haggin's canal had transformed wastelands into vineyards, orchards, and gardens. To recognize Miller and Lux's claims would deprive these lands of water and render them once again "utterly barren, desert, and worthless."

Similarly, when the cattlemen appealed Brundage's decision, three of the seven members of the state supreme court rejected riparianism as inappropriate to the needs of the state and denied that it had been received as part of the common law. Erskine M. Ross, the only justice from southern California, argued that the state and federal governments had nullified riparian rights when they recognized prior appropriation on the public lands. Even the common law, he insisted, did not countenance riparianism in an arid state: the two most important qualities of the common law were flexibility and rationality; but it was a perversion of human reason to require that California's waters, its very "lifeblood," continue to flow in natural channels to be wasted in the sea.

However, in 1884, the four-man majority tersely rejected these entreaties. To them the law was "plain enough": the common law of waters had never been revoked, riparian rights were part of property in land, and riparian owners were entitled to the continued flow and benefit of the stream. The chief problem in *Lux v. Haggin* lay instead in arriving at the facts, and Brundage's decision was overturned because he had not allowed the cattlemen to present rebuttal evidence essential to determining if they had valid claims to water. However, acknowledging the crescendo of antiriparianism, the court agreed to rehear the appeal and to entertain arguments from others interested in the issue of water rights. The reargument changed no minds. In 1886, still divided 4-3, the California Supreme Court again threw out Brundage's verdict and ordered a new trial. Now the court issued a 200-page decision, the longest in its history, directing that broad color of title be given to assertions of riparian rights.

The essence of this opinion lay in a heartfelt commitment to rule of law and to protecting vested rights. Property, including that in water, could be taken only by following established eminent domain procedures and paying compensation. While Brundage had seized upon every insinuation of weakness to strike down the cattlemen's claims, the court's majority presumed their title was good. Only convincing and conclusive proof, which had not been provided during the earlier trial, not inference, justified the rejection of the traditional privileges of ownership. Similarly the majority denied that the recognition of prior appropriation had stripped land along the state's rivers of riparian rights. While Haggin argued that in accepting appropriation the legislature had bestowed its waters on all the people, the court saw this statute as a limited "concession" to those fulfilling its requirements. With this exception, state-held lands retained their attached water rights, both because the same statute protected existing riparian interests and because it did not explicitly donate them to the public. At the same time, federal lands and those in private hands, even if title had not been perfected, retained water rights: the state could not give away what it did not own.

Throughout, the court abjured an activist role. Once law was settled, in this instance by the adoption of the common law in 1850, courts could not annul it but must apply it as consistently as possible. The majority found no legal principle negating riparian property rights in the Spanish and Mexican codes that had earlier governed California and dismissed as preposterous the notion that geography or public policy should deter the application of established rules. Though eschewing a concern with policy, they did evaluate Haggin's argument that prior appropriation nourished economic democracy, concluding that, on the contrary, it spawned water monopoly. Only in accepting irrigation as a use of riparian waters did the court depart from traditional doctrine. However while this was an accommodation to local needs, the court perceived the ruling as a natural application of precepts of reasonable use found in

decisions of judges such as Lemuel Shaw of Massachusetts. Like many other jurists in the late nineteenth century, the four here upholding riparian rights denied that courts made law. Rather, in applying the rules of law to each circumstance, the judiciary provided certainty, stability, and security, protecting individual freedoms (and property) from all threats, especially threats with popular support.

An outcry of protest, much of it funded and organized by Haggin and Carr, greeted this decision. The governor was induced to call a special session of the legislature to overturn the ruling and to oust the justices who had supported it as old men out of step with the times. Quickly branded a threat to judicial independence, the proposed restructuring of the court failed, and efforts to revise the water code foundered with it. During the next regular session in 1887, lawmakers adopted the Wright Act, a seminal bill providing for popularly organized irrigation districts with the power to tax and to employ eminent domain. The legislature also rescinded that portion of the 1872 water code that acknowledged riparian rights. However, with riparian rights recognized as vested under the common law, this last action was an empty, symbolic gesture. Meanwhile negotiations, not the second trial provided for in *Lux v. Haggin,* settled the original conflict. In 1888, Miller and Haggin signed a contract partitioning the waters of the Kern between them. With control of the river secured, both the riparian and the appropriator continued to amass land within the county.

Though the bitter refrain of antiriparianism continued to reverberate through the legislature, public debate, and legal briefs, *Lux v. Haggin* was not overturned. Irrigation expanded rapidly, most often under the favored doctrine of appropriation; but where riparian owners asserted their rights, they were successful. Henry Miller used *Lux v. Haggin* as a powerful weapon, repeatedly suing those who infringed on his claims to rivers such as the San Joaquin, the second largest in the state. In the mire of subsequent litigation, the divided decision of 1886 hardened into rigid doctrine. Riparian owners were entitled to the full flow of the stream even if they squandered water that upstream appropriators might put to beneficial use. Such broad prerogatives were only limited, and at that timidly, with the amendment of the state constitution in 1928. Following *Lux v. Haggin*, succeeding jurists treated water as a part of land, not as a separate resource to be governed by independent principles. They accepted boundaries set by four men who had rejected all serious consideration of water policy out of a belief that only the strict rule of law could protect property rights.

Selected Bibliography

Freyfogle, Eric T. "*Lux v. Haggin* and the Common Law Burdens of Modern Water Law." *University of Colorado Law Review* 57 (1986): 485–525.

Miller, Gordon. "Shaping California Water Law, 1781–1928." *Southern California Quarterly* 55 (1973): 9–42.

Miller, M. Catherine. "Riparian Rights and the Control of Water in California, 1879–1928: The Relationship Between an Agricultural Enterprise and Legal Change." *Agricultural History* 59 (1985): 1–24.

Pisani, Donald J. *From the Family Farm to Agribusiness: The Irrigation Crusade in California and the West, 1850–1931*. Berkeley: University of California Press, 1984.

Shaw, Lucien. "The Development of the Law of Waters in the West." *California Law Review* 10 (1922): 444–460.

Wiel, Samuel C. "Public Policy in Western Water Decisions." *California Law Review* 1 (1912–13): 11–31.

The Hydraulic Society of the Colorado River

—◦—

Gordon Morris Bakken

Department of History
California State University, Fullerton

Arizona v. California, 373 U.S. 563 (1963) [U.S. Supreme Court]

◦ THE CASE IN BRIEF ◦

Date
1963

Location
Arizona
California
Nevada
Colorado River

Court
U.S. Supreme Court

Principal Participants
State of Arizona; State of California;
Federal courts

Significance of the Case
After years of litigation, the Supreme
Court settled a dispute over the division
of water from the Colorado River, thus
beginning a new era of federal
involvement in the development of
water power in the West.

Construing the Boulder Canyon Act of 1928 to evidence a congressional intent to create a federal scheme of water apportionment, the U.S. Supreme Court in this case decided a multistate dispute over the division of water from the Colorado River among its claimants and launched a new era of increased federal involvement in the evolving hydraulic "society" of the American West. The Court held that Congress intended to authorize the secretary of the interior to apportion and to regulate water flowing from federally financed Colorado River projects in California, Arizona, and Nevada. Prior to this decision, multistate water rights disputes had been settled only by interstate compacts and federal court decisions. Now the Court held that Congress had decided the exact amounts of water that each state would receive and, in a far-reaching element of decision, determined that the secretary of interior had the authority to apportion surplus waters and regulate water allocations in periods of shortage. This authority extended beyond decisions relating to states to individual water users within the state.

This case grew out of decades of litigation and multistate disputes over the use of water in the Colorado River basin. Water law prior to federal statutory intervention had been the province of state and territorial law. One of the federal government's first ventures into the field was the Carey Act of 1894. This statute authorized the secretary of interior to donate up to one million acres to arid states, provided they improve, irrigate, and reclaim tracts. Individual settlers could occupy and eventually own improved parcels of 160 acres. State finances hindered the success of the plan, and by 1899 only Wyoming had actually developed land under the statute. The Reclamation Act of 1902 continued the expansion of the hydraulic society, but now the federal government was the administrator of the law. The statute set aside land-sale receipts for the construction of reservoirs in the arid states, authorized the secretary of interior to survey and construct such facilities, and designated the Reclamation Service as administrator of the program. More acres received water from bigger and bigger projects. Litigation by the states were increasingly replaced by interstate compacts dividing the waters.

With the infusion of federal reclamation dollars into the region, and with increased water demand due to urbanization, industrialization, and intensive irrigation, competition for water and federal money increased among the states. In 1922 Congressman Phil Swing and Senator Hiram Johnson, both of California, introduced the Boulder Canyon Bill calling for the construction of a dam in the Boulder Canyon of the Colorado. The dam would create a huge storage reservoir for irrigation and hydroelectric power generation.

That same year, the U.S. Supreme Court held that the rule of prior appropriation in water law applied to interstate streams and controversies. The ruling denied Colorado's argument that it alone possessed the right to waters arising within the state's borders. Clearly, agreements among the states appeared to be a means to resolve the growing volume of water controversies in the arid West.

One such attempt at resolution was the Colorado River Compact of 1922. On November 24, 1922, the Colorado River Commission, chaired by Herbert Hoover, issued the compact document making allocations by basins and settling use priorities. California, Utah, Wyoming, Nevada, Colorado, and New Mexico ratified the compact within five months, but Arizona balked, precipitating six years of bitter haggling leading up to the Boulder Canyon Act of 1928.

The Boulder Canyon Act's implementation positioned southern California for tremendous growth. The Hoover Dam was completed in 1935, and hydroelectric power arrived in California the next year. In 1941 water flowed into southern California and Los Angeles and the Imperial Valley started converting desert into crops, cash, and condominiums.

California's growth based upon Colorado River water and power was at the expense of Arizona. Arizona responded with law suits. Arizona went to the U.S. Supreme Court arguing that the Boulder Canyon Act was unconstitutional. In a 1931 decision, the Court rejected the state's claims and held that the statute was a "valid exercise of congressional power." Three years later the state mounted another legal stratagem: it asked the Court to "perpetuate" some oral testimony that was intended for use in future litigation to prove that one million acre feet of water under the compact was intended for Arizona. On May 21, 1934, the Court unanimously ruled that the proposed testimony was not relevant and could never be relevant because Arizona had refused to ratify the compact. In November 1935 the state went back yet a third time. Now it asked the Court to determine Arizona's equitable share of the water. In 1936 the Court explained an elementary concept of jurisdiction to the state's attorneys. To come before the Court, the state would have to allege and prove that a "justifiable controversy" existed. The state could only show such a controversy if it could demonstrate that it was being harmed in some way. The Court noted that there were millions of acre-feet of water flowing down the Colorado unused. The jurisdictional hint was that Arizona would be hard pressed to show harm under the circumstances. The Court also noted that the United States should have been made a party to the suit. Not doing so was an equally fatal jurisdictional error.

Arizona's losses in the federal courts turned it to negotiation. In 1944 the state ratified the compact. Then the state went to Congress. Arizona's senior U.S. senator, Carl Hayden, started a campaign for a federal project to bring water to the interior of the state, particularly for Phoenix and Tucson. From 1947 on, Hayden was successful in getting the Senate to approve a billion-dollar Central Arizona Project. Every year the California delegation in the House of Representatives blocked the legislation, arguing that there was simply not enough water. The reason there was not enough water was California's excessive use.

Thwarted in Congress, Arizona went back to the United States Supreme Court in 1952. The suit lasted eleven years, necessitated the services of a special master, cost nearly $5 million, recorded the testimony of over 300 witnesses, and demanded the services of over four dozen attorneys. In *Arizona v. California*, Arizona finally emerged victorious. It was awarded 2.8 million acre-feet of water. In addition, Native American water rights received important legal recognition. Indian water rights (which were measured by irrigable acreage rather than use) dated from the creation of the various reservations, were superior to subsequent non-Indian use, and were not subject to abandonment rules for nonuse. The decision put Indian tribes, particularly the Navajo, into the irrigation and water rights litigation business. Law suits regarding the extent and nature of Native Americans' rights continue to be a feature of Western water development.

Congress put Arizona into the hydraulic society business with this 1963 decision. The Colorado River Basin Project Act of 1968 gave the state the Central Arizona Project. The federal government built Parker Dam, creating Lake Havasu and a network of pipes, channels, and aqueducts servicing Phoenix and Tucson. The water started to flow in 1985. The Colorado River, as historian Donald Worster has so aptly put it, "had been transmogrified into an industrial artifact, an almost perfectly realized expression of the new imperial West." The federal government's money and the U.S. Supreme Court made it possible for the Colorado to become the West's leading river of empire.

Selected Bibliography

August, J., Jr. *Vision in the Desert: Carl Hayden and the Hydropolitics in the American Southwest.* Fort Worth: Texas Christian University Press, 1999.

Bakken, Gordon Morris. *The Development of Law on the Rocky Mountain Frontier: Civil Law and Society, 1850–1912.* Westport, Connecticut: Greenwood Press, 1983.

Fradbin, P. *A River No More: The Colorado River and the West.* Berkeley: University of California Press, 1996.

Hundley, Norris, Jr. *The Great Thirst: Californians and Water, 1770s-1990s.* Berkeley: University of California Press, 1992.

Hundley, Norris, Jr. *Water and the West: The Colorado River Compact and the Politics of Water in the American West.* Berkeley: University of California Press, 1975.

Pisani, Donald J. *To Reclaim a Divided West: Water, Law, and Public Policy, 1848–1902.* Albuquerque: University of New Mexico Press, 1992.

Worster, Donald. *Rivers of Empire: Water, Aridity, and the Growth of the American West.* New York: Pantheon Books, 1985.

Controversy over a Fast-Breeder

—◦—

George T. Mazuzan

History Office
National Science Foundation

Power Reactor Development Company, Petitioner, v. International Union of Electrical, Radio and Machine Workers, AFL–CIO, et al. and *United States et al., Petitioners v. International Union of Electrical, Radio and Machine Workers, AFL–CIO, et al.,* 364 U.S. 889 (1960) [U.S. Supreme Court]

◦ THE CASE IN BRIEF ◦

Date
1960

Location
Michigan

Court
U.S. Supreme Court

Principal Participants
Power Reactor Development Company
International Union of Electrical, Radio, and Machine Workers, AFL-CIO
Government of the United States

Significance of the Case
The ruling allowed the civilian nuclear power program to continue with fewer bureaucratic delays, but it also contributed to a growing credibility problem facing the Atomic Energy Commission.

Few judges are qualified to determine the safety of a technology. They are qualified, however, to determine if the established legal procedures used to influence the safety of the technology are correct. In so doing, judges shape the direction the technology takes. The federal courts did this in the *PRDC* case.

The commercial application of nuclear energy was in its infancy in the mid-1950s when different types of reactors were being proposed for a new American nuclear power industry. The revised federal Atomic Energy Act of 1954 gave regulatory power over construction and operation of privately owned nuclear facilities to the Atomic Energy Commission (AEC). The act also established a two-step licensing procedure for each nuclear plant and required adherence to a statutory standard of assuring "public health and safety." A company planning to build a plant first had to apply to the AEC for a construction permit and submit detailed plans as to how the facility would be constructed to assure public health and safety. Once constructed, the company could apply for an operating license to run the plant. To promote the development of this new industry, the AEC implemented new regulations under the act. The agency also used its already established Advisory Committee on Reactor Safeguards (ACRS), a part-time group of highly respected reactor experts, for advice on the safety of any proposed facility.

Taking advantage of the revisions under the 1954 act, a group of privately owned power utilities and industrial corporations, led by Detroit Edison, formed a consortium, the Power Reactor Development Company (PRDC), to build and operate an advanced-design fast-breeder power reactor at Lagoona Beach, about 30 miles south of Detroit, Michigan. Fast-breeder technology, showing great promise, was nonetheless still fairly experimental compared to the more developed light-water reactors that were adopted by many utilities and which would become the mainstays of the American nuclear power industry. But in this incubation stage of the industry, the AEC encouraged development of different reactor types.

The PRDC submitted its application to the AEC for a construction permit in early 1956. In a letter to the commission on June 6, 1956, the ACRS, after reviewing the PRDC application, unfavorably commented on the company's plan. The experts suggested that a construction permit not be issued until more characteristics of the dangerous fast-breeder technology could be determined through an ongoing AEC experimental program. The letter concluded that "there is insufficient information available at this time to give assurance that the PRDC reactor can be operated at this site without public hazard." The letter, not publicly issued but "leaked," became the catalyst for a series of events. The commission, despite the misgivings of the ACRS, granted a construction permit to the PRDC on August 4, 1956. Agency officials felt that, during the lengthy construction period, the technical problems underscored by the ACRS could be worked out so that a license eventually could be issued for safe operation of the facility.

Three labor unions of the American Federation of Labor–Congress of Industrial Organizations (AFL–CIO)—the International Union of Electrical, Radio, and Machine Workers, the United Paperworkers of America, and the

United Automobile, Aircraft, and Agricultural Implement Workers of America—each of which had substantial memberships in the Detroit area, soon submitted intervention petitions to the AEC for a hearing on the PRDC construction permit. The AFL–CIO, while a supporter of development of a nuclear industry, was also concerned about the way the AEC appeared to be disregarding its obligation to assure public health and safety. The petitions to intervene were the first to be directed against the agency.

A protracted public hearing and commission review drew considerable media interest. The talented general counsel of the machinists' union, Benjamin Sigal, represented the unions; the PRDC retained W. Graham Claytor Jr., a senior partner in Covington and Burling; and the AEC established a "separated" legal staff to represent the agency. On December 10, 1958, the AEC issued its long-awaited initial decision. It continued the construction permit and dismissed the unions' charge that the AEC had failed in its obligation to assure public health and safety. After allowing time for filing of exceptions, the commission issued a final decision on May 26, 1959, reiterating its December decision. The unions, to the surprise of no one, petitioned for review by the U.S. Court of Appeals of the District of Columbia.

A three-member appeals court panel heard oral arguments on March 23, 1960. Sigal argued, as he had done before the commission, that the AEC had not met the requirements of the 1954 law establishing the two-step licensing procedure and the implementing regulations. Citing the legislative history of the act, Sigal said that the Congress intended that an applicant who received a construction permit should also have assurance that he would receive a permit to operate the reactor as long as he constructed it according to the conditions of the construction permit. Therefore, the essential finding with respect to safety had to be made at the time the construction permit was issued and that that finding would also be made at the time of the granting of an operating license. This protected the paramount interest of the public in safety.

The commission brief countered by drawing a clear dichotomy between the standards applicable to construction permits and those applicable to operating licenses. The implementing regulation carried out that distinction, the commission argued. It prescribed safety standards for construction permits on the "basis of the developmental nature of nuclear power technology, of which Congress was aware." The commission had issued the PRDC construction permit on that acknowledgment.

On June 10, 1960, the panel, in a 2-1 opinion, upheld the unions by declaring the PRDC construction permit illegal. Circuit Judges Henry W. Edgerton and David L. Bazelon formed the majority; Judge Warren E. Burger wrote a dissenting opinion. In deciding for the unions, Judge Edgerton's majority opinion found that the AEC had an obligation to use the same standards in judging a construction permit application as it did for a subsequent operating license. On the basis largely of a detailed review of the 1954 act, Edgerton concluded: "It seems certain that if the Act did not require, as a condition to the issuance of a construction permit, a finding that the proposed facility can be operated without undue risk to the health and safety of the public, the Act would not require the issuance of a license when the permitted construction permit is carried out." His opinion went on to find inconsistencies in the commission's findings in this case. Taken together, they implied that while it seemed reasonable that scientific research would eventually establish that the PRDC reactor could be operated safely, the evidence currently available did not establish the fact. The court disliked the existing uncertainty.

In his dissent, Judge Burger wrote that, in a technological area such as the development of nuclear energy in which so much scientific uncertainty prevailed, the AEC must be allowed to proceed on a step-by-step basis. He suggested that his colleagues, in their majority opinion, were "undertaking to assume responsibilities which Congress vested in the Commission." They were, in effect, telling the agency it had made an unwise decision. The majority assumed, Burger charged, that once the commission had "permitted PRDC to invest its millions in the plant, they are 'bound' or 'likely' to relax their notion of what is safe or dangerous in order to bail out the investors." Burger refused to believe that the AEC would act "to make a

finding of safety which is not supported by substantial scientific evidence."

Reactions, naturally, were mixed. The unions were highly pleased. A United Automobile Workers spokesman said the decision showed "that no one, the AEC especially, should brush aside the opinions of atomic scientists who serve on the Advisory Committee on Reactor Safeguards." The ruling stunned officials at both the AEC and PRDC. At the agency, the commission started the wheels in motion to overturn the decision through an appeal. To not do so would jeopardize construction permits issued to other companies. In addition, the whole licensing scheme that the agency had developed would be undermined. After being denied by the appeals court for a rehearing *en banc*, the AEC and the Justice Department filed a petition for *certiorari* with the U.S. Supreme Court asking it to review the court of appeals record. On November 19, 1960, the Supreme Court issued a writ granting the review and placed the case on its docket.

The High Court agreed to consider two main questions and a subsidiary one. One was whether the AEC had the legal authority to license a power reactor near a large city without showing compelling reasons for the location, and the other was whether the 1954 act permitted the AEC to license the construction and operation of nuclear power plants in two steps. The subsidiary question related to the latter one: had the commission really addressed the safety issues as required by its own regulations, or were its findings as ambiguous as the court of appeals had found.

Two aspects of the Supreme Court proceeding are noteworthy. First, the justices avoided the question of whether the PRDC reactor could be proved to be sufficiently safe. Although a main issue on which the commission originally granted a hearing was the sufficiency of information available to provide assurance that the reactor could be operated without undue risk to the health and safety of the public, the High Court would not resolve that matter. But the second issue that the unions pressed—that the AEC violated its own regulations in initially issuing the construction permit—the Court decided to review.

On June 12, 1961, the Supreme Court announced a 7-2 vote in favor of the AEC and the PRDC. Justice William J. Brennan Jr. wrote the majority opinion, while Justice William O. Douglas filed a dissent.

Brennan wrote that the main question before the Court was whether the AEC, in issuing a construction permit, must make the "same definitive finding of safety of operation" as it would have to make before it issued an operating license. After reviewing the 1954 act and the AEC regulations, the Court determined that Congress "contemplated a step-by-step procedure." Second, the Court found that, before licensing the operation of a reactor, the commission "will have to make a positive finding that operation of the facility will 'provide adequate protection to the health and safety of the public.' " But the statute did not make it clear, and so it became "the center of controversy in this case" whether the commission "must also have made such a finding when it issued PRDC's construction permit."

Brennan reviewed the AEC regulation that elaborated upon and described the step-by-step procedure contemplated by the statute. The Court found that the regulation "was a valid exercise of the rule-making power" granted to the AEC. And it required that "some finding as to the safety of operation be made before a provisional construction permit is granted." The real question, Brennan wrote, "is whether the first finding must be backed up with as much conviction as to the safety . . . as the second, final finding must be." Brennan and the majority thought the weight of the argument permitted the AEC "to defer a definitive safety finding until operation is actually licensed." Brennan offered common sense reasoning for this: "For nuclear reactors are fast-developing and fast-changing. What is up to date now, may not, probably will not, be as acceptable tomorrow. Problems which seem insuperable now may be solved tomorrow, perhaps in the very process of construction itself." Based on that, the Court held that the AEC had complied with the statute and its own regulations fully.

Justice Douglas's short dissenting opinion found the AEC's interpretation that "safety findings can be made after construction is finished" to be socially irresponsible. The commission's interpretation was, Douglas wrote, "a light-hearted approach to the most awesome, the most deadly, the most dangerous process that man has ever conceived."

The *New York Times* highlighted the decision as "an important test case for the atomic energy program." Indeed it was, for had the AEC not been sustained by the Supreme Court, it would have meant, at the very least, significant delays in the civilian nuclear power program while the Congress and the agency developed new procedures to license private power reactors. The decision, of course, did not resolve any of the safety questions raised by the ACRS. By implication, the decision of the Court affirmed that it lacked the technical expertise to evaluate such issues. The law gave that responsibility to the AEC, and, if the Court had attempted to answer safety questions, it would have been second-guessing the commission. The justices correctly avoided that role because they did not view it as a judicial function.

Although the AEC "won" the case, the manner in which it handled the early proceedings undermined public confidence in its judgment on safety issues. The whole proceeding contributed to the beginning of a credibility problem over the agency's role as a regulator while also acting as a promoter of nuclear power.

Selected Bibliography

Fuller, John G. *We Almost Lost Detroit*. New York: Reader's Digest Press, 1975.

Mazuzan, George T. "Atomic Power Safety: The Case of the Power Reactor Development Company Fast Breeder, 1955–1956." *Technology and Culture* 23 (July 1982): 341–371.

Mazuzan, George T., and J. Samuel Walker. *Controlling the Atom: The Beginnings of Nuclear Regulation, 1946–1962*. Berkeley: University of California Press, 1984.

Morrisson, James L., and B. John Garrick. "What We Learned from the PRDC Case." *Nucleonics* 17 (July 1959): 60–63.

Walker, J. Samuel. *Containing the Atom: Nuclear Regulation in a Changing Environment, 1963–1971*. Berkeley: University of California Press, 1992.

The Atomic Energy Commission and the Environment

—◄◦►—

J. Samuel Walker

History Office
U.S. Nuclear Regulatory Commission

Calvert Cliffs Coordinating Committee, Inc. et al. v. United States Atomic Energy Commission and United States of America, 449 F. 2d 1109 (1971) [U.S. Court of Appeals]

◄◦► THE CASE IN BRIEF ◄◦►

Date
  1971

Location
  Maryland

Court
  U.S. Court of Appeals

Principal Participants
  Calvert Cliffs Coordinating Committee
    and interested environmental groups
  Atomic Energy Commission
  Government of the United States

Significance of the Case
  The ruling thrust a reluctant Atomic Energy Commission into an era of environmental awareness and had a profound impact on the substance and process of nuclear regulation.

During the latter half of the 1960s, the decline of environmental quality in the United States took on growing urgency as a public policy issue. A series of controversies over the effects of substances such as DDT, asbestos, mercury, and phosphates, ecological disasters such as a huge oil spill off the coast of California and fish kills in the Mississippi River, and easily visible evidence of foul air and dirty water fueled public alarm about the deterioration of the environment.

At the same time that the environmental crisis commanded increasing attention, questions about the availability of electrical power triggered deepening concern. Since the early 1940s, the use of electricity had expanded by an average of 7 percent per year, which meant that it roughly doubled every decade. Utility and government planners found no indications that the pace of growth was likely to slow in the near future.

The growing public concern with environmental quality and the continually increasing demand for electricity put utilities in a quandary. Electrical generating stations were major polluters. Fossil fuel plants, in particular, which provided over 85 percent of the nation's electricity in the 1960s, spewed millions of tons of noxious chemicals into the atmosphere annually. The concurrent demands for sufficient electricity and clean air created, in the words of a leading environmental group, "a most vexing dilemma: How do we protect the environment from further destruction and, at the same time, have all the electricity we want at the flick of a switch?"

After the mid-1960s, utilities increasingly viewed nuclear power as the answer to that dilemma. It promised the means to produce electricity without fouling the air, and environmental concerns were a major spur to the rapid growth of the nuclear industry. Officials of the U.S. Atomic Energy Commission (AEC) actively promoted the idea that nuclear power provided the answer to both the environmental crisis and the energy crisis. Under its statutory mandate, the AEC was responsible both for encouraging the use of atomic energy for peaceful purposes and for regulating its safety. The AEC saw the energy/environment dilemma as an opportunity to enhance the attractiveness of nuclear power. Chairman Glenn T. Seaborg declared in 1966, that in light of expanding demand for electricity and deteriorating air quality, "we can be grateful that, historically speaking, nuclear energy arrived on the scene when it did."

Within a short time, however, some environmental groups, members of Congress, and other government agencies were suggesting that nuclear power plants, while reducing air pollution, threatened water quality by discharging large quantities of heated water used to cool the steam that drove the turbines to produce electricity. This incited a major controversy over the effects of "thermal pollution" and eventually over the general issue of the impact of nuclear power on the environment. Much of the debate centered on the role of the AEC in requiring nuclear plants to meet environmental standards, and differing perspectives and priorities inevitably led to court.

The AEC was reluctant to regulate environmental hazards other than radiation. It asserted that it sympathized with efforts to curb environmental abuse, but that it had no authority to take action against thermal pollution or other non-radiological environmental effects. The AEC's position elicited sharp criticism from those who thought it should do more to combat thermal pollution. The agency's legal claim received support, however, from the U.S. Court of Appeals for the First Circuit, which agreed in a January 1969 ruling that the AEC lacked the statutory jurisdiction to regulate the thermal effects of its licensed plants. The court denied the petition of the state of New Hampshire, which asserted that the AEC had the obligation to force the Vermont Yankee plant, under construction across the Connecticut River, to meet water quality standards. Nevertheless, the court expressed "utmost sympathy with the appellant" and urged Congress to grant the AEC the necessary authority over non-radiological environmental effects.

Congress appeared to fulfill that request when it passed the National Environmental Policy Act (NEPA) in December 1969. NEPA gave federal agencies a broad mandate to weigh the environmental impact of their activities and to take corrective measures when necessary, though it left unclear the precise boundaries of their authority and responsibilities.

The AEC took a narrow view of its jurisdiction under the new law. Although NEPA clearly expanded its responsibilities, the agency was cautious and restrictive in applying its environmental mandate. It was particularly concerned that an expansive interpretation of its authority would cause unwarranted delays in licensing new plants. The flood of orders for plants had already increased the time required to review applications, and the AEC worried that NEPA would cause a "quantum leap" in the length of the process. If this occurred, it would aggravate the shortage of electrical power, which the AEC considered a more serious and immediate threat to public welfare than the environmental consequences of operating nuclear plants. It attempted to strike a balance between environmental concerns and energy needs in writing its regulations to carry out NEPA.

In December 1970, the AEC published the final version of its environmental regulations. They required that applicants for licenses submit a detailed statement on the environmental impact of proposed plants. The statement would become a part of the licensing process and could be challenged in licensing hearings. The AEC would not make an independent appraisal of the anticipated environmental effects of nuclear plants, but would rely instead on the evaluations and standards of other federal and appropriate state agencies. On questions of water quality, the AEC would follow the provisions of the Water Quality Improvement Act, passed three months after NEPA, which required that applicants for federal licenses present certification from appropriate state or interstate agencies (or, in the absence of adequate state regulations, the secretary of the interior) that the proposed facility could meet existing standards. Once again, the AEC would accept the judgment of certifying agencies without undertaking an analysis of its own. The AEC's regulations also specified that environmental issues under NEPA could not be raised in licensing proceedings for which a notice of hearing was published before March 4, 1971. This was done, it explained, "to avoid unreasonable delays in the construction and operation of nuclear power plants."

The AEC's regulations went further than ever before in accepting responsibility for nonradiological effects of nuclear plants, but they met stern opposition from environmentalists. Within a few days after they were issued, three groups, the National Wildlife Federation, the Sierra Club, and the Calvert Cliffs Coordinating Committee, challenged the rules in a suit filed in the U.S. Court of Appeals for the District of Columbia Circuit. The litigation focused on the twin Calvert Cliffs nuclear plants under construction by the Baltimore Gas and Electric Company on the Chesapeake Bay. The suit not only called on the AEC to consider immediately the environmental costs of the plants and to halt construction if necessary, but also disputed its entire approach to NEPA. The petitioners' brief, written by Anthony Z. Roisman, a thirty-three-year-old Harvard Law School graduate who had recently joined with two other young attorneys to establish a public interest law firm, argued that the AEC's regulations fell far short of full compliance with

NEPA. It emphasized that the agency had failed to carry out the purposes of the act because it planned to rely on the standards of other agencies in evaluating environmental issues. This would "foreclose any examination of adverse environmental effects which will occur even when the standards and requirements are met." The petitioners also strongly objected to the AEC's deferral of consideration of NEPA issues until after March 4, 1971.

The AEC responded that it was attempting to take a "balanced approach" to environmental and energy needs, and it stressed that its policy on NEPA was necessarily influenced by the serious shortage of power that the nation faced. It pointed out that the major environmental effects of nuclear plants, radiation emissions and thermal discharges, were covered by statutes other than NEPA, which made the petitioners' charge that the AEC was ignoring environmental problems "hyperbole." It further suggested that to rely on the judgement of other agencies on NEPA matters was "wholly reasonable," since its own expertise focused heavily on radiological health and safety.

The AEC's brief made the strongest possible case for its plan to implement NEPA, but staff lawyers feared that the arguments would not fare well in court because they emphasized policy considerations rather than legal precedents. The concerns arising from the frailty of the AEC's legal position were heightened by revelations of the identity of judges on the panel selected to decide the case. They seemed likely to give the environmentalists a sympathetic, or at least an open-minded, hearing. "The luck of the draw was with us," Roisman commented later.

The court's decision, handed down on July 23, 1971, was a crushing defeat for the AEC. Not only did the ruling categorically reject the agency's arguments, but it did so in language that was extraordinarily harsh. Judge J. Skelly Wright, who wrote the opinion, faulted the agency for not doing more to consider environmental issues in its licensing process. In his most widely quoted phrase, he declared: "We believe that the Commission's crabbed interpretation of NEPA makes a mockery of the Act." He further submitted that the law required the

AEC to conduct independent evaluations of the environmental effects of proposed plants rather than relying solely on the standards of other agencies. He agreed that their views should be solicited, but he denied that NEPA authorized a "total abdication to those agencies." Wright sharply reproached the AEC for its plan to postpone consideration of NEPA requirements. He described it as "shocking," and added: "Whether or not the specter of a national power crisis is as real as the Commission apparently believes, it must not be used to create a blackout of environmental consideration."

The court's ruling did not come as a surprise to those who had followed the case, but the tone of Wright's language and the totality of the AEC's defeat was unexpected. Once it recovered from its initial shock, the AEC acted promptly to comply with the decision. Within a month, it decided not to file an appeal and drafted new regulations that broadened its approach to carrying out NEPA. Ironically, in light of the AEC's efforts to prevent NEPA from causing licensing delays, the *Calvert Cliffs* decision led to a *de facto* licensing moratorium of several months to allow time to rewrite regulations, revise environmental impact statements, review applications, conduct hearings, and train new staff members. The ruling had a decisive impact on both the substance and the process of nu-

clear regulation. It thrust the AEC, grudgingly, into an era of environmental awareness and anxiety in which full consideration of the impact of power plants on their natural surroundings was an absolute imperative.

As a result of *Calvert Cliffs*, other federal agencies assumed the same obligations as the AEC in applying NEPA. Although later decisions modified or bypassed *Calvert Cliffs*, as the first comprehensive judicial ruling on NEPA, it was the landmark that established the broadranging effects of the law and the responsibilities of the federal government to carry out its purposes.

Selected Bibliography

Duffy, R. J. *Nuclear Politics in America: A History and Theory of Government Regulation.* Lawrence: University Press of Kansas, 1997.

Liroff, Richard A. *A National Policy for the Environment: NEPA and Its Aftermath.* Bloomington: Indiana University Press, 1976.

Melosi, Martin V. *Coping with Abundance: Energy and Environment in Industrial America.* Philadelphia: Temple University Press, 1985.

Walker, J. Samuel. *Containing the Atom: Nuclear Regulation in a Changing Environment, 1963–1971.* Berkeley: University of California Press, 1992.

Insuring Against Nuclear Plant Accidents

—◦—

John W. Johnson

Department of History
University of Northern Iowa

Duke Power Company v. Carolina Environmental Study Group, Inc., et al. and
United States Nuclear Regulatory Commission v. Carolina Environmental Study Group, Inc., et al.,
438 U.S. 59 (1978) [U.S. Supreme Court]

◦ THE CASE IN BRIEF ◦

Date
1978

Location
North Carolina

Court
U.S. Supreme Court

Principal Participants
Gayl Waller
Duke Power Company
Carolina Environmental Study Group
U.S. Nuclear Regulatory Commission
Judge James B. McMillan
Chief Justice Warren E. Burger

Significance of the Case
Although the Supreme Court upheld a federal law limiting the liability of the nuclear industry in the event of an accident, it began an era in which nuclear power construction virtually ceased.

It is not often that a private citizen with a complaint is able to convince the U.S. Supreme Court to devote a major decision to its resolution. But for Gayl Waller, a diminutive southern club woman who did not want to see a nuclear power plant built next to her lake home, this is exactly what happened.

In the early 1970s, Mrs. Waller joined with a handful of environmentalists near Charlotte, North Carolina, in an attempt to stop the local utility, Duke Power Company, from embarking upon an ambitious program of nuclear construction in the Carolina Piedmont. Their efforts sparked confrontations with Duke Power and the federal body charged with regulating nuclear power in the United States, the Nuclear Regulatory Commission (NRC).

Mrs. Waller and her fellow activists called themselves the Carolina Environmental Study Group (CESG). Taking advantage of volunteer legal assistance, they sought in various ways to stop Duke Power from building nuclear plants in the western Carolinas. Yet, every issue they raised was eventually thrown out by regulatory panels or the federal courts—save one. The claim that allowed the CESG to have its day in court was a challenge to the constitutionality of an important but little known law, the Price-Anderson Act.

The Price-Anderson Act limits the liability of licensed nuclear power plant operators to the American public in the event of catastrophic nuclear accidents. It was passed by Congress in 1957, has been amended several times over the last forty years, and is still in force. The Price-Anderson Act's most important provision established a scheme to compensate the public for damages from a serious nuclear accident, such as a reactor core melt—the often mentioned "China Syndrome." When the CESG brought its lawsuit in the mid-1970s, the Price-Anderson Act provided that the total available compensation pool would be $560 million.

At first glance, $560 million might appear to be adequate compensation. However, the $560 million is a ceiling amount, no matter how many individuals—fifty or 50,000—suffer injury to person or property. Furthermore, government-sponsored studies of the potential damages from a serious nuclear plant accident have estimated that damage claims for the consequences to lives and property could run into tens of billions of dollars. It was because of estimates such as these that companies interested in owning and operating nuclear power plants insisted on the establishment of a statutory scheme to limit their liability to the public in the event of serious accidents. These companies continue to demand such protective legislation. The present liability limits under amended versions of Price-Anderson are more than ten times higher than they were in the seventies, but not high enough to suit those critical of nuclear power.

Admittedly, the chances of a serious accident taking place at a single location are minuscule, but the Three Mile Island accident in 1979 and the Chernobyl accident in 1986 demonstrate that serious nuclear accidents can and do happen. Although the accident at Three Mile Island did not result in the release of significant radiation into the atmosphere, had the core melt there continued for another hour or so, the containment structure might have been breached and the health and financial consequences could have been catastrophic. The Chernobyl accident did

lead to a substantial release of radiation. The West will probably never know the full health and financial consequences of Chernobyl, but rough estimates placed the total damages at more than $5 billion.

For the United States, supporters and critics of nuclear power agree: without the Price-Anderson Act, there would be no commercially generated nuclear power. Therefore, the CESG challenge to the constitutionality of the Price-Anderson Act was not only a device to test the legality of one aspect of nuclear power regulation. It was also an assault upon America's large and powerful nuclear industry. Thus, the case of *Duke Power Company and the Nuclear Regulatory Commission v. Carolina Environmental Study Group* and its companion case hold an important place in American business, economic, and legal history.

The main legal argument the CESG raised against Price-Anderson's limitation on liability clause was that it denied "property" of CESG members. This claim was based upon the Fifth Amendment to the U.S. Constitution that protects individuals against the deprivation of life, liberty, or property without due process of law or the taking of private property for public use without just compensation. The CESG, represented in federal court by attorneys employed by Ralph Nader's Public Citizen Litigation Group, maintained that, should a catastrophic accident occur, Price-Anderson's ceiling on liability made it likely that some of the individuals residing near the defective reactor would not be fairly compensated for their losses. The arbitrarily low ceiling amount, the Nader lawyers stressed, violated the Fifth Amendment. Also, the CESG attorneys argued that those living near reactors faced greater financial dangers from nuclear power than other groups in the population because of the Price-Anderson limitations. This, they maintained, offended the "equal protection" feature of American law gleaned from the Fourteenth Amendment.

These claims were interesting, but few legal scholars gave the CESG much chance to have its case heard on the merits in federal court. No accident had occurred to damage the CESG plaintiffs in North and South Carolina. In fact, the plants that Mrs. Waller and her friends were worried about were years from completion when her lawsuit was initiated. Thus, Duke and the NRC argued that the plaintiffs lacked "standing" (that they had not suffered any measurable loss) and that the case was not "ripe" for decision (that because no accident had taken place there was no need to decide the legal questions advanced).

However, one federal district judge, James B. McMillan of the Western District of North Carolina, found the CESG's arguments worthy of consideration and scheduled a hearing in 1976 to test their validity. Judge McMillan, a 1968 appointee of President Lyndon Johnson, was the first federal judge in the country to order busing to achieve racial balance in a public school district. His ruling was upheld in the landmark Supreme Court decision of *Swann v. Charlotte-Mecklenburg Board of Education* in 1971.

For a week in September 1976, Judge McMillan listened to witnesses and accepted exhibits from the CESG, Duke Power, and the NRC relating to the constitutionality of the limitation of liability feature of the Price-Anderson Act. Because of the fundamental relationship between the liability statute and the existence of commercial nuclear power in the United States, it can be justifiably said that the country's nuclear industry was on trial in Judge McMillan's courtroom. Evidence was submitted and witnesses testified on all aspects of nuclear energy—scientific, engineering, environmental, financial, and social. Appearing along with health physicists, NRC staff members, actuaries, Duke Power executives, and nuclear engineers were Gayl Waller and selected CESG members.

During the pretrial skirmishing and at the hearing itself, it was clear that Judge McMillan was uncomfortable with aspects of the Price-Anderson Act. Just how uncomfortable was not revealed until he issued his decision in 1977. In his fifty-page opinion, distinguished as much by well-turned phrases and literary allusions as by legal analysis, McMillan not only ruled that the CESG had satisfied the standing and ripeness tests for having their claims adjudicated in court but he also found the limitation of liability clause of the Price-Anderson Act unconstitutional. Although he was unwilling to speculate as to the chances of a nuclear accident at an American plant (he said "the court is not a bookie"), he did conclude that the likelihood of an accident causing damages above the Price-Anderson ceiling was "not fanciful but real." Thus, the plaintiffs had standing and the case was ripe for decision.

In his discussion of the merits of the CESG's suit, he found the Price-Anderson Act wanting on several grounds. In terms of due process and just compensation, he concluded that the amount of compensation authorized by the statute was not rationally related to the possible upper level of damages (he cited a 1975 NRC estimate of $17 billion for a major nuclear accident). He also found some of the technical features of the act deficient. For example, he criticized the mechanism for disbursing compensation in the aftermath of an accident because of the delays built into the law. He also cited what he felt was the unfairness of the Price-Anderson Act absorbing the entire pool of insurance money wagered on nuclear accidents, thus making it impossible for property owners to purchase individual nuclear liability insurance policies. In terms of "equal protection," the judge ruled that the act placed an unreasonable burden upon those living close to nuclear power plants.

The CESG and other antinuclear groups greeted Judge McMillan's decision with resounding approval. The attorneys for the plaintiffs said that the decision went beyond the wildest hopes. But Duke Power and the rest of the nuclear industry found it very disturbing. Although the decision technically had validity only in the western third of North Carolina, the major organizations in the nuclear industry (e.g., the Atomic Industrial Forum, nuclear construction and engineering firms, and licensed nuclear utilities) recognized that if the Supreme Court were to affirm Judge McMillan's ruling then the Price-Anderson Act would no longer protect licensed reactors anywhere in the country. So the industry quickly mounted a campaign to overturn the decision. The leading groups in the nuclear industry met several times in 1977 under the rubric of a "Price-Anderson Appeal Project" to coordinate appellate strategy and to draft *amicus curiae* ("friend of the court") briefs for submission to the Supreme Court on behalf of Duke Power and

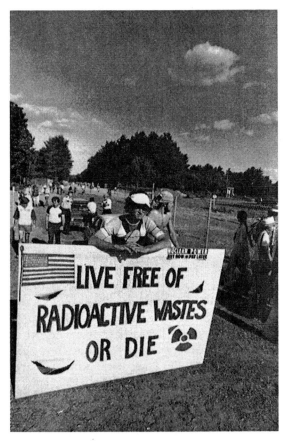

An anti-nuclear power demonstration in Seabrook, New Hampshire, June 1978. *Marty Levick.*

the NRC. Ultimately, the major nuclear industry groups submitted seven long briefs.

The case was argued before the Supreme Court in March 1978. On June 25, 1978, the Supreme Court handed down its decision. As predicted, the Court reversed Judge McMillan and upheld the constitutionality of the Price-Anderson Act. Surprising to many legal experts, however, was the fact that a majority of the Court—six justices—voted for reversal on the merits. That is, they felt that the CESG had satisfied the legal requirements for standing and ripeness. Even without a showing of appreciable physical damage to the plaintiffs and in the absence of a serious nuclear accident, the Court held that this was the time to pass muster on the constitutionality of the Price-Anderson Act. The Court quoted with approval Judge McMillan's aphorism, "the time to put on the roof is before it starts raining."

The opinion of the Court in *Carolina Environmental Study Group v. Duke Power Company* was written by Chief Justice Warren Burger. The chief justice's main point in support of the constitutionality of the Price-Anderson Act was that Judge McMillan did not accord the law the appropriate presumption of constitutionality. The attorneys for the CESG had tried to convince the Supreme Court that the Price-Anderson Act should be evaluated as a law affecting the rights and liberties of individuals and thus seen as "suspect" for its arbitrary liability limit. The Supreme Court disagreed. Relying upon a line of cases reaching back to the New Deal, Burger submitted that courts must respect the validity of congressional enactments relating to the economy so long as there is "a reasonable basis" for the legislation. Studies citing the infinitesimal chances of a serious nuclear accident that Judge McMillan had criticized, the Supreme Court found reasonably well founded.

Reactions to the opinion in the case were predictable. Nuclear industry and most general business publications supported the decision, while antinuclear and environmental organizations were critical. Much of the law review commentary on the case focused on the surprising willingness of the Court to brush aside procedural barriers and rush to a consideration of the merits of the case. Because of the case's complexity and because it was decided in the shadow of the more newsworthy *Bakke* decision on affirmative action, it did not receive as much media coverage as perhaps might have been expected given the momentous issues involved in the litigation.

In June 1978, when the *Duke Power* decision was issued, the justices and most of the public believed that the chances of a serious nuclear accident were remote. Within nine months after the decision, however, the NRC had discredited a crucial section of one of its safety studies for underestimating the chances of a nuclear accident and, shortly following that, the accident at Three Mile Island took place, significantly souring the American public's view of nuclear energy. If the High Court had been faced with the CESG suit against Duke Power in the spring of 1979 rather than the spring of 1978, would the Court's majority have been so confident in the safety of nuclear power upon which the limitation of liability features of Price-Anderson is predicated? Several law review commentators and some of the principals in the CESG suit expressed doubt that the decision would have been the same.

When the Supreme Court decided the *Duke Power* case in 1978, myriad financial problems were just beginning to afflict the nuclear industry. In fact, it has now been over two decades since an American utility has placed an order for a nuclear reactor. And over 100 orders have been canceled since the *Duke Power* decision. In the early 1980s a number of bills were introduced in Congress to amend, extend, or otherwise refine the Price-Anderson Act. The intensifying controversy over nuclear power in the United States frustrated hope of easy compromise over nuclear liability legislation. And the 1986 Chernobyl accident further polarized and prolonged the debate over nuclear power legislation. Finally, in 1988, Congress passed amendments to the Price-Anderson Act that extended the limitation of liability feature into the early twenty-first century. Although the constitutionality of Price-Anderson is now settled law, the wisdom and policy implications of the limitation on liability remain controversial.

Selected Bibliography

Green, Harold P. "Nuclear Power: Risk, Liability and Indemnity." *Michigan Law Review* 71 (January 1973): 479–510.

Johnson, John W. *Insuring Against Disaster: The Nuclear Industry on Trial.* Macon, GA: Mercer University Press, 1986.

Maleson, Diane Carter. "Historical Roots of the Legal System's Response to Nuclear Power." *Southern California Law Review* 55 (March 1982): 597–640.

Mazuzan, George T., and J. Samuel Walker. *Controlling the Atom: The Beginnings of Nuclear Regulation, 1946–1962.* Berkeley: University of California Press, 1985.

Meek, Daniel W. "Nuclear Power and the Price-Anderson Act: Promotion over Public Protection." *Stanford Law Review* 30 (January 1978): 393–468.

Nichol, Gene R. "*Duke Power Company v. Carolina Environmental Study Group.*" *Santa Clara Law Review* 20 (Spring 1980): 381–404.

Varat, Jonathan D. "Variable Justiciability and the *Duke Power Case.*" *Texas Law Review* 58 (February 1980): 273–327.

Walker, J. Samuel. *Containing the Atom: Nuclear Regulation in a Changing Environment, 1963–1971.* Berkeley: University of California Press, 1992.